THE HANDBOOK OF
INSTITUTIONAL RESEARCH

THE HANDBOOK OF INSTITUTIONAL RESEARCH

Richard D. Howard, Gerald W. McLaughlin, William E. Knight, and Associates

JOSSEY-BASS
A Wiley Imprint
www.josseybass.com

Copyright © 2012 by John Wiley & Sons, Inc. All rights reserved.
Published by Jossey-Bass
A Wiley Imprint
One Montgomery Street,
Suite 1200
San Francisco, CA 94104-4594
www.josseybass.com

Jossey-Bass books and products are available through most bookstores. To contact Jossey-Bass directly call our Customer Care Department within the U.S. at 800-956-7739, outside the U.S. at 317-572-3986, or fax 317-572-4002.

Wiley also publishes its books in a variety of electronic formats and by print-on-demand. Some material included with standard print versions of this book may not be included in e-books or in print-on-demand. If the version of this book that you purchased references media such as CD or DVD that was not included in your purchase, you may download this material at http://booksupport.wiley.com. For more information about Wiley products, visit www.wiley.com.

Library of Congress Cataloging-in-Publication Data

The handbook of institutional research / [edited by] Richard D. Howard, Gerald W. McLaughlin, William E. Knight. — First edition.
    pages cm. — (The Jossey-Bass higher and adult education series)
    Includes bibliographical references and index.
    ISBN 978-0-470-60953-8; ISBN 978-1-118-25901-6 (mobipocket);
    ISBN 978-1-118-23451-8 (epub); ISBN 978-1-118-22074-0 (pdf)
      1. Education, Higher—Research—Handbooks, manuals, etc. I. Howard, Richard D. II. McLaughlin, Gerald W. III. Knight, William E., 1965–
  LB2326.3.H36 2012
  378.007—dc23

                          2012016806

Printed in the United States of America

FIRST EDITION
HB Printing 10 9 8 7 6 5 4 3 2 1

The Jossey-Bass Higher and Adult Education Series

CONTENTS

PART 1: THE HISTORY, THEORY, AND PRACTICE OF INSTITUTIONAL RESEARCH   1

PART 2: SUPPORTING CAMPUS LEADERSHIP AND MANAGEMENT   131

PART 3: BRIDGING INTERNAL AND EXTERNAL REQUIREMENTS FOR IR   295

PART 4: INSTITUTIONAL RESEARCH TOOLS AND TECHNIQUES 455

TABLES, FIGURES, AND EXHIBITS

List of Tables

List of Figures

List of Exhibits

APPENDICES

PREFACE

The purpose of this *Handbook* is to give practitioners, administrators, faculty members, and students a single source that provides an overview of the core aspects of institutional research—its history and theoretical foundations; its role in support of planning and decision making; its role in responding to external accountability mandates; the data sources built by, and available to, institutional research professionals; and the tools and techniques used to study our institutions and to inform all members of the academy.

The last comprehensive discussion of the theory and practice of institutional research in higher education was more than 40 years ago. In 1971 Paul Dressel, a professor at Michigan State University, worked with his associates to write *Institutional Research in the University: A Handbook,* a volume that described a burgeoning practice that was much more of an art than a profession, and a newcomer to academic institutions. Since that time, the art described by Dressel has turned into a profession, practiced in virtually every postsecondary institution in the United States and at many others around the world. As a profession, it has a published set of ethics and standards, organizations of practitioners, an evolving language, and a unique and expanding knowledge base. Over the years, as the profession has grown, there have been many publications addressing various aspects of the practice of institutional research. However, since Dressel's publication in 1971 there has been no attempt to comprehensively describe and discuss the concepts, processes, and methodologies used in the practice of institutional research. That is why this *Handbook* was written.

Our first task was to try to answer the perplexing question: What exactly is institutional research? Although a number of definitions have been put forward to describe the function of institutional research, Joe Saupe's (1990) definition clearly and succinctly defines the profession: "Institutional research is research conducted within an institution of higher education to provide information which supports institutional planning, policy formation and decision making" (p. 1). Earlier, in Asa Knowles's *Handbook of College and University Administration* (1971), John Stecklein outlined three fundamental purposes of institutional research that we believe are still relevant today. Paraphrasing Stecklein, the purposes of institutional research are: (1) provide service to faculty members, (2) provide service to the administration, and (3) provide services to coordinating groups and other outside agencies (pp. 4–125). He also notes a wide range of activities by which we provide these services, such as

- Providing a research basis for critical examinations of teaching procedures and practices
- Creating a better understanding of the purpose of a course or curriculum
- Determining a basis for comparative judgments concerning instruction and curriculum building
- Obtaining a better understanding of admissions practices, examinations procedures, grading practices, and workloads
- Obtaining a better understanding of the role of the faculty member in the administration of a college or university
- Developing a better understanding of the factors that influence costs
- Obtaining a better understanding of the way in which curricular decisions can impact the use of resources such as space utilization, building costs, and other routine operations
- Providing up-to-date statistics on the characteristics of the institution, identifying trends in any of these characteristics, providing data and information useful in obtaining financial support, and providing data useful in explaining the mission and achievements of the institution

It is an amazingly broad list of activities and responsibilities. It is also very similar to the list developed by Chambers and Gerek (2007). Adding to this list, Randy Swing (2009), executive director of the Association for Institutional Research, recently stated that institutional research professionals also need to support and manage change on their campuses; IR practitioners need to develop their technical skills, critical thinking and reasoning skills, understanding of campus systems and divisional cultures, and management skills. A short description of the Association is on page xxxi.

Overview and Organization of the Handbook

The *Handbook* is made up of four parts that describe the breadth of the core knowledge and techniques that make up the profession of institutional research. In organizing the topics covered in this volume, we used Pat Terenzini's (1993) conceptual model, which defines three tiers, or major types, of knowledge as a framework for ordering the chapters. In the first part, the authors set a context for the practice of the profession of institutional research (Terenzini's third tier of knowledge: *contextual intelligence* or *institutional wisdom*), looking at the development of the profession and its current practice, and offering some thinking about future directions on our campuses. In the second part, Terenzini's second tier of knowledge, *issues intelligence,* is reflected in a series of chapters that address specific planning and decision support activities on our campuses. In the third part, the focus is on the development and use of different data sources that support both external accountability and institutional studies. In this part, Terenzini's aspects of issues intelligence are combined with his first tier of knowledge—*technical and analytical intelligence*—and reflected in the activities and processes discussed as IR bridges the internal and external environments. Chapters in the final part focus on technical and analytical topics that reflect Terenzini's first tier of intelligence. Topics include research and management tools and techniques typically used by institutional research professionals.

The following is a short description of each part:

- In Part One—*The History, Theory, and Practice of Institutional Research*—the reader is introduced to the profession, its history, how the function is organized and practiced, and new roles and expectations that are emerging on our campuses.
- In Part Two—*Supporting Campus Leadership and Management*—the focus of the chapters is the support of institutional leadership and the processes that institutional research is often asked to inform and assess. Topics include support of executive and academic leadership and governance, monitoring and analysis of faculty and student success, strategic and operational planning and management, facilities management, and campus sustainability.
- The third part—*Bridging Internal and External Requirements for IR*—includes chapters in which various data sources (federal, state, specially created, and campus) and their use by institutional researcher professionals are discussed.
- The focus of the fourth part—*Institutional Research Tools and Techniques*—includes discussions of the analytic tools, techniques, and methodologies used by institutional research professionals in the practice of institutional research. Topics include research activities such as statistical applications; comparative analyses; quality control systems; measuring student, faculty, and staff opinions; and management activities such as being strategic in improving organizational effectiveness.

Handbook Development

This *Handbook* was developed in several steps. Initially, the editors developed a proposed outline of topics to be covered. This outline was then reviewed by two sets of IR professionals—the first set made up of individuals representing different sectors of higher education, the second set including experts in various aspects of institutional research. Based on comments and suggestions from these professionals, topics were identified. The resulting outline was then sent in a *call for volunteer authors* to all members of the Association for Institutional Research. In response to the call, some two hundred individuals volunteered to write—some volunteering to write on a specific topic, others volunteering to write wherever they might be needed. Lead authors for each chapter were selected by the editors. These authors were then given a list of individuals who had volunteered to write on their topics, as possible coauthors. Some authors chose to write their chapters by themselves; others selected colleagues for coauthors and recruited coauthors from the list of other volunteers. Through this process, we believe this volume can accurately be characterized as a discussion of the roles, knowledge, and methods of institutional research, written by practicing institutional research professionals and scholars.

Summary

In summary, this volume covers a broad array of topics reflecting the diverse nature and multitude of tasks in which institutional research practitioners find themselves engaged. Some of the discussions are conceptual and give extensive references to other works. Other discussions are more technical, but they also provide a substantive list of supporting references. As was the case in *Institutional Research in the University: A Handbook* (Dressel & Associates, 1971), "Chapters overlap somewhat, but differences in focus and in points of view justify this. Institutional research simply cannot be divided into a completely independent set of discrete topics" (p. xii). This *Handbook* is not, however, a final authority on the practice of institutional research, nor a compendium of all institutional research activities; rather, it is intended to be a starting place in which the interested person will find a road map to more topics, advanced discussions, and examples of how we can do what we do.

References

Chambers, S., & Gerek, M. L. (2007, February 26). *IR activities, IR applications,* vol. 12. Association for Institutional Research.

Dressel, P. L., & Associates. (1971). *Institutional research in the university: A handbook.* San Francisco: Jossey-Bass.

Knowles, A. S. (Ed.). (1971). *Handbook of college and university administration.* New York: McGraw-Hill.

Saupe, J. P. (1990). *The functions of institutional research.* Tallahassee, FL: Association of Institutional Research.

Stecklein, J. E. (1971). *Institutional research.* In A. S. Knowles (Ed.), *Handbook of college and university administration* (pp. 4-123–4-134). New York: McGraw-Hill.

Swing, R. (2009). Institutional researchers as change agents. In C. Leimer (Ed.), *Imagining the future of institutional research* (pp. 5–16). New Directions for Institutional Research, no. 143. San Francisco: Jossey-Bass.

Terenzini, P. T. (1993). On the nature of institutional research and the knowledge and skills it requires. *Research in Higher Education, 34*(1), 1–10.

ACKNOWLEDGMENTS

First, we would like to thank our wives, Josetta, Adriene, and especially Pat, for their patience and support as we worked to make this *Handbook* a reality.

The *Handbook* reminds us of how important networking is for our profession. Over the years we have profited from the wisdom and guidance of many mentors. We are thankful that their doors were always open, with special thanks to Jim Montgomery, Chuck Elton, and Cameron Fincher.

We would also like to express our appreciation to those authors who wrote chapters, contributing their wisdom and energy to the creation of this *Handbook*. In addition, we would like to thank Jossey-Bass and the Association for Institutional Research for the support and advice provided during the development of this volume.

Finally, we would like to recognize Jean Chulak, who, as AIR's administrative director from 1974 to 1991, was the heart and soul of the Association in its formative years. We cannot imagine where we would have been without her energy and dedication.

Richard D. Howard
Gerald W. McLaughlin
William E. Knight

ABOUT THE EDITORS

Richard D. Howard currently serves as a consultant in higher education. He recently retired from his positions as director of institutional research and professor of educational policy and administration at the University of Minnesota. Before this he served as director of institutional research and held faculty positions at West Virginia University, North Carolina State University, and the University of Arizona. Howard also was a tenured professor of higher education at Montana State University, teaching graduate courses and directing student research, and served as chair of the University's faculty council. For the Association for Institutional Research, he is a past president and served as chair of the professional development committee, forum chair, and editor of the *Resources in Institutional Research* monograph series, and has taught continuously at the Foundations Institute since its inception. Howard has also taught in the Statistics Institute and the Data and Decisions Institutes and has presented papers and workshops at the annual meetings of various professional associations, including the Association for Institutional Research (AIR), the Society for College and University Planning (SCUP), EDUCAUSE, the Southern Association of Colleges and Schools (SACS), and the American Educational Research Association (AERA). He has also been awarded the Outstanding Service Award and is a Distinguished Member of the Association. In addition, Howard is a past president and Distinguished Member of SAIR. His professional interests include strategic planning, higher education administration, data administration, and mixed methods methodologies.

Gerald W. McLaughlin is an associate vice president for enrollment management and marketing at DePaul University. He was formerly director of institutional planning and research at DePaul and also director of institutional research and planning analysis at Virginia Tech. McLaughlin has taught courses in management and education and was a professor at Virginia Tech, where he also sat on master's and doctoral committees. For the Association for Institutional Research, he has served as president, forum chair, and chair of the publications board. McLaughlin was forum chair and president and a founding member of the Southern Association for Institutional Research (SAIR). He has served as editor of the AIR Professional file and IR Applications. McLaughlin has taught in the Foundations Institute since its inception and has also taught in the Statistics Institute and the Data and Decisions Institutes and has given papers and workshops at various professional associations, including AIR, SCUP, EDUCAUSE, SACS, SAIR, and the Association of Governing Boards. He has received the Sidney Suslow Award as well as the Outstanding Service and Distinguished Member Awards from AIR and SAIR. McLaughlin's areas of professional interest include methodology, strategic management, and data management.

William E. Knight is executive director of institutional effectiveness and an adjunct faculty member at Ball State University. He leads and teaches in Ball State's institutional research certificate program. Knight was previously an institutional researcher and faculty member at Bowling Green State University and Georgia Southern University and an institutional researcher at Kent State University. He received the BG Best Award in 1998 and the BGSU Timothy D. King Friend of Student Affairs Award in 2009. Knight is past president, past forum chair, and a past member of the board of directors of the Association for Institutional Research. His scholarly interests include the impact of college on students and effectiveness in institutional research. Knight has authored or coauthored twenty-five peer-reviewed and invited publications, edited the *Primer for Institutional Research,* served as associate editor of the *Resources in Institutional Research* monograph series, delivered one hundred peer-reviewed and invited conference presentations and workshops, and served as a member of fifty-five dissertation and thesis committees. He also serves as a consultant-evaluator, team chair, and member of the Accreditation Review Council for the North Central Association Higher Learning Commission.

LIST OF CONTRIBUTORS

Lisa M. Amoroso, Associate Professor of Management, Dominican University

Sandra J. Archer, Director for University Analysis and Planning Support, University of Central Florida

Kim K. Bender, Director of Assessment, Colorado State University

Tom R. Bohannon, Analytical Consultant, SAS Institute Inc.

Rachel D. Boon, Associate Director, Higher Education Data Sharing Consortium, Wabash College

Victor M. H. Borden, Professor, Educational Leadership and Policy Studies, Indiana University Bloomington

Paul T. Brinkman, Associate Vice President for Budget and Planning, University of Utah

Corbin M. Campbell, Graduate Assistant, Office of Institutional Research, University of Maryland—College Park

Julie W. Carpenter-Hubin, Director of Institutional Research and Planning, The Ohio State University-Main Campus

Rebecca E. Carr, National Coordinator, Association of American Universities Data Exchange

John J. Cheslock, Associate Professor, Dept. of Ed. Policy Studies and Senior Research Associate, Center for the Study of Higher Education, The Pennsylvania State University

Michael J. Dooris, Director of Planning Research and Assessment, The Pennsylvania State University

Mardy T. Eimers, Director of Institutional Research, University of Missouri-Columbia

Ann S. Ferren, Senior Fellow, Association of American Colleges and Universities

Jonathan D. Fife, Visiting Professor, Educational Leadership and Policy Studies, Virginia Polytechnic Institute and State University

Joseph W. Filkins, Senior Research Associate, Institutional Research and Marketing Analytics, DePaul University

Gayle M. Fink, Assistant Vice President for Institutional Effectiveness, Bowie State University

Carol H. Fuller, Consultant

Denise C. Gardner, Assistant Provost and Director, Office of Institutional Research & Assessment, The University of Tennessee

Charles F. Harrington, Professor of Management, The University of North Carolina at Pembroke

Rosemary Q. Hayes, Director of Consortia for Student Retention Data Exchange, Consortium of Student Retention Data Exchange

Teri L. Hinds, Director of Institutional Planning, Assessment & Research, Winona State University

Richard D. Howard, Consultant

Glenn W. James, Director of Institutional Research, Tennessee Technological University

Elizabeth A. Jones, Director of the Doctoral Program and Professor, School of Education, Holy Family University

Daniel R. Jones-White, Analyst, Office of Institutional Research, University of Minnesota

Christine M. Keller, Voluntary System of Accountability Executive Director and Director of Research and Policy Analysis, Association of Public and Land-grant Universities

Heather A. Kelly, Director of the Office of Institutional Research, University of Delaware

Adrianna J. Kezar, Associate Professor, Rossier School of Education, University of Southern California

Beverly R. King, Assistant Vice Chancellor for Institutional Effectiveness, The University of North Carolina at Pembroke

Jang W. Ko, Assistant Professor, Department of Education, SungKyunKwan University, Korea

Dennis A. Kramer II, Graduate Assistant, Institute of Higher Education, University of Georgia

Paula S. Krist, Assistant Dean, Assessment Support, University of San Diego

Rick J. Kroc, Associate Vice Provost for the Office of Institutional Research and Planning Support, The University of Arizona

Marsha V. Krotseng, Vice Chancellor for Strategic Planning and Executive Director of the College Technical Education Council, North Dakota University System

Thulasi Kumar, Director of Institutional Research and Assessment, Missouri University of Science and Technology

Cathy J. Lebo, Assistant Provost for Institutional Research, Johns Hopkins University

Ying J. Liu, Research Analyst, Dartmouth College

Jing Luan, Vice Chancellor for Educational Services and Planning, San Mateo County Community College District

Andrew L. Luna, Director of Institutional Research, Planning and Assessment, University of North Alabama

Jan W. Lyddon, Principal, Organizational Effectiveness Consultants

Bruce E. McComb, Principal, Organizational Effectiveness Consultants

Gerald W. McLaughlin, Associate Vice President for Enrollment Management and Marketing, DePaul University

Josetta S. McLaughlin, Associate Professor of Management, Walter E. Heller College of Business Administration, Roosevelt University

Martha C. Merrill, Associate Professor of Higher Education, Kent State University

John H. Milam, Director of Planning and Institutional Effectiveness, Lord Fairfax Community College

J. Patrick Mizak, Director of Institutional Research, Canisius College

John A. Muffo, President, John A. Muffo and Associates

Chad Muntz, Director of Institutional Research, University System of Maryland

Daniel W. Newhart, Associate Director of Student Life Research and Assessment, The Ohio State University-Main Campus

Julie P. Noble, Principal Research Associate, ACT, Inc.

Gita W. Pitter, Associate Vice President for Institutional Effectiveness, Florida A&M University

John D. Porter, Associate Provost for Institutional Research and Analysis, The State University of New York

James T. Posey, Associate Vice President for Institutional Research and Planning, College of Charleston

James Purcell, Commissioner of Higher Education, Louisiana Board of Regents

Jerome S. Rackoff, Assistant Vice President for Planning and Institutional Research, Bucknell University

Donald J. Reichard, Senior Advisor to the President, Emory & Henry College

Gary A. Rice, Associate Vice Provost for Institutional Research, University of Alaska Anchorage

John J. Rome, Deputy CIO and BI Strategist, Arizona State University

Sharron L. Ronco, Assessment Director, Office of the Provost, Marquette University

Patrick M. Rossol, Senior Research Analyst, National Higher Education Benchmarking Institute, Johnson County Community College

Maryann S. Ruddock, Retired, University of Texas at Austin

Alene B. Russell, Senior State Policy Consultant, American Association of State Colleges and Universities

Patricia C. Ryan, Director of Institutional Research, Southeast Missouri State University

Liz Sanders, Assistant Vice President for Institutional Research and Market Analytics, DePaul University

Richard L. Sawyer, Senior Research Scientist, ACT, Inc.

Jeffrey A. Seybert, Director of the National Higher Education Benchmarking Institute, Johnson County Community College

Sean Simone, Associate Research Scientist, National Center for Education Statistics, Institute of Education Sciences

Stephen D. Spangehl, Vice-President for Accreditation Relations, The Higher Learning Commission

Sutee Sujitparapitaya, Associate Vice President for Institutional Research, San José State University

Daniel Teodorescu, Director of Institutional Research, Emory University

Kimberly A. Thompson, Director of Institutional Effectiveness, University of Colorado-Denver

Robert K. Toutkoushian, Professor, Institute of Higher Education, University of Georgia

J. Fredericks Volkwein, Emeritus Professor of Higher Education, Pennsylvania State University

Richard A. Voorhees, Principal, Voorhees Group LLC

Allison M. Walters, Assistant Director of Institutional Research, University of Delaware

Catherine E. Watt, Director of the Master of Public Administration Program, Clemson University

James Woodell, Director, Innovation and Technology Policy, Association of Public and Land-grant Universities

THE ASSOCIATION FOR INSTITUTIONAL RESEARCH

The Association for Institutional Research (AIR) is the world's largest professional organization for institutional researchers (IR). Formed in 1965, the organization provides educational resources, best practices, and professional development opportunities for its more than 4,000 members worldwide. Its primary purpose is to support high-quality, data-informed decisions for the enhancement of higher education and student success.

AIR is a membership organization governed by a board of directors elected from the membership. Board members are IR practitioners who represent postsecondary institutions, higher education associations, and other related organizations. In addition to governance, AIR members are active participants in the development of publications, like this *Handbook*. Most of the chapter authors are AIR members, and all three of the *Handbook* editors are past presidents of the association.

AIR is a comprehensive source of IR education and professional development, offering a wealth of online resources and training opportunities to ensure that members are fully equipped to perform their jobs at the highest levels. Educational opportunities include the *Data and Decisions Academy,* a series of self-paced, online professional development courses for institutional researchers; AIR's exclusive workshops and tutorials in the use of Integrated Post Secondary Education Data System (IPEDS) surveys and data tools; and a number of online publications that introduce IR processes and models and share applied practical knowledge with institutional researchers.

Each spring, AIR serves as host of the field's premier conference, the AIR Forum—the world's largest gathering of higher education professionals working in institutional research, assessment, planning, and related postsecondary education fields. The four-day event includes more than 450 presentations, representing all sectors of higher education, and an exhibit hall featuring the latest tools and resources to support data use for decision making.

We hope you will agree that the *Handbook* is the premier publication in the field and your must-have professional resource. In addition, we invite readers to continue their professional development through active involvement in the AIR network of peers and colleagues representing all sectors of higher education.

THE HANDBOOK OF
INSTITUTIONAL RESEARCH

PART ONE

THE HISTORY, THEORY, AND PRACTICE OF INSTITUTIONAL RESEARCH

The practice of institutional research has evolved into a recognized professional activity in higher education over the past fifty years in the United States and Canada, and during the past several decades it has appeared in many other countries across the globe. In the seven chapters that make up Part One, the reader is introduced to the theory and practice of the profession of institutional research. For newcomers to the field of institutional research, the authors provide an overview of the profession—its history and how it is practiced at our colleges and universities—providing a context for the specific discussions of institutional research activities in subsequent parts. For both IR professionals and those interested in the profession, the authors provide a set of discussions about the role that an institutional research unit and IR professional might play, nationally and internationally, in reaction to and in anticipation of changing demands and opportunities, both internal and external.

In the first chapter, Don Reichard outlines the history of the profession through emerging institutional research functions and the creation of the Association for Institutional Research. Notably, he identifies the individuals who played key roles in the profession's development and the Association for Institutional Research's establishment and growth, as well as some of their key contributions that were instrumental in shaping the profession. Reichard credits seminal publications that have defined and described the theory and practice of institutional research over the past fifty years. These publications described the natural tension between "institutional" (administrative responsibilities) and "research" (scholarly opportunities). They helped clarify functions that have become the foundation of our profession.

The three chapters that follow describe the structure and practice of institutional research. In Chapter 2, Fred Volkwein, Ying

(Jessie) Liu, and James Woodell present a comparative overview of the structures and activities of institutional research offices derived from national surveys conducted over the past thirty years. Volkwein analyzes the different roles of institutional research based on its internal and external focuses. In Chapter 3, Mardy Eimers, Jang Wan Ko, and Denise Gardner discuss the practice of institutional research in relation to the types of skills required to be effective. This discussion includes the *AIR Code of Ethics and Professional Standards,* which sets the standards for the profession. Types of professional development for institutional research available through AIR are also discussed. The chapter concludes with a discussion of the types of practices conducted in an institutional research office, illustrating that although there are common responsibilities, specific planning and activities related to decision support are institutionally dependent. In Chapter 4, Ann Ferren and Martha Merrill describe the cultural and political realities affecting the practice of institutional research at international universities. The practice of institutional research in these institutions often is complicated by international accords and multinational agreements that require reporting to national and international agencies. Often the multiple reporting demands require the use of different definitions and data requirements. Many of the challenges at these institutions will also be faced by our colleges and universities as higher education becomes more global.

In Chapter 5, Rick Voorhees and Teri Hinds challenge institutional research professionals to be activists on their campuses, and they discuss moving beyond external accountability reporting to providing actionable information that helps position the campus to proactively respond to current and future threats and opportunities.

These challenges must be viewed in the context of the capabilities discussed in the preceding three chapters, as they describe the practice and structure of institutional research. How these challenges are met must also be viewed as a potential next step in the evolution of our profession.

The final two chapters in this part of the *Handbook* discuss the notions of organizational learning and change management. In Chapter 6, Victor Borden and Adrianna Kezar explore the theories and concepts related to collaborative organizational learning and how they can inform the purpose and practice of institutional research. This includes a discussion of the different theories of collaborative organizational learning. This chapter concludes with how these different types of organizational learning theories can inform institutional research practice. In Chapter 7, Kim Bender describes change management, discusses it in the context of organizational learning, and provides an example of how these concepts are being used by the institutional research office at one university to manage change. Both chapters explore how institutional research can change and enhance their influence on a campus.

As readers move through this part of the *Handbook,* they will note that the practice and theory of institutional research has a historical foundation. It will become clear that the knowledge and skills required are complex and the importance of specific activities depends heavily on the institutional context in which institutional research is performed. Finally, the reader will find that the profession is continuing to evolve and change. Effective institutional research requires an understanding of how these changes can be managed. This part sets the context for the rest of the volume, in which specific institutional research activities, functions, tools, and techniques are discussed.

CHAPTER 1

THE HISTORY OF INSTITUTIONAL RESEARCH

Donald J. Reichard

This chapter provides an overview of the historical origins of the field of institutional research and the circumstances that led to the establishment of the Association for Institutional Research (AIR) in 1965. Publications cited are intended not to represent an integrated literature review or bibliographical essay, but to identify significant sources that readers may wish to examine in their original form.

Early Beginnings of the Profession

The origins of what might come to be termed "institutional research" are found in (1) self-studies conducted on an ad hoc basis by individual institutions interested in investigating issues pertaining to their unique circumstance; (2) surveys conducted by external groups or associations across institutions; and (3) the establishment of specialized research committees, bureaus, or research-oriented offices in large public universities charged with investigating relevant issues on an ongoing basis.

College Self-Study

College Self-Study: Lectures on Institutional Research (Axt & Sprague, 1960) was perhaps the first well-integrated series of papers focusing primarily on institutional research. Published by the Western Interstate Commission on Higher Education (WICHE), it contained papers given at a week-long July 1959

Note: The author is indebted to William Lasher for conversations and insights that led to the selection of the accompanying resources on which this chapter is based.

workshop at Stanford University attended by 130 college and university officers from thirteen Western states and twelve states outside the WICHE region. The opening lecture—presented by W. H. Cowley, the distinguished historian of higher education at Stanford—bore the title "Two and a Half Centuries of Institutional Research." Cowley's paper identified 1701, the year in which Yale was founded, as the first example of an "institutional research" study, because the founders of Yale, after reviewing the single governing board structures of Scottish universities and the University of Dublin, had adopted a similar structure, which differed from the dual governing board structures of Harvard and William and Mary, the only two American colleges then in existence. Cowley went on to identify several other studies conducted in the 1700s, studies conducted by various Harvard committees in the 1820s, and the Yale Curriculum Study of 1828 as important forerunners of institutional research. He indicated that A. Lawrence Lowell succeeded Charles Eliot as president of Harvard in 1909, "largely because of his institutional research activities" that began in 1902 when Lowell became a member of the Committee on Improving Instruction in Harvard College (Cowley, 1960, p. 6).

Cowley's lecture cited such works as an 1899 paper by William Rainey Harper, president of the University of Chicago, titled "Waste in Education," and a study published by the Carnegie Foundation for the Advancement of Teaching titled *Industrial and Academic Efficiency* (Cooke, 1910). Such works preceded efficiency expert F. W. Taylor's publication of *The Principles of Scientific Management* in 1911.

Surveys

In his dissertation on the origins of institutional research, Tetlow (1973) cited the period 1908–1943 as "The Survey Era," which began with a comprehensive investigation of strategic questions initiated by Oberlin College president Henry C. King. Abraham Flexner's 1910 critical study of medical education was also particularly notable at the beginning of this period. Indeed, Walter Crosby Eells identified more than 500 studies and authored a special report on 240 of them in a publication titled *Surveys of American Higher Education,* issued in 1937 by the Carnegie Foundation for the Advancement of Teaching. Eells went on to note ten main reasons why surveys had become a predominant tool of analysis including: "(1) the development of the scientific spirit in education; (2) the efficiency movement in business and industry; (3) the social survey movement; (4) the growth of higher education; (5) the complexity of higher education; (6) the cost of higher education; (7) the criticisms of higher education; (8) the development of accrediting agencies; (9) the influence of the general educational survey movement; and (10) self-protection" (Eells, 1937, 54–68).

If Eells was the principal chronicler of the survey movement, it may be argued that Floyd W. Reeves of the University of Chicago was among the most prominent initiators of surveys that had an enormous impact on higher education in the late 1920s and early 1930s. Reeves's work in this regard is summarized in a chapter titled "Surveys of Colleges, Universities, and Other Educational Institutions and Work with the North Central Association of Colleges and Schools, 1927–1936" (Niehoff, 1991, pp. 29–65). Eells noted ninety-six surveys of all types of institutions in which Reeves was involved, including sixty-four surveys in which Reeves served as the principal investigator. Among those done for the North Central Association were surveys of the *Costs of Education in Liberal Arts Colleges* (1927), *Financial Standards for Accrediting Colleges* (1928), *Standards for Accrediting Colleges* (1928), and *The Evaluation of Higher Education Institutions,* a series of studies released in the period 1929–1936.

Reeves's most well-known works were a series of twelve volumes reflecting studies undertaken from 1929 to 1933 as part of a comprehensive self-survey of the University of Chicago. Reeves and his doctoral student and protégé, John Dale Russell, served as principal authors and collaborators in nine of the twelve volumes (Niehoff, 1991, pp. 7–8.) From 1930–32, Reeves also directed a survey of some thirty-five colleges related to the Methodist Episcopal Church which resulted in a more than 700 page volume published in 1932 titled *The Liberal Arts College.* It should be noted that two of his more junior collaborators in that study were John Dale Russell and A. J. Brumbaugh, who would become the first two recipients of the Distinguished Membership Award from the Association for Institutional Research in 1966, the year in which AIR held its first Forum.

The clearest precursor of a study defining areas and methods of inquiry that might evolve into the field of institutional research appears to have been developed in a dissertation by Schiller Scroggs that was completed at Yale University in 1935 but not published until 1938. The purpose of the study, titled *Systematic Fact-Finding and Research in the Administration of Higher Education,* was "to ascertain how an office of administrative statistics and research in an institution of higher education should systematically determine upon and present its data" and "to serve as a concrete aid to college executives interested in setting up within their institutions a system of fact-finding and research as an administrative agency" (Scroggs, 1938, iii).

Scroggs' general bibliography contained a listing of 259 references, including many study documents obtained in response to his "field inquiries" that were completed by sixty college and universities of varying size and complexity.

Research Committees/Bureaus

Cowley notes that larger-scale multi-institutional studies in the first twenty to thirty years of the twentieth century tended to be funded by foundations that were reluctant to fund self-studies within a single institution. In the absence of single institution funding, a few presidents of larger institutions sought to encourage educational and administrative research on their own. Cowley referenced the existence of a Bureau of Institutional Research at the University of Illinois in 1918, a Division of Educational Reference at Purdue in 1920, and a Department of Personnel Study at Yale in 1921. A Bureau of Educational Research at Ohio State, which was largely concerned with secondary school surveys, was established in 1918. By 1928, a Division of Achievement Tests was also created at Ohio State, headed by Ralph W. Tyler, and a parallel post in student affairs research headed by Cowley was added at Ohio State in 1929. A Bureau of University Research was established at the University of Michigan about 1927; during the period 1929–1945 it was retitled the Office of Educational Investigations (Cowley, 1960, pp. 13–14).

The University of Minnesota created a University Committee on Educational Research in 1924; it became the Bureau of Institutional Research in 1948. As described in the Faculty Handbook, the role of the bureau was to serve as "a special research unit maintained by the University for the study of its own educational and administrative problems" (Stecklein, 1960, p. 32). "Priorities of the Bureau's work were first problems of the University, second higher education in Minnesota, and third, higher education in the nation" (Stecklein, 1960, p. 33).

Advocacy for Establishment of Institutional Research Offices

The most prominent advocates for the establishment and training of institutional research personnel were the American Council on Education (ACE) at the national level, and the regional compacts—including the Southern Regional Education Board (SREB), the Western Interstate Commission on Higher Education (WICHE), and the New England Board for Higher Education (NEBHE)—which were established in the period 1948–1955 to cooperatively address state-level higher education issues and concerns. The array of national meetings and workshops conducted in the period 1956–1960, and the National Institutional Research Forums held from 1960 to 1965, in turn led to the formal creation of the Association for Institutional Research in 1965. These activities are described in detail by Schietinger (1968, 1979) and Tetlow (1973).

It is estimated that prior to 1955 only ten colleges and universities had established offices of institutional research. By 1964, there were 115 institutions with a bureau or official charged with responsibility for conducting institutional research; 21 of these offices were created in the year 1966 alone (Rourke and Brooks, 1966, pp. 45–46). The creation of institutional research offices would help to answer increased demands for accountability in line with vastly increased expenditures of public funds for higher education during this period.

With the aid of a $375,000 grant from the Carnegie Corporation in 1956, ACE established an Office of Statistical Information and Research (OSIR). Following a February 1957 conference of college and university presidents, Elmer West, the acting director of OSIR, was particularly influential in urging presidents to appoint staff who would engage in systematic institutional research. The subsequent development by OSIR of a series of workshops on topical areas encouraged further workshop activities sponsored by SREB and the 1959 WICHE workshop, previously cited, in which Cowley (1960) implored: "Someone needs to state the case for institutional research more convincingly than it seems to have thus far been stated. Indeed, I know of no adequate address, article, or book to which one might refer a president or faculty member whose interest in it he might want to arouse" (p. 15).

The document that served to answer Cowley's challenge, more than any other at the time, was authored by A. J. Brumbaugh. Titled *Research Designed to Improve Institutions of Higher Learning*, it was issued by ACE in 1960. Topics addressed in the monograph included: (1) The Need for Institutional Research, (2) Areas of Institutional Research, (3) The Conduct of Institutional Research, and (4) The Effects of Institutional Research. Additionally, appendices noted (A) Institutional Problems on Which Boards Must Make Policy Decisions, (B) Examples of How Institutional Research May Be Organized, and (C) Changes Attributed to the Impact of Institutional Research. Two key paragraphs from the document, including the last paragraph, which was italicized, noted:

> The difference between higher educational institutions and business enterprises in no sense relieves the colleges and universities of the responsibility for operating efficiently. But they must develop their own methods of evaluating their own goals and functions.
>
> *The key to effective administration is the ability of the president and those who work with him to ask the right questions and then find the right answers. But the right answers to the right questions, whether they are specific in relation to a given institution or whether they are more comprehensive, must take into account all the relevant, factual data—the kind of data that only institutional research can provide.*
> (Brumbaugh, 1960, p. 2)

A second publication that greatly encouraged the establishment of institutional research offices was *The Managerial Revolution in Higher Education* by Rourke and Brooks (1966). The volume devoted chapters to the effects of increases in bureaucracy, the increasing computerization of campuses, and the need for effective processes in allocating resources, as well as chapters on newer developing styles of university management and managerial innovations. Most important in the Rourke and Brooks volume was a chapter on the growth of institutional research, which traced the origins of institutional research, cited emerging patterns of organization, and speculated on the prospects for increased influence on the part of the field of institutional research in the future (see also Stickler, 1968). The role that these sources played in increasing the awareness, recognition, and necessity for the establishment of effective institutional research units cannot be underestimated.

Practitioners Begin to Organize

The history of the organizational efforts leading to the formation of AIR has been reported in detail by several individuals (Lins, 1966; Stecklein, 1966; Tetlow, 1973; Doi, 1979; Saupe, 2005; Howard, 2011; Lasher, 2011). The following is a description of the five National Institutional Research Forums that led to the creation of AIR (Lins, 1966, pp. i–iii).

National Institutional Research Forums

As a result of various advocacy efforts, an increasing number of campus-based individuals began to feel the need to meet and share common interests, leading to the establishment of the National Institutional Research Forum, a predecessor of what would in time become the Association for Institutional Research.

The National Institutional Research Forum (NIRF) was conceived at a luncheon meeting in Tallahassee, Florida, on July 14, 1960, during a week-long "Institute on Institutional Research" sponsored by SREB. It was agreed that it would be worthwhile to hold an informal national meeting the next spring to discuss methodological problems in institutional research. Attendance would be by invitation only. John Folger, associate director of research at SREB, served as forum chair for the first NIRF meeting, held in Chicago March 4–5, 1961, just prior to the annual meeting of the American Association for Higher Education (AAHE). The meeting had forty-six participants, with sixteen from the Northeast, ten from the South, nine from the West, nine from the Midwest, and two from the United States Office of Education (USOE) in attendance.

The second NIRF meeting was again held in Chicago, March 3–4, 1962, prior to the AAHE meeting, with fifty in attendance and a registration fee of one dollar. John Stecklein of the University of Minnesota served as chair of the Planning Committee. John Dale Russell and A. J. Brumbaugh, the "deans" of institutional research, were honored at the dinner meeting "for their long service to the principles of and their major contributions to institutional research" (Lins, 1966, p. i).

The third NIRF meeting, offering both general and workshop sessions, was held at Wayne State University, May 5–7, 1963. A ten-person Planning Committee, selected nationally rather than regionally, was chaired by L. Joseph Lins of the University of Wisconsin. This meeting was open to "all persons actively engaged and/or vitally interested in institutional research work in colleges or universities or in associations with colleges and universities" (Lins, 1966, p. i). The meeting had 196 in attendance, with representation from thirty-six states as well as the District of Columbia, Hawaii, the Philippines, and Puerto Rico. This was the first meeting for which Proceedings were published, edited by Lins and titled *The Role of Institutional Research in Planning*.

The fourth NIRF meeting was held at the University of Minnesota and Hotel Leamington on May 17–20, 1964, with 146 in attendance. The Proceedings were titled *A Conceptual Role for Institutional Research.* At this meeting it was decided to establish a formal institutional research organization, and a Constitution Committee was formed.

The fifth and final NIRF meeting was held at SUNY Stony Brook, May 3–5, 1965, with 201 in attendance. The Proceedings were titled *Design and Methodology in Institutional Research.* John Stecklein presented the constitution for approval (which it received) and was elected the first president of AIR.

The Association for Institutional Research

The first annual meeting of AIR and the sixth Forum were held at the Hotel Somerset in Boston, May 2–5, 1966, with 257 in attendance. The Forum Proceedings were titled *Research on Academic Input.* AIR was incorporated as a non-profit corporation in the state of Michigan and had, at the time of the meeting, 371 paid members, 282 of whom were Full members and 89 of whom were Associate members.

With the formal establishment of AIR accomplished, Doi (1979) observed that the "old guard" who had been involved in the early workshops and NIRF meetings made an interesting decision with regard to the role they would play in the future of the Association:

> Rather than controlling the new association, as they readily might have done, they chose to turn the reins over to the new corps of institutional researchers as quickly as possible. Their intent was to hasten the development of a broad base of leadership for institutional research.
>
> By 1970, none of the forty or so individuals who had participated in the first forum in 1961 occupied a leadership position in AIR; for a professional association, this must have been something of a record. True, not all forty were active in institutional research in 1970, but a number were. More to the point, however, the decision by the older, more experienced leaders to take a back seat in the affairs had two unintended consequences. First, for a least a half dozen years, the AIR conferences were dominated by a concern for identity and utility. What is institutional research? Who are we? Does what we do have significant impact upon decision making? These are obviously questions of importance to recently appointed institutional research directors, but they are hardly those that would advance the state of the art. Second, the technical papers themselves, by and large, reflected ignorance of historical antecedents. As Paul Jedamus of the University of Colorado remarked on more than one occasion, it was as if the profession had no memory. (Doi, 1979, pp. 36–37)

Although AIR was formally established as an organization in 1965, no central office existed until 1974. Therefore the earlier presidents of AIR essentially conducted the Association's business with significant support from their home institutions. Officers were elected from a double slate of candidates suggested by the Executive Committee until an elected Nominating Committee was established in 1976–77. Individuals elected as vice-president would become president the following year and were faced with the additional obligation of serving as Forum chair during their year as vice-president. This practice would continue until separate Forum chair and associate Forum chair positions were established in 1980.

Establishment of AIR Affiliated Regional, State, and Special Interest Groups

While ACE and the regional compacts were the leading advocates for the establishment of Offices of Institutional Research, AIR members took primary responsibility for the establishment of affiliated state, regional, and special interest groups of IR practitioners. AIR strove to encourage the formation of such groups through the establishment of an Affiliated Groups Committee in 1978–79. The first formal listing of Affiliated Regional/Special Interest Groups, appearing in the *1981–82 AIR Directory and Proceedings* of the Association (pp. 134–135), identified thirteen state or regional affiliated groups in the United States and two community college oriented groups—the National Council for Research and Planning (NCRP) and the Southern Association of Community College Researchers (SACCR).

In contrast, in 2010, the AIR website listed fifty-six groups formally affiliated with AIR, including seven international associations, six multistate regional associations, and twenty-nine single-state associations in the United States. Also included among the AIR Affiliated Groups were seven specialized subgroupings of institutional researchers within a single state, such as the City University of New York Council on Institutional Research, and seven mutual interest associations, including such groups as the Traditionally Black Colleges and Universities (TBCU), Institutional Research Faculty, and the New England Educational Assessment Network.

Among the first state-level organizations, the Florida Association for Institutional Research has held annual conferences since 1968, although it did not formally adopt a constitution until 1987. California held its first conference in 1971, with Sidney Suslow of the University of California at Berkeley as the keynote speaker. In 1973, the North Carolina Association for Institutional Research (NCAIR) was among the first groups to formally adopt a constitution and to formally affiliate with AIR. At the multistate regional level, regional interstate associations such as Rocky Mountain AIR and the Association for Institutional Research in the Upper Midwest (AIRUM) began to hold conferences in 1971 while the Southern Association for Institutional Research

(SAIR) and North East Association for Institutional Research trace their first meetings and origins back to 1974.

Establishment of AIR Affiliated International Groups

Theoretically, in terms of methodological and analytic approaches, AIR has seen and continues to see itself as truly international in scope. In reality, AIR's membership base and programmatic offerings have become more and more responsive to issues and forces affecting American higher education. Forums held in Canada, including those in Vancouver (1973), Montreal (1977), and Toronto (1983, 2002, and 2011), have become less common as membership and attendance at the AIR Forum from Canada and other countries have decreased in both numbers and percentage over the past twenty years.

Decreases in non-U.S. AIR membership and Forum participation stem primarily from the formation and growth of seven institutional research associations in other parts of the world that have become affiliated with AIR. The oldest and largest of these associations is the European Association for Institutional Research (EAIR), which held its first Forum in 1979. EAIR has since changed its name to the European Higher Education Society. It has nearly 500 members, and maintains its Secretariat in Amsterdam. Like AIR, the Society publishes its own journal and monograph series.

More recently established international associations include the Australasian Association for Institutional Research (1988), which has published the *Journal of Institutional Research* since 1991; the Southern African Association for Institutional Research (1994); the Canadian Institutional Research and Planning Association (CIRPA, 1994); the Higher Education Research and Policy Network based in Nigeria (2000); and the South East Asian Association for Institutional Research (2001). In addition, the Overseas Chinese Association for Institutional Research was established in 1996. As a "virtual" organization, it discusses issues over the Internet and meets face to face annually at the AIR Forum. Brief profiles of each of these international associations are available online in CIRPA's April 2010 newsletter at http://www.cirpa-acpri.ca/images/newsletter_pdfs/vol 12no2eng.pdf. For a comparison of common external conditions shaping management and institutional research in the United States and Europe at the time of the twenty-fifth anniversary forums of EAIR and AIR, see Peterson, 2003.

Alternative Views of IR: Research, Administrative Support, or Self-Study?

Embedded in AIR's origins and continuing to the present is a fundamental question: Was the association to be theoretical in nature, intended to contribute to basic understandings of the higher education enterprise, or was it to be concerned with problems of a purely operational nature? Could it serve both purposes? References to several key publications highlight important sources that helped to frame the debate and set the stage for further discussion in other chapters of this *Handbook.*

In his article "Can Institutional Research Lead to a Science of Institutions?" Dyer (1966) summarized the fundamental debate—whether institutional research should be theoretical or operational in nature—by indicating the seemingly polar opposite positions taken by Nevitt Sanford and John Dale Russell.

The theoretical perspective is perhaps best stated in the last chapter of Sanford's monumental work *The American College: A Psychological and Sociological Interpretation of the Higher Learning* (Sanford, 1962, 1009–1034). The operational views of John Dale Russell appear in many places but are perhaps most succinctly summarized in a presentation, "The Purpose and Organization of Institutional Research," made at the same 1959 Stanford workshop sponsored by WICHE in which Cowley traced the history of institutional research back more than 250 years (Russell, 1960, pp. 17–22).

Dyer concludes that both views must be integrated because "either approach if used by itself is almost certain to be sterile; used together they have an outside chance of changing things for the better" (Dyer, 1966, p. 454). The centrality and relevance of Dyer's article to the debate over the role of institutional research is further highlighted in the first AIR presidential address (Stecklein, 1966) and the fact that these discussions continue to the present.

Paul Dressel, founder of the Office of Institutional Research at Michigan State University, took the middle ground in the Sanford-Russell debate, arguing for institutional research as an independent force empowered to objectively look into all aspects of an institution, especially the self-study and long-range planning processes (Dressel, 1964). Later, in *Institutional Research in the University: A Handbook,* Dressel states: "The basic purpose of institutional research is to probe deeply into the workings of an institution for evidence of weakness or flaws which interfere with the attainment of its purposes or which utilize an undue amount of resources in so doing. In the search for flaws, no function, individual, or unit should be regarded as off limits" (Dressel & Associates, 1971, p. 23).

Interpreting and Providing Examples of IR to IR Practitioners

Prior to the vote to formally establish AIR in 1965, examples of institutional research of interest to would-be practitioners or those already engaged in institutional research were limited, by and large, to the fugitive publishing of occasional workshop proceedings. A rare exception is a monograph published at the University of Wisconsin, *Basis for Decision: A Composite of Institutional Research Methods and Reports of Colleges and Universities* (Lins, 1963). In the Foreword, the editor indicated that the publication was "presented as a service to persons interested in and concerned with institutional research. It is hoped that it will, in at least a small way, fill a felt need—that of providing an avenue for exchange of methods and results of research" (Lins, 1963, p. iii). Among the 29 complete or summarized studies contained in the document are a study of Faculty Satisfactions and Dissatisfactions by John Dale Russell and a study of College Preparatory Course Work coauthored by James Montgomery, the second president of AIR. Indeed, it was the discovery of the Lins document that led the author of this chapter to pursue a doctoral program and career with an emphasis on institutional research.

As a fledgling organization and field of endeavor, AIR needed to explain what institutional research was all about to a growing number of interested administrators, as well as to AIR members and potential members. A publication titled *A Look at the Charter Members of AIR* (Bureau of Institutional Research, 1966) helped to serve this need through an analysis of the characteristics of AIR's 382 charter members. The survey noted, among other things, memberships in other professional organizations, the types and sizes of institutions employing AIR members, levels and fields of academic preparation, age, sex (90 percent were male), academic rank (held by 42 percent), and the types of duties and studies in which charter members were engaged.

The study of the 1966 Charter Members of the Association was updated by Tincher (1970). By 1970, membership in AIR had increased 136 percent, from 382 in 1966 to 902. Four years after its founding, 223 of the 382 (58 percent) of AIR's original charter members had retained their membership. In 1970, approximately 84 percent of the membership was employed in college and university settings, while about half of the remaining membership was employed by state-supported agencies or coordinating groups. The number of AIR members employed in state agency, non-campus settings was the most rapidly growing group, increasing from 19 to 50 in the four-year period. AIR membership would increase to 1,765 in 1980, 2,485 in 1990, 3,097 in 2000, and approximately 4,200 in 2010. A much more detailed account of the development of the Association for Institutional Research, decade by decade, over the last fifty years is provided by Howard (2011) and Lasher (2011).

A second type of publication of the Association, titled *Memo to a Newcomer to the Field of Institutional Research* (Saupe, 1967), provided advice to administrators and those charged with setting up Offices of Institutional Research. It suggested a range of higher education associations with related interests, journals or other publications to which an office might wish to subscribe, and academic centers for the study of higher education that might offer courses or programs of interest (four were listed), and it included a brief bibliography on institutional research.

Memorandum to a Newcomer in the Field of Institutional Research (Lyons, 1976) essentially updated Saupe's earlier document. Its purpose was to "provide the newly appointed institutional research officer with a descriptive compendium of available resources" (p. i). Lyons lamented that institutional research in the preceding decade had become more subject to a management orientation, so that "most institutional researchers find themselves spending more and more time compiling data about current institutional operations" (p. 1). The number of academic research centers for the study of higher education had increased from four to ten. There were additions to the list of periodic publications that AIR recommended an Office of Institutional Research subscribe to: *Change Magazine* and the New Directions for Institutional Research, New Directions for Higher Education, and New Directions for Community Colleges series published by Jossey-Bass, which did not exist at the time of Saupe's 1967 publication.

An important question, regularly discussed at the Forums from their inception, related to whether institutional research is truly a profession and whether it possesses a code of ethics particular to the craft (McLaughlin & Howard, 2001). The "annual angst" of such discussions and the process of developing a code of ethics for AIR practitioners is reflected in *Ethics and Standards in Institutional Research* (Schiltz, 1992). Much of the material in this particular volume was the work of AIR's Committee on Standards and Ethics of the Association, which led to the development of a Code of Ethics adopted initially by the membership in 1992, and subsequently updated in 2001. Major sections of the Code speak to competence, practice, confidentiality, as well as relationships to the community and to the craft.

Interpreting IR to the Broader Higher Education Community

Institutional researchers sometimes have enough difficulty explaining to their own families and institutions the somewhat esoteric nature of what they do for a living. It is even more challenging to explain the nature and benefits of institutional research to broader audiences. The first such attempts, as previously noted, were made by advocates for the establishment of such offices not directly employed in campus-based institutional research settings (Brumbaugh, 1960; Dyer, 1966; Rourke & Brooks, 1966). Of the subsequent efforts by the Association for Institutional Research or individual IR practitioners to articulate to broader audiences the needs, benefits, and challenges facing institutional research, those especially worthy of note are described in this section.

The first statement prepared for AIR that was intended to interpret institutional research to a wider audience than those already in the choir was *The Nature and Role of Institutional Research* (Saupe and Montgomery, 1970). The questions addressed included:

- What is institutional research?
- How pure can institutional research be?
- What can institutional research do for the institution?

- Should institutional research be administratively or educationally oriented?
- How should institutional research relate to long-range planning?
- How should institutional research be organized?
- What are the requirements for effective institutional research?

A more current version of Saupe and Montgomery's 1970 monograph bears the title *The Functions of Institutional Research*, second edition (Saupe, 1990). This monograph is actually a revision of a similar document produced by Saupe in 1981.

Mindful of Cowley's (1960) plea for institutional research to be stated more convincingly, AIR obtained a grant from the Esso Education Foundation to support an invitational conference with fifteen participants that met at Shakertown in Pleasant Hill, Kentucky, in 1971. The result of the conference was *A Declaration on Institutional Research* (Suslow, 1972).

Occasionally, individual practitioners are asked to provide brief introductions to the field for external audiences. An entry in the *International Encyclopedia of Higher Education*, "Institutional Research," provides an example of this type of overview (Sheehan & Torrence, 1977). Although primarily reflecting North American patterns in the conduct of institutional research, the article indicates that in Europe institutional research functions are often circumscribed by the nature of the state's control over institutions of higher education. Both continental and British institutions also noted a tendency to co-opt faculty for ad hoc studies rather than developing permanent analytical staff (p. 2184). For those willing to accept information at face value the "institutional research" entry in Wikipedia may suffice. Like all Wikipedia entries, the authorship is unknown, but the Wikipedia entry does direct individuals to several other sources, including the AIR website.

Among the most recent and notable publications that help to interpret institutional research to those in the broader higher education community is an entry in the New Directions for Higher Education (NDHE) series titled *Institutional Research: More Than Just Data* (Terkla, 2008). This volume helps demonstrate—to a wider audience than the institutional research community alone—that institutional researchers are more than "bean counters" who are sometimes reputed to know the cost of everything and the value of nothing.

Adding Perspective: Some Key Sources

All too seldom does a profession or practitioners of that profession take the opportunity to reexamine where their profession has been and where it is going, unless there is a specific occasion to do so or the practitioners choose to take time out for reflection. In this regard, three primary resources that provide perspective on the development of the field of institutional research are *Institutional Research in the University: A Handbook* (Dressel & Associates,

1971), *Improving Academic Management: A Handbook of Planning and Institutional Research* (Jedamus & Peterson, 1980), and the *ASHE Reader on Planning and Institutional Research* (Peterson & Associates, 1999).

Persons choosing to search the Web on the term *institutional research* would find many references to the web pages for specific offices of institutional research or studies produced by such offices, but surprisingly few entries that focus specifically on the field of institutional research. Indeed, the New Directions for Institutional Research (NDIR) series, which has produced more than 150 quarterly sourcebooks since its inception in 1974, includes only two issues that provide integrated retrospective views of the profession (Peterson & Corcoran, 1985; Volkwein, 1999b). In a third NDIR volume, future possibilities for the redesign and transformation of institutional research are examined (Leimer, 2009).

Faced with an unprecedented period of two successive years of decline in AIR membership—from 1,869 members in 1981–82 to 1,627 members in 1982–83 and to 1,544 members in 1983–84—in September 1982 the Association appointed a twelve-member Commission to Reassess the Purposes and Objectives of the Association. The Commission examined the role of institutional research in the higher education environment of the 1980s, the purposes of the Association, and the visibility of the profession and the Association in postsecondary education. Also examined were AIR's membership base, international activities, input into policy development, and AIR's service to its members (Reichard, 1984).

The Commission made ten recommendations. Its report spoke of the need to develop a year-round array of professional services that would serve its members between forums; the need to recruit "invisible" institutional researchers employed outside of formally designated offices of institutional research; and the need to understand more fully how the efforts of AIR and affiliated regional, state, provincial, and international groups might best complement each other. The Commission's report led to a substantially increased commitment by the Association to enhancing the professional development of its members and expanded input by the Association and its members in the development of federal and state data collection policies.

A special volume of NDIR that coincided with AIR's twenty-fifth anniversary Forum was both retrospective and prospective (Peterson & Corcoran, 1985). The lead chapter by Peterson (1985) identified three main periods for institutional research development: (1) the emergence of the profession in the 1950s and1960s, (2) a period of growth and consolidation in the 1970s, and (3) a period of fragmentation and uncertainty in the 1980s. For each of these periods, forces affecting higher education were examined in relation to the practice of institutional research, the profession of institutional research, and developments within the Association for Institutional Research.

The second chapter in the NDIR volume, coinciding with the twenty-fifth anniversary Forum, traced the various theoretical bases, methods of inquiry, and empirical findings that might suggest that the field of institutional research was predominantly either an art or a science. Fincher (1985) concluded that the merits of institutional research were less dependent on its scientific underpinnings than on its relevance in decision and policy making.

Of special interest for its substance and clarity is the keynote address at the 1995 Forum in Boston, titled "Evolution and Revolution in Institutional Research" (Terenzini, 1995). This presentation expands on Terenzini's conception of the nature of institutional research (1993) and traces the emergence of institutional research in the 1950s and 1960s; the growth, consolidation, and analytical developments of the 1970s; as well as the assessment, planning, and quality assurance emphases, which led to the dispersion of institutional research functions in the 1980s and beyond.

The chapter titled "The Role of Institutional Research: From Improvement to Redesign" (Peterson, 1999) extends Peterson's earlier (1985) work by expanding the analyses of evolutionary forces affecting institutional research through the last fifteen years of the twentieth century. This chapter is the last chapter in the NDIR volume titled *What Is Institutional Research All About? A Critical and Comprehensive Assessment of the Profession* (Volkwein, 1999b). It analyzes twenty-first-century challenges and the forces reshaping the postsecondary knowledge industry. Institutional research is seen as a force for institutional redesign. Peterson concludes that "institutional research has flourished as an institutional function and a profession because it has contributed to institutions' *adaptive function* and has played a major role in fostering and assisting institutional change" (p. 84).

The chapter titled "The Foundations and Evolution of Institutional Research" (Volkwein, 2008) expands on Volkwein's earlier work (1999a, 1999b) and presents an overview of the evolution of institutional research, as well as a description of the many different topics addressed by institutional research practitioners in highly varied organizational settings. This chapter, and the entire NDHE volume of which it is a part, provides valuable insights for those new to the profession of institutional research as well as those with responsibilities for supervising the institutional research function who may not have had previous professional experience in the area.

Concluding Note

From an informal invitational meeting with forty-six in attendance at the first National Institutional Research Forum in 1961, to a vibrant professional organization with over four thousand members some fifty years later, the Association for Institutional Research and the profession of institutional research, wherever practiced throughout the world, have continued to grow and adapt to changing roles and conditions.

More than thirty years ago, Doi (1979) attributed the viability of institutional research to the confluence of actors and events with reciprocal interests, including (1) the regional interstate compacts for higher education, which served as the first advocates for establishing institutional research offices; (2) the spread of state-wide coordination of higher education, from nine states in 1954 to forty-eight states in 1978; and (3) the growth of research into the higher education enterprise and development of instruments of interest to individual institutions by organizations such as the Educational Testing Service, American College Testing Program, or the National Center for Higher Education Management Systems (NCHEMS); and (4) the growth of graduate programs in higher education whose professors expand the perspectives of institutional research practitioners, and whose academic departments occasionally provide a home base for practitioners who seek a more contemplative life later in their careers.

Today, although the names of actors, issues, and technology have changed, the factors identified by Doi still exist. Integrated Postsecondary Education Data System (IPEDS) reporting and the need for institutional research involvement in assessment, accreditation, and institutional effectiveness processes (Reichard & Marchese, 1987) have created what some refer to as the "First and Second Full-Time Employment Acts for Institutional Researchers." Meeting such needs, as described in other portions of this *Handbook*, may account in part for the continued growth of the Association for Institutional Research. However, we need to be continually reminded that institutional research is, indeed, about more than just data.

Whether institutional research is destined to play a leading or a supporting role in addressing the postsecondary knowledge industry's future needs is open to debate. If institutional researchers and those concerned with the profession can add perspective to the institutional issues at hand and contribute meaningfully to the further development of analytical processes at their institutions, the prospects for the next fifty years will most likely be bright for the institutional research profession and its professionals.

References

Axt, R. G., & Sprague, H. T. (Eds.). (1960). *College self-study: Lectures on institutional research.* Boulder, CO: The Western Interstate Commission for Higher Education.

Brumbaugh, A. J. (1960). *Research designed to improve institutions of higher learning.* Washington, DC: American Council on Education.

Bureau of Institutional Research, University of Minnesota. (1966). *A look at the charter members of AIR.* Minneapolis, MN: University of Minnesota.

Cooke, M. L. (1910). *Academic and industrial efficiency.* New York: Carnegie Foundation for the Advancement of Teaching.

Cowley, W. H. (1960). Two and a half centuries of institutional research. In R. G. Axt and H. T. Sprague (Eds.), *College self studies: Lectures on institutional research.* Boulder, CO: Western Interstate Commission on Higher Education, 1–16.

Doi, J. L. (1979). The beginnings of a profession. In R. G. Cope (Ed.), *Professional development for institutional research* (pp. 33–41). New Directions for Institutional Research, no. 23. San Francisco: Jossey-Bass.

Dressel, P. L. (1964). A comprehensive and continuing program of institutional research. In E. McGrath (Ed.), *Cooperative long-range planning in liberal arts colleges* (pp. 37–49). New York: Teachers College, Columbia University,.

Dressel, P. L., & Associates. (1971). *Institutional research in the university: A handbook.* San Francisco: Jossey-Bass.

Dyer, H. S. (1966). Can institutional research lead to a science of institutions? *Educational Record,* 452–466.

Eells, W. C. (1937). *Surveys of American higher education.* New York: Carnegie Foundation for the Advancement of Teaching.

Fincher, C. (1985). The art and science of institutional research. In M. W. Peterson and M. Corcoran (Eds.), *Institutional research in transition* (pp. 17–37). New Directions for Institutional Research, no. 46. San Francisco: Jossey-Bass.

Howard, R. D. (2011). AIR History—Governance, Policies, and Services—Perspectives of Past Presidents 1965–2010. In M. A. Coughlin & R. D. Howard (Eds.), *The Association for Institutional Research: The First 50 Years.* Tallahassee, FL: Association for Institutional Research.

Jedamus, P., & Peterson, M. W. (Eds.). (1980). *Improving academic management: A handbook of planning and institutional research.* San Francisco: Jossey-Bass.

Lasher, W. F. (2011). The history of institutional research and its role in American higher education over the past 50 years. In M. A. Coughlin & R. D. Howard (Eds.), *The Association for Institutional Research: The first 50 years.* Tallahassee, FL: Association for Institutional Research.

Leimer, C. (Ed.). (2009). *Imagining the future of institutional research.* New Directions for Institutional Research, no. 143. San Francisco: Jossey-Bass.

Lins, L. J. (1963). *Basis for decision: A composite of institutional research methods and reports of colleges and universities.* Madison, WI: Dembar Educational Research Services. Also in *Journal of Experimental Education,* 1962, *31*(2), 88–234.

Lins, L. J. (1966). The Association for Institutional Research: A history. In C. H. Bagley (Ed.), *Research on academic input.* Proceedings of the Sixth Annual Forum of the Association for Institutional Research, Boston, Massachusetts, i–iii.

Lyons, J. L. (1976). *Memorandum to a newcomer to the field of institutional research.* Tallahassee, FL: Association for Institutional Research.

McLaughlin, G. W., & Howard, R. D. (2001). Theory, practice, and ethics of institutional research. In R. D. Howard (Ed.), *Institutional research: Decision support in higher education* (pp. 163–194). Tallahassee, FL: Association for Institutional Research.

Niehoff, R. O. (1991). *Floyd W. Reeves: Innovative educator and distinguished practitioner of the art of public administration.* Lanham, MD: University Press of America.

Peterson, M. W. (1985). Institutional research: An evolutionary perspective. In M. W. Peterson and M. Corcoran (Eds.), *Institutional research in transition* (pp. 5–15). New Directions for Institutional Research, no. 46. San Francisco: Jossey-Bass.

Peterson, M. W. (1999). The role of institutional research: From improvement to redesign. In J. F. Volkwein (Ed.), *What is institutional research all about? A critical and comprehensive assessment of the profession* (pp. 83–103). New Directions for Institutional Research, no. 104. San Francisco: Jossey-Bass.

Peterson, M. W. (2003). Institutional research and management in the U.S. and Europe: Some EAIR-AIR comparisons. In R. Begg (Ed.), *The dialogue between higher education research and practice* (pp. 1–15). Dordrecht, the Netherlands: Kulwer Academic Publishers.

Peterson, M. W., & Associates (Ed). (1999). *ASHE reader on planning and institutional research.* Needham, MA: Pearson Custom Publishing.

Peterson, M. W., & Corcoran, M. (1985). Proliferation or professional integration: Transition or transformation. In M. W. Peterson and M. Corcoran (Eds.), *Institutional research in transition* (pp. 99–112). New Directions for Institutional Research, no. 46. San Francisco: Jossey-Bass.

Peterson, M. W., Dill, D. D., Mets, L. A., & Associates. (1997). *Planning and management for a changing environment.* San Francisco: Jossey-Bass.

Reichard, D. J. (Chair). (1984). Final report of the commission to reassess the purposes and objectives of the Association. *AIR 1984–85 Directory* (pp. 16–39). Tallahassee, FL: Association for Institutional Research.

Reichard, D. J., & Marchese, T. J. (1987). Assessment, accreditation, and institutional effectiveness: Implications for our profession. Presidential Session in *Managing Education Better: Technology and Tomorrow* (pp. 27–42). 27th Annual Forum of the Association for Institutional Research, Kansas City, MO.

Rourke, F. E., & Brooks, G. E. (1966). *The managerial revolution in higher education.* Baltimore, MD: Johns Hopkins University Press.

Russell, J. D. (1960). The purpose and orgainization of institutional research. In R. G. Axt & H. T. Sprague (Eds.), *College self studies: Lectures on institutional research.* Boulder, CO: Western Interstate Commission on Higher Education, 17–22.

Sanford, N. (1962). Research and policy in higher education. In N. Sanford (Ed.), *The American college: A psychological and sociological interpretation of the higher learning* (pp. 1009–1034). New York: Wiley.

Saupe, J. L. (1967). *Memo to a newcomer to the field of institutional research.* Tallahassee, FL: Association for Institutional Research.

Saupe, J. L. (1990). *The functions of institutional research* (2nd ed.). Tallahassee, FL: Association for Institutional Research.

Saupe, J. L. (2005, November 10). How old is institutional research and how did it develop? Presentation made at the Annual Mid-America Association for Institutional Research (MIDAIR).

Saupe, J. L., & Montgomery, J. R. (1970). *The nature and role of institutional research: Memo to a college or university.* Tallahassee, FL: Association for Institutional Research.

Schietinger, E. F. (Ed.). (1968). *Introductory papers on institutional research.* Atlanta: Southern Regional Education Board.

Schietinger, E. F. (1979). Origins of IR. *Research in Higher Education, 10,* 371–374.

Schiltz, M. E. (Ed.). (1992). *Ethics and standards in institutional research.* New Directions for Institutional Research, no. 73. San Francisco: Jossey-Bass.

Scroggs, S. (1938). *Systematic fact-finding and research in the administration of higher education.* Doctoral dissertation, Yale University. Ann Arbor, MI: Edwards Brothers.

Sheehan, B. S., & Torrence, L. E. (1977). Institutional research. In A. S. Knowles (Ed.), *International Encyclopedia of Education* (pp. 2184–2193). San Francisco: Jossey-Bass.

Stecklein, J. E. (1960). Institutional research at the Universities of Colorado, Wisconsin, and Minnesota. In R. G. Axt & H. T. Sprague (Eds.), *College self-studies: Lectures on institutional research.* Boulder, CO: Western Interstate Commission on Higher Education, 31–35.

Stecklein, J. E. (1966). President's address: The birth of a profession. In C. H. Bagley (Ed.), *Research on academic input* (pp. 9–13). Proceedings of the Sixth Annual Forum of the Association for Institutional Research, Boston, MA.

Stickler, W. H. (1968). The role of institutional research in the managerial revolution in higher education: An overview. In E. F. Schietinger (Ed.), *Introductory papers on institutional research* (pp. 1–15). Atlanta: Southern Regional Education Board.

Suslow, S. (1972). *A declaration on institutional research.* Esso Education Foundation and Association for Institutional Research.

Terenzini, P. T. (1993). On the nature of institutional research and the knowledge and skills it requires. *Research in Higher Education, 34,* 1–10.

Terenzini, P. T. (1995). Evolution and revolution in institutional research. Keynote address at AIR Forum, Boston, MA.

Terkla, D. G. (Ed.). (2008). *Institutional research: More than just data.* New Directions for Higher Education, no. 141. San Francisco: Jossey-Bass.

Tetlow, W. L. (1973). *Institutional research: The emergence of a staff function in higher education.* Doctoral dissertation, Cornell University.

Tincher, W. A. (1970). *A study of the members of the Association for Institutional Research.* The Association for Institutional Research.

Volkwein, J. F. (1999a). The four faces of institutional research. In J. F. Volkwein (Ed.), *What is institutional research all about? A critical and comprehensive assessment of the profession* (pp. 9–19). New Directions for Institutional Research, no. 104. San Francisco: Jossey-Bass.

Volkwein, J. F. (Ed.). (1999b). *What is institutional research all about? A critical and comprehensive assessment of the profession.* New Directions for Institutional Research, no. 104. San Francisco: Jossey-Bass.

Volkwein, J. F. (2008). The foundations and evolution of institutional research. In D. G. Terkla (Ed.), *Institutional research: More than just data* (pp. 5–20). New Directions for Higher Education, no. 141. San Francisco: Jossey-Bass.

CHAPTER 2

THE STRUCTURE AND FUNCTIONS OF INSTITUTIONAL RESEARCH OFFICES

J. Fredericks Volkwein, Ying (Jessie) Liu, and James Woodell

"What is institutional research?" Almost every IR professional who has been in the field for more than a couple of years can tell a story of being in a crowded elevator between floors at a conference hotel, when another passenger notices our name badges and asks this magic question. Many of us have given stammering, perhaps even humorous responses to that question. But two of the most widely accepted definitions are Joe Saupe's (1990) notion of IR as *decision support*—a set of activities that provide support for institutional planning, policy formation, and decision making—and Cameron Fincher's (1978) description of IR as *organizational intelligence.*

Pat Terenzini has elaborated on this idea by describing three tiers of organizational intelligence (1993). The first, most basic tier of organizational intelligence is *technical and analytical.* This is the type of intelligence that you need in order to produce the facts and figures that describe the basic profile of an institution: admissions, enrollment, degrees awarded, faculty workload, and finances. Technical and analytical intelligence also includes the entry-level tools that you need, in the form of spreadsheets, knowledge of statistics, software packages like SPSS, and survey research skills, among others.

Terenzini's second level, on which the first tier is built, is *issues intelligence.* This includes knowledge not just about the technical aspects of the job but also about the particular issues that the institution faces—student and faculty diversity, resource allocation priorities, the need for program evaluation and improvement, enrollment goal setting, and capital construction. Issues intelligence also requires knowing about the key people at the institution and working with them to address these issues.

Thus tier one is more basic than tier two, and tiers one and two are both more basic than tier three: contextual intelligence. The context involves knowing the institution not only internally, but also externally—its history, its culture, its evolution, and its external environment. The sum total of contextual intelligence understands all the relevant trends in the external environment—financial, social, political, and demographic. (Several chapters in this volume draw on Terenzini's framework; see, in particular, Chapter 3 for a more detailed discussion.)

The Organizational Characteristics of Institutional Research

Much of what we know about the profession of institutional research comes from several multistate and national surveys of AIR and regional members (Peterson, 1985; Volkwein, 1990; Knight, Moore, & Coperthwaite, 1997; Lindquist, 1999; Muffo, 1999). To update these surveys from the 1980s and 1990s, the Center for the Study of Higher Education at Penn State undertook a National Survey of Institutional Research Offices in 2008–09. We received responses from over 1,100 IR offices employing over 3,300 professional staff. Although this survey indicates that IR offices on average employ three professional staff, the range is quite broad—from offices with a single part-time person to offices of twenty-two professional full-time employees (see Figure 2.1).

What does the national survey tell us about professional identity? We know that 38 percent of the offices in colleges and universities use traditional titles containing words like *institutional research, analysis, information, reporting,* or *studies.* A second large group (35 percent) of offices falls under the umbrella represented by words like *assessment, accountability, accreditation, evaluation, effectiveness,* and *performance.* We see that there is a wide array of other titles as well. Institutional researchers and IR functions are imbedded in offices of strategic planning, enrollment management, budget, policy analysis, even registration and information technology. But it is important to recognize that institutional research, whatever is called, is not necessarily limited to colleges and universities. We know from these surveys that foundations, government bureaus, state education departments, and research-oriented organizations of many varieties also hire people with training in research and analysis, and that this constitutes about 10 percent of AIR membership. We conclude that the professional identity of the profession is diverse and complex.

If you look across the American higher education landscape, you will see that at most institutions there are strong connections, if not formal organizational arrangements, that unite the people in these three analytical functions: (1) institutional reporting and administrative policy analysis; (2) strategic planning, enrollment and financial management; and (3) outcomes assessment, program review, accountability, accreditation, and institutional effectiveness. These constitute the golden triangle of institutional research (Figure 2.2) because they dominate most of the practice of IR in the United States. As we shall see in the discussion that follows, campuses differ in the extent to which they combine these functions or keep them separate.

FIGURE 2.1   IR OFFICE SIZE: FTE PROFESSIONALS

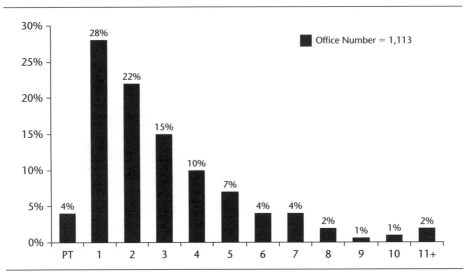

Source: Volkwein, Liu, and Woodell, Penn State University.

FIGURE 2.2   THE GOLDEN TRIANGLE OF INSTITUTIONAL RESEARCH

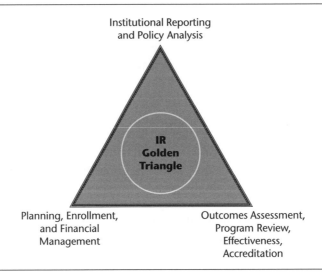

The Evolution of IR

Volkwein (2008) and Peterson (1985, 1999) summarize the evolution of institutional research and place IR in the context of the larger changes that are taking place in society and in higher education. Certainly, the changes in higher education over the decades have been remarkable.

In Chapter 1 of this volume, Reichard provides a detailed description of the evolution of the institutional research as a profession. The IR profession was born five decades ago when its primary role required it to produce accurate numbers, descriptive statistics, and fact books. It quickly evolved during a period where there was much more analysis and evaluation, both quantitative and qualitative. Now we are in a period where demands for IR skills require multivariate analysis and modeling skills: projecting admissions yield, identifying the student experiences that produce beneficial outcomes, modeling alternative scenarios of tuition and financial aid and their impact on enrollment and revenue. Certainly, we see growth in the emphasis on accountability and performance, technology and information systems, outcomes assessment, and studies of persistence and retention. Institutional researchers report all of these as increasingly important to their job responsibilities.

Driven by the winds of accountability, accreditation, quality assurance, and competition, institutions of higher education throughout the world are making large investments in their analytical and research capacities. This is reflected in the growth of AIR membership, from under 1,000 in the mid-1970s (with about 500 at the annual conference) to around 4,000 in recent years (with 1,700 at the annual conference). State and regional affiliates of AIR have experienced similar growth.

Organizational arrangements and assigned tasks for IR are highly variable from campus to campus. Figure 2.3 shows the organizational arrangements

FIGURE 2.3 IR OFFICE ORGANIZATIONAL LOCATION AND REPORTING LEVEL

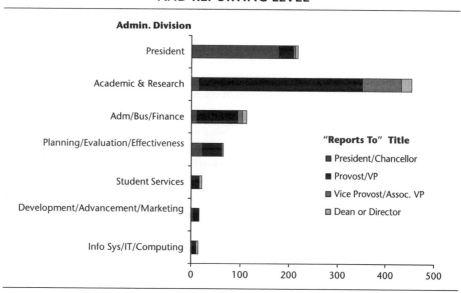

for the campus-based offices in our 2008 study. The length of each bar indicates the number of offices in each administrative division. The shading in each bar designates the title of the person to whom the office reports. We found that about 84 percent of responding offices report to senior management, someone with the title of president, chancellor, provost, or vice president. Only 16 percent report to those with lesser titles.

Figure 2.3 also shows that the most common organizational location for IR is in the academic affairs division, reporting to the chief academic officer, provost, or vice president. In these situations the typical office is heavily engaged in studies that are directly connected to the instructional and academic side of the institution—studies of faculty instructional workload and salary equity, student ratings of instruction, and faculty research and scholarship. Many other IR offices report to the president or chancellor, and this is especially true in relatively small institutions and on larger campuses where the title of planning is in the title of the office or in the person's job description. If the IR function is located in finance and business, it is much more likely to be carrying out studies that support the resource allocation process and making enrollment and revenue projections.

Development and alumni operations increasingly hire researchers to engage in activities and analysis to support fundraising and alumni development. Chief student affairs officers need professionals to help them engage in studies of campus climate, residential life, the first-year experience, retention and diversity, and the effectiveness of student services and how they might be improved. So these are other growth areas within the larger picture of IR.

There is inconclusive evidence about the maturity of the profession based on the degree attainment and the experience levels of members of AIR as reported in various surveys during the past three decades. Table 2.1 aggregates the results of several national and regional surveys in the 1980s and 1990s and compares them with our 2008 survey. IR directors and others with the highest-ranking title in each office make up consistently higher proportions of those with doctoral degrees and years of experience, and they are more likely to have received their training in the social sciences and education fields, from which the profession still draws about half of its personnel. However, judging by the 2008 percentages for "all staff," growth in the field appears to be occurring among those without doctorates majoring in scientific fields, technology, engineering, math, business administration, and accounting.

In the aggregate, the degree credentials of the IR workforce appear rather modest. Three in ten working IR professionals (and one in ten IR office heads) have a bachelor's degree or less. In the largest offices, the proportion of IR professionals with no graduate degree is often above 50 percent. This does not give staff much legitimacy (nor career advancement potential) in an academic organization.

TABLE 2.1 HIGHEST DEGREE AND YEARS EXPERIENCE

	1980s	1990s	2008	2008
	All Staff	All Staff	All Staff	Office Heads
Highest Degree				
Doctorate	33%	38%	25%	46%
Masters	46	50	45	44
Field of Highest Degree				
Social Sciences	39	34	30	33
Education	26	31	19	30
STEM Fields	14	13	23	15
Business and Accounting	11	16	18	16
Humanities/Other	8	6	10	6
Years of Experience in IR				
0–2	20	19	26	14
3–5	20	16	22	19
6–10	21	25	23	26
11+	39	40	29	41
20+	na	na	12	19

An Institutional Research Ecology

Building on the work of Peterson (1985), Volkwein (1990, 2008) has been collecting information since the 1980s about the structures and functions of IR offices. In addition, Muffo (1999) summarized the regional and state studies of IR offices. Confirming the diversity of IR as a profession, several studies in separate years show dramatically different IR office sizes, with an average of five people per office in Canada and four people in the South, whereas one- and two-person offices are quite common in New England and the Northeast.

Some IR offices are fairly new and underdeveloped, sometimes with a single person who has been pulled out of the faculty and given the IR assignment by the president or provost. We also see large mature offices that are relatively well established and have gained the confidence of the president and the provost over time. In other cases, institutional research is highly fragmented and IR activities take place in many different pockets and corners of the campus. A four-part ecology reflects and describes what we see in the field (Volkwein, 1990, 2008).

Craft structure is the term used for the surprisingly large number of one- and two-person offices that are highly burdened by mandated routine reporting and a modest amount of number-crunching for the institution. These people and these offices dominate the ranks of institutions with enrollments under five thousand, but they also characterize the fragmented model on large campuses where every vice president and many deans have their own IR person. The work agendas for craft structures are highly responsive to their administrative hosts.

Many craft structures evolve and grow into *small adhocracies*, especially if the institution is not fragmented into silos. These are the two- and three-person offices that have grown into an intermediate stage of development. These offices have a flat hierarchy, a simple division of labor, and only the beginnings of specialization. The tasks of small adhocracies and the credentials of the staff vary highly from one campus to another. Most are engaged in applied research projects and modest policy analysis, as well as routine reporting. Some of their staff members have doctoral degrees, but most have master's degrees and work experience. Small adhocracies account for more than one-third of IR offices in the United States, and they frequently carry out analytical activities collaboratively with other administrative offices.

Small adhocracies often grow into *professional bureaucracies*, particularly in larger institutions. The professional bureaucracy most commonly develops when most analytical functions and activities are centralized in a single office. This represents a more formal IR arrangement of at least four and usually more professionals. Our 2008 survey found over 150 offices with six to 22 professional staff. The professional bureaucracy is nearly always headed by those who have doctorates and years of experience. These offices have developed a modest bureaucratic structure in terms of a hierarchy and division of labor into specialties. The professional bureaucracy frequently has several entry-level positions, occupied by graduate assistants or others with a master's degree who may be just getting started in the field. These offices are the ones that carry out the most sophisticated research projects, and these projects are likely to be centralized in the IR office rather than carried out by another office with IR participation. We know from national meetings that these offices constitute the model that most of us picture when we think about the American version of IR. However, professional bureaucracies account for barely one-quarter of the IR arrangements nationally.

The other arrangement, *elaborate profusion*, is most common at research universities, and especially at private research universities. It results from an autonomous culture in which the deans and vice-presidents feel that each needs his or her own staff to carry out analytical activities. Thus these offices are decentralized and fragmented, often operating in silos, but sometimes they are loosely coordinated. Under conditions of elaborate profusion, large analytical studies—like enrollment modeling or budget projections, or multivariate longitudinal studies of student outcomes—are likely to be assigned to a lone researcher, if carried out at all. However, in the professional bureaucracy these studies frequently involve teams of researchers.

In one of the online IR courses that I teach each year, I ask students to place their IR operations within this ecology, and the results appear in Figure 1.7 of *NDHE* #141 (Volkwein, 2008). Obviously, not all offices fit neatly into one part of this framework; some are a borderline mix, and others may be in transition. However, these descriptions seem to capture the dominant patterns that we observe in the field of IR today. Roughly two-thirds of the

FIGURE 2.4   IR ORGANIZED BY MAJOR FUNCTION, TYPICAL FOR THE PROFESSIONAL BUREAUCRACY VERSION OF IR

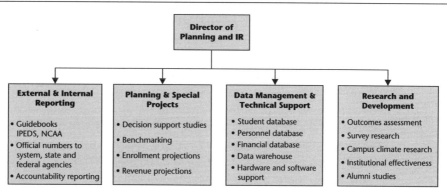

colleges and universities in our national survey have IR operations that are in the craft structure or adhocracy stages of evolution. However, the other institutions that are able to support a larger IR and planning operation seem to face a clear choice between a relatively centralized professional model versus a relatively decentralized one.

These conclusions about the evolution of IR are supported not only by the quadruple growth in AIR membership since the mid-1970s, but also by the growth in resources reported by most respondents to our national survey. Almost 37 percent of IR offices grew by at least one FTE in the two years preceding the survey, compared to only 10 percent reporting a reduction. Moreover, about 65 percent of offices report corresponding increases in staffing and budget in the decade between 1998 and 2008, compared to less than 14 percent reporting a reduction in resources.

Figure 2.4 shows a common model for IR office organization. This centralized IR professional bureaucracy is usually more efficient and more effective than other arrangements because it takes advantage of natural economies of scale associated with a larger resource base, shared expertise, cross-training, and methodological diversity. A centralized arrangement better protects the institution from the inefficiency of narrow specialization and the service gaps resulting from staff turnover, health problems, and family emergency. Any particular function or task that you can identify—student tracking, survey research, instructional workload analysis, or enrollment forecasting—can be better supported in a centralized operation because of the backup that comes with cross-training and teamwork. What is the likelihood that in a given office, in the course of any particular day or week, someone will be absent due to an illness, vacation, or family emergency? In cases of absence, whatever that person is working on comes to a halt, *except* in a large office where you have cross-training and teamwork and many people involved in the project instead of just one. Effective teamwork usually takes place in a relatively large centralized operation—and is usually missing from a fragmented one where IR is scattered across the institution in a series of smaller offices.

The model organizational chart in Figure 2.4 shows the core functions of institutional research divided into areas that are each the responsibility of a well-trained if not experienced analyst. Someone needs to be the lead person for compiling the official facts and figures about the institution, both internally and externally. Someone needs to be the "go-to" person for key decision-support studies, especially those that support campus planning. Someone needs to be the center of gravity for ongoing data management and technical support, and to act as the office's liaison with tech support and the many offices that supply data to the campus data warehouse. And someone needs to provide the research design and multivariate statistical skills for the office and to act as the local expert on survey research, evaluation, and assessment. Naturally, the director of the office should also have some of these skills. Most effective offices have full-time analysts in each of these areas, allowing the director to lead, coordinate, and be an important contributor to the campus management team—in addition to also being a researcher him- or herself. This works only when there are other people around in a centralized operation to pick up the ball during temporary absence or turnover.

Not only is a centralized professional bureaucracy the most efficient and effective organization, but it is even better if this office reports to the president or the chief executive officer of the institution—that is, the chief information customer. Thus an ideal arrangement for centralized IR and planning combines organization by function with organization by major information customer. The benefit of this arrangement is that each of the major parts of the organization knows there is a person they can go to if they want information. If the provost needs a study of faculty workload, or a salary equity analysis, or indicators of faculty activity and effort, there is an IR contact person to serve that need, regardless of whatever background they may have in other areas—like survey research or multivariate statistics. Similarly, the chief financial officer knows there is an analyst available if the officer wants to do a tuition pricing analysis and to look at the balance between tuition and financial aid and what that might do to revenue. There is an enrollment management person who works with various offices, like admissions and student affairs, and does follow-up studies of retention and graduation, perhaps even alumni research. An IR analyst is also available to work with student affairs on everything from satisfaction surveys to studies of campus climate and diversity, athletics, and the quality of residential life. When needed, each of these persons takes the lead for a project, or they may work as a team because they have cross-training and research expertise that cuts across these areas. This alternative arrangement emphasizes customer service and makes sure that all the key campus decision makers are receiving the information they need.

Other nations, from Europe to Asia, are beginning to establish campus offices of institutional research. A few of them have translated our IR survey, collected the data, and compared their findings to those in the United States. For example, the Middle East and North Africa Association for Institutional Research (MENA-AIR) last year produced some very interesting findings. Although many IR Office characteristics and responsibilities in MENA institutions are similar to those in the United States, we found some significant differences.

- About half of MENA IR offices have been established in the last five years.
- The majority of MENA offices have centralized IR reporting to the president rather than to the provost.
- MENA IR Offices have, on average, 4.4 staff compared with 3 in the United States.
- More MENA offices are headed by a person with a doctoral degree (60 percent versus 46 percent in the United States).
- MENA has a higher percent of staff with educational credentials and training in science, engineering, computer science, and IT.
- MENA IR offices do more database management than their U.S. counterparts.

This suggests that most universities in developing nations may be skipping the craft structure and adhocracy stages of IR evolution and moving right to the professional bureaucracy model. In any case, we appear to have an effective model for the conduct of campus decision support and organizational intelligence endeavors. Larger institutions are evolving toward that model, while others struggle to attain it.

Measuring the Maturity of Institutional Research

Based on earlier studies, we entered the 2008 study with ideas and beliefs about the relative maturity of IR offices based on their organizational location, staff size, years of experience, and degree preparation (Volkwein 1990, 1999a). We expect that larger offices reporting to senior management and staffed by more experienced professionals with higher levels of degree preparation are likely to indicate a relatively more developed and mature institutional research and planning function on the campus. Thus, in the 2008 survey, we sought to examine these and other characteristics for evidence of such maturity. As shown in Figure 2.5, our measure of "IR maturity" is a combination of IR staff size, reporting level, years of experience, and highest level of degree preparation. Much to our surprise, IR maturity is only weakly associated with other organizational variables, such as institution type, institution size, and Carnegie Classification. For example, some community colleges rate very high on IR maturity while some research universities are fragmented into a series of craft structures.

FIGURE 2.5   CALCULATION OF IR MATURITY

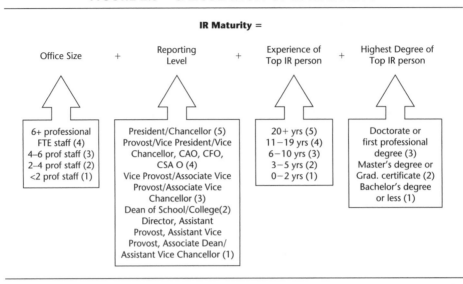

IR Maturity =

| Office Size | + | Reporting Level | + | Experience of Top IR person | + | Highest Degree of Top IR person |

| 6+ professional FTE staff (4)
4–6 prof staff (3)
2–4 prof staff (2)
<2 prof staff (1) | President/Chancellor (5)
Provost/Vice President/Vice Chancellor, CAO, CFO, CSA O (4)
Vice Provost/Associate Vice Provost/Associate Vice Chancellor (3)
Dean of School/College(2)
Director, Assistant Provost, Assistant Vice Provost, Associate Dean/ Assistant Vice Chancellor (1) | 20+ yrs (5)
11–19 yrs (4)
6–10 yrs (3)
3–5 yrs (2)
0–2 yrs (1) | Doctorate or first professional degree (3)
Master's degree or Grad. certificate (2)
Bachelor's degree or less (1) |

Source: J.F. Volkwein, "The Foundations and Evolution of Institutions," Chapter 1 in New Directions for Higher Education, # 141, Spring 2008, Dawn Terkla (ed). Jossey-Bass, San Francisco. Reprinted with permission of John Wiley & Sons, Inc.

Hierarchy of IR Tasks

We also approached the 2008 survey design with questions about the array of tasks performed by IR offices. We developed an inventory of 77 analytical responsibilities and built them into our survey response scale (leaving spaces for other entries as well). The inventory included:

- Fourteen types of general reporting responsibility
- Nine types of technology and database administration
- Seven types of academic affairs research and analysis
- Twelve types of administration and finance analysis
- Twelve types of strategic planning and enrollment management studies
- Twenty-three types of assessment, effectiveness, evaluation, and accountability studies

We asked offices to indicate whether each separate responsibility is conducted or not in IR and whether it is shared with some other office or offices. Moreover, we evaluated each activity as high, medium, or low in terms of its analytical complexity and skill required. We gave a high rating to those IR activities requiring high levels of educational preparation and analytical skill (for example, enrollment projection modeling, multivariate outcomes studies, peer benchmarking). On the other hand, we gave a low rating to each activity requiring less training and skill (for example, maintaining or producing the campus fact book; responding to guidebooks and federal/state data requests; reporting student characteristics, enrollments, and degrees awarded).

FIGURE 2.6   CALCULATION OF TASK HIERARCHY SCORE

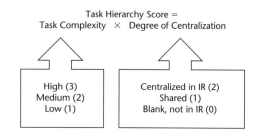

Task Hierarchy Score =
Task Complexity × Degree of Centralization

High (3)
Medium (2)
Low (1)

Centralized in IR (2)
Shared (1)
Blank, not in IR (0)

Note: Based on responses to seventy-seven survey items.

Based on the sum of these high, medium, and low ratings, we created a "task hierarchy" score for each IR office (see Figure 2.6).

Our analysis of responses from over 1,100 offices in 2008 reveals a core of relatively centralized analytical tasks that are conducted by the vast majority of IR offices around the country. The majority of these centralized IR activities relate to collecting and reporting campus and national data: coordinating national survey data collection (77 percent); maintaining or producing the campus fact book (73 percent); responding to guidebook (67 percent) and federal or state data requests (67 percent); exchanging data (61 percent); and reporting student characteristics (63 percent), enrollments (54 percent), and degrees awarded (58 percent). These general reporting responsibilities involve expertise that we judge to be largely descriptive in nature, as distinct from analytical. The centralized IR activities that are perhaps more analytical than descriptive include using the IPEDS peer analysis system (73 percent); analyses of attrition, retention, and graduation (66 percent); peer benchmarking (65 percent); analyzing national databases (65 percent); and studying student engagement (59 percent) and student satisfaction (58 percent). Thus IR appears to "own" a cluster of tasks that are a mix of analysis and routine reporting.

A more complete picture of IR work appears when we examine the responsibilities that IR offices share with others across the campus. Combining the centralized and shared IR tasks, we see not only a higher proportion of IR office involvement, but also a larger array of analytical challenges. For example, over 90 percent of IR offices are engaged in activities related to institutional and departmental self-study and accreditation. About eight of every ten IR Offices collaborate with relevant others or themselves conduct studies of student tracking, performance, progress, engagement, and satisfaction. In addition, they study performance indicators and institutional goal attainment. About seven of every ten offices participate in administrative policy research, engage in environmental scanning, supply data for marketing and recruitment, and study faculty instructional workload. Sixty-two percent of offices report their involvement in campus planning and enrollment management and projections.

Other areas of frequent IR involvement and collaboration include many evaluation and assessment tasks, like student outcomes research (64 percent), assessment of student general education skills (62 percent) and personal growth (55 percent), studies of employee satisfaction (59 percent), CQI (56 percent), alumni studies (56 percent), and evaluation of student services (60 percent) and administrative offices (52 percent). Overall, this profile suggests that teamwork is becoming increasingly necessary and valuable in IR work. Also, because about 70 percent of IR offices have three or fewer professional staff, these results may reflect the need for teamwork as a healthy coping mechanism for sparse staffing.

To what extent are these task hierarchy scores related to the maturity of the campus IR operation? The results confirm our expectations (see Figure 2.7). Our measure of IR maturity accounts for important office-to-office differences in the task hierarchy scores. In every area of IR activity, the offices rated low on maturity have lower task scores than the offices rated medium or high. In the aggregate, the most mature 339 IR offices exhibit significantly higher task hierarchy scores than the others.

The Characteristics of a Mature Profession: Does IR Enjoy These?

We know from the most mature professions—fields like medicine, law, theology, and engineering—that each has its own hierarchy of job titles and

FIGURE 2.7 AVERAGE TASK HIERARCHY SCORES FOR THE THREE LEVELS OF IR OFFICE MATURITY

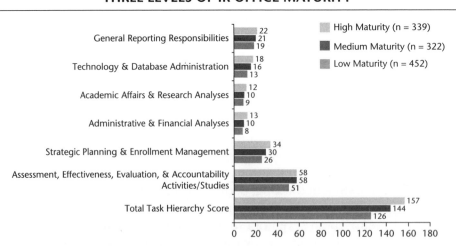

Source: Volkwein, Liu, and Woodell, Penn State University.

common nomenclatures for the subspecialties in that field. There is similar training and curricula for each degree title, as well as a dominant pattern for career paths. In each of these mature professions, the people holding these titles perform relatively common tasks, and there are relatively well-established quality assurance mechanisms, such as curricular accreditation, professional examination for licensure, and ethical review boards.

So what's the verdict? Is IR a mature profession? We see from the preceding evidence that IR appears in many different organizational arrangements. Although we see a slow evolution from small to larger offices, professional identity in terms of office titles and job titles is both inconsistent and diverse. There is a core of relatively common tasks, but office responsibilities depend substantially on the part of the organization in which IR is lodged. People come into the field with highly variable training, background, and earned degrees. Also, career patterns and career paths are unclear, especially because a high proportion of the IR workforce is relatively new to the field and only about 12 percent of the professionals have been in IR for as long as twenty years. Although there is a general consensus about the skills that IR practitioners need, this shapes hiring practices only indirectly, and there is no IR curriculum, nor "accreditation."

On the other hand, IR has begun to develop its own training and quality assurance mechanisms through summer institutes and Forum workshops, and through the IR certificate program, like ours at Penn State. Moreover, AIR does have, and has had for many years, an effective and thorough statement of ethics for the profession. In addition, we have several mature AIR publications that form the knowledge base for the field. The official scholarly journal for AIR, published since 1972, is *Research in Higher Education,* which is now perhaps the most selective journal in the field of higher education. Another enduring publication resource is *New Directions for Institutional Research,* a topic-based source book, published by Jossey-Bass since 1974 under the sponsorship and policies of AIR and its publications committee. Started in 1985, the *Higher Education Handbook* publishes one annual volume and is jointly sponsored by AIR and the Association for the Study of Higher Education. *Electronic AIR* is the single oldest, still-publishing email newsletter on the Internet, having been regularly published since October 1987. It still serves as a model for other organizations. Additional publications resources include the *AIR Professional File, Applications for Institutional Research,* and *Resources in Institutional Research,* a series of AIR monographs like the *Primer for IR,* and *Assessment in the Disciplines.* For more information about these publications, see http://www .airweb.org/?page55.

Thus we have to be cautious in making generalizations about the practice of institutional research. Both internationally and domestically, the profession is still developing at a high rate of growth, and we see great variations in office sizes, staff degree preparation, reporting lines, and assigned responsibilities from campus to campus. The work agendas of IR offices are variable and shaped more by organizational location than by type of institution. The most mature IR offices tend to perform more—and more complex—analytical tasks and responsibilities. So it may be safe to say that the field is gradually evolving toward a state of a greater maturity from its infancy of forty to fifty years ago when it began as a field of practice, and it now continues as both a field of increasingly defined practice and a field of study.

The Faces of Institutional Research

Thus we conclude that IR is an evolving profession, and one of its realities is the tension between the IR administrative role, in which one acts as a member of the administration and a member of the management team, contrasted to the professional role, which is more academic and scholarly and emphasizes the need for impartial and objective research. In addition, the functions and tasks of IR are frequently divided between the internal need for improvement (a more formative role) and the external need to demonstrate accountability (a more summative role). These contradictory dualities and tensions force institutional researchers to play a medley of different roles that we have been calling the *faces of institutional research* (Volkwein, 1999b, 2008), shown in Table 2.2.

The heading above the two columns on the right first distinguishes between those IR purposes, roles, and activities that are more internal, formative, and improvement oriented versus those that are more external, summative, and accountability oriented. The far left column divides the organizational culture and value system into two rows: the administrative and institutional, and the academic and professional. This produces a typology of four overlapping yet distinguishable types of IR purposes and roles. These are not pure types, but they reflect dominant tendencies, and they can be applied either to the office as a whole, or to the separate individuals and functions within them.

TABLE 2.2   THE FOUR FACES OF INSTITUTIONAL RESEARCH

IR Organizational Role and Culture	IR Purposes and Audiences	
	Formative and internal—for improvement	Summative and external—for accountability
Administrative and Institutional Role	To describe the institution—IR as information authority	To present the best case—IR as spin doctor
Academic and Professional Role	To analyze alternatives—IR as policy analyst	To supply impartial evidence of effectiveness—IR as scholar and researcher

Source: J.F. Volkwein, Chapter 1 in *New Directions for Institutional Research*, # 104, Winter 1999, J.F. Volkwein (ed). Jossey-Bass, San Francisco. Reprinted with permission of John Wiley & Sons, Inc.

IR as Information Authority. The internal and more administrative purpose and support role calls on institutional research to describe the shape and size of the institution, its students and staff, and its activities. Here the institutional researcher educates the campus community about itself in terms of data on admissions, enrollment, faculty, finances, and degrees awarded. Of the many challenging IR tasks, this one probably requires the least preparation in the form of education and experience. The role requirements roughly corresponds to Terenzini's technical intelligence (1993).

IR as Policy Analyst. The internal and more professional purpose calls on IR to study and analyze the institution and its policies. In this role the institutional researcher works with top management as an analyst or consultant by providing support for planning and budget allocation decisions, policy revision, administrative restructuring, or other needed change. Here the institutional researcher is the policy analyst who educates the management team. Falling into this category are studies that give alternative enrollment and revenue scenarios, comparative cost analyses, student survey research, and studies of admissions yield and salary equity. This role requires relatively high levels of education and training, as well as both analytical and issues intelligence.

IR as Spin Doctor. Of the two external types, the more administrative style is visible when IR assembles descriptive statistics that reflect favorably on the institution. Many of us are called on to play this advocate role frequently, and we need to protect against carrying this style to an unethical extreme. Here, the IR staff presents the "best case" for the campus, describing the glass as half full rather than half empty. We certainly perform this role when we assist campus admissions, fund-raisers, and government relations staff in presenting a positive image. Some experience on the job and knowledge of the institution is usually needed for success in this role.

IR as Scholar and Researcher. The more professionally oriented and analytic version of the external/accountability role is that of the impartial researcher and scholar who investigates and produces evidence so that institutional effectiveness, legal compliance, and goal attainment can be judged. Conducting outcomes studies and performance reports when the primary audience is external to the campus falls into this category, and this requires advanced training and years of experience.

IR as Knowledge Manager. In her *NDIR* volume 113, Serban (2002) improved on Volkwein's four faces by adding a fifth: IR as knowledge manager, gathering and transforming data into information and knowledge, collaborating in the creation and maintenance of information repositories. This is a good enhancement because creating and managing knowledge is a form of organizational intelligence that fertilizes all the others.

Some IR activities are difficult to classify because they overlap several categories. The campus statistical profile is produced for both internal and external audiences. Compliance reporting has both descriptive and analytical aspects. When we score and report student ratings, we act as the information authority, but we become the research analyst when we carry out studies based on student ratings data. Faculty workload and instructional analysis can appear in all four boxes, depending on the audience and the complexity of the task.

Nevertheless, most of what we do forces us to play one or another of these roles, sometimes daily. Although the boundaries around these faces of institutional research may blur from time to time, and the transition from one to the other can be as rapid as a telephone call, we are convinced that every institution needs IR to play all these roles effectively. At its best, institutional research is the center of gravity for all of the university's analytical and decision support activities—the internal and the external, the formative and the summative, the administrative and the academic. By filling these needs, IR illuminates all the institution's endeavors.

References

Fincher, C. (1978). Institutional research as organizational intelligence. *Research in Higher Education, 8*(2), 189–192.

Knight, W. E., Moore, M. E., & Coperthwaite, C. A. (1997). Institutional research: Knowledge, skills, and perceptions of effectiveness. *Research in Higher Education, 38*, 419–433.

Lindquist, S. B. (1999). A profile of institutional researchers from AIR national membership surveys. In J. F. Volkwein (Ed.), *What is institutional research all about? A critical and comprehensive assessment of the profession* (pp. 41–50). New Directions for Institutional Research, no. 104. San Francisco: Jossey-Bass.

Muffo, J. A. (1999). A comparison of findings from regional studies of institutional research offices. In J. F. Volkwein (Ed.), *What is institutional research all about? A critical and comprehensive assessment of the profession* (pp. 51–60). New Directions for Institutional Research, no. 104. San Francisco: Jossey-Bass.

Peterson, M. W. (1985). Institutional research: An evolutionary perspective. In M. Corcoran and M. W. Peterson (Eds.), *Institutional research in transition* (pp. 5–15). New Directions for Institutional Research, no. 46. San Francisco: Jossey-Bass.

Peterson, M. W. (1999). The role of institutional research: From improvement to redesign. In J. F. Volkwein (Ed.), *What is institutional research all about? A critical and comprehensive assessment of the profession* (pp. 83–104). New Directions for Institutional Research, no. 104. San Francisco: Jossey-Bass.

Saupe, J. L. (1990). *The functions of institutional research* (2nd ed.). Tallahassee, FL: Association for Institutional Research. Available at http://www.airweb.org/page.asp?page585

Serban, A. M. (2002). Knowledge management: The fifth face of institutional research. In A. M. Serban and J. Luan (Eds.), *Knowledge management: Building a competitive advantage in higher education* (pp. 105–112). New Directions for Institutional Research, no. 113. San Francisco: Jossey-Bass.

Terenzini, P. T. (1993). On the nature of institutional research and the knowledge and skills it requires. *Research in Higher Education, 34,* 1–10.

Volkwein, J. F. (1990). The diversity of institutional research structures and tasks. In J. B. Presley (Ed.), *Organizing effective institutional research offices* (pp. 7–26). New Directions for Institutional Research, no. 66. San Francisco: Jossey-Bass.

Volkwein, J. F. (Ed.). (1999a). *What is institutional research all about? A critical and comprehensive assessment of the profession.* New Directions for Institutional Research, no. 104. San Francisco: Jossey-Bass.

Volkwein, J. F. (1999b). The four faces of institutional research. In J. F. Volkwein (Ed.), *What is institutional research all about? A critical and comprehensive assessment of the profession* (pp. 9–19). New Directions for Institutional Research, no. 104. San Francisco: Jossey-Bass.

Volkwein, J. F. (2008). The foundations and evolution of institutional research. In Dawn Terkla (Ed.), *Institutional research: More than just data* (pp. 5–20). New Directions for Higher Education, no. 141. San Francisco: Jossey-Bass.

CHAPTER 3

PRACTICING INSTITUTIONAL RESEARCH

Mardy T. Eimers, Jang Wan Ko, and Denise Gardner

The practice of institutional research has evolved over the past fifty years into a profession defined by a set of standards and ethics. And although the precise tasks and responsibilities of the institutional research function are specific to each institution, certain types of skills and knowledge are required to be effective at all of them. In this chapter we discuss four topics that define necessary skills and knowledge for the effective practice of institutional research: (1) gaining a foundation of ethical understanding and practice, (2) knowing which skills or intelligences are necessary in order to excel in the field of institutional research, (3) understanding the avenues and opportunities for professional skill advancement, and (4) understanding how the topics of interest vary across institutional types and reporting lines.

Standards of Professional Practice and Codes of Ethics in Institutional Research

The Association for Institutional Research (AIR) has defined institutional research as "research leading to improved understanding, planning, and operating of institutions of postsecondary education" (Peterson, 1999, p. 84). In the past two decades, institutional research has become more analytical, anticipatory, and proactive. Institutional research is "evolving toward a unique blend of data skills, strategic planning, outcomes assessment, and advocacy for improvement" (Swing, 2009, p. 5). The primary function of institutional research professionals is to assist administrators at their colleges and universities by creating information for planning and decision support. Thus the institutional research professional is often in a position to influence senior leaderships' decision making. To protect the integrity of IR professionals and their work, it is important to have the guidance of a set of professional standards and ethics appropriate for the higher education setting and the requirements of their specific duties.

Standards of Professional Practice

Every profession needs a set of standards and ethics from which to operate. There is no set understanding of what should be included in standards of professional practice, but many seem to include at least one section that addresses professional ethics. Although there are many commonalities between professions, each also has its unique definitions and operating protocol. In addition, individuals employed in these professions should be guided by both their own ethical standards as well as standards for the practice of their duties and obligations to their employer.

Many educational organizations have their own statement of ethics or standards. The American Association of University Professors' Statement on Professional Ethics details a set of responsibilities (not just ethics) of the academic profession. The American Educational Research Association has a set of standards designed specifically to guide the work of researchers in education. The Association for the Study of Higher Education has a statement of Principles of Ethical Conduct, which are broad standards. NASPA, an association of Student Affairs Administrators in Higher Education, has a set of Standards of Professional Practice (including research and assessment).

Standards for professional practice usually include general guidelines and standards relevant to the specific skills and duties of the professions. Standards may include sections on ethics; separate ethical codes may also exist.

Codes of Ethics

The word *ethics* evolved from the Greek words *ethos,* denoting personal character, and *ta ethika,* used to refer to the philosophical inquiries into the nature of good and evil. A code of ethics is an attempt to define basic rules or principles for determining what constitutes "good" or "right" behavior—in other words, to determine what we "ought" to do (Burns, n.d.).

The Center for the Study of Ethics in the Professions (CSEP, n.d.) was established in 1976 to promote research and teaching on practical moral problems in the professions. The first interdisciplinary center for ethics to focus on the professions, CSEP continues to be one of the nation's leading centers for practical and professional ethics. Quoting Luegenbiehl, the Center defines the significance of a code in defining a profession: "The adoption of a code is significant for the professionalization of an occupational group, because it is one of the external hallmarks testifying to the claim that the group recognizes an obligation to society that transcends mere economic self-interest" (Luegenbiehl, 1991, p. 138).

The Association for Institutional Research developed a Code of Ethics "to provide members of the association with some broad ethical statements with which to guide their professional lives and to identify relevant considerations when ethical uncertainties arise" (2001). A committee began drafting the Code in the early 1990s, first by examining many existing codes and pertinent ethnical issues (such as those in survey research). However, the group soon realized that institutional research needed its own specific standards (Schiltz, 1992).

Professionals who are employed as institutional researchers come from a variety of academic backgrounds and experiences. As such, the profession is composed of individuals with a multidisciplinary mix of perspectives—education, statistics, history, political science, business, and others. The practice of institutional research is often not pure academic research, but instead practical and applied, with a specific institutional focus. In addition, the actual duties performed by institutional researchers will vary depending on the institutional mission and structure.

AIR's Code of Ethics lists ethical principles and standards to guide the work of institutional researchers. It provides not a set of rules, but rather standards to which individuals should aspire and against which their actions can be judged. It should be treated as a living document, amenable to adaptation to changing environments. The AIR code has five sections, addressing *competence, practice, confidentiality, relationships to community,* and *relationships to craft.*

The code of competence, as addressed in the first section, states that institutional researchers should not claim or imply competence that they don't possess, either in the course of their work or on job applications. They should seek appropriate training for themselves and provide professional development for others in the field.

Section two, concerning the specifics of practicing institutional research, states that institutional researchers should be objective and unbiased and avoid personal conflicts of interest. Individuals should understand what they are being asked to do and always ensure that all data used are accurate. Reports should be clear, concise, and well documented. This section does not go into detail about the many technical standards required for the broad array of skills and duties of an institutional researcher.

Confidentiality of data and information is vital to an institutional researcher's job; this is the focus of section three. Data should be securely stored and transmitted, and written standards must exist. It is vital that privacy rights be protected.

Sections four and five of the Code deal with relationships to the community and to the craft. Community includes the actual office as well as the whole institution. All employees should be treated fairly, the institutional research office and its functions should be regularly evaluated, and all information and reports should be secure, accurate, and properly reported. The craft of institutional research should be upheld by a responsibility to the integrity of the profession. Institutional researchers have a unique perspective on institutional data and practices, which should be shared with institutional administrators as well as their colleagues in the field.

AIR's Code of Ethics was most recently revised in 2001. It is referred to in AIR-sponsored training such as the Foundations for Institutional Research Institute, newcomers workshops at AIR Forums and regional conferences, and the curriculum of most graduate certificate programs focused on institutional research–related skills. Institutional research professionals should periodically discuss the code with their colleagues and consider carefully how it applies to their own responsibilities.

Description, Synthesis, and Assessment of Skills Needed in Institutional Research

To be effective, institutional researchers should have an appreciation for the basic tenets of professional practice and should demonstrate ethical behavior in their professional lives. This foundation undergirds the skills necessary to succeed in the field. In the institutional research literature, the most recognized perspective on these skills was introduced by Terenzini in 1993. Using Terenzini's three organizational intelligences as a framework, we present the skills necessary to function at each level of intelligence in Exhibit 3.1 and describe them in the text that follows.

EXHIBIT 3.1   TERENZINI'S THREE ORGANIZATIONAL INTELLIGENCES OF INSTITUTIONAL RESEARCH

I. Technical and Analytical Intelligence
   a. Factual knowledge
   b. Methodology skills
   c. Understanding computing and computing software
II. Issues Intelligence
   a. Understanding key issues in higher education especially the internal issues most germane to your institution (for example, faculty workload, time to degree)
   b. How your institution functions including the formal and informal decision-making process
   c. Ability to work with and through others to accomplish goals
III. Contextual Intelligence
   a. Understanding the culture of higher education, including your own institution's culture and history (such as institutional memory)
   b. How business is done at your institution (for example, who the key players and the key processes are at your institution)
   c. Respecting the perspectives of all constituencies
   d. Knowledge of the environment in which your college operates

Source: Adapted from Terenzini, 1993.

Technical and Analytical Intelligence

Terenzini's first level of intelligence, technical and analytical intelligence, requires competence in three areas. First, the institutional researcher should have a firm understanding of *factual knowledge or information*. This includes knowing various definitions, terms, key acronyms, data fields, usable databases in different systems (for example, student, human resources), and the limitations of these databases and data structures. It also includes knowing how to calculate basic derived measures such as student-faculty ratio, the number of FTE students, and section credits per faculty member taught.

A second area encompasses procedural knowledge regarding *methodological skills.* These skills include developing quantitative and qualitative research studies, creating and administering surveys, understanding techniques to examine student retention, and conducting enrollment projections.

The third area of technical and analytical intelligence encompasses the ability to effectively use *computing and computing software*. Examples in this area include writing program code for a computing process, understanding technical nomenclature and procedures, developing spreadsheets, facilitating pivot tables, formatting data into a usable data structure, and using statistical packages to analyze data.

Similar skills were cited by Joe Saupe and James Montgomery in *The Nature and Role of Institutional Research: Memo to a College or University* (1970). They stressed the importance of having skills in quantitative methods and research methodologies, modeling, statistics, oral and written communication, tabular and graphic presentation, and "information processing machinery" (p. 13). Although the technical capabilities and nomenclature of computing has evolved profoundly since 1970, knowing how to use computing in institutional research has remained a critical skill for an institutional research office.

Technical and analytical intelligence is considered both "fundamental and foundational." That is, it is essential before one can fully realize the other organizational intelligences defined by Terenzini. However, the work using technical and analytical intelligence has limited value, in and of itself, beyond providing descriptive profiles in support of planning and decision making.

Issues Intelligence

The first area of issues intelligence centers on knowing and understanding the *key issues in higher education and those issues that are most germane to your institution.* Issues intelligence also includes knowing how your institution operates and how decisions are made. What are *the formal and informal decision-making processes?* What areas or individuals possess power and influence on your campus? What are the norms of operation at your institution, and how do they affect decision making, how priorities are established, and what gets accomplished? What gets rewarded at your institution? Because this subcomponent relies so much on understanding the informal processes and structure at an institution, it requires a combination of intuition and experience working with the decision makers in order to fully grasp how decisions are made at a given institution.

Another subcomponent of issues intelligence involves the ability of the institutional research office to *work with and through others to accomplish goals.* For an institutional researcher, learning to work with colleagues across campus to accomplish institutional goals is a key component of issues intelligence. Saupe and Montgomery (1970) emphasized that institutional researchers should work to establish good relationships across campus and strive to become an accepted member of the administrative team. In particular, institutional research professionals should establish good relationships with colleagues in those units that the campus institutional research office interacts with most, such as the admissions, registrar, business affairs, financial aid, human relations, and other offices. Furthermore, the authors stressed the importance of having "access to knowledge of current problems and the issues facing the institution" (p. 11) and "keeping abreast of the more recent studies in higher education so that they can be adapted to your institution if necessary" (p. 12).

Contextual Intelligence

Terenzini's third level of organizational intelligence, contextual intelligence, includes understanding *the culture of higher education,* both in general and more specifically within your sphere of work. Having a historical and philosophical understanding of your institution and a context for why certain choices were made is part of contextual intelligence. Terenzini uses the term *institutional memory* to capture this aspect of contextual intelligence. "It includes *knowledge of how business is done in this particular college or university and who the key players are in both organizational and governance units"* (Terenzini, 1993, p. 6). Contextual intelligence also encompasses acknowledging and *respecting the perspectives of all constituencies*—students, parents, alums, legislators, faculty, business leaders, staff, the community, and others.

Some of the subcomponents of contextual intelligence were written about prior to Terenzini's article, and they have certainly been reinforced by several authors in the field since 1993. For example, Saupe and Montgomery (1970) recommended that it might be worthwhile for the institutional research professional to occasionally teach a college course. Among other things, teaching a course enables the institutional researcher to better understand the faculty perspective and academic environment. In addition, Sheehan's three-hat theory (Sheehan, 1975) puts a slightly different twist on knowing and respecting different constituencies. According to this theory, institutional research professionals must have the skills to assume three different perspectives when they receive a request for management information. First, the analyst must assume the perspective (or wear the hat) of the person requesting the information. Second, the analyst must assume the role of the analyst (for example, himself or herself) in being able to carefully interpret the request, identify available data, use the tools and techniques available, and know how best to address the request in light of the resources at the analyst's disposal. Finally, the analyst must wear the hat of the technician or programmer to understand exactly what data are available and what limitations this might place on the analyst's ability to address the decision maker's request.

Institutional researchers who have obtained contextual intelligence *know the environment in which their college or university operates and fully grasp the opportunities and constraints presented*. In Marvin Peterson's chapter, "The Role of Institutional Research: From Improvement to Redesign" (1999), he underscored institutional researchers' responsibility to understand the changing landscape of higher education and to think intentionally about how it will impact their institutions.

Fred Volkwein (1999) introduced four roles or purposes of institutional research and dubbed them the "four faces" of institutional research: (1) information authority, (2) policy analyst, (3) spin doctor, and (4) scholar and researcher (for a complete description, see Chapter 2). In terms of the education and experience required to fulfill each role effectively, the *scholar and researcher* role requires the most educational training and experience, followed in order by the *policy analyst, spin doctor,* and *information authority* roles (Volkwein, 1999). In terms of Terenzini's intelligences, the following would be minimally required for each face of institutional research (Volkwein, 1999): *information authority* requires technical intelligence, the *policy analyst* and *spin doctor* roles require issues intelligence, and the *research and scholar* role necessitates contextual intelligence. Serban (2002) recommended adding a fifth face: institutional researcher as *knowledge manager*. Although this role leans heavily on technical and analytical intelligence, an argument could easily be made that the institutional research professional must possess contextual intelligence before assembling and organizing data as required of the *knowledge manager*.

In summary, the skills necessary to be effective in the field of institutional research have been written about by scholars and practitioners for the past forty years. The increasing complexity of the internal and external environment will require both individuals and the office as a whole to improve their mastery of the three institutional research intelligences.

It is important to reinforce the notion that contextual intelligence cannot be fully developed without having a foundation of technical and analytical as well as issues intelligence, and issues intelligence cannot be fully realized without technical and analytical intelligence (Terenzini, 1993). The institutional research personnel at a college or university should strive as an organizational unit to enhance their collective intelligences, in order to provide the best institutional research value.

An Assessment of the Profession's Skills and Intelligences

It appears that there has not yet been a systematic, general assessment of where the institutional research profession, as a collective organization, might place particular strengths or weaknesses in regard to the three intelligences. Using Terenzini's three levels of intelligence as a framework, in this section we evaluate the institutional research professionals and the profession in terms of where strengths are likely to exist and where there may be opportunities for improvement or professional development. We do so for three reasons. First, it suggests areas where improvements could be made to enhance the institutional research profession as a whole. Second, it encourages individuals in the profession to assess their own skill sets and work to build those skills, especially if they have aspirations to advance to positions of increased responsibility. Third, it provides a means whereby institutional research directors could assess their own unit's skill set and work to develop a staff that collectively encompasses the skills necessary to function at each level of intelligence.

An assessment of the profession would likely find strengths particularly in technical and analytical intelligence, and in certain areas of issues and contextual intelligence. With technical and analytical intelligence, our profession tends to attract individuals who are extremely strong from an analytical and technological perspective. Either we have been drawn to the profession initially because our skill set fits well with the skills required to be successful in institutional research, or mentors and colleagues have steered us in this direction because of the congruence between our skill set and the requirements of the profession. Furthermore, for many institutional researchers with master's and doctoral level training, we have been socialized to appreciate the academic and professional value of analytical and technical mastery.

With regard to issues and contextual intelligence, the professional would likely receive high marks from his or her colleagues for understanding the issues facing higher education, recognizing the importance of the culture and history in higher education, and having knowledge of the local college environment. These three components of issues and contextual intelligence represent *the environmental context* in which a higher education institution operates. We argue that the vast majority of IR professionals are well versed in these environmental context areas, for it is an essential component of institutional research work. These points support, at least in part, the rationale for why the profession is likely to be strong in the analytical, technical, and environmental areas of Terenzini's levels of intelligence.

Having said this, however, there may also be aspects of Terenzini's intelligences that challenge institutional researchers more significantly than others. Issues and contextual intelligence require institutional researchers to work with colleagues across campus, respect and appreciate the perspectives of multiple constituencies, grasp the intricacies of knowing who the key players are across campus, and appreciate the informal decision-making processes unique to a particular campus. From our personal experience as well as through discussions with colleagues, we notice that many institutional research professionals tend to find these aspects of Terenzini's intelligences particularly challenging.

This conclusion can be further supported if one examines personal preferences based on personality assessments. The well-known Myers-Briggs Type Indicator (MBTI) assesses an individual on four personality dimensions, based on the logic that an individual has a preference (either A or B) in each dimension (Isachsen & Berens, 1988; Schnell & Hammer, 1997). It would not be unreasonable to postulate—given the basic requirements and the advanced training necessary to perform the fundamentals of the job—that many of those individuals who consider institutional research their profession lean toward the bolded preferences in the MBTI dimensions presented in Exhibit 3.2.

Of the four dimensions of the MBTI, the results of informal surveys of institutional research professionals suggest that many of those drawn to the profession tend to lean toward *introversion, sensing, thinking,* and *judging.* What this

EXHIBIT 3.2   MYERS-BRIGGS TYPE INDICATOR DIMENSIONS: AN INSTITUTIONAL RESEARCH PERSPECTIVE

Dimension 1: Gaining energy
A. Extroversion: As an institutional researcher, you prefer to focus on projects and relationships in your external world. These interactions stimulate and energize your efforts.
B. **Introversion: As an institutional researcher, you prefer to focus on aspects of your internal world. Reflecting independently on information, ideas, and thoughts stimulates and energizes your efforts.**

Dimension 2: Interpreting information
A. **Sensing: In your institutional research role, you prefer to process information by examining the facts, details, and data within the current context of higher education.**
B. Intuition: In your institutional research role, you prefer to nurture and trust interrelationships and adhere to theories; you are future-oriented.

Dimension 3: Making decisions
A. **Thinking: When confronted with a decision at work, you tend to take a logical, measured approach that is straightforward and objective.**
B. Feeling: When confronted with a decision at work, you strive to create harmony among the ranks and carefully consider the impact on individuals.

Dimension 4: Living in the higher education environment
A. **Judging: Your preference as an institutional researcher is to be organized and systematic and to make decisions quickly.**
B. Perceiving: Your preference as an institutional researcher is to be flexible and adaptable and to keep various options open.

Source: Adapted from Schnell and Hammer, 1997.

suggests—certainly, there are exceptions—is that the very talents, skills, and preferences that make us effective in the profession of institutional research, particularly at the core level (technical and analytical intelligence), may also inhibit our ability to fully realize key subcategories of other intelligences. As such, many of us tend to gain energy through reflection with an internal focus, in contrast to getting our energy through relationships; we tend to trust information that is factual and detailed, instead of using our intuition; we prefer to make decisions using logic and analysis and typically are less concerned with others' feelings; and we prefer to be organized and orderly rather than adaptable and flexible. These very tendencies also may limit our effectiveness as institutional researchers on our campus.

Emotional intelligence, a concept coined nearly two decades ago, captures some of the higher-order subintelligences that Terenzini described and to which institutional researchers may need to give greater attention. Emotional intelligence is related to one's ability to manage oneself and one's relationships in mature and effective ways (Goleman, Boyatzis, & McKee, 2002). Emotional intelligence consists of personal competence and social competence. Personal competence includes, among other aspects, careful self-reflection and thoughtfulness, trusting your "gut feeling" once you have considered all of the data, and the ability to be adaptable and flexible. If, for example, you test as an ISTJ (that is, inclined toward introversion, sensing, thinking, and judging), then as an institutional research professional you may need to trust your intuition more as well as try to be less structured and more flexible.

Social competence is also considered to be part of emotional intelligence. Leimer and Terkla (2009) emphasized the importance of social intelligence in a recent chapter in *New Directions in Institutional Research*. Social competence includes, among other things, sensing and understanding others' emotions and perspective; having an organizational awareness of the internal politics, currents, and decision networks; and cultivating relationships (Goleman, Boyatzis & McKee, 2002). These three aspects of social competence are closely connected to the aforementioned areas in Terenzini's framework—and increased attention to them may be beneficial, particularly issues intelligence (*learning how to work with and through others*) and contextual intelligence (*having respect for the perspectives of different constituencies*) (see Exhibit 3.1).

Whether we focus on the potential areas of weakness in the profession based on Terenzini's framework or identify these areas under the rubric of emotional intelligence, there is further justification for focusing on these areas as a profession. First, the skills connected to emotional intelligence are not typically taught in graduate school, an environment in which most of us have spent considerable time. Second, the skills associated with emotional intelligence have not been overly stressed in conference sessions, workshops, institutes, or other professional development opportunities typically associated with AIR or other associations. Third, institutional researchers might be able to get specialized training or professional development in emotional intelligence and similar areas if their institution offered such opportunities (for example, leadership programs, leadership training). Fourth, developing these qualities is more than likely closely tied to one's ability to advance in the field; that is, those institutional research professionals who hone these skills are more likely to advance to leadership positions in institutional research or hold these leadership positions, in part because of their talent in these higher-order, emotional intelligence aspects of their work.

In summary, there are good reasons why we should each assess our own skills and strive to enhance those areas in which we find limitations. We may also, as a profession, consider adding seminars, workshops, and institutes dedicated to improving the *comprehensive array of skills and intelligences* described and discussed in this section. As it currently stands, a more intentional focus on offering professional development opportunities that address the skills and abilities that manifest issues and contextual intelligence could further advance those in the profession. The next section focuses on educational and training opportunities currently available to professionals who wish to improve their skills as institutional researchers.

Acquiring Skills for Effective Institutional Research

Institutional researchers acquire the skills necessary to function at each level of Terenzini's three intelligences through various means. First, AIR addresses the professional development and continuing education needs of members of the Association through various summer institutes, webinars, pre-forum workshops at the annual forums, and publications. Second, sponsored by National Center for Education Statistics (NCES) and the National Science Foundation (NSF), the AIR certificate programs provide formal coursework for institutional researchers or persons who aspire to be IR professionals. Third, IR practitioners enhance their knowledge and skills by actively engaging in special interest groups (SIGs) and regional IR associations. These educational and training opportunities are discussed in detail in this section.

AIR launched the Graduate Certificate in Institutional Research program to provide academic and professional development opportunities for institutional researchers, administrators, graduate students, and faculty in higher education. There are currently a handful of institutions that offer the institutional research graduate certificate, including Penn State University and Florida State University, two of the original certificate programs. Courses in the certificate programs are delivered in both traditional and online formats. In general, the certificate programs consist of a minimum of eighteen credit hours of graduate-level coursework, with many students electing to take additional courses in a specific area (for example, enrollment management, program review and assessment). Although each university provides its own particular courses, the programs generally offer basic courses (such as foundations and fundamentals of IR), research method courses (such as educational research methods and design), and special topics in IR or higher education (for example, faculty workload, assessment). In addition to the courses, the programs offer IR practicums or internships allowing the participants to apply theory to practice. The certificate programs tend to focus on knowledge and skills defined in the framework of analytical and technical intelligence, providing the core and foundation of IR knowledge and skills. However, participants have an opportunity to develop issues and contextual intelligence through an IR practicum or internship, which is required by each of the four programs.

Second, AIR summer institutes, which consist of four institutes—Foundations I Institute, Foundations II Institute, Statistics Institute, and Assessment Institute for Institutional Research Practitioners—reflect well AIR's efforts to provide extensive knowledge and skills for IR practitioners. The AIR Foundation Institute, established in 1990 to provide a focused, intensive, structured learning environment for new IR practitioners, has been offered each summer.

Due to increasing demand, AIR launched a second foundation institute in 2006 (AIR, 2008). The Foundations II Institute is designed for established IR practitioners with two or more years of experience to advance their career toward senior leadership or for additional professional development experience. Topics include strategic planning, institutional effectiveness, office management, and advanced statistics. The instructional modules focus on concepts, theories, and IR best practices, with a combination of lecture, discussion, hands-on activities, and small-group exercises to illustrate practical applications of the featured methods and strategies. Many institutional researchers and practitioners have participated in the Foundation II; in some years as many as eighty professionals have participated in the Foundation II institute (AIR, 2008).

The Applied Statistics Institute centers on advancing participants' skills in statistical concepts, applications, and research methodologies. The Institute focuses on statistical methods, such as analysis of variance, multivariate analysis, and nonparametric analysis statistics. These techniques are closely tied to technical and analytical intelligence, and participants learn how to apply them appropriately in higher education settings.

The Assessment Institute was established in 2007 to meet the continuous demand for institutional accreditation and assessment activities. The Assessment Institute is designed to help IR or assessment professionals acquire knowledge about the assessment field and to expand their knowledge and skills regarding the assessment needs at their respective institutions.

Third, from the initial forums, AIR has provided pre-forum workshops for the members to enhance knowledge and practical skills at the annual AIR Forums. The number of workshops and participants has increased over time, with as many as thirty-six workshops offered to over eight hundred participants (AIR, 2007). The workshops cover a multitude of topics, from basic technical skills with hands-on training, to advanced statistical and research methods, to planning strategies. Although the workshops lean more toward developing technical and analytical intelligence, there are certainly workshops that include issues and contextual intelligence–related topics. Also, each year there is a Newcomers workshop for first-time AIR Forum participants to learn about the practice of institutional research and AIR.

Fourth, with increasing demand for professional training and the rapid development of technology, webinars have become an effective way of delivering knowledge and skills for IR practitioners. AIR initially provided a webinar cosponsored with Statistical Package for the Social Sciences (SPSS) for the application of the AMOS structural equation modeling software and two webinars on the Integrated Postsecondary Education Data System (IPEDS), in 2004 (AIR, 2005). The demand for webinars has dramatically increased over the years (AIR, 2005, 2006, 2007, 2008, and 2010). Currently, AIR's webinars include on-demand professional development services such as the statistical webinar series and AIR Connections. AIR also provides new NSF webinars related to the Scientists and Engineers Statistical Data System (SESTAT) and the WebCASPAR data system, in partnership with the NSF.

Fifth, special interest groups (SIGs) and affiliated IR associations are sources not only for gaining technical knowledge and skills but also for exchanging experiences among IR practitioners and addressing related higher education issues. The SIGs vary from technical groups to highly issue-oriented groups. They usually hold their annual or regular meetings at the AIR annual forum each year. Affiliated associations or groups are another good example of how to enhance knowledge and networking among IR practitioners. AIR has seven regional and twenty-seven state-affiliated groups in the United States. These affiliated groups have their own meetings to enhance members' knowledge and experience. There are also seven international affiliated groups. Active networking and knowledge exchanges among the SIGs and affiliated groups are good ways to develop issues intelligence as well as technical and analytical intelligence. Because these groups are formed on the basis of common interests, they tend to maximize their efforts toward acquiring pertinent knowledge.

Finally, AIR publishes or directly supports a number of periodicals that can help IR professionals enhance their knowledge and skills. Several of these publications specifically target the IR profession (see AIR [n.d.] for a full overview). The *Professional File* introduces new models, techniques, and processes that can be used in a number of higher education settings. *IR Applications* is an electronic publication that focuses on the application of specialized methodologies to support higher education management.

In addition, AIR supports a number of publications that bridge theory and practice. *New Directions in Institutional Research* comprehensively addresses a single topic or issue relating to institutional research. *The Journal of Research in Higher Education* (published by Springer Science) and *Higher Education: The Handbook of Theory and Research* (a joint effort by AIR and the Association for the Study of Higher Education [ASHE] published by Kluwer Academic) are also examples of AIR publications that connect theory with higher education practice.

In an effort to keep up-to-date with current changes in the profession, the Association also provides regularly published information on student assessment (*Assessment Update*) and federal data and reporting concerns (*AIR Alerts*), as well as a monthly newsletter (*Electronic AIR*) that keeps members abreast of key happenings, new techniques, and opportunities in institutional research.

Skills' Relation to Institution Types and IR Office Locations

Fred Volkwein and his colleagues wrote extensively about the organizational structure of institutional research offices, the size of these offices, and their organizational locations. Volkwein describes how these three factors can significantly influence the type of work required in the institutional research office and the subsequent skills necessary to complete this work. (For a more comprehensive review, we suggest revisiting Chapter 2 in this volume.) However, the key points as they pertain to this chapter include the following. First, Volkwein (1990, 2008) described four types of IR offices based on institutional size and degree of development or centralization: craft structure, adhocracy, professional bureaucracy, and elaborate profusion. The educational level of the staff, the training necessary, and the skills required tend to differ greatly based on how an institutional research office might be classified in Volkwein's schema. Second, the organizational location of the institutional research office (for example, academic affairs, president's office, finance and budget) also shapes the types of projects assigned and the skills necessary to complete those projects (Muffo, 1999; Lindquist, 1999; Volkwein & Woodell, 2008; Leimer & Terkla, 2009). For example, an office housed in the finance and budget administration division is likely to engage in different projects from an IR office reporting to academic affairs or the president's office.

From a different perspective, Ko (2008, 2009) provided insights into the qualifications and use of skills by positions in IR offices. Using job descriptions of institutional researchers, Ko analyzed 93 positions and titles for the chief IR officers and 112 positions for staff, such as an assistant and associate director, research analyst, senior researcher, and coordinators. According to Ko (2008), the most desired qualification for chief IR officers in four-year universities is experience in the IR area, followed by interpersonal skills, communication skills, and use of database software. The desired qualifications in two-year colleges were the use of database software and statistical software and the design and implementation of research models and surveys. In the Ko (2008) study, large institutions tended to require more technical skills, whereas medium-size institutions tended to require more experience in IR or in higher education. The responsibilities of chief IR officers vary by institutional level and size.

At four-year institutions, IR directors tend to conduct general tasks (that is, providing reports to internal or external agencies) and to lead research and assessment activities. At two-year colleges, chief IR officers tend to support strategic planning as well as perform general tasks. Although chief IR officers' primary responsibilities are similar across institutional sizes, those in medium-size universities apparently tend more to support program reviews and accreditation activities than those in small and large institutions.

Staff qualifications vary by position (Ko, 2009). IR offices require both technical skills (that is, use of databases and statistical software, data management system) and IR competencies (that is, interpersonal skills and project management skills) for assistant or associate directors. Research analysts, a predominant position in an IR office, are required to have all dimensions of IR knowledge and skills, including use of desktop software and databases, communication skills, and statistical analysis. Research analysts at four-year institutions are generally expected to have more interpersonal skills and project management abilities than those at two-year colleges. Senior researchers also need technical experience in research and assessment and the implementation of research design. The primary skills for the coordinator are interpersonal skills, use of databases, and experience in research.

Conclusion

This chapter has focused on four major areas: (1) establishing a foundation of ethical understanding and practice, (2) knowing what skills or intelligences are necessary in order to excel in the field of institutional research, (3) understanding the avenues and opportunities for professional skill advancement, and (4) understanding how the necessary skills and topics of interest vary across institutional type and reporting lines.

The AIR Code of Ethics was most recently revised in 2001. As the nature of institutional research evolves, it may be time for the Association to reexamine the Code and make the appropriate updates. An empirical analysis of how well the institutional research profession does in terms of having the skills to function effectively at each level of intelligence would be a substantial contribution to our field. Understanding the work preferences of those involved in institutional research, using the MBTI or some other battery, could significantly shape the curricula offered by AIR via its many venues (for example, institutes, workshops, webinars). AIR offers a tremendous number of professional development and training opportunities, which vary by level of commitment and focus, suggesting that there are educational opportunities for nearly all members in one area or another. Finally, the nature of institutional research work is shaped in important ways by the type of institution and the administrative area for which one works. Although the skills required are reasonably consistent across institutional types and reporting lines, knowing the subtle nuances will help institutional researchers find the best match for a successful career.

References

Association for Institutional Research. (2005). *2004–05 annual report.* Tallahassee, FL: Association for Institutional Research.

Association for Institutional Research. (2006). *2005–06 annual report.* Tallahassee, FL: Association for Institutional Research.

Association for Institutional Research. (2007). *2006–07 annual report.* Tallahassee, FL: Association for Institutional Research.

Association for Institutional Research. (2008). *2007–08 annual report.* Tallahassee, FL: Association for Institutional Research.

Association for Institutional Research. (2010). *2009–2010 annual report.* Tallahassee, FL: Association for Institutional Research.

Association for Institutional Research. (n.d.). Publications. Retrieved from www.airweb .org/?page=5

Association for Institutional Research Code of Ethics. (2001). Retrieved from http://www .airweb.org/?page=140

Burns, S. A. (n.d.). Evolutionary pragmatism: A discourse on a modern philosophy for the 21st century. Retrieved from http://www3.sympatico.ca/saburns/pg0401.htm

Center for the Study of Ethics in the Professions (CSEP). (n.d.). Retrieved from http:// ethics.iit.edu/index1.php/Programs/Codes%20of%20Ethics

Goleman, D., Boyatzis, R. E., & McKee, A. (2002). *Primal leadership: Realizing the power of emotional intelligence* (1st ed.). New York: Harvard Business School Press.

Isachsen, O., & Berens, L. (1988). *Working together: A personality centered approach to management.* Coronado, CA: Neworld Management Press.

Ko, J. (2008). Chief institutional research officers: Their qualifications, occupational duties, and implications for institutional research. Presented at the Association for Institutional Research (AIR) 2008 Annual Forum. Seattle, Washington, May 24–28.

Ko, J. (2009). The qualifications and occupational duties of institutional researchers. Presented at the Association for Institutional Research (AIR) 2009 Annual Forum. Atlanta, GA, May 30–June 3.

Leimer, C., & Terkla, D. (2009). Laying the foundation: Institutional research office organization, staffing, and career development. In C. Leimer (Ed.), *Imagine the future of institutional research* (pp. 43–58). New Directions for Institutional Research, no. 143. San Francisco: Jossey-Bass.

Lindquist, S. B. (1999). A profile of institutional researchers from AIR national membership surveys. In J. F. Volkwein (Ed.), *What is institutional research all about? A critical and comprehensive assessment of the profession* (pp. 41–50). New Directions for Institutional Research, no. 104. San Francisco: Jossey-Bass.

Luegenbiehl, H. C. (1991). Codes of ethics and the moral education of engineers. *Business and Professional Ethics Journal, 2,* 41–61. Also in Johnson, D. G. (Ed.). (1991). *Ethical issues in engineering.* Englewood Cliffs, NJ: Prentice-Hall, 137–154. Retrieved from http://ethics.iit.edu/index1.php/Programs/Codes%20of%20Ethics/Function%20 and%20Value%20of%20Codes%20of%20Ethics

Muffo, J. A. (1999). A comparison of findings from regional studies of institutional research offices. In J. F. Volkwein (Ed.), *What is institutional research all about? A critical and comprehensive assessment of the profession* (pp. 51–60). New Directions for Institutional Research, no. 104. San Francisco: Jossey-Bass.

Peterson, M. W. (1999).The role of institutional research: From improvement to redesign. In J. F. Volkwein (Ed.), *What is institutional research all about? A critical and comprehensive assessment of the profession* (pp. 83–103). New Directions for Institutional Research, no. 104. San Francisco: Jossey-Bass.

Saupe, J., & Montgomery, J. (1970). A memo to a college or university. *Association for Institutional Research.* Retrieved from http://www.airweb.org/page.asp?page=84

Schiltz, M. E. (1992). An introduction to the draft code of ethics. In M. E. Schiltz (Ed.), *Ethics and standards in institutional research* (pp. 3–9). New Directions for Institutional Research, no. 73. San Francisco: Jossey-Bass.

Schnell, E. R., & Hammer, A. L. (1997). Integrating the FIRO-B with the MBTI: Relationships, case examples, and interpretation strategies. In C. Fitzgerald and L. K. Kirby (Eds.), *Developing leaders: Research and applications in psychological type and leadership development* (pp. 439–464). Palo Alto, CA: Davies-Black.

Serban, A. M. (2002). Knowledge management: The "fifth face" of institutional research. In A. M. Serban & J. Luan (Eds.), *Knowledge management: Building a competitive advantage in higher education* (pp. 105–111). New Directions for Institutional Research, no. 113. San Francisco: Jossey-Bass.

Sheehan, B. (1975). The question of a synthesis in higher education management. In P. J. Plourde and C. R. Thomas (Eds.), *Innovative systems: Solution or illusion?* Proceedings for College and University Systems Exchange 1974 CAUSE National Conference, Boulder, CO: College and University Systems Exchange, *1,* 135–155.

Swing, R. L. (2009). Institutional researchers as change agents. In C. Leimer (Ed.), *Imagine the future of institutional research* (pp. 5–16). New Directions for Institutional Research, no. 143. San Francisco: Jossey-Bass.

Terenzini, P. (1993). On the nature of institutional research and the knowledge and skills it requires. *Research in Higher Education, 34*(1), 1–10.

Volkwein, J. F. (1990). The diversity of institutional research structures and tasks. In J. B. Presley (Ed.), *Organizing effective institutional research offices* (pp. 7–26). New Directions for Institutional Research, no. 66. San Francisco: Jossey-Bass.

Volkwein, J. F. (1999). The four faces of institutional research. In J. F. Volkwein (Ed.), *What is institutional research all about? A critical and comprehensive assessment of the profession* (pp. 9–19). New Directions for Institutional Research, no. 104. San Francisco: Jossey-Bass.

Volkwein, J. F. (2008). The foundations and evolution of institutional research. In D. G. Terkla (Ed.), *Institutional research: More than just data* (pp. 5–20). New Directions for Higher Education, no. 141. San Francisco: Jossey-Bass.

Volkwein, J. F., & Woodell, J. (2008). AIR survey fact. *The Electronic AIR, 28*(10). Tallahassee, FL: Association for Institutional Research.

CHAPTER 4

THE ROLE OF INSTITUTIONAL RESEARCH IN INTERNATIONAL UNIVERSITIES

Ann S. Ferren and Martha C. Merrill

In the first decade of the twenty-first century, institutions throughout different regions of the world have been adjusting to the impact of globalization on the flow of ideas, peoples, products, and technologies across borders, which has stimulated a transformation of higher education (Knight, 2006). In many cases, change has been driven by government influence aimed at regulating and coordinating institutions in order to increase region-wide economic competitiveness; to extend access, both national and international; and to create standards for quality assurance. These reform efforts vary in their procedures, degree of transparency, methodologies, and relation to funding (Billing, 2004). The best-known example is the Bologna Process, designed to set standards for a European Higher Education Area and make European education more competitive with the rest of the world (Gaston, 2010). Consequently, institutional research in a global context is far more policy and management oriented than in U.S. institutions.

We will reference four types of international universities in this chapter. A "world-class university" is a highly-renowned international university, such as Oxford and the Ecole Polytech, which shows up in the rankings as one of the top one hundred universities in the world (Levin, Jeong, & Ou, 2006). Another type of international university, from a U.S. perspective, is defined as simply any university in a country outside the United States, and includes both public and private institutions. Although institutional research is not well developed in many areas of the world, the topics for institutional research in both of these types of international universities are similar to those outlined throughout this *Handbook*. What is different is that researchers in some contexts will need to be aware of the political uses to which data may be put.

Two other types of "international universities"—(1) private universities patterned after U.S. educational models, and (2) U.S. public and private institutions functioning abroad in a variety of forms, including online, branch, and joint operations with another institution in the host country—require a somewhat different role for institutional researchers. These two forms of international higher education aim to follow the best practices and requirements of U.S. institutional research, while at the same time they must meet local expectations and legal requirements. With two procedures for accreditation, institutional researchers often find they are working in two cultures with different standards. In many cases, IR staff are confronted with challenges to their independent analyses, limitations on availability of data, and lack of a comparison group, as well as a whole host of issues that emerge when conducting research in unfamiliar cultural contexts, such as local norms related to integrity and transparency (Crossley & Watson, 2003).

In this chapter, we give primary attention to the major issues facing higher education throughout the world, namely: (1) the increased emphasis on quality assurance as governments move toward deregulation of higher education; (2) the call for cooperation as a result of regionalization; (3) the challenges institutions face as they compete for the best students and, at the same time, expand access; and (4) the impact of market forces as higher education has become a commodity, with new providers taking advantage of developments in technology and trade agreements (Knight, 2006). Where appropriate, we reference policy documents, relevant associations, and sources of data. Institutional researchers need to understand not only the drivers of change affecting all international higher education, but also the specific political, social, and economic contexts in which their work is situated.

World-Class Universities

Although rankings are often criticized for their methodology, scholars have identified traits that most would agree set world-class institutions apart. Salmi (2009) notes "three complementary sets of factors at play in the top universities: (a) a high concentration of talent (faculty and students), (b) abundant resources to offer a rich learning environment and to conduct advanced research, and (c) favorable governance features that encourage strategic vision, innovation, and flexibility and that enable institutions to make decisions and to manage resources without being encumbered by bureaucracy" (p. 7). Such a list of factors makes it clear that world-class universities are most likely to thrive in nations where autonomy trumps regulation and resources are abundant. In the most widely recognized world rankings, U.S. institutions hold the majority of places in the top one hundred, followed by institutions from nine European nations, Japan, Australia, Canada, and Israel (Academic Rankings, 2009).

World-class universities and "aspiring" world-class universities present institutional researchers with three unique challenges. The first is that such universities, by definition, address international rather than national audiences. Institutional researchers will need to gather both student and faculty data in a greater variety of categories than if they were based in a nationally focused university. Maintaining up-to-date contact information on alumni to collect statistics on career placement and graduate school enrollment is more difficult. Even furnishing data for institutional marketing purposes is more complex, because, as researchers in the field of contrastive rhetoric have documented, what is considered persuasive varies from one culture to another. For example, in one cultural setting statistics are meaningful, whereas in another, statements from authorities are deemed more reliable. To be responsive to all stakeholders, IR staff in world-class universities may be expected to understand intercultural communication as well as to either be multilingual or have access to translators and cultural informants.

The second unique challenge, particularly in aspiring world-class universities, is the degree to which institutional researchers need to collect data in categories that will help a university move up in international rankings, such as the Academic Rankings of World Universities (formerly the Shanghai Jiao Tong rankings) and QS World University Rankings (formerly the *Times* Higher Education Rankings). Although other systems are being developed by practitioners concerned about the emphasis these two systems place on publications in English, and particularly on publications in the hard sciences, research productivity and citations are the hallmark of elite universities. Deemed to be an external validation of quality, rankings are taken so seriously by senior administrators and even political figures that IR staff must stay current with the criteria and methodologies for different ranking systems if they are to help position their institutions favorably. Those involved in computing rankings have an association—the International Ranking Expert Group (IREG)—a regular conference, a code of ethics, and a set of principles for the design of ranking systems (Berlin Principles, 2006).

The third unique challenge for IR staff working in world-class universities is that the generally accepted goal of increasing student access is not an objective of such universities. Although increasing the *diversity* of its elite student population may be a goal, increasing *access* or increasing enrollment works against the interests of world-class universities. They gain by limiting access: the more selective the institution, the more prestigious it is, giving students advantages in jobs, income, and social status. Elite education is a positional good—one that gains value by being scarce (Marginson, 1997). For some institutional researchers, gathering data that emphasize an institution's exclusivity may cause some rethinking of values. The emphasis on exclusivity may also come into conflict with national mandates for accepting secondary school graduates in certain categories. The sometimes internally contested goals of universities and their increasingly diverse stakeholders and cultural environments mean that institutional researchers in the twenty-first century need political acumen to judge and juggle demands.

Universities Outside the United States

Universities that serve primarily national audiences also are dealing with new external demands prompted by globalization and the resulting reform efforts. The most prominent is mass student access, defined by Trow (2007) as a situation in which 16 to 50 percent of the relevant age cohort of a nation attends higher education institutions. Both individual institutions and national systems are encountering increasing diversity as traditional age students as well as adults see the social and economic value of higher education in a "knowledge economy" that requires a skilled workforce. Because massification has occurred without significant increases in financial and human resources, observers note the positive effect of greater social mobility and the democratization of education, but they also fear a lowering of standards and inadequate numbers of trained faculty (Altbach, Reisberg, & Rumbley, 2009). The task for IR staff is to document gains in both participation and quality as evidence of capacity building in the region they serve.

Just as in the United States, diversity in economic groups, age groups, and ethnic groups requires IR staff to move beyond adding new rows to Excel spreadsheets analyzing the impact of increasing diversity on, for example, retention, faculty productivity, and course-taking patterns. In the United States, the term *swirling* is used to describe the attendance patterns of many of these new students, who see higher education institutions as service providers and in the course of one semester, often while working full or part-time, may take a math course at a university, a computer class at a community college, and a distance education course in business from a for-profit institution. Such students expect to put all of the pieces together into some kind of coherent whole at a later date. Tracking student progress or measuring institutional efficiency in these new circumstances requires new techniques and definitions, just as "graduation rate" needed to be redefined by the National Center for Educational Statistics (NCES) from four to six years.

The implications of massification have moved beyond the idea of "build more buildings and hire more professors" to rethinking how these varied students are, in fact, reshaping higher education policy and forms (Altbach, Reisberg, & Rumbley, 2009). Although higher education is increasingly recognized as not only a public good but also a basic human right, there remain dramatic differences in participation rates around the world. Consequently, the pressure to expand educational opportunities not only affects the activities at individual institutions, but also leads to institutional diversity and, unfortunately, creates opportunities for unscrupulous providers to enter the market. Governments are strengthening barriers to recognition of private and for-profit higher education to reduce the possibility of diploma mills, even as they facilitate the entry of new providers to meet increasing demand.

The Kyrgyz Republic—which, at the time of independence in 1991, had one full-fledged university—is, as of this writing, home to over fifty universities, including the American University in Central Asia, the Kyrgyz-Russian Slavonic University, a Turkish university supported by the Turkish government and a Turkish university supported by a Sufi religious order, a university sponsored by Kuwait, branch campuses of five Russian universities, five Bologna Process centers, a Confucius Institute, and a technical university—one division of which is actively seeking to offer dual degrees with a university in Germany. Some universities there use the bachelor's/master's system; some use the Soviet-era *diplom, kandidat nauk,* and *doktor nauk;* some use credit hours, some use contact hours, and some use both. This is but one example of the rapidly changing landscape of international higher education that makes it challenging for institutional researchers to collect, analyze, and compare data to meet institutional and government needs.

Fulfilling the reporting requirements of the countries' ministries of education, who oversee public institutions and some private institutions, requires systematic data gathering and standardized reporting. Changes in governments, reforms in higher education laws, and new requirements to protect data and encourage integrity in reporting are just a few of the elements that put pressure on IR staff with limited experience, especially in countries with relatively undeveloped infrastructures. Even experienced IR staff benefit from the professional development opportunities and publications that are available through such organizations as the European Association for Institutional Research (EAIR) and the European Association for Quality Assurance (ENQA). IR professionals may also want to be familiar with various sources of information on higher education in other countries such as the Higher Education Statistics Agency (HESA) in the UK, the United Nations Educational, Scientific and Cultural Organization (UNESCO) Institute for Statistics: Global Education Digest, the Stocktaking reports of all Bologna countries, and the analytic reports sponsored by UNESCO and the World Bank.

Regional Cooperation to Improve Higher Education

In many parts of the world, what is known as "regionalization" is taking place. Nations are forming regional groupings to coordinate their higher education systems, to reduce bureaucratic regulation, to facilitate the movement of students and scholars, and to make it easier to transfer credits and recognize degrees. These efforts require respect for the diversity of cultures and systems. As these regional systems develop and mature, there is demand for more and more data in support of both making processes more transparent and providing data for quality assessment. The most pressing fundamental question is how to define quality—a question faced by U.S. higher education as well. "I know it when I see it" is no longer a sufficient answer in an environment in which choices about government funding, expectations of employers, or demands of students and parents reflect conflicting definitions of academic quality, such as excellence, fitness for purpose, transformation, or value for money (Harvey, 2006).

Despite efforts to establish a fixed definition, academic quality remains a multidimensional and somewhat culture-specific concept. At the first level, because very few can be "the best," attention is given to the degree to which an institution achieves its own mission and objectives. At a second level, measuring a program or institution against the standards of the discipline, the national educational system, or accreditation criteria ensures that minimum standards are met and allows comparisons among institutions and programs. At an even broader level, quality is measured in the societal context, such as producing individuals with the special skills and attitudes employers expect and the ability to be life-long learners, consistent with the principle that education is essential to economic development and civic participation. In any discussion of quality, there will be differences of opinion as to whether to measure inputs, processes, or outcomes; which categories to address, such as academic programs, faculty, services, facilities, and management; and whether quality assessment should be only internal or require external review as well. Institutional researchers must anchor their work in both the institutional and the international conversation about quality.

In this complex environment, regionalization increases the pressure to reduce the variations in definitions and procedures and strive toward convergence in quality assurance systems supported by centralized authority, good communication, and cooperation across borders. The most advanced regionalization effort is among institutions complying with the Bologna Process policies and regulations. Harmonizing forms of education and degree requirements was the first step, followed by clearly defined quality assurance processes. The website of the European Higher Education Area, which the Bologna Process was said to have achieved in 2010 (European Higher Education Area, 2010), is a well-organized and comprehensive resource, and Paul Gaston's *The Challenge of Bologna* (2010) is a readable introduction to the process, particularly for those who are familiar with the U.S. higher education system. Eaton (2009, paragraph 7) succinctly contrasts the "international emphasis on government authority for quality assurance" with the United States' effort to "maintain an appropriate balance of accountability to government and the historic independence of both accreditation and higher education institutions."

Although the Bologna Process may appear to be monolithic and well supported, it is, above all, a political process initiated by ministers of education interested in the economic competitiveness of the European Union, and it has met with some resistance at the institutional level (de Wit, 2002). The focus on the instrumental uses of higher education has been strongly protested by a variety of stakeholders involved in higher education who resist letting specific workforce requirements be the *raison d'être* for major change. Alternative cases for education reform, such as the importance of promoting social cohesion and supporting innovation networks, are less well represented in the criteria.

Any institutional researcher in the Bologna Process region needs to be aware of the political contexts and attitudes toward the Bologna Process on his or her specific campus or risk lack of cooperation in gathering data and conducting studies. As Reichert and Tauch (2003) have pointed out, what is promulgated in a declaration at a biannual ministerial meeting differs from what a minister responsible for higher education is able to implement at home, and what that minister is able to have accepted at a national level may differ from what is valued and financed at a campus level. Indeed, some of the elite universities believe the Bologna Process is only for universities serving the European region, not for "world-class" universities serving the world.

One aspect of the Bologna Process to be emulated is the clear national-level data reporting requirements. The template for the required biannual National Reports (Bologna Process Stocktaking, 2009) includes indicators of progress, and these indicators require institutional-level data that then must be aggregated nationally. For example, each nation must report on the percentage of its students who are enrolled in "two-cycle" degree programs (usually bachelor's and master's); on the degree of student participation in five levels of quality assessment processes; on the proportion of students receiving diploma supplements in addition to transcripts; on the degree to which the European Credit Transfer System (ECTS) credits are linked to student learning outcomes; and on the status of the creation of procedures for assessing prior learning—an issue of great interest in the European Union, which needs a nimble workforce but whose population is aging.

To further reduce national differences, all quality assessment under the Bologna Process must meet carefully spelled out guidelines. The *Standards and Guidelines for Quality Assurance in the European Higher Education Area* (ENQA, 2009) focuses on three categories: for internal assessment, for external assessment, and for quality assessment agencies themselves. These include seven standards for internal reviews, eight for external reviews, and eight for agencies. The internal standards address everything from assessment of students, periodic program reviews, and assessing faculty qualifications to ensuring that relevant information is collected regularly and is publicly available. IR staff will recognize that these standards are similar to the standards used by the regional accrediting bodies in the United States.

A brief look at two other regionalization efforts is also instructive in demonstrating the need for institutional research to reflect its context and set realistic goals. A system that is even more audacious in some ways than the Bologna area—given the speed with which reforms and coordination are envisioned to take place, the diversity of both the secondary and higher education systems, the vast numbers of students involved, the geographic distances to be covered, and the relative poverty of the countries involved—is that of Southeast Asia, coordinated by the South East Asian Ministers of Education Organization

Regional Centre for Higher Education and Development. Among the cooperating nations are Indonesia, Malaysia, Singapore, the Philippines, and Thailand. Powell (2008, paragraph 1) comments, "Arguing the case for an extensive overhaul of co-operation and compatibility involving 6,500 higher education institutions and 12 million students in 10 widely differing nations is no easy task; and it's particularly onerous if the deadline for implementation is 2015."

This regional initiative shows both the pressures of worldwide trends in higher education and the needs for region-specific responses. Writing two years before the process was initiated, Lee and Healy (2006) note a series of characteristics of Southeast Asian higher education, similar to those in the Bologna Process nations: massification, system diversification, internationalization, marketization and privatization, institutional restructuring, and trading of autonomy for accountability. Of particular interest is the fact that a group of Asian countries, working with UNESCO, created a convention on the mutual recognition of academic credentials nearly a decade and a half before the Lisbon Recognition Convention was signed in 1997. Population increases, global trade, and increased student mobility within the region are cited as drivers behind the Southeast Asian regionalization effort (Cabreza, 2010). Although the region differs dramatically from Europe in a number of ways—population size, the youthfulness of the population, the economic and political diversity of the nations involved, and, for some, colonial legacies that continue to affect higher education—a number of the challenges and responses are the same, including the value of collective efforts and a focus on quality. Institutional researchers in this region find support and resources through the South East Asian Association for Institutional Research (SEAAIR).

The continent of Africa is also an instructive case study of a region where efforts to integrate and revitalize higher education are essential to addressing challenges of poverty, underdevelopment, and gender and racial inequality. However, comprehensive educational reform is hampered by many of the same challenges that the national governments face, including political instability, corruption, and lack of human and financial resources. The African Association of Universities, with the support of the UNESCO-ADEA Task Force for Higher Education in Africa, African Development Bank, and the World Bank, is guiding initiatives to encourage the more developed African countries to help the less developed countries; to focus the curriculum on both basic needs, such as agriculture and natural resources, as well as new areas of study that can diversify African economies; and to attract international partners, providers, and donors to address the challenges of lack of infrastructure and capacity (Mohamedbhai, 2008). Even with steady increases in enrollment in the last decade, overall only 5 percent of African youth attend college, many in substandard conditions.

Despite significant societal barriers, African nations are working together to expand institutional capacity with the same commitment to quality assurance and the same management challenges as in other regions of the world. Materu (2007) notes that "Systematic quality assurance systems are in place in about one third of African countries" (p. 63). Quality assurance criteria must embrace all forms of education, including the established research universities and technical universities, as well as the growing private sector, branch campuses, and entrepreneurial forms of education such as virtual universities and franchised institutions. Institutional research in a traditional type of higher education institution may focus on research productivity, effective teaching, and student services, whereas in other types the focus may be on training needs, marketing, and expanding enrollment (Emetarom & Enyi, 2007).

The numerous quality assurance agencies recognize the benefits of regionalization, including recognition of degrees, mobility of faculty, and involvement of external peer reviewers in their processes. However, their efforts are increasingly difficult because the new cross border initiatives, such as e-learning, can reach students directly and not be audited for quality. For example, the Higher Education Quality Committee in South Africa, a national agency, tries to oversee the setting up of branch campuses, but acknowledges its limited success in dealing with distance education from abroad (Knight, 2006).

This rapidly changing and challenging environment requires leadership, collaboration, and human capacity at both government and institutional levels. The recently developed Regional Higher Education Management Information Network System (RHEMINS) aims to support a collaborative approach for the "acquisition and management of information as a strategy for strengthening higher education management in the African region" (Emetarom & Enyi, 2007, p. 4). Given resource constraints, one can assume that there are few trained institutional researchers to support the collection, interpretation, and dissemination of information to support accreditation and quality assessment. The Southern African Association for Institutional Research (SAAIR) aims to provide guidance to build capacity. Whether in the wealthier or the poorer nations, higher education institutions are cooperating and striving to overcome challenges and adapt to globalization in order to achieve quality higher education outcomes—employable graduates, responsible citizens, and economic and social development.

U.S. Institutions Functioning Abroad

When U.S. campuses open branches abroad or form partnerships with institutions in other countries, they do so because of a commitment to extending higher education abroad for social, economic, and political reasons (de Wit, 2002)—however, not without self-interest. These U.S. institutions aim to contribute to areas with insufficient higher education resources; in return, they anticipate new markets, revenue from new enrollments, overseas experiences for U.S. faculty, greater control over instruction than if provided by distance education, and enhancement of their reputation as a "global university." The host country adds to its portfolio of quality offerings at a lower cost than sending students abroad and reduces the possibility of brain drain. The challenge for institutional researchers is to establish an office with staff trained in traditional research methodologies who understand both U.S. higher education requirements and local and regional requirements. The types of tools they need and studies they might conduct are outlined throughout this *Handbook*. The external pressures they may face are not.

For any overseas initiative to be sustainable, U.S. institutions must be realistic about the challenges they will face in the host country. Many sources have covered in detail the pitfalls and problems that are similar to those faced by multinational businesses as they learn to do business in another culture (Rumbley & Altbach, 2007). Among the difficulties for higher education institutions are different cultural perspectives on the importance of autonomy and integrity in institutional operations, nondiscrimination in admissions and employment, and academic freedom in the classroom and curriculum. Administrators must learn to deal with the inevitable culture clashes in the work environment and with student expectations, confusing regulatory and legal issues, and complicated labor laws. For the host country, the branch may create tensions with other in-country campuses and be seen as undermining their viability or perpetuating elitism, or the branch may be suspected of recruiting students who later will transfer out to the home campus in the United States (McBurnie & Ziguras, 2010). To manage all the subtleties, IR staff should be competent in the local language, willing to monitor the environment as it changes, and sensitive about how best to gather, interpret, and present information.

Although 48 percent of current international branch campuses are sponsored by U.S. institutions, there are other major providers, including Australia, United Kingdom, France, and India, with China and the United Arab Emirates as the leading host countries (Becker, 2010). In this competitive environment, IR may be asked to help with market research to determine whether there is sufficient demand and sufficient resources for the partnership or new initiative to be successful. Once the branch campus is established, IR will address issues of quality assurance and recognition of degrees; for example, by working with agencies such as the University Quality Assurance International Board (UQAIB) in Dubai to achieve validation to complement U.S. accreditation (Ahmed, 2010). One interesting question not addressed in the international quality standards is whether local students enrolled in a branch campus gain the benefits of internationalization. If students and staff are primarily local and the curriculum is not global in design, the international branch campus may provide good education but not give its graduates "an international outlook," thus not realizing this increasingly important goal of U.S. higher education (McBurnie & Ziguras, 2010).

Depending on one's perspective and definition, globalization is either positive—that is, stimulating educational opportunity around the world—or negative—that is, reducing quality and diversity. The inclusion of education as a "service" under the WTO's General Agreement on Trade in Services (GATS) awakens many of these fears: that all sorts of for-profit ventures will crowd out underfunded public institutions in developing countries, make it difficult to validate courses or programs, and create unintended consequences due to lack of regulation (Scott, 2007). Monitoring trade negotiations may not be a common activity for most IR staff, but it is essential for those living in WTO countries, as the results of such negotiations can impact institutional operations and are legally binding. For example, Knight (2008, p. 155) lists several instances in which elements of accreditation processes have been called "barriers to trade." In addition, because most licensing and quality assessment processes were designed to evaluate national providers and not providers from abroad, the opportunity for degree mills and other questionable providers to set up shop, either physically or virtually, around the world, is an issue of real concern (Knight, 2008, pp. 174–178). Not only credential evaluators but also students, ministries of education, and other higher education agencies need to be aware of the possibilities of unethical practices as national assessment regulations designed with one set of assumptions await the revisions needed for a new era. To address this issue, UNESCO/OECD (2005) have written *Guidelines for Quality Provision in Cross-Border Higher Education.*

International Universities Based on the U.S. Model

The final type of international university is an independent private institution based on the U.S. model of higher education, and in most cases carrying both U.S. accreditation and local recognition. These private American-style universities range from the well established, such as the American University in Beirut, founded in 1862, to those founded in the post-Soviet period of the early 1990s to help with the transition to democracy, such as Central European University in Budapest, to the even more recent U.S.-government-supported American University in Afghanistan. Not all of these universities include "American" in their name, but all of them share a common commitment to effective education based on a liberal arts foundation, instruction in English, and student-centered pedagogy, characterized by the values of integrity and respect for others. Because of the different histories, governance and financial structures, and political and social contexts, it is not possible to generalize about the role of institutional researchers, except to note that they must function under two quality assurance systems and find their place in the host country, often without the full support that is accorded to the public institutions. In some cases, sustainability is as challenging as maintaining quality.

The Association of American International Colleges and Universities (AAICU), founded in 1971, serves as a support group for its twenty-five members and associate members. An annual meeting for the presidents and chief academic officers, workshops on accreditation, and recent efforts to share data are designed to promote quality. The American International Consortium of Academic Libraries (AMICAL), founded in 2004, serves a similar function to ensure that library professionals in these institutions, located in seventeen different countries and serving students from well over one hundred nations, have access to the latest developments in information resources. Although these American-style institutions can learn from each other, they are not comparable enough in admissions standards, faculty composition, size, or resources to provide comparison data. These cooperative efforts do not have a formal role in quality control, but they do provide perspective and advice, which is especially important for newly founded institutions that may want to receive U.S. accreditation.

A large part of the IR staff workload in these institutions consists of conducting studies and reporting data to meet local requirements. The extensive guidelines of the ministries of education sometimes have IR staff trying to fit new "round pegs" into old "square holes." Reporting quantitative measures such as the number of volumes in the library per student is no longer meaningful when electronic resources replace print materials. Reporting the number of public computers available to students does not indicate technology access if many students have their own personal computer. In the Kyrgyz Republic, as in much of the former Soviet Union, one of the pieces of data that must be supplied to the ministry of education is the number of square meters per student. The required number is nine. This requirement makes sense under a contact hour system wherein students are on campus and in class thirty-five hours a week, but not under the American-style credit hour system wherein they may be in class twelve to fifteen hours a week and working independently at other times. Thus the same space can accommodate more students. Over time such discrete input measures may be replaced by a greater emphasis on outcomes and evidence of a process for continuous improvement, thus making reporting requirements more congruent with U.S. accreditation requirements.

Two concepts that are often handled differently in these American-style institutions than they are in the other higher education institutions in the host country are integrity and transparency, both accepted values in U.S. higher education. Integrity in the United States is reflected in all aspects of the institution, ranging from admissions, student assignments, and grading to employment, research, and management of resources. In some areas of the world, hiring based on relationships, accepting a student along with a gift to the university, or a faculty member earning supplemental pay directly from a student is a matter of course. Similarly, standards with regard to confidentiality of information may clash with local notions about transparency and what information should show up in the newspaper. Institutional researchers will need clear ethical standards, and they must regularly scan the kinds of statistics that are collected, try to determine how reliable they are, get advice about which data requests to meet, and be prepared to say "no" when information requests are inappropriate.

One of the most challenging issues for U.S. institutions abroad is the recruitment and retention of faculty. Recruiting sufficient expatriate faculty for these American-style campuses is difficult because job security is not the same as in the United States, and not everyone is interested in—or suited to—being an expatriate. Faculty working abroad soon become experts on salary comparisons, benefits, taxation, currency fluctuation, and a host of other issues ranging from security to local traditions. Designing a compensation plan is particularly challenging when the local salaries and cost of living are significantly different from that in the home country of the newly recruited faculty member. On some campuses, U.S. faculty, local faculty, and third country nationals each have a different compensation program.

The IR staff may be asked to conduct salary analyses, taking into consideration cost of living, comparative information on higher education salaries, and income studies in the country. Unlike in the United States, where administrators rely on American Association of University Professors (AAUP) reports on salary averages by rank and type of institution or the College and University Personnel Association (CUPA) studies that provide salary ranges by discipline and type of institution for both new hires and continuing faculty, overseas campuses have little information to guide them in setting competitive salaries. A comprehensive study conducted by Rumbley, Pacheco, and Altbach (2008) provides comparative data on academic salaries in sixteen countries, but also demonstrates just how difficult it is to conduct such an analysis. As a stable faculty is important for continuity in programs and services to students, IR staff will want to study turnover, not just statistically but through qualitative methods, to help the institution improve hiring, transition support, faculty development, and other essential aspects of life abroad.

Conclusion

The role of institutional research in international universities, as described in this chapter, varies according to the type of "international university," but no matter the type—world-class, national, a branch of a U.S. campus, or an American-style university—the institutional researchers must attend to both the institution's needs and the global context. If the institutional researchers are from the United States, effective work will require adapting through conscientious reflection about assumptions, values, and methodologies appropriate to the new location. If the researchers are nationals of the country where the institution is located, they must learn as much as possible about data sources and research methodologies in other contexts to give perspective for the changing governmental and societal framework in which the institution functions. As noted throughout this chapter, each type of institution requires of the researcher skills and knowledge particular to the situation and quite different from what is needed for a university located in the United States.

In addition, an institutional researcher working abroad will want to take time for professional development in order to handle the plethora of rapidly changing issues: the effects of massification in a time of limited resources; new forms of quality assessment, as nations deal with regionalization of standards and diversification of institutional types; mobility of not only students but also professors and staff; educational services negotiated under rules of international trade; and more. Institutional research in international universities is challenging and changing—an ideal environment for professional growth and learning.

References

Academic Rankings of World Universities 2009. (2009). Retrieved from http://www.arwu .org/ARWU2009.jsp

Ahmed, A. (2010). Quality check for foreign universities. *Khaleej Times.* Retrieved from http://www.khaleejtimes.com/DisplayArticleNew.asp?col=&section=theuae&xfile= data/theuae/2010/April/theuae_April481.xml

Altbach, P., Reisberg, L., & Rumbley, L. (2009). *Trends in global higher education: Tracking an academic revolution.* Chestnut Hill, MA: Boston College Center for International Higher Education.

Becker, R. (2010). International branch campuses: New trends and directions. *International Higher Education.* Retrieved from http://www.bc.edu/bc_org/avp/soe/ cihe/newsletter/Number58/p3_Becker.htm

Berlin Principles (2006). Berlin principles on ranking of higher education institutions. Retrieved from http://www.che.de/downloads/Berlin_Principles_IREG_534.pdf

Billing, D. (2004). International comparisons and trends in external quality assurance of higher education: Commonality or diversity? *Higher Education, 47*(1), 113–137.

Bologna Process Stocktaking: List of Indicators 2009. (2009). Retrieved from http://www .ond.vlaanderen.be/hogeronderwijs/bologna/actionlines/documents/Stocktaking_ indicators_final.pdf. Available from the "Action Lines" section of the 2007–2010 official Bologna Process website: http://www.ond.vlaanderen.be/hogeronderwijs/Bologna/

Cabreza, V. (2010). Global university standards pushed. *Inquirer.net.* Posted February 14, 2010. Retrieved from http://business.inquirer.net/money/topstories/view/20100214– 253183/Global-university-standards-pushed

Crossley, M., & Watson, K. (2003). *Comparative and international research in education globalisation: Context and differences.* London: RoutledgeFalmer.

de Wit, H. (2002). *Internationalization of higher education in the United States of America and Europe: A historical, comparative, and conceptual analysis.* Westport, CT: Greenwood Press.

Eaton, J. (2009). Quality assurance and the world conference on higher education. *Inside Accreditation, 5*: 5. Retrieved from http://www.chea.org/ia/IA_ 2009.07.23.html

Emetarom, U., & Enyi, D. (2007). Strengthening the management of the higher education system in Africa: The role of a regional higher education management information network system (RHEMINS). Retrieved from http://www.airweb.org/webrecordings/publications/africanreview/EMETARON.pdf

European Association for Quality Assurance in Higher Education. (2009). *Standards and guidelines for quality assurance in the European higher education area.* Retrieved from http://www.enqa.eu/files/ESG_3edition%20(2).pdf

European Higher Education Area. (2010). Official website. Retrieved from http://www.ehea.info/

Gaston, P. (2010). *The challenge of Bologna: What United States higher education has to learn from Europe and why it matters that we learn it.* Sterling, VA: Stylus.

Harvey, L. (2006). Understanding quality. In L. Purser (Ed.), *EUA Bologna handbook: Making Bologna work.* Brussels European University Association and Berlin: Raabe. http://www.bologna-handbook.com/

Knight, J. (2006). *Higher education crossing borders: A guide to the implications of the General Agreement on Trade in Services (GATS) for cross-border education.* Paris: Commonwealth of Learning and UNESCO.

Knight, J. (2008). *Higher education in turmoil: The changing world of internationalization.* Rotterdam: Sense Publishers.

Lee, M.N.N., & Healy, S. (2006). Higher education in South-East Asia: An overview. In *Higher Education in South-East Asia* (pp. 1–12). Asia-Pacific Programme of Educational Innovation for Development, United Nations Educational, Scientific and Cultural Organization. Bangkok, Thailand: UNESCO Bangkok.

Levin, H., Jeong, D., & Ou, D. (2006). What is a world class university? Paper presented at the Conference of the Comparative and International Education Society. Retrieved from http://www.tc.columbia.edu/centers/coce/pdf_files/c12.pdf

Marginson, S. (1997). *Markets in education.* Sydney: Allen and Unwin.

Materu, P. (2007). *Higher education quality assurance in Sub Saharan Africa: Status, challenges, opportunities, and promising practices.* Washington, DC: World Bank.

McBurnie, G., & Ziguras, C. (2010). The international branch campus. Retrieved from http://www.iienetwork.org/page/84656/

Mohamedbhai, G. (2008). *The effects of massification on higher education in Africa.* Ghana: Association of African Universities.

Powell, S. (2008, November 12). Asian nations aim to harmonize systems. *Australian.* Retrieved from http://www.theaustralian.com.au/higher-education/asian-nations-aim-to-harmonise-systems/story-e6frgcjx-1111118006196

Reichert, S., & Tauch, C. (2003). *Bologna four years after: Steps toward sustainable reform of higher education in Europe.* European University Association Trends III: Progress Toward the European Higher Education Area. European Directorate for Education and Culture. Retrieved from http://www.ond.vlaanderen.be/hogeronderwijs/bologna/documents/EUA_Trends_Reports/TRENDS_III-July2003.pdf

Rumbley, L., & Altbach, P. (2007). International branch campus issues. Retrieved from http://democrats.science.house.gov/Media/File/Commdocs/hearings/2007/full/26jul/altbach_appendix_1.pdf

Rumbley, L., Pacheco, I., & Altbach, P. (2008). *International comparison of academic salaries.* Chestnut Hill, MA: Boston College Center for International Higher Education.

Salmi, J. (2009). *The challenge of establishing world-class universities.* Washington, DC: International Bank for Reconstruction and Development/The World Bank. Retrieved

from http://siteresources.worldbank.org/EDUCATION/Resources/
278200–1099079877269/547664–1099079956815/547670–1237305262556/WCU.pdf

Scott, P. (2007). The external face of the Bologna Process: The European Higher
Education Area in a global context. In L. Purser (Ed.), *EUA Bologna handbook: Making
Bologna work*. Brussels European University Association and Berlin: Raabe. http://www
.bologna-handbook.com/

Trow, M. (2007). Reflections on the transition from elite to mass to universal access: Forms
and phases of higher education in modern societies since WWII. In J.J.F. Forest and
P. Altbach (Eds.), *International handbook of higher education* (pp. 243–280). Dordrecht,
Netherlands: Springer (e-book edition).

UNESCO/OECD (2005). Guidelines for quality provision in cross-border
higher education. Paris: UNESCO/OECD. Retrieved from www.oecd.org/
dataoecd/27/51/35779480.pdf

CHAPTER 5

OUT OF THE BOX AND OUT OF THE OFFICE

Institutional Research for Changing Times

Richard A. Voorhees and Teri Hinds

Institutional research should serve as the institutional nexus not merely for providing data, on request, to units across the institution, but also—on much higher ground—as the hub for institutional strategy. In this chapter we argue for an activist role for institutional research as well as vigorous contributions to overall institutional health by the professionals who work in this critical field. Too often, in our experience, institutional research is viewed as a passive pursuit, populated by office-bound actors who prepare routine reports for external agencies. Although the authors suggest that preparation of required external reports is *one* legitimate product of institutional research, we also argue that there are other opportunities that require institutional research skills that can be much more exciting and certainly more useful to an institution.

The financial crisis in higher education that began in the first decade of the twenty-first century is a strong signal that higher education as it was once known will never be the same. The demands placed on institutions and those who work inside institutions to be innovative have never been this loud. In fact, those who believe that public higher education will return to "normal" after the 50 U.S. states run out of stimulus dollars to fill funding gaps—roughly predicted for the time this *Handbook* is published—are increasingly hard to find. Kelderman (2010) reported that half of the states would have spent all of their stimulus money for education by the end of June 2010 and that 40 states would experience revenue shortfalls in the following fiscal year. Clearly, something has to give in the short term, and much more is predicted to give in the long term. Our purpose, however, is not to restate the obvious sea change that is now occurring or to dwell on an unstable future for higher education. Rather, we point out the profound need for institutional researchers to engage directly in the challenges ahead and to position their institutions to move ahead with creating actionable data that can spell the difference between being passive recipients of unprecedented change or intelligent actors trying to create a more manageable future.

Institutional researchers have the skills to buttress innovative thinking. Where else in a given organization do individuals presumably know best about the quantitative and qualitative methodologies used to create knowledge about higher education and how to apply this knowledge to higher education's problems and opportunities? Where else can knowledge about harvesting primary data, accessing institutional data, and using external databases to support hard management decisions be found? Clearly, institutional researchers come to their work with many advantages. But are these advantages deployed in ways that serve both the institution and the individual who has the skills?

Other chapters in this *Handbook* speak directly to the attributes required of successful institutional researchers. In Chapter 2, for example, Volkwein, Liu, and Woodel examine Terenzini's (1993) three tiers of organizational intelligence. Terenzini's hierarchy presents a clear way for institutional researchers to engage in self-examination, especially to ensure not only that they have technical expertise, but also that they understand issues facing higher education and can place their own work within institutional culture and context. In Chapter 3, Eimers, Ko, and Gardner argue that the profession needs to better understand the work preferences of its members, perhaps by using a standardized approach to measuring personality types. Those authors conclude that the skills required for institutional research are reasonably consistent across institutional types and reporting lines, but that knowing subtle nuances can help institutional researchers accelerate their careers. In this chapter, we urge institutional researchers to go beyond cognitive skill sets and their own personality orientations to engage widely and purposefully with others throughout their institutions. Simple awareness of an ideal collection of skills or other attributes—without a corresponding roadmap or plan of action to bring those skills to bear—is a glass only half full. We call on institutional researchers to *animate* higher-order skills to support innovation—a meme we call "out of the box and out of the office."

Context for Innovation and Leadership

We suggest that institutional research needs to be actively engaged across the institution, while acknowledging that the institutional climate can either promote or discourage the efforts of institutional research to make that engagement meaningful. No one factor distinguishes an organizational context that is ready for innovation and leadership. Certainly, those institutions that have buy-in for data and information from top administrators are likely to bolster the role of institutional research. We also acknowledge that top administrators who discourage the engagement of institutional research and who choose to operate in a political model are increasingly rare in higher education, if for no other reason than the increased external demand for data and accountability.

Institutions that make a commitment to providing transparent data and information are institutions that will prosper in tough times. But it is not enough to make information transparent. Institutions must show that they are not only making data and information accessible but also *acting* on what they know. It is usually up to the institutional research function to lay out how an institution's data can be used to make actionable decisions. Institutional researchers can accelerate the development of actionable data, but this requires a commitment to open dialogue across the campus and, often, a willingness to visit other units to form a deep understanding of the issues they face.

A critical waypoint in the organizational context is a meaningful strategic plan. One can tell much about an institution's inertia and opportunities for institutional research by a quick scan of an institution's strategic plan. Does it, for example, contain *measurable* strategies or just strategies by themselves? Is there evidence that the plan is tied directly to a planning and budgeting cycle? What targets does it set for institutional performance? Are those targets set in reference to an institution's history? Does the strategic plan consider actions by the institution's competitors? Without establishing the definitive criteria for separating an effective strategic plan from a public relations piece, it should be obvious that there are many opportunities for institutional researchers to vastly improve most strategic plans.

Individual Context

What can institutional research professionals do to align themselves with an organizational agenda that stresses innovation? Although the core skills of institutional research are increasingly important to establish competence within an institution, so, too, are interpersonal skills and personal attributes important to success. Knight, Moore, and Coperthwaite (1997), in a study of the effectiveness of institutional researchers, found minimal relationships between their background characteristics, knowledge, and skills in institutional research and perceptions of others' effectiveness. This led the researchers to suggest that institutional culture, expectations, and leaders' personalities are alternative predictors of effectiveness.

The next section of this chapter explores the interaction of the institutional researcher as key actor in institutional culture. We also explore—albeit indirectly—the personality attributes that our experience suggests are associated with success in institutional contexts. Together, these concepts support our argument that an effective institutional researcher is also an individual who is "out of the box and out of the office." We don't mean to suggest that the *sine qua non* for leadership of an institutional research function is for introverts to reinvent themselves as snappy, perky, and outwardly ebullient.

We do, however, suggest that there are touchstone practices that all institutional researchers can adopt that will serve them well in the pursuit of helping their institutions innovate.

Navigating the Terrain

To be effective, we believe, requires a certain cognitive dissonance between the institution and the institutional research director. It is often desirable to maintain some distance from the conventional wisdom in place at an institution so as to play a role in shaping that wisdom later. To some, a purposefully dispassionate stance may be mistaken for noninvolvement. However, not automatically choosing sides in institutional debates and being able to avoid the appearance of toeing the "party line" can be beneficial in the long run. Fence-sitting is generally viewed somewhat negatively as a state of indecision; however, it can also be a state of mediation, capable of seeing what lies on both—or many—sides of an issue and to communicate those views to advance the best interests of the institution. Institutional researchers should be comfortable existing at, and reaching across, boundaries to help the institution accomplish its strategic goals. It is paramount that those in institutional research offices see the larger picture of institutional effectiveness and be able to act on this vision.

Organizational Skills

Understanding and acting on issues. At a macro level, it is critical to understand the issues facing higher education as an industry as well as those issues that are of current import on a given campus to frame data and analysis in context. Seeing how their institution fits in this broader social and political landscape will enable practitioners to anticipate the needs of key stakeholders on campus and to give them appropriate information in a timely manner. For instance, increasing the number of baccalaureate degrees has recently received great attention in national public policy discussions; knowing the details of this national conversation allows institutional research practitioners to provide information and analysis to decision makers on our campuses that help them demonstrate how the institution contributes to that goal as well as to create performance models that can estimate the effect of institutional actions on graduation goals. Here, a forward-thinking institutional research office might be able to estimate the effect of producing more degrees on an institution's recruitment and retention strategies.

Environmental scanning is critical and has become increasingly easier to execute through technology and increasing access to information. Scanning national, regional, and local headlines should become a daily practice, but it can be a difficult habit to start, particularly if the institutional researcher is not already tracking at least some trends. The ubiquity of electronic communications, especially social media, has given us access to instantaneous information. At the same time, keeping up with a barrage of headlines, tweets, and blog postings can quickly overwhelm even the most adroit practitioners. Learning how to sort through headlines—what to pass over quickly and what to read in more detail—is a skill that improves over time. Frequency of headlines for a given topic is a good indicator of its importance to an institution. Sharing analyses of why a given topic is important to your institution is a time-honored way of positioning the institutional office as a player in institutional decisions and creating dialogue that can be very helpful to institutional strategy. Examples of blogs that practitioners might find helpful include the Chronicle of Higher Education Ticker (http://chronicle.com/blog/The-Ticker/1/), Inside Higher Ed (http://www.insidehighered.com/), the *New York Times* Education section (http://www.nytimes.com/pages/education/index.html?partner=rss), and the *Washington Post* Campus Overload (http://voices.washingtonpost.com/campus-overload/) and College Inc. (http://voices.washingtonpost.com/college-inc/). Regional and local resources will vary depending on where you are, but you can look for feeds from state system offices (both in your state and in neighboring states), and major newspapers from surrounding cities (such as state capitals and major employer hubs).

Cultural Skills

Because institutional research exists at the organizational borders between units, practitioners should learn the vocabulary of all sides and use this language to facilitate both communication and efficiencies among institutional actors. In this context, efficiency refers to bringing data to the table and being able to explain that data in ways that are understandable to diverse audiences to instigate productive and sustained conversations. The very nature of institutional research work occurs in those in-between spaces. Simply by being far-reaching both within and across an institution—especially because institutional research should touch data produced or maintained by nearly every office on campus—the institutional research office can proactively bridge cultural gaps.

Key informants. Institutional research is most often the only unit in an institution that can navigate cultural boundaries with both internal institutional knowledge and a broader external view that can be employed to clarify questions and to reveal motivations behind institutional processes. Bridging these gaps can be a prime role for an activist institutional researcher. The opportunity to critically observe processes across the institution places institutional research professionals in an optimal position to help the institution understand where processes work and don't work to improve or replace them.

Trust. To be a successful interlocutor requires the institutional researcher to be viewed by the institution and its key decision-making bodies as an active and trusted participant in campus-wide discussions. It is therefore necessary to actively work toward improving trust and respect among a wide variety of campus constituencies. There are many levels of the institution with which institutional research personnel should work to establish the networks necessary to support these activities. For small offices to establish and supply these networks requires uncommon stamina. Large offices may be better able to supply expertise to an institution's networks. Regardless of size, however, a fundamental obligation is to gain trust through ethical participation in networks. In our experience, the key elements of trust building are frankness, the ability to see both sides of an argument, and forbearance in sometimes difficult and protracted discussions.

Functional offices. Developing a network of relationships with offices across the enterprise should occur naturally, as institutional research relies on a range of functional areas (for example, admissions, records, financial aid, and information technology) to supply data and insight. Data don't exist without context, and these offices know and live within that context. Siloed thinking is endemic to most organizations, and the institutional research professional will want to explore ways to break down persistent boundaries to efficiency. One fruitful way in which institutional research can promote collaboration is to review an institution's data dictionary with those offices that have a stake in data as either collectors or users. Rarely does a data dictionary—even a well-maintained one—capture the full flavor and nuance of an given unit's data, so periodic reviews can help to maintain strong relationships across the institution, especially by those units whose day-to-day work is data.

Key decision-making bodies. The institutional research office will be well served by active and regular participation as a consultant to key committees and deliberative bodies such as the dean's council, faculty senate, and university planning and budget groups. Institutional research personnel who can engage these bodies in the role of policy analyst and impartial advisor can elevate not just the role of institutional research but the entire dialogue among group members. If the institutional researcher enters this role purposefully, to facilitate group work, rather than as a participant with a specific agenda, then much can be accomplished in the resulting atmosphere of trust. The guiding philosophy should be one of servant leadership, focused on helping the institution meet their goals as defined through the strategic planning process.

Fortunately, the approach to starting relationships with any group can and should be the same: seek out the key personnel in each office or on each committee and ask to meet for the purpose of better understanding how they use data—how they obtain them, the business processes involved, and most important, the meaning of that unit's data to that individual. It's important to recognize—and acknowledge—that functional office personnel are the experts when it comes to their data; establishing that up front will go a long way toward building trust between institutional research and the functional areas. Institutional researchers are frequently asked to report data in ways that are at least marginally different from the purpose for which the data were gathered, so understanding the life cycle of the data will help institutional research professionals ensure that data are used appropriately by other campus decision makers.

Functional offices should be expert in their own data; although many committees may have a solid understanding of the types of data they use regularly, there are truly very few offices in an institution of higher education that understand enough of what's happening across campus as a whole. No other unit has the perspective that institutional research can bring to the table. At the same time, institutional research practitioners must have enough visibility across each area to make appropriate connections, but they rarely possess the depth of knowledge held in each area to make the ultimate decision on behalf of the institution. By being in the middle, however, and peeking into each area to see what's happening, institutional researchers can facilitate efficiencies and understandings others may be unable to see. Although all units of the institution can be omniscient, each can understand enough about their own data and how all units' data can come together to create a mosaic, especially if that pattern is the same data framework that supports a strategic plan. The strategy behind knowing enough without drowning in extraneous information can help individuals throughout the institution see how the big pieces fit together.

Interpersonal Skills and Leadership

When sufficient contextual knowledge and cross-institutional trust are established (or the process has at least been started, such that initial conversations are productive), the role of institutional research transforms slightly into one that places more emphasis on the leadership portion of the servant leader role. Diplomacy and honesty are key traits in both the establishment and maintenance of the trust essential for a centralized institutional research function to intentionally lead campus discussions toward continual performance assessment and evaluation of progress toward strategic planning goals.

Higher education institutions are human organizations. Although many in the institutional research profession may believe that their institutions operate rationally, our experience as institutional research officers in higher education institutions has not been quite so linear. An adroit professional understands the difference between formal and informal power structures in an institution. In fact, to not understand how decisions are made, who makes decisions, and how data can influence decisions is tantamount to organizational suicide for the institutional researcher. Couple this with the need to understand how resources are allocated, who determines the priorities for resource allocation, and the process by which those priorities are established, and a frame of reference emerges for understanding institutional interactions and the intersections where leadership can make a difference.

It is beyond the scope of this chapter to review the organizational literature of higher education as it applies to the performance of institutional research offices, but there are nonetheless some touchstones in that litera-ture. Birnbaum (1988) argues that there are four political models under which institutions operate: bureaucratic, collegial, anarchical, and political. The *bureaucratic* institution prides itself on a rationalizing structure and its ability to make decisions. Although the authors believe that this is the model with which institutional research may feel most comfortable, it is important to note that Birnbaum's models are not mutually exclusive. In fact, any insti-tution is likely to experience multiple models in operation at any given time, which adds to the complexity faced by institutional researchers and gives them pause to ascertain which model is currently in play and what leader-ship is required to advance institutional interest at that time. According to Birnbaum, the *collegial* institution is most focused on sharing power and val-ues in a community of equals. An *anarchical* institution, on the other hand, is a community of autonomous actors united by little, including common data. Last, the *political* institution is marked by a competition for power and resources. Viewed from Birnbaum's perspective, all institutions respond to internal and external political environments. For institutional researchers, the question becomes one of elevating debates with actionable data, the shape of which is determined by the model in use at any given time by any given audience.

Bringing It Together

In our experience, there are several areas in which institutional researchers can use their interpersonal and leadership skills for the benefit of the institution. To illustrate these attributes, we pick four areas that challenge institutional researchers and the institutions they serve: assessment, strategic planning, accreditation, and curriculum development.

Assessment

Unfortunately, assessment has become a "four-letter word" on many campuses, and even though many faculty and staff incorporate assessment work into their daily activities, it seems the mere mention of the word is enough to raise defenses. One of the greatest gifts an effective institutional research function can bring to campus is the ability and willingness to start conversations with campus constituencies about the importance of evaluation and performance monitoring. To borrow from the language of social workers, understanding the idea of "person-in-environment" (Meyer, 1983) and starting where each group is in terms of their level of acceptance for these processes is essential to success-fully implementing and maintaining useful assessment activities.

Some departments may be willing to share their assessment data, yet not understand how to gather or summarize it in a meaningful way. Others may be resistant to the idea of assessment from the start and thus need to be helped to understand that they're already engaging in at least some assessment activities and simply need to start documenting what they're doing. Still others are shining examples of cultures of assessment that may need occasional encouragement but will be mostly self-sufficient. The key to success is being able to recognize where any given unit is along the continua of both acceptance of assessment and skill in conducting meaningful assessment. Although there will always be those opposed to assessment, much of the resistance can be overcome by adapting the "person-in-environment" philosophy and taking the time to develop the trust and understanding within each unit.

Strategic Planning

Throughout this chapter we have made the case for institutional researchers to help their institutions advance their current strategic plans. But what role should institutional research have in helping institutions *shape* strategic plans? The difference between passivity and leadership, as argued in this chapter, is a starting point. So, too, is the acknowledgment that the skill set of the institutional researcher is critical for constructing a strategic plan that can be much more than a public relations piece.

A meaningful strategic plan must integrate external data and an institution's own data in actionable ways. Most institutions don't suffer from a lack of data but suffocate from a lack of *actionable* data that can point to alternative futures. Too often an institution's own data are arrayed in routine reports, factbooks, accreditation studies, and meager strategic plans that—although perhaps skillfully developed—do not serve as a basis for practical institutional action. We term these data "wallpaper" because they are interesting to look at but don't really cause anyone to arrive at next steps that could be taken to improve the institution. In our experience, most participants in a strategic planning process are hungry for not just data, but data that have been prepared so that a clear status of the institution can be gained and a sense of the likely future, based on institutional choices, can be grasped.

Most strategic plans usher forth lofty goals and sweeping visions, but fall short in sketching out how the institution will make progress toward these ends and who will be responsible for achieving them. In other words, accountability is often missing in strategic planning documents. Institutional researchers can assist by helping their colleagues from across the institution to arrive at action statements that describe in practical terms how that unit will support a strategic plan and how the unit will know its own progress by specifying those actions in measurable terms. This is an area that requires considerable finesse, because most organizational units may have little experience in evaluating their own actions in the context of the institution. Where such work is new, the institutional researcher can also anticipate much consternation about publically stating accountability measures.

Institutional researchers can also shape a strategic plan by reaching outside the institution to identify key stakeholders and to test their perceptions of the institution and its future with public meetings and interviews. We suggest that external participants—like their internal counterparts—are hungry for data, especially actionable data. Many external participants will not understand the inner workings of an institution and may not understand how the institution touches or potentially could touch their businesses, organizations, or communities. Gathering external audiences is important to strategic planning processes, but the proactive institutional researcher will want to ensure that fresh and meaningful data are available so the sum of these meetings is more than a collection of unguided perceptions.

Accreditation

The six regional accreditation agencies operate a compliance certification process in which institutions participate in an in-depth self-study to evaluate their progress against a set of preestablished criteria or standards. This process is typically animated on a ten-year cycle, although two of six regional accrediting agencies have established processes outside this cycle that provide pathways for institutions to participate in an quality improvement cycle (see, for example, Manning, n.d.). Typically, a team drawn from across the institution spends significant time determining where the institution stands with respect to accreditation criteria and prepares a report for inclusion in the self-study. Colleges and universities are finding that they can no longer gear up for the self-study process a few years before an accreditation visit, but instead must demonstrate ongoing and integrated institutional processes.

A remarkable shift has occurred in the focus of accreditation, away from compliance and toward student learning and the use of outcome data to improve learning delivery. The documentation of student learning is a prime area for institutional researchers to become involved, but it requires an extension of the traditional institutional research skill set and invites new learning in the areas of cognitive design, measuring seemingly abstract learning concepts, and acquiring a new vocabulary. To be helpful, institutional research personnel should be prepared to help faculty and staff establish appropriate benchmarks for their courses and programs and to determine realistic ways of measuring whether these benchmarks have been met. An understanding of what commercial instruments measure and what they don't measure further expands the skill set. The nimble institutional researcher will want to use her or his knowledge of instrumentation to ensure that the institution's curriculum does not become subservient to commercial testing, but rather that testing is seen as the logical endpoint to a well-designed curriculum. In the next section, we review competency-based models as an overarching technique to bring these skills together.

Curriculum Development

One often-overlooked area in which institutional researchers can help their institutions is that of curriculum development. Although faculty have general prerogatives in designing and delivering the curriculum, they can benefit from the expertise of institutional researchers in understanding how students flow into and out of their programs, the capability that students bring with them from previous schooling, program graduation rates, and data on the success of graduates in employment and further education. These tasks are quite conventional and fall into the realm of an organized program review cycle at most colleges and universities. Institutional researchers can also proactively add value in several other key leadership areas, especially by helping their institutions understand the role of competency-based learning models and performance-based learning.

Recent interest by educational foundations in determining what a degree in a given field means in learning and competency for students presents an opportunity for institutional researchers. As a project allied with the Bologna Process in Europe, called "Tuning" in the United States, the focus is on ensuring that degrees awarded by institutions are comparable and to provide a basis for defining quality. Tuning also advances the goal of developing flexible curricula based on student needs. State study teams recently have been implemented in Indiana, Minnesota, and Utah to study these issues (Lumina Foundation for Education, 2010).

In the past, curriculum development may have been regarded as an inward-looking institutional activity. However, given the stunning growth of electronic learning options, no institution can be a curricular island. The pathways created by technology no longer lead automatically to institutions of higher education. Competitor organizations outside of postsecondary education have made significant inroads by providing performance-based learning opportunities built on competencies. Potential students and undergraduates are becoming more sophisticated educational consumers and quickly grasp the concept of acquiring skills and competencies through various means and at times they prefer. By understanding how the curriculum can be bundled and unbundled and translated across institutions in a common vocabulary and how competencies can be used to compare learning outcomes between an institution and its competitors, institutional researchers can position the institution well for the future.

Shaping the curriculum through use of competencies appears to be an idea whose time has arrived for most institutions. Regional accreditors' interest in improving student success and graduation rates—as well as institutions' own efforts to achieve these ends—have given rise to using competencies as building blocks for an institution's curriculum (Voorhees, 2001). For example, most institutions publish catalog descriptions of their courses, but many fail to require faculty to specify a common set of learning outcomes for these courses.

Under these circumstances, content can be changed based on an individual faculty member's interpretation of what that course should accomplish and that faculty member's perception of his or her own teaching strengths and weaknesses. By understanding the need to document learning outcomes and why those outcomes should be specified in the same way across common courses, the institution can better standardize learning experiences; this can also lead to discussions about sequencing the curriculum in ways that promote student success. This, in turn, helps students to see the patterns in their course taking at the institution and to identify those competencies that the curriculum seeks to impart. It also ensures students that their learning experience embraces all competencies—not just those that individual faculty believe are important.

An institutional researcher would do well not to mistake the definition and assessment of competencies for easy work. Efforts to define and assess competencies face a number of challenges. For example, what methodologies will be used to assess performance? Researchers must choose among tests, portfolios, teacher or employer ratings, and benchmarks or exemplars of performance. Who will be responsible for assessment? Stakeholders and recipients of results must be defined among individual faculty, departments, schools, admission offices, employers, and accrediting bodies. How will assessments of competencies be used? The potential uses (and misuses) by credentialing bodies, admissions and placement offices, and the recruitment arms of employers need careful consideration. These issues have ramifications for new data priorities, as states and education and training providers enter uncharted territory in developing performance standards and assessing competencies.

Synthesis

It is simply not enough to be "out of the box and out of the office" in a rapidly shifting higher education environment. Increased visibility for institutional research personnel and new thinking about possibilities must be accompanied by the confluence of interpersonal skill and a deep understanding of what is possible in current institutional culture. We also suggest that "out of the box" is not synonymous with being a "Jack-in-the-box." The need for dispassionate thinking and preserving impartiality in presenting data and converting those data to actionable information will always be paramount, regardless of the press of business. At the same time, we have made the case for using institutional research skills in activist ways to guide innovation. It is up to the individual institutional researcher to balance these attributes with the pace of work at her or his institution in ways that engender trust.

As trust grows across campus and institutional research professionals become established as unbiased providers of information, interpretation, and guidance, institutional researchers can capitalize on that trust to introduce new topics in campus conversations. The trust that produced these opportunities can be extended further by continuing to understand when and where, and to whom, such overtures will be most effective and where additional pressure will (or won't) yield results. Reading the social and political mood of a campus is always more art than science; fortunately, it's a trainable skill that develops over time through active participation in the life of an institution and the institutional researcher's commitment to be out of the box and out of the office.

References

Birnbaum, R. (1988). *How colleges work: The cybernetics of academic organization and leadership.* San Francisco: Jossey-Bass.

Kelderman, E. (2010, January). Stimulus money staved off deep cuts in state appropriations. Retrieved from http://chronicle.com/article/Stimulus-Money-Staved-Off-Deep/63544/

Knight, W. E., Moore, W. E., & Coperthwaite, C. A. (1997). Institutional research: Knowledge, skills, and perceptions of effectiveness. *Research in Higher Education, 38*(4), 419–433.

Lumina Foundation for Education. (2010). TUNING USA. Retrieved from http://www.luminafoundation.org/our_work/tuning/

Manning, T. M. (n.d.). Using Achieving the Dream to meet accreditation requirements: Principles and practices of student success. Retrieved from http://www.achievingthedream.org/CAMPUSSTRATEGIES/GUIDES/default.tp

Meyer, C. H. (Ed.). (1983). *Clinical social work in the eco-systems perspective.* New York: Columbia University Press.

Terenzini, P. T. (1993). On the nature of institutional research and the knowledge and skills it requires. *Research in Higher Education, 34*, 1–10.

Voorhees, R. A. (E.d.) (2001). *Measuring what matters: Competency-based models in higher education.* New Directions for Institutional Research, no. 110. San Francisco: Jossey-Bass.

CHAPTER 6

INSTITUTIONAL RESEARCH AND COLLABORATIVE ORGANIZATIONAL LEARNING

Victor M. H. Borden and Adrianna Kezar

This chapter examines how theories and concepts related to collaborative organizational learning inform the purpose and practice of institutional research (IR). We begin by identifying the pervasive decision-support ethos in the profession. We examine the limitations of this approach to IR in complex higher education institutions. We then examine a modest range of organizational learning concepts and perspectives, noting their specific implications for shifting the purpose of IR from one that informs decisions to one that contributes to organizational learning and thereby facilitates improvements in organizational effectiveness. Finally, we consider the implications of this shift in perspective for the requisite knowledge, skills, and abilities of the IR practitioner.

The Uses and Limits of IR as a Decision-Support Activity

Joe Saupe (1990) began his classic treatise on the nature and purpose of institutional research by declaring as its purpose "to provide information which supports institutional planning, policy formation and decision making" (p. 1). Institutional research has been defined in a variety of ways over time, but, as Terenzini (1999) noted, the definition always relates the conduct of research and analysis to the practice of administering higher education programs, institutions, and systems: practices that are characterized by decision making as a core process (Chaffee, 1983). The institutional research profession has developed and flourished at a time when higher education institutions have adopted increasingly professionalized models of administration and management. With this shift in management culture came the attendant rise in quantitatively driven, rational approaches to decision making (Swenk, 1999) and related management processes like strategic planning, resource allocation modeling, and program evaluation and assessment.

To claim that members of any professional group have common dispositions, attitudes, or skills is to overlook vast individual differences and, in the case of institutional researchers, the diverse nature of the higher education institutions and organizational cultures in which they work. Acknowledging this diversity, we suggest a prototypical affinity among IR professionals for quantitative analysis in support of rational decision-making processes. The focus on quantitative methodology for decision support is evident in the titles of the *Resources in Institutional Research* monograph series published by the Association for Institutional Research, including *Applications of Intermediate/Advanced Statistics in Institutional Research* (Coughlin, 2005), *People, Processes, and Managing Data* (McLaughlin & Howard, 2004), *Institutional Research: Decision Support in Higher Education* (Howard, 2001), and *Questionnaire Survey Research: What Works* (Suskie, 1996). Only one title in the series, *Using Mixed Methods in Institutional Research* (Howard, 2007), directly acknowledges the potential use of qualitative research methodologies, but does so as a complementary enhancement to quantitative methods, not as a potential alternative.

A range of attributes, skills, and dispositions enables effective IR practice as exemplified by Terenzini's (1999) characterization of the three forms of organizational intelligence required for effective IR practice (technical and analytical, issues, and contextual), and Volkwein's (1999) four faces of institutional research (information authority, policy analyst, spin doctor, and scholar/researcher). However, we suggest that the quantitative or rational ethos has had a more explicit influence in shaping the literature and culture of the profession, and we seek to demonstrate how concepts of collaborative organizational learning can enrich our understanding of and approaches to institutional research.

Although rationality is a desirable quality and goal, institutional researchers are limited if they operate purely from this perspective. These limitations were recognized by Herbert Simon and colleagues (Simon et al., 1987) as arising from "the incompleteness and inadequacy of human knowledge, the inconsistencies of individual preference and belief, the conflicts of value among people and groups of people, and the inadequacy of the computations we can carry out, even with the aid of the most powerful computers" (p. 13). Simon (1991) coined the term *bounded rationality* to characterize both the importance of rationality as well as its limitations.[1]

The organization and operation of higher education institutions introduces further complications to rational decision-making processes and corresponding modes of constructing institutional research. Higher education institutions have been characterized as composites of hierarchical or bureaucratic and collegial models of administration and governance—often termed a *professional bureaucracy* (Swenk, 1999). The decision-making culture of the administrative hierarchy often comes into conflict with core principles of collegial academic governance. As Swenk notes, "The professionals (the faculty) maintain superior authority to decide the major goals, while the authority of the administrators is limited to deciding the means to achieve those goals and to setting performance standards" (1999, p. 5). The institution is further embedded in political and market systems that bring into play a variety of interests and agendas of varying degrees of compatibility.

As professional bureaucracies, higher education institutions are typically characterized by highly decentralized and loosely coupled authority structures. The highly educated, domain-specific expert employees of professional bureaucracies have more authority and control than do the less skilled and less educated staff in a traditional hierarchical bureaucracy. This brings up issues regarding who should be involved in decisions, what information is relevant, and how it will be transmitted and interpreted at various levels in the organization, not just among those in senior positions.

Institutional researchers are also often involved with institutional processes that focus on what we characterize throughout this chapter as "collaborative organizational learning." As Milam (2005) notes, they participate with institutional and professional colleagues in such activities as "accreditation procedures, national association activities, the search for best practices, quality improvement initiatives, accounting standards, and program review" (p. 63). We are not suggesting that institutional researchers (or higher education institutions) are not deeply invested in the less rationally constrained, more interactive, and more creative processes of constructing organizational knowledge. Instead, we hope to provide a framework for involving institutional research and the institutional researcher more intentionally and effectively in promoting more extensive and deeper organizational learning.

The basic premise of our collaborative organizational learning perspective is that decision making in higher education can be viewed as occurring in the context of an interactive learning experience in which two or more people work together to develop a deeper understanding of complex phenomena through inquiry and analysis. Questions are posed and posed again in an iterative fashion, as increasingly well-honed evidence is considered and varying perspectives are reconciled. This characterization has implications for the design, conduct, and dissemination of institutional research products and services that, if accommodated, will help practitioners produce more useful information and put that information to better use. Conversely, a lack of proper attention to these learning processes can marginalize the institutional research function and staff at a higher education institution.

There are several anticipated benefits of applying this perspective to the processes and products of institutional research. One is that increased collaboration creates greater buy-in, ownership, and engagement in the learning process, which in turn facilitates transfer of learning. Research demonstrates that it is difficult to transfer knowledge gains to those who did not participate in the process (Elkjaer, 1999). Institutional researchers often encounter a simple form of resistance to organizational learning when the accuracy of the data they provide is questioned. However, when departmental colleagues are engaged in developing the kinds of census snapshots that institutional research work requires, they appreciate and accept the inherent limitations of such snapshots and move beyond questioning the data to using the data to assess processes and programs. This engagement can also benefit the quality of the data, as colleagues then realize the implications of communicating changes through appropriate channels to ensure data integrity.

Another benefit of collaborative organizational learning is the greater collective intelligence potential among groups of individuals learning together. A variety of studies have demonstrated the cognitive strength of teams (Bensimon & Neumann, 1993). The focus on team and community provides the opportunity for more complex and powerful solutions to organizational problems. Engagement in such teams' efforts also enables institutional researchers to understand with greater nuance the kinds of information and analysis that would further stimulate constructive engagement among team members.

Yet another benefit to involving larger numbers of individuals in learning processes is the opportunity to question limiting organizational assumptions. When a more select group of individuals processes information, they are often less likely to challenge belief systems and often develop group-think or operate under conforming assumptions (Argyris & Schön, 1978). As organizations take a collaborative learning approach, people are more likely to question traditional values and assumptions if others around them are also questioning existing beliefs (Brown & Duguid, 1991; Weick & Westley, 1996). Collaborative approaches to organizational learning increase the likelihood for organizational assumptions to be challenged, which facilitates learning (Dixon, 1999).

In the next two sections of this chapter, we explore some concepts and perspectives of organizational learning (OL) that support this paradigmatic shift. Within the constraints of this chapter, we can provide only a basic introduction to a modest range of concepts.

Defining OL and Understanding a Collaborative Approach

There is no standard definition of organizational learning, but most scholars agree that it relates to a change in awareness, practice, or both among organizational actors for the purpose of improving organizational performance (Fiol & Lyles, 1985; Huber, 1991). Huber's definition is recognized as being inclusive of various fields: "an organization learns if any of its units acquires knowledge that it recognizes as potentially useful to the organization" (p. 89). Organizational learning emerged from the common observation that decisions taken do not always lead to desired changes, but decisions associated with learning processes were found to change the way people think about problems and processes and facilitate the kind of change sought through decisions. Consequently, individuals who contribute to decision-making processes, such as institutional researchers, should expand their thinking to include facilitation of and involvement in organizational learning.

Because organizational learning has been studied from so many different disciplinary perspectives, varying definitions and approaches have emerged, focusing on different aspects of the phenomenon.[2] Organizational psychologists, for example, focus on how individuals learn—examining mental models, underlying values, and learning styles. This literature places notable emphasis on individual barriers to learning, such as the way habits and routines deter new thinking or how people rationalize their current behavior in order to address errors. Studies arising from a management science perspective focus on issues that are important for organizations, rather than for individuals, as well as on information processing. Examples of aspects considered from this perspective include organizational networks for learning and knowledge transfer, the way leaders can help challenge assumptions to promote deeper learning, or the way that the environment can bring information into the organization to increase learning. In contrast, studies from a sociological or organizational theory perspective focus on the impact of hierarchy, politics, power, and structures on learning. They also examine aspects of the organization that facilitate and enhance learning, such as incentives or a culture of risk. Essentially, these disciplines have studied organizational learning at different levels—individual, group, and organization—each looking at the interplay of these levels but focusing on the level most related to the discipline.

The variety of disciplinary approaches to organizational learning has led to the emergence of differing philosophical traditions. Early studies are characterized by a functionalist perspective that focuses on organizational learning as acquiring, storing, and managing data. More recently, an interpretive perspective has emerged, which focuses more on the use and interpretation of data rather than on its production, dissemination, and management. From this perspective, data themselves do not generally have meaning; to create knowledge, they need to be digested and combined with other forms of information, such as experience or intuition (Easterby-Smith, Aráujo, & Burgoyne, 1999). Scholars in this camp also emphasize that knowledge is constructed between individuals and focus on the way groups interact in community contexts to make meaning and sense of data (Brown & Duguid, 1991).

Interpretive approaches also suggest that new ideas and information can emerge throughout the organization and do not need to come from leaders or research units (Easterby-Smith, Aráujo & Burgoyne, 1999; Kezar, 2005). Knowledge is emphasized over information, and organizational learning becomes a process focused on people rather than databases or storehouses of knowledge or leaders at the top (Milam, 2005). Conflict, misunderstanding, and politics are seen as inherently part of organizations and not something that can be minimized or controlled. Interpretive approaches to organizational learning are inherently collaborative.

We use the term *collaborative organizational learning* rather than *interpretive organizational learning* for several reasons. First, we do not want this work to be seen as resting entirely in the interpretive philosophical tradition. The functionalist "camp" is more compatible with what we have characterized as the traditional decision-support ethos of institutional research. Moreover, there are considerable "functionalist" pressures on IR offices and practitioners that, if disregarded, can lead to unfulfilled expectations among the senior administrative staff that sponsor and rely on IR support. We believe the practice of IR can be enhanced by adopting new assumptions and concepts. This means not abandoning existing practices and beliefs but rather incorporating them into a more elaborate approach that can enrich the learning environment. Second, the term *collaborative* reflects the aims and goals shared among institutional researchers and their faculty and staff colleagues that support the notion of teams working together to identify and pursue improvements and more effective practice. The interpretive aspects of organizational learning focus on the processes by which individuals develop knowledge in organizational contexts through the sharing of information, ideas, and experiences. Collaboration entails a more intentional focus on the complex range of interrelated but sometimes competing goals and objectives that underpin effective organizational practice.

Concepts to Facilitate Collaborative Organizational Learning

In this section, we review three contrasting concepts that derive from varying disciplinary traditions in the organizational learning literature and describe how they inform the practice of institutional research. First, we consider Argyris and Schön's (1978, 1996) concepts of single-loop and double-loop learning, which derive from organizational psychology underpinnings of Christopher Argyris, albeit with clear influence from the more interpretive leanings of philosopher Donald Schön. We next employ Huber's (1991) taxonomy for organizational learning—a management science perspective—to assess the role of institutional research within broader organizational processes for procuring, distributing, interpreting and storing information to support organizational management and operations. Finally, we consider a perspective from the interpretive tradition, situated learning, and communities of practice (Brown & Duguid, 2002; Lave & Wenger, 1991; Wenger, 1998), to understand how institutional research can contribute to the interpersonally dynamic and highly interactive processes that characterize learning and decision making at postsecondary institutions.

Argyris and Schön's Single- and Double-Loop Learning

Argyris and Schön's core concepts of organizational learning (1978, 1996) revolve around the idea that individuals develop theories of action; that is, a set of beliefs and expectations regarding how certain behaviors lead to certain predictable results in specific contexts. Individuals do not need to learn anything new as long as these beliefs and expectations are met. Learning opportunities arise out of "error detection"; that is, when individuals experience or witness anomalous outcomes of behavior. When faced with an anomaly, they must make some kind of adjustment in their thinking to put things back into order. Argyris and Schön distinguish between two types of adjustment to such anomalies: single-loop learning—that is, superficial adjustments in action strategies—and double-loop learning—that is, more fundamental changes in underpinning values, assumptions, and beliefs. They further distinguish between Model I and Model II theories-in-use, which represent clusters of principles, strategies, and consequences that advance from single-loop and double-loop processes, respectively. Models I and II are particularly useful for characterizing organizational capacities. In a Model I organization, adhering to rules, regulations, and traditions is as important as achieving goals—or sometimes more important. Things are done because that's the way they were always done, even if they may not make sense anymore. The Model II Learning Organization has values, policies, and practices that promote double-loop learning. Members of the organization share their information and their thinking. Ideas for improvement and change are tested publicly, and people work together to achieve higher and more profound levels of understanding while continuously monitoring the responsiveness of the organization to changing external environments.

Single- and double-loop learning and the Model I and Model II counterparts describe "ideal types" that are not generally experienced in pure form. Individual learning involves a constant interplay between superficial and deeper learning processes. To the degree that the environment and organizational operations are stable and predictable, it is likely that single-loop learning processes will dominate and that Model I principles and strategies will suffice. However, if current processes are not producing desired results or if conditions are changing in a way that warrants a reconsideration of organizational policies and practices, more disruptive double-loop learning is needed, as facilitated by Model II principles and strategies.

Single-loop, Model I learning is supported by such common IR products as standard management reports, performance indicators, and enrollment profiles; that is, information that is recurrent and consistent and does not require significant time to process. The information contained in such reports may reveal anomalous outcomes, such as an unexpected drop in enrollment or revenues below projected levels. But these reports do not generally provide insights into the causes of these anomalies and so do not support well the types of actions and interactions required to deal with them.

The information that best supports double-loop learning differs from these examples in two respects. First, it includes more in-depth analysis and interpretation, facilitated by explicit identification and critical review of assumptions and values. Second, it generally requires iteration. When core values and assumptions are questioned, the individuals involved in the process do not have a "rational basis" for making sense of information. The purpose of information and analysis in double-loop learning is to help participants in the learning process build new rational bases that accommodate the changed outcomes or consequences that were observed or reported. This often requires several inquiries that build on each other.

Institutional research that stimulates double-loop learning can occur in the context of supporting a specific committee or task force. Questions arise that the institutional researcher can address with evidence and analysis, which in turn leads to more questions that invoke further study. For example, an impending shortfall in entering students might bring together colleagues to find reasons for the shortfall. Data and analysis can be used to scrutinize expectations and assumptions. With careful and systematic inquiry in a trusted setting, the individuals who are responsible for various processes are more likely to accept information that suggests that certain processes might need to be rethought and reworked.

The ability to lead individuals through a process of questioning core assumptions and developing new ways of thinking goes well beyond the technical skills of reporting, research, and analysis that are the underpinnings of most institutional research job descriptions. The "issues" and "contextual" forms of organizational intelligence described by Terenzini (1999) and the "policy analyst" and "spin doctor" faces of institutional research described by Volkwein (1999) capture some components of the skills and abilities that are required for this type of organizational development process. In addition, skills associated with such activities as meeting facilitation, conflict resolution, contract negotiation, and diplomacy are essential.

Accommodating the interpretive perspective of organizational learning into institutional research can be characterized as a double-loop learning process. Focusing on how organizational players "make meaning" from information, and the sources of information that support such interpretive processes, requires more fundamental rethinking of core assumptions and beliefs as to how an institutional research operation might operate.

Huber's Taxonomy for Organizational Learning

Huber (1991) offered a taxonomy for organizing the broad base of literature that had developed in organizational learning by the early 1990s. Huber's more inclusive definition of organizational learning, described earlier, departed from conceptions popular in the organizational science literature, such as those of Argyris and Schön (1978), which viewed organizational learning as an intentional process directed at or, even more restrictedly, leading to improved effectiveness. Consonant with DiBella's (1998) notion that organizational learning occurs constantly and at multiple levels in an organization, Huber's inclusive definition suggests that one does not create or control organizational learning; rather, it is an ongoing phenomenon that can be more or less intentionally guided toward desired outcomes, but never completely controlled. Huber further posits that "more organizational learning occurs when more of the organization's components obtain . . . knowledge and recognize it as potentially useful . . . more and varied interpretations are developed . . . [and] more organizational units develop uniform comprehensions of the various interpretations" (p. 90). He labels the three attributes defined by these statements as breadth, elaborateness, and thoroughness, respectively. Although distinctive, these three attributes together highlight the strong, positive association between collaboration and organizational learning.

Huber (1991) describes four primary processes of organizational learning: knowledge acquisition (how knowledge is obtained), information distribution (how information is shared), information interpretation (how it is given meaning), and organizational memory (how it is stored). Three of the four primary processes have subprocesses, some of which have further subprocesses. Figure 6.1, excerpted from Huber (1991, p. 90), depicts the full organizing framework.

FIGURE 6.1   CONSTRUCTS AND PROCESSES ASSOCIATED WITH ORGANIZATIONAL LEARNING

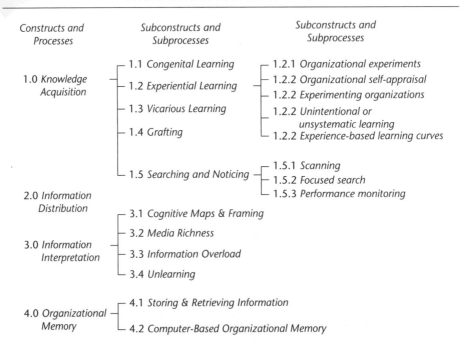

In Huber's terms, we posit that institutional research has focused primarily on knowledge acquisition and secondarily on information distribution. There has been some notable focus in recent years on organizational memory in the guise of knowledge management (Serban & Luan, 2002a; Milam, 2005). We contend that a collaborative organizational learning lens focuses our attention on information interpretation as an essential element of the productive use of the products and services of an institutional research office. An effective institutional research office will shape its products, services, and modes of interacting with colleagues throughout the organization to promote information interpretation in a way that facilitates progress on organizational goals and objectives. We now review the four aspects of Huber's taxonomy of organizational learning.

Knowledge Acquisition. The range of institutional research processes described by McLaughlin and Howard (2004)—deciding which data to collect, collecting and storing data, restructuring and analyzing the data into usable information, delivering the information, and, ultimately, using the information to "influence" knowledge—places institutional research within a fairly narrow range of Huber's model; primarily in the "experiential learning" branch of knowledge acquisition, although also touching on the "searching and noticing" branch, as well as the less-differentiated "information distribution" node. Huber places these processes within a larger domain: the organization's collective knowledge base and ongoing learning processes. In a higher education institution, this can be a daunting context, given the institution's primary function of knowledge creation and dissemination. Even within the administration and management activities of the organization, the knowledge domains are broad, complex, and intricately intertwined (for example, academic program management and planning, physical plant and facilities, finance, human resources, student records management, student financial aid, alumni relations, development). Administrative staff are hired based, in large part, on their knowledge base, prior experience, and demonstrated abilities. They work together in various combinations of organizational units, committees, teams, and so on to bring together their prior knowledge and experience (congenital learning); to review together various forms of data and information that emerge from their operational and managerial processes (experiential learning); to attend conferences and visit other institutions to learn from what others are doing (vicarious learning and searching and noticing). They will occasionally reorganize or create new units and processes to better manage a process or function (grafting).

Huber's construct of knowledge acquisition provides insights into how the institutional research practitioner can better leverage the vast knowledge store and ongoing processes to contribute more effectively to the larger mosaic. The construct suggests that the IR practitioner should devote time and attention to understanding what colleagues already know, what kinds of operational data they review together, and who they look to as examples of best practice. This can serve as a useful context for deciding what other kinds of information might best stimulate learning, as it reveals predispositions and prospective biases, as well as areas of incomplete or misaligned understanding.

This expanded perspective is obtained primarily through collaboration: work on committees, talking with colleagues in formal and informal settings, attending department meetings of other units, and so on. Such activity is often requisite for the director of an institutional research operation but less likely among research analysts and other support staff. Increasing opportunities among institutional researchers for interaction and participation with colleagues, especially as related to domains intended as clients or audience, will promote more useful institutional research that can better inform organizational learning.

Information Distribution. Huber suggests that information distribution directly influences the occurrence and breadth of organizational learning. He summarizes the literature regarding obstacles related to getting needed information from wherever (or whomever) it happens to be available to where it is useful. Among these obstacles are the lack of understanding of the relevance of information to different individuals and groups, power and status differentials, the workload of providers and recipients, and the number of sequential links in the communication chain. These logistical issues often result in the organization's not completely knowing what it knows, which in turn often leads to duplication of effort in assembling information and inconsistency in the information that emerges from those redundant compilation efforts.

The traditional focus for institutional researchers regarding information distribution is on deciding who should receive the information that is produced or otherwise known to be available. Huber's discussion suggests further consideration of determining when information created for one purpose might be useful to others in the organization, being respectful of the organization's protocols for communication. Given the vast quantities of information that are now available, attention needs to shift from distributing information when *available* to distributing it when *needed*. Many IR operations use restricted or unrestricted computer network–based systems to store and make available information. However, users do not necessarily know where to look or even the likelihood of finding something relevant to a particular need.

Huber's discussion of information distribution also highlights the usefulness of broader coordination among an organization's information provider offices and functions to better serve the needs of a wide array of academic and administrative users. The institutional research operation is often in a good position to serve in a coordinating role regarding the availability of information resources across the spectrum of functions and services. This "brokering" role has been highlighted as an important aspect of the institutional research function for many years (for example, Borden & Delaney, 1989; Delaney, 2009), but it appears to be gaining greater significance with the advance of technologies that have enabled more members of an organization to create reports and analysis that might be useful to others in the organization.

Information Interpretation. Huber's discussion of the literature related to interpretation focuses on how new information relates with what people already know and think, how the medium through which it is conveyed influences interpretation, the focus or lack of focus created by the amount of information that is flowing, and the particular difficulties that arise when what is already believed conflicts with what is learned (which is the basis for double-loop learning). His discussion highlights the importance of being more aware of what happens to the information produced by an institutional research operation in relation to other sources of information. He notes that, because individuals are bombarded with information from a variety of sources, it is essential to focus on how information is communicated most effectively, which requires paying attention to what recipients already know and what garners their attention. Huber suggests that it is important to attend to the richness with which information is conveyed (for example, multimodal or visual display issues) and to structure information in a way that does not further contribute to overload (for example, small pieces up front with available backup detail, information about what is relevant, avoiding questions that are not asked, and so on).

Institutional researchers often have opportunities to "sit at the table" in committees, task forces, and unit meetings when the information is used and are able to contribute significantly to the responsible and effective use of the information by noting its implications and limitations. However, some of the traditional practices of institutional research separate the institutional researcher from the processes of interpretation engendered by its products and services. It is therefore important to contextualize provided information with guidance for interpretation. IR practitioners are generally comfortable with describing the sources and known issues related to the reliability and validity of information. Including more explicit interpretation and especially recommendations for actions with information and analysis presents a potential both for contributing positively to ensuing organizational learning and for overstepping one's role in the organization.

Organizational Memory. Huber discusses organizational memory issues related to the limitations of human memory (for example, learning biases and incomplete recall), difficulties in knowing what is worth storing for unknowable future needs, and the uneven and partly unknown distribution of useful information and knowledge among organizational members. Although he uses an outdated distinction between hard copy and computer-based memory, the primary point of this distinction remains pertinent and informative. A more relevant terminology for this distinction is between documents (that is, formulated text, tables, or graphical files that include both qualitative and quantitative information in a highly processed but irregularly structured form) and more elemental data that are structured and organized for reporting and analysis.

Institutional researchers focus primarily on the more elemental forms of stored data as the basic input into research and analysis. The administration, warehousing, and mining of institutional data are frequent topics of presentations at national, regional, and state forums. These topics are also addressed in several volumes of the Association for Institutional Research series, *Resources in Institutional Research* (for example, Borden, Massa, & Milam, 2001; McLaughlin & Howard, 2004), as is use of the increasingly abundant array of external data resources (Milam, 2003).

Managing and analyzing information, as stored in documents and other more highly processed forms, is less prevalent in institutional research practice. The literature includes at least one highly relevant treatment of this topic: the volume of *New Directions for Institutional Research* devoted to knowledge management (KM) (Serban & Luan, 2002a). Serban and Luan (2002b) define knowledge management as "a systematic effort to capitalize on the cumulative knowledge that an organization has" (p. 5). The KM movement relates closely to the issues that Huber describes in the organizational memory section of his taxonomy. It embodies efforts to create, capture, organize, access, and use highly processed forms of information or knowledge. Serban and Luan cite, as an example relevant to higher education institutions, "information related to pedagogy and assessment techniques, student evaluations, and curriculum revision efforts" (p. 13). Many institutions are now grappling with what to do with the large quantity of amassed archival electronic records, including the vast number of e-mail messages, many of which contain prospectively useful information.

In the same volume of *New Directions for Institutional Research*, Petrides (2002) describes the close relationship between knowledge management and organizational learning. She suggests that institutional research offices are well-positioned to play a central role in the development of institutional knowledge-based systems because of their roles in public accountability; as a general repository for institutional information and a central point in its flow throughout the organization; and as a catalyst for internal research and analysis to support decision making.

Effective use of the broad range of information resources encompassed by the KM movement is also central to business intelligence (BI) and business analytics trends that are gaining momentum throughout the corporate world as well as in higher education (for example, Campbell, DeBlois, & Oblinger, 2007; Norris, Baer, Leonard, Pugliese, & Lefrere, 2008). Whereas KM expands the information horizon to highly processed documents, BI expands into the realm of transactional data systems—that is, the day-to-day flow of operational data. Institutional research has traditionally focused on point-in-time extracts of data to represent broad periods of time (for example, a semester or a year) and have left operational information concerns to their colleagues in the functional offices from which these data emanate (for example, admissions, registrar, human resources, accounting).

These KM and BI considerations, like the entire Huber taxonomy, place the traditional domain and sphere of institutional research practice as a modest component of far larger organizational information and learning processes. They highlight the need for IR practitioners to consider how their work integrates with these other sources to serve institutional information needs and organizational learning. They further highlight the importance of collaboration as a foundation of organizational learning.

Situated Learning and Communities of Practice

Knowledge management and business intelligence trends are associated with a view of institutional information as part of an ecology or ecosystem in which the data and individuals using the data are constantly interacting and inseparable (Davenport & Kusak, 1997). Situated learning theory posits that "knowledge is dynamically constructed as we conceive of what is happening to us, talk and move" (Clancey, 1995, p. 49); that is, learning is situated in our roles as members of various groups and communities and occurs as a function of our activities in these cultures and contexts (Lave, 1988).

In higher education institutions, as in most organizations, the individuals who conduct the core business operations develop and hone their work through guided practice: the individuals and units that institutional researchers support with information and analysis are constantly learning and evolving in the social context of their work. Lave and Wenger (1991; Wenger, 1998) coined the term *communities of practice* to describe these dynamic social contexts that focus on common work goals and objectives; rules, norms, and roles that bind the members of the community together as a social entity; and the communal resources that the members develop over time. Brown and Duguid (1991, 2002) describe the essential role of situated learning and communities of practice in the development of professional practice. The knowledge gained through these social learning processes is characterized as *know-how* because of its close tie to practice.

These concepts imply that the information produced by institutional research, or from any other source, becomes usable knowledge (know-how) only when it is integrated into and processed by a community of practice or other social context. This means the information is not, in itself, knowledge; rather, knowledge results from the social interaction of the community around the information. A member of a community of practice understands how information might be digested and interpreted in that social context; a nonmember is not likely to have that understanding.

Although information developed by institutional researchers is likely at some point to enter into such social contexts, it is often not possible to know, at the time of its creation, the extent to which this will occur. Moreover, many of the recurrent information products of an IR operation serve as generic resources that are used across a wide variety of such contexts. However, IR offices and practitioners are often called on to provide support directly to specific situated learning contexts—such as committees, task forces, and organizational units—that intend to use the requested information as part of a social process aimed at coming to a consensual decision. Increasingly, campuses are developing more explicit learning communities that IR professionals can work with to collaboratively develop research. For example, many campuses have a community of practice around engaged learning, community engagement, diversity and multiculturalism, internationalization, or assessment. Institutional researchers can work directly with these various communities to acquire, disseminate, participate in, and help to store their knowledge as membership evolves.

IR as Collaborative Organizational Learning: Implications for Future Work

In this final section, we provide some summative and thematic observations, give examples of approaches to institutional research that accommodate collaborative organizational learning, and comment on the skills and dispositions that are essential for promoting these modes of construction.

Implications for IR Products, Processes, and Services

Institutional researchers and IR offices provide a range of products and services to support evidence-informed practice and decision making. For this discussion, we set aside the reports and services related to external accountability requirements and focus primarily on the products and services that serve internal administration and management. In this realm, we consider three types of products: standard (recurrent) management reports, responses to *ad hoc* requests for information, and research and analysis that serves more in-depth inquiries.

Factbooks, enrollment reports, student profiles, department profiles, and student survey reports are common examples of standard management reports produced by IR offices. As recurrent reports, these products are relatively stable in terms of their content and structure, with changes made periodically based on input from colleagues, changes in the environment, and, more generally, the evolving priorities of the institution. These reports can be useful information resources but are often underutilized because they are produced on a schedule based on when information is available rather than when it is needed. The concepts reviewed in this chapter emphasize the importance of understanding when and how colleagues might need this information, how they would search for it, and how it is then interpreted. Search engines and indexes become more critical to the effective use of such information, as does the form and format by which the information is presented. It is also important for IR practitioners to talk with colleagues about how the information is interpreted and used. Finally, institutional researchers should be attuned to the anomalies that can often be revealed through standard reports, and how these can be significant organizational learning triggers. Given that the scarcest resources available are time and attention, the skilled institutional researcher must be able to surmise when an anomaly is worth pursuing and the types of further analysis that would assist colleagues in determining how much time and attention to devote.

Ad hoc requests for information, ranging from very simple to complex, occupy a significant amount of time and resources for most IR operations. IR practitioners acknowledge that success in serving an ad hoc request is dependent on the quality of the question posed. Adept institutional researchers help colleagues hone their question and determine what information will best serve their need. These lines of inquiry usually involve defining the problem at hand and what the requester wants to find out. The concepts reviewed in this chapter suggest that this process is best aided when the question is framed according to the context in which the response will be used. Ideally, an institutional researcher would confer with at least a few of the individuals who may be involved in using the results. Argyris and Schön's concepts also highlight the potential that provided information will raise new questions that require additional information. Rather than seeking to satisfy an ad hoc information need, collaborative organizational learning considerations suggest that we think about how the stated need fits into a broader inquiry process. Taking a more collaborative approach may also lead to fewer ad hoc requests that come out of the blue, as IR professionals become part of committees and groups and have a better sense of information needs.

Institutional researchers are called on to apply more advanced research and analysis skills to serve essential institutional objectives. Student progress, faculty workload, program evaluation, and campus climate studies are examples of common topics for such research. Hansen and Borden (2006) describe an action research model for engaging in institutional research that is built on the collaborative organizational learning ideas reviewed in this paper. They characterize a traditional approach, wherein a request is received "from outside the office" and perhaps clarified through questions, and the research proceeds through a process that is largely controlled by the researcher until results are sent to the client. In contrast, the action research approach requires the researcher to engage with the individuals or groups that will use the results at the start of the process, when the research question and methodology is being formulated. The collaboration continues throughout the research process, involving the stakeholders in data collection and analysis at some level. Preliminary findings are shared and reviewed in a group context to obtain input into the interpretation and need for additional inquiry. When more complete results are obtained, the researcher works with the stakeholders to interpret the results and devise a plan of action, including provisions for collecting and evaluating data to determine whether the actions produced desired results.

Implications for the Skills and Dispositions Useful to IR

Terenzini's (1999) and Volkwein's (1999) characterizations of IR skill sets capture in a general way both the technical and methodological skill set that serves the more traditional, rational decision-support ethos, as well as the more interpretive and collaborative modes of work on which we have focused. However, more detailed descriptions of required IR skills, knowledge, and abilities, such as the information executive, information architect, and information engineer roles described by Borden, Massa, and Milam (2001), focus more on methodological and technical aspects than on the kinds of skills and disposition that facilitate collaborative organizational learning. Missing from these specifications are the facilitation, negotiation, and political dispositions and skill sets needed when one shifts the focus from information production and analysis to interpretation and, most important, when one works with the vast and varied organizational dynamics common to higher education institutions.

In a Delphi study of senior institutional research professionals and higher education researchers, Polk (2001) identified 10 skill areas reflecting the breadth of skills that encompass the technical, contextual, and human relational dimensions that emerge from infusing the collaborative organizational learning framework on top of the traditional rational, decision-support approach. These skill areas include communication; critical thinking and questioning; statistical reasoning; technical knowledge within specific information and methodological domains; contextual knowledge regarding higher education administration in general and the culture of one's own institution; ethical, moral, and professional conduct; and interpersonal relations.

The knowledge, skills, and abilities (KSAs) needed for effective practice was an ongoing topic of discussion at annual meetings of a grant program, in which the first author participated, to design institutional research graduate certificate programs at five universities. Each participating institution team could readily describe how its curriculum addressed the technical, methodological, and issues skills. The skills found most difficult to address as an outcome of course curriculum were the political and human relational ones—the very ones that we suggest are crucial to facilitating collaborative organizational learning. It became apparent to the participants in this project that the skills required to promote the effective production and use of institutional research to support organizational learning arise from learning that occurs in the socioorganizational contexts of the actual work. In other words, the concepts of situated learning and communities of practice apply as much to the development of skills needed to facilitate collaborative organizational learning as they do to the context in which institutional researchers can most productively support

TABLE 6.1   THE TENETS OF INSTITUTIONAL RESEARCH: SHIFTING FROM A DECISION SUPPORT TO A COLLABORATIVE ORGANIZATIONAL LEARNING ETHOS

Decision-Support Approach to IR	COL-Informed Approach to IR
Rational, data-driven decision-making processes yield more informed and successful decisions.	Learning-driven organizational development improves institutional and educational effectiveness.
Improved access to well-managed institutional data sources gives decision makers the tools they need to inform decision processes.	Institutional data sources provide useful but limited input into the learning process.
To be useful, data must be turned into information, and information into knowledge.	Data and information are useful learning resources.
Data, information, and knowledge need to be managed.	Knowledge is accrued through guided social interaction in organizational contexts.
The primary purpose of institutional research is to provide information needed by decision makers and decision-making groups.	The primary purpose of institutional research is to facilitate organizational learning.

collaborative organizational learning. This suggests that participation in communities of practice—in both one's own organization as well as those related specifically to the practice of institutional research—are essential contexts for learning to become effective institutional researchers, as Brown and Duguid (2002) describe for other work groups.

Shifting the Tenets of Institutional Research

In closing, we offer Table 6.1 to characterize the shift in mindset that we suggest emerges from overlaying a collaborative organizational learning framework on top of the traditional rational, decision-support ethos that has dominated the field of practice.

Notes

1. More formal theoretical and empirical explorations of these limits are exemplified at the intrapersonal (cognitive) level as biases and anomalies in information processing (Kahneman & Tversky, 1979; Kahneman, Slovic, & Tversky, 1982), at the interpersonal level as coordination problems in group dynamics (for example, Steiner, 1972; Thibaut & Kelley, 1986), and at the social system level as the heightening of emotional response related to inherent conflicts in varying perspectives and agendas (for example, Mazur, 1968; Louis, Taylor, & Douglas, 2005).

2. The discussion that follows summarizes fuller descriptions, with accompanying citations provided by Easterby-Smith (1997). The literature on organizational learning is vast and varied (Kezar, 2005). By the early 1990s the popularity of OL had grown to the extent that more academic papers were produced in one year (1993) than in the entire preceding decade (Crosson & Guatto, 1996). Easterby-Smith (1997) outlines six

disciplines that have actively undertaken studies on organizational learning, including (1) psychology and organizational development; (2) management science; (3) sociology, and organizational theory; (4) strategy; (5) production management; and (6) cultural anthropology. Therefore OL is becoming the core area of study in a variety of disciplines that see its central role in understanding how organizations operate.

3. Although leaving accountability-related practices aside, Petrides (2002) notes that public accountability and organizational learning can be constructively linked through the evidence-based practices in which many institutional researchers engage, such as program review and evaluation. She further notes, citing Volkwein (1999), that institutional researchers are well positioned to serve their institutions as a bridge among academic, administrative, and governmental cultures.

References

Argyris, C., & Schön, D. (1978). *Organizational learning: A theory of action perspective.* Reading, MA: Addison Wesley.

Argyris, C., & Schön, D. (1996). *Organizational learning II: Theory, method and practice.* Reading, MA: Addison Wesley.

Bensimon, E., & Neumann, A. (1993). *Redesigning collegiate leadership.* Baltimore, MD: Johns Hopkins University Press.

Borden, V.M.H., & Delaney, E. L. (1989). Information support for group decision making. In P. Ewell (Ed.), *Enhancing information use in decision making* (pp. 49–60). New Directions for Institutional Research, no. 64. San Francisco: Jossey-Bass.

Borden, V.M.H., Massa, T., & Milam, J. (2001). Technology and tools for institutional research. In R. Howard (Ed.), *Institutional research: Decision support in higher education. Resources in Institutional Research, 13,* 195–222. Tallahassee, FL: Association for Institutional Research.

Brown, J. S., & Duguid, P. (1991). Organizational learning and communities of practice: Toward a unified view of working, learning, and innovation. *Organizational Science, 2*(1), 40–57.

Brown, J. S., & Duguid, P. (2002). *The social life of information.* Boston, MA: Harvard Business School Press.

Campbell, J. P., DeBlois, P. B., & Oblinger, D. G. (2007). Academic analytics: A new tool for a new era. *EDUCAUSE Review, 42*(4), 40–57.

Chaffee, E. E. (1983). *Rational decisionmaking in higher education.* Boulder, CO: National Center for Higher Education Management Systems.

Clancey, W. J. (1995). A tutorial on situated learning. In J. Self (Ed.), *Proceedings of the International Conference on Computers and Education* (Taiwan) (pp. 49–70). Charlottesville, VA: AACE.

Coughlin, M. A. (Ed.). (2005). *Applications of intermediate/advanced statistical applications in institutional research. Resources in Institutional Research, 16.* Tallahassee, FL: Association for Institutional Research.

Crosson, M. M., & Guatto, T. (1996). Organizational learning research profile. *Journal of Organizational Change Management, 9*(1), 107–112.

Davenport, T. H., & Kusak, L. (1997). *Information ecology.* New York: Oxford University Press.

Delaney, A. M. (2009). Institutional researchers' expanding roles: Policy, planning, program evaluation, assessment, and new research methodologies. In C. Leimer (Ed.), *Special issue: Imagining the future of institutional research* (pp. 29–41). New Directions for Institutional Research, no. 143. San Francisco: Jossey-Bass.

DiBella, A. (1998). *How organizations learn: An integrated strategy for building learning capability.* San Francisco: Jossey Bass.

Dixon, N. M. (1999). *The organizational learning cycle: How we can learn collectively.* Hampshire, UK: Gower.

Easterby-Smith, M. (1997). Disciplines of organizational learning: Contributions and critiques. *Human Relations, 50*(4), 1085–1113.

Easterby-Smith, M., Aráujo, L., & Burgoyne, J. (Eds.). (1999). *Organizational learning and the learning organization: Developments in theory and practice.* Thousand Oaks, CA: SAGE.

Elkjaer, B. (1999). In search of social learning theory. In A. Smith, J. Burgoyne, and L. Araujo (Eds.), *Organizational learning and the learning organization* (pp. 75–92). London: Sage Publications.

Fiol, C., & Lyles, M (1985, July-August). Organizational learning. *Academy of Management Review, 71*(4), 81–91.

Friedlander, F. (1983). Patterns of individual and organizational learning. In S. Srivastva and Associates (Eds.), *The executive mind: New insights in managerial thought and action.* San Francisco: Jossey-Bass.

Hansen, M. J., & Borden, V.M.H. (2006). Using action research to support academic program improvement. In E. P. St. John & M. Wilkerson (Eds.), *Reframing persistence research to improve academic success* (pp. 47–62). New Directions for Institutional Research, no. 130. San Francisco: Jossey-Bass.

Howard, R. D. (Ed.). (2001). *Institutional research: Decision support in higher education. Resources in Institutional Research, 13.* Tallahassee, FL: Association for Institutional Research.

Howard, R. D. (Ed.). (2007). *Using mixed methods in institutional research. Resources in Institutional Research, 17.* Tallahassee, FL: Association for Institutional Research.

Huber, G. (1991). Organizational learning: The contributing processes and the literature. *Organization Science, 2*(2), 88–115.

Kahneman, D., Slovic, P., & Tversky, A. (Eds.). (1982). *Judgment under uncertainty: Heuristics and biases.* New York: Cambridge University Press.

Kahneman, D., & Tversky, A. (1979). Intuitive prediction: Biases and corrective procedures. *Management Science, 12,* 313–327.

Kezar, A. (Ed.). (2005). *Higher education as a learning organization: Promising concepts and approaches.* New Directions for Higher Education, no. 131. San Francisco: Jossey-Bass.

Lave, J. (1988). *Cognition in practice: Mind, mathematics, and culture in everyday life.* Cambridge, UK: Cambridge University Press.

Lave, J., & Wenger, E. (1991). *Situated learning: Legitimate peripheral participation.* New York: Cambridge University Press.

Louis, W. R., Taylor, D. M., and Douglas, R. L. (2005). Normative influence and rational conflict decisions: Group norms and cost-benefit analyses for intergroup behavior. *Group Processes & Intergroup Relations, 8*(4), 355–374.

Mazur, A. (1968). A nonrational approach to theories of conflict and coalitions. *Journal of Conflict Resolution, 12(2),* 196–205.

McLaughlin, G., & Howard, R. D. (2004). *People, processes, and managing data* (2nd ed.). *Resources in Institutional Research, 15.* Tallahassee, FL: Association for Institutional Research.

Milam, J. (2003). Using national datasets for postsecondary education research. In W. Knight (Ed.), *Primer for institutional research* (pp. 123–149). *Resources in Institutional Research, 14.* Tallahassee, FL: Association for Institutional Research.

Milam, J. (2005). Organizational learning through knowledge workers and infomediaries. In A. Kezar (Ed.), *Organizational learning in higher education* (pp. 61–73). New Directions for Higher Education, no. 131. San Francisco: Jossey Bass.

Norris, D., Baer, L., Leonard, J., Pugliese, L., & Lefrere, P. (2008). Action analytics: Measuring and improving performance that matters in higher education. *EDUCAUSE Review, 43*(1), 42–67.

Petrides, L. A. (2002). Organizational learning and the case for knowledge-based systems. In A. M. Serban & J. Luan (Eds.), *Knowledge management: Building a competitive advantage in higher education* (pp. 69–84). New Directions in Institutional Research, no. 113. San Francisco: Jossey Bass.

Polk, N. E. (2001). Key competencies for institutional researchers in the first decade of the twenty-first century: A Delphi technique for curriculum planning. (Doctoral dissertation). Retrieved from ProQuest Dissertations and Theses. (Accession Order No. AAT 3028478)

Saupe, J. L. (1990). *The functions of institutional research* (2nd ed.). Tallahassee, FL: Association for Institutional Research.

Serban, A. M., & Luan, J. (Eds.). (2002a). *Knowledge management: Building a competitive advantage in higher education.* New Directions in Institutional Research, no. 113. San Francisco: Jossey Bass.

Serban, A. M., & Luan, J. (2002b). Overview of knowledge management. In A. M. Serban & J. Luan (Eds.), *Knowledge management: Building a competitive advantage in higher education* (pp. 5–16). New Directions in Institutional Research, no. 113. San Francisco: Jossey-Bass.

Simon, H. A. (1991). Bounded rationality and organizational learning. *Organization Science, 2*(1), 125–134.

Simon, H. A., Dantzig, G. B., Horgarth, R., Plott, C. R., Raiffa, H., Schelling, T. C., & Winter, S. (1987). Decision making and problem solving. *Interfaces, 17*(5), 11–31.

Steiner, I. D. (1972). *Group processes and productivity.* New York: Academic Press.

Suskie, L. A. (1996). *Questionnaire survey research: What works* (2nd ed.). *Resources in Institutional Research, 9.* Tallahassee, FL: Association for Institutional Research.

Swenk, J. (1999). Planning failures: Decision cultural clashes. *Review of Higher Education, 23*(1), 1–21.

Terenzini, P. T. (1999). On the nature of institutional research and the knowledge and skills it requires. In J. F. Volkwein (Ed.), *What is institutional research all about? A critical and comprehensive assessment of the profession* (pp. 21–29). New Directions for Institutional Research, no. 104. San Francisco: Jossey Bass.

Thibaut, J. W., & Kelley, H. H. (1986). *The social psychology of groups.* New York: Wiley.

Volkwein, J. F. (1999). The four faces of institutional research. In J. F. Volkwein (Ed.), *What is institutional research all about? A critical and comprehensive assessment of the profession* (pp. 9–19). New Directions for Institutional Research, no. 104. San Francisco: Jossey-Bass.

Weick, K. E., & Westley, F. (1996). Organizational learning: Affirming an oxymoron. In S. R. Clegg, C. Hardy, & W. R. Nord (Eds.), *Handbook of organization studies* (pp. 440–458). London: Sage Publications.

Wenger, E. (1998). *Communities of practice: Learning, meaning, and identity.* New York: Cambridge University Press.

CHAPTER 7

DEVELOPING INSTITUTIONAL ADAPTABILITY USING CHANGE MANAGEMENT PROCESSES

Kim Bender

Institutions have practiced change management for decades, but they have not managed it well. Now, however, environmental complexity has outstripped institutional capacity to respond with simplistic, episodic planning and evaluation methods. Change management has emerged as a means to intentionally strengthen an institution's resiliency and adaptive capacity. Technology innovations are providing institutions with better tools to manage change. Planning and evaluation processes at most institutions are shifting from paper formats to interactive database activities, which enable institutions to systematize, coordinate, and share this work. Even in a time of diminishing resources, institutions can significantly improve their capacity to manage change and become more adaptable by using a renewable resource: continuous human learning about how their organizations work and how they can work better. Institutional research/assessment (IR/A) offices can and should play a critical role in strengthening this resource.

The Expanding Role of IR Units: The New Frontier of Managing Change

Randy Swing, executive director of the Association of Institutional Research (AIR), sees institutional research as evolving toward a blending of data skills, strategic planning, outcomes assessment, and advocacy for improvement. He argues that institutional researchers should begin developing competencies in change management theory. Additionally, IR/A offices need to provide professional development to gain skills in organizational change, while graduate programs in higher education leadership need to develop courses in change management. Institutional research professional associations should organize training opportunities for researchers to acquire the needed skills to become change agents at their institutions (Swing, 2009).

The journal *New Directions for Institutional Research* added definition to role expansion with its 2009 special issue focused on the future of institutional research. Issue editor Christine Leimer wrote that the necessity and practice of institutional researchers to work in multiple areas of an institution qualify them to encourage a culture of collaboration among decentralized academic and support units. Instead of just providing these units with data, Leimer suggests that IR/A offices proactively support transformation and change using features of organizational learning (Leimer, 2009). A few years earlier, John Milam recommended that IR/A staff members be the grassroots leaders of knowledge management. Strategies for knowledge management include distributing best practices, online "help" training, search engines, use of taxonomies, data warehousing, and display of learning histories. The IR/A role should include connecting information users with the information they seek (Milam, 2005).

Change management is emerging as a new frontier for many IR/A offices. Assisting the exploration and professionalization of this area, this chapter presents the following categories of information to help IR/A staff (1) recognize the context of change management, (2) understand processes of change management and ways to mitigate change barriers, and (3) learn how institutions can apply change management theory and practices on their own campuses for enhancing institutional resiliency and adaptability.

Context of Change Management: Motivation and Theory

Effective change management needs to be comprehensive and decentralized, meaning large numbers of faculty and staff will be involved. Motivation is key to developing the kind of participation required and for developing a supportive culture. Knowing the various theories and types of change can guide those who are responsible for supporting change processes at an institution.

Motivation: Philosophy, Social-Ecological Systems, and the Pressures of Change

IR/A offices can implement change management more effectively if they communicate *why* it is important to the core essence of their institutions. Two American philosophies and recent studies in social-ecological systems support similar characteristics of institutional change management: (1) quality and managed change are closely related, (2) diversity of planning and evaluation efforts strengthen institutional adaptability, and (3) decentralized and continuous self-examination and exploration verify the truth and accelerate development of unit quality.

Pragmatism, as defined by William James in *Pragmatism, A New Name for Some Old Ways of Thinking*, is an optimistic and melioristic philosophy, supporting the belief that human beings can aid the betterment of the world by exercising their free will to change reality (James, 1907/1981). Pragmatism is an empowering philosophy based on action and continuous testing of truths for verification of knowledge.[1] IR/A staff support this action when they develop continuous improvement or change management processes.

Robert Pirsig developed his thoughts on quality into a philosophy called the metaphysics of quality (MOQ), which he defined in his 1991 novel *Lila: An Inquiry into Morals*. MOQ defines quality as value. The development of value, or improvement through change, strengthens quality (Pirsig, 1991, p. 58).[2] Institutional unit or departmental improvement is based on the attainment of the values its faculty or staff share. Because values are seldom uniform, designs of change or planning for units must remain decentralized if substantive quality is to be achieved. Systematic management of change, or planning and evaluation, accelerates this attainment of values. Pirsig claims that quality attainment is a driving force in the universe, much like gravity. It is present in the theory of evolution. Activity that seeks a movement toward higher quality is inherent in most people.

There are periods of *static quality*, in which change is consolidated and firmed up. There are also times of *dynamic quality*, in which an organization is in the state of becoming, is flexible, is open to change (Pirsig, 1991, pp. 115). Higher-quality institutions will build capacity that sustains their flexibility and adaptability so that they can respond more quickly to environmental change and can lead change in their direction. Using continuous planning and evaluation at the decentralized unit level manifests value and strengthens the propensity for dynamic quality or constructive evolution.

Recent social-ecological systems literature reinforces decentralized adaptive management as a means to strengthen institutional resiliency and subsequent sustainability. An institution's adaptive management includes decentralized action planning and evaluation processes that serve as sensing or feedback mechanisms for local units to learn about themselves and their environment. Diversity of units and functions is a critical factor in developing resiliency, which is the ability to bounce back after experiencing challenges from the environment; for example, external policy changes or a state budget crisis (Gunderson & Holling, 2002). The degree of demographic and functional diversity can positively impact change processes. Organizational diversity encourages creativity, leads to more effective problem solving, and strengthens adaptability to change (Cao et al., 1999).

A common dilemma for change managers is balancing functional diversity and subsequent redundancies with concepts of efficiency and centralization. However, when IR/A staff develop feedback or sensing resources for decentralized units, they can argue that they are building adaptive capacity, which strengthens their institution's resiliency for responding to the pressures of change.

As complexity deepens, institutions are confronting greater pressures for change. David Nadler offers a prophetic statement in his book *Champions of Change*. His reference to business organization complacency can be applied to higher education. "A company that enjoys a monopoly or oligopoly can get away with doing more of the same for quite some time. But add disequilibrium and a destabilizing event to the mix and then throw in an environmental factor such as a new competitive force, technological innovation, or governmental involvement, and all of a sudden the outcomes of decreased customer focus, increased costs, loss of speed, and so on start manifesting themselves in sharply declining performance" (Nadler, 1998, p. 73).

The beginning of the twenty-first century brought an environment of deep change to higher education. Technology has connected the people of nations around the world with continuously expanding information resources. The global distribution of wealth is shifting significantly. The electronic distribution of education and publishing favors market entry by those with smaller pockets. Public concern about higher education performance has strengthened expectations for accountability. The instructional labor of institutions is shifting from tenured faculty to temporary instructors. The student body is becoming more diverse. Increased federal regulation is expanding compliance activities. This watershed of change—functional, social, and political (Dacin, Goodstein, & Scott, 2002)—is exceeding the change-managing capacity of those institutions that are still using old methods such as episodic evaluation and disconnected planning (Bok, 2006).[3]

Accrediting bodies are responding to these pressures and encouraging institutions to adopt adaptability processes to improve the quality of their operations. Recently, agencies like the Higher Learning Commission (HLC) of the North Central Association began offering alternatives to compliance criteria. HLC's new Open Pathway (2014–15) accreditation model contains an assurance process for compliance and a quality initiative process to stimulate change. In addition, the Southern Association of Colleges and Schools (SACS) recently added the Quality Enhancement Plan to its core requirements (2.12) and comprehensive standards (33.2), making change management at institutions a higher-stakes activity (Southern Association of Colleges and Schools, 2009). Institutions will need change management processes to implement quality enhancing projects. Furthermore, regional accrediting bodies are beginning to incorporate federal compliance programs into their criteria. This is another growth area of change management, as IR/A offices help their institutions adapt to changing policies and reporting requirements.

Change Process Theories, Models, and Types

Quantum physics and chaos theory suggest that change is unpredictable, non-linear, and uncertain. The emerging connectivity of systems and subsystems contributes to environmental complexity; a small change in one area can lead to unpredicted change in other related areas. Long-term strategic planning that is linear and teleological and operates by a succession of steps is becoming obsolete. Command and control methods of implementing change are becoming ineffective (Wheatley, 2005). Change management at the institutional level may even be a contradiction in terms, unless it develops a meaning that supports managing the conditions that encourage change rather than determining its direction and content. The decentralized departments and support units will become more responsible for managing the content of change in the future (Simsek & Louis, 1994). As complexity expands, IR/A staff members can use their knowledge of change theory to better inform their design of change management infrastructure.

One of the more comprehensive works that surveys the theory of change is Marshal Poole and Andrew H. Van de Ven's *Handbook of Organizational Change and Innovation*. They define organizational change as "a difference in form, quality, or state over time in an organizational entity" (Poole & Van de Ven, 2004, p. xi). According to Poole and Van de Ven, four theories dominate description of the change process. The Evolutionary, Dialectic, Life Cycle, and Teleological theories are briefly described in Table 7.1. In addition, Table 7.1 presents four central models of change management—Lewin's action research, cyclical/iterative, transformation management, and the emergent approach to change—and reveals the situations in which they are appropriate to use (Lewin, 1948/1999). The social-ecological systems literature relates most closely with elements in column three (transformative). Table 7.1 is a quick reference to the theory, modeling, and context of change management dynamics.

The Range of Change Types: From Simple to Complex

The types of change range along a continuum from easy one-time alterations to difficult, ongoing transformative change that becomes institutionalized (Burnes, 2000). Change can be short-run, episodic, first-order, linear, and incremental at one end of the change continuum, and at the other end it can be long-run, continuous, second-order, multifaceted, and transformative (Poole & Van de Ven, 2004). Episodic change is more easily managed and less disruptive to organizations. It is associated with institutional reaction to change or aspects of problem solving and uses a local, closed system that is buffered from outside interference. This first-order change can impact institutional structures, processes, and activities. In contrast, transformative change is more complex and involves a planning process that is multidimensional and ongoing and eventually affects the institutional culture—changing assumptions, behaviors, and values (Boyce, 2003). It embraces uncertainty and uses open systems that invite the complexity of engaging multiple campus subcultures and outside community groups in implementing change.

TABLE 7.1   SUMMARY OF CHANGE MANAGEMENT
CHARACTERISTICS, THEORIES, AND MODELS

Dynamics	Episodic/One-Time	Incremental/ Continuous	Transformative/ Radical
Anticipatory	Scanning	Tuning	Redirecting
Reactive	Problem solving	Adapting	Overhauling
Time Frame	Short-term	Short- and long-term	Continuous
Process Theories (Poole & Van de Ven, 2004, p. 7)	*Teleological/lifecycle theory* views the organization as a living organism that moves through the stages of start-up, growth, harvest, and termination.	*Teleological theory* is based on a philosophical concept where change moves along a direct line of progress ranging from dissatisfaction, search, and goal setting, to implementation of planning. It is continuous, as an achieved set of goals is replaced with a new group.	*Evolutionary theory* portrays change as a biological process based on the competitive survival of the fittest or adaptability. *Dialectic theory* respects pluralism and views the world as a series of colliding events or forces with opposing values that create conflict. Occasionally the conflict of two opposing groups generates a third variety or a synthesis of the two.
Model Type	*Lewin's three-step process,* unveiled in the 1940s by Kurt Lewin, involves using a three-step process of (1) unfreezing— preparing the environment; (2) change implementation; and (3) refreezing— institutionalizing the change (Burnes, 2000, p. 270). Lewin's development of "action research" parallels this as a means to implement.	*Cyclical/Iterative* model of change implementation is (1) recognizing the change imperative, (2) developing a shared vision, (3) implementing change, (4) consolidating change, and (5) sustaining change with emphasis on recognizing the next change initiative (Nadler, 1998, p. 75). *Transition management* includes four stages for the change process: (1) trigger layer— opportunity, threat, crisis; (2) vision layer—defining the future; (3) conversion layer—persuasion, recruitment; and (4) maintenance—sustaining, reinforcing (Paton & McCalman, 2008, p. 11).	*Emergent change approach* denies that change can be solidified or can be manifested through a linear process of steps. Instead, change is viewed as a continuous process and cannot be planned per se. It relies on a bottom-up approach of local unit change-management empowerment. Its focus is on establishing the conditions of adaptability (Burnes, 2000, p. 283).
Complexity	Isolated, simple, certainty/confidence	High and low cycles of certainty	Multiple interconnected parts High uncertainty
Learning Levels	Single loop: simple reactive thinking	Combinations of single and double loop	Double loop: continuous examining, rigorous organizational inquiry

Direction of Change	Linear	Progressive	Nonlinear
Organization Type and Size	Small single purpose cohesive unit/dept. Personal relationships	Mid-size division or college	Large, multifaceted institution, loose coupled system of organizations Impersonal, structured relationships
Institutional Impact	Isolated practice or activity changed	Process, policy, or structure changed	Culture values, behaviors, assumptions changed
Change Intensity	Contained or controlled	Metamorphosis or evolution	Revolution
Leadership Style	Directing plan content and acting as change agent	Collaborative team leadership	Vision-building role and supporting change processes and capacity, such as organization learning

Note: Social-ecological systems literature relates most closely with items in column three (transformative).

Sources: Parts of this table rely on D. Nadler, 1998, and Kezar, 2001.

Change Management Process Steps and Mitigation of Its Barriers

Institutional research and assessment staff can help their institutions become more receptive to change, provide them with options for implementing change, and support their efforts to mitigate the barriers that frustrate change.

Exciting Change by Encouraging Doubt: Placing Data in High-Use Areas

Various terms are used to describe this first phase of creative destruction, such as *de-institutionalization* (Dacin et al., 2002), or *disconfirmation* (Schein, 1992, p. 299). Mary Boyce claims that institutions need to introduce stress in order to overcome the inertia that challenges change. The change features should be presented as a means to reduce the stress (Boyce, 2003). Schein (1992) states that all forms of learning and change start with some form of dissatisfaction or frustration, generated by data that disconfirm our expectations or hopes. Whether change is sought to adapt to environmental shifts (reaction) or to implement a change identified by generative organizational learning (proactive), disconfirmation functions as a primary driving force in motivating change. This step must include the realization that institutional or unit-level values are threatened by the new information, to the extent that it generates a critical mass of "anxiety" (pp. 51, 299).

IR/A offices play a critical role at this step, because they generate much of the data that can be used to contradict expectations. Some develop interactive data resources that other units can interact with; for example, online survey results. Many IR/A offices systematically launch data or information disclosures on the adaptive management (planning and evaluation) platforms that they manage or service; for example, assessment plans, program reviews, accreditation self-studies, or strategic planning projects. Frequently, data challenges assumptions and encourages doubt, especially if it is placed in areas where faculty and staff routinely need to work.

Implementing Change: Selecting the Mode of Change

Once the will to change is established, institutions review the options available to manage it. Resources such as Table 7.1 and change management handbooks such as Poole and Van de Ven's (2004) are good starting points.

When working in a stable environment toward incremental or episodic change, institutions will likely use a simple change model that can be implemented by change agents or leaders. Plans might resemble Lewin's (1948) model of unfreeze, implement, and refreeze and seek to produce linear change that runs on a teleological or life cycle process (see Table 7.1 for definitions). Data gathering will inform the institution or unit whether the change is working and validate the change itself.

Institutions operating in a more complicated, volatile environment will seek change that is more revolutionary, large-scale, and long-term. They will implement a slower, more complex change process that is multifaceted, whereby alterations are made in the diverse arenas of process, political organization, and culture (Cao et al., 1999). Institutions will design complex change holistically, engaging all or most of the organizational parts rather than isolating change to one area at a time. Leadership is more focused on developing vision, creating feedback capacity, and empowering decentralized units with skills and responsibility to manage their own incremental change. This kind of change cannot be driven from the top down (Senge, 1999).

No implementation of significant change is sustainable without a plan to institutionalize it. For linear, well-focused plans for change, institutionalization is less demanding. Stabilizing this kind of change can be achieved through adjustments in institutional policy guidelines, for example. However, with complex, transformative change initiatives, institutionalizing change becomes more challenging. To change campus-wide assumptions and behaviors, repetitive processes and organizational learning must be implemented. (See the "Case Study" section for a discussion of how to institutionalize a change management system.) As IR/A offices work to implement change management processes, they will encounter resistance on many fronts.

Barriers to Change: How IR/A Units Can Mitigate Their Impact

Peter Senge (1999) uses a biological concept to illustrate the "dance of change." "Every movement is being inhibited as it occurs" (p. 10). Senge adds that there is an inevitable interplay between growth processes and limiting processes. Business scholar John March (2008) claims that the more institutionalized an area is, the more robust are its structures against reform.

The intellectual historian Lewis Menand writes: "Trying to reform the contemporary university is like trying to get on the Internet with a typewriter or like riding a horse to the mall" (2010, p. 17).

Traditional management practices still used by some higher education institutions offer functional barriers that frustrate change management initiatives. Many institutions still use episodic planning and evaluation processes whereby faculty in departments organize to develop program review or special accreditation self-studies once every five or six years, then disband and forget about this activity until the next evaluation. Feedback systems are episodic as well, with occasional requests for data going to the institutional research office only when a crisis develops or a new program proposal is written. Planning is often disjointed, with assessment planning, program review action planning, college planning, and institutional strategic planning all running on separate tracks of development and monitoring. Information or knowledge management is not systemized at many institutions, so administrative turnover depletes institutional memory and even leads to development of dysfunctional memory that distorts planning. Moreover, the evaluation guidelines for department heads, and perhaps for deans, are not always explicit about the quality of change management leadership.

IR/A offices can often mitigate functional barriers using recent technology for developing interactive electronic planning and evaluation databases. They can be constructed to regularly monitor institutions' continuous improvement activity for process continuity, thereby minimizing the harmful effects of administrative disruptions and discontinuity of self-evaluation. Furthermore, regular peer-review processes and subsequent reports make lags in change management participation more visible across campus. Institutional researchers can provide continuous data feeds into online departmental self-studies or other unit venues to strengthen feedback continuity. Archiving planning and connecting current and past planning in seamless online formats illustrates planning evolution and reduces the administrative loss of memory. The embedding of multiple tiered levels of planning into units' action plan goals enables classification that visually shows planning integration. IR/A offices can work directly with peer-review committees to provide system reporting resources and to develop peer evaluation rubrics that help reviewers manage the quality of planning and evaluation so that it optimally delivers change patterns; for example, diagnostic planning encourages change activity better than monitoring goals. Planting the language of change management and its best practices in online assessment plans or program review self-study templates works to level steep learning curves. Raising the visibility of leadership evaluation criteria in program review self-studies can show the emphasis placed on change management skills.

Some change barriers are culture oriented. Some organizations or suborganizations avoid sharing information for fear of exploitation by competitors; others fear contamination of the culture. Academic departments resist ideas of market determination, consumerism, and instrumentalism that serve the corporate sector. Other units fear loss of status or budget resources if institutional strategic shifts occur. Some will argue that current resources will not support the change or that the evidence or data encouraging the change is flawed (Paton & McCalman, 2008).

An institution's culture can act as a barrier to change or as a resource for implementing change. To avoid unnecessary conflict, change managers must know their cultures well and introduce change strategies that use their strengths (Tierney, 1988). Cultures vary by educational tier—and, often, by individual institutions. Many larger institutions have subcultures that interact with one another, making change management more complex (Chaffee & Jacobson, 1997).

Using policy and the design of online interactive planning systems, IR/A offices can emphasize localism to reduce cultural resistance to change. IR/A staff members can design change management processes to encourage decentralization and exploit the loosely coupled structure of higher education institutions. This emphasis on localism reduces anxieties over centralized structures or policies that might otherwise contradict cultural norms. For example, policy guidelines, such as program review, can require faculty and staff to base their planning and evaluation activity on their own local unit values. The decentralization of planning and experimenting reduces risk levels, countering those who argue for the status quo based on the uncertainty of adopting a change. Mistakes can be tolerated.

Application of these mitigation tactics and others appear in the next "Case Study" section. The section demonstrates how IR/A offices can apply the theories and models just discussed, engage process steps, mitigate barriers, and strengthen institutional resiliency by supporting the characteristics of resiliency—systems thinking, decentralized self-organization, functional diversity, adaptive management, and organizational learning.

Applying Theory to Practice: Case Study of an Operating Change Management Process

Using a case study approach, this section illustrates application of change management theory and systems thinking, describes tactics for mitigating barriers to change, and shows how institutions can build the unit resiliency and adaptive capacity that support institutional sustainability.

IR/A Role in Building Institutional Resiliency and Adaptive Capacity

IR/A offices can intentionally strengthen the resiliency of their institutions by (1) raising the comfort level with uncertainty and complexity, (2) nurturing functional diversity, (3) creating resources that support self-organizing of decentralized units, and (4) strengthening organizational learning (Berkes Colding, & Folke, 2003, p. 383).[4] Early articulation of complexity appeared in Peter Senge's book *The Fifth Discipline*. Later, Senge (1999) explained that living systems thinking assumes that human groups are self-organizing. There are no designers to control the flow of information, but ". . . information courses rapidly through the organization in its own natural patterns" (Senge, p. 144). Adrianna Kezar (2001) reinforces this perspective: "In general, it is wiser for institutions to invest in innovation throughout the campus and to let great ideas bubble up" (p. 117). Offering a design for this kind of change management, David Nadler (1995) advocated a federal configuration that requires coordination of planning at the center and decentralized plan implementation at the periphery (p. 276).

Developing institutional adaptability through decentralization of change management is an area ripe for IR/A service activity. For example, developing interactive data resources for local departmental use contributes to local feedback systems (Mets, 1997).[5] Effective central design of planning databases (assessment and program review) assists the integration of institutional planning and enables unit-based organizational learning. Institutional researchers can play a role in identifying the "bubbling up" of ideas or emergent change if they help form electronic planning and evaluation resources that monitor and report planning activity and that share the local strategies being used to solve problems.

The CSI Change Management Process

The case study research university, Change State Institution (CSI), has developed a change management process called Attain Quality Faster (AQF) that applies theories of change management. It combines aspects of the emergent change model for transformation at the institutional level with the Lewin model at the localized department level (see Table 7.1). The change theory that most closely applies at the institutional level is the evolution process, whereas the teleological cycle is more applicable at the department level where action planning occurs. Making environmental variation, selection, and retention a process at the institutional level, AQF identifies and makes visible the best practices of unit change management; when replicated, this increases the value of the institution and strengthens its resiliency. By decentralizing change management responsibility, variation and diversity are encouraged. AQF collaboration in change management with other institutions expands the pool of best practices, accelerating CSI's rate of change and strengthening its adaptability. The evolution theory nicely parallels Pirsig's metaphysics of quality, whereby disposition to change leads to greater value and quality.

When IR/A units design change management systems, what components should they consider integrating? The possibilities include human organizations, databases, planning and process connections, continuous information flow patterns, and institutional collaborations. The AQF uses ten interrelated parts, ranging from a home-grown assessment database management system that operates multilevel feedback mechanisms to a public transparency site that shares evaluation information with constituents. Consistent with open systems theory, it attempts to make connections to other systems, expanding the complexity of its interactions; for example, with institutional strategic planning and with other institutions using AQF. Organized to work on the principle of federalism, the database planning platforms and organizational learning are managed centrally, while adaptive management (design of change planning and performance evaluation processes) is delegated to localized departments and units. Each unit is intended to attain a critical mass of self-organizing capacity—such as planning and evaluation skills—to effectively manage its own destiny. Figures 7.1 and 7.2 offer a view of the AQF model and its system components.

Adaptive Management: Evoking Change by Creating Platforms for Provoking Doubt

Attaining unit values and quality requires a regular pattern of change that is provoked by doubt or disconfirmation of accepted truths. Since it became operational in 2003, the AQF has provided opportunities for routine

FIGURE 7.1   THE AQF CONCEPT MODEL FOR CHANGE MANAGEMENT PROCESS

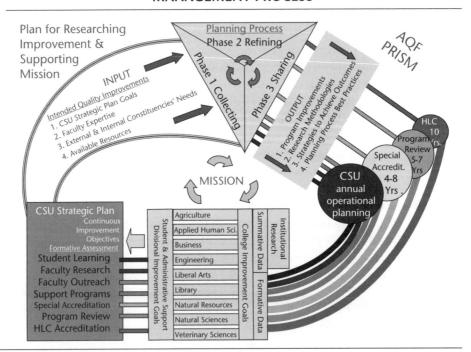

FIGURE 7.2   THE TEN-PART AQF PROCESS AND INFORMATION FLOW

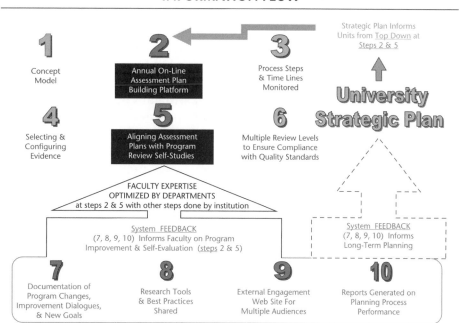

disconfirmation at the localized department level. About 170 academic programs and 30 student affairs units developed online assessment plans in the AQF database, which define action planning for student learning, faculty research, and student support efficiencies. These are annually peer-reviewed by standing committees representing each academic college and student affairs division. The AQF annual time line has departments/units regularly collect, present, and analyze data and peer-review information. Periodically, these data contradict faculty expectations for student learning, making faculty more receptive to changes—in accordance with Pirsig's state of dynamic quality. This leads to improvements in curriculum, professional development, and the assessment process. Centrally, CSI tests the truthfulness (pragmatism) of its four-part strategic plan by having four institution-wide committees annually scrutinize and change its content while monitoring its metrics, which IR/A staff members inform with data reports that occasionally challenge assumptions and expectations.

The IR/A office staff serve on CSI peer-review committees and help develop and use rubrics that define the institution's quality planning and evaluation standards. Annual use of the rubric for review encourages change through valuing and recognizing plans that identify unit strengths and weaknesses, making the best practices of diagnostic capacity visible for sharing across campus. Diagnostic performance research more effectively challenges existing practice than does research that merely monitors activity.

When working with the online program review piece of AQF, IR/A staff place institutional research data into applicable sections of the departmental self-study narratives; for example, inserting class-size data into a student learning environment section. Data are in a position to support or contradict claims of quality. In addition, the program review team members insert their online feedback comments into the self-study. These also support or contradict program claims and challenge assumptions. The template design that an IR/A office applies can increase a department's opportunities to question its own practices. A change management process can increase the number of times faculty members discuss issues of program quality. It can expand their exposure to current and meaningful analytic data feedback systems. Before AQF, there was less systematic generation of concerns and thus change moved more slowly.

Monitoring the Continuity of Change Mitigates Change Barriers

The IR/A office plays a role in developing accountability for implementing identified changes, using tactics of visibility and recognition. Each department or unit is responsible for implementing the changes it identifies through planning. IR/A staff members develop easy-access, interactive reporting resources on the AQF database that show levels of unit planning participation and their frequency of implemented improvements at the department level. Each year, the IR/A office sends an agenda item to the CSI board of governors that shows how well departments did in achieving their program review action plan goals. The annual peer review for the assessment action planning and the peer reviewers for program review evaluate the record of change implementation and provide feedback questioning nonperformance. The IR/A office rewards those departments that implement significant changes in performance by giving them recognition on AQF's public transparency site, which highlights CSI improvements. Peer review also includes recognizing departments' best practices in program improvements made as a result of assessment planning. Recognition is made visible in two places—by announcing it in the program assessment plan itself and by adding it to a best practices pool that is accessible campus-wide. The IR/A uses an interactive time line feature to monitor completion of planning and evaluation steps. Its subsequent reporting of change management activity sustains continuity, helping to mitigate the negative impact of episodic planning. Maintaining a historical record of planning and evaluation shows its evolution over time and reduces the impact of administrative turnover.

Institutionalizing Change Management: Strengthening Institutional Resiliency

After creating the AQF originally to satisfy student learning outcomes criteria for regional re-accreditation in 2004, CSI realized that transformative change, or successful adoption of AQF, would take an additional five to ten years. It had developed a nascent change management system—decentralized unit action planning with centralized learning resources—but it needed to be institutionalized. The IR/A office began implementing strategies that would make the process more valuable to more people for more reasons. It shifted from a teleological to an evolutionary model that could encourage and recognize emergent change. Systems thinking—a federal division of responsibility that nurtured self-organization and organizational learning—drove the change management design.

Systems Thinking: Integrating AQF Planning with More Areas of Accepted Cultural Practice. The change management strategy included increasing the value (quality) of continuous learning outcomes assessment planning by expanding its use across many existing activities. With the support of the provost, the IR/A office extended assessment beyond student learning to include both faculty research and outreach service. This way student learning would be included in the other traditional pursuits of academic departments. With leadership from IR/A staff, CSI integrated annual assessment planning with its six-year program reviews, revising its program review guidelines so that assessment plans would automatically appear in AQF's new online self-study templates. Furthermore, IR/A technology staff embedded the institution's strategic plan into program review action plans so that faculty could establish recorded relationships through a classification exercise. The AQF database now more closely integrates annual assessment, program review action planning, and institutional strategic planning, to the point that reports can more accurately show the distribution of human efforts to manage change. IR/A staff also worked with provost staff to amend the new program proposal policy to further expand AQF's usefulness as an evaluation method.

To further strengthen the value of AQF, the institution's IR/A staff worked to expand its scope and national visibility. IR/A personnel worked with student affairs personnel to encourage their use of AQF online assessment planning and program review functions. Their unit planning now integrates with the academic side to inform strategic planning. The IR/A office shared its AQF assessment database management software with other research institutions to develop collaborations in support of the open systems concept. The IR/A office also believed that expanding the visibility of AQF nationally would strengthen its reputation on the CSI campus. Varying features of AQF have been presented at conferences with national coverage, multiple journal publications feature its characteristics, and non-CSI websites provide additional AQF exposure. Knowledge distribution of this kind helps integrate the AQF system into the culture of a research university.

Complexity and Self-Organizing Units: Tactics of Decentralization and Centralization. Exploiting the culture of decentralization and the loosely coupled structure of higher education institutions, the IR/A office helped shape CSI change management policy and developed the technology infrastructure to support localized planning and evaluation. Karl Weick argues that loosely coupled organizations make good systems of localized adaptation, as "they potentially can retain a greater number of mutations and novel solutions . . . and preserve more diversity in responding to a wider range of changes" (Weick, 2000, 40–41).

The CSI goal is to have local units become self-organizing groups capable of engineering their own self-perpetuating change. Participants are to articulate the goals they would like to achieve, experiment with new projects and initiatives, learn from their successes and mistakes, and talk with each other candidly about the results (Senge, 1999). To further support institutional resiliency, the IR/A office integrated multilevel department feedback resources to the planning and evaluation components of AQF; for example, two regular peer-review processes (one for annual assessment and one for six-year cycle program review), interactive student course survey information, and institutional data at the department level that are continuously fed into tables used in the online program review self-studies. This gives faculty constant data feedback resources at the unit level and sustains use of the self-studies over time. Furthermore, the IR/A office purchased a license to use a sensing or feedback mechanism known as Academic Analytics to generate data analytics for local units that need customized, continuous metrics for indicating scholarship and research performance. Staff built the AQF database to generate bottom-up planning reports that reveal emergent change or change developing at the periphery of the institution. The reports reveal patterns forming within the decentralized planning that support or do not support central strategic planning implementation. Patterns that do not support strategic planning are legitimate formations of human effort that could merit resources.

Developing Organizational Learning. IR/A offices can explore several options for expanding organizational learning, such as (1) views of systematic problem solving, (2) experimentation with new approaches, (3) learning from experience and past history, (4) learning from the experiences and best practices of others, and (5) transferring knowledge quickly and efficiently throughout the organization (Kezar, 2005). (More information on organizational learning can be found in Chapter 6.)

One tactic IR staff members used is to capture organizational dialogues or online faculty conversations that result in mutual learning on which an organization can act. Institutions should create "carrying vehicles" for these dialogues to form and be distributed (Boyce, 2003). Vehicles or platforms can include learning assessment plans and program review self-studies or other activities in which faculty interact. Senge (1999) adds, "If the right people meet in diverse, frequent interactions, with a variety of patterns to those interactions, a beneficial reframing will emerge on its own" (p. 144).

CSI used several learning tactics when centrally building its organizational learning capacity into the AQF. It wanted to support a local unit, self-organizing approach while strengthening institutional adaptability. For example, AQF's concept map works as a knowledge management tool to establish brand identity and communicate how the continuous improvement process works on campus (Milam, 2005). The information distribution capacity of AQF includes interactive database resources that encourage campus-wide, on-task learning, such as the faculty and staff viewing of best practices in planning and evaluation at CSI while they form plans. Additionally, database viewers can effectively search through hundreds of evaluation instruments, including student learning rubrics, internship evaluation forms, exit surveys, graduate committee forms for dissertations, and more. Staff inserted several Help button features into the planning database to inform users of high-quality practices, such as how to write effective learning outcomes that are measurable. (For examples of these features, go to http://prism.colostate.edu; in the "PRISM" Login, enter "demo" for both UserName and Password.)

For program review, captive audiences—such as the department faculty who prepare their self-studies and the CSI reviewing faculty who read them (about 88 rotating faculty per year)—have access to the best practices embedded into the sixteen online self-study sections. This resource exposes them to the high-quality expectations for each section. Departments report that operating changes result from these challenges to improve. Conversation spaces are formally provided in both the assessment and program review sections of the AQF database; here, faculty can develop written dialogues about quality and improvement of change management processes. Hundreds of dialogues are generated each year. The change management database contains classification exercises for faculty to link annual operational assessment planning to six-year program review action plan goals and to link these action goals to broader institutional strategic goals. AQF visually helps campus personnel realize how local and central planning are mutually supportive, and it provides search options for looking up the department-level strategies that support the institution's goals. The IR/A office also has faculty or staff set the priority levels for action goals in AQF to help administrators make budget allocations.

John Milam wrote, in "Ontologies in Higher Education," that taxonomies represent the most promising approach to solving the growing problem of informative overload (Milam, 2006). IR/A staff at CSI embed taxonomies into the AQF planning platforms to assist classification of planning that generates reports on the decentralized and locally emergent change activity. The resulting interactive system reports help campus viewers and accrediting teams learn about the change management system's output, such as the number and types of outcomes, the types of assessment methods, capacity to identify strengths and weakness of program performance, and the number and types of improvements. The percentage of planning outcomes that use diagnostic analysis partly reveals the degree of dynamic quality or level of challenge to accepted practice posed by the data.

To expand the number of those who can learn from change management activity, CSI includes external constituents within its organizational learning network. The IR/A office developed a public website, Planning for Improvement and Change (http://improvement.colostate.edu), that connects varying types of constituents with the information they seek. Each population group has a distinct pathway to assessment feedback information. For example, parents can view benchmarked survey results showing the safety of CSI residence housing relative to its peers. Expanding its organizational learning still further, CSI joins multiple change management systems. Three other universities collaboratively use AQF, with the potential to share assessment plans, best practices, and performance evaluation tools. The organizational learning capacity for all collaborators expands with the increased diffusion of change. Interesting research questions result; for example, What kinds of change are happening at other institutions? In what areas is change occurring, and how frequently is change happening? Which institutions are more adaptable, and why?

Continuously Developing Value for Change Management Processes

IR/A offices must look for multiple ways to make change management valuable to their campuses. For example, their planning and evaluation processes and databases should generate evidence that satisfies the continuous quality improvement criteria of regional and specialized accrediting bodies. AQF does this effectively when documenting all faculty peer-review dialogues, reporting types and number of program improvements, visually showing the integration of planning at all levels, quantifying the percent of program participation in AQF, demonstrating transparency with constituents—for example, sharing learning outcomes with students—and storing the evolution of planning over time. Regional accrediting bodies, such as HLC, will soon require institutions to regularly maintain electronic files that demonstrate compliance with standards on a four- to five-year cycle. IR/A offices must include this kind of compliance infrastructure as a feature of their change management process. The AQF offers this electronic file storage capacity in its online program review self-study template design and can scale it up to the institutional level. It can also be adapted to serve special accreditation.

To meet the definition of transformative change, evidence must show that characteristics of institutional culture have changed or that culture has absorbed the changes. This demonstrates the value of the change management process. In addition, an effective change process should help an institution learn about itself; for example, by identifying units that are most successful at adapting and implementing change.

Evidence of System Impact on Academic Culture

The following examples from CSI demonstrate that AQF is affecting faculty culture, gradually moving it toward valuing a systematic change management process. After long delays in participation, two colleges recently began using the AQF planning database; one of these added a part-time assessment coordinator to support the use of AQF. The number of program review action plan goals for student learning has increased dramatically, which is significant at a research university. References to AQF in the institution's strategic plan have more than tripled. Policies on program review and for new program proposals now mention AQF processes. Some departments are beginning to use AQF references in their specialized accreditation self-studies and in their grant proposals to federal agencies, such as the NSF. In 2011, CSI selected AQF as a central resource for developing evidence for its 2014 regional accreditation evaluation.

Evidence of Change Activity and Success: An Index That Monitors Change Characteristics

Frequencies of best practices and program improvements partly indicate levels of change activity underway at the institution, college, and department levels. Percents of programs practicing diagnostic planning can reveal the receptivity to change. IR/A staff developed a planning and evaluation index tool that scores each department's process effectiveness for planning and evaluation (see Table 7.2).

TABLE 7.2   PLANNING AND EVALUATION EFFECTIVENESS: ANNUAL REPORT FOR 2003–2004[6]

	INDICATOR	ART	ENGLISH	FOR LANG	MUSIC	PHIL	SPEECH	AVG. HUM.
Student Learning	Indicator 1 Range of Outcomes	5.0	3.0	3.0	4.0	3.0	4.0	3.7
	Indicator 2 Intensity of Exploration × .50*	4.9	4.8	6.7	4.6	5.9	5.8	5.4
	Indicator 3 Measuring Methods	6.0	9.0	4.0	6.0	5.0	4.0	5.7
	Indicator 4 Measuring Frequency	4.0	11.0	4.0	3.3	5.0	3.0	5.1
	Indicator 5 Measuring Points in Time	3.0	2.0	1.0	3.0	1.0	2.0	2.0
	Indicator 6 Diagnostic Capacity	1.6	2.3	2.3	0.1	1.5	1.0	1.5
	Indicator 7 Improvement Range	2.0	1.0	4.0	2.0	0.0	4.0	2.2
	Indicator 8 Improvement Frequency	1.2	2.0	2.5	1.7	0.0	3.0	1.7

(continued)

TABLE 7.2 PLANNING AND EVALUATION EFFECTIVENESS:
ANNUAL REPORT FOR 2003–2004[6] (*Continued*)

	INDICATOR	ART	ENGLISH	FOR LANG	MUSIC	PHIL	SPEECH	AVG. HUM.
System Engagement	Indicator 9 Feedback—best practices	4.0	3.0	2.8	0.3	1.0	3.5	2.4
	Indicator 10 Feedback— comments × .50 *	−5.6	−6.3	−8.6	−9.4	−5.8	−10.0	−7.6
	Indicator 11 Low Participation Level	0.0	0.0	0.0	−1.4	−1.5	0.0	−0.5
	Indicator 12 Low Participation Level	0.0	0.0	0.0	−1.6	−1.5	0.0	−0.5
Research and Service	Indicator 13 Range of Exploration Research	3.0	2.0	2.0	4.0	2.0	4.0	2.8
	Indicator 14 Use of Impact Indicators Research	3.0	0.0	3.0	1.0	0.0	4.0	1.8
	Indicator 15 Range of Exploration Service	4.0	2.0	2.0	3.0	1.0	0.0	2.0
	Indicator 16 Use of Impact Indicators Service	1.0	0.0	1.0	0.0	0.0	0.0	0.3
Indicator Groups	A) Performance Research Range/Intensity:	16.9	11.8	0.0	15.6	11.9	13.8	13.9
	B) Measuring Frequency:	13.0	22.0	13.7	12.3	11.0	9.0	12.7
	C) Changes/Improvements:	3.2	3.0	9.0	3.7	0.0	7.0	3.9
	D) Diagnostic Capacity:	5.6	2.3	6.5	1.1	1.5	5.0	3.6
	E) Peer Review Feedback:	−1.6	−3.3	6.3	−9.1	−4.8	−6.5	−5.2
	F) Reporting Participation:	0.0	0.0	−5.8	−3.0	−3.0	0.0	−1.0
	Department Level EFFECTIVENESS / INDEX SCORE >>	37.1	35.8	29.7	20.6	16.7	28.3	28.0

*Indicators 2 and 10 include weighting features that reduce their impact on the index. If left with its full weight, indicator 2 would reward programs that merely write a good research plan or intend to study in depth, but do not gather any data and do not report findings. Additionally, while peer-review feedback is defined as a negative indicator—as this appears only if something is wrong with a plan—the system does not want to inhibit the peer-reviewers from making comments in the plans. The table shows Philosophy as performing at a lower level (16.7), with weakness in the areas of improvements (7, 8) and low participation (11, 12).

Source: Bender, *Planning and Evaluation Effectiveness Index.* Colorado State University Continuous Improvement Activity. Department of Assessment. Reprinted with permission.

Conclusion

Institutions that are helping communities and the world attain a more sustainable environment should themselves work systematically on their own sustainability. IR/A offices will play a leading role in developing change management processes that simultaneously support the decentralization of diverse, self-organizing units for adaptive management and the centralization of infrastructure for developing organizational learning.[7] Mostly, change management addresses the institution's problem-solving needs—which are mainly how to attain unit values faster (decentralization) and ensure their relation to institutional priorities (central governance). Many institutions want to reduce class size, strengthen the diversity of faculty and students, develop new revenue streams, and strengthen student retention of learning outcomes. This happens only with change and its effective management. One certainty in an increasingly uncertain and complex environment is that IR/A staff will have more work to do as those features contributing to an institution's adaptive capacity steadily increase in value.

Notes

1. Charles S. Peirce brought pragmatism to notice in an 1878 *Popular Science Monthly* article, "How to Make Our Ideas Clear." The chapter section on process uses Peirce's 1877 essay on the "Fixation of belief" for the emphasis on doubt as a vital element for changing beliefs.
2. Robert Pirsig first presented questions about quality in his 1974 book *Zen and the Art of Motorcycle Maintenance: An Inquiry into Values.*
3. Bok (2006, pp. 316, 331) supports development of organizational learning at institutions that supports continuous self-evaluation and criticizes the poor methods institutions use to improve themselves.
4. Berkes and others define adaptive capacity as the capacity to respond to and shape change.
5. Mets wrote that organizational change itself is viewed as organizational learning.
6. Some of the sixteen effectiveness indicators in Table 7.2 are defined as follows: (1) *Range of Outcomes* relates to the breadth of learning research—whether a program only researches writing skills or also measures problem solving, project planning skills, application of knowledge, or others. (2) *Intensity of Exploration* relates to the depth of research—whether a program researches writing holistically or also measures the subcomponents of writing, such as organization, thesis development, transitions/flow, mechanics, synthesis, documentation, and others. (3) *Measuring Methods* relates to the variety of instruments used to gather data—whether a program uses only a graduating exit survey or also uses a culminating project with a rubric and uses an internship form for skills application, and uses a pre-test to assess incoming skills and others. (4) *Measuring Frequency* relates to how many times the program uses its assessment instruments in an academic year; for example, once per year, once per semester, or more. (5) *Measuring Points in Time* relates to how many times during a student's career the

program makes measurements of learning; for example, beginning, middle, end, and postgraduate. (7) *Improvement Range* and (8) *Improvement Frequency* relate to the number of program categories improvements cover, e.g., assessment, curriculum, professional development, technology or others, while frequency refers to the number of improvements implemented per year. A program earns negative numbers if it receives repeated and excessive peer-review (9) *Feedback* and if it fails to (11) *Participate* or report data findings. For faculty research and service, programs earn positive numbers if they demonstrate planning that uses (14) *Impact Indicators,* such as a citations index for publications or volume of leadership positions on editorial boards, grant review boards, or professional associations. Taken all together, these sixteen indicators make up a single process-effectiveness index. The index serves as an overall diagnostic indicator, in that its measure of process and activity identifies potentially low-performing departments and reveals what process areas seem to most require improvement. A complete analytic indexing table is available from the author.

7. J. Burke, in his 2007 book *Fixing the Fragmented University: Decentralization with Direction,* advocated decentralization with a unifying direction.

References

Bender, K. (2003). Planning and evaluation effectiveness index. Colorado State University Continuous Improvement Activity. Department of Assessment.

Berkes, F., Colding, J., and Folke, C. (2003). *Navigating social-ecological systems: Building resilience for complexity and change.* Cambridge: Cambridge University Press.

Bok, D. (2006). *Our underachieving colleges: A candid look at how much students learn and why they should be learning more.* Princeton: Princeton University Press.

Boyce, M. (2003). Organizational learning is essential to achieving and sustaining change in higher education. *Innovative Higher Education, 28,* 119–36.

Burnes, B. (2000). *Managing change: A strategic approach to organizational dynamics.* London: Pearson Education.

Cao, G., Clarke, S., and Lehaney, B. (1999). Towards systemic management of diversity in organizational change. *Strategic Choices, 8,* 205–216.

Chaffee, E., & Jacobson, S. (1997). Creating and changing institutional cultures. In M. Peterson, D. Dill, & L. Mets (Eds.), *Planning and management for a changing environment: A handbook for redesigning postsecondary institutions* (pp. 230–245). San Francisco: Jossey-Bass.

Dacin, M., Goodstein, J., & Scott, W. (2002). Institutional theory and institutional change. *Academy of Management Journal, 45,* 43–56.

Gunderson, L., & Holling, C. (2002). *Panarchy: Understanding transformations in human and natural systems.* Washington: Island Press.

James, W. (1907/1981). *Pragmatism, a new name for some old ways of thinking.* Indianapolis, IN: Hackett Publishing.

Kezar, A. (2001). Understanding and facilitating organizational change in the 21st century: Recent research and conceptualizations. *ASHE-ERIC Higher Education Report, 28*(4). San Francisco: Jossey-Bass.

Kezar, A. (2005). What campuses need to know about organizational learning and the learning organization. In A. Kezar (Ed.), *Organizational learning in higher education* (pp. 7–22). New Directions for Higher Education, no. 131. San Francisco: Jossey-Bass.

Leimer, C. (2009). Taking a broader view: Using institutional research's natural qualities for transformation. In C. Leimer (Ed.), *Imagining the future of institutional research* (pp. 85–93). New Directions for Institutional Research, no. 143. San Francisco: Jossey-Bass.

Lewin, K. (1948). Group decision and social change. In T. M. Newcomb (Ed.), *Readings in social psychology* (pp. 330–341). New York: Henry Holt; later in Gold, M. (Ed.). (1999). *The complete social scientist: A Kurt Lewin reader* (pp. 265–284). Washington, DC: American Psychological Association.

March, J. (2008). *Explorations in organizations.* Stanford, CA: Stanford University Press.

Menand, L. (2010). *The marketplace of ideas.* New York: Norton.

Mets, L. (1997). Planning change through program review. In M. Peterson, D. Dill, & L. Mets (Eds.), *Planning and management for a changing environment: A handbook for redesigning post secondary institutions* (pp. 340–359). San Francisco: Jossey-Bass.

Milam, J. (2005). Organizational learning through knowledge workers and infomediaries. *New Directions for Higher Education, 131,* 61–73.

Milam, J. (2006). Ontologies in higher education. In A. Metcalfe (Ed.), *Knowledge management and higher education: A critical analysis* (pp. 34–62). Hershey, PA: Information Science Pub.

Nadler, D. (1995). *Discontinuous change: Leading organizational transformation.* San Francisco: Jossey-Bass.

Nadler, D. (1998). *Champions of change: How CEOs and their companies are mastering the skills of radical change.* San Francisco: Jossey-Bass.

Paton, R., & McCalman, J. (2008). *Change management: A guide to effective implementation.* Los Angeles: Sage.

Pirsig, R. (1991). *Lila: An inquiry into morals.* New York: Bantam Books.

Poole, M., & Van de Ven, A. (2004). *Handbook of organizational change and innovation.* New York: Oxford University Press.

Schein, E. (1992). *Organizational culture and leadership.* San Francisco: Jossey-Bass.

Senge, P. (1999). *The dance of change: The challenges of sustaining momentum in learning organizations.* New York: Doubleday/Currency.

Simsek, H., & Louis, K. (1994). Organizational change as paradigm shift: Analysis of the change process in a large public university. *Journal of Higher Education, 65,* 670–95.

Southern Association of Colleges and Schools. (2009, December). *Summary of modifications to the principles of accreditation.* Retrieved from http://sacscoc.org/

Swing, R. (2009). Institutional researchers as change agents. In C. Leimer (Ed.), *Imagining the future of institutional research* (pp. 5–16). New Directions for Institutional Research, no. 143. San Francisco: Jossey-Bass.

Tierney, W. (1988). Organizational culture in higher education. *Journal of Higher Education, 59,* 2–21.

Weick, K. E. (2000). Educational organizations as loosely coupled systems. In M. Christopher Brown II (Ed.), *Organization and governance in higher education* (5th ed.) (pp. 36–49). Boston: Pearson.

Wheatley, M. (2005). *Finding our way: Leadership for an uncertain time.* San Francisco: Berrett-Koehler.

PART TWO

SUPPORTING CAMPUS LEADERSHIP AND MANAGEMENT

As described in the first chapter of this volume, initial institutional research activities were conducted to create information to inform senior campus leaders' decision making. In this part, topics are discussed that reflect the support of institutional governance and leadership and specific institutional management activities. It is important to note that in these discussions the activities of institutional research are conducted in support of the function without formal authority or responsibility for its success. The first three chapters in this section (Chapters 8 through 10) address roles that institutional research often fills in support of campus and system-wide leadership and governance. In Chapters 11 through 16, specific institutional management responsibilities and the ways in which institutional research support can make them effective are discussed.

Focusing on the support of institutional governance, in Chapter 8 James Purcell, Charles Harrington, and Beverly King present the realities of decision making

at executive levels and the kinds of information required. The role and realities of shared governance in leadership and management of today's institutions of higher education are also discussed in this chapter. Although shared governance is a topic not often discussed in institutional research circles, the authors posit that when effective it greatly enhances the functioning and productivity of the institution. The notion that institutional leaders must have *trust* in the institutional research function to be effective is key to successful support of institutional governance.

In Chapter 9, James Posey and Gita Pitter address the support of the chief academic affairs officer or provost. In particular, they focus on supporting the leadership and management of instructional and research activities at the institutional level. As the demands on the academic officer are often intense and always complex, these authors (like those in earlier chapters) argue that effective support must include the creation of Terenzini's issues and contextual intelligence. The authors provide examples of the demands on the provost and types of effective institutional research support. Focusing on one particular responsibility of the provost's office, in Chapter 10, Daniel Teodorescu discusses the data and systems that an institutional research office might build to support management and monitoring of faculty, from recruitment through retention and into retirement. This chapter presents data collection and analyses strategies that provide the provost with information about the institution's ability to recruit and retain faculty that reflect the overall faculty profile needed to make the institution effective.

The four chapters that follow discuss specific campus-wide issues that require data-based support. In Chapter 11, Michael Dooris and Jerome Rackoff outline processes for institutional planning and resource allocation, as well as the support that institutional research can provide. They suggest that "intentionality" characterizes effective strategic planning, requiring both institutional knowledge and data-based analyses. In Chapter 12, John Milam and Paul Brinkman discuss the development of cost models that can be built to support budgeting and resource allocations. Both of these chapters present the contributions of institutional research in the creation of useful data and information.

In Chapter 13, John Cheslock and Rick Kroc discuss enrollment management in the context of student flow through the institution and the types of support that institutional research can provide to help an institution meet its enrollment goals. They then expand the discussion to reflect enrollment management concerns about specific types of students, different types of institutions, and various types of educational delivery. In Chapter 14, Gary Rice and Alene Russell present the issues associated with the reporting and interpreting of graduation rates in the context of student success. They follow this discussion with a model for measuring student success that expands the current use of graduation rates by also including the total graduate productivity of the institution in the context of student goals and academic performance.

The final two chapters in this section address the topics of space management and sustainability. Catherine Watt, in Chapter 15, presents a model for managing academic space through the use of data, reflecting not only the physical aspects of the space but also its use and who is using it. In Chapter 16, Josetta McLaughlin and Lisa Amoroso provide an overview of the concept of sustainability, expanding the notion beyond facilities to include issues associated with leadership and management, community relations, and the curricula. These authors argue that the future of our campuses will be influenced by the sustainability efforts put in place today.

In this part, topics discussed take the reader from the support of institutional leadership and management to the management of specific institutional issues. The authors provide detail about the issues and the support that institutional research can provide to make them effective. We recognize that not all institutional functions and programs are presented in these chapters. However, we feel that some of the more traditional functions supported by institutional research are presented, as well as several newer issues that are being or will be addressed on our campuses.

CHAPTER 8

SUPPORTING INSTITUTIONAL GOVERNANCE

James Purcell, Charles Harrington, and Beverly King

Institutional "governance concerns power: who is in charge; who makes decisions; who has a voice; and how loud that voice is" (Rosovsky, 1990, p. 261). Shared governance as a system of organizational control and influence is predicated on two distinctly different forms of authority, one legal and the other professional (Birnbaum, 2003). Legal authority is the basis for the role and responsibilities of the institutional governing board, and the board has ultimate responsibility for decisions made for an institution or a system. Commonly, governing boards transfer authority to the institution's president or chancellor for operational and strategic decision making (Lazerson, 1997).

Professional authority justifies the role of the faculty; that is, as recognized by both precedence (Tappan, 1961) and pronouncement (American Association of University Professors [AAUP], 1966), faculty members possess the expertise to be considered the authority on academic matters such as instruction and the curriculum. Although shared governance is present to some extent in most American colleges and universities, the ways in which the principles of shared governance are applied vary from institution to institution (Veit, 2005).

Ideally, the term *shared governance* can be thought of as a mutual sharing of responsibility by faculty, administration, staff, appointed personnel, and students, for making both operational and strategic decisions about institutional mission, policies, and budget and finance priorities. Under shared governance, each stakeholder endeavors to think and act in terms of the good of the institution as a whole and to work collaboratively in order to reach agreement or consensus before making final decisions.

In this chapter, we examine the role that institutional research can play in supporting both the specific information needs of the president and shared governance on a campus. Key in this discussion is the notion that effective shared governance requires the support and leadership of the president, bringing various stakeholder representatives into discussions about institutional direction and performance. As such, all information developed to support shared governance is by definition relevant to the president. However, all information that might be created for the president is not relevant to shared governance. The institutional research professional must recognize the difference between information that legitimately falls under the umbrella of shared governance and that which is the president's responsibility to share or not to share.

Supporting the President/CEO

Many institutional researchers would describe their most memorable interaction with a campus leader as involving a hurried request for information on an obscure institutional subpopulation needed for a presentation within the hour. Although this type of request does occur, it is the long-term relationship, built on trust, between the institutional research office and the campus president that makes the experience effective.

Special Relationship

No other interdepartmental interaction can impact an organization's success more than the sharing of quality information and perspective between the IR staff and the chief executive officer of the campus, system, or coordinating board. In the relationship with the campus chief executive officer (CEO), an IR staff member should serve more as a futurist than as someone assessing current action. Daily operations of a campus are more often delegated to divisional vice presidents, provosts, and department heads, but the future direction of the campus—the institutional vision—is the dominating purview of the campus president. The president will be judged most on the ability to develop a plan, articulate the plan, and implement the plan.

McLaughlin and Howard (2004) assert that institutional success "depends on an information support structure that assures the quality and availability of relevant data that can be restructured for use by the decision makers" (p. 8). Most plans fail not because they lack content but because they lack implementation or focus. Institutional research offices, when performing their best support for the institutional CEO, will provide information and trends that identify possibilities for the future, help in determining the appropriate institutional actions that become a part of the intervention plan, and assist in monitoring and evaluating the plan itself. Thus the true measure of an IR office is the success of the institution, the president, and the institutional plan.

The dialogue between the IR office and the president should be constant and steady, and as the relationship develops it should be the IR office's goal to predict the information needs for the CEO rather than waiting for a request.

Depending on the incumbent's route to the presidency, his or her approach to being presidential will vary, but the common purposes and realities of all leaders and higher education institutions should direct both the work of the president and IR staff.

Presidential Realities

Regardless of the campus, there are common realities regarding presidential leadership. All presidents are talented individuals in their own professional or academic careers and have the intellect to excel, especially if they are open to input and insight from campus practitioners.

Reality 1. More often than not, the campus president will not have leadership experience in governing all aspects of a campus. Of college presidents in 2006, only about one in five (21 percent) had served as a college president prior to becoming president at a current campus. Academic vice presidents and provosts account for 43 percent of presidents and another 13 percent come from outside higher education (Chronicle of Higher Education, 2008). Often the presidential vision of the world and solutions for issues are heavily influenced by previous experiences. When faced with low student success, the academic may seek to increase the quality of instruction, whereas the student affairs practitioner may seek additional student support. A president with a business background may seek to maximize productivity or eliminate waste. Watkins (2003) admonishes new leaders for trying to apply the paradigm of their old jobs to CEO. Watkins further highlights the importance of learning the essential skills of executive decision making. Filtering information is the key to successful leadership. The IR staff should understand the context of the president's past experiences and buttress the many talents they bring to the position with information that can direct future action.

Reality 2. New presidents are especially vulnerable to unfettered enthusiasm for change. The rationale—and the strategy—for change both need to be developed based on facts. A seasoned IR director can be an ideal source for identifying issues and suggesting effective approaches for success. The common role of the organizational leader is to create the future. It is by serving in this unique role—as sage and futurist—that an IR staff member will enable a successful journey into the future. Trends and projections are more important to a campus CEO than the day-to-day managerial assessments provided to vice presidents and deans.

Projecting the impact of proposed changes is essential for presidential success. For example, a new president of an open-admissions university with historically low graduation rates may advocate for selective admission standards, or not admitting students requiring developmental education, or both. Identifying the percentage and characteristics of students who would be impacted by the new standard and projecting the impact on enrollment, funding, and student success will greatly inform strategy and implementation, and potentially impact ultimate success.

In the mid-1990s, Georgia College & State University, which had served as a regional nonselective university, was designated by the university system of Georgia to become the state's public liberal arts university. In order to transform the university in accordance with the new mission, the new president sought to increase admissions standards, reduce remediation levels of the freshman class from 40 percent to less than 5 percent, alter the student recruitment strategy, revise the curriculum toward a more liberal arts–based foundation, and develop a revenue stream that allowed for reduced student-to-faculty ratios. In addition, on-campus housing needed to be expanded to 40 percent of enrollment, and the campus library and a few academic buildings required extensive renovation. Collateral issues also had to be addressed. Because of greater selectivity, many local and minority students would not be admitted, and the university needed to articulate appropriate bridge programs with a local community college to ensure community support for the transition. Based on the projected future impacts of the desired aspects of the institutions, the president and her leadership team were able to implement a plan that thoughtfully addressed all these issues over a period of seven years, and the institution is now recognized as an educational destination of choice for many in-state and out-of-state students and for its solid liberal arts experiences in and out of the classroom, increased *U.S. News and World Report* rankings, and greater student success.

Reality 3. Time is short. Although introspection and contemplation make a good leader, the time pressures and eclectic roles of modern institutional presidents often limit the opportunities to discover on their own the relevant information from a multitude of reports. It is essential that IR staff readily identify the pertinent points from data provided and suggest implications for current policy and future planning. Because of computer technology, the amount of information available to a college president today is expansive (Coughlin, 2005). The role of the IR staff should be to examine the plethora of data, synthesize it into the essential points, and reveal points of opportunity and concern. Presidents welcome conclusions and informed recommendations. The role of the IR office is to determine which information indicates institutional success and which indicates failure. It's the president's role to create an institutional vision and inculcate a transformational mindset among the campus trustees, faculty, and staff (Pelletier, 2009).

Clearly, identifying trends in data that illustrate a change in the campus milieu keeps the president informed of potential future issues. For example, a review of student, faculty, and staff satisfaction assessments can identify areas in which particular aspects of the institution are improving and which need to be addressed. A president's intervention on the lowest-rated items on a survey of satisfaction can mitigate future problems. Success in addressing these issues can easily be determined in future satisfaction surveys.

Reality 4. Trust is a terrible thing to waste. Presidential confidence in the information provided by the IR office is crucial to institutional, presidential, and IR staff success. Can the data be trusted? Are the recommendations based on the facts and the professional literature? This need for trust applies to not only the reliability and viability of the data but also the ability of the IR staff to present the information in a usable context. Accuracy of information is very important when it is publicly articulated from behind a podium and when speaking to alumni, trustees, or the legislature. Certainly leadership skills, fund-raising ability, political savvy, and good board relations are criteria on which a president is judged, but all of these should be supported by a strong institutional research function.

The IR office should always serve as an honest broker of information. The Association for Institutional Research (AIR) articulates the importance of objectivity in maintaining the integrity of the IR office and of the information provided (Association for Institutional Research, 2001). Fundamentally, what is provided to a campus president should be information—rather than mere data—that is suggestive of future institutional direction.

Having served as a state higher education executive officer in both Arkansas and Louisiana, one of the chapter authors (Purcell) relies heavily on data from a multitude of sources to make decisions that impact students, faculty, academic programs, funding, and institutions. When difficult issues are being debated, questions about the appropriateness or the quality of the data used in analyses often become the focus of the discussion rather than the policy or action initially under discussion.

Reality 5. Things look different from the other side of the desk. Phenomenological absolutism is a term used to describe the fact that people have unique perspectives of the same phenomena. Although new presidents have a view of the world based on their career paths, all presidents will view the world from the position of being campus CEO. Presidents will be privy to many aspects of the campus milieu that influence decision making as much as or more than facts and figures. Decision making and futurism are not fully data-based rational processes (Leslie and Fretwell, 1996). Wallin (2009) states that "the CEO must communicate a vision of what can be—what should be—for the benefit of the college, its students, and its community" (p. 33). IR staff should know that their role is to provide quality information for decision making, but that ultimately the decision will be made at the presidential or board level. IR staff need to find comfort in the fact that good information and advice is given, rather than in the direction that is ultimately taken.

Because of the nature of the unspoken factors that influence executive decision making, no specific examples are provided, but a literary example is provided to give context. James Baldwin (1961), author and civil rights icon, said "the price one pays for pursuing any profession or calling is an intimate knowledge of its ugly side" (p. 240). As with all complex human endeavors, executive decision making in higher education is influenced by unspoken factors such as political intrigue, potential litigation, financial considerations, interpersonal relationships, and personnel issues. Not all contributors in the decision-making process need to know all of the factors in order for the president to make the decision. Applying rational information to decision making in such a world is helpful, but it does not diminish the existence of other factors.

Types of Executive Requests

From a practical perspective, there is information that will always be of benefit to campus leaders. Managing a campus can be a daunting task unless the essential components are consistently monitored. Working with the campus leadership, IR staff should identify information that is most essential to monitoring progress.

Dashboards. Institutional "dashboards" that highlight essential mission-critical information help give campus leadership a common focus and understanding. Providing this information on a timely and routine basis is essential. Dashboard measures should be benchmarked and trend based and have a connection to the institutional mission and institutional plan. For example, new student enrollment can be monitored by application trends based on previous year experiences and a projected yield. Similarly, monitoring graduation rates can be derived from previous retention rates and tracking of demographic population historical successes. Dashboard contents vary depending on the institution, but all should be concise and to the point.

Ad Hoc Requests. Even the best dashboards will not reduce the necessity of responding to ad hoc requests for information. It is essential that the IR staff develop a data extraction process that allows for a prompt and trustworthy response to such requests. There is great risk of error with ad hoc and time-sensitive requests. Information provided must be accurate and most appropriate for the inquiry. Staff should always clarify the nature of the inquiry and check the results to assure accuracy. Trust and confidence in the IR staff can often be lost through the provision of poorly constructed ad hoc reports. The IR staff should highlight the important aspects of the report and suggest its impact on the institution.

On occasion, the president may need data meant for his/her eyes only. This is often done in response to a constituent inquiry or a complaint regarding services or an individual. It is important that such information requests be kept confidential and handled with utmost care. The merits of complaints can be determined only by gathering additional information. Discretion is an essential trait for those serving campus leaders.

Planning. Because a president is most concerned about the future, the institutional plan and related benchmarks are crucial to articulating presidential vision. A solid plan connects the past, present, and future. IR staff can develop processes for monitoring progress in achieving organizational goals by assessing trends and calculating the pace and the trajectory of monitored data points. It is helpful to illustrate the connection between the institutional plan, institutional budgets, and accreditation requirements. Determining staff and faculty awareness of future plans and their level of buy-in is essential to maintaining institutional progress. Flack (1994) identifies three critical elements in strategic planning that, by their nature, involve both the president and the IR office:

- A solid, honest assessment of the college or university's . . . situation (p. 25)
- Having an acceptable process to develop action priorities (p. 27)
- The college or university's president taking ownership of the plan and the process and seeking support of campus stakeholders

Institutional Budgeting and Finance. The most significant means of communicating the commitment for change is the reallocation of institutional resources toward the revised institutional vision. Wellman (2009) advises institutions to consistently ask "how strategic priorities translate into goals for spending" (p. 12). Determining which items are mission-critical should be the primary criteria for determining institutional budgets—especially in times of financial constraints. Trend data on expenditures can be helpful in determining true institutional priorities.

Building an Information Timeline. IR offices should work with the president to determine when particular information is needed. The IR cycle of state and federal reporting can serve as the fundamental base, but presidential events usually do not coincide with traditional data collection cycles. Most common of these events is a president's desire to provide a state-of-the-institution report to faculty in August prior to the beginning of the fall academic term. In August, every student data point is subject to change; thus reliance on history and trend data is important. Footnotes are important when developing preliminary information for large audiences.

The timeline for providing information to new presidents can be unique in that information is often requested prior to the official hiring day. This eagerness and desire to prepare is a good sign of leadership. Watkins (2003) argues that new leaders should have a plan for their first ninety days and they should have information on the condition of their new organization as early as ninety days prior to their first official day of employment in order to make those plans. Providing the incoming leader with information as early as possible can help improve the president's ability to have the desired initial impact.

Regardless of whether or not data are requested prior to employment, the year prior to a president's ascendancy will more often than not be an important source of baseline data and will need to be tracked over time. Both the president and the organization's board will look at progress on key institutional indicators when determining the president's effectiveness. Institutional data as well as peer institution and other national comparable data will be the key components of baseline data.

Converting Management Data into Public Relations Information. Presidents are constantly seeking opportunities to highlight institutional successes. Although the IR office can certainly help in providing data, it is important that information be provided in a manner that it is accurate and in context. The AIR code of ethics delineates that data be truthful. Although sometimes not appreciated, it is perfectly appropriate for the director of IR to scrutinize the use of data in press releases and campus promotional materials and call attention to any facts that are stretched to the point that they border on fiction.

Board of Trustees. In most college and university organizational structures, the president reports to the board of trustees. In the case of state institutions, trustees are often appointed by the governor. When addressing an inquiry from a board member, an IR office should work through the president. The president is more aware of the issues and concerns of the board. Including the president in the response to an inquiry will ensure that the IR office is not working at cross purposes with the president. Because trustees are not involved in the everyday operation of the college, information provided may need additional explanation.

Shared Governance

As described at the beginning of this chapter, shared governance is an institutional activity in which each stakeholder endeavors to think and act in terms of the good of the institution as a whole and to work collaboratively in order to reach agreement or consensus before making final decisions. This is often a messy process, as stakeholders typically bring different perspectives, values, and priorities to the table. For instance, when one of the greatest leaders of the twenty-first century, Dwight Eisenhower, was serving as president of Columbia University, he once referred to faculty as employees of the university. He was quickly admonished with the response, "Mr. President, faculty are not employees of the university, they are the university" (Devons, 2001, p. 46). The key to successful shared governance is mutual respect of all stakeholders and an understanding of the mission of the institution and how it is performing this mission. And, like the role of the president, the role of shared governance should be primarily that of safeguarding the institution's future and the progress it is making to reach the goals that define the mission.

What Is Shared and with Whom?

Three areas most often considered germane to shared governance are budget and strategic planning, academic and academic personnel policies, and selection and review of academic administrators.. Most institutions recognize faculty authority over academic policies and procedures. Faculty exercise primary control over the academic curriculum, policies regarding student admission criteria, standards for academic progress, and the conferral of degrees. At many colleges and universities, the faculty also set criteria for faculty evaluation, including those for promotion and tenure. However, there is disagreement on the role of shared governance in institutional budgeting and strategic planning. When presidents and institutional governing boards see strategic agenda setting and the allocation of institutional resources as their responsibility, the viability of shared governance will often be challenged by faculty and other campus stakeholders.

There is no ideal composition of who should or should not be involved directly in shared governance. The depth and breadth of stakeholder involvement varies as dramatically as the institutions of which they are a part. Most typically involved are instructional faculty (often represented by a faculty governance body and excluding part-time or non–tenure track faculty), executive level administrators, key midlevel management and support staff, collective bargaining unit representatives (if the institution has collective bargaining agreements for faculty, staff, or both), boards of trustees or similar governing bodies, and often other constituencies. Other stakeholders may include university alumni, student governance body leadership (president), institutional affiliated foundation representatives, and, in some instances, community representatives. When the institutions in question are religiously affiliated, principals and laypersons from the specific denomination are often involved.

IR Support of Shared Governance

Misunderstandings about the definition of shared governance and variability among schools in its practice may lead IR professionals to question their ability to identify, and successfully implement, mechanisms by which to support shared governance. However, as stated in the opening paragraph of this chapter, shared governance, at its most basic, is about collective decision making. Thus the ways in which IR professionals can support shared governance are not all that dissimilar from the ways in which they support other activities related to decision making in their institutions. Examples given in this section are aligned with typical functions of an IR office: assessment, planning, and data management.

According to Terenzini (as cited in Chambers & Gerek, 2007), IR professionals must have competency in three intelligences to be valuable and useful to their organizations: technical/analytical, issues, and context. Issues and context intelligence includes a thorough understanding of issues in higher education (both ongoing and emerging) in general and in the context (climate, culture, and history) of one's local institution and region. Given the differences among institutions' governance structures and processes, it is critical for IR professionals to be familiar with not only the issues of shared governance in general but also how those play out on their own campuses. The same is true of other members of the university community. One way of understanding these issues is through assessment. Whether it is suggested by or to an IR professional, conversations about shared governance may lead to a request for information about how it is working on a particular campus. In that instance, the professional may want to make use of an assessment instrument such as that available on the American Association of University Professors (AAUP) website, http://www.aaup.org/AAUP/issues/governance/goveval.htm. This instrument is intended to measure how well an institution is complying with standards for shared governance. According to AAUP, the survey questions (and the reference materials on which they are based) "can provide a useful framework for building and improving shared governance in colleges and universities" (paragraph 4).

A key component of institutional variation comes with the creation of each institution's unique mission. As Hamilton (1999) advocates, governance models should be aligned with the overall mission of institutions (for example, a primarily teaching institution may have a governance structure different from that of a more research-oriented university, and two-year schools will have a focus different from that of baccalaureate and beyond schools). All governance units or other parties involved in shared decision making should be involved in formulating an institution's mission statement as well as its short- and long-term goals and objectives; that is, they should be involved in strategic planning. Although the AAUP and the Association of Governing Boards (Association of Governing Boards, 2001) allocate key responsibility for strategic decisions and comprehensive planning to governing boards (Hamilton, 1999), Rhoades (2005) recommends a new model with "wider deliberations" and "trickle up mechanisms for strategic initiatives" (p. 42). Although strategic planning within academia has been referred to as "managerialism run rampant" (Low, 2002), no other activity in higher education can profit more from collaboration among stakeholders. Additionally, no other activity can involve institutional researchers as fully, from surveying both the external and internal environments to assessing the successful implementation of processes to meet strategic goals.

Perhaps the most important role that IR professionals can play in support of shared governance is in the area of data management. Collaborative engagement in shared governance assumes that all parties have equal and unfettered access to the data and information necessary to make informed decisions. Each group should be using the same metrics and benchmarks in developing their decision plans. It is not entirely unheard of to find important decision making being founded on assumptions, assertions, and anecdotal evidence. Additionally, some stakeholders may collect data and information from a wide variety of sources in order to support their own cases for particular decision outcomes. Good decision making demands accurate, reliable, and timely data. Offices of institutional research serve as custodians of data at their colleges or universities and as brokers of those data. McLaughlin and Howard (2004) define a data broker's role as adding value by transforming data into meaningful information. Whether or not IR professionals add the title of "data broker" to their business cards, they are responsible for not only maintaining reliable data but also knowing which data are necessary and which will be helpful (and not divisive), delivering that data, and translating into formats appropriate for each audience. Empathy in understanding people's need to be heard and to have a say in how their institution is run can help achieve consensus among individuals and group members of all campus communities.

Conclusion

At the forty-fifth annual AIR Forum, a panel of CEOs spoke about the role an IR office could play in promoting institutional effectiveness (Chambers & Gerek, 2007). Two of the presidents on that panel agreed that having an institutional researcher present for executive team meetings was "sound management practice." This is so because IR professionals are in a position to offer ideas and information based on their particular positions in the university structure. The very nature of the diversity (breadth and depth) of activities that take place in an IR office tends to develop, in those who work there, an ability to see the university from both a macro and a micro level. This unique perspective means that IR practitioners have a tremendous opportunity to support both the campus CEO and other shared governance structures. They, more than anyone else, can observe—and facilitate interaction among—the various campus constituencies that need to play a role in effective shared governance and provide those constituencies with the tools needed for sound decision making; that is, decision making in the interest of a university's mission and students.

It is the role of IR staff to develop information delivery processes that alert the campus leadership to positive and negative trends that could impact the institution. The establishment of a trusting relationship between IR staff, the CEO, and other shared governance stakeholders is critical in determining institutional staff success. The building of this relationship is dependent on the IR staff's ability to create a multidimensional view of the institution. The IR staff's ability to provide various perspectives—academic, financial, student support, and fund-raising, among others—in a relevant and concise format when requested and to anticipate data needs will help to ensure maximum institutional success.

Good institutional governance is built from a collective concern for what is best for the campus and the academy. Although there is no argument that the president is ultimately responsible for defining the institution's future, shared governance—from setting academic standards and processes to providing advice about institutional policies and priorities—can only enhance the quality of the institution. An active and engaged institutional research function creates and provides information about the effectiveness of the institution's policies and practices—information that will ultimately describe the institution's future.

References

American Association of University Professors. (1966). *Statement on the governance of colleges and universities*. Washington, DC: American Association of University Professors.

Association of Governing Boards. (2001). *Governing in the public interest: External influences on colleges and universities*. Washington, DC: Association of Governing Boards.

Association for Institutional Research. (2001). Code of ethics. Retrieved from http://www.airweb.org/?page=140

Baldwin, J. (1961). *Nobody knows my name*. New York: Vintage International.

Birnbaum, R. (2003). The end of shared governance: Looking ahead or looking back. *New Directions for Higher Education, 127*, 5–22. Retrieved from ERIC database.

Chambers, S., & Gerek, M. L. (2007). IR activities. *IR Applications, 12*. Retrieved from http://www.airweb.org/images/irapps12.pdf

Chronicle of Higher Education. (2008). A profile of college presidents, 2006. *Chronicle of Higher Education, Almanac Issue 2007–8*, LIV, 1.

Coughlin, M. A. (2005). *Applications of intermediate/advanced statistics in institutional research*. Tallahassee, FL: Assocation for Institutional Research.

Devons, S. (2001, Summer). I. I. Rabi: Physics and science at Columbia, in America, and worldwide. *Columbia Magazine: Living Legacies; Great Moments and Leading Figures in the History of Columbia University Series*. Retrieved from http://www.columbia.edu/cu/alumni/Magazine/Summer2001/Rabi.html

Flack, H. (1994, Fall). Three critical elements in strategic planning. *Planning for Higher Education, 23*, 24–31.

Hamilton, N. (1999). Are we speaking the same language? Comparing AAUP and AGB. *Liberal Education, 85*(4), 24–31.

Lazerson, M. (1997, March/April). Who owns higher education? *Change*, 10–15.

Leslie, D. W., & Fretwell, E. K., Jr. (1996). *Wise move in hard times: Creating and managing resilient colleges and universities*. San Francisco: Jossey Bass.

Low, B. (2002). The future role of the institutional researcher in Australian universities, or "Never let the facts interfere with a good theory." *A primer on institutional research in Australasia*. Retrieved from http://www.aair.org.au/jir/Primer/Low.pdf

McLaughlin, G. W., & Howard, R. D. (2004). *People, processes, and managing data* (2nd ed.). Tallahassee, FL: Association for Institutional Research.

Pelletier, S. (2009, March/April). Toward transformative change: Finding a path to systemic reform. *Trusteeship, 17*, 2.

Rhoades, G. (2005). Capitalism, academic style, and shared governance. *Academe, 91*(3), 38–42.

Rosovsky, H. (1990). *The university: An owner's manual*. New York: Norton.

Tappan, H. P. (1961). The idea of the true university. In R. Hofstader & W. Smith (Eds), *American higher education: A documentary history, Vol. II* (pp. 515–545). Chicago: University of Chicago Press.

Veit, R. (2005). Some branches were more equal than others. *Academe, 91*(6), 42–45.

Wallin, D. (2009). Fast-paced environment creates new leadership demands. *Community College Journal, 79*, 6.

Watkins, M. (2003). *The first 90 days. Critical success strategies for new leaders at all levels*. Boston, MA: Harvard Business School Press.

Wellman, J. (2009, May/June). Connecting spending and results: Tying dollars to national, campus goals. *Trusteeship, 17*, 3.

CHAPTER 9

SUPPORTING THE PROVOST AND ACADEMIC VICE PRESIDENT

James T. Posey and Gita Wijesinghe Pitter

In this chapter, the role of institutional research (IR) to support the provost and academic vice president is discussed. The traditional three pillars of academia are teaching, service, and research; this chapter will focus on the IR support functions for teaching and research, with the understanding that many of the principles and techniques discussed can be applied to support of service. The chapter is organized into three major components: theoretical understanding, support for teaching activities, and support for research activities.

Context for Supporting the Provost

Colleges and universities have faced increasing expectations of accountability based on externally established performance indicators since the 1990s (Ruppert, 1994). In the United States, federal and state governments are the primary forces promoting the accountability movements in education (Ewell, 1991). As global competition in higher education increases the need for transformational leadership, the roles of the president and provost grow more complex and their need for information grows concomitantly. The provost or vice president for academic affairs, generally considered the individual responsible for academic leadership at higher education institutions, plays a pivotal role in accountability, as many of the metrics for accountability revolve around outcomes and the use of resources in the academic areas.

Some argue that the traditional role of the provost and academic vice president is changing. Whereas historically this role has been focused primarily on supporting and promoting the academic mission of instruction and learning, in today's world of higher education, other concerns—such as college rankings,

SAT scores, unfunded mandates from government, and accountability or institutional competiveness requirements—are consuming much of a provost and academic vice president's time (Paradise & Dawson, 2007).

In the remainder of this chapter, we refer to the provost and academic vice president or the chief academic officer as "provost."

The Importance of IR in Supporting Academic Institutional Effectiveness

The placement of the IR office in an institution influences the types of analyses it is called on to perform. In the most common organizational structure, the IR office reports to the chief academic officer (Volkwein, 2008). An IR office that reports to, or supports, the provost may be engaged in assessing student learning, providing accreditation support, planning for new academic programs, conducting surveys of graduates, and analyzing research productivity and the relationship of faculty resources to students (Saupe, 1990).

IR professionals need to provide the provost with data to inform multiple perspectives and complex connections. For example, when faced with revenue shortfalls, the president and provost will need to examine many alternative courses of action. Therefore they may require varied information, such as the likelihood of being able to increase revenue through increased tuition, the potential for increased financial aid to assist students to meet the additional costs, and the possible impact on student retention. They may also want to explore areas to be cut, identified by lack of productivity on specified metrics, and the numbers of tenured faculty and other staff who may be affected. The increasing complexity of issues that provosts must face requires "complicated" understanding; that is, the ability to comprehend organizational and environmental events from multiple, rather than single, perspectives (Bartunek, Gordon, & Weathersby, 1983). Providing data alone is insufficient. IR professionals themselves must develop complicated understandings in order to know what data may be useful for given complex situations and to produce nuanced analyses or data-based information that will be helpful to the provost. Complicated understandings may also be thought of as encompassing Terenzini's issues intelligence and contextual intelligence (Terenzini, 1993). For example, if the data indicate a decline in graduation rates, the effective IR professional must ascertain how a web of factors—including admissions characteristics of incoming students, policy changes at the institution, changes in high enrollment majors, and availability of courses—may have impacted the graduation rates. Explicit data requests from the provost may not be the most helpful trigger for IR providing data to the provost, who may not realize exactly which data would be helpful to explore an issue. It is the job of IR to understand issues facing the university in general, or the provost in particular, and suggest what data they may provide to help address the issue. To know what issues will need the attention of the provost, IR needs to be at the table when issues are discussed, such as being at regular meetings of the academic affairs leadership.

In his book *The View from the Helm* (2007), James Duderstadt, former president of the University of Michigan, identifies establishing priorities among academic programs as the most difficult and controversial actions the leaders of an institution must make. This is particularly true in the face of resource constraints. Supporting leaders in making such important and controversial decisions, IR professionals must know which data are relevant and must also be astute about campus politics and how and when to divulge information to a wider audience.

At the forty-fifth annual AIR Forum, a panel of CEOs identified several areas they want IR to address, including assessment of student learning and helping to address emerging issues such as access, time to degree, and costs of higher education. They also suggested the following means of increasing IR's usefulness to the CEO: "1) maintain objectivity; 2) be ahead of the curve . . . 3) stay aware of trends at the national, state, local and institutional levels; 4) break out of the routine; 5) understand the context of your institution by collaborating with senior administrators, and 6) participate in self-assessment practices" (Chambers, 2007, p. 6).

Institutional effectiveness (IE) has become a critical component for regional accreditation of institutions. In a nutshell, IE addresses how well the institution is meeting its stated mission. This includes assessment of the various functions of the institution (particularly its academic functions), demonstration that resources are used in a manner consistent with the strategic goals of the mission, and establishment of performance measures to indicate the institution is making continuous progress in meeting its mission (New England Association of Schools and Colleges, Commission on Institutions of Higher Education, 2011; Higher Learning Commission, 2003; North Central Association of Colleges and Schools, The Higher Learning Commission, 2003). At many institutions it has become the responsibility of IR to help demonstrate institutional effectiveness.

Keys to Providing Timely and Distilled Information to the Provost

The chief academic officer of a complex organization is a busy person, with demands for the officer's attention coming from many internal and external sources. IR professionals need to be cognizant of the types of information and analyses that are most useful and also how best to present them (Howard, 2001). The following are some guidelines to help the IR director establish a productive relationship with the provost:

- IR professionals should become knowledgeable about the institution though data collection and analyses, meetings, and individual contacts in academic units. And they should become knowledgeable about current issues in higher education. This will help IR to develop Terenzini's issues intelligence and contextual intelligence. For example, if the institution wants to increase its standing in research, what is the most effective strategy for investing resources in order to meet the goal? This calls for knowledge not only about one's own institutional strengths in research but also the areas of national growth in research funding and the lessons learned from the experience of other institutions who have undertaken a similar challenge.

- IR should provide not just information, but also analyses (McLaughlin & Howard, 2004). Staff must think through issues from multiple perspectives. For example, if the institution experiences a significant drop in student retention from spring to the next fall, what are the possible reasons and what interventions may be effective in increasing the retention in the future?
- With data, as with jokes, timing is everything. If the provost needs data today for making a decision, it will not be much use to provide it the following day. The provost often does not control the timeline of external demands, threats, or opportunities that call for immediate action on her part.
- Information should be presented on one page whenever possible. Combined verbal, written, and visual elements have the greatest impact (using multiple lenses). Bullet points, charts, and other clear graphics are effective. The most important information should appear first or last, so the provost does not have to search for the answer. The bottom line should be obvious (Henry, 2009).

Today's provosts do not live in a well-ordered world in which events proceed in a linear fashion. The complex requirements of leadership in higher education are often unpredictable and chaotic, due to the nature of both internal dynamics and external influences. Therefore IR must be prepared for ad hoc requests from the provost with very short deadlines. The IR professional who uses the following strategies to respond quickly is likely to become a valued resource to inform decision making:

- Ensure that data needed to deliver frequently requested information is readily available
- Know where to obtain other relevant data
- Anticipate issues through knowledge of both the institutional context and higher education

Relevance to the Mission of the Institution

The types of information that IR is expected to convey to the provost will of course depend on the mission of the institution (Coughlin, Hoey, & Hirano-Nakanishi, 2009). Data related to transfer rates to four-year institutions will be important to two-year community colleges, and transfers from two-year colleges will be important to four-year universities. Data reflecting research activities will be important for research universities, but not for community colleges or teaching institutions. The IR professional must be mindful of the mission of the institution and the institutional context at a particular point in time in order to assess the relative importance of information to the provost.

Delaney (1997) found that an institution's size had a strong relationship with institutional research functions: "Larger, four-year and private institutions were more likely to engage in projects involving social science research methodology, such as planning, forecasting, and research on faculty and academic issues. Also, compared with public institutions, private institutions were more likely to engage in advanced research projects and in studies focused on academic issues" (p. 6).

Framework for Academic Support

The role of the provost is complex and intricately woven throughout a campus. There are two basic frameworks that IR should understand in order to effectively support a provost: (1) the complexity of interactions between the provost and other constituents, and (2) the complexity and multiple levels of data required.

The Balancing Act of Complex Interactions

Weick (1979), in his theory of complicated understanding, suggests that administrators need to see and understand organizational and environmental events from multiple frames rather than a singular perspective. Because many situations are sufficiently complex to be subject to a wide variety of interpretations and understandings, the ability to perceive multiple interpretations of a situation will benefit the administrator, whereas a narrow framework or understanding can result in ineffective solutions or reactions. Weick elucidates that successful administrators use multiple frames to find solutions and benefit from providing multiple approaches to solutions.

The driving force behind the complex data needs of a provost can be understood within the intricate overlapping of distinct organizations that exist in an institution of higher education. Birnbaum (1988) posits that there are three distinct and competing levels of organization at a college or university: (1) the technical level of teaching, research, and service, which is primarily the responsibility of faculty, (2) the institution level, which must respond to external social forces and is the responsibility of presidents and boards, and (3) the managerial or administrative level, which must mediate between the other two levels and find solutions to balance the often conflicting missions of faculty and boards. The provost functions at this administrative level.

Because a provost reports to the president, is responsible for the academic mission, and is dependent on faculty to meet that mission, she is required to examine data from multiple perspectives. Faculty and trustees perform different functions at an institution and often have very different backgrounds. According to Birnbaum (1988), faculty often see administration as synonymous with red tape, constraints, and bowing to outside pressures, while trustees can see faculty as self-absorbed and unwilling to pay attention to necessary requests for accountability. The provost's battle is to navigate between these competing perspectives, providing both with support. The provost can accomplish this through accurate and thorough data-based information.

To satisfy the president and trustees, the provost must analyze data from the perspective of the institutional mission, vision, and priorities. Data need to inform not only internal planning and quality improvement but also accountability measures relevant to external audiences. Often, one difficulty of the provost's role is to obtain faculty buy-in on the importance of institutional effectiveness measures. In contrast to employees in a business, faculty are seen as constituents rather than followers. Nichols (1995) cites faculty resistance as the most significant factor impeding the implementation of institutional effectiveness activities. Ryan (1993, as cited in Welsh and Metcalf, 2003) noted that faculty often see IE efforts as "(1) attacks on tenure and academic freedom, (2) attempts to reduce faculty lines, (3) selling out to business ideologies, and/ or (4) caving in to governmental bureaucracies" (p. 448). Just as important, accountability measures are seen by faculty as loss of control over curriculum.

Ehrenberg (2005) talks about the need to get faculty involved in conducting institutional effectiveness studies, and the methods for doing so. Because many institutional IE measures are based on resources and inputs not concerning faculty, the collection and analysis of the data often does not require faculty involvement. However, the recent emphasis on student learning outcomes as a definition of quality does require faculty involvement. In fact, faculty involvement is integral in order to establish a collaborative approach rather than an "us versus them" paradigm. Faculty support for IE activities is likely to be increased by ensuring that faculty are personally involved in institutional effectiveness activities (Welsh & Metcalf, 2003). Institutional researchers should take advantage of faculty expertise on campus to conduct collaborative studies.

To be useful to a provost, data must be structured to allow users to drill down to schools and colleges, programs, and individual faculty. Provosts interact frequently with deans, and discussions often revolve around the need for resources, which are seen as finite and in competition with other schools or programs. Deans have to balance the expectations of faculty, academic departments, and central administration and are therefore interested in data to facilitate the negotiations around competing interests (Wolverton, Wolverton, & Gmelch, 1999). These data are often integral to generating necessary political support for a provost's decisions related to resource allocations.

A quote attributed to Winston Churchill exemplifies today's world of higher education: "Gentlemen, we are out of money. Now we must think" (Clark, 2009). No one is more affected by current budget concerns than the provost, who has a strong need for data that are linked to finance—data that support budgeting and resource allocation decisions. Provosts are required to make tough choices, to set priorities and develop strategies. Kotler and Murphy (1981) detail three levels of planning necessary in higher education: (1) budgeting and scheduling, (2) short-range planning such as recruiting students and curricular program modifications, and (3) long-range planning, which requires ". . . both quantitative and qualitative assessments of the external environment" (p. 471).

Efficiency Versus Effectiveness

Colleges and universities often focus on efficiency measures such as how to provide quality education for less money. *Efficiency* can be defined as the ratio of costs to some output, or as the amount of energy lost in the production of organizational output. Cost per full-time equivalent (FTE) student, student-faculty ratios, cost per faculty member, and cost per degree are examples of efficiency measures, which can be equated to quantifiable key performance indicators. *Effectiveness*, in contrast, focuses on demonstrating the effective use of resources to produce an output (Cameron, 1978). The competency skills of graduates fall into this effectiveness category. Effectiveness measures might be seen as critical success factors, which, when successfully met, will ensure the success of an organization (Martin, 1982).

Various budgeting models are used in higher education today to measure efficiency and effectiveness, including activity-based budgeting (ABB) and decentralized budgeting such as responsibility center management (RCM). Both of these budgeting models are performance-based models that require examination of evidence to determine the need for funding. Conversely, other traditional funding models were often based on how much funding was received in previous years rather than on performance.

ABB is a system in which every cost-incurring activity must be accounted for and analyzed in relation to the mission and strategic goals of a college or university. ABB in essence is the allocation of resources to individual activities, while maintaining central control. ABB aligns activities with objectives by first looking at results rather than raw inputs (Investopedia, 2010). The ABB model creates transparency in understanding the full cost of programs and services.

Decentralized budgeting was implemented by the University of New Hampshire in 2000 as responsibility center management (University of New Hampshire, 2010). This financial management system empowers deans and other directors to create appropriate incentives for revenue generation and cost efficiency. Decentralized budgeting, in contrast to traditional budgeting, distributes control of resources and their distribution to deans and vice presidents rather than through university-level executive management. Both ABB and RCM are mentioned here in brief in order to underscore the necessity of providing the provost with data that are linked to financial decision making at the institution. We should note that both of these systems require timely data that are easily shared in order to facilitate common understanding. Required data might include student credit hour and degree production, student tuition and fees, other earned income, endowments and gifts, enrollment projections, and faculty productivity.

Transactional and Transformational Leadership Activities

Burns (1978) expounded a concept of transactional rather than transformational leadership, which is extremely apropos to role of the provost. In brief, a transactional leader maintains power by producing rewards and fairly distributing them; that is, fulfilling expectations. A transformational leader expresses new and better values, producing intended change. Transactional leadership involves an exchange of value, which could be economic, political, or psychological. According to Burns, "Each party to the bargain is conscious of the power resources and attitudes of the other . . . Their purposes are related" (p. 19). Birnbaum (1988) further states that higher education administrators receive their power in exchange for filling the expectations and needs of constituents. There are abundant examples of provost engagement in transactional leadership, such as addressing budget requests, securing desired office space for a department, or allocating new faculty lines.

Transformational leadership is also critical to the success of a provost. This type of leadership occurs when leaders and followers raise one another to higher levels of motivation (Burns, 2003). The two parties unite for a common purpose. Examples of transformational leadership are introducing new degree programs, reshaping schools or colleges, introducing a campus-wide assessment initiative, implementing new program or policy initiatives, or attempting to change an established culture or system.

Institutional researchers should understand these two types of leadership activities and strive to provide data for either as the situation demands. Whether transactional or transformational, it is important to not simply provide data but instead provide value-added information that informs and illuminates leadership activities and resulting impacts.

Academic Support: Teaching and Research

Although teaching and research are seen as pillars of academia and are often interrelated, these activities can be performed by various people in overlapping but competing structures (Birnbaum, 1988). Additionally, a college or university may focus primarily on one of these aspects as the core mission, thereby becoming known as either a teaching or a research institution (Terpstra & Honoree, 2009). The focus of effective IR in supporting the provost will therefore be related to the type and mission of the institution. The importance of providing data about teaching and research is fundamental to the institution's management because rewards such as institutional recognition, merit pay, tenure and promotion, and performance funding are tied to the success of these activities at the individual and institutional levels. Core measures of concern to a provost for academic support include assessment of student learning and competency, student satisfaction, faculty satisfaction, faculty research quality and quantity, levels of service, retention of students and faculty, existing program review, new program development, accreditation, strategic planning implementation, and the development of extension services and continuing education.

IR Support of Teaching

Although teaching and academic support remain critical functions of provosts, they are also heavily concerned with institutional effectiveness while supporting academic programs. Cameron (1978) identified nine dimensions of effectiveness and their respective criteria, of which the following five are particularly applicable to the data needs of a provost: student educational satisfaction, student academic development, student career development, faculty satisfaction, and professional development and quality of the faculty.

This section regarding teaching is organized into two primary areas. The first deals with data and information pertaining to existing conditions, including faculty, students, academic support, and progress on meeting strategic plan goals and accreditation. The second area suggests how IR may help the provost in developing new initiatives and creating transformational change.

Accountability and Productivity Data for Academic Support. Although institutional researchers should always consult closely with the provost as to required data, the following are examples of academic data commonly required on many campuses, depending on the institution's size and mission.

Institutional Data. A provost requires institutional-level data mainly for accountability measures to report to external constituencies who are not interested in program- or faculty-level data but who want to see how the institution compares to other institutions in a broad sense. This is where institutional research can assist in establishing peer institutions and benchmarks. Institutional researchers should be aware that the establishment of peer institutions is one of the most political undertakings on a campus because of the previously mentioned reality of separate organizations in a college or university. Faculty, administrators, and board members may all have differing perspectives on which institutions should be considered peers. However, providing comparative data about peer institutions can be extremely valuable to a provost when considering resource allocation. Such data can include tuition levels, faculty credit hour production, faculty salaries, staffing levels, and student/faculty ratios. These comparative data can be used to justify tuition increases, budget requests, teaching loads, or salary increases (Teeter & Brinkman, 2003). See Chapter 36 for a detailed discussion of creating a comparison group of institutions.

Program Data. Although a provost needs to see institution-level data in order to benchmark against peer institutions, invariably, for purposes of internal accountability and evaluation, the institution-level data must be broken out by program and ultimately by individual faculty. Program-level data are crucial to informing budget and policy decisions. Examples of important program-level data are:

- Application and enrollment trends
- Percent of degrees awarded within minimum credits required
- Counts of majors
- Six-year and/or three-year graduation rates
- Data on courses, such as barrier courses, course availability, average class size, and course enrollments
- Number of degrees awarded by level (including high-demand and state-need areas, such as science, math, and engineering graduates)
- Funding per FTE
- Student/faculty ratios
- Number of programs ranked nationally
- Faculty salary analyses
- Total student credit hours generated
- Student and faculty retention rates
- Number and percentage of students who obtain an advanced degree after graduation
- Sponsored research expenditures per faculty member and total

Faculty Data. Accountability and productivity data for faculty involve both quantity and quality measures, such as the number of faculty, which leads to student/faculty ratios; faculty demographics, with an eye on diversity; breakout of faculty by tenure, tenure track, and adjunct; breakout of faculty by administrative faculty and instructional faculty; faculty status by full-time, part-time, sabbatical, and release time; courses taught, including enrollments; percentage of courses taught by full-time versus part-time faculty; student evaluations; citations of scholarly work; faculty awards received; faculty elected to national academies; number of patents awarded; and the amount of research and development funds received.

Student Data. These data can include student demographics, such as diversity (with detailed analyses of underrepresented minorities); age; residence; entering test scores; first-generation status; and financial aid recipients by percent of scholarships, grants, and loans; student satisfaction rates, including perceptions and needs from local and national surveys such as NSSE or CCSSE; percent who agree they would choose the program or institution again; quarterly and one-year retention rates; transfer rates; graduation rates; and the number of students with internships, research, or service experience.

Academic Support Data. Colleges and universities provide, to varying degrees, academic support services such as teaching and learning centers, federal TRIO programs, testing centers, and tutoring. The provost needs data to evaluate how well the support areas are functioning. These data might include the number of students using the services; their demographics; and analyses of use by topic, frequency, time of day, and impact or outcomes, such as improvements in GPA, retention, or graduation rates.

Information from Processes Leading to Quality Assurance and Evidence of Improvement. Processes leading to quality assurance and improvement include assessment, program review, strategic planning, and accreditation. In this section, we focus on the information from these activities that is most helpful to the provost.

Assessment, Including Survey Data from Students, Alumni, and Employers. An important role the provost plays in assessment is regularly keeping assessment activities in the minds of faculty and administrators. Assessment is a difficult activity to sustain even when institutionalized, so it is necessary to give the provost periodic summary reports on the good (units that are engaging in and reporting on assessment), the bad (units that are not reporting on assessment), and the ugly (units that are reporting on assessment but only in a perfunctory, meaningless way). IR should assist the provost in getting the attention of the units that are not reporting or not truly engaging in assessment. The types of assessment information the IR professional needs to provide the provost are:

- Identify common issues or themes evident in several assessment results in academic units or in surveys.
- Provide information on the level of effectiveness of academic support services; do they in fact improve student learning?
- Identify those issues requiring institutional-level attention that are larger than individual units can address.
- Identify major improvements in assessment results over time; celebrating success helps sustain assessment efforts and provides necessary information for accreditation.
- Summarize general education outcomes: areas in which students excel and areas needing improvement
- Identify gaps in compliance with regional accreditation assessment criteria.

Program review. Identify major issues needing the provost's attention. Program reviews take several forms, depending on the institution. Whatever the model, it is likely to identify some urgent issues that need the provost's attention, such as safety concerns in laboratories or dramatic declines in enrollment or degrees awarded in particular programs. There may also be happier findings that the provost should be informed of, such as programs of exceptional quality and potential for making a leap to prominence or initiating a higher degree level in the program.

IR should identify common issues evident in multiple program reviews. As in assessment, common themes or issues emerging across several program reviews may merit institutional attention. For example, several programs may have problems attracting graduate students because of insufficient tuition waivers that make the overall packages offered noncompetitive, or the equipment in the teaching laboratories of several programs may be found to be thoroughly inadequate. The provost will need to be informed of these issues so that institutional plans can be made to address them.

IR should summarize improvements made as a result of reviews. As with assessment, the provost will want to be informed of improvements resulting from previous program reviews that reflect well on the institution and on particular programs. Summaries of such improvements are essential in demonstrating institutional effectiveness to accrediting bodies.

Strategic Planning. The roles IR can play in the institution's strategic planning efforts are discussed in Chapter 11. Once the strategic plan is implemented, IR needs to keep the provost informed of the contribution of various units to the institutional goals and progress made on the goals.

A matrix crosswalk of unit goals mapped to institutional strategic plan goals can document which units are addressing each of the institutional strategic planning goals and will help the provost assess whether all relevant units are doing their share to contribute to the institutional goals. This will also make any gaps in addressing institutional goals evident; that is, identifying which institutional goals no one appears to be addressing.

IR should report on progress made on key strategic planning goals by units. Annually, they should compile data and give the provost a summary of progress made in achieving the strategic planning goals. It is useful for the institution to create a tactical work plan with specific measures and target performance criteria to address each goal on the strategic plan. Comparing the actual results each year to the targets will enable the provost to determine whether some goals need special attention or other goals were unrealistic and should be modified in a strategic plan revision.

Specialized Accreditation Information. Specialized accreditation and how IR professionals may help in this endeavor is discussed in Chapter 18. One of the most important functions of deans and the provost is to ensure continued accreditation of academic programs. IR can assist the provost to monitor programmatic accreditation activities through the following two activities:

1. Compile and annually update information on specialized accreditation. Most institutions have a number of academic programs that periodically undergo specialized accreditation reviews. (For a listing of specialized accreditation agencies in the United States, see Council for Higher Education Accreditation, 2010.) It is essential that the provost knows, in any given year, which programs are scheduled for review and which programs are accredited. Informing the provost of the programs coming up for accreditation during the current year may lead to discussions with the respective deans to ensure that the units are well prepared. The units themselves may be urged to complete a gap analysis in relation to each of the accreditation criteria.
2. Assist the provost in monitoring progress on accreditation issues through action plans. An action plan that summarizes the areas of noncompliance and actions that must be completed in order to come into compliance will not only keep the provost informed but will also be a useful tool for the dean to ensure that corrective actions are proceeding at a pace that will ensure compliance before any upcoming deadlines.

Identifying and Supporting New Initiatives. Crucial to continuous improvement and transformation is information that will help identify the right initiatives at the right time. This is particularly important in the academic arena because it is through the implementation of new academic programs that institutions most often transform themselves.

Need and Demand Data for New Programs and New Priorities. New academic programs are most successful when the ideas flow from the faculty who are involved in the program. Administrators who see an opportunity in a field may ask a faculty committee to look into the possibility of a university initiative, but ultimately it will take the enthusiasm of faculty who are themselves convinced of the exciting possibilities in the field to carry the new program to successful implementation. IR may provide labor market information for the program. Alternatively, faculty who want to implement the program may be asked to provide need and demand data as part of a proposal, which can then be evaluated by IR. The advantages of this approach are that the faculty, in collecting and analyzing the data, will themselves be convinced of either the need or lack of need. Faculty members are most likely to know the sources of good data specific to their field. IR can supplement this with IPEDS data to determine whether other institutions have similar programs and how productive those programs are. If other programs at comparative institutions tend to be small, the IR staff could question the viability of such a program at their institutions. If there are no other such programs, and literature in the field (provided by faculty) indicate this is a new field that is likely to come into high demand, the provost will need to determine whether the institution is ready to take on the challenging task of developing and supporting a cutting-edge program. There are some programs for which there is a market need but student demand is dwindling. However attractive the market need, the provost should be convinced of both sufficient student demand and budget resources to move forward on a new program. IR, departmental faculty, or both can conduct a survey of current or potential students in the community to determine the strength of student interest in such a program. The particular mission of the institution will determine whether need and demand are gauged at a local, state, or national level. Proposals for new academic programs should contain, at a minimum, information on congruity with institutional mission, need and demand, the curriculum, whether there are qualified faculty at the institution to offer the program or additional faculty will be needed, programmatic accreditation requirements (if relevant), and projected enrollment and costs, which would form a business plan to ensure the viability of the program.

As with new programs, new priorities envisioned by the university administration and the governing board should be supported by data-based analyses. IR can provide data and objective analyses that can convince administrators either that the ideas are sound and likely to enhance the institution, or that there are potentially challenging issues that must be taken into consideration before making a decision. If the president or provost is enthusiastic about a potential new initiative but IR finds information that indicates it may be damaging to the institution, IR should diplomatically convey this information to the administrators. The AIR Code of Ethics (Association for Institutional Research, 2001) is a valuable resource in these situations.

Another area may be the need for new or expanded academic support services. This will often become evident as IR analyzes data from various sources, such as student characteristics, both demographic and academic; data from surveys such as NSSE, CCSSE, or Noel-Levitz and exit surveys; grade patterns that reveal courses with a high failure rate; and results of standardized tests such as the ETS Proficiency Profile (previously the Measure of Academic Proficiency and Progress or MAPP) and the Collegiate Learning Assessment (CLA). If a need for a new academic support service is strongly indicated through one or more of these sources or from faculty and student affairs input, the provost should be informed not only of the need, but also of how meeting this need will impact student success. (See Chapters 14 and 30 for detailed discussions of these and other instruments.)

Data to Inform Transformational Change. Transformational change is seldom instantaneous. It often begins with an idea that emerges from the president or provost. It can also begin with the vision of a dean or other individual who sees a unique opportunity and seizes it. There are many opportunities that may sound like an exciting chance for transformational change, but IR professionals and others need to ferret out as many pertinent facts as possible. This would include an analysis of the probability of success and necessary resources for success. Individuals who present opportunities to the provost may be too enthusiastic to have considered all the costs or pitfalls; that job often falls to IR. IR should cultivate an evenhanded approach, so other parties know they can count on them to provide unbiased information from several relevant perspectives, suggesting positive and negative aspects of the proposal and its potential.

Leadership unaccustomed to strong or proactive IR resources may not think of asking IR for assistance when considering a significant change. IR staff can build their value to the university leadership by providing essential information on an important topic being considered without waiting to be asked. (Chapter 4 provides more information on being proactive in IR.)

The following types of data can inform vision for transformational change:

- Cost analyses
- Analysis of the institution's capability to mount the change
- Analyses of the potential impact of the change, both positive and negative
- Profile of lessons learned from other institutions that instituted the kind of change being considered

IR Support of Research

The centrality of the research enterprise varies considerably by institutional mission. For universities in which it is a key component of the mission, research is essential to competitiveness, prestige, and standing in the hierarchy of research universities. An international perspective on research universities may be gleaned through publications of organizations such as the Organization for Economic Cooperation and Development (Connell, 2004). Institutions that benefit most from the national interest in research fall within the research-extensive, research-intensive, and research/doctoral institutions of the Carnegie classification system (Carnegie Foundation, 2005). Even for institutions in other categories, such as master's, with aspirations to be research institutions, performance on various metrics of research productivity is of great interest to the provost.

The following section provides suggestions for metrics that may be useful to analyze research productivity and summarize notable findings (either positive or negative) for the provost. Some or all of these should be part of the key performance indicators produced annually by IR at research institutions.

Data for Accountability and Productivity.

Trends in Sponsored Research Productivity by Academic Units. Useful trend data to track productivity by unit may include

- Trends in number and ratio per faculty of grant proposals submitted, by school or college and by department
- Trends in annual research revenues and expenditures, by source of funds (such as federal, state, or other) by college or school and by department, available from sources such as Webcaspar (National Science Foundation, 2010)

Patents, Licenses, Royalties, or Licensing Income by College, School, or Department. The Association of University Technology Managers (AUTM) Licensing Survey (Association of University Technology Managers, n.d.) is a good source of information on patents, licenses, and licensing income.

Other useful data include information on start-up companies, jobs created, and outcomes of technology transfer from the institution's research. The NSF Webcaspar website (National Science Foundation, 2010) provides a wealth of data that may be used by IR to provide the kinds of analyses useful to the provost. This and other sources of data are discussed in Chapter 21.

Scholarship as Cited from a Nationally Reputable Source. Although scholarship is considered easier to measure than teaching, because one can "count" publications, it is by no means a simple matter. Questions abound, such as whether the publications are in reputable peer-reviewed journals, how multiple authorship should be treated, and whether journals are more prestigious than books or vice versa, depending on the discipline. Scholarship in the visual and performing arts brings its own particular challenges, as creative works are included in scholarship. One means of counting peer-reviewed journal articles is to use a source such as the *Web of Knowledge* (2010), which compiles citations in peer-reviewed articles in premier journals in most disciplines. Institutional membership is necessary in order to use these services, and they have their limitations, as the premier journals in particular disciplines may not be included. Also, if an institution is at a point in the evolution of its research enterprise where faculty are publishing but not in the most prestigious journals, these services may be of little use to IR staff there. Given the complexities of measuring productivity in scholarship, it is essential that faculty participate in developing a methodology for assessing scholarship measures and compiling the data.

Return on Investment Data. Justifying the research function of the university is a challenge that presidents and provosts face. The public and public officials expect the research engine of universities to drive economic development for the region, the state, and the nation, particularly as nations transform to knowledge economies. Justifications for investment in research can be bolstered by these measures:

- Data on the numbers of students involved in the institution's research efforts and the numbers of presentations and publications from undergraduate and graduate students
- Ratio of dollars generated through sponsored research and license income for every dollar spent on research programs
- Data on technology transfer, the number of start-up companies spawned by university research, and the jobs created through them.

Rankings with Respect to Peers, and Key Metrics. Research performance in relation to peers and aspirational peers may be tracked using data from various sources. One source for identifying peers is the Carnegie classification system (Carnegie Foundation, 2005), which enables researchers to search for peer institutions by one or more of the metrics used in the system, such as enrollment, size, and setting, and the basic classification, which is the metric usually referred to in categorizing the research activity of institutions. Peers may also be identified through the various rankings systems, such as the National Research Council (NRC), the Center for Measuring Performance, *U.S. News and World Report* rankings, and the University of Illinois-Urbana Champaign research ranking site, which allows one to customize the NRC rankings. The major metrics generally focus on peer-reviewed publications, sponsored research activities, and patents and royalty income (Keith, 2001; University of Illinois, 2009; National Research Council, 1995; Center for Measuring Performance, 2008; *U.S. News and World Report*, 2011).

Setting Targets for Transformational Change. The provost may wish to create transformational change in the research enterprise of the university. IR could help map the path for that transformation. The transformation may encompass the entire university, targeting all disciplines for significantly increased research and scholarship. Or, more likely, the transformation could begin with research niches in which the institution already has some strength; these are areas of strategic emphases in funding opportunities, in which the university could realistically hope to make a significant contribution to the advancement of knowledge. IR would need to provide an array of information, including:

- Demographic data of the institution
- Research productivity data
- Information from program reviews conducted for this specific purpose, obtaining the services of experts in the areas targeted, to ascertain what would realistically be required for the desired transformation
- Information on significant investments the institution may need to make over a period of time in order to create the transformation
- Congruence between the selected areas for transformation and state or regional interests and strengths that may be leveraged

- Analysis of policies such as teaching loads, tenure and promotion criteria, and the provision of start-up funds for faculty that may need to be revisited
- Standing in relation to peers in the selected disciplines
- External funding opportunities.

Conclusion

It is well known that institutional research has an identity crisis when it comes to describing the specific functions all IR offices perform. There should be no identity crisis for IR when it comes to supporting the provost and academic mission of the institution; the need for data-based decision support is evident and abundant. The pressures on a provost are vast, as more people see higher education through the lens of accountability that often reflects conflicting values. There are growing demands for greater productivity in teaching and learning; institutions are expected to confer a greater volume of degrees with more competent graduates. This increased emphasis on academic institutional effectiveness is placed squarely on the shoulders of the provost.

The word *productivity* is often applied to performance related to funding. State legislatures are responding to the argument that without more state support, tuition and fees must be raised, with calls for productivity measures to determine how well institutions are performing with current resources. However, there are challenges to standardizing measures of productivity—in particular, when trying to address the unique value-added impact of an institution. Initial efforts to define productivity often involve academic outcomes such as graduation rates and the cost of producing a college degree (Kelly, 2009). The provost is required to monitor academic programs and therefore needs to regularly review data to determine whether programs are functioning at an acceptable level. Because the issue of funding is of such critical importance in higher education, IR should make support of the provost a top priority by providing data on academic outcomes linked to revenues and expenditures. A provost cannot accurately evaluate performance or effectively allocate resources without accurate and detailed information. Such information can lead to effective use of resources, formulation of sound policies, increased productivity, and demonstrable value to the constituents that an institution serves.

References

Association for Institutional Research. (2001). *Code of ethics.* Retrieved from http://www.airweb.org/?page=140

Association of University Technology Managers. (n.d.). *AUTM statistics access for tech transfer (STATT).* Retrieved from http://www.autm.net/Home.htm

Bartunek, J. M., Gordon, J. R., & Weathersby, R. P. (1983). Developing "complicated" understanding in administrators. *Academy of Management Review, 8*(2), 273–284.

Birnbaum, R. (1988). *How colleges work: The cybernetics of academic organization and leadership.* San Francisco: Jossey-Bass.

Burns, J. M. (1978). *Leadership.* New York: Harper Torchbooks.

Burns, J. M. (2003). *Transforming leadership.* New York: Grove Press.

Cameron, K. (1978, Dec.). Measuring organizational effectiveness in institutions of higher education. *Administrative Science Quarterly, 23*(4), 604–632.

Carnegie Foundation for the Advancement of Teaching (2005). *Carnegie classification of institutions of higher education.* Retrieved from http://classifications .carnegiefoundation.org/

Center for Measuring Performance (2008). *The top American research universities annual report.* Retrieved from http://mup.asu.edu/research.html

Chambers, S. (2007, February 26). Insights from the institutional research knowledge base on understanding chief executive needs in IR applications. *Association for Institutional Research, 12.*

Clark, T. B. (2009). Management matters: Now we must think. *Government Executive.* Retrieved from http://www.govexec.com/dailyfed/0809/081909mm.htm

Connell, H. M. (Ed.). (2004). *University research management: Meeting the institutional challenge.* Paris, France: Organization for Economic Cooperation and Development.

Coughlin, M. A., Hoey, J., & Hirano-Nakanishi, M. (2009). Sector differences in the role of institutional research in informing decision making and governance in higher education. *Asia Pacific Education Review, 10*(1), 69–81.

Council for Higher Education Accreditation (CHEA). (2010). *Recognized accrediting organizations.* Retrieved from http://www.chea.org/pdf/CHEA_USDE_AllAccred.pdf

Delaney, A. M. (1997). The role of institutional research in higher education: Enabling researchers to meet new challenges. *Research in Higher Education,* AIR Forum Issue, *38*(1), 1–16.

Duderstadt, J. J. (2007). *The view from the helm: Leading the American university.* Ann Arbor, MI: University of Michigan Press.

Ehrenberg, R. G. (2005, May). AIR research and practice: Why universities need institutional researchers and institutional researchers need faculty members more than both realize. *Research in Higher Education, 46*(3), 349–363.

Ewell, P. T. (1991, Nov.–Dec.). Assessment and public accountability: Back to the future. *Change, 23*(6), 12–17.

Henry, D. P. (2009). *The art and psychology of effective presentations.* Paper presented at the Association for Institutional Research, Atlanta, GA.

Higher Learning Commission. (2003). *Institutional accreditation: An overview.* Retrieved from http://www.ncahlc.org/download/2003Overview.pdf

Howard, R. D. (Ed.). (2001). *Institutional research: Decision support in higher education.* Tallahassee, FL: Association for Institutional Research.

Investopedia. (2010). Activity-Based Budgeting—ABB. Retrieved from http://www.investo pedia.com/terms/a/abb.asp

Keith, B (2001). Organizational contexts and university performance outcomes: The limited role of purposive action in the management of institutional status. *Research in Higher Education, 42*(5).

Kelly, P. J. (2009). *The dreaded "P" word: An examination of productivity in public postsecondary education.* Delta Cost Project white paper series. Retrieved from http://www.deltacostproject.org/resources/pdf/Kelly07–09_WP.pdf

Kotler, P., & Murphy, P. E. (1981, Sept.–Oct). Strategic planning for higher education. *Journal of Higher Education, 52*(5), 470–489.

Martin, E. W. (1982, June). Critical success factors of chief MIS/DP executives. *MIS Quarterly, 6*(2), 1–9.

McLaughlin, G. W., & Howard, R. D. (2004). *People, processes, and managing data* (2nd ed.). Tallahassee, FL: Association for Institutional Research.

National Research Council (NRC). (1995). *Research doctorate programs in the United States.* Washington, DC: National Academy Press.

National Science Foundation. (2010). *Webcaspar.* Retrieved from https://webcaspar.nsf.gov/

New England Association of Schools and Colleges, Commission on Institutions of Higher Education. (2011). Standards for accreditation. Retrieved from http://cihe.neasc.org/downloads/Standards/June_2011_Standards_revisions_in_color.pdf

Nichols, J. O. (1995). *A practitioner's handbook for institutional effectiveness and student outcomes assessment implementation.* New York: Agathon Press.

North Central Association of Colleges and Schools, The Higher Learning Commission. (2003). *Handbook on Accreditation* (3rd ed.). Retrieved from http://www.ncahlc.org/

Paradise, L. V., & Dawson, K. M. (2007). New peril for the provost: Marginalization of the academic mission. *About Campus, 12*(1), 30–32.

Ruppert, S. (Ed). (1994). *Charting higher education accountability: A sourcebook on state level performance indicators.* Denver, CO: Education Commission of the States.

Saupe, J. L. (1990). *The functions of institutional research* (2nd ed.). Tallahassee, FL: Association for Institutional Research.

Teeter, D. J., & Brinkman, P. T. (2003). Peer institutions. In W. E. Knight (Ed.), *The primer for institutional research* (pp. 103–113). Resources in Institutional Research, no. 14. Tallahassee, FL: Association for Institutional Research.

Terenzini, P. T. (1993). On the nature of institutional research and the knowledge and skills it requires. *Journal of Research in Higher Education, 34*(1), 1–10.

Terpstra, D. E., & Honoree, A. L. (2009, Jan.–Feb.). The effects of different teaching, research, and service emphases on individual and organizational outcomes in higher education institutions. *Journal of Education for Business, 84*(3), 169–176.

University of Illinois. (2009). *College and university rankings.* Retrieved from http://www.library.illinois.edu/edx/rankings/index.html

University of New Hampshire. (2010). Responsibility center management. Retrieved from http://www.unh.edu/rcm/

U.S. News and World Report. (2011). *Best colleges 2011.* Retrieved from http://www.usnews.com/education/slideshows/best-colleges-2011

Volkwein, J. F. (2008). *The foundations and evolution of institutional research.* New Directions for Higher Education, no. 141. San Francisco: Jossey-Bass. Retrieved from www.interscience.wiley.com

Web of Knowledge. (2010). Retrieved from http://isiwebofknowledge.com/

Weick, K. E. (1979). *The social psychology of organizing* (2nd ed.). New York: McGraw-Hill.

Welsh, J. F., & Metcalf, J. (2003. Jul.–Aug.). Faculty and administrative support for institutional effectiveness activities: A bridge across the chasm? *Journal of Higher Education, 74*(4), 445–468.

Wolverton, M., Wolverton, M. L., & Gmelch, W. H. (1999, Jan.–Feb). The impact of role conflict and ambiguity on academic deans. *Journal of Higher Education, 70*(1), 80–106.

CHAPTER 10

EXAMINING FACULTY RECRUITMENT, RETENTION, PROMOTION, AND RETIREMENT

Daniel Teodorescu

Colleges and universities invest considerable resources in faculty, but how successful are they in their recruitment efforts? And how successful are they in tenuring, promoting, and retaining the faculty they hire? Unlike student data, data on faculty are relatively scant in many IR offices, and such questions often go unanswered. Because faculty satisfaction is a strong predictor of retention, IR professionals must conduct periodic assessments of an institution's academic workplace and the level of satisfaction among faculty. At the same time, with support from the provost's office, they should develop and maintain data collection systems that can describe and explore their institution's success at recruiting, promoting, and retaining faculty. In this chapter, I discuss approaches to collecting and reporting the information that is necessary to understand faculty flow—from recruitment success to tenure and promotion rates, to retention analysis, to retirement projections and projections of new faculty. (See also Chapter 9 concerning support for academic affairs.)

Evaluating Faculty Recruitment

With support from the provost's office, IR professionals should engage in an annual analysis of information on new faculty searches and outside offers in order to allow academic leaders to examine the success of faculty recruitment efforts across the campus. The information collected should be consistent across all schools and colleges and should capture the relevant information as each offer occurs. Because information on faculty recruitment processes is not usually captured by HR data systems, these data collection activities might be initiated by the IR Office with the support of the provost. Although the IR office might play a significant role in designing the collection templates and analyzing the data, it is usually the staff in the provost's office that handle the collection of data from the academic units. Because all deans report directly to the provost, the request for annual updates usually will be addressed more efficiently if it comes directly from the provost. Ideally, the faculty data collection templates should be incorporated within the annual reporting process that schools/colleges regularly use to submit their information on past year activities to the provost. It is recommended that the information on recruitment success be presented by discipline and campus (at a multi-campus university), and by recruitment type (open search or administrative appointment). Table 10.1 offers an example of how such information could be organized at the university level.

Institutions are often interested in gauging their success in hiring underrepresented faculty, such as minority and women. A major obstacle that may be encountered when embarking on an analysis of equity in hiring decisions is that complete records on the gender and race/ethnicity of applicants for all searches are often not available at most institutions. To be able to document equity in hires, IR should collaborate with other offices on campus to organize a centralized, uniform process for data collection that will ensure that key demographic data are available from each search committee.

Because tracking equity in hiring decisions is a critical goal for the office that ensures compliance with all applicable federal and state antidiscrimination laws, including laws addressing equal employment opportunity and affirmative action, the design of data collection systems and processes should be a collaborative project between the IR office and the office of equal opportunity programs (EOP). The EOP office monitors the institution's hiring processes and procedures and assists departments with recruiting and hiring practices designed to support access, equity, and inclusion. As part of this monitoring, the EOP office requires that all search committees submit a search activity report (SAR) form for every faculty search. Approval by the EOP office must be obtained before an official employment offer can be made. The IR office might assist the EOP staff with the design of the SAR form and the database that stores the data collected through that form. It could also help the EOP staff with the analysis of the data collected for each search.

TABLE 10.1 TENURE TRACK FACULTY RECRUITMENTS AND SUCCESS RATES, FALL 1999–2009

	1999	2000	2001	2002	2003	2004	2005	2006	2007	2008	2009
Searches	891	441	302	504	486	504	511	759	889	937	1,142
Appointments	526	237	184	371	367	401	388	543	616	704	845
Success Rate	59%	54%	61%	74%	76%	79%	76%	72%	69%	75%	74%

Using the SAR form, a "faculty search" data collection system could track for each faculty search the following data elements: college/school/division, department/section and chair, year, date of advertisement, level advertised, level hired, search chair, gender and race/ethnicity distribution of the search committee members, gender and race/ethnicity distribution of the applicant pool, gender and race/ethnicity distribution of the availability pool for the specific discipline, ethnic/racial diversity and gender distribution of the candidates on the short list, and the final outcome for each candidate on the short list (position offered, offer accepted, or offer declined), as well as reasons for the selection or nonselection of the candidate.

Analysis of these data will help academic leaders identify stages in the hiring process at which gender and race/ethnicity disparities occur, which is critical information for departments as they review their recruiting and hiring practices. Based on these data, IR should be able to answer the following questions: (1) What is the trend in the number and percentage of women hired into tenure track positions over the past ten years? (2) Have women been hired in nontenured positions to a greater extent than male faculty? (3) Adjusting for national availability pool statistics in the discipline, which departments or schools have made progress in hiring women over the past ten years? Similar questions could be answered to examine advances in the representation of minorities.

Having collected descriptive data on recruitment success rates, IR analysts should also plan to conduct an analysis of the factors associated with highly successful recruitment activities. Of course, recruitment success varies depending on the academic area in which a search is conducted and the location of the campus; therefore the analysis should examine success rates by school, discipline, and/or campus (if the institution has more than one campus). The data needed to help explain which factors are associated with high success rates usually come from two sources: academic units (through deans and department chairs) and recruited faculty.

Data from Academic Units

Because detailed information about the outcomes of faculty searches is rarely collected on campuses, the provost's office might need to initiate such data collection processes. The office that is most likely to provide these data is that of the associate dean of faculty at each school. Again, although the provost's office will be responsible for collecting the data regularly from schools and colleges, the IR analysts may be called on to design the data collection system and analyze the recruitment data. An effective way to track recruitment success is to gather data at the time of a recruitment offer, when the data will be more accurate than it would be if trying to reconstruct it after the fact. In terms of data needed, IR needs to design a spreadsheet to record information on faculty recruitment, including successful and unsuccessful offers made to potential faculty members. In the case of unsuccessful recruitments, data should be collected on the reasons the offer was not accepted.

The template used by the academic planning and analysis office at the University of Wisconsin-Madison (2009) provides an example of requirements for this data collection process. A more complex data collection strategy is used by California State University (2006), which also collects information from administrators in the hiring units on average moving expenses, start-up funds, and workload reduction by discipline. These are important factors that faculty typically consider when deciding whether to join another institution.

Data obtained from the units can be analyzed in many ways. For all the searches that failed, a simple tabulation of reasons for declining an offer would reveal whether compensation or other institutional characteristics were major impediments to achieving recruitment targets. In addition to constructing simple frequency tabulations of these factors, IR should consider developing regression models that aim to identify the most significant predictors of recruitment success. In a multi-campus environment, regression analysis will help answer important research questions such as these: (1) What is the relationship between recruitment success at the campus level and starting salaries? (2) What is the relationship between recruitment success at the campus level and housing costs? (3) In science fields, what is the relationship between start-up packages and recruitment success, after controlling for salary offers? Another revealing analysis is the examination of hiring of minority and women faculty by school and department. Specifically, such analysis would determine the percentage of offers made to targeted minority and female faculty and the percentage of offers accepted. With these data, one could establish, for instance, whether the acceptance rate for offers is comparable for minority and white male faculty. The report on faculty recruitment produced by California State University (2006) illustrates many other types of analyses that could be undertaken to examine recruitment success.

Data from Recruited Faculty Members

Most colleges and universities survey their admitted students to identify factors that influence students' decisions whether to enroll at their campuses (through in-house surveys or the Admitted Student Questionnaire administered by ACT). However, very few institutions survey the faculty they recruited, including those who declined offers. To better understand what may cause faculty being recruited to accept or reject an offer, IR should consider working with the provost's office to supplement periodically the data received from the hiring units with surveys of both faculty who accepted offers as well as faculty who rejected offers from the institution. This direct feedback will yield more in-depth information about why faculty accept or decline offers.

California State University (2006) provides an example of a survey used to collect data from recruited faculty. The survey gathered information across six domains: (1) reasons given for accepting an offer, (2) ratings of the recruiting process by respondents, (3) competing offers—salary of accepted offer compared to other offers received, (4) reasons given for declining an offer, (5) institution where the respondent who declined an offer will be working, and (6) difference in salary between accepted offer and declined offer. The data gathered through the "recruited faculty" survey allows IR to answer important recruitment questions such as these:

- What are the most important reasons cited by faculty who accept an offer from the institution?
- What do faculty think of recruitment processes at the institution?
- Were the interviews perceived as fair?
- Was the process timely?
- Were questions about compensation and benefits answered completely?
- What are the top reasons cited for individuals declining offers?
- How do average salaries differ between the accepted offer and other offers received?
- Where do faculty who declined an offer go?

The indicators discussed thus far measure the quantity of hires, not the quality. An additional level of detail could be added to the analysis of recruitment success by recording whether the hire was the "first," "second" or "third" choice candidate, as determined by the search committee. Again, such information should be collected via the SAR submitted to the EOP office for each faculty search. The NRC rank of the Ph.D. program completed by the new hire could be another crude indicator to gauge the quality of the faculty for those hired at junior ranks. For faculty who come in at the associate professor and professor rank, the national ranking of their former employer could serve as a proxy for quality. Finally, for those institutions that have implemented a strategic plan, it is important to be able to document how each hire relates to the institution's strategic goals and initiatives.

Analyzing Faculty Retention

The ability to recruit high caliber faculty is only one dimension of an institution's academic strength. Equally important to the future of an institution is its ability to retain faculty and allow their careers to flourish. Faculty turnover rates at major research universities vary from approximately 2 percent to 10 percent per year (Harrigan, 1999). Two-year colleges and smaller public institutions lose faculty at a slightly higher rate, and turnover rates are higher for women than for men. In the 2004–05 Higher Education Research Institute (HERI) faculty survey, one-third of respondents indicated that they had considered leaving academe for different jobs, and 28 percent received at least one firm offer. These findings suggest that the issue of faculty retention requires examination by IR professionals. Data on faculty retention typically originate from two sources: academic units and faculty.

Data from Academic Units

As with the issue of recruitment, current HR data systems at most institutions do not provide sufficient information to permit a thorough analysis of faculty departure. The reasons for faculty departure captured in HR databases frequently are too general to allow meaningful interpretation. As such, in addition to establishing data collection tools to examine recruitment success, IR offices should also design systems for collecting annual data on outside offers and the outcomes of faculty retention efforts. As with other faculty data, collecting retention data requires strong and visible support from the provost. Although the IR office may design the collection templates, the staff members in the provost's office are usually the ones collecting the data. Once the data are collected, the IR staff build the files and conduct the required analyses.

The template used by the University of Wisconsin-Madison (2009) provides a model for organizing such data collection efforts. The template collects information on both "preemptive" and "responsive" retention offers as well as cases in which no retention offer was made. "Responsive" retention offers are made to faculty who have received an actual outside offer, either orally or in writing, or are about to receive such an offer. Included in this category are also faculty members who the school wanted to retain but to whom it didn't actually make a counteroffer because the faculty member indicated they didn't want a counteroffer or because the outside offer was so attractive that it clearly could not be matched.

"Preemptive" retention offers are made to faculty who are "looking around." The schools do something explicitly to keep the faculty member (for example, increased salary, more space, a research assistant) even though they may not have received an actual offer or even gone for an interview. The distinction between responsive and preemptive offers may be difficult to identify in some cases, and the persons providing the annual data should be advised to use their best judgment when deciding on the type of offer. A third possibility, "no counteroffer," refers to cases in which the faculty member has an outside offer but the campus decides against making a counteroffer; these are individuals that the dean or chair did not want to retain or who were leaving for a career change (for example, to take an administrative or industry position elsewhere).

Once data on the institution's reaction to outside offers have been collected for a few years, the IR office can generate several valuable analyses. The main point to keep in mind is that there is no other place in the institution more appropriate than the IR office for assessing the institution-wide success of retention efforts, working with strong support from the provost's office.

EXHIBIT 10.1   TYPICAL QUESTIONS RELATED TO FACULTY RETENTION ANALYSIS

- What universities and colleges do we lose faculty to?
- Has the number of outside offers increased in the past three years? If so, in which fields? (An increase in the number of outside offers could signal the university leaders that they have to put together a larger number of retention packages, and this is expensive.)
- What percentage of faculty with outside offers have we successfully retained during the last academic year? Has this percentage declined over the past three years?
- Which fields appear to be most vulnerable in terms of low retention?
- Is compensation a major reason in faculty decisions to leave?
- What are the main non-financial reasons for faculty departure?

Although such information may be known within each department or school, it will remain highly fragmented at the university level unless the IR office takes the initiative to organize a centralized data collection system. Exhibit 10.1 presents a list of questions one could answer at the school and university level using the data gathered from academic units.

The reasons faculty members leave university or college employment before retirement can be grouped into two general categories: involuntary (fiscal emergency, did not earn tenure, dismissed for cause) and voluntary (dissatisfied with position, found better career opportunity, higher salary elsewhere). The retention analyses just discussed are limited to voluntary resignations caused by outside offers. However, a complete analysis of retention should include an examination of nonvoluntary departures—tenure denials, nonreappointments, nonrenewals, and retrenchments (see the California State University Report on Faculty Recruitment Survey, 2006).

Data from Faculty Members

As with recruitment analyses, asking faculty directly why they leave the institution can provide valuable information, particularly about personal reasons that might not be captured by the templates discussed earlier. In addition, exit surveys or interviews will give IR more comprehensive data regarding faculty opinions of the university, not only reasons for leaving. Many institutions conduct regular exit interviews or surveys of their departing faculty, and have established systematic processes for managing these efforts.

Once IR decides that learning directly from departing faculty is a worthy enterprise, staff must consider the relative advantages of interviews (with their potential for in-depth and open-ended discussion of factors in departure) versus surveys (with their potentially lower costs, more standardized indicators, and comprehensiveness). Although surveys may be the preferred approach for larger institutions, in campuses with only a handful of faculty leaving in any given year, survey data are likely to be skewed by individual cases (even if the data are aggregated over a number of years), and so interviews may prove to be a better alternative. Some institutions conduct both surveys and exit interviews.

For those considering surveys as a method of data collection, the exit survey used by Penn State (2009) provides a good example. Most exit surveys are sent only to tenured and tenure-track faculty, but that does not mean that IR should not consider surveying other employee groups. Also, some universities deploy the surveys on an ongoing basis—as faculty leave—whereas others choose to conduct periodic studies, focusing on faculty that left the institution within the past three years. An ongoing survey (while faculty members are still at the institution) may produce not only better response rates but also more accurate data. One useful analysis that IR staff could consider is a "gap" analysis, which compares perceived importance of various factors that influence faculty careers and satisfaction with these factors. The largest gaps indicate areas of "weaknesses" where intervention may be needed (see Table 10.2).

Although surveys let faculty provide feedback on their experiences anonymously, the exit interview report allows each departing faculty member to speak in detail and on the record. Although they involve more staff time and analysis effort, interviews can uncover the need for more personal attention and concern about faculty departure. Interviews can be conducted by faculty representatives or ombudsmen within each school, or they can be centralized and assigned to staff in the equal opportunity programs, human resources office, or provost's office. When the interviewing process is decentralized, the provost's office may consider requiring schools to use a standard set of questions so that the annual reporting of findings from various parts of the university can be accomplished by IR using a common format. Again, the process

TABLE 10.2　LARGEST GAPS BETWEEN IMPORTANCE AND SATISFACTION FOR INFLUENCES ON FACULTY CAREERS

Survey Item	Importance/ Satisfaction Gap
1. Sense of collegiality, inclusiveness, and shared decision making	2.07
2. University's commitment to your department or discipline	2.00
3. Balanced workload assignments for faculty in the department	1.91
4. University's commitment to your area of research	1.80
5. Effective departmental leadership	1.79
6. Healthy social climate within the department	1.72
7. Availability of time for research/scholarship, relative to other demands	1.71
8. Effective departmental management	1.67
9. Your annual salary	1.66
10. Fairness of review processes for annual merit increases	1.58

Source: Hearn, Jensen, & Gustafson (2001). Leaving the University of Minnesota: Results of an Exploratory Survey of Departed Faculty, 1997–2000, December 2001. Posted at: http://www1.umn.edu/usenate/scfa/exitsurveyreport .html. Reprinted with permission.

established by Penn State (2009) offers a good example of how a decentralized approach to faculty exit interviews might be implemented.

Regardless of the method IR chooses to collect feedback from departing faculty, staff should be aware that the information provided by this group may not describe the attitudes of retained, current faculty. Therefore it is important that the institution periodically conduct a satisfaction survey to gauge the faculty climate and intent to leave among faculty, as well as other employee populations.

Aside from hiring patterns, an important factor that may impact the representation of women faculty at the campus is the retention of tenured women. The institution's HR database should be used to determine the numbers of departures for male and female associate professors and full professors during a period covering at least three to five years. Usually the numbers of female full professors in many departments, particularly in science and engineering fields, are too small to provide a statistically meaningful analysis at the department level. The retention analysis should differentiate between retirement and nonretirement departures. Because most recent NSOPF data indicate that approximately 35 percent of full-time faculty across U.S. institutions are fifty-five years or older, a major part of faculty attrition within the next decade will be caused by retirements. And because the majority of faculty approaching retirement are men, it is important to build retirement projections that will estimate the male/female ratio assuming that new hires reflect national faculty availability ratios. The tricky part when projecting retirements is factoring in "phased" retirements, whereby some faculty may continue teaching one course or even maintain a research agenda for five to ten years after retirement. The following is a list of possible attrition-related questions IR might consider in designing an equity study:

1. Do tenured women leave the university at rates higher than their male peers?
2. Are men and women equally likely to experience a retention effort by the institution upon receipt of an outside offer?
3. After controlling for rank and number of years at the institution, are women less likely than men to receive an outside offer?
4. Are senior male and female faculty projected to retire at the same rates? What will faculty aging do to the male/female ratio in the next five years?

When interpreting the results of a retention analysis, one should keep in mind that a certain amount of turnover is necessary and healthy for any institution. Retirements and other terminations often create opportunities for needed changes in the focus of academic programs or development or expansion of new curricular areas. However, faculty replacement is expensive, so turnover above a certain threshold produces excessive costs to an institution. Furthermore, higher turnover rates, especially for women or minority faculty, may signal university problems with overall climate, salary equity, department leadership, poor mentoring, or the tenure process.

The methods presented in this section do not require complex statistical analysis. If time allows, IR should use logistic regression or survival analysis to estimate the probability of not being retained. Harrigan (1999) shows how to use survival analysis to model faculty retention behaviors. Those interested in examining faculty retention issues at the national level can use data from the National Study of Postsecondary Faculty (NSOPF) study. The Zhou and Volkwein (2004) article illustrates the use of logistic regression with NSOPF data to study the predictors of faculty intended departure.

Analyzing Promotion and Tenure Decisions

IR professionals may be asked by the provost's office to be actively engaged in analyzing and sharing data that can inform judgments about the effectiveness, rigor, and fairness of the tenure and promotion process. Again, the data collection responsibilities in this area rest with the provost's office. Here are some basic questions that IR could answer when analyzing faculty career progression:

- What percentage of new assistant professors achieve tenure? How does the tenure rate compare to peer institutions? What are the tenure success rates by discipline, gender, and minority status?
- What percentage of associate professors are promoted to professor within five years?
- How does the average time at the associate professor level vary by discipline, gender, and minority status?

Although the methodology employed to calculate tenure rates is fairly simple, creating a longitudinal database to allow such analysis could be a labor-intensive endeavor. The method requires tracking one or more cohorts of newly appointed assistant professors on tenure track appointments over a period of seven years or so. The tracking system IR designs will need to adjust the cohort for those faculty members whose tenure clock was stopped to provide elder or dependent care and those who switched to nontenure track appointments. Such tracking can be challenging, because HR databases at many campuses are not structured to allow longitudinal analysis of the faculty cohorts. In the absence of an HR data warehouse, IR will have to merge the initial cohort file with faculty files for each subsequent year to determine a faculty member's status, year by year.

Another potential challenge is that many institutions are unable to gather data regarding decisions affecting promotion and tenure at the level of the department and/or school; their data reflect only those files that reach the provost's office. However, an accurate assessment of the outcomes of tenure track hires requires information about all cases, including those that do not formally reach the provost's office. With support from the provost's office,

TABLE 10.3 SAMPLE TEMPLATE FOR TRACKING TENURE/PROMOTION DENIALS

Faculty Name	School	Dept	Rank	Review Type (mark with "X")			Review Date	The decision not to proceed with promotion/ tenure was taken at: (mark with "X")	
				Promotion	Tenure	Third Year or Other Pre-tenure Review		Dept Level	Dean's Level
John Smart	Arts & Science	Sociology	Assistant Professor		X		9/15/2011	X	

IR professionals should work with the deans to establish a systematic data collection system at the level of department and school. A possible data collection template is shown in Table 10.3.

IR can also conduct multivariate analysis to identify significant predictors of tenure for new assistant professors and promotion to professor for associate professors at various points in time, both across cohorts and for each cohort. Knight and Zhang (2005) illustrate the use of these techniques at Bowling Green State University to estimate retention, tenure, and promotion rates. They used gender, ethnicity, and college affiliation as independent variables. Harrigan (1999) employs survival analysis to estimate the probabilities of promotion to tenure separately for men and women. Becker and Toutkoushian (2003) employ a probit model designed to explain whether a faculty member is a full or associate professor. Their set of independent variables includes experience, three variables for highest degree (bachelor's, master's, and doctorate), years of seniority, citations to publications, days of nonprofessional leave, college affiliation, and gender. Also, Perna (2001) uses logistic regression and data from the National Study of Postsecondary Faculty to explore sources of the lower representation of women and minorities among tenured than among tenure track faculty and among full professors than among lower ranking faculty. One of the most frequent uses of multivariate analysis is in studies of equity in promotion and tenure decisions. Institutional researchers should resist the temptation to conduct equity studies of tenure or promotion decisions if measures of faculty productivity are not available. Colleagues' votes are influenced most by the candidate's productivity in teaching, research, and service, rather than by their sex, highest degree, and length of service. Ignoring this reality may invite irrational policy making—or even litigation. As Dooris and Guidos (2006) note, data on tenure success rates or time in rank that would enable interinstitutional comparisons are rarely available. In the absence of a standard multi-institution survey, IR professionals should seek comparative data by approaching colleagues at peer institutions directly. They should be aware, however, that tenure rates vary by discipline, so they should avoid making comparisons among institutions that differ markedly in the mix of disciplines. As Harrigan (1999) notes, at the University of Wisconsin-Madison, only about 50 percent of the assistant professors in the social sciences achieve tenure, compared to about 70 percent in the physical sciences.

Projecting Retirements

With the recent "graying of the faculty," the number and rate of faculty retirements have become areas of increasing concern to many higher education institutions. Across all institutional types in the United States, 36 percent of all full-time and part-time faculty members are at least fifty-five years old. As Table 10.4 shows, half of all tenured faculty members at four-year institutions are at least fifty-five years old.

Although most faculty members will retire around the age of sixty-five, the more healthy, academically successful, and better-paid faculty are likely to remain employed until the age of seventy. The numbers presented in Table 10.4 suggest that in order to be prepared for the significant wave of retirements in the next decade, institutions need to build projections of faculty retirements into their hiring plans.

TABLE 10.4   AGE DISTRIBUTION FOR FULL-TIME FACULTY AT FOUR-YEAR INSTITUTIONS, 2003

Age	Not on Tenure Track/No Tenure System	On Tenure Track	Tenured
<35 years	15.6	18.3	0.3
35–44 years	29.1	47.0	13.3
45–54 years	31.4	23.9	35.9
55–64 years	20.1	9.6	39.6
65–69 years	2.7	1.1	7.9
70+ years	1.2	0.2	3.0

Source: U.S. Department of Education, National Center for Education Statistics, 2004.

TABLE 10.5 PROJECTED PROPORTIONS OF FACULTY: RETIRED AND ELIGIBLE TO RETIRE

FY	Number of Faculty Retired	Average Age	Number of Faculty Eligible to Retire	Retired Faculty as a Percentage of Those Eligible to Retire
FY06	21	63.2	245	8.6%
FY07	25	63.4	296	8.4%
FY08	26	68.1	312	8.3%
FY09	28	66.3	340	8.2%
FY10	30	66.5	376	8.0%
Overall	**26**	**65.5**	**314**	**8.3%**

At a minimum, projections of faculty retirements should be based on past retirement patterns and the age and other eligibility conditions of the current faculty (see analysis reported by Huhn, 2003). Preferably, these estimations should be done for each college or school and department. The first step in this analysis is determining the average retirement rate for the preceding five years. In the example in Table 10.5, only 8.3 percent of faculty eligible to retire have retired over the past five years. Next, the average retirement rate is multiplied by the size of the cohort of eligible faculty in each projection year.

The data projections in the table are descriptive; if the goal is to understand what factors explain retirement decisions, then more complex estimations, such as logistic regression models, are needed. Harrigan's model (1997) for the University of Wisconsin retirements includes the following variables: age, years as a faculty member, whether the individual held a UW position prior to the faculty appointment, divisional committee affiliation, school or college, race, gender, rank, department size, whether the faculty member held a terminal degree, and the ratio of the individual's salary to average faculty salary. Perhaps additional data reflecting teaching loads, research activity, and scholarly productivity would produce an even more robust model.

Aside from preparing projections of future retirements, IR professionals may be called on to measure faculty interest and participation in early retirement incentives and/or phased retirement programs. Surveying faculty on these issues could provide valuable information leading to more accurate retirement projections and estimates of savings from participation in such programs.

Although the methods discussed thus far to project or explain retirement decisions involve the use of institutional data, there are studies that examine these issues at the national level using National Study of Postsecondary Faculty (NSOPF) data. Conley (2004) illustrates the use of NSOPF 1999 data to explore retirement issues for faculty at two-year colleges.

Projecting Number of Hires, Salary Outlays, and Faculty Mix

The large number of retirements expected to occur over the next decade will create both challenges and opportunities for colleges and universities in recruiting new faculty members. The major challenge is that one has to begin planning for a market in which, nationally, other colleges and universities also are going to be competitively recruiting to replace retiring faculty. A compounding problem is that colleges and universities will face increased competition from other professional career fields available to new Ph.D. graduates, particularly from industry, and even from the government. There is evidence—especially in biomedical and life sciences, health sciences, and engineering fields—that graduates pursue academic careers less often in recent years than they have in the past. Additionally, federal, state, and even local governments increasingly hire environmental scientists, social scientists, survey researchers, and demographers, among others, to conduct research on policies and programs.

The implications of increasing competition and turnover can be devastating for an institution if it does not plan carefully in advance for necessary replacement hires. A sizeable wave of retirements within a short period of time, for instance, can create excessive costs. In addition to the costs of the actual search, there are often costs associated with hiring temporary replacements until a faculty position can be filled. The costs of hiring a new scientist at a research university can exceed a half million dollars for laboratory equipment, space, and funding for graduate assistants as part of a start-up package.

Even more important than the budgetary impact is the realization that both the strength and the reputation of academic programs can drop significantly if most of their senior faculty retire within a short period of time. It is evident that deans and department chairs need to be informed about retirement projections and budgetary implications so that they can plan accordingly for course offerings, space, and salaries.

When estimating the number of new hires, institutions should consider in their projections not only the number of faculty needed to replace those who retire or leave but also the number needed to meet new enrollment demands. These projections have implications for search committees, too. The actual number of searches can be estimated based on past recruitment success rates and the expected number of hires.

To estimate the impact of new hires, voluntary resignations, and retirements on salary outlays, IR professionals can use faculty flow modeling, as illustrated by Kelly (1998). The basic models typically use simulations in Microsoft Excel spreadsheets and provide multiyear projections of the number of faculty and anticipated attrition and replacement hires. The cost estimate model described by Kelly allows testing of a number of different scenarios by varying parameters, such as retirement rates for ages fifty-five through seventy, termination rates by years of service, age distribution of newly hired faculty, average starting salary, and promotion rates. For instance, one could model the cost savings to the institution as a result of higher retirement rates for faculty aged fifty-five to sixty-four to determine the effect of early retirement programs.

Although Kelly's model aims to estimate a future salary structure, faculty flow models can also be used to estimate the effect of policies on faculty mix by rank, tenure status, gender, ethnicity/race, and age. Using faculty flow modeling, questions such as the following can be asked:

1. How will the mix of faculty demographics (such as gender ratio, age, race or ethnicity, and rank) be affected by the upcoming wave of retirements?
2. What will the ratio of tenure to nontenure track positions look like ten years from now if the number of nontenure track hires increases each year by 5 percent?
3. What effect would varying promotion rates have on faculty turnover? Alternatively, is there a statistical connection between departmental promotion rates and turnover?
4. How many years will it take the institution to achieve gender parity in the representation of women among tenured and tenure track faculty?

Assessing Faculty Job Satisfaction

At many institutions, faculty satisfaction is often unknown until a professor chooses to leave a position in search of a better setting for his or her professional work and personal situation. Faculty members' satisfaction—and, implicitly, their decisions to stay or leave—are influenced by a variety of factors. Without conducting periodical studies of current faculty satisfaction, an institution's leaders most likely will not understand the causes of attrition.

Although exit interviews or surveys of former faculty can reveal sources of faculty dissatisfaction for those who left, typically they will not reveal much about the satisfaction of retained faculty. The opinions of former faculty may not characterize the opinions of current faculty. A former faculty member's views might be influenced by a sense of nostalgia, feelings of regret, or a need to justify his or her decision. Regularly assessing the current faculty climate is more valuable to organizational intelligence.

IR can design its own survey or choose to participate in one of the national studies of faculty such as the HERI Faculty Survey or the Collaborative on Academic Careers in Higher Education (COACHE) Survey of Pre-Tenure Faculty. The NSOPF surveys also collect data on satisfaction, but they are designed to be nationally representative and draw on only a small sample of faculty from each institution. The small institutional sample is not representative for individual institutions. Of course, participation in a national survey will enable IR to compare job satisfaction at the institution to national

EXHIBIT 10.2   CORRELATES OF JOB SATISFACTION

- Interactions with and support from the institution's administration
- Department's overall climate (such as positive interactions with colleagues, teamwork, and perceived sense of community)
- Salary and benefits
- Recognition for one's work
- Autonomy and perceived control over one's career
- Sense of accomplishment with one's work and professional growth
- Workload and time constraints
- Adequate and equitable access to campus resources

benchmarks. If IR decides to develop its own questionnaire, it should aim to be as comprehensive as possible and include possible correlates of job satisfaction. Research shows that faculty job satisfaction is influenced by the factors, listed in Exhibit 10.2, among others.

Regarding the last factor listed in Exhibit 10.2, past studies have included resources such as secretarial and office support, technical support, library services, support for teaching, quality of graduate assistants, support for research activities in general, and support for professional development. The typical faculty satisfaction questionnaire asks a question about overall satisfaction with the employing institution and separate questions for the factors that are believed to influence overall satisfaction. Some institutions also include questions related to workloads (total hours worked per week) and sources of stress. In the 2004–05 Faculty HERI Survey (Lindholm, Szelenyi, Hurtado, & Korn, 2005), faculty cited the following as important sources of stress: lack of personal time (73.8 percent), managing household responsibilities (73.5 percent), institutional procedures and red tape (68.5 percent), tenure- and promotion-review process (44.4 percent), physical health (51.4 percent), care of an elderly parent (32.9 percent), and child care (29.5 percent). Once IR has gathered faculty satisfaction data through either a locally developed or a national survey, there are several useful reports to consider in addition to producing a simple frequency distribution of responses.

Strengths and Weaknesses

Senior administrators find this type of reporting extremely useful because it identifies areas for immediate intervention. Assuming that the satisfaction-related questions use a five-item Likert scale, IR could group the findings into the following three categories:

1. *Strengths to Build On* are areas in which a substantial majority of the faculty report themselves highly satisfied (that is, 60 percent or more with ratings of 4 or 5).

2. *Issues to be Mindful Of* are those in which the majority of the respondents judged themselves satisfied or better, but a significant minority of respondents reported being less than satisfied (that is, 25 to 39 percent with ratings of 1 or 2).

3. *Areas That Need Improvement* are those in which a significant fraction of the faculty were dissatisfied (that is, over 40 percent with ratings of 1 or 2).

Differences in Satisfaction Levels Across Subpopulations

Women and minorities tend to express less satisfaction with certain aspects of their work than do white men. Analyzing HERI data, Lindholm et al. (2005) found that women are less satisfied than men with their teaching loads, salaries and benefits, opportunities for advancement, and opportunities for scholarly pursuits. Institutional researchers should test whether the same differences can be observed in their institution's data. If the institution participates in COACHE or HERI, it will receive a report that presents the results separately for men and women.

Correlates of Satisfaction

To identify the factors that contribute most to faculty job satisfaction at an institution, IR professionals will need to conduct a multiple regression analysis. A strong correlation between overall satisfaction with being a faculty member and specific aspects of the work environment would suggest that those domains are particularly important to pay attention to. Separate regression equations could be run for men and women to determine whether the correlates of faculty satisfaction vary by gender. Those interested in developing a model of job satisfaction will find the Zhou and Volkwein (2004) study extremely valuable. Chapter 29 provides a detailed discussion of measuring opinion and behavior.

References

Becker, W. E., & Toutkoushian, R. K. (2003). Measuring gender bias in the salaries of tenured faculty members. In R. K. Toutkoushian (Ed.), *Unresolved issues in conducting gender equity studies* (pp. 5–20). New Directions for Institutional Research, no. 117. San Francisco: Jossey-Bass.

California State University. (2006). Report on faculty recruitment survey. Retrieved from http://www.calstate.edu/HR/FacRecSurvRep05.pdf

Conley, V. M. (2004, May 30–June 2). Exploring faculty retirement issues in public 2-year institutions. Presented at the annual meeting of the Association for Institutional Research, Boston, MA.

Dooris, M. J., & Guidos, M. (2006, May). Tenure achievement rates at research universities. Presentation at the Annual Forum of the Association for Institutional Research Chicago, IL.

Harrigan, M. (1997). Faculty retirement issues at UW-Madison. Retrieved from http://apa.wisc.edu/facultyretirements.htm

Harrigan, M. (1999, May 30–June 2). An analysis of faculty turnover at the University of Wisconsin-Madison. Paper presented at the 39th Annual AIR Forum, Seattle, WA.

Hearn, J. C., Jensen, S. K., & Gustafson, K. L. (2001, December). Leaving the University of Minnesota: Results of an exploratory survey of departed faculty, 1997–2000. Retrieved from http://www1.umn.edu/usenate/scfa/exitsurveyreport.html

Huhn, C. (2003). UW-Madison faculty retirement patterns and projections: Faculty retirements from October 1990 through September 2002. Retrieved from http://apa.wisc.edu/FacultyRetirement/FacultyRetirementProjections_2003.pdf

Kelly, W. (1998). Studying faculty flows using an interactive spreadsheet model. *AIR Professional File* (69). Retrieved from http://www.airweb.org/page.asp?page=73&apppage=85&id=69

Knight, W. E., & Zhang, R. W. (2005). Developing and using a faculty flow model. Presented at the Association for Institutional Research Forum, San Diego, CA. Retrieved from http://www.bgsu.edu/downloads/finance/file31713.pdf

Lindholm, J. A., Szelenyi, K., Hurtado, S., & Korn, W. S. (2005). *The American college teacher: National norms for the 2004–05 HERI faculty survey.* Los Angeles: Higher Education Research Institute, UCLA. Retrieved from http://www.gseis.ucla.edu/heri/PDFs/ACT-Research%20Brief.pdf

Penn State University. (2009). Faculty exit survey and exit interviews for department faculty members. Retrieved from http://www.psu.edu/vpaa/exitinterview.htm

Perna, L. W. (2001). Sex and race differences in faculty tenure and promotion. *Research in Higher Education, 42*(5), 541–567.

University of Wisconsin-Madison. (2009). Faculty hiring and retention. Retrieved from http://apa.wisc.edu/faculty_hire.html

U.S. Department of Education. National Center for Education Statistics. (2004). National Study of Postsecondary Faculty, 2004 Data Analysis System. Washington, DC: National Center for Education Statistics. Retrieved from http://www.nces.ed.gov/DAS/

Zhou, Y., & Volkwein, F. (2004). Examining the influences on faculty departure intentions: A comparison of tenured and nontenured faculty at research universities using NSOPF-99. *Research in Higher Education, 45*(2), 139–176.

CHAPTER 11

INSTITUTIONAL PLANNING AND RESOURCE MANAGEMENT

Michael J. Dooris and Jerome S. Rackoff

The introduction to this volume makes an important point: that colleges and universities expect institutional research to link with other key organizational processes such as assessment, program evaluation, quality improvement, and accreditation. To that end, institutional research can and should connect with planning and budgeting.

Institutional Research, Planning, and Budgeting

In a 1999 volume of the journal *New Directions for Institutional Research*, Patrick Terenzini wrote "On the Nature of Institutional Research and the Skills It Requires." He offered a view of institutional research as "organizational intelligence"—construing IR "to refer to the data gathered about an institution, to their analysis and transformation into information, and to the insight and informed sense of the organization that a competent institutional researcher brings to the interpretation of that information" (p. 23).

Terenzini laid out three tiers of organizational intelligence-*cum*-IR, introduced in Chapter 2 of this *Handbook*. Tier one is *technical and analytic intelligence*, encompassing factual information and methods that provide the basic building blocks of defining, counting, and measuring. That category includes computer skills such as database management, familiarity with data coding structures and conventions, and the use of software applications. Tier two is *issues intelligence*, which involves knowledge of the substantive problems (say, developing budgets or evaluating programs) to which tier one information can be brought to bear. Tier three is *contextual intelligence*—knowledge of higher education in general and of the particular college or university where the IR practitioner works.

Tier three adds to tiers one and two skills that Terenzini calls "organizational savvy"—enabling prudent and intelligent application of technical knowledge to locally pertinent versions of more general issues and developments (such as external economic, political, and demographic changes). It is this third tier of skills—which allows institutional researchers to have the most pronounced impact on institutional effectiveness—that is most directly relevant to this chapter.

All three of Terenzini's tiers matter, of course, because the contextual use of information assumes that data are accurate and accessible. The point here is that, although institutional researchers usually do not have specific responsibility or authority for institutional budgeting per se, IR is inextricably bound together with informed planning and decision making. Thanks to the growing power of enterprise information systems and business intelligence tools, the tier three aspects of IR are even more germane now than when Terenzini introduced the concept in 1999.

Conceptions of Strategic Management

A college or university constantly shapes itself through decisions about hiring faculty and staff, recruiting students, building and renovating facilities, adding or eliminating programs and services, setting tuition, establishing salary levels, and upgrading the information technology infrastructure.

Most such choices involve the allocation of scarce resources—time, money, facilities, and people—among competing demands. Alternatives may be selected carefully or casually, deliberately or nonchalantly, by design or by coincidence, but choices must be made. The field of economics studies the allocation of scarce resources among competing demands; we find that conception to be one helpful way to think about planning and budgeting.

John Bryson (1995) defined *strategic planning* as a disciplined effort to produce fundamental decisions and actions that shape and guide what an organization is, what it does, and why it does it. That too is a useful definition.

In the business literature, a distinction is often made between strategic *planning* and strategic *management*. The idea is that strategic management is more encompassing than just planning, because it links strategy formulation, implementation and evaluation, adaptation, and goal achievement. That definitional divide is less distinct in the non-profit and higher education sectors (think of the ubiquitous term *planning and budgeting* in colleges and universities), and in this chapter we mostly use the terms interchangeably. Reducing both notions to their essence, we suggest that one idea—*intentionality*—lies at the heart of strategic planning and management.

Strategic management can be done well. It can also be done poorly. The late George Keller is informally recognized as the father of planning in higher education; both the *New York Times* and *Change* magazine named Keller's

1983 book *Academic Strategy: The Management Revolution in American Higher Education*—which eventually went through seven printings—as the most influential higher education book of that decade. In a typically thoughtful essay, Keller in 1997 posed an implicit challenge to anyone who would see himself or herself as a strategic planner in a college or university. Keller observed that the standard management-guru advice on how to effect change is to involve everyone and create buy-in, thereby ensuring that consensus for change will "magically" emerge. Keller argued, "That no such process has ever resulted in a major change at any university, or is likely to ever do so, does not prevent the proponents of this theory from continuing to advocate it often and with astonishing confidence" (Keller, 1997, p. 18).

Keller's argument, as he made clear in the rest of his article, was not that institutional planning is worthless, but that it needs to be approached intelligently, and that it means different things in different institutions, or in different parts of a given institution. In short, there is no one magic formula for successful planning and resource management, but lessons from experience can help college and university leaders to intentionally and systematically shape decision making and enhance mission attainment.

Multiple Institutions, Multiple Contexts

Over the past three decades, thinking about planning and resource management in higher education has clearly become increasingly sophisticated. One aspect of this has been recognition of the limits of cookie-cutter methodologies, and movement away from planning per se and toward management approaches that enable creativity and tough decision making (Rowley & Sherman, 2001; Keller, 1999–2000). Higher education planning needs to challenge assumptions and catalyze radical change to existing structures and processes; to have real value, it must lead to action.

The authors' own backgrounds are rooted in different higher education sectors and mostly in two quite different institutions: Penn State University, a huge multi-campus public research university, and Bucknell University, a selective private liberal arts college. Our varied perspectives have illuminated two shared assumptions that we have incorporated into this chapter: (1) each college or university is unique, and (2) mission, history, culture, and institutional context matter.

It is useful to understand and appreciate the experiences of other colleges and universities, and the strengths, weaknesses, successes, and failures of various management approaches. On the strategic planning dimension, a 2004 *New Directions in Institutional Research* monograph presents planning experiences in such diverse settings as Los Angeles City College, Villanova University, Carroll Community College, the University of Wisconsin-Madison, and the school of medicine at Northwestern University (Dooris, Kelley, & Trainer, 2004).

On the resource allocation dimension, *Prioritizing Academic Programs and Services* includes institutional examples from the University of Saint Francis, Drake University, and Seattle Central Community College, along with cross-sectional information from the Association of Governing Boards, the Carnegie Foundation for the Advancement of Teaching, and the National Center for Education Statistics (Dickeson, 2010). In this chapter, we draw on our understanding of all of these institutions as well as our decades of personal experiences at Bucknell and Penn State.

Reflecting on this variety of institutional types and cultures, we are struck not only by their differences, but also by some of the commonalities in the nature of the problems they face, and the tools at their disposal.

Setting Priorities, Making Choices

As this chapter is written, in 2011, higher education faces a remarkably difficult environment of converging challenges. Broad economic turmoil is accompanied by shifting demographics, rising costs of operation, a changing competitive landscape, erosion of states' willingness or ability to provide operating support, pressures for accountability, and national and state efforts to boost college completion rates and educational attainment—while shifting the burden of paying for higher education from society to students and families.

It may be discomfiting for those of us in the academy to admit, but some of our institutions' choices have probably exacerbated the external pressures and challenges. In the years leading up to the recession of 2008, colleges and universities hurt themselves to the extent that they took on risky investments; relied excessively on endowment income; overbuilt facilities, thanks to the availability of cheap credit; positioned themselves clumsily in relation to other social-political priorities (such as health care, K–12 education, and jobs); allowed the undisciplined proliferation of programs at the expense of core competencies; overcommitted optimistically projected income streams to capital projects and operating expenses; and failed to optimize faculty workloads.

The point is that colleges and universities have some control over their own destinies. In good times and bad, planning, evaluation, and resource allocation should center on vision, mission, and values. Planning and budgeting, poorly conceived and executed, can exacerbate problems. Done well, they can keep an institution attuned to the realities of the external environment and help it to evolve and improve, to become more efficient, effective, and responsive. Indeed, according to Rumelt (2011), "A strategy is a way through a difficulty, an approach to overcoming an obstacle, a response to a challenge."

Institutions can use data to inform decision making. They can align budgeting with planning, use technology wisely, and commit to doing fewer things well rather than doing many things expensively and poorly. IR that helps build organizational intelligence can make a key contribution to the important job of strategic management. That job is, more than ever, being recognized as *setting priorities, making smart choices,* and *selectively allocating resources* based on those priorities.

From Planning to Action

Little genius is required to write lofty mission or vision statements or to come up with a list of impressive-sounding goals. In our experience, the key difference between ineffective and effective planning most often lies in whether plans are implemented. Change occurs when plans break high-level goals into specific action steps, delineate individual responsibilities, and clearly define timelines and performance metrics.

Action Strategies and Responsibilities. Any list of goals takes on a more realistic tone if accompanied by clearly defined assigned actions and responsibilities. For example, a college could operationalize an abstract goal such as "enhancing student success" by specifying that "Outcomes assessment will be strengthened. Every academic program will have defined learning outcomes in place by [a given date], with assessment procedures operational one year later. The dean for academic affairs is assigned primary leadership and reporting responsibility." Reports might be required on an annual or semi-annual basis. Or a university might make a goal such as "Use technology to enhance access and opportunities" more concrete by specifying that "Online offerings will be expanded. The goal is to achieve [specified targets] for online enrollments, numbers of courses offered, and numbers of degrees awarded over each of the next five years. The vice president for continuing education is assigned primary leadership and reporting responsibility, with the council of deans and the faculty senate in supporting roles."

Strategic Review of Academic Programs

To illustrate how this can work in practice, let us walk through a hypothetical case that will probably be relevant to many if not most colleges and universities.

A typical higher education strategic plan might contain five to ten goals. We suggest that any goal should be accompanied by a handful of action strategies—perhaps three to five. A responsibility matrix might thus include 30 or so action strategies. It would name the individual, usually at the vice president level, responsible for leading each action. The responsibility matrix would also define respective timelines, along with one or two high-level performance metrics (such as financial impact, enrollment counts, or other appropriate indicators, depending on the nature of the action strategy). The responsibility matrix would also mandate progress reports (probably to the office of the president) on each action at specified dates.

For illustrative purposes, let's focus on an academic quality goal that many colleges or universities, irrespective of institutional type, would include in their strategic plans.

To wit: Penn State is a public land-grant research university that enrolls 96,000 students and has an operating budget in excess of $4 billion. Bucknell is a highly selective private liberal arts college that enrolls 3,600 students and has an operating budget of $180 million. Despite such marked differences, one of Penn State's seven strategic goals—to "advance academic and research excellence"—is very similar to one of Bucknell's five goals—namely, to "strengthen the academic core."

It is not a stretch to posit that a hypothetical institution would have a similar goal—say, to "enhance academic excellence." Let's illustrate how tough-minded, intentional strategic planning and resource management could contribute toward achievement of this goal.

As already stated, effective planning and resource management must help in *setting priorities, making smart choices,* and *selectively allocating resources* based on those priorities. The driving idea is that if our hypothetical college or university wishes to enhance academic excellence, it must do so by intelligently redirecting resources from weaker programs and redundant or less valuable activities toward academic programs with the potential to be stronger and more closely aligned with institutional mission, vision, and goals.

Action Strategy, Responsibility, and Impact

One action strategy to advance progress toward the goal of enhancing academic excellence could be defined as "conducting efficient, effective, and focused reviews of all academic degree programs. The desired end is to maximize academic potential, reduce redundancy, and free resources to support greater academic excellence and enable new strategic investments." For this action, it's likely that the institution's chief academic officer would be identified as having primary responsibility. A realistic timeline, perhaps eighteen months, would need to be defined, along with some performance target. That metric would vary greatly depending on the institutional context, but it might involve some specific, permanently budgeted amount that could be redirected as the result of the review.

An important part of leadership's responsibility for any action strategy would, of course, be creating a mechanism and organizing the key players. For this particular action strategy, it is likely that the chief academic officer would rely on a small committee of some sort—perhaps an existing planning committee, or perhaps an ad hoc, high-level academic review council convened expressly for this task.

A Role for Institutional Research

In the scenario described here, the message should be that all activities are on the table. Thus, first-cut screening data, applied to *all* academic programs, can identify those in need of further, in-depth analysis. Clearly, no decisions would be based solely on screening data alone. But when every program is placed under the same lens and evaluated according to the same metrics, some compelling and sometimes startling insights are likely.

Compiling and interpreting such data will draw heavily on institutional research expertise and capabilities. Because most colleges and universities have never before embarked on this sort of comprehensive academic program review, a rigorous, data-based evaluation may well require new analyses of program efficiency and effectiveness.

A practical way to organize the data aspects of such a review is by academic unit (school or department) and by program (degrees in various majors). Obviously, the specifics will vary by institution, but institutional researchers probably would compile, at a minimum, data more or less as follows:

Department level screening data:

> Faculty counts
>
> Student credit hours per faculty member
>
> Cost per student credit hour
>
> Organized research $ per faculty member

Academic program screening data:

> Student enrollments (five-year trends)
>
> Degrees awarded (five-year trends)
>
> Entering student test scores (SAT, GRE, and so on)
>
> Percentage of under-enrolled courses
>
> Course section sizes
>
> Operating budget (for the department)
>
> As appropriate, rankings (such as NRC) and/or benchmarks (such as size, structure, and trends of competing programs)

The Review and Recommendation Process

The chief academic officer and his or her review council could examine data such as these to get some tentative sense of where the likely targets for reorganization or consolidation might lie. Institutional researchers almost certainly would play an important role in this phase of the review. The need to clarify definitions and interpretation will inevitably arise, along with additional data-oriented questions. Ideally, the IR office would provide staff support to the review council.

Results of the initial screening would be shared with deans and other senior administrators. Recommendations would need to be developed through a back-and-forth process, allowing knowledgeable stakeholders to participate and further inform ultimate decisions about programs in which the institution should selectively invest and disinvest.

The hypothetical model just described draws heavily from Penn State's experience with an extensive change-oriented review of academic programs and administrative undertaken in 2010 and 2011. Details are available online (Penn State, 2011).

College and University Budgeting

Budgeting is the realization of planning. Implicitly or explicitly, budgeting enacts strategy, and strategy brings life to budgeting.

It is easy to parrot language about not reinventing the wheel, balancing centralization and decentralization, not working at cross-purposes, eliminating overlap and duplication, and so on. There is often truth to such generalizations, but unless based on solid information, they become vacuous. Institutional researchers' ability to strengthen planning and resource allocation will be much greater if they can move beyond clichés. Institutional researchers should develop a substantive understanding of budgeting concepts and principles, knowledge of how to interpret relevant program and performance information, and a genuine appreciation of the ways in which budgeting works at their institutions.

We like two higher education budgeting books in particular, and we recommend both to colleagues. Goldstein's *College & University Budgeting* (2005) covers well the nuts and bolts of budget processes, terminology, and definitions. Dickeson's *Prioritizing Academic Programs and Services* (2010) suggests approaches for setting priorities and reallocating budgets. We have also seen a prepublication draft of what promises to be another excellent budgeting primer, directed at planners, from the Society for College and University Planning (Rylee, in press).

Any institutional researcher with responsibilities that touch on strategic management should understand basic concepts such as what fund accounting is and how it differs from business accounting; the distinction between operating budgets and capital budgets; the definition and uses of general funds, restricted funds, auxiliary enterprises, contingency and reserve funds, and endowment funds; and ways to integrate planning across these various types of budgets.

Space does not permit exploration of these topics in this chapter, but we emphasize the need to connect planning in different spheres—academic programs, student affairs, enrollments, information technology, interdisciplinary research, diversity, and facilities. Although capital budgeting is distinct from operational budgeting, strategic management should be and can be connected to both. Otherwise (to pose an obvious hypothetical difficulty), campuses might begin creating programs and admitting students that existing infrastructure and staffing could not support.

Budget Planning Is a Balancing Act. Conceptually, the rationale for linking strategic planning with budget planning is that resources are limited and choices must be made. Pragmatically, it can be helpful to explicitly state—in writing—the major tradeoffs involved in building a budget. This provides a useful reference point for central administrative leadership, and it also can be a frank reminder to faculty, staff, and other stakeholders of the difficult choices that budgeting entails. A concise presentation of this balancing act might build around a few main points (supplemented with appropriate dollar and/or percentage figures), such as these:

- Holding tuition increases to the lowest feasible level
- Remaining competitive in faculty and staff salaries
- Paying for unavoidable increases in health care, fuel and utilities, and maintenance
- Setting aside funds for targeted strategic initiatives

Planning and Resource Allocation: Lessons of Experience

In the sixteenth century, Niccolò Machiavelli (ca. 1513/1964) wrote, "There is nothing more difficult to carry out nor more doubtful of success nor more dangerous to manage than to introduce a new system of things; for the introducer has as his enemies all those who benefit from the old system, and lukewarm defenders in all those who would benefit from the new system" (pp. 43–45).

It's Still a People Problem

Since Machiavelli's day there has of course been a torrent of books, videos, articles, websites, and consultants offering advice on how to facilitate organizational change. Literature reviews make clear that many of the propositions for how to lead strategic change and improvement are not research-based and have not been conclusively validated. Organizational behavior scholars Bolman and Deal (2003) have warned that "leadership is a word that has risen above normal workaday usage as a conveyor of meaning and has become a kind of incantation" (p. 336), and they warn against thinking that there is any magic formula or single prescription (pp. 336–340). Simplistic thinking about strategic management may be *too* simplistic. The challenge is not trivial, but there are useful principles and helpful lessons to be gained from experience.

There is no substitute for judgment, attention to context and culture, leadership, and sustained work and attention over time. Not only is every college, university, school, or department unique; higher education itself is, in many respects, an especially challenging culture. We will return to matters of community and collegiality, but here we emphasize one simple fact: colleges and universities are people-intensive enterprises. At both Penn State and Bucknell, about 70 percent of the education and general (E&G) budgets go toward salaries and benefits. Thus decisions to change programs are really decisions to change people's lives. Naïve approaches that are not sensitive to this reality are unlikely to result in happy long-term outcomes for anyone. It is necessary to organize planning efforts well, identify opinion leaders early and engage them in the process, formulate key messages and ideas, and concisely represent those messages for presentation in ways that people around the institution can understand and support.

Institutions Can't Be All Things to All People

No college or university has sufficient resources to do everything well. Trying to be the best at everything is neither cost-effective for individual institutions nor beneficial for the higher education enterprise writ large. According to the planning language that the institutional research office has introduced at Bucknell University, institutions should aim to be "distinctive and distinguished." They should seek to identify capacities that distinguish them in the marketplace and pursue strategies that will make them recognized leaders in those endeavors. In short, educational institutions must make critical choices about their market strategy and the services they can best provide for particular groups of students.

Across-the-Board Cuts Lead to Mediocrity

Adverse economic situations require difficult campus decisions and hard choices to achieve balanced budgets. The easy solution to this problem—across-the-board budget cuts—is likely to take away funds equally from programs that are distinguished and those that are not, and from programs that are strong revenue generators and those that are not profitable. The probable long-term outcome from that approach is mediocrity.

The more difficult path—reallocating dollars strategically—can allow an institution to advance critical objectives and even make gains in spite of constraints and challenges. Fundamentally, this involves privileging certain budgets that are pivotal to the advancement of clearly defined institutional strategic goals. Even in times of institutional growth overall, certain budgets should receive higher rates of increase than the overall budget increment.

Create Strong Resource Allocation Tools Before They Are Needed

Sound resource allocations rest on well-conceived fiscal policies—and such policies are best developed and/or updated *before* a pressing need is widely recognized. Strategic planning should help anticipate categories of events that can impact institutional finances and prepare thoughtful policies and guidelines when heads are cool. This truism applies equally well to situations that are challenging to the organization and those that present enticing opportunities.

In the first category—challenges—it is helpful to have clear guidelines for budget cutting in anticipation of austerity. What is the institutional perspective on staff positions? What strategic budgets will be protected? What principles will be applied in the decision-making process? Is there an institutional policy on debt financing? Under what conditions, and with what limits, will additional debt be incurred? What is the capacity for additional debt, before Moody's ratings will be downgraded? It is much more stressful to respond to these questions at the time of a crisis than it is to address them deliberatively through normal governance processes.

In the second category—opportunities—suppose that, for example, a declining real estate market offers favorable opportunities for purchasing properties adjoining the campus. What guidance does the board provide on such acquisitions, and what principles will be followed in deciding what constitutes a wise purchase? Unusual offers of big-ticket gifts-in-kind also present challenging questions for a higher education institution. Should a gift of a racehorse be accepted? A yacht? A piece of former industrial property? What are the costs to the institution of holding such assets until they can be sold? What are the liabilities? Does the industrial property have a buried gasoline tank that will require expensive environmental remediation? These are fundamental questions of risk management—a collective issue that requires ongoing awareness and careful attention from both the board and the administration.

Planning to Plan

Considerable background work may be needed to prepare a campus for a new strategic planning process. The challenge is to develop a robust common understanding of foundational planning issues that promote engaged and informed community participation. At the initiation of Bucknell's last planning process in January 2005, this preparation took the form of a preplanning document, prepared by the Office of Planning & Institutional Research and distributed to the entire campus community. The contents of that document included:

- A *common vocabulary for planning*. The diversity of planning terminology and usage—goals, objectives, tactics, outcomes, and so on—demands a clear set of definitions to guide public discussions from the outset.
- An *environmental scan*. An analysis of the factors in the current external environment that can strongly influence the efforts of the institution to achieve its strategic goals. Individual environmental factors may be threats or opportunities—or sometimes both. Such analyses are often structured into broad categories of factors, such as governmental/regulatory, economic/financial, demographics (student, faculty, and staff), technological, social, and the like. One of the most salient aspects of an institution's external environment is the set (or sets) of institutions with which it competes for students, faculty, financial resources, and prestige in the marketplace.

- A reminder and/or revision of the school's *official peer group*, and a commitment to hold that peer group constant for the duration of the planning period. It is impossible to gauge progress in achieving plan goals if the peer group is continuously changing.

- A reminder of the institutions that are the *most prominent competitors*. Although this list may overlap the peer group, it is a set that is not really determined by the institution. It is defined by the realities of the marketplace; for an institution such as Bucknell, key competitors are those institutions with the greatest overlap in applications and in offers of admissions, those that prospective students say they prefer in head-to-head comparisons, and those that have greater win rates with competing admissions offers. Unlike the peer group, this competitive set *can* change during the planning period, and win rates may be appropriate metrics to gauge the progress of the strategic plan.

- A review and analysis of *peer strategic plans*. Typically available on institutional websites, peer plans are a rich resource for evaluating current and emerging competitive threats and opportunities. What are the goals of competitors' plans? To what extent do they overlap the direction of your own institution? What are the competitors *not* doing that is within the range of your institution's competencies? What market niche are the competitors targeting, and what groups are they seeking to serve?

- A review of *best practice in the development of strategic plans*. Looking beyond the plans of the peer group and competitors, what institutions have planning documents that represent the state of the art? What are the characteristics of such plans? How many goals are established? What are the major categories of goals? How are such plans named, framed, and structured? What plans best capture a reader's imagination, and why?

- Finally, a review of any *previous or ongoing planning processes*. What is the base on which the proposed new planning process will rest? What goals already have broad acceptance by the community? What unmet goals or needs carry over from the last planning process? What focused planning efforts, recently completed, can be incorporated into an institution-wide strategic planning process? Plans build on a foundation of prior planning. Synthesizing these aspects of institutional planning history prepares the community to respect and learn from the past while focusing attention on the future.

Import-Export Model: The Orienting Role of the Environment

It is common in biology to liken the nucleus of a single cell to the brain of a higher organism. However, cell biologist Bruce Lipton has made the controversial assertion that it is not the nucleus (or the genes, which are housed within the nucleus), but the cell membrane that is the real "brain" of the cell (Lipton, 2008). It is this membrane that senses its external environment, mediates the exchange of information and material into or out of the cell, and allows it to react adaptively to positive and negative stimuli.

Imagine a similar boundary separating educational institutions from their external environments. Outside this boundary lies an external world awash in a sea of information and populated by a variety of resources (students, money, technology, and so on) and processes that can either assist or impede the institution. As with a single cell, the survival and prosperity of an educational institution depend on the effectiveness of the systems it has established to discriminate and capture (import) that which is useful and avoid that which is harmful. As with the single cell, such information allows the organization to react adaptively to its environment.

As Figure 11.1 suggests, educational institutions do not simply respond to their environment; they also have the capacity to act on and change the environment to their advantage. They do so through their decisions about what to *export* across the institutional boundary into the external world. Most commonly, what is exported is information. This information may be highly structured and objective and even mandated, as in Integrated Postsecondary Education Data System (IPEDS) submissions or Higher Education Act disclosures. On the other hand, the information may be very subjective and nuanced, and designed to associate the institution with particular images, values, or feelings. In this category, one might consider public relations material, admission brochures, and institutional websites. Hybrids of these two categories are also possible, as with purportedly objective net revenue calculators, which, though mandated, can be framed in ways that present an institution in the most favorable light possible. Such informational exports aim to influence the educational environment to attract more resources to the institution (more and better students, talented faculty, institutional prestige, higher grant revenues, and the like). One must also remember that one of the most vital exports of an educational institution is its annual production of satisfied graduates. This growing population also changes the external environment of the organization by attracting greater gift revenues, volunteer support, admissions referrals, and general improvement in institutional prestige via the careers and personal successes of graduates.

The external boundary of an educational institution is normally porous; it tends to be very open to the two-way passage of data and materials. This characteristic is essential to the educational aims of promoting dialogue and teaching diverse perspectives. Yet there are times when it is crucial to keep certain information in, and times when other information must be kept out. Policies rating the sensitivity of different categories of institutional information typically determine what information resides on the external website (open to the public), what information is available only to members of the academic community on an intranet, and what information is restricted (legally or otherwise) on a need-to-know basis. Similar restrictions are necessary for inputs; institutions employ technology and institute policies to eliminate spam from mail systems and bar solicitors from campuses.

The message again is that this interface should be *intentionally* managed in a planned, comprehensive, and collaborative way by those offices that have

FIGURE 11.1   IMPORT-EXPORT MODEL: THE ORIENTING ROLE OF THE ENVIRONMENT

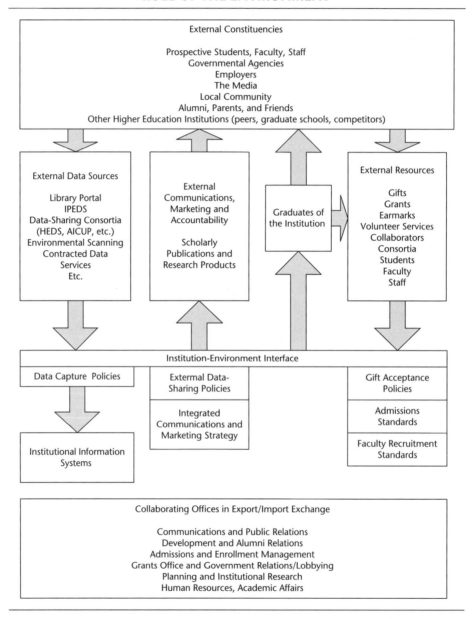

the primary responsibility for "import" and "export" functions: institutional research, admissions, public relations and communications (including those responsible for institutional websites), development and alumni relations, sponsored research, and other functions such as lobbying. As with all other institutional processes, these import and export plans should be driven by institutional strategic goals.

Never Waste a Crisis

As this chapter is written, it appears that higher education should be bracing for tough years ahead. It should be apparent to all faculty, staff, students, and other stakeholders that it is not enough to muddle along and survive one tough, but temporary, crisis. External challenges can clarify the need for intentional, action-oriented planning that is meaningfully connected to resource allocations, for tough choices, and for strong leadership.

Benchmarking Budget Allocations

Chapter 36 of this *Handbook* addresses the topics of benchmarking and peer groups; it is not necessary to revisit these in great detail here. However, one aspect of benchmarking that is often overlooked, and that is especially relevant to this chapter, pertains directly to budgeting.

Even in effective institutions, all parties want assurance that the allocation of financial resources across divisions (academic affairs versus student affairs, for example) falls within the normal range of variation for peer institutions. Analyzing data for a carefully selected peer group can be very instructive, but it is fraught with problems of interpretation. IPEDS financial data alone does not provide sufficient detail for accurate comparisons. Audited financial reports provide a richer picture of institutional practices, particularly if one pays careful attention to the footnotes. Institutional practice can be particularly varied and idiosyncratic, for example, in the location of athletic expenditures and in the handling of auxiliary enterprises.

Focusing on a Limited Number of Goals

Effective strategic management requires organizational focus—that is, concentrating on a few (usually no more than a half dozen or so) strategic goals. Such focus is critical for two reasons.

First, in effective organizations, individuals in all divisions and at all levels must remember and understand shared goals and be clear about their roles in fulfilling them. Most people cannot retain more than five or six goals in their minds at one time, so focused plans contribute to campus-wide buy-in and engagement in plan implementation.

Second, with large numbers of institutional goals, it is impossible to optimize all of them at the same time. If thirty goals have been publicly endorsed, will an institution decide (and justify to its constituents) that some goals are of higher priority than others? Large numbers of goals thus have an effect opposite from the one intended in strategic planning: they complicate rather than facilitate institutional resource allocation decisions. Even with a few goals, priority setting is difficult, but it is at least easier and more transparent than when too many goals are included.

Integrated Planning

It makes sense to connect various dimensions of planning and resource management. Changes in academic programs, athletics, facilities, information technology, enrollments, diversity, and so on all obviously impact on one another. Integrated planning can happen in different ways and across several dimensions. In this section we offer some ideas based on real-world practices that can be adopted, adapted, or both.

Integrated Vertical Hierarchy of Goals. Institution-level goals often can and should be vertically mapped to goals and objectives at lower levels of the organization (college, division, department, or program). This is best done by developing unit action plans—plans that define the initiatives that the unit will undertake to contribute to the advancement of specific strategic goals of the organization. Bucknell structures two broadly defined sets of goals in parallel. One concerns educational outcomes; the other deals with administrative goals. Both are derived from and consistent with Bucknell's mission and strategic direction.

Institutional goal statements should be framed in fairly broad terms, while referring to operational initiatives. The selection of tactics is thus a critical activity for a college or university, and it requires a disciplined review process. At Bucknell, proposals for strategic actions must be accompanied by a completed business plan, including the identification of funding sources, clearly defined outcomes or success measures, and a plan for assessing the achievement of outcomes.

Funding strategies for new strategic initiatives or tactics include a menu of support options:

- Current operating funds
- Reallocation of current operating funds
- New funds, raised either in comprehensive alumni fund drives or through grant proposals
- Self-funding, with an appropriate project structure
- Partnerships with other entities, such as government or the local community
- Outsourcing (as with residence halls built by outside investors)
- Debt financing

Clarity of funding strategies assists in the process of tactical review and approval, and it promotes collaboration between budgeting and advancement functions.

Integrated Financial Models. It is insufficient to develop a balanced budget for the coming year alone. Strategic management is driven by a longer time horizon needed to achieve ambitious institutional goals. Multiyear financial projections are essential, and they should help decision makers discriminate between different decision scenarios in their full complexity. Typically, this requires input from multiple models maintained by different offices—enrollment models, financial aid models, endowment models, residence hall models, and so on. Some of these may be run out of the enterprise software system of the institution, but others, particularly at smaller institutions, may exist on the hard drives of particular staff members outside of the college or university's finance office.

It is cumbersome and labor-intensive to get such diverse models to work together in an analysis of alternate resource allocation scenarios. At Bucknell, integrated financial modeling software (FuturePerfect, from the PFM Group) provides a powerful tool for bringing together these diverse components of financial planning and generating instantaneous answers—the net revenue consequences—to complex financial modeling scenarios.

Useful Techniques

Institutional researchers are often called on to participate in or facilitate strategic planning activities at their respective colleges or universities. There are several tools that we have found to be especially helpful. These include:

- SWOT analysis (strengths, weaknesses, opportunities, and threats)
- Nominal group technique and affinity diagrams (two brainstorming techniques)
- SMART language (an acronym for *specific, measurable, achievable, results-oriented,* and *time-bound,* which can help when writing strategic goals)
- Responsibility matrixes (a tool to keep track of who has responsibility for what, and when)
- Goal attainment teams (successfully employed at Villanova and elsewhere to engage stakeholders in shaping and realizing a vision)

These and other useful techniques and resources have been concisely summarized by Trainer (2004).

Implications and Conclusion

We began this chapter with the notion of *intentionality.* We return to that idea now. Especially in complex institutions, major organizational activities should be synchronized in order to fuse intuition and creativity with information and disciplined decision making, and to move the organization intelligently toward desired ends. As Mintzberg wrote more than a decade ago in what remains one of the landmark works on strategic management, "The outcome of strategic thinking is an integrated perspective of the enterprise" (1994, p. 108).

Connecting Planning, Assessment, Improvement, and Resource Allocation

The values, mission, vision, and goals of a college or university (and of schools, departments, and administrative units) should lie at the intersection of planning and budgeting, which are most usefully viewed not as ends in themselves but as catalysts that can support and enable the achievement of mission. Thus planning and resource allocation should be ongoing and continuously linked to each other and to other major management processes such as professional development, hiring and promotion decisions, marketing, IT and facilities planning, and accreditation.

Participative Processes and the Soft Side of Strategic Management

The phrase "influence without authority" (from Cohen and Bradford's 2005 book by that name) captures a fundamental challenge of leadership and shared governance in higher education. An organizational trait not unique to colleges and universities, but one that is nonetheless noteworthy, is that often leaders attempt to gain influence over people and situations that they do not control. This is a culture that prizes collegiality, shared governance, academic freedom, disciplinary norms, professional autonomy, and the marketplace of ideas. Consensus often must be built on a foundation of extensive institutional conversations, and leaders must be able to package goals into a vision that is viewed as legitimate, responsive, and exciting (or at least acceptable) to the broad community. Change processes should respect organizational history, reflect institutional values, and address what are perceived as the needs and collective ambitions of the community. Across all constituencies, vision statements should help people to answer *both* "What's in it for me?" and "What is in the best interest of the organization?"

To those experienced in corporate planning, the shared governance path to strategic planning in higher education may appear cumbersome. However, this discounts the extraordinary power of a process that, when properly conceived and executed, can draw on a broad and deep pool of collective wisdom and mobilize the minds, hearts, and energies of an entire community.

The need to nurture support does not end with the production of a strategic plan. As a plan is translated into action, decisions must be transparent and be perceived broadly as legitimate and rational. A communications plan should define ongoing approaches that will be employed to inform campus and external audiences of progress toward shared goals and to sustain their ongoing support and commitment.

Plan Implementation

The mantra for success in real estate—location, location, location—has a powerful analog in planning: execution, execution, execution. Successful planning is a process, not a document. The commitment of energy must continue, and probably expand dramatically, after a plan is completed, as messages reverberate throughout the organization in a succession of unit plans and the selection of supportable initiatives to achieve institutional goals. As the reach of planning grows, so too does the challenge of tracking and monitoring the success of myriad initiatives and of evaluating the extent to which overall goals have been achieved.

Because one of the principal challenges in strategic management is the assignment of line responsibility for tracking overall implementation of the plan, after Bucknell's most recent strategic plan was approved in 2006, the University created a new position: director of strategy implementation. One of the director's first tasks was to create a database to record and track the hundreds of strategic plan tactics that had been proposed by members of the Bucknell community. This resource was posted publicly for the campus community on the intra-university website. A tactical review committee evaluated and classified each proposal based on criteria made publicly available to the campus community.

Strategic Management and Transformative Change

In this chapter we have tried to concisely present pragmatic and realistic ideas about how institutional researchers and other college or university leaders can usefully approach planning and resource management. Reflecting on the material presented, and distilling the lessons of our own experience, we conclude that when done well, strategic planning and resource management can help a college, university, school, department, or administrative unit to define itself and carry out its mission more efficiently and more effectively.

In some cases this may mean protecting existing strengths; in others it may involve embarking on positive transformative change. In either case, the result can be a culture that Schwartz (1996, p. 235) so aptly described as "living in a permanent strategic conversation." In this conception, very human abilities and aspirations—to explicitly define goals, to deliberately and realistically consider alternatives, to challenge ourselves, to innovate, to solve problems, to act purposefully, and to create—live at the core of institutional planning and resource management.

References

Bolman, L. G., & Deal, T. E. (2003). *Reframing organizations: Artistry, choice, and leadership.* San Francisco: Jossey-Bass.

Bryson, J. (1995). *Strategic planning for public and nonprofit organizations.* San Francisco: Jossey-Bass.

Cohen, A., & Bradford, D. (2005). *Influence without authority* (2nd ed.). Hoboken, NJ: Wiley.

Dickeson, R. C. (2010). *Prioritizing academic programs and services.* San Franciso: John Wiley & Sons.

Dooris, M. J., Kelley, J. M., & Trainer, J. E. (Eds.). (2004, Fall). *Successful strategic planning.* New Directions for Institutional Research, no. 123. San Francisco: Jossey-Bass.

Goldstein, L. (2005). *College & university budgeting.* Washington, DC: National Association of College and University Business Officers.

Keller, G. (1983). *Academic strategy: The management revolution in American higher education.* Baltimore: Johns Hopkins University Press.

Keller, G. (1997). Planning, decisions, and human nature. *Planning for Higher Education, 26*(2), 18–23.

Keller, G. (1999–2000). The emerging third stage in higher education planning. *Planning for Higher Education, 28*(2), 1–7.

Lipton, B. (2008). *The biology of belief.* Carlsbad, CA: Hay House.

Machiavelli, N. (1964). *The prince* (M. Musa, Trans.). New York: St. Martin's Press. (Original work published ca. 1513)

Mintzberg, H. (1994). The fall and rise of strategic planning. *Harvard Business Review, 72*(1), 107–114.

Penn State. (2011). Academic and administrative services review core council. Retrieved from http://www.psu.edu/president/cqi/strategic_planning/corecouncil/index.html

Rowley, D. J., & Sherman, H. (2001). *From strategy to change: Implementing the plan in higher education.* San Francisco: Jossey-Bass.

Rumelt, R. (2011). The perils of bad strategy. *McKinsey Quarterly.* Retrieved from http://www.mckinseyquarterly.com/article_print.aspx?L2=21&L3=37&ar=2826

Rylee, C. (Ed.). (In press). *Integrated resource and budget planning at colleges and universities.* Ann Arbor, MI: Society for College and University Planning.

Schwartz, P. (1996). *The art of the long view.* New York: Doubleday Division, Bantam Doubleday Dell Publishing Group.

Terenzini, P. T. (1999). *On the nature of institutional research and the knowledge it requires.* New Directions for Institutional Research, no. 104. San Francisco: Jossey-Bass.

Trainer, J. F. (2004, Fall). Models and tools for strategic planning. In M. J. Dooris, J. M. Kelley, & J. E. Trainer (Eds.), *Successful strategic planning* (pp. 129–138). New Directions for Institutional Research, no. 123. San Francisco: Jossey-Bass.

CHAPTER 12

BUILDING COST MODELS

John Milam and Paul Brinkman

It is often assumed that anyone can build a cost model, if the question at hand is understood and the appropriate data are gathered. Although this is sometimes the case, the reader is warned that the process of building cost models is more complicated than it may seem at first glance. Fortunately, there is an extensive knowledge base dealing with cost models, particularly those that address the cost of instruction. This chapter presents an introduction to the literature, research, methodologies, and data structures for building cost models. Instructional cost models are discussed in greater detail, because they are likely topics of interest to institutional researchers.

Why build cost models? There are at least five major reasons. First, cost analyses can be the basis for an institution's request for funding. Notable examples are many state funding formulas and the cost analyses that are fundamental to the A-21 negotiations that determine indirect cost recovery rates for research universities. Second, institutional administrators may use cost analyses as the basis for allocating resources—for example, to one program versus another. Third, an institution or a funder (primarily states) may be interested in achieving greater efficiencies. Understanding the costs of an outcome or a process is foundational to crafting strategies to reduce costs. Fourth, the public can become concerned over the prices charged by higher education institutions, which may lead to an examination of supplier costs. Finally, someone may simply be interested in knowing what the costs are, have been, or will be, under various circumstances, as when economists look to test a theory.

Who conducts cost studies? Within institutions, cost studies are typically conducted by offices for budget, institutional research, data and information technology systems, academic affairs or planning and policy, financial aid, and sponsored research. Topics include instructional costs, the indirect costs of conducting research, academic program costs, program delivery costs, and various administrative activity costs. External consultants may focus on facilities, information technology, benefits plans, branch campuses, financial aid, utilities, changes in enrollment, and bond financing or debt service. Economists examine costs more often than not to determine their behavior, for example, when output increases or decreases.

In a study addressing state capacity for cost studies, Milam, Coutts, Bosacco, Golliday, and Simpson (2008) found that only half of the states conduct them. For those that do, a variety of topics are covered, including capital projects, new construction, and renovation; creating a new degree program or major; space utilization; increasing or decreasing enrollment; financial aid planning; implementing new software; and hospitals. Although states may or may not conduct cost studies themselves, many state resource allocation models are based on underlying cost data at the institutional level. The recent Four-State Cost Study (Conger, Bell, & Stanley, 2009) undertaken by the State Higher Education Executive Officers (SHEEO) reflects the interest on the part of that influential organization in costs and cost containment from a state perspective.

Higher education costs are of interest nationally as well, as reflected in the work of special commissions such as the congressionally mandated three-year Study of College Costs and Prices by the National Center for Education Statistics (National Center for Education Statistics, 2001) and the secretary of education's Commission on the Future of Higher Education (Dickeson, 2006). A similar, non-federal effort is the National Association of College and University Business Officers (2002) Explaining College Costs: NACUBO's Methodology for Identifying the Costs of Delivering Undergraduate Education.

More recently, the Delta Project on Postsecondary Education Costs, Productivity, and Accountability reports on Trends in College Spending (Wellman, Desrochers, Lenthan, Kirshstein, Hurlburt, & Honegger, 2009), using the metrics of revenue and expense categories per student FTE. Subsidy patterns reflect differences in institutional mission and help address broad questions such as "who pays, and who benefits from higher education—as well as the balance of financial responsibility among a student, an institution, and a state" (Delta Project, 2009, p. 2).

Few of these national studies involve cost models per se, although there is much information about the factors and drivers that may be included in such models. Reindl (2000) provides an overview and assessment of several of these studies. McPherson and Shulenburger (2010) and Wellman (2010) reflect on some of the assumptions and findings of these studies. Increases in tuition, along with the ongoing confusion between prices charged and supplier costs, virtually guarantees continued national interest in those costs. A case in point is the congressional enactment in 2008 of the Higher Education Opportunity Act, which requires higher education institutions with large increases in tuition and fees to develop cost containment strategies.

The Basics: Types of Cost Models and Types of Cost

In common parlance, the term *cost* is used freely, often without recognition of the nuances and subtleties that surround the term in more analytical contexts. In reality, the term has many meanings, or at any rate there are many types of cost. It is important, then, when undertaking a cost study to begin by carefully determining the question or questions to be addressed. As noted in the New Millennium Project on Higher Education Costs, Pricing, and Productivity, "costs are complicated and there is an internal incentive structure that leads institutions to avoid being clear about them. There are several subsets to this overarching problem, including issues of measurement, audience, and culture" (Institute for Higher Education Policy, 2000, p. 7).

Once the question or purpose of the study is agreed on, the analyst is then in a position to select an appropriate type of cost model. Brinkman and Allen (1986) catalog five types of studies based on the work of Carlson (1976); also see Witmer (1972). The first type consists of studies that simply provide cost calculations, using some form of statistics, but with "no attempt to relate variables statistically." An example is cost per credit hour across departments. Most cost studies are of this nature.

A second set of cost studies "statistically estimate average behavior between two or more cost-related variables" using some type of regression analysis. Most of these studies try to understand "how average or marginal costs behave in response to changes in enrollment or credit-hour production" (Brinkman & Allen, 1986, p. 2); that is, *scale economies.* A few address the question of whether products, such as undergraduate and graduate education or graduate education and research, can be produced more cheaply jointly than separately; that is, *scope economies.* Cohn, Rhine, and Santos (1989) and Dundar and Lewis (1995) examine both scale and scope. See Toutkoushian (1999) and Brinkman (1990, 2000, 2006) for demonstrations and overviews of how these studies, which typically estimate an econometric cost model known as the "cost function," can be useful for institutional research. The studies can be particularly helpful when seeking advice about the likely behavior of costs when institutions are contemplating major changes in the number of students they enroll or in their mission, such as adding graduate programs or developing research capabilities. (See also the discussion of cost and quantity of output in the later section on Factors and Drivers in Cost Models.)

A third type of study, admittedly quite rare, focuses on efficient behavior. In this approach, techniques such as data envelopment analysis, a form of linear programming, or constrained residuals regression are used to compute a convex hull; that is, fitting a line or plane around a scatter of points (see, for example, Carlson 1975; Sperry, 1995). One would think that these efforts to locate the "efficient frontier" would appear more frequently in an era of increasingly scarce resources and a focus on efficiency. A likely impediment is the difficulty inherent in adequately defining and measuring output as well as controlling for qualitative differences among production units.

In contrast to the first three procedures, which take an accounting or a statistical approach to cost estimation, a fourth type features an engineering methodology, which "consists of modeling a production process by decomposing the process to a very basic level and then studying alternative ways of putting the pieces back together to achieve alternative ends" (Brinkman & Allen, 1986, p. 3). Among these simulation modeling studies, also known as "constructed" cost models, the analysis of liberal arts education by Bowen and Douglass (1971) is perhaps the best-known example, examining how production relationships in class size, mode of instruction, and other factors impact costs. A familiar example is the difference in costs per student between construct one, wherein one professor teaches a large class of hundreds of students with the help of teaching assistants who lead discussion sections, and construct two, wherein a cadre of professors teaches the same material but in classes of thirty students each. Gonyea's (1978) study of medical education costs is another example, as is Massy and Wilger's (1998) relatively early analysis of the various ways in which technology can affect the cost of instruction, now a matter of concern for virtually all colleges and universities. (See the later section on Cost Models for Technology.)

Finally, in a fifth type of model, the analyst combines accounting and engineering approaches to focus on three categories of cost drivers: "volume of the activity, environment within which the activity is carried out, and decisions that might affect the cost of the activity" (Brinkman & Allen, 1986, p. 3). As the volume of activity changes, costs can be affected by changes in the proportion of inputs to outputs. Examples of environmental factors affecting costs are inflation in the price of inputs and regulations regarding the use of hazardous materials. Among many decisions affecting costs, the use of part-time rather than full-time faculty is an obvious example. Additional examples, along with further elaboration on the methodology, can be found in Robinson, Ray, and Turk (1977).

Based on Adams et al. (1978), Brinkman and Allen (1986) delineate seven ways to define costs: (1) cost objectives (input, output, activity, organizational unit); (2) cost basis (historical, projected, standard, imputed, replacement); (3) cost assignability (direct, indirect, full); (4) cost variability (fixed, variable, semi-variable); (5) cost-activity relationship (total, average, marginal); (6) cost-determination method (specific service, continuous service); and (7) cost-time relationship (time period, accrual or cash, deflated). Some combination of these alternatives will be featured in any cost model. One frequent combination is historical full costs of an activity such as instruction, typically focusing on average costs over an academic year. (See Chapter 11 for more discussion on budgets and costing.)

Focus on Cost Accounting Procedures to Determine Instructional Costs

This section focuses on instructional costs as determined through various cost accounting procedures. It is helpful to take a historical view, going back several decades. Over that period, although individual scholars contributed to the cumulative knowledge base, two organizations have played a major role— the National Association of College and University Business Officers (NACUBO) and the National Center for Higher Education Management Systems (NCHEMS). Their efforts provide a framework for the discussion that follows.

National Association of College and University Business Officers (NACUBO). Meisinger (1994) and Jenny (1996) detail the NACUBO approach to cost accounting, with its focus on determining the full cost of academic programs and disciplines, using various schemes to allocate costs to objectives such as instruction, and incorporating a three-tiered approach. Tier one includes all direct costs for a specific cost center or cost objective of interest. The second tier adds indirect costs that can be attributed to the same cost center or objective, related to support services and other forms of overhead such as administration. The third tier builds in assignable depreciation or use charges for facilities and capital equipment. In building a model with this approach, five basic steps are taken: (1) specify the objective or cost center, (2) determine the categories of information, (3) assign tier one costs, (4) assign tier two and three costs, and (5) calculate the output measure or unit cost.

One of the aims of the NACUBO Cost of College Project was to present "a simple methodology to explain college costs" (National Association of College and University Business Officers, 2002, p. 16). The principles of the methodology are as follows: use basic averaging techniques, focus on undergraduate costs, use accepted allocation methods, and attempt simplicity. Various data issues are addressed, including the definition of price, calculations of student FTE, weighting of graduate education, departmental research, institutional and community costs, financial aid, and facilities and capital costs. Further complexities are identified as a result of accounting practices and governance structures. The data collection template "identifies three categories of expenditures: instruction and student services, institutional and community costs, and undergraduate financial aid costs. Under each category, the cost per undergraduate is recorded for the various expense items and then subtotaled . . ." with an optional section on facilities capital costs (National Association of College and University Business Officers, 2002, p. 25).

National Center for Higher Education Management Systems (NCHEMS). The NCHEMS cost of instruction model, developed in conjunction with NACUBO, is detailed in NCHEMS (1977) and NCHEMS-NACUBO (1980) and discussed by many others. The NCHEMS model "received substantial publicity, evaluation, and, in many states, acceptance as the costing system that most effectively minimizes methodological differences" (California Postsecondary Education Commission, 1980, p. 5).

The NCHEMS cost of instruction model is based on the premise that all administrative information systems are essentially built on the same data structures (Hample, 1980). Typically, cost of instruction models incorporate data on student enrollment, courses, faculty, space utilization or room inventory, financial aid, and finances. These and other data structures originate in the 1971 NCHEMS Data Element Dictionary and are documented in 1996 and 2004 editions of the Consortium for Higher Education Software Services (CHESS) Data Definitions for Colleges and Universities, published by NCHEMS (Thomas, 2004).

Built when the mainframe computer first made possible the complex simulation of resources, the NCHEMS Resource Requirements Prediction Model (RRPM) was designed to help planners estimate budgets based on enrollment and to model the impact of institutional policies (Gamso, 1977). The Educom Financial Planning Model (EFPM) was completed in 1978 and continued to evolve, with funding from the Lilly Foundation (Heterick, 1998). EFPM let users "build and operate budget models through a question and answer routine that requires no computer sophistication"; by 1981 it was used by over 120 institutions (U.S. Office of Technology Assessment, 1982).

For a Delta Cost Project white paper, Johnson (2009) asks "What does a college degree cost?" and outlines five methodologies: (1) catalog cost, (2) transcript cost, (3) full cost attribution, (4) regression-based cost estimates, and (5) student's cost of a degree (p. 5). Data for these come from the IPEDS finance categories of expenses and are allocated by student credit hour, based on the level of instruction and two-digit Classification of Instructional Programs (CIP) Code discipline. Average expenses per credit by level and discipline are used to construct the estimated catalog versus transcript total for a degree program. The full cost attribution calculation tries to be sensitive to productivity measures with both the number of majors and degree recipients, providing insight into the cost of attrition and transfer behavior. The "out-of-pocket" and "net economic" cost to students are calculated, using net tuition and fees, expenses, room and board, and forgone wages. These methods move away from the use of more sophisticated allocation schemes, faculty workload data, discipline-level expenditures, facilities use or opportunity costs, and the consumption and contribution relationships of majors and departments that are part of other evolving models; instead, they promote the use of standardized IPEDS derived variables about finance to higher levels of institutional comparison.

Activity-based costing (ABC) in higher education involves identifying activities and costs at an activity level rather than at a unit level, then reengineering processes and concepts for more efficient planning and management of funds (National Association of College and University Business Officers, 2004; Cox, Smith, & Downey, 2000). Both ABC and other process approaches to costing are based on the realization that traditional accounting structures typically focus on costs within a particular budget center. Understanding process costs can be the basis for reengineering to achieve greater efficiencies. For examples, see Coopers & Lybrand & Barbara S. Shafer & Associates (1995).

Factors and Drivers in Cost Models

Generally speaking, there are two very different types of cost drivers. One type involves factors that are external to the instructional process itself such as the tendency of people to identify price with quality, the benefits of a college education, mores and expectations within the higher education community, and the quest for prestige and improvement in rankings—all of which influence the resources available to higher education overall, individual institutions, and individual departments and programs (for example, see Bowen, 1980). The other type, the focus of the remainder of this chapter, involves factors internal to the instructional process (for example, see Hoenack, 1990).

There are just three key drivers of cost in the instructional process itself: inputs, input prices, and the relationship between inputs and outputs (the production technology). For example, direct instructional cost per student is heavily influenced by faculty workload, faculty compensation, compensation for departmental support staff, and class size. As Jones (2000) argues, there are some variables that explain institutional costs better than others, especially data on "human assets—the number of employees of various kinds, compensation levels, and their utilization" (p. 82).

Not surprisingly, there is a significant amount of research on faculty workload, including sample survey data such as the NCES National Study of Postsecondary Faculty (NSOPF), which provides benchmarks on faculty activity (Abraham et al., 2002). Although faculty workload can be focused entirely on one activity, it is often spread across multiple activities, including instruction, research or other scholarly activities, and service. In the case of multiple activities, it is important to attribute only a portion of faculty salaries to the cost of any one of those activities. This task of apportioning salaries (and sometimes related support costs as well) can be daunting, especially when joint production is present (for example, when graduate instruction and research occur together), but it needs to be done or assigned costs will be inflated. Workload is central to ABC models, which rely to some degree on time tracking to document the true expenditures of human esources. Workload is a central component in the NCES Study of College Costs and Prices, which uses national survey data to "identify those factors that are associated with the variation in direct instructional costs between and across academic disciplines, and to identify those cost factors that are tied to the magnitude of instructional expenditures in a given discipline" (Middaugh, Graham, & Shahid, 2003, p. 7). McLaughlin, Fendley, Winstead, Montgomery, & Smith (1983) and Seybert and Rossol (2010) provide additional context for cost differences by discipline. Simpson and Sperber (1984) focus on variations in the use of tenured or tenure track faculty from an opportunity cost perspective.

Faculty compensation has two components: earnings of regular, full-time faculty and the ratio of full-time to part-time faculty, as both pay rates and labor substitution strategies make a difference in costs (for example, see Seybert & Rossol, 2010). Some equipment costs may be treated as a direct cost of instruction, but most will likely be treated as indirect costs.

If full costs rather than just direct costs of instruction are the objective, the analyst will have to choose which indirect costs to include and the method for doing so. Indirect costs related to administration, libraries, and operation and maintenance of the plant are typically included. Standard allocation procedures have been set forth by NACUBO (Hyatt, 1983). An alternative proposed by Winston (2000) allocates the cost of space by treating it as an opportunity cost, calculated as the revenue forgone by not renting the same amount of space. The determination of full costs is a critical component of responsibility center management (RCM). Useful discussions of the cost allocation procedures underlying RCM can be found in Whalen (1991) and Curry and Strauss (2002). Looking to the future, it is safe to assume that technology costs will loom ever larger as a component of the full cost of instruction; more on this in the next section.

Another cost driver is the relationship between cost and the quantity of output. This relationship has long been of interest to economists, especially in regard to the possibility of economies of scale. See Brinkman and Leslie (1986) for a review of research findings on scale economies in higher education. The most direct approach to examining the cost-quantity relationship is embedded in the concept of marginal cost; that is, the change in total cost accompanying an additional unit of output. Although knowing what marginal costs are in a given situation can be helpful for a variety of management decisions, marginal costs are not as readily accessible as are average costs. Indeed, it is fair to say that marginal costs cannot be calculated directly; they can only be estimated. Allen and Brinkman (1983) compare the strengths and weaknesses of alternative approaches to estimating marginal costs.

Toutkoushian's (1999) article on the utility of cost functions for institutional research is a good example of how to estimate the marginal costs of instruction in the standard econometric fashion, which entails estimating a cost function using some form of multiple regression analysis. As is typically true for such statistical techniques, lots of data points are required. Options with respect to the form of the cost function, which directly affects how the estimated marginal cost coefficients are allowed to behave, need to be considered carefully.

Although a researcher could attempt to calculate directly the relationship between small changes in the quantity of output and changes in total costs, there is little likelihood that such changes will behave in a theoretically consistent manner (Allen & Brinkman, 1983). In the microcosm of a single program, for example, total costs could as easily go down or up not so much in response to, but in association with, a change in one unit of production, such as an additional student taught. Short-term swings in cost per student or per credit hour are particularly susceptible to changes in revenue.

Another way to examine the cost-output quantity relationship is to determine whether, as the quantity of output changes, all costs are variable or some are fixed. If any costs happen to be fixed, then scale economies are likely. Brinkman notes, "As production increases, only the variable portion of total cost increases, which means that average total cost will decrease over some range of increased output in most circumstances. If all costs are fixed, then marginal cost will be zero. When some costs are variable, average variable costs can be used as an estimate of marginal cost across some portion of the range of output" (2006, p. 52). Whether a particular cost is fixed or variable, however, may be subject to interpretation and even negotiation. A good example of the latter would be a negotiation between a department chair and a faculty member regarding a class-size limit.

Cost Models for Technology

There are interesting variations in the methodologies used for the study of technology costs and potential cost savings through the use of technology. This is to be expected as different technologies tend to have different cost structures.

Sponsored research efforts have contributed to this effort, including those of the Carnegie, Andrew W. Mellon, Ford, and Alfred P. Sloan foundations, the Pew Charitable Trust, the Lumina Foundation for Education, and Annenberg/CPB. Annenberg/CPB developed the Flashlight Toolkit and Flashlight Program, with technology surveys of students and faculty, technology roundtables for institutional change, and the "Flashlight Cost Analysis Handbook." The Alfred P. Sloan Foundation's Asynchronous Learning Network developed findings about the cost-effectiveness of online education (Bishop, 2006). The Andrew W. Mellon Foundation funded twenty five projects as part of its Cost-Effective Uses of Technology in Teaching (CEUTT) program that measured pedagogic effectiveness, teaching costs, and cost-effectiveness (Ehrmann & Milam, 1999; Fisher & Nygren, 2006). This program also spearheaded, with Fund for the Improvement of Post-Secondary Education (FIPSE) funding, the Costs Project, and the Technology Cost Measurement (TCM) project. The Joint Funding Councils of Great Britain and KPMG (1997) present a model with data about staff costs, depreciation, other operating expenses, and overhead.

The WICHE (Western Interstate Commission for Higher Education) Cooperative for Educational Technologies (WCET) partnered with NCHEMS to develop standards for TCM, which included case studies and spreadsheet software called the "TCM Tabulator" and a simpler "TCM Tabulator-EZ."

The TCM methodology is based on the NCHEMS Cost Funding Principles (Jones, 2001). TCM focuses on direct costs allocated to instruction, with the course as the unit of analysis. Costs are calculated per student and per credit hour. Various white papers, such as Opper and Mathews's (2002) "Funding and Cost Containment of Educational Technology: Shifting Policy and Practices," were produced. Jewett (2002) assisted WCET in developing the TCM, creating the Bridge Model to compare the cost of instruction by mediated versus traditional delivery. The Lumina Foundation on Education funded many efforts for understanding and controlling costs in the national Making College Affordable initiative, such as the Delta Project.

Another approach to course costs and technology was funded by the Pew Grant Program in Course Redesign and conducted by the Center for Academic Transformation at Rensselaer Polytechnic Institute. The purpose of the Program in Course Redesign was to encourage the use of technology in redesigning instructional approaches to save costs and enhance quality. Institutions use a Course Planning Tool or spreadsheet to compare cost results before and after implementing a course redesign (see Graves, 2004; Twigg, 2003).

Building One Type of Instructional Cost Model

Up to this point, the focus has been on reviewing basic concepts of cost and providing a map to major components of the literature on higher education costs. The chapter concludes with a how-to-do-it section dealing with a foundational type analysis of instructional costs, the induced course load matrix (ICLM), developed initially by Suslow (1976).

The ICLM is a two-dimensional array of student majors against departments. It allows administrators to understand two critical types of enrollment behavior: (1) consumption—the amount and type of student credit hours that different majors take; and (2) contribution—the types of students and majors that are served by departments (Meisinger, 1994). By modeling different scenarios in consumption and contribution, managers may predict the impact of increasing enrollment in a major, including what courses will be needed to serve these new majors and therefore what amount of faculty resources will be needed to offer courses. See Allen and Brinkman (1983), however, for the difficulty of determining the impact on costs of changes in enrollment.

The ICLM can be helpful in analyzing the effect of enrollment behavior on resource allocation, whether the resource being allocated is money, space, faculty, or infrastructure. For the purposes of building a typical cost of instruction model, one needs unit record data about courses, students, expenditures, faculty, faculty workload, and, depending on the question asked, space. A database tool is required to generate the many different types of reports of interest. Different levels of aggregation are needed for reports that examine costs at the major, program, degree, department, school, college or university, system, and state level. A model based on unit record data may be more readily updated with the addition of new extracts, which will allow the model to evolve and meet a variety of needs over time.

To prepare the ICLM, data need to be aggregated from the basic student data files for one academic year. Typically, these files contain one record per student per course per term. Ideally, these should be end-of-term census files in order to capture as much accurate and complete course activity as possible. Each record should include a student identifier, student level, course discipline, course level and number, number of credit hours earned, course department, course division, department of student major, division of student major, student major, term of course, and other data of interest. Student typology is also relevant for examining variations in course-taking behavior. For example, course-taking patterns may vary for traditional college age, nontraditional, part-time only, and nonmatriculated students.

Using the image of a spreadsheet matrix, one can write reports that document student credit hour (SCH) data for each division, department, and discipline in the left axis and the name of each major in the column headers. Read from left to right, the reports document how much a specific department contributes to the SCH taken by each major. Read from top to bottom, they illustrate how many SCH a specific major consumes from each different department. These consumption and contribution ratios are then tied to expenditure data to calculate costs. These steps are shown in Tables 12.1 through 12.4.

TABLE 12.1 STEP 1: GET SCH BREAKOUT WITH ICLM

| | Division 1 | | | | |
| | Department 1 | | Department 2 | | |
	Major 1	Major 2	Major 3	Major 4	Row total
Division 1	20	20	7	7	54
Department 1	12	6	3	3	24
Discipline A	6	0	3	0	9
DiscA 100–001	3	0	3	0	6
DiscA 100–002	3	0	0	0	3
Discipline B	6	6	0	3	15
DiscB 100–001	3	3	0	3	9
DiscB 100–002	3	3	0	0	6
Subtotal	12	6	3	3	24
Department 2	8	14	4	4	30
Discipline C	0	6	0	0	6
DiscC 100–001	0	3	0	0	3
DiscC 100–002	0	3	0	0	3
Discipline D	8	8	4	4	24
DiscD 100–001	4	8	4	0	16
DiscD 100–002	4	0	0	4	8
Subtotal	8	14	4	4	30
Division total	20	20	7	7	54

TABLE 12.2 STEP 2: CONVERT TO PERCENTAGES

| | Division 1 | | | | |
| | Department 1 | | Department 2 | | |
	Major 1	Major 2	Major 3	Major 4	Row total
Division 1					
Department 1					
Discipline A					
DiscA 100–001	12.5%	0.0%	12.5%	0.0%	25.0%
DiscA 100–002	12.5%	0.0%	0.0%	0.0%	12.5%
Discipline B					
DiscB 100–001	12.5%	12.5%	0.0%	12.5%	37.5%
DiscB 100–002	12.5%	12.5%	0.0%	0.0%	25.0%
Subtotal					
Department 2					
Discipline C					
DiscC 100–001	0.0%	10.0%	0.0%	0.0%	10.0%
DiscC 100–002	0.0%	10.0%	0.0%	0.0%	10.0%
Discipline D					
DiscD 100–001	13.3%	26.7%	13.3%	0.0%	53.3%
DiscD 100–002	13.3%	0.0%	0.0%	13.3%	26.7%
Subtotal					
Division total					
Grand total					

In considering the availability of cost data, budget reports are a useful source. These reports display expenditures by department or unit and type of expenditure. Instructional expenditures are documented in a chart of accounts clearly separated from other expenditures—such as for research and public service—by ledger codes or numbers. Although expenditures occur at the transaction level, they are rolled up or aggregated for routine reports to an object code or class level to represent categories or types of expenses. Object codes may be grouped by administrative faculty salaries, classified salaries, work study, fringe benefits, full-time faculty salaries, graduate assistants, services other than personnel, part-time faculty salaries, and other salaries and wages. Expenditures by department are then arrayed by object code.

To tie the ICLM data to the expenditure data, the departmental or unit mapping must be comparable between the student and course systems and those of financial and human resource administrative information systems. Often this is not the case, and the model builder needs to develop an appropriate crosswalk. This process can, at times, seem quite limiting.

Operating units that are not primarily instructional in nature need to be examined for their potential impact on the cost of instruction. If they support instruction, and if determining full costs is the goal, then their associated costs

TABLE 12.3 STEP 3: ALLOCATE BUDGET DATA BASED ON SCH

| | Division 1 | | | | |
| | Department 1 | | Department 2 | | |
	Major 1	Major 2	Major 3	Major 4	Row total
Division 1					
Department 1					
Discipline A					
DiscA 100–001	7,375.00	0.00	7,375.00	0.00	14,750.00
DiscA 100–002	7,375.00	0.00	0.00	0.00	7,375.00
Discipline B					
DiscB 100–001	7,375.00	7,375.00	0.00	7,375.00	22,125.00
DiscB 100–002	7,375.00	7,375.00	0.00	0.00	14,750.00
Subtotal					
Department 2					
Discipline C					
DiscC 100–001	0.00	7,000.00	0.00	0.00	7,000.00
DiscC 100–002	0.00	7,000.00	0.00	0.00	7,000.00
Discipline D					
DiscD 100–001	9,333.33	18,666.67	9,333.33	0.00	37,333.33
DiscD 100–002	9,333.33	0.00	0.00	9,333.33	18,666.67
Subtotal					
Division total					
Grand total					

must be allocated across the instructional departments. There are many standard methods for allocation. For example, library expenses may be allocated based on student headcount, with breakouts by undergraduate versus graduate. Another basis for allocation is square footage, in which costs for expenses such as utilities are assigned based on the amount of space used. Other factors relevant to program costs include space utilization, equipment, and other types of expenses that support instruction but are not recorded as direct costs within a department.

Sometimes expenditures can be totaled only at the division or school level, not at the department or unit level. If those expenditures take the form of direct costs, they will need to be prorated accordingly, based on SCH at different levels. If they consist of indirect costs, the allocation methodology will depend on whether decision making can be tied to specific program activities or the indirect expenditures are more diffuse.

The results of the model allow users to examine costs associated with a major as seen in coursework across a variety of disciplines. The addition of enrollments to an existing major or the creation of new majors or a program may have a significant impact on departments other than the one responsible for the major's home. The costs per SCH per major and program are documented and may be sorted to identify the most expensive program, differences by

TABLE 12.4 STEP 4: SUM BREAKOUT CELLS FOR SUBTOTALS

| | Division 1 | | | | |
| | Department 1 | | Department 2 | | |
	Major 1	Major 2	Major 3	Major 4	Row total
Division 1	48,166.67	47,416.67	16,708.33	16,708.33	129,000.00
Department 1	29,500.00	14,750.00	7,375.00	7,375.00	59,000.00
Discipline A	14,750.00	0.00	7,375.00	0.00	22,125.00
DiscA 100–001	7,375.00	0.00	7,375.00	0.00	14,750.00
DiscA 100–002	7,375.00	0.00	0.00	0.00	7,375.00
Discipline B	14,750.00	14,750.00	0.00	7,375.00	36,875.00
DiscB 100–001	7,375.00	7,375.00	0.00	7,375.00	22,125.00
DiscB 100–002	7,375.00	7,375.00	0.00	0.00	14,750.00
Subtotal	29,500.00	14,750.00	7,375.00	7,375.00	59,000.00
Department 2	18,666.67	32,666.67	9,333.33	9,333.33	70,000.00
Discipline C	0.00	14,000.00	0.00	0.00	14,000.00
DiscC 100–001	0.00	7,000.00	0.00	0.00	7,000.00
DiscC 100–002	0.00	7,000.00	0.00	0.00	7,000.00
Discipline D	18,666.67	18,666.67	9,333.33	9,333.33	56,000.00
DiscD 100–001	9,333.33	18,666.67	9,333.33	0.00	37,333.33
DiscD 100–002	9,333.33	0.00	0.00	9,333.33	18,666.67
Subtotal	18,666.67	32,666.67	9,333.33	9,333.33	70,000.00
Division total	48,166.67	47,416.67	16,708.33	16,708.33	129,000.00

program, and other comparisons of interest. The results may be analyzed over multiple terms to identify heavy consumers of certain types of resources, and the impact of possible reallocation of resources may be studied. It is important to realize that, although the initial results of building a cost of instruction model are informative, the true potential for the model lies in being able to tweak the drivers and units of measure to examine different scenarios.

Additional work may need to be done if there is a great deal of noncredit course activity, which fails to be captured if SCH is the unit of measure. Milam (2005) found that noncredit and workforce activity can be very significant at a community college or land-grant institution, for example, and that this makes other productivity measures suspect.

A basic cost of instruction model illustrates, in a spreadsheet matrix format, how ICLM data by discipline and major can be arrayed and used in conjunction with budget data to calculate consumption and contribution ratios, average cost per program, and average cost per major. Additional tiers of costs, such as space utilization and administrative overhead, must be added. It is up to the institutional researcher how elaborate or complicated the model needs to be. Its development, however, is a balance between the accuracy and availability of data to meet the user's needs and what is already known about the institution.

If the model is not complex enough and sensitive to tweaking based on contextual factors and drivers such as faculty salary increases or enrollment demand, it will get picked apart as inadequate. If it is too complex, it will not be adequately understood and will get mired in efforts to assemble and update the data. The way to overcome this problem of competing demands and expectations is to make the model-building work as an integral and routine function of institutional research, and the only way to do that is to ensure that the results are used. It is at this point that issues of organizational change come into play, which is beyond the scope of this chapter. While these dynamics occur, with or without change agents to champion the use of cost models, the reader is left to the interesting and worthwhile literature discussed herein.

References

Abraham, S. Y., et al. (2002). *1999 national study of postsecondary faculty (NSOPF:99) Methodology Report.* U.S. Department of Education, National Center for Education Statistics. Washington, DC: U.S. Government Printing Office.

Adams, C. R., et al. (1978). A study of cost analysis in higher education. *The literature of cost and cost analysis in higher education.* Washington, DC: American Council on Education.

Allen, R., & Brinkman, P. (1983). Marginal costing techniques for higher education. Boulder, CO: National Center for Higher Education Management Systems.

Bishop, T. (2006). Research highlights: Cost effectiveness of online education. The Sloan Consortium. Retrieved from http://www.sloan-c.org/publications/books/pdf/ce_summary.pdf

Bowen, H. R. (1980). The costs of higher education: How much do colleges and universities spend per student and how much should they spend? San Francisco: Jossey-Bass.

Bowen, H. R., & Douglass, G. K. (1971). Efficiency in liberal education. New York: McGraw-Hill.

Brinkman, P. T. (1990). Higher education cost functions. In S. A. Hoenack and E. L. Collins (Eds.), *The economics of American universities: Management, operations, and fiscal environment* (pp. 107–128). Albany, NY: State University of New York Press.

Brinkman, P. T. (2000). The economics of higher education: Focus on cost. In M. F. Middaugh (Ed.), Analyzing costs in higher education: What institutional researchers need to know (pp. 5–18). New Directions for Institutional Research, no. 106. San Francisco: Jossey-Bass.

Brinkman, P. T. (2006). Using economic concepts in IR on higher education costs. In Toutkoushian, R. (Ed.), Applying economics to institutional research (pp. 43–58). New Directions for Institutional Research, no. 132. San Francisco: Jossey-Bass.

Brinkman, P. T., & Allen, R. H. (1986). Concepts of cost and cost analysis for higher education. AIR Professional File, no. 23. Tallahassee, FL: Association for Institutional Research.

Brinkman, P. T., & Leslie, L. L. (1986). Economies of scale in higher education: Sixty years of research. *Review of Higher Education, 10,* 1–28.

California Postsecondary Education Commission. (1980). Determining the cost of instruction in Sacramento: California Postsecondary Education Commission.

Carlson, D. (1975). Examining efficient joint production processes. In R. A. Wallhaus (Ed.), *Measuring and increasing academic productivity* (pp. 39–59). New Directions for Institutional Research, no. 9. San Francisco: Jossey-Bass.

Carlson, D. (1976). A review of production function estimation for higher education institutions. Cambridge, MA: Harvard Graduate School of Education.

Cohn, E., Rhine, S.L.W., & Santos, M. C. (1989). Institutions of higher education as multi-product firms: Economies of scale and scope. *Review of Economics and Statistics, 71*, 284–90.

Conger, S., Bell, A., & Stanley, J. (2009, November). *Four-state cost study.* Boulder, CO: State Higher Education Executive Officers.

Coopers & Lybrand & Barbara S. Shafer & Associates. (1995). Benchmarking for process improvement in higher education: Process costing workbook FY 1994. Washington, DC: National Association of College and University Business Officers.

Cox, K. S., Smith, L. G., & Downey, R. G. (2000). ABCs of higher education—Getting back to the basics: An activity-based costing approach to planning and financial decision making. *AIR Professional File,* no. 77. Tallahassee, FL: Association for Institutional Research.

Curry, J. R., & Strauss, J. C. (2002). Responsibility center management: Lessons from 25 years of decentralized management. Washington, DC: National Association of College and University Business Officers.

Delta Project on Postsecondary Education Costs, Productivity, and Accountability. (2009). Issue brief #2: Metrics for improving cost accountability. Washington, DC: Delta Project. Retrieved from http://www.deltacostproject.org/resources/pdf/issuebrief_02.pdf

Dickeson, R. C. (2006). Frequently asked questions about college costs. Issue paper released by the Secretary of Education's Commission on the Future of Higher Education. Washington, DC: U.S. Department of Education. Retrieved from http://www.ed.gov/about/bdscomm/list/hiedfuture/reports/dickeson2.pdf

Dundar, H., & Lewis, D. R. (1995). Departmental productivity in American universities: Economies of scale and scope. *Economics of Education Review, 14*(2), 119–44.

Ehrmann, S. C., & Milam, J. H. (1999). *Flashlight cost analysis handbook: Modeling resource use in teaching and learning with technology.* Washington, DC: The TLT Group.

Fisher, S., & Nygren, T. I. (2006). Experiments in the cost-effective uses of technology in teaching: Lessons from the Mellon Program so far. New York: Andrew W. Mellon Foundation. Retrieved from http://www.immagic.com/eLibrary/UNPROCESSED/Unprocessed%20eLibrary/COMPLETE/ICLT-CEUTT.pdf

Gamso, G. (1977). The RRPM guide: A primer for using the NCHEMS Resource Requirements Prediction Model (RRPM 1.6). National Center for Higher Education Management Systems Technical Report 104. Boulder, CO: National Center for Higher Education Management Systems.

Gonyea, M. A. (Ed.). (1978). *Analyzing and constructing cost.* New Directions for Institutional Research, no. 17. San Francisco: Jossey-Bass.

Graves, W. H. (2004). Academic redesign: Accomplishing more with less. *Journal of Asynchronous Learning, 8*(1), 27–38.

Hample, S. R. (1980). Cost studies in higher education. *AIR Professional File* #7. Tallahassee, FL: Association for Institutional Research.

Heterick, R. C. (1998). Educom: A retrospective. *Educom Review, 33*(5), 42–47. Retrieved from http://net.educause.edu/ir/library/html/erm/erm98/erm9853.html

Hoenack, S. A. (1990). An economist's perspective on costs within higher education institutions. In S. A. Hoenack & E. L. Collins (Eds.), *The economics of American universities: Management, operations, and fiscal environment.* Albany, NY: State University of New York Press.

Hyatt, J. A. (1983). *A cost accounting handbook for colleges and universities.* Washington, DC: National Association of College and University Business Officers.

Institute for Higher Education Policy. (2000). Higher education cost assessment: Public policy issues, options, and strategies. The New Millennium Project on Higher Education Costs, Pricing, and Productivity. Washington, DC: Institute for Higher Education Policy.

Jenny, H. H. (1996). *Cost accounting in higher education: Simplified macro- and micro- costing techniques.* Washington, DC: National Association of College and University Business Officers.

Jewett, F. (2002). *TCM/BRIDGE Project: Applications of the Mini-BRIDGE model to TCM cost data.* Boulder, CO: Western Interstate Commission for Higher Education/ WICHE Cooperative for Educational Telecommunications.

Johnson, N. (2009). What does a college degree cost? Comparing approaches to measuring cost per degree. Washington, DC: Delta Project. Available at http://www.deltacostproject.org/resources/pdf/johnson3–09_WP.pdf

Joint Funding Councils of Great Britain & KPMG. (1997). Management information for decision-making: Costing guidelines for higher education institutions. Scottish Higher Education Funding Council, Higher Education Funding Council for England, Higher Education Funding Council for Wales. Produced by KPMG. Retrieved from http://www.shefc.ac.uk/shefc/publicat/others/costing/contents.htm

Jones, D. P. (2000). An alternative look at the cost question. In *Higher education cost measurement: Public policy issues, options, and strategies.* Washington, DC: Institute for Higher Education Policy.

Jones, D. P. (2001). *Technology costing methodology handbook—Version 1.0.* Boulder, CO: Western Cooperative for Educational Telecommunications.

Massy, W. K., & Wilger, A. K. (1998). Technology's contribution to higher education productivity. In H. M. Levin and W. S. Koski (Ed.), *Enhancing productivity: Administrative, instructional, and technological strategies* (pp. 49–60). New Directions for Higher Education, no. 103. San Francisco: Jossey-Bass.

McLaughlin, G. W., Fendley, W. R., Winstead, W. H., Montgomery, J. R., & Smith, A. W. (1983). Evaluating the reliability of indices from IEP. Paper presented at the Annual Forum of the Association for Institutional Research, Toronto, ON.

McPherson, P., & Shulenburger, D. (2010). Understanding the cost of public higher education. *Planning for Higher Education Planning, 38*(3), 15–24.

Meisinger, R. J., Jr. (1994). *College and university budgeting: An introduction for faculty and academic administrators* (2nd ed.). Washington, DC: National Association of College and University Business Officers.

Middaugh, M. F., Graham, R., and Shahid, A. (2003). *A study of higher education instructional expenditures: The Delaware study of instructional costs and productivity: Research and development report.* NCES 2003–161. U.S. Department of Education, National Center for Education Statistics. Washington, DC: U.S. Government Printing Office.

Milam, J. (2005). The role of noncredit courses in serving nontraditional learners. In Brian Pusser (Ed.), *Arenas of entrepreneurship: Where nonprofit and for-profit institutions compete* (pp. 55–68). New Directions for Higher Education, no 129. San Francisco: Jossey-Bass.

Milam, J. Coutts, C., Bosacco, E., Golliday, A., & Simpson, A. (2008). The cost of not knowing: State capacity for postsecondary cost studies. Stephens City, VA: HigherEd.org.

National Association of College and University Business Officers. (2002). Explaining college costs: NACUBO's methodology for identifying the costs of delivering undergraduate education. Washington, DC: National Association of College and University Business Officers. Retrieved from http://www.nacubo.org/public_policy/cost_of_college/final_report.pdf

National Association of College and University Business Officers. (2004). Managerial analysis and decision support: A guidebook and case studies. Washington, DC: National Association of College and University Business Officers.

National Center for Education Statistics. (2001). Study of college costs and prices, 1988–89 to 1997–98. Washington, DC: National Center for Education Statistics. NCES 2002–157. Retrieved from http://www.nacubo.org/public_policy/cost_of_college/final_report.pdf

National Center for Higher Education Management Systems. (1977). *Procedures for determining historical full costs: The costing component of the information exchange procedures* (2nd ed.). Technical Report #65. Boulder, CO: National Center for Higher Education Management Systems.

National Center for Higher Education Management Systems–National Association of College and University Business Officers. (1980). Costing for policy analysis. Boulder, CO: National Center for Higher Education Management Systems.

Opper, J., & Mathews, J. B. (2002). Funding and cost containment of educational technology: Shifting policy and practices. *Technology Costing Methodology*, White Paper #2. Boulder, CO: WICHE Cooperative for Educational Technologies (WCET).

Reindl, T. (2000). To lift the veil: New college cost studies and the quest for the perfect formula. In M. F. Middaugh (Ed.), *Analyzing costs in higher education: What institutional researchers need to know* (pp. 89–101). New Directions for Institutional Research, no. 106. San Francisco: Jossey-Bass.

Robinson, D., Ray, H., & Turk, F. (1977). Cost behavioral analysis for planning in higher education. NACUBO Professional File, *9*, 1–51.

Seybert, J. A., & Rossol, P. M. (2010). What drives instructional costs in two-year colleges: Data from the Kansas study of community college instructional costs and productivity. *Planning for Higher Education, 38*(3), 38–44.

Simpson, W. A., & Sperber, W. E. (1984). A new type of cost analysis for planners in academic departments. *Planning for Higher Education, 12*, 13–17.

Sperry, R. J. (1995). The use of data envelopment analysis to study the economic efficiency of academic anesthesiology departments. (Unpublished doctoral dissertation). Department of Educational Administration, University of Utah.

Suslow, S. (1976). Induced course load matrix: Conception and use. In T. R. Mason (Ed.), *Assessing computer-based systems models* (pp. 35–51). New Directions for Institutional Research, no. 9. San Francisco: Jossey-Bass.

Thomas, C. R. (2004). CHESS data definitions for colleges and universities. Boulder, CO: National Center for Higher Education Management Systems.

Toutkoushian, R. K. (1999). The value of cost functions for policy making and institutional research. *Research in Higher Education, 40*(1), 1–15.

Twigg, C. (2003). *Improving learning and reducing costs: Lessons learned from round I of the Pew Grant Program in Course Redesign*. Troy, NY: Center for Academic Transformation, Rensselaer Polytechnic Institute. Pew Learning and Technology Program. Retrieved from http://www.thencat.org/PCR/Rd1Lessons.pdf

U.S. Office of Technology Assessment. (1982). *Information technology and its impact on American education* (p. 234). U.S. Office of Technology Assessment, Congress. Washington, DC: U.S. Government Printing Office.

Wellman, J. V. (2010). Improving data to tackle the higher education "cost disease." *Planning for Higher Education, 38*(3), 25–37.

Wellman, J. V., Desrochers, D., Lenthan, C., Kirshstein, R., Hurlburt, S., & Honegger, S. (2009, January). *Trends in college spending: Where does the money come from? Where does it go?* Washington, DC: Delta Cost Project.

Whalen, E. L. (1991). *Responsibility center budgeting: An approach to decentralized management for institutions of higher education*. Bloomington, IN: Indiana University Press.

Winston, G. C., (2000). A guide to measuring college costs. In M. F. Middaugh (Ed.), *Analyzing costs in higher education: What institutional researchers need to know* (pp. 31–46). New Directions for Institutional Research, no. 106. San Francisco: Jossey-Bass.

Witmer, D. R. (1972). Cost studies in higher education. *Review of Educational Research, 42*(1), 99–127.

CHAPTER 13

MANAGING COLLEGE ENROLLMENTS

John Cheslock and Rick Kroc

Enrollment management, for the purpose of this chapter, is defined as an institutional research and planning function that examines and seeks to manage the flow of students to, through, and from college. We view the enterprise using an "educational pipeline" view, considering key institutional research needs associated with the flow of students from the time they become prospects to their exit as alumni and into the workforce. Beyond the pipeline view, we discuss how enrollment management varies by type of institution, type of student, and form of educational delivery. We also consider some key central issues within the EM domain. Finally, we reflect on the future of enrollment management as it intersects institutional research.

A Common Theme

Institutional leaders wish to enroll underrepresented and economically disadvantaged students, well-prepared students with high test scores and grades, and students who can contribute large amounts of tuition and fees—all at the same time. Most enrollment management policies, however, do not advance all three objectives; instead, they lead to gains in some areas and declines in others (Humphrey, 2006; Schulz, 2008). Consequently, the simultaneous achievement of student access, preparation, and revenue is the Holy Grail of the enrollment management pursuit.

Enrollment management has become more important and more visible because these three goals have grown in importance and will continue to do so in the future. Governmental funding has not kept pace with rising educational costs, so higher education institutions increasingly rely on students to pay the bills. The growing importance of institutional rankings has led to institution's reputations being increasingly determined by their level of selectivity and the incoming credentials of their student body. The incentive to enroll students with strong academic preparation is also being increased by rising accountability pressures, which are leading to examinations of students' academic and workforce success. At the same time, schools are increasingly scrutinized for low levels of diversity due to low enrollment of underrepresented minorities or low-income students.

The difficult nature and growing importance of enrollment management presents an opportunity for institutional researchers. Institutions can substantially improve enrollment management policies through quality data analysis, and IR offices that can produce such research will grow in value. Although many researchers will not help their institution obtain the Holy Grail—simultaneous achievement of student access, academic preparation, and revenue—they can help schools balance these conflicting objectives as well as possible.

Research Within the Educational Pipeline

The term *educational pipeline* is often used to describe the flow of students through the educational system. At various points, students will enter or exit this pipeline, providing numerous opportunities for research and analysis. The following eight sections describe research issues and opportunities, from the recruitment of undergraduate students through their attainment of degrees and beyond.

Recruiting Students

Institutional researchers are often asked to help answer three questions related to student recruitment:

- Who is available?
- Whom would we like to enroll?
- How do students make their college choice?

To answer these questions, a solid understanding of the educational pipeline is essential. This pipeline will vary according to the type of institution and level of student. A community college, for example, will depend on a pipeline defined from a local population with a wide range of ages, whereas a research university graduate school will draw from an international population of students who have previously earned undergraduate degrees. For many state universities, where access is a fundamental goal and the Hispanic population is growing rapidly, understanding that part of the pipeline is critical. Figure 13.1 illustrates the pipeline for Hispanic students in one southwestern state. If the goal is to recruit, retain, and graduate more Hispanic students, then it is important to have a thorough understanding of who is in the pipeline and the reasons

FIGURE 13.1 ARIZONA HISPANIC POPULATION PIPELINE: 1,880,000 TOTAL HISPANICS IN 2008

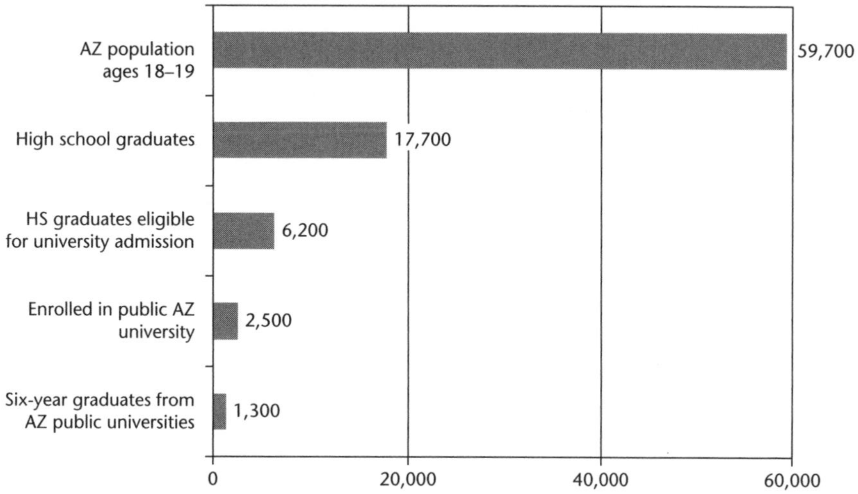

Source: U.S. Census Bureau, AZ High School Report Card.

for "leakage" from this pipeline at various junctions. If increased tuition revenue is another goal, then enrollment managers will need an analysis of how the demographic profile (and pipeline) of potential students who can afford to pay full tuition differs from that of students for whom access is a key goal.

Effective student recruitment requires an understanding of how students choose a college (Hossler, 1999). Hossler, Schmitz, and Vespar (1999) and McDonough (1997) provide useful, empirically based descriptions of this process. The efficiency and effectiveness of recruitment activities depends heavily on this process and its impact on the enrollment pipeline. Market research, high school outreach, prospect identification, student group profiling, and predictive modeling can all help to target students for recruitment (DesJardins, 2002). Profiles of individual high schools can also be useful. Some institutions develop their own systems and staff to provide these analyses; in addition, many external instruments, services, and vendors are available (described in detail in Chapter 30). The institutional researcher can make substantial contributions in this area by working closely with the admissions office staff to help match the most important needs with the appropriate tools, databases, and services. (See Chapter 27 for a discussion of national efforts to improve consumer information.)

Admitting Students

At many institutions, nearly all applicants are accepted, so student admission is a relatively minor activity and there is little need for admission analysis. But for selective institutions, this part of the enrollment management process can substantially alter the composition of an institution's student body. The IR office can help admissions staff set enrollment objectives, develop policies to meet the chosen objectives, and effectively measure progress toward these objectives.

IR offices are often asked to help develop an index of academic success that can be used to select "high-quality" students who are likely to succeed. Variables such as standardized test scores and high school GPA are often used in a regression model to calculate an index for each applicant, using first-year college GPA or retention as the dependent variable. Using more detailed high school transcript–level data, including number of AP courses and highest-level math course taken, may provide even better prediction (Adelman, 1999). Some researchers have explored the validity of "noncognitive" data for admissions (Sedlacek, 1993).

The impact of admissions criteria on the enrollment of underrepresented minorities and low-income students is a highly contentious issue in the admissions field. IR offices may be asked to predict how enrollment levels of certain groups vary across different admissions criteria. Diversity considerations can often be illuminated by conducting research for specific subgroups. For example, the predictive power of a specific academic success index might vary by the race, ethnicity, or socioeconomic characteristics of the applicants. If the researcher determines this to be true, multiple academic success indices will need to be developed.

Some institutions choose to consider financial need in admissions so that their eventual student body produces a certain level of net tuition revenue. At these institutions, sophisticated projections are required to estimate the revenue projections for various sets of admissions decisions. As the next two sections further demonstrate, enrollment management research support increasingly examines the revenue implications of available policies.

Awarding Financial Aid

The tensions underlying the distribution of institutional aid help demonstrate why the simultaneous achievement of student access, academic preparation, and revenue is so difficult to obtain. If an institution awards substantial aid to increase access and improve the academic preparation of their incoming students, then net tuition revenue will decline over time. Institutions can most easily maximize prior academic preparation by concentrating on higher socioeconomic status (SES) high schools, but such targeting will result in reduced access for low-income students and underrepresented minorities.

Historically, the purpose of institutional financial aid was to promote access, and these considerations remain an important, although less dominant, part of aid distribution. Financial aid is thought to promote access when financial need—the gap between cost of attendance (COA) and expected family contribution (EFC)—is minimized. Major changes in tuition levels or other sources of aid can substantially alter the level of student need, and institutional researchers can help institutional policy makers realize the impact of these changes on institutional aid budgets and the diversity of the student body. The complex intersection of federal aid, state aid, institutional aid, listed tuition, and enrollment levels for particular groups makes sound decision making without research almost impossible (Kurz & Scannell, 2004). This same complexity, however, makes the required analysis quite difficult. IR offices may also be asked to incorporate student indebtedness into the analysis; for example, how debt levels relate to tuition, aid, and other college costs.

Higher education institutions often compete for students with strong levels of pre-college academic preparation through offers of merit-based financial aid. To support this activity, institutional researchers may be asked to create measures, such as an index of academic success, that can be used to determine the criteria of merit-aid allocation. After implementation, merit-aid programs need to be continually refined, which is best done when supported by research that examines how the level and distribution of merit-aid programs alter yield rates for targeted students.

As institutions increasingly rely on their students to cover educational costs, the economic implications of institutional aid have grown in importance. Cheslock (2006) explains how economic considerations have also altered the measures analysts use to chart aid offerings. Historically, total institutional aid was the primary metric; budgets were set and aid offerings were not allowed to exceed the budgeted amount. Over time, net tuition revenue (NTR) became the metric of choice, and the goal was to generate a specific level of NTR. This measure, which equals gross tuition minus institutional aid, alerts institutional leaders to the amount of revenue students are providing to the institution.

Examination of net tuition revenue has long been essential in private education, but it is a relatively new pursuit in public higher education (McPherson & Shapiro, 1998). Public institutions have increasingly sought to increase net tuition revenue by increasing enrollment, particularly of out-of-state students, through the provision of relatively small amounts of institutional aid. In developing these policies, they often ask the IR office to answer the following question: "What is the minimum scholarship that we need to offer a student with a particular set of background and academic characteristics, such that she enrolls and pays sufficient tuition to benefit the institution?" Because this often involves complex analyses, a number of third-party vendors provide this service, as well as help with other areas of financial aid and enrollment management analysis. In light of the complexity of financial aid data and analysis, it can be useful to contract with a vendor to help with the initial establishment of these analyses and processes, such that data and analyses can subsequently be managed entirely locally.

Predicting Enrollment and Tuition Revenue

Understanding the needs and context for enrollment projections is essential. Increasingly, the budget process of the institution drives the need for projections, adding estimates of net tuition revenue as an essential dimension. Other needs include identifying instructors and course enrollments, evaluating and planning student recruitment efforts, and strategic and capital planning. Each of these needs may require different data, methods, and time horizons. Course planning tends to be shorter term and more granular, usually looking at two- to three-year patterns of course enrollments, disaggregated by student level, and sometimes cross-tabulated with student majors. In contrast, strategic and capital planning often have long time horizons, and data are aggregated into larger groups. Tuition revenue projections add complexity by necessitating an understanding of tuition payment patterns and institutional aid disbursements.

After determining the need, institutional researchers need to identify variables and levels. Likely candidates may include graduate or undergraduate, tuition domicile (critical for budgeting), ethnicity, class level, new or continuing, and academic preparation. A careful consideration of the variables can help reduce errors in the projection. Because each variable in a projection has some statistical variability or measurement error, a model with many variables can have considerable uncertainty, particularly if projected out several years or more. Providing a range of estimates (for example, most likely, high, and low) is best, although not always easy to do or politically acceptable.

A variety of quantitative methods can be used for projecting enrollments. Brinkman and McIntyre (1997) compare and contrast many of these methods, providing useful descriptions of strengths and weaknesses. In some cases, especially for long-range planning, qualitative methods may be useful. An example is scenario development; according to Roger Caldwell, in a personal communication with the authors, this "describes a situation in common terms that represents what might happen in the future. It is not a prediction, but a way of putting a lot of ideas and possibilities together."

Placing Students

Appropriate placement of students in entry-level courses, especially gateway courses, is a critical first curricular step toward retaining and graduating students. Indicators of academic preparation that have been used to select students may also be used to place students in appropriate levels of a college curriculum, but it is important to understand that selection and placement uses are very different (Kroc & Hanson, 2001). The effectiveness with which measures of academic preparation can help us to place students appropriately can be evaluated using three indicators. First, how many of the students we expect to pass their courses do so? Second, how many of the students that we judged to be ready for a particular course fail the course? Finally, how many of the students we judged to be underprepared could have successfully completed a more difficult course without taking the prerequisite course? IR offices can often assist with these types of analyses.

In addition, often more detailed diagnostic information about areas of strength and weakness is needed than is available from, say, an overall standardized test score. This is especially true at community colleges, where developmental or remedial coursework is usually a significant part of the mission. In addition to use of standard admission indicators, an array of other published placement instruments is available (see Chapter 30). Some institutions develop their own instruments to ensure that the content is tailored to their curriculum. This is a challenging task, though—from the writing of good test questions that reflect course prerequisite expectations to ensuring an appropriate array of easy and difficult questions to the setting of the placement cut scores.

Measuring Student Enrollment

The measurement of student enrollment has a number of dimensions. Simple headcount is best for most public and media consumption, because it is the most obvious and understandable metric. For their state appropriations funding, though, many public colleges and universities depend on full-time equivalent (FTE) enrollments. This is usually calculated formulaically from student credit hours (SCH), a more direct measure of teaching activities. Graduate and professional SCH are usually weighted most, whereas lower division undergraduate SCH are weighted least, reflecting the relative cost of education at different course levels.

For institutions adopting a responsibility center management (RCM) budgeting model, measuring student enrollment has become critical to internal funding allocations. If net tuition revenue follows students through either their enrollment in an academic degree program (their major) or their course enrollment, or both, then it is vital to measure NTR and how it tracks directly to responsibility centers through the credit hours taught and students' majors.

Retaining and Graduating Students

Retention and graduation rates not only are direct internal measures of student success, but they also may be the most commonly used measures for accountability reporting and national rankings. Moreover, the link between recruitment and graduation rates is complex and strong. Returning to our theme, if a strong commitment to access leads to enrollment of more students with lower levels of academic preparation, then grad rates may decrease in spite of robust institutional retention efforts. Conversely, of course, achieving higher levels of "quality" in the recruitment process is likely to increase graduation rates, even without any changes in retention efforts.

Input characteristics shape retention, but so does the student experience after enrollment. For an IR analyst, it is important to use an array of data and methods to help the institution develop realistic expectations about improving graduation rates. How much of the variance is explained by pre-college characteristics, how much is within the institution's control, and how much is just not known? In his chapter in Hossler, Bean, and Associates (1990), "Using Retention Research in Enrollment Management," John Bean describes and compares different methods for researching retention, making recommendations about using the various methods and about implementing research findings.

The following are a few of the important current issues facing colleges and universities:

- Increasing degree production by increasing retention and graduation rates
- Increasing transfer rates and baccalaureate degree completion of community college students
- Reducing time-to-graduation
- Closing the gap in graduation rates between underrepresented groups and other students
- Increasing academic preparation—the link between recruitment and retention
- Implementing and evaluating efficient and effective retention programs
- Improving the curriculum to facilitate learning and student success

The IR analyst needs to begin with solid descriptive data that can be sliced and diced in many ways; for example, by gender, ethnicity, major or discipline, freshman or transfer, resident or nonresident, and level of academic preparation. Beyond simple descriptive data (and in conjunction with campus learning assessment efforts), it is critical to analyze the flow of students through the curriculum. Such issues as the impact of poor grades in gateway courses, changing majors, advanced standing requirements, and transfer shock are important areas for study. Also, IR offices are sometimes asked to assist program coordinators with the evaluation of their programs, either by helping to design the evaluation or by providing basic institutional data for the evaluation. In some cases, IR offices have staff whose primary responsibility is program evaluation.

In addition to understanding local concerns, the researcher needs to be informed about the national context. A number of sources for national graduation rate data exist, including the Consortium for Student Retention Data Exchange (CSRDE) and IPEDS. Also, the National Student Clearinghouse provides its clients with a service to determine enrollment and degree completion for students who have left the institution.

Beyond Graduation

Enrollment management should not end when students graduate. Valuable insights can be gained from alumni as well as from employers of former students, often using survey data. These insights may help institutions to better recruit and retain students and enrich students' college experience. There is strong convergence here between student assessment and enrollment management. Student outcomes assessment has encouraged researchers to gather information after graduation, which may also be useful for managing enrollments. IR can complete the cycle that begins with student prospects by understanding the outcomes and by using this knowledge to improve their ability to attract new students, thus completing the feedback loop.

In some states, wage and earnings data are available using social security numbers as the link to student data. These data can be useful to demonstrate the economic impact of a college degree; to examine changes over time in wages and employment; and to assess patterns of employment by region, job type, major, and other factors. Extending the educational pipeline beyond graduation can be very useful.

Varying Types of Enrollment Management

The basic structure of the educational pipeline does not vary across contexts; however, many other aspects of enrollment management vary widely. In this section, we discuss important considerations for specific institutional types, student types, and forms of educational delivery.

Differences by Institutional Type

Reflective of the authors' experience, this chapter has focused primarily on issues and examples from the four-year public sector. In this section, we briefly discuss issues of concern to other sectors.

Community colleges often have multiple missions and open enrollment policies, so student "recruitment" may be more like marketing research designed to discover the effectiveness of various advertising and other outreach activities. IR may be able to help identify target markets and to assist with market survey design. As discussed earlier, IR may also be able to help identify students and analyze the effectiveness of developmental education. In another enrollment management area, as community colleges become increasingly important in the production of baccalaureate degrees, in both transfer articulation and sometimes direct conferral of some four-year degrees, detailed analysis of the effectiveness of the transfer pipeline is essential. Unit record data—including majors, courses taken, and course grades—are required to provide adequate analyses.

Enrollment management first grew in the private sector (Coomes, 2000; Duffy & Goldberg, 1998). With the exception of a small set of institutions with large endowments, most *private colleges* rely primarily on students for revenue. For those with small student bodies, enrollment management projections become incredibly important. Relatively small errors in projected enrollment or net tuition revenue can lead to major financial difficulties for an institution. At selective institutions, admissions play a major role because demand far exceeds enrollment capacity. At nonselective privates, financial aid allocation is often quite complex, because extensive and differentiated tuition discounts are required to meet enrollment targets while still providing the desired levels of net tuition revenue.

Proprietary institutions enroll a rapidly growing share of postsecondary students. The revenue base at these institutions is heavily reliant on federal financial aid programs, as students use Pell Grants and federal loans to cover much of the costs. Enrollment management at these institutions often focuses heavily on marketing and student recruitment efforts.

Differences by Student Type

Defining a particular "type" of undergraduate student for a cohort level of analysis is becoming increasingly difficult. For example, a student may be a freshman at both a community college and a university in the same semester. As students move more freely and frequently among institutions, understanding "student swirl" becomes critical. Most states now have unit record statewide longitudinal data systems that enable such analyses to be done within a state. The National Student Clearinghouse provides services to look at where high school graduates, admitted college students, and nonretained undergraduates attend and graduate in other states. As more institutions become Clearinghouse clients, these services have become increasingly comprehensive and useful.

Graduate education is another growing area in enrollment management. Until recently, costs and revenues in this area were not carefully analyzed. Except perhaps for MBA programs, graduate education was not considered for revenue generation. In the current economic climate, however, more universities are examining ways to generate revenue from their graduate programs, particularly at the master's level. Institutions that have RCM budget models provide detailed data for responsibility centers to examine graduate program revenues and costs. Working closely with graduate colleges, IR offices can often assist with analyses in this area by examining enrollment patterns, financial aid, and tuition (and program fee) flow.

New Forms of Educational Delivery

As online and distance delivery of courses and programs increases, enrollment management must expand to accommodate this type of delivery and the enrollment swirling that this often produces. In many cases, issues related to the quality of delivery and student learning outcomes are at the center of interest, which may engage IR analysts. Online education may require a new set of enrollment management tools and approaches. This form of education does not face the same physical space constraints as residential education, and it may require marketing and recruitment efforts that are more geographically dispersed.

Organizing for Enrollment Management

In their book *Strategies for Effective Enrollment Management*, Kemerer, Baldridge, and Green (1982) describe an instructive framework for understanding structures for managing college enrollments. They describe four models: the enrollment management committee, the enrollment management coordinator, the enrollment management matrix, and the enrollment management division. In some institutions with EM divisions, there may be a separate enrollment management research unit apart from the central IR office. Understanding the structure at a particular institution can be essential to guide effective support from the central IR office. As described by Terenzini (1993), a contextual understanding of the particular campus where the institutional researcher works is critical. Without this understanding of the organizational structure, people, and political context, even the best IR studies may not be heeded.

Targeting Resources for Maximum Effect

Enrollment management consultants and texts rely heavily on one recommendation from microeconomic theory: target funds on those students who will be most influenced by additional resources. Figure 13.2 demonstrates this principal in the context of financial aid. The horizontal x axis measures a student's interest in attending institution Z; the vertical y axis measures the impact of institutional financial aid on a student's enrollment decision. Student A has little interest in institution Z even if a general aid package was offered, whereas student C is so attracted to institution Z that he or she would attend even in the absence of aid. Between the two, student B is ambivalent about enrollment, and the aid offer will substantially increase her likelihood of enrollment. An institution will achieve larger enrollments when it concentrates its aid offers on applicants like student B. Similar results occur in many other contexts. For example, retention rates will be improved most by efforts that target students at risk of dropping out but whose fate is not yet sealed.

Although simple in theory, the application of this principle is difficult, as it requires one to identify which students are on the fence. If institutional researchers can effectively identify those students who are on the fence, their value to higher education institutions will be considerable. Such identification

FIGURE 13.2 PRICE RESPONSE AND STUDENT INTEREST

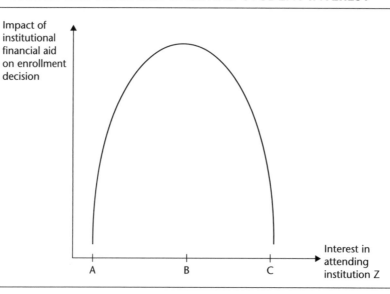

requires sound statistical analysis that effectively predicts which students will be most influenced by offers of aid, extra academic support, or other resources.

Ubiquitous Data

In a recent interview, Hal Varian predicted that "the sexy job in the next ten years will be statisticians" (Varian, 2009). The logic he used to reach this conclusion is highly relevant to institutional researchers supporting enrollment management: "The ability to take data—to be able to understand it, to process it, to extract value from it, to visualize it, to communicate it—that's going to be a hugely important skill in the next decades. . . . Because now we really do have essentially free and ubiquitous data. So the complementary scarce factor is the ability to understand that data and extract value from it" (Varian, 2009).

Higher education institutions are awash in enrollment management data. The rise of geographic information systems allows schools to predict many characteristics of prospective students merely from their home address. Sophisticated software allows enrollment management professional to track every contact they have with prospective students. If students enroll, greater amounts of information are being collected about their educational experiences as they progress in their studies. So extensive data are now available for each student, but, as Varian notes, these data are of little use unless analysts can extract value from them. Institutional researchers who can effectively navigate large quantities of data will become extremely valuable.

Ethical Issues

Institutional researchers will increasingly be asked to use large amounts of data to identify those students who can be most influenced by resources. Such requests will raise a number of ethical concerns. Many feel that higher education institutions should not differentiate prices across students in the same manner as car dealerships and airlines. Institutional researchers will have little influence over these sorts of overarching questions, but they will face numerous technical decisions that present ethical dilemmas.

A classic example is information on the number of campus visits a prospective student takes. One can effectively predict a student's enrollment propensity using a campus visit variable, but do we really want to decrease a prospective student's aid offer every time that student attends a campus tour? If institutional researchers focus solely on the predictive power of their statistical model, they will help produce enrollment management policies that produce better "numbers." Institutional leaders, however, may wish to forgo these gains, because the method for producing them conflicts with the core mission of the institution. Institutional researchers may be the only professionals with a knowledge of the ethical concerns underlying the statistical analysis, and they must effectively communicate the trade-offs that come with improved predictive power. When vendors are used, IR professionals need to ensure that the variables used in prediction are appropriate.

College Rankings and Accountability Metrics

Ethical issues must be scrutinized, because institutional policy makers face numerous pressures that conflict with the core mission of their school. For example, rising costs in combination with declining or stagnating governmental funding can lead policy makers to focus on net tuition revenue, which often conflicts with other goals. The most notorious pressures, however, emanate from competition to move up in published rankings of colleges, such as those produced by *U.S. News and World Report*, which are based heavily on student and enrollment data (Ehrenberg, 2002). The stakes are high, as demonstrated by the incentive bonuses given to some college presidents for increasing their institutions' rankings, so providing the "right" data is critical. In many cases, especially when data definitions are clear, the valid and correct data are obvious, and they should be provided. When definitions are less clear, however, the IR professional often has some choices. In these cases, it is best to provide multiple views of the data, along with descriptions of the pros and cons of each view to assist with the final decision. Ranking and accountability metrics are an increasing part of the IR office's responsibilities.

The Future of Enrollment Management

A number of trends related to enrollment management will have important implications for the IR profession:

- *Enrollment management will become increasingly central to college and university missions.* Managing enrollments will grow in importance as institutions compete for students in an environment in which funding is often insecure. This will extend a trend that began for some institutions in the 1980s or even earlier.

- *Institutional researchers will become increasingly important in enrollment management.* As institutional policy makers increasingly seek to manage enrollments, they will need research support to improve their decision making. At the same time, computing innovations will make data collection easier, which will result in greater amounts of data on prospective, current, and past students. Institutional researchers will consequently have greater opportunities for improving institutional decision making, and those who can make meaning from large quantities of data will be increasingly valuable.

- *There will be better integration with strategic planning and budgeting processes.* Enrollment growth will become a more critical avenue for maintaining the revenue stream and developing discretionary funds for many institutions. Tuition increases, which can be expected to continue at public institutions due to state budgetary problems, will forge stronger linkages with the budgeting and planning processes. Enrollment researchers who understand key economic principles and how they relate to enrollment management will be vital. DesJardins and Bell (2006) provide an introduction to many of these concepts.

- *The partnership between enrollment management and student assessment will strengthen.* As described in this chapter, assessment programs and enrollment management share a variety of common interests. Assessment studies and data will help colleges understand how students move through the curriculum—and may also help us to design better recruitment strategies as we get to know our students better.

- *Collaborations with other sectors and other institutions will increase.* Higher education boundaries are becoming less distinct. Technology-delivered education, development of new higher education pathways, and increased swirling of students across sectors will increase collaborative efforts across sectors and among institutions.

References

Adelman, C. (1999). *Answers in the toolbox: Academic intensity, attendance patterns, and bachelor's degree attainment.* Washington, DC: U.S. Department of Education, Office of Educational Research and Improvement.

Arizona Board of Regents (2010). *AZ High School Report Card.* Retrieved from https://azregents.asu.edu/ABOR%20Reports/2009-10%20High%20School%20Report%20Card.pdf

Brinkman, P., & McIntyre, C. (1997). Methods and techniques of enrollment forecasting. *New Directions for Institutional Research, 24*(1), 67–80.

Cheslock, J. (2006). Applying economics to institutional research on higher education revenues. In R. Toutksoushian & M. Paulsen (Eds.), *Applying economics to institutional research* (pp. 25–41). New Directions for Institutional Research, no. 132. San Francisco: Jossey-Bass.

Coomes, M. (2000). The historical roots of enrollment management. In M. Coomes (Ed.), *The role student aid plays in enrollmeng management* (pp. 5–18). New Directions for Student Services, no. 89. San Francisco: Jossey-Bass.

DesJardins, S. (2002). An analytic strategy to assist institutional recruitment and marketing efforts. *Research in Higher Education, 43*(5), 531–553.

DesJardins, S., & Bell, A. (2006). Using economic concepts to inform enrollment management. In R. Toutksoushian & M. Paulsen (Eds.), *Applying economics to institutional research* (pp. 59–74). New Directions for Institutional Research, no. 132. San Francisco: Jossey-Bass.

Duffy, E. A., & Goldberg, I. (1998). *Crafting a class: College admissions and financial aid, 1955–1994.* Princeton, NJ: Princeton University Press.

Ehrenberg, R. (2002). Reaching for the brass ring: The U.S. News & World Report rankings and competition. *Review of Higher Education, 26*(2), 145–162.

Hossler, D. (1999). Effective admissions recruitment. In G. Gaither (Ed.), *Promising practices in recruitment, remediation, and retention* (pp. 15–30). New Directions for Higher Education, no. 108. San Francisco: Jossey-Bass.

Hossler, D., Bean, J., & Associates. (1990). *The strategic management of college enrollments.* San Francisco: Jossey-Bass.

Hossler, D., Schmitz, J., & Vespar, N. (1999). *Going to college: How social, economic, and educational factors influence the decisions students make.* Baltimore: Johns Hopkins University Press.

Humphrey, K. (2006). At the crossroads of access and financial stability: The push and pull on the enrollment manager. *College and University Journal, 82*(1), 11–16.

Kemerer, F., Baldridge,V., & Green, K. (1982). *Strategies for effective enrollment management.* Washington, D.C.: American Association of State Colleges and Universities.

Kroc, R., & Hanson, G. (2001). Enrollment management and student affairs. In R. Howard (Ed.), *Institutional research: Decision support in higher education.* Tallahassee, FL: Association for Institutional Research.

Kurz, K., & Scannell, J. (2004). Aid-award pitfalls: Why intuition is not enough. *Chronicle of Higher Education, 50*(34), B18.

McDonough, P. (1997). *Choosing colleges: How social class and schools structure opportunity.* Albany: State University of New York Press.

McPherson, M., & Shapiro, M. (1998). *The student aid game: Meeting need and rewarding talent in American higher education.* Princeton, NJ: Princeton University Press.

Schulz, S. (2008). Mastering the art of balance: An analysis of how private master's institutions pursue institutional quality, access, and financial stability through their enrollment practices. *Enrollment Management Journal, 2*(1), 65–100.

Sedlacek, W. (1993). Employing noncognitive variables in admissions and retention in higher education. In National Association of College Admissions Counselors (Eds.), *Achieving diversity: Issues in the recruitment and retention of underrepresented racial/ethnic students in higher education* (pp. 33–39). Alexandria, VA: National Association of College Admission Counselors.

Terenzini, P. (1993). On the nature of institutional research and the knowledge and skills it requires. *Research in Higher Education, 34*(1), 1–10.

Varian, H. (2009). Hal Varian on how the Web challenges managers. *McKinsey Quarterly.* Retrieved from http://www.mckinseyquarterly.com/Hal_Varian_on_how_the_Web_challenges_managers_2286

CHAPTER 14

REFOCUSING STUDENT SUCCESS

Toward a Comprehensive Model

Gary A. Rice and Alene Bycer Russell

Since the passage of the federal Student Right-to-Know Act of 1990 (SRTK), the graduation rate has taken center stage as an indicator of student success, and it has been a subject of much debate and controversy. Given the paucity of comparable, widely accepted outcome measures for postsecondary education, state and federal policy makers have latched on to student persistence and graduation measures as key accountability indicators. At the same time, critics have denounced simple graduation rates as inadequate and misleading metrics. Despite the many limitations of these measures, graduation rates have gained attention and influence in the media, in college ranking systems, and among consumers. As a result, many higher education administrators are concerned that this narrowly focused concept of student success does not adequately reflect all that they do, and that it deflects attention and resources from broader institutional concerns.

Why all the fuss? The simple truth is that graduation from college does matter, but it is not all that matters. From the societal perspective, the United States is falling behind other nations in the production of college graduates, and in order to remain competitive in the global marketplace, we need many more workers with postsecondary credentials. However, we also need workers to acquire advanced training and job-related skills, independent of whether they are seeking degrees. From this perspective, it does not matter whether individuals meet their education goals at the institutions they first enroll in, nor how long it takes. Further, federal and state investment in higher education has never been higher, and poor completion rates may be viewed as a waste of public resources. However, individuals derive value from the postsecondary courses they complete, and employers derive value from the knowledge and skills their workers acquire through postsecondary coursework—not from their degrees. From the individual perspective, it is clear that students enroll in college with very varied life circumstances and with many different goals. Such diversity calls for a broader conception of student success and better metrics to describe institutional performance.

This chapter argues that data on student progress can and should be used to improve institutional accountability, consumer information, and institutional performance, but that one size cannot fit all. It is time to move away from a narrowly conceived, institutionally focused measure of student success and refocus on a more wide-ranging, student-centered model.

The first part of this chapter explores the federal role in shaping where we are today, limitations of current definitions, and progress that has been made on several fronts. The remaining section of the chapter describes a comprehensive model that has been implemented at the University of Alaska Anchorage, a model that is inclusive of all students and that incorporates diverse measures of student success.

The Federal Role in Shaping Current Metrics of Student Success

The federal Student Right-to-Know Act of 1990 (SRTK) established in law the requirement that all institutions participating in Title IV programs must annually report their graduation rate for first-time, full-time, degree- or certificate-seeking students at 150 percent of normal time. To carry out this requirement, the National Center for Education Statistics (NCES) developed the Graduation Rate Survey (GRS) as part of its Integrated Postsecondary Education Data System (IPEDS) (National Center for Education Statistics, n.d.). GRS was different from other IPEDS surveys because it required the tracking of individual students over a period of time, a requirement that challenged the capacity of many existing data systems.

The 1998 Higher Education Act (HEA) Amendments went further, charging NCES with making specific consumer information, including graduation rates, available online. The NCES release of the first GRS data was significant in the sense that institutional graduation rates for the entire nation had not previously existed. This further solidified the primacy of the graduation rate—as defined in GRS—as an indicator of student success.

The passage of the Higher Education Opportunity Act (HEOA) in 2008 contains several sections related to graduation rates, but it did not significantly change the landscape on student success measurement. Among the new consumer information that must be made available on the College Navigator website (section 132), there is a requirement for a graduation rate for first-time, full-time students who graduate within 200 percent of normal time—an expansion of the existing GRS time frame of 150 percent. Also, Title IV (section 488) requires institutions to annually disclose a graduation rate that is disaggregated by financial aid category, broken down into three categories:

recipients of federal Pell Grants, recipients of federal subsidized loans who do not receive Pell Grants, and students who do not receive either a Pell Grant or a federal subsidized loan. While the intent was to recognize that student socioeconomic status affects the likelihood of college graduation, the requirement for *disclosure* only, rather than *reporting* to NCES for posting on College Navigator, somewhat lessens the potential impact of this provision. All in all, not much had changed.

Limitations of the Traditional Graduation Rate Measure in Today's Environment

The traditional measure is based on a narrowly defined cohort. Specifically, the GRS cohort (the "denominator") includes only first-time, full-time, degree- or certificate-seeking students who begin in fall term. This cohort excludes an increasingly large proportion of today's undergraduate students:

- Students who begin college as part-time students
- Those who transfer in from other postsecondary institutions
- Adults who earned postsecondary credits at an earlier stage in their lives
- Students who begin college spring term
- Individuals who are not seeking a degree or certificate but are attending college for a variety of other reasons

As a result of this narrow cohort definition, the traditional graduation rate measure fails to examine the vast majority of undergraduate students at many non-elite institutions, particularly at community colleges. By definition, it can account for only a small portion of what these institutions do.

The traditional measure is based on a narrow definition of student success and an artificial time frame. Specifically, the GRS definition of "success" (the "numerator") includes only those students who earn a degree or certificate and only those who do so in 150 percent of normal time. By this definition, each of the following would be considered a failure, even though there is success from the student's point of view:

- A four-year-college student who graduates in six and a half years
- A student who transfers and attains a bachelor's degree at another institution in four years
- A community college student who begins full-time, switches to part-time, and attains an associate degree in five years
- A student who achieves documented successful learning, including acquiring desired postsecondary knowledge and/or higher-order skills and competencies, but no credential
- All graduate and professional students; in fact, these students are typically excluded from discussions of institutional performance and student success (and not part of the denominator), though they represent a significant portion of the work of many institutions

The traditional measure fails to take into account variation in institutional mission and in the characteristics of entering students. It holds institutions accountable for students' life circumstances and personal goals that are beyond higher education's ability to control, and it does not recognize higher education's contributions to students' learning progress. This is a problem because it may lead policy makers, the media, and students and their families to draw incorrect conclusions about institutional performance.

In particular, the current measure effectively blames institutions whose missions are more student access–oriented, and that have less selective admissions criteria. Research has repeatedly shown that students with certain "risk factors" are less likely than others to graduate within a defined period of time (Horn & Premo, 1995). For example, the NCES longitudinal study Beginning Postsecondary Students identified seven characteristics associated with leaving postsecondary education without a degree: delayed enrollment, enrolling part time, working more than 35 hours per week, financial independence, having children, being a single parent, and not having a high school diploma.

To the extent that institutions disproportionately serve "at-risk" students, they demonstrate, on average, lower graduation rates. NCES reports that the average six-year graduation rate for institutions with 20 percent or less low-income students was 70 percent, compared to a graduation rate of 42 percent for institutions with more than 40 percent low-income students (Horn, 2006).

The traditional measure oversimplifies and distorts reality by reducing institutional success to a single number. In our fast-paced, high-stress, multitasking world, a common expectation is that the answer to every question is found in a single number. Examples abound: one's credit score or cumulative GPA, the *U.S. News & World Report* rankings, the cost-of-living index, and so on. Unfortunately, student success is no different, and an entire institution's success may be judged today on the very narrow and simplistic current graduation rate measure.

In sum, our current graduation rate metric is based on an outmoded model of student behavior that assumes linear and timely progression through a single institution. This model fails to recognize the increasingly common "swirling" behavior that involves alternating full- and part-time attendance, enrollment in multiple institutions, transfer, and stopping out. By not taking into account students' actual enrollment behavior, and by failing to encompass much of what institutions do, current graduation rate data lead to misleading conclusions about institutional performance.

Progress in Data System Development Facilitating Improved Graduation Rate Measures

When SRTK was passed two decades ago, many institutions had no way of knowing what happened to their students who failed to re-enroll. Such students were counted as "failures" for no better reason than a lack of good data about what happened next. Since that time, postsecondary education has seen the rise of data systems that cross institutional and even state lines, creating opportunities for improved measurement.

A growing number of statewide and system-wide higher education boards make it possible to track students across institutional lines. Such agencies have been collecting, reporting, and using institutional data for decades, but the passage of SRTK stimulated the development of state student unit record databases. Since that time, such databases have grown in number, in types of data collected, in the number of institutions included, and in cross-agency linkages.

Forty states now have student unit record databases in place covering at least the public institutions in their states, for a total of 47 such databases (Ewell & Boeke, 2007). Seven of these states have more than one such database, corresponding to different postsecondary systems, but in most cases they can share data across databases. Seventeen states have at least some information from independent institutions, and six have at least some information from proprietary institutions.

The most common use of these databases is the calculation of graduation rates (Ewell & Boeke, 2007). All use a methodology consistent with GRS, but some states have additional capabilities, such as tracking students for longer periods of time, following part-time cohorts, and measuring transfer to other institutions in the state. These features are extremely valuable in terms of expanding the meaningfulness of graduation rates.

As attention has shifted away from the possibility of a federal unit record database, there is increasing interest in the question of whether a "national" (not federal) system can be developed based on existing state databases. Ewell and Boeke (2007) focused on this question and determined that it is feasible to harness state databases into a national system. By analyzing 33 key data elements, they found that the nation is close to having a consistent "common core" of data elements. The report recommends the creation of "a national capacity to link unit record data quickly and securely" (p. 18), noting that it would be most effective if managed by a third-party, non-governmental organization.

Supported by the Lumina Foundation, the National Center for Higher Education Management Systems (NCHEMS) conducted a study in 2003–04 to test the feasibility of linking data across states (National Center for Higher Education Management Systems, 2008). NCHEMS worked with only two states—Ohio and Kentucky—but did find value in the effort. In 2004–07, an expanded project unfolded that involved data exchange among four states: Kentucky, Ohio, Tennessee, and West Virginia. Researchers concluded that "it is feasible to exchange records from multiple state SUR [student unit record] systems to create more accurate estimates of cohort retention and completion" but that "political issues trump data issues and will slow the effort down" (National Center for Higher Education Management Systems, 2008, p. 9). It remains to be seen whether states will have much interest in interstate data exchange efforts in the future.

The National Student Clearinghouse (NSC), founded in 1993 to document student enrollment for lenders, represents a different kind of data system, with a potential not yet fully realized (National Student Clearinghouse, n.d.). This system is based on voluntary participation by institutions, but it now covers over 90 percent of college students. Through it, records are matched across institutions, and institutions can learn what happens to their students who do not re-enroll—if they enroll and/or graduate elsewhere. Though not founded for this purpose, the Clearinghouse has also provided limited information for researchers pertaining to inter-state student transfer. The Alaska model, described shortly, uses NCS annually for tracking all cohorts' transfer entry over a decade after their initial entry.

Promising Initiatives to Expand or Improve on Existing Graduation Rate Measures

Several recent initiatives illustrate creative and meaningful usage of the graduation rate metric as it relates to student success. These include the following:

- Using data from the Cooperative Institutional Research Program (CIRP), Freshman Survey, the Higher Education Research Institution at the University of California at Los Angeles has developed an "actual-to-expected" graduation rate model that allows comparison of institutions based on the characteristics of entering freshmen (Astin, 2004).
- Building on the efforts of the Joint Commission on Accountability Reporting (JCAR) of the mid-1990s, the Voluntary System of Accountability (VSA) has established the College Portrait website, which provides a more complete picture of student advancement (American Association of State Colleges and Universities & the Association of Public and Land-Grant Universities, n.d.). College Portrait contains data on two cohorts—the GRS-defined first-time, full-time cohort, and an additional transfer cohort—and it presents multiple measures of student progress: graduation from that institution, graduation from another institution, still enrolled at that institution, and still enrolled at another institution.
- Using GRS data, The Education Trust has developed the College Results Online web-based tool that enables actual-to-peer comparison, as well as comparison of graduation rates by race or ethnicity and gender, and graduation rates over time (The Education Trust, n.d.).
- Many states are tracking students more broadly than required under SRTK, and states can be innovative in how they use their data in order to meet particular policy goals related to student success. In 2009, an NGA Center for Best Practices policy brief addressed how state leaders could design student achievement measures to meet their unique policy needs (NGA Center for Best Practices, 2009). It called for governors to track four key milestones: successful completion of remedial and core courses, advancement from remedial to credit-bearing courses, transfer from a two-year institution to a four-year

institutions, and credential attainment. It also called for states to provide more disaggregated measures by grouping achievement rates by student subpopulation; among them, part-time and full-time students, transfers, Pell-eligible students, underrepresented ethnic minorities, and students over age 21 when first enrolled.

These and other examples offer promise, but they do not replace the predominant way of thinking defined at the federal level by SRTK and GRS.

Emerging Applications of Improved Data Systems and Metrics for Measuring Student Success

A number of organizations and researchers are pushing the envelope in their research as they make use of some of the advances just described. Because these efforts are data-based and focused on specific institutional issues, they have enhanced potential for bringing about change.

Research by HigherEd.org, Inc., made use of the NCHEMS interstate data exchange described earlier to explore issues related to nontraditional students (Milam, 2009). This work is especially significant because GRS data are ill-suited to examining policy questions related to these students. This work built on the four-state database already established and added two additional databases (Virginia and the State University of New York) for a six-state analysis. The study was able to identify factors that are linked to improved student outcomes for nontraditional students.

With support from The Education Trust, the National Association of System Heads (NASH) initiated the Access to Success Initiative (A2S) with 24 leaders of public higher education systems (National Association of System Heads & The Education Trust, 2009). Committed to increasing the number of college graduates in their states and reducing racial and socioeconomic gaps in enrollment and graduation, by conscious design this initiative incorporated both part-time and transfer students in order to more fully document what happens to different groups of students as they progress through college; it specifically tracked the progress of low-income students.

Expanding and Refocusing What Constitutes Student Success

It is safe to conclude that established conventions pertaining to graduation rate reporting are not likely to disappear in the foreseeable future and that this will remain a contentious issue for some time to come. The challenge is to find ways to expand and refocus this metric to maximize its usefulness and minimize potentially detrimental or unforeseen consequences. On the one hand, there needs to be wider recognition of alternative and multiple measures of student success, including various concepts of retention, transfer, and documentation of student learning. On the other, the time-to-degree issue must be addressed, with expansion of conventional time frames. At the same time, work must continue on the development and effective use of disaggregated graduation rates that offer more meaningful comparisons.

In the following section, we present the work that is being done at the University of Alaska Anchorage (UAA) to address many of the issues described above. The model that has been designed at UAA provides the capacity to measure student learning from several different perspectives, reflecting both the university mission and the realities of the people it serves.

University of Alaska Anchorage (UAA) Model Overview

Institutional Profile. The University of Alaska higher education system has a composite bipartite mission: open-access (two-year) and a traditional instruction, research, outreach university mission. UAA is the largest of three public universities in the system. Its primary service area is south-central Alaska, home to about two-thirds of the state's population. UAA is composed of the lead Anchorage main campus, offering certificates and degrees from associate to the doctorate. Four community campuses (community colleges), offering certificate and associate degree programs, report to the main campus. As of this writing, the university's total enrollment is approximately 21,500 students, with a total budget approaching $300 million. (For a complete profile of UAA, its enrollment, finances, and human recourses, see the UAA Fact Book, http://www.uaa.alaska.edu/ir/publications/factbook/index.cfm.)

Why Was the Model Built? Two primary, interrelated drivers were the genesis for the development of a model to measure and evaluate student success or student learning progress. First, the current metric (graduation rates as defined for IPEDS reporting) has many significant limitations that this model sought to address. This has already been amply documented in the first section of this chapter. The second driver was a recognized need for an expanded recognition and definition of what constitutes "student success"—a definition that reflects accountability in serving all students in today's global higher education world. The following "beliefs" about student success guided the development of the model and define the philosophy behind its use:

- Student success should be viewed from a learner's perspective, not an institution's.
- There is no single, homogeneous student body.
- We serve all students who enroll, not just full-time, first-time, undergraduate degree seekers.
- Student learning is progressive, not just success or failure.
- Acquiring knowledge is the single common reason all students enroll. An institution is responsible for optimizing that process within its capability and resources.

Institutionally, the model supports planning, program assessment, and decision making by addressing the most fundamental student success question: For *whom* and where should resources be distributed to realize the most efficient and effective student success outcomes for all students we serve? The model bases determination of student success on what all institutions have in common within the instructional component of their respective missions—how well does the institution assist all of its various student subgroups to acquire essential and desired knowledge, skills, and/or capabilities? The traditional graduation rate metric cannot answer this question.

Model Design, Assumptions, and Decision Rules

The model operates at two levels. First, the simple surface appearance, by design, creates a communication bridge between higher education and its various stakeholders. Key is the ability to effectively communicate to a diverse stakeholder population that successful learning has occurred in its students while enrolled at the university. Second, the model provides the data and structure to analyze underlying inherent complexity of interaction between two dynamic and complex systems: the student and the institution.

Underlying model development is the assumption that, regardless of declared or undeclared intent(s), every student seeks to acquire knowledge and improved skills/competencies to reach personal goals. Each student demonstrates successful knowledge acquisition and learning progress relative to predefined learning outcome criteria, as assessed by the instructor.

Data Design and Operational Methodology

The UAA model has been designed to be implemented using an institution's current student databases by existing staff. Essential data to operate the model are routinely gathered on every student each term, including summer, at colleges and universities across the country. Data are extracted from existing census freeze point data sources. The model requires low maintenance and can be handled by an IR office with limited resources. Although it required about 2.5 years to originally design and implement at UAA, it should take an institution with an IR office with one technical support analyst, using our knowledge and guidance, eight to ten days spread over two months to initially implement the model while maintaining regular IR operations. Once operational, identifying each new cohort takes two to four hours plus two to three days once a year to update the current status of each student in the ten cohorts. Initial implementation required no additional resources—human, financial, or equipment.

The following steps represented the basic core activities in building the Model at UAA:

1. The process starts by determining the "life cycle" of the vast majority of first-time students. At UAA it was determined to be ten years. Within that time, 95 percent either (a) earned their intended award (met their degree/certificate

goal for attending the University), (b) transferred to another institution, or (c) left the university, could not be found at another university, and never returned to UAA. The life cycle of non-degree-seekers also fit within this time frame, as did the current 200 percent time frame allowable for degree seekers to complete degrees within the traditional graduation rate definition.

2. Next, the process selects those student characteristics currently captured electronically that will be important to analyze and evaluate in relation to student success on a recurring basis over the years. Additional characteristics can be added as they are captured. These characteristics can be used to define various cohorts or student groups. Characteristics might include various demographic attributes, academic preparation, transfer status, and the like. *Caution*: Decisions about what to include and track must be made with significant deliberation, with a focus on "need to know" versus "nice to know." The latter is a function of who is making the decision, so consensus needs to be sought. The model's operation is based on student success from the student's perspective, not the institution's. Also, selecting characteristics that result in small subcohorts will produce information based on just a few students. That will likely be unreliable and result in bad decisions. One suggested subcohort that will be of interest is the first-time, full-time freshman cohort that is used to calculate the traditional graduation rate metric. Comparison of and profiling the graduation rate success of this subcohort with the model outcomes may challenge conventional wisdom about their success. Another subcohort of broad importance for many institutions is the "underprepared" student.

3. *Cohort Selection.* This step is *critical,* as it is the foundation of the model: to identify all students who are entering the institution for the first time at a particular point each year to track forward. UAA decided to use the fall semester as the single annual master cohort selection point. Alternatives for the cohort selection point could include all or any of the academic semesters, quarters, or academic sessions in which a significant number of students are first admitted. From the total student body, there is just one selection criterion for inclusion in the tracking cohort: "Is this the first time we have ever enrolled this student?' High school students taking college courses are not tracked unless or until they graduate from high school or are at least 19 years old and did not graduate when they enroll. Only first-time students are tracked—not the total student body—for a particular year. Once the student is selected into a particular master cohort, he or she can be further categorized into several subcohorts, such as undergraduate-graduate, degree seeker or non-degree seeker, primary campus (for multi-campus institutions, traditional metric student, and so on). However, the student will always remain with the same initial master cohort for tracking every term for ten years from initial entry. At UAA, each fall another master cohort is created. Ultimately, ten separate master cohorts are concurrently being tracked for ten years at any given time. Within those ten separate cohorts every student that has ever been served by the institution will be included in a specific master cohort and tracked for a decade. Traditional metric first-time,

FIGURE 14.1 TEN-YEAR MAP OF THE FALL 1998 FIRST-TIME UNDERGRADUATE ENTRY COHORT

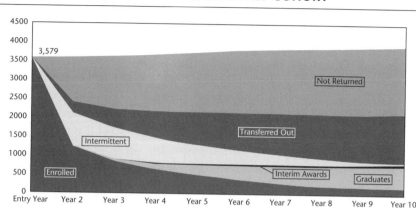

full-time baccalaureate students continue to be tracked but now become a separate subcohort rather than the proxy for total institutional student success.

4. *Student Status Tracking.* At UAA, every fall term the academic status of each student in each of the ten master cohorts is compared to his or her academic status the previous fall semester. There are six student status categories. A student can be in only one category in any given academic period, but can be identified in more than one status point during the decade. At this point, the model is actually tracking status change over the decade for each student in a subcohort. There are six primary student status decision rules that define the academic status of each student at each term snapshot point—Enrolled (Retention), Intermittent (Stopout), Interim Award, Graduated, Transferred, or Not Returned (Dropout)—and two student progress measures: Course Grades and Level of Goal Progress. (See Appendix 14.1.)

5. *Create a Student Flow Map.* Scientists have never seen an ion, but they study them by putting them in a cloud chamber and observing behavior by the tracks they leave. Similarly, the student flow map (see Figure 14.1), created from the student status tracking tables, represents the "cloud chamber" of students as they flow through the institution over a decade.

This map tells the story of the fall 1998 first-time undergraduate, term by term, over a ten-year period. The Not Returned category may include Non-Degree Seekers that met their goal; however, when looking at a student term by term, the Non-Degree Seeker has not returned since attending for just one term. The Enrolled, Intermittent, and Non-Returned categories are not cumulative term after term; the Transferred Out, Interim Awards, and Graduates categories are cumulative. The apparent increase in the number of students in this map stems from students being placed in multiple categories at each snapshot.

Note the continued growth of students after six years. Three of the categories are quite noteworthy:

1. There is a large drop-off after the first year.
2. The number of graduates continues to grow after six years.
3. Our students continue to transfer out.

The map encourages researchers to focus on changing patterns rather than numbers, because each status tells a story. The map's gestalt reveals something greater than the sum of its parts. Stable map patterns for a single subcohort over time reveal the movement and, subsequently, the underlying successful learning progress of that group, which can be compared to the learning patterns of other subcohorts. Each subcohort has a unique pattern, and the study of student "churn" by different student groups over time, placed side by side, can be very revealing.

6. *Create the Ten-Year Final Tracking Status Profile.* At the decade endpoint, a final portrait of each master cohort is created and moved to archives; concurrently, a new cohort is being created to begin its journey. Table 14.1 presents the unduplicated headcount difference between degree seeking and non-degree seeking students' successful learning (Learning Goal Met, Learning Progress, and Learning Goal Not Met) after ten years. It also separately reports the levels of Successful Learning Progress among progressing degree seekers who did not earn a UAA award for several reasons over the decade.

7. *Determine the Successful Learning Rate (SLR) for Each Subcohort Annually and at Decade's End.* The model described thus far reveals important insights during the tracking process, but its real strength lies in determining successful learning progress of various student subcohorts. Although course grades are the basis of the model, what is tracked is not grades per se, but rather, what the grades represent (see Figure 14.1). This model defines and accepts SLR progress in terms of grades received for learning outcomes in coursework and will continue to use them until there is majority consensus across the academy and general public that creates a better way to define and assess student learning progress. Aggregate levels of successful learning within a cohort or across a variety of subcohorts are established by determining the SLR; that is, the proportion of courses successfully passed in relation to total courses attempted throughout a decade. To illustrate, a student who successfully passes three courses out of five taken (60 percent) is equally successful in his or her learning progress as a student who successfully passes six out of ten courses (60 percent). From the institution's perspective, they are making equal learning progress relative to the learning they attempted. Thus the learning progress of part-time students and non-degree students are evaluated with the same metric as that used to evaluate the progress of full-time students.

8. *Optional.* Cohorts defined by specific demographic characteristics can be captured in the model at initial entry to the institution, allowing learning progress analysis and comparison across different subgroups of interest. This provides information about the changing composition of first-time cohorts

TABLE 14.1 LEARNING GOAL STATUS AFTER TEN YEARS: UAA FIRST-TIME UNDERGRADUATES, FALL 1998 ENTRY COHORT

Learning Goal Met	Degree Seeker		Non-Degree Seeker		Total	
	N	% Total	N	% Total	N	% Total
Graduated Within 6 years	100	6.7			100	2.8
Graduated Within 10 years	258	17.2	167	8.0	425	11.9
Non-Degree: Progress with Distinction			552	26.5	552	15.4
Non-Degree: Substantial Progress			108	5.2	108	3.0
Goal Met Total	358	23.9	827	39.7	1185	33.1
Progressing						
Non-Stop Enrollment	1	0.1			1	0.0
Received Interim Awards	26	1.7			26	0.7
Intermittent	349	23.3			349	9.8
Transferred Before Graduating	402	26.8	719	34.6	1121	31.3
Non-Degree: Moderate Progress			272	13.1	272	7.6
Non-Degree: Minimal Progress			43	2.1	43	1.2
Progressing Total	778	51.9	1034	49.7	1812	50.6
Learning Goal Not Met						
No Return After Year 1	362	24.2			362	10.1
Non-Degree: No Progress			220	10.6	220	6.1
Goal Not Met Total	362	24.2	2081	10.6	582	16.3
Total	1498	100	2081	100	3579	100.0

"PROGRESSING" DEGREE SEEKERS' LEVELS OF SUCCESSFUL LEARNING PROGRESS

Progress Status	Distinction		Substantial		Moderate		Minimal		No Progress		Total	
	N	%	N	%	N	%	N	%	N	%	N	%
Non-stop Enrollment												
Rec. Interim Awards												
Intermittent												
Transfer Degree Seeker												
Progressing Degree Seeker												

Note: Levels of Successful Learning Progress are determined by the percentage of courses taken with passing grades.

Progress with Distinction: 90–100 percent

Substantial Progress: 75–89 percent

Moderate Progress: 31–74 percent

Minimal Progress: 11–30 percent

No Progress: 0–10 percent

*The row "Graduated Within Six Years" includes only traditional metric, full-time, four-year-degree-seeking students.

over time and how this change may be related to academic performance. It also allows the institution to evaluate the effectiveness of programs designed to support specific types of students or to identify particular student groups that are underperforming.

9. *Optional.* Some important student subcohorts cannot be identified initially but are uncovered and documented at the final decade status point. These students include transfers, intermittent students, and nonreturning students. They can be extracted from the master cohort and passed through the model again as a new cohort to seek additional insights.

Note that all data used in the model are currently available in virtually all institutions' student databases. As such, institutions can create the databases to support the use of the model without waiting for the full ten years. At UAA, historical data were accessed to create a ten-year trend history at the outset.

Model Design or Implementation Challenges

There were myriad issues, large and small, that surfaced during the model design and initial implementation at UAA. Recognizing that each institution is unique and will have to address its own set of challenges, we present five of the most challenging issues here.

1. Addressing the paradigm shift about what constituted student success required faculty and administrators to think about and accept student success as successful learning by all students rather than only degrees granted to a very select subset. Although degrees granted are a component in the model, what is really tracked is the underlying successful learning that the official degree or certificate represents. This required shifting the focus on student success to a student's demonstrated learning performance rather than viewing success through the institution's lens: graduation rates. It required expanding the tracking time frame to ten years from six years. Gaining consensus across the university about the eight fundamental status-determination rules was challenging but essential for outcomes of the model to be useful to campus leadership in planning and curricular decision making.

2. UAA researchers had to identify and address pockets of passive or active resistance to the use of course grades, especially D grades, to represent levels of successful learning. People had to recognize that D grades are defined as "minimal pass," not failure (F). They also had to accept the use of grades, as used in the model, as the only currently accepted proxy for successful learning (A, B, C, D, P) compared with unsuccessful (F) learning. The model does *not* try to resolve the intractable debate about the meaning of grades.

3. The student flow map proved to be a challenge in itself, because people were not used to seeing and understanding a student body in motion and changing character over time. Patterns were more important than absolute numbers. Once people understood what the map revealed about student

"churn" and underlying successful learning, they found that comparing maps of several student subcohorts in visual form over time revealed relationships and insights that would otherwise be very difficult to uncover.

4. The emerging understanding of the model at UAA rapidly gave rise to a large number of information requests that quickly inundated the IR staff. Both IR office staff and the provost recognized that priority-setting guidelines needed to be developed to distinguish "need to know" from "nice to have." Obviously, this distinction might be seen as a function of who is making the decision, and this set of guidelines is still being debated. Standardized reports were developed annually to provide a campus-wide picture of student learning progress. As these were developed and automated, more attention could be directed to student learning progress related to specific institutional concerns.

5. Once the model is fully operational, it is very challenging to establish strategies to get model findings incorporated into the institution's decision-making and institutional culture. Creation of a model incorporation plan—with tangible goals, small incremental but coordinated steps, and personal responsibility or accountability—is key to success.

Model Findings

The model has been in initial existence for the past three years but is still a work in progress at UAA. Standardized reports have been developed and analyses conducted. Space limitations in this chapter do not permit the presentation of examples of additional figures and tables that have been developed. The interested reader is referred to the UAA OIR website (http://www.uaa.alaska .edu/ir/reports/success) for examples of the output formats and Topic Paper analyses of selected subcohorts at UAA.

Model Status To Date

The model is in its initial stages of development and implementation into the university's planning and decision-making processes. However, several significant indications have surfaced that the model has been accepted by senior leaders at the university; among them:

- A university-wide model integration plan is being implemented.
- The UAA chancellor and cabinet are already individually taking specific internal and external action steps to fully understand, communicate, and use model findings in the governance of the university and to share its potential with peers and throughout their spheres of influence.
- Findings have been introduced into the current reaccreditation self-study process.
- The UAA faculty senate adopted an unsolicited official model endorsement and has formed an ongoing joint subcommittee with the OIR to monitor model findings, impacts, or issues.

- Degree program coordinators are studying ways to incorporate findings as part of required program review documentation.
- Requests for internal research funds that seek to improve student success must include model findings as part of their project outcomes documentation.
- UAA staff members are seeking to learn more about the impact of their contributions to assist student learning.
- The OIR has received numerous requests for model information about a variety of subcohorts, resulting in workload demands that outstripped its capacity to meet. The model integration plan, which includes guidelines for determining "need to know" and priorities, has provided accepted guidelines for prioritizing information and data requests.
- A series of foundation student success questions is being refined as a contextual framework for further analysis and use of the model across the university.
- The SLR and learning progress metrics for degree seekers and non-degree seekers are being developed and considered for inclusion as state-wide performance metrics.

Beyond UAA and the Future

What does the future hold? It is clear that higher education and the students being served have evolved over the past fifty years, but the academy and its stakeholders have not been adapting to stay relevant in assessing and communicating student success in this changing environment. The following are some anticipated short- and long-term strategies being initiated that are intended to address this state of affairs. Others will be emerging as the impacts of these strategies become apparent.

- Expand beta testing of the model capabilities and potential nationwide to include all types and levels of higher education.
- Expand national and international awareness of the model's existence and capabilities through national, regional and invited presentations. This would include state and federal legislators, U.S. Department of Education, state higher education systems, professional higher education associations, and private industry leaders.
- Involve and solicit external funding support necessary to make the model an operational reality throughout U.S. higher education and internationally.
- Initiate and facilitate dialogue throughout the academy and general public leading to an expanded paradigm shift in what constitutes student success that is in concert with today's students, national higher education priorities, and each institution's instructional mission.

References

American Association of State Colleges and Universities & the Association of Public and Land-Grant Universities. (n.d.). College portrait of undergraduate education website. Retrieved from http://www. collegeportraits.org/

Astin, A. (2004, October 22). To use graduation rates to measure excellence, you have to do your homework. *Chronicle of Higher Education.* Retrieved from http://chronicle .com/article/To-Use-Graduation-Rates-to/27636/

Ewell, P., & Boeke, M. (2007). *Critical connections: Linking states' unit record systems to track student progress.* Indianapolis, IN: Lumina Foundation for Education.

Horn, L. (2006). *Placing college graduation rates in context: How 4-year college graduation rates vary with selectivity and the size of low-income enrollment* (NCES 2007–161). Washington, DC: U.S. Department of Education, National Center for Education Statistics.

Horn, L. J., & Premo, M. D. (1995). *Profile of undergraduates in U.S. postsecondary education institutions: 1992–93, with an essay on undergraduates at risk* (NCES 96–237). Washington, DC: U.S. Department of Education, National Center for Education Statistics.

Milam, J. (2009). Nontraditional students in public higher education: A multi-state, student unit record study. Retrieved from http://highered.org/docs/ NontraditionalStudentsinPublicInstitutions.pdf

National Association of System Heads & The Education Trust. (2009). *Charting a necessary path: The baseline report of public higher education systems in the Access to Success initiative.* Washington, DC: Authors.

National Center for Education Statistics. (n.d.). College navigator website. Retrieved from http://nces.ed.gov/collegenavigator/

National Center for Higher Education Management Systems. (2008). Tracking postsecondary students across state lines: Results of a pilot multi-state data exchange initiative. Retrieved from http://www.nchems.org/c2sp/documents/ResultsofMulti-StateDataExchange.pdf

National Student Clearinghouse. (n.d.). National Student Clearinghouse website. Retrieved from http://www.studentclearinghouse.org/

NGA Center for Best Practices. (2009, November). *Measuring student achievement at postsecondary institutions.* Washington, DC: National Governors Association.

The Education Trust. (n.d.). College results online. Retrieved from http://www .collegeresults.org/

Appendix 14.1: UAA Decision Rules for Student Status Determination

Cohort Selection Criterion: A student is placed in a master cohort/ subcohort(s) and tracked forward for a decade from that point. UGRAD: The sole selection criterion each fall semester is [that] the student is enrolling at UAA for the first time as an undergraduate. GRAD: Initial selection is based on the first time (term and year) any student enrolls in a UAA 600+ level course. Separate cohorts are identified each semester. Undergraduates who become graduate students are tracked separately for a decade in both cohorts.

RULE #1: Course Completion: Any successful grade (UGRAD = A, B, C, D, or P) and (GRAD = A, B, C, or P) earned is considered to represent goal learning progress and some level of "value-added" by the university. Auditors (AU) are also included for undergraduate non-degree seekers only if initial declared and sustained intent was to audit.—GOAL PROGRESS

RULE #2: Graduated—UGRAD & GRAD: All degree-seeking students who receive an award (degree or certificate) at or above the level of their initial declared intent are considered to have met their learning goal. Non-degree seekers who change their mind and earn any award are also considered to have met their learning goal. (See Rule #8)—GOAL MET

RULE #3: Interim Award—UGRAD & GRAD: Degree-seeking students who receive awards (degree or certificate) lower than initial intent are considered to have made UAA-assisted progress.—GOAL PROGRESS

RULE #4: Transfers Out—UGRAD & GRAD: All students who transfer out before earning a UAA award (degree or certificate) and are admitted and enroll at another college/university are considered to have made UAA-assisted progress to the extent the student has earned successful grades.—GOAL PROGRESS

RULE #5: Tracking Student Behavior/Performance—UGRAD & GRAD: It is assumed student behavior and academic course performance are directly attributable to the student's underlying intent. Goal progress/attainment is reflected in such behavior.—GOAL PROGRESS

RULE #6: Intermittent (Stopouts)—UGRAD & GRAD: All students who attend more than one term but less than all terms, summers excluded, throughout the decade are considered to be "Intermittent Enrollees." Note: At the decade point, degree seekers in "Intermittent" status remain there but are no longer tracked annually. All NDS intermittent students at that point are classified into "Goal Progress Levels" based on the course completion criteria. (See Rule #8)—GOAL PROGRESS

RULE #7: Non-Returning (Dropouts)—UGRAD & GRAD: All students who enroll for the initial term only but do not return for ten years and do not transfer to another institution are considered to have not met their goal—GOAL NOT MET. Note: Any non-degree seeking student who enrolls for the initial term only is ultimately classified into "Goal Progress Levels" at the decade final status report.—GOAL PROGRESS

RULE #8: Levels of Goal Progress: It is considered that all students are making levels of learning progress toward their goal to the extent they are earning "Success" grades in their courses. It is further considered that grades issued symbolize the extent to which each student has demonstrated mastery of the expected academic learning outcomes the instructor has identified to the student and assessed through student performance throughout the term.

The model distinguishes among levels of Successful Learning Progress ranges based on the number of courses taken with "success" grades: (0–10 percent = No Progress; 11–30 percent = Minimal Progress; 31–74 percent = Moderate Progress; 75–89 percent = Substantial Progress; 90+ percent = Progress with Distinction.—GOAL PROGRESS

CHAPTER 15

ACADEMIC SPACE MANAGEMENT AND THE ROLE OF INSTITUTIONAL RESEARCH

Catherine Watt

The importance of academic facilities and the space contained therein for colleges and universities cannot be understated. Figures from 2009 put construction costs for a science or engineering building at more than $300 per square foot (Abramson, 2010). At this time, facilities are the second greatest investment that an institution makes, second only to faculty and staff. What is remarkable is that although we hold faculty members accountable for almost every aspect of their work, most institutional leaders and their respective state counterparts do not often ask questions about how their facilities are used.

There are multiple contemporary information needs that suggest institutions could benefit from enhanced facilities data. Among the reasons:

- The information needs are challenging because of our loosely coupled, complex organizations.
- Institutional cultures often reinforce college independence and decentralized decision making, which reinforces the idea that space "belongs" to a department or even to an individual.
- Measurement of academic planning objectives requires accurate and quantifiable information to assess progress.
- Leased space, multiple campus locations, and sharing of faculty all present another layer of complexity to management and planning.

The purpose of this chapter is to explore the role of institutional researchers in analyzing and tracking the use of space, using a concept referred to as *academic space management* (ASM). This concept does not replace the data typically

---

The original content of this chapter was developed in the author's unpublished dissertation, and is reprinted with permission.

collected by an institution's physical plant; rather, it expands the importance of physical plant data to the senior administration. ASM is an innovative construct for developing criteria for assessment of current space allocation to academic programs, defining benchmarks relative to program needs, and using those benchmarks as a foundation for setting expectations and making management decisions. It involves the use of a web-based system in which authority for space accuracy is delegated down to the colleges and departments. ASM also suggests using more detailed text-based room descriptors (for example, *bench laboratory* rather than only *laboratory*) as well as assigning individuals to offices and laboratories. The more detailed information can then be used in productivity reporting about research activities and planning for future needs, and can contribute to decision making at the senior management levels. ASM addresses space needs that are complex and multifaceted. It includes defining benchmarks relative to program needs—and using those benchmarks as a foundation for setting expectations can improve academic planning. Institutional research is positioned well to take a lead in AMS, because it is the single institutional source for merging databases from multiple departments and turning those pieces of data into information for senior leaders.

Why Does Space Matter?

Space has been recognized in the literature as a finite resource requiring careful management. Administrators across all types of institutions have acknowledged this need for at least two decades (Castaldi, 1987; Kaiser, 1989; Ehrenberg, 2000). Unfortunately, the traditional information resource—the typical physical plant generic inventory—seldom is useful for management purposes. The focus of the inventory tends to be on the physical attributes of rooms, with references to fixed, overarching function codes. An inventory's use of codes and its lack of fields that can be linked with other databases make it of limited utility for those outside of physical plant administration. Lacking sufficient detail of function and assigned faculty, these inventories can rarely be used by the institution's academic administration for immediate management decisions or long-term planning.

Academic leaders and governing boards are increasingly aware of both the importance and the difficulty of managing physical plants as finite resources. In the 1960s, operation and maintenance of facilities represented only 3 to 10 percent of an operating budget, but that percentage jumped to 20 to 30 percent by 1985 (Montgomery, 1989). The National Science Foundation (2007) suggests that research space will become even more important as institutions are faced with increases in long-deferred maintenance costs coming due. The finances currently required to renovate or build facilities represent a substantial challenge to institutional leaders. In 2006, colleges and universities spent $15.1 billion on new construction and renovation, with the expenditures varying significantly by state. As an example, the median cost per square foot for a specialized science building was $290 in 2006 (Abramson, 2007).

Improved information should be of interest to all sectors of higher education. All institutions face substantially greater financial pressure and must justify building new or renovating facilities. Although many states do require accountability in terms of classroom or laboratory use percentages, space used for research, administration, and other services goes unreported. As our physical spaces become increasingly specific for issues related to information technology, new medical specialties, and even entirely new disciplines, we must build databases that can adapt to meet specific administrative needs.

An academic space management system involves the use of an accessible web-based system to track both occupation and use of academic space. Again, the tool adds much when presidents must go before their boards or legislatures to request funds for new buildings or significant renovations. Being able to graphically and financially detail how demands on a current facility exceed its capacity is a powerful weapon that most institutions do not possess. Similarly, the case for using federal funds for infrastructure changes must be very convincing, and the ASM construct allows such arguments to be made with facts, not just persuasive stories. This type of system provides a new tool for senior administrators, deans, and department chairs who need information about institutional space at their fingertips.

Moving from Traditional Systems to Databases

For most institutions, traditional facilities inventories are maintained for cataloging, for listing maintenance and renovation orders, and for tracking individual classrooms. At public institutions, such inventories also support state reporting of facilities use. An inventory is, by definition, simply a listing of items, a catalog. An inventory is not usually designed with either management or decision making in mind. It serves the purpose of simple reporting to states and federal agencies that then report data related to insurance, room use, and overall research capacity. For research institutions, these inventories can easily include over 15,000 individual rooms, even when excluding residence halls. During visits to several institutions and in collaboration with other facilities professionals, the author discovered that as a general rule, facilities inventories are stand-alone systems that have a focus on maintenance and repair rather than overall use or even occupancy. Technology-based systems, such as ARCHIBUS or Bricsnet, can make the information more accessible by those in the physical plant and even link architectural drawings to rooms. However, according to those institutions visited by the author, the primary purpose of these database systems remains maintenance and upkeep of rooms and buildings.

For example, traditional inventories have only one code designating classrooms—110—but today's classrooms come in greater variety. How would

FIGURE 15.1   EXAMPLE OF CODE USE IN A SPACE DATABASE

Building	Room	Department	Room Function	Room Use	Stations	Empl ID	Employee	Assignable Area
000023-Earle Hall	100	0909-Chemical Engr	11-Instruction	111-Smart Classroom	76			1468
000023-Earle Hall	103	0909-Chemical Engr	11-Instruction	110-Classroom	28			577
000023-Earle Hall	207	0909-Chemical Engr	11-Instruction	110-Classroom	30			568
000023-Earle Hall	G023	0909-Chemical Engr	11-Instruction	310-Office				392
000023-Earle Hall	209	0909-Chemical Engr	11-Instruction	311-Faculty Office		002780	Gooding, Charles H	181
000023-Earle Hall	G016	0909-Chemical Engr	11-Instruction	311-Faculty Office		000359	Hirt, Douglas E	186

one delineate which rooms are "smart classrooms"—those fully equipped with current technology? Perhaps there is also a need for specialized classrooms for nursing, for drafting? As disciplines incorporate different teaching techniques into their pedagogical styles, it would seem that the traditional 110 code becomes increasingly uninformative to decision makers. The foundation of ASM posits that it is possible—and actually preferable—to break these traditional codes into greater detail and to use text in the database to facilitate use by those outside of the physical plant. Institutional researchers can be the leader in this effort to merge traditional inventory systems with more informative database elements while continuing maintenance of roll-up codes for summary reports. Using the information in Figure 15.1, professionals inside and outside of institutional research could make use of the variables to analyze and plan for facility needs. In Figure 15.1 is an example of what is possible in a space management database.

One of the strengths allowed in designing a space *database* is that one can better discuss issues of space "ownership"—which is part of the initial challenge in developing a space management system. For most of us, the more time we spend in a particular space, the more we consider it *ours*. When space is not part of an institution's management portfolio, individuals (professors, chairs, or deans) can start to think that all space is theirs to manage as they wish. Designing a system that is open to institutional leadership and is queried regularly diminishes the idea that institutional space belongs to individuals. The task of articulating ownership is discussed in greater detail later in this chapter.

Leaders of complex enterprises require tools that integrate data and allow them to become useful information. Information today must be accessible at a moment's request, and all information must be linkable with other institutional databases, such as personnel, finance, and enrollment. Good database design principles require standardized fields for use in merging with other data resources, and these fields must have content that can be understood by those who use the database. Designing a database that encompasses an institution's needs is best accomplished by those who need the information. In addition, a facilities database that encourages use by other professionals outside of physical plant tends to increase the accuracy and thoroughness of the data.

Developing and maintaining an institution's information system is a primary challenge for today's institutional leaders, given that technology changes almost daily, concerns about security abound, and costs are added annually. Databases designed to support the personnel, student, and financial operations of a complex college or university cost millions of dollars to purchase and unknown millions in management and annual fees. Institutions require massive amounts of detailed information to manage their complex endeavors, and those requirements are only increasing with demands for compliance, financial accountability, and potential conflicts of interest.

Institutions that start down the path of developing a space database can think about how to incorporate various pieces of information in their systems. The rest of this chapter will take institutional researchers through the process of building collaborations within their institutions as they prepare to implement a space management system designed to respond to twenty-first-century needs. The overall process is depicted in Figure 15.2, which illustrates how most institutions move through the space management process, starting with the traditional inventory and evolving to a knowledge system capable of linking with multiple institutional databases.

Acquiring new information from space data usually means adopting changes—integrating innovative data techniques and philosophies into the institutional culture. It is the blending of technical methodology with the nuances of organization culture that leads to holistic ASM. The technical portion of ASM is relatively well defined, whereas the factors affecting its

FIGURE 15.2   INSTITUTIONAL KNOWLEDGE PHASES

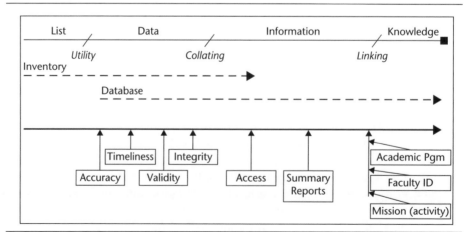

integration (consistent use) into the organization are more difficult to assess and categorize. It is essential to establish accountability standards for the support of investigators in order to attract and retain the most productive researchers. Although two institutional types—academic medical centers and research universities—may seemingly have different nonresearch missions, they share in recognizing the importance of good space management practices. Community colleges, for example, are being pressed for classroom space and office space as their enrollments swell. In other cases, schools may need to do what could be termed a "space audit" as they reevaluate where traditional classrooms may need to be renovated for computer space or new student social space.

The Metrics of Academic Space Management

The approach behind ASM involves developing criteria for assigning space to faculty members and academic units as well as assessing existing assigned space. One of the few common characteristics across multiple science and engineering fields is the use of specialized laboratory space. The costs of using this space are usually not calculated and charged directly to a researcher in the same manner that a person is charged for utilities at a home residence. Without that usual reminder of costs, it can become easy to take this immense resource for granted. The need for and use of specialized space, as well as the grants garnered for research, vary significantly across the disciplines. However, all researchers in engineering and science have in common the need for laboratory space and external dollars. Therefore the integration of institutional research space assignment data with sponsored research data would be a measure of general interest when assessing how effectively this expensive and specialized space is being used.

A quantitative assessment can be made by integrating data on research funds generated or expended per unit of research-dedicated space. Results typically are expressed in dollars per net assignable square foot (NASF) of space ($/NASF). Usually $/NASF are first evaluated at the level of individual investigators, but summative information is useful to assess department, college, center, or institutional values as well. This measure is an attempt to quantify how effectively a faculty member uses his or her assigned space. Effectiveness is defined as using assigned specialized research space in a manner at least as well as one's peers or at a level set through internal standards or expectations, perhaps using a trend analysis to consider fluctuations over time. An evaluation of a faculty member's ability to garner external awards in a set amount of space assesses the effectiveness with which each uses limited resources and provides a common definition for other comparisons. The resulting "effectiveness metric" ($/NASF) can be used to improve resource allocation across the institution in both personnel time and actual dollars saved. For example, this information can be invaluable for department chairs as they assess space assignment

FIGURE 15.3   INDIVIDUAL FACULTY MEMBER'S SPACE ASSIGNMENTS IN A SPACE DATABASE

Faculty Member (can be Searched)

Name on Award Data	Name on Space Data
NORRIS, JAMES S.	Norris, James S. (PhD)

Assigned Rooms

Buillding	Room	Center or Shared	Dept.	Description	Area	Research Area
Basic Science	BS203A		Microbiology and	Office, Faculty	190	
Basic Science	BS206C		Microbiology and	Lab, Research Bench	945	945
Basic Science	BS206C1		Microbiology and	Lab, Research Bench	119	119
Basic Science	BS206C2		Microbiology and	Lab, Research Bench	110	110
Basic Science	BS206D		Microbiology and	Lab, Research Bench	879	879
Basic Science	BS206D1		Microbiology and	Lab, Research Bench	119	119
Basic Science	BS206D2		Microbiology and	Lab, Research Bench	110	110
				Totals:	**3,567**	**2,674**

effectiveness, for deans reviewing departmental space requests, for university officers convincing boards to approve construction, and for assigning work order priorities to laboratories that generate the most indirect costs.

Administrators at the Medical University of South Carolina (MUSC) created this effectiveness metric beginning in the early 1990s when a dean of the College of Medicine and his department chairs needed detailed space utilization information to compete for federal dollars and justify the subsequent need for research space. Using an open source program, the university created a database that included all academic and administrative space. Gradually, the system also decentralized space edits, so that designated employees can now edit the database to ensure updates and accuracy (Watt, Higerd, & Chrestman, 2004). Although once used only by the departments within the College of Medicine, the process is now used across the university. The effectiveness metric, along with concurrent research award information, is produced at least annually for use by department chairs to demonstrate to their deans how well their departments are performing compared with a college or university standard. The report details, for chairs, an individual's space assignments (Figure 15.3) and sponsored awards (Figure 15.4), and the report to the dean summarizes each department's space and awards (Figure 15.5).

Figure 15.3 shows an individual faculty member's space assignment, totaled at the bottom. It is important to note that there is no inclusion of technicians or graduate students who may occupy the space, because the faculty member is accountable for the research in that space, and he or she may move graduate students and staff around as needed for the research. In addition, the faculty member's office space is not included in the research space total. For the institutions in South Carolina that have adopted ASM, the philosophy is that all faculty members are entitled to office space, but lab space is not an entitlement.

FIGURE 15.4   INDIVIDUAL FACULTY MEMBER'S RESEARCH AWARDS, INCLUDING FUNDING PER SQUARE FOOT

Total Awards in Sponsored Programes

Sponsorer	Award No.	Budget j.r Start/End	Project Start/End	Title	Awarded ($1 Budget j.r)		
					Direct	Indirect	Total
HEXAL		10/1/1997 3/31/2000	10/1/1997 3/31/2000	RIBOZYME GENE THERAPY	247, 301	0	247, 301
HEXAL		10/1/1999 9/30/2000	10/1/1997 9/30/2000	RIBOZYME GENE THERAPY	773, 046	359,558	1,132,604
NIH/NCI	2RO1 CA49949-0	4/1/1999 2/29/2000	9/1/1998 9/28/2002	STEROID MODULATION OF TUMOR CELL GROWTH	196, 689	83.363	280,052
NIH/NCI	5RO1 CA49949-1	4/1/1999 2/29/2000	9/1/1988 9/28/2002	STEROID MODULATION OF TUMOR CELL GROWTH	194, 802	85,713	280,515
NIH/NCI	5RO1 CA69598-0	7/1/1999 6/30/2000	9/1/1997 9/30/2002	INDUCTION AND ANALYSIS OF PROSTATE CANCER	166,289	72,776	239,065

Totals: **1,578,127 601,410 2,179,537**

Total Funding per Assigned Space

Direct $/NSF	Indirect $/NSF	Total $/NSF
$590	$225	$815

Figure 15.4 shows some of the research awards for the same faculty member shown in Figure 15.3, again totaled at the bottom. The award dollars have been annualized and broken out into direct award, indirect award, and total award. This is because of the importance that some institutions place on garnering indirect dollars, and the perspective that the direct portion is simply a "pass through," going only to specific costs associated with the research project. At the bottom of the table, the research dollar totals have been divided by the research space from Figure 15.3 to generate the "effectiveness metric" in dollars awarded per square foot of assigned research space.

Figure 15.5 illustrates what can be summarized for department level analysis and, perhaps, given to a Dean or Provost for assessing the research needs of a department. This type of summary can be useful to Deans and Provosts as they assess needs for a coming year or evaluate institutional emphasis areas for research. A summary of this type also allows administrators to assess internal changes to a department over time, given that it is easier to re-allocate space within a department rather than "take over" space allocated to another department.

Although the forms shown in these figures are best used at research institutions, it is hoped that they may provide a springboard for additional ideas from other institutional types. For example, community colleges can use the number of majors enrolled in programs such as nursing or drafting, noting that those programs require high-cost facilities that may take longer to pay for themselves based on student tuition. Similarly, colleges may want to evaluate space based

FIGURE 15.5   DEPARTMENTAL SUMMARY OF SPACE

Biochemistry and Molecular Biology, College of Medicine-Basic Sciences

	Direct	Indirect	Total
Total Awards:	4,620,847	1,558,535	6,179,382
Lab-requiring Awards:	4,595,587	1,557,757	6,153,344

Research-dedicated Dept NSF: 24,889

	Direct	Indirect	Rate	Total
Award $/Research NSF:	$184.64	$62.59	25.3%	$247.23

Biometry and Epidemiology, College of Medicine-Basic Sciences

	Direct	Indirect	Total
Total Awards:	4,410,514	1,035,782	5,446,296
Lab-requiring Awards:	3,147,193	993,039	4,140,232

Research-dedicated Dept NSF: 4,027

	Direct	Indirect	Rate	Total
Award $/Research NSF:	$781.52	$246.60	24.0%	$1,028.12

Cell Biology and Anatomy, College of Medicine-Basic Sciences

	Direct	Indirect	Total
Total Awards:	7,034,476	2,229,128	9,263,604
Lab-requiring Awards:	6,899,681	2,229,128	9,128,809

Research-dedicated Dept NSF: 18,380

	Direct	Indirect	Rate	Total
Award $/Research NSF:	$375.39	$121.28	24.4%	$496.67

on the faculty members as well as student majors. The bottom line for institutional researchers is to evaluate the strategic goals for their institutions and determine how space can be used in decision making.

The Role of Institutional Research in Space Management

Once an institutional research office embarks on building a space management system, there will be challenges along the way. It is important for the IR staff to proceed, asking specific questions: what purpose will the system serve, and who will the primary users be? The author strongly recommends working closely with department chairs in particular, because they are the ones closest to the space and they have operational responsibility for its use. One strength of institutional research offices across the country and around the world is their connectedness with departments throughout an institution and their knowledge of various institutional data.

Exhibit 15.1 presents a set of suggested questions to consider asking when initiating the space database discussions. As with other aspects of the system, these will depend on the needs and goals of an individual institution. Above all, these discussions are *not* considered optional. Involvement with other offices and leadership is essential to the success of the project.

As mentioned earlier, institutions can purchase a space management package—a system that costs from $3 to $5 million, depending on specific capabilities. It is also possible to use an open-source database system using components of MySQL, Perl, and a standard Microsoft Access database to develop a system that can manage facilities at a large research university. Depending on the

EXHIBIT 15.1 QUESTIONS TO ASK IN SPACE MANAGEMENT IMPLEMENTATION

Who will use your database and what are their issues?
- Department chairs and faculty tasked committees
- College deans
- Administrative support, such as institutional research, sponsored programs
- Senior administrative officers, such as BOT, presidents, provosts, CEOs

What data elements and attributes do you want included in your database?
- All buildings versus only academic buildings
- Research intensive facilities anticipating F&A audits
- Specialty use rooms, such as smart classrooms
- Personnel information

What do you need to accomplish? (Program planning is important!)
- List the high-priority information needs.
- Identify champion(s) to drive and coordinate objectives.
- Build in methods to update and to assess the accuracy of the information.
- Be sure constituents have access to the information as well as the data.

capacity of a school's institutional research office, it is possible to collaborate with information technology staff, physical plant directors, and department chairs to create a space database. The open source system can be a good option, because few institutions can afford a million-dollar investment during tough times, and the senior administration will be more willing to move ahead with a space database if the up-front costs are low and the returns are high.

The recommended database elements can be as simple or as complex as the institution needs—another reason for institutional researchers to tackle the new initiative. It is important to keep in mind certain specific recommendations when building the web-based system:

- Ensure use of the authenticated data source for all elements and that the links are active and regularly updated.
- Do not allow use of "free text" fields in the web system except as comments; it is recommended that drop-down boxes be used for all fields.
- Not all fields should be open for edits by institutional personnel. Determine which fields will be editable; other changes can be recommended in a comments box.
- Depending on the size of your institution, appointing one person in each college as the designated space person can be very useful. The institutional research office should work closely with these appointees to manage and pull data from the new space system.

FIGURE 15.6   ELEMENTS OF A BASIC WEB-BASED SPACE DATABASE

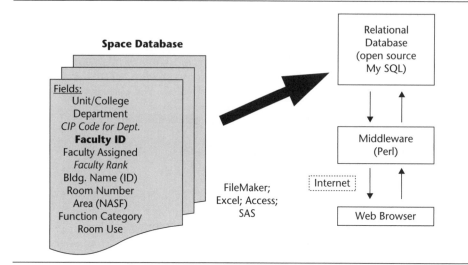

- Overall, the sooner reports can be generated and shared with multiple parties, from chairs to the president, the better the system will become integrated into the institutional culture.

Readers interested in learning more about two existing space management systems can view more at the Clemson website (http://www.clemson.edu/oirweb1/fb/OIRWebpage/) or the MUSC website (http://academicdepartments.musc.edu/oipa/planning/space%20inventory/space.htm).

Institutional research offices can prepare for managing space information with some simple steps that will make the process move more smoothly:

- Provide simple space summaries to department chairs and center directors as the change process starts.
- Seek out the greatest critics and give them a way to have input into the system.
- Open access to the new space system when it is approximately 80 percent complete.
- Understand that building a space management system will take a significant amount of time and is unlike usual IR endeavors.
- Build contacts at other institutions in order to build comparable information systems and make space even more relevant.

Overall, IR offices will be able to maximize the usefulness of space information by merging multiple databases and building peer comparisons. There is no other office in an institution that possesses this capability.

Space management is an ever-growing concern for institutions large and small. There is little money available from state or local budgets for new buildings, and the deferred maintenance bill continues to escalate. Room use is an evolving issue, with courses being offered online or classes scheduled during what used to be considered off hours. Finally, as institutions construct buildings that are LEED certified or green, institutions will seek to evaluate yet another aspect of energy costs and use (see Chapter 16 for a more detailed discussion of these topics). Only institutional research offices are prepared to manage the myriad databases required for the ASM construct to work at their institutions and to add vital information to the decision-making process.

References

Abramson, P. (2007). *College construction report. College Planning & Management 10,* C2(7). Retrieved from *InfoTrac oneFile* via Thomson Gale, http://find.galegroup .com/itx/infomark.do?&contentSet=IAC-Documents&type=retrieve&tabID=T00 3&prodId=ITOF&docId=A160590810&source=gale&userGroupName=clemson_ itweb&version=1.0

Abramson, P. (2010). College Construction Report. *College Planning & Management 10,* C2(7). Retrieved from Google Scholar, www.peterli.com/cpm/pdfs/CPM-Construction-Report.pdf

Castaldi, B. (1987). *Educational facilities: Planning, modernization, and management.* Boston: Allyn and Bacon.

Ehrenberg, R. G. (2000). *Tuition rising: Why college costs so much.* Cambridge, MA: Harvard University Press.

Kaiser, H. H. (Ed.). (1989, Spring). *Planning and managing higher education facilities.* New Directions for Institutional Research, no. 61. San Francisco: Jossey-Bass.

Montgomery, D. A. (1989). Organizing for space management. In H. H. Kaiser (Ed.), *Planning and managing higher education facilities* (pp. 21–36). New Directions for Institutional Research, no. 61. San Francisco: Jossey-Bass.

National Science Foundation. (2007). *Scientific and engineering research facilities at colleges and universities, 2005.* NSF 01–301. Arlington, VA: Division of Science Resources Studies.

Watt, C. E., Higerd, T. B., & Chrestman, R. E. (2004, May). *Academic space management: An initial report from the SPACE Consortium.* Association for Institutional Research national conference, Boston, MA.

CHAPTER 16

MANAGING SUSTAINABILITY

Josetta S. McLaughlin and Lisa M. Amoroso

The most commonly used definition of sustainable development is one articulated by the Brundtland Commission in its report titled *Our Common Future*: "development that meets the needs of the present without compromising the ability of future generations to meet their own needs" (1987). Sustainability advocates are looking to colleges and universities to put this definition into practice by playing a pivotal role in shaping the attitudes of students, faculty, staff, and others affiliated with their organizations. Furthermore, the discussions about education's role in sustainable development are taking place in all sectors of the global society, indicating that there is a worldwide expectation that colleges and universities should work to bring societal attitudes into greater alignment with the Brundtland Commission definition. Response to this expectation can have immediate positive consequences, in that college and university campuses have historically been major contributors to unsustainable practices. With respect to facilities alone, a college campus leaves a significant ecological and carbon footprint (*The Princeton Review's Guide*, 2010). Lowering this footprint requires redesigning shared spaces, developing curriculum, partnering with community, and conducting research—all of which are consistent with sustainability values.

Expectations about higher education's role in creating a social consciousness about sustainable development are not passing whims, and they are likely to result in new perspectives on what students should be learning and how campuses should operate. These expectations are both philosophical and operational. At a philosophical level, education can help individuals overcome cognitive and normative obstacles standing in the way of reaching sustainability goals (Edwards, 2005). Educators can thus play a decisive role in establishing sustainability as a value in society's existing structures and in supporting identification of solutions to systemic global problems (UNDESD, 2002, Resolution 57/254). At an operational level, higher education practitioners are called to lead through actions, including retrofit of facilities, waste and emissions management, and modification of college curriculum. Current operational discussions tend to focus on environmental or "green" initiatives or on use of sustainable development in institutional branding. This focus is being broadened to include the two additional pillars of sustainability—economic sustainability and social justice. Inclusion of all three pillars of sustainability in college and university life, from student cocurricular activities to classroom management to research to operations, elevates the role of education in creating a more sustainable future.

Institutional researchers who recognize the evolving societal expectations of higher education's role in creating a sustainable future can play a critical role in supporting sustainability initiatives at their colleges and universities. For example, they can develop auditing and reporting frameworks to monitor sustainability outcomes. Furthermore, they can position themselves strategically to support implementation of processes and procedures that ensure transparency and accountability in all aspects of institutional operations.

This chapter focuses on information that can assist institutional researchers in supporting sustainability initiatives at their institutions. It provides examples of both the major catalysts that drive higher education sustainability initiatives and the frameworks that support auditing and reporting on sustainable development. We begin by identifying catalysts for sustainability planning at colleges and universities, including global initiatives that articulate a role for higher education in creating a more sustainable world. This is followed by a description of initiatives that focus on identification of sustainability frameworks and indicators being used for evaluating, reporting, and ranking sustainable development outcomes. We conclude with a discussion of how institutional researchers can strategically prepare to support college and university sustainability initiatives.

Understanding the Context

Expectations concerning the role of higher education in sustainable development have been evolving for more than 30 years. Two of the earliest calls for sustainability education (in particular, environmental sustainability) came from sources external to higher education—the Stockholm Declaration (1972) and the Tbilisi Declaration (1977). Principle 19, one of the twenty-four Stockholm Declaration principles, stressed that achieving environmental sustainability requires education "for the younger generation as well as adults" (Stockholm Declaration, 1972). This sentiment was echoed in 1977 with the crafting of the Tbilisi Declaration at the first United Nations Educational, Scientific and Cultural Organization/United Nations Environment Programme–sponsored Intergovernmental Conference on Environmental Education (Tblisi Declaration, 1978). The declaration advocated for environmental education

EXHIBIT 16.1   SUSTAINABILITY-RELATED CODES FOR USE BY COLLEGIATE INSTITUTIONS

- Stockholm Declaration on the Human Environment (1972)
- Tbilisi Declaration (1977)
- Talloires Declaration (1990)
- Halifax Declaration (1991)
- Rio Declaration on Environment and Development, Chapter 36 of Agenda 21 (1992)
- Swansea Declaration (1993)
- CRE Copernicus Charter (1993)
- Kyoto Declaration (1993)
- Blueprint for a Green Campus (1994)
- The Essex Report (1995)
- Declaration of Thessaloniki (1997)
- World Declaration on Higher Education for the 21st Century (1998)
- Dutch Charter for Sustainable Development in Vocational Training (1999)
- Earth Charter (2000)
- Luneburg Declaration (2001)
- Ubuntu Declaration (September 2002)
- Cape Town Declaration on Research for Sustainable Development (2002)
- Declaration of Barcelona (2004)
- The Graz Declaration (2005)
- Declaration on the Responsibility of Higher Education for a Democratic Culture—Citizenship, Human Rights and Sustainability (2006)
- Lucerne Declaration on Geographical Education for Sustainable Development (2007)
- Charter for Alliance of French Universities Fostering Sustainable Development (2008)
- Tokyo Declaration of HOPE (2009)

Source: Various websites, including the International Association of Universities and the United Nations.

through the formal and nonformal education systems. Subsequent declarations have further clarified sustainable development in higher education as including all three pillars of sustainability—economic, social, and environmental.

Major intergovernmental declarations passed since 1972 have acted as major drivers for action by professional associations and nongovernmental organizations (NGOs) representing the higher education sector. They have also provided roadmaps for both new and preexisting associations on how to develop and implement sustainability initiatives (see Exhibit 16.1). Most declarations have a dedicated website; additional information on major declarations is thus readily available through the Internet.

Forces driving higher education institutions to adopt sustainability initiatives are also internal and evolve out of initiatives of individuals holding top executive positions in colleges and universities. Two initiatives—one developed by the Association of University Leaders for a Sustainable Future (ULSF) and one by the American College & University Presidents' Climate Commitment (ACUPCC)—are especially important to understanding the higher education commitment to sustainable development. These initiatives demonstrate the commitment made by the most influential leadership groups in higher education sectors, both nationally and internationally. They signal an acceptance of the values and ideals associated with the sustainability movement. They are described in more detail in the following section.

Understanding the Tone at the Top

College and university presidents and chancellors representing many institutions have made public commitments to work towards a sustainable future; the most widely discussed and perhaps most influential commitment is the Talloires Declaration (1990). It was articulated at a meeting of 22 universities convened by John Mayer, then president of Tufts University, in Talloires, France. The meeting's purpose was to define higher education's role in achieving a sustainable future. The end product was a ten-point action plan for revisions to teaching, research, and outreach. The plan—the Talloires Declaration—is shown in Appendix 16.1. ULSF is the Secretariat for this Declaration. Presidents and chancellors who sign the Declaration—currently more than 400—agree to follow the action plan and to encourage education, research, policy formation, and information exchange that raise public awareness about moving toward a sustainable future (About ULSF, n.d.).

As part of its global outreach effort, ULSF assists colleges and universities in assessing their performance on sustainability through use of a qualitative questionnaire, the Sustainability Assessment Questionnaire (SAQ) (n.d.). Findings from the SAQ provide institutions with a snapshot of the state of sustainability on their campus as well as information on which to base their next steps. The eight categories covered in the survey are: (1) curriculum, (2) research and scholarship, (3) operations, (4) faculty and staff development and rewards, (5) outreach and service, (6) student opportunities, (7) institutional mission, and (8) structure and planning.

ULSF partners on numerous sustainability initiatives, including the Global Higher Education for Sustainability Partnership (GHESP) (UNESCO, n.d.). GHESP was formed to support sustainable development in response to Chapter 36 of Agenda 21, 1992 Earth Summit, held in Rio de Janeiro (Agenda 21, 1992). Chapter 36.1 builds on the fundamental principles laid out in the Declaration and Recommendations of the 1977 Tbilisi Intergovernmental Conference on Environmental Education.

A second initiative that reflects a somewhat narrower commitment of higher education top leadership to sustainable development is the American College & University Presidents' Climate Commitment (ACUPCC). Like the ULSF, ACUPCC is an organization made up of higher education leaders; unlike the ULSF, it focuses more narrowly on problems associated with climate change, in particular emissions (Mission and History, n.d.). Participating presidents and chancellors publicly support the need to reduce the global emission of greenhouse gases. (See Chapter 8 for more discussion of supporting executives.)

ACUPCC supports its signatory institutions through provision of resources, most importantly, the *Implementation Liaison Handbook* (Reporting System, n.d.). The Handbook provides information to assist institutions in fulfilling the terms of the president's climate commitment. The ACUPCC uses a web-based reporting mechanism to provide information on performance of signatory institutions. It is available to the public and provides statistics on average gross emissions by Carnegie class, average gross emissions by source, tangible action statistics, and stakeholder group statistics (Resources & Events, n.d.). Other resource information provided by ACUPCC includes links to information ranging from examples of climate action plans to energy, green building, gas emission inventories, transportation, procurement, and recycling and waste management (Resources & Events, n.d.).

USLF and ACUPCC are two of many organizations that support sustainability initiatives in higher education. However, because their memberships are composed of top university leadership teams, they are especially influential. An important group of NGOs has also formed to support USLF and ACUPCC initiatives and those of other higher education entities that are promoting sustainable development. Global and national groups include (but are not limited to) the International Institute for Sustainable Development, the Global Higher Education for Sustainability Partnership (GHESP), Second Nature, ecoAmerica, the National Association of Environmental Law Societies (NAELS), the Clinton Climate Initiative, the Aspen Institute, Philippine Association of Tertiary Level Educational Institutions in Environmental Protection and Management (PATLEPAM), and the Association for the Advancement of Sustainability in Higher Education (AASHE). Each of these organizations has a dedicated website that contains information on collaborations and other networks that have formed to support higher education sustainability efforts. AASHE is discussed in greater detail later in this chapter.

Auditing and Tracking the Context

Colleges and universities will be held accountable by key stakeholders and the general public for answers to three broadly stated questions that represent the three pillars of sustainability. First, do our activities promote sustainable economic health for the university, the local community, and the global community? Second, do we conduct operations in a manner that contributes to the well-being of our employees, our students, and the worldwide civil society? And third, do we manage operations in a way that is protective of the environment (Blackburn, 2007)? To accurately address these questions, institutional researchers need to capture the progress and outcomes of institutional sustainability efforts from multiple functions at the college or university. Institutional researchers face the strategic and formidable challenge of determining how to ensure data availability through data management activities. This includes identification of data currently available, data needed in the future, data coding for consistency over time, design and development of a sustainability database, collection and integration of data, and reporting of sustainable development performance outcomes (McLaughlin & Howard, 2004). Such efforts can be informed by the use of frameworks being developed to specifically guide sustainability initiatives by colleges and universities.

Broadly Focused Auditing Frameworks

Broadly focused sustainability auditing frameworks are developed for use by multiple industry sectors and types of organizations. At the global level, the most widely used framework is the Reporting Framework developed by the Global Reporting Initiative (GRI) (Reporting Framework, n.d.). It is available for free and online for voluntary adoption by organizations of any size, type, or geographic region (About GRI, n.d.). GRI's *G3 Guidelines,* the foundation of the framework, identify both sound reporting principles and triple bottom line (economic, social, and environmental) performance indicators as part of its user support (G3 Guidelines, n.d.). GRI is currently developing *sector supplements* that provide unique industry indicators and *national annexes* that identify unique country-level information. As of May 2010, a sector supplement had not yet been developed for colleges and universities.

GRI uses economic, social, and environmental performance categories to organize its triple bottom line performance indicators. Due to the complexities associated with social performance, this category is broken down into four subcategories—labor practices and decent work, human rights, society, and product responsibility—yielding six indicator categories. Categories and indicator codes are shown in Table 16.1. Indicators are then assigned "Indicator Aspects," headings that more specifically reflect the issue to be measured. For example, Performance Indicator EN8 (water withdrawal) falls under the Water Aspect in the Environment Category. Indicator EN11 on protected areas also falls under the Environment Category but is found under the Biodiversity Aspect. One or more indicators may be assigned to each Indicator Aspect.

Higher Education Auditing Frameworks

Professional associations, following the lead of the 1990 Talloires initiative, are developing sustainability auditing frameworks to evaluate performance outcomes for higher education sustainable development initiatives. Collaboration among NGOs and higher education institutions is widespread, global, and

TABLE 16.1   GRI INDICATORS

Indicator Code	Performance Indicator Category	# of Aspects	Aspects Labels	
EC	Economic	3	Economic Performance Market Presence	Indirect Economic Impacts
EN	Environmental	9	Materials Energy Water Biodiversity Emissions, Effluents, & Waste	Products and Services Compliance Transport Overall
LA	Social Performance: Labor Practices & Decent Work	5	Employment Labor/Management Relations Occupational Health & Safety	Training & Education Diversity & Equal Opportunity
HR	Social Performance: Human Rights	8	Investment & Procurement Practices Non-Discrimination Freedom of Association & Collective Bargaining	Child Labor Forced &Compulsory Labor Security Practices Indigenous Rights
SO	Social Performance: Society	5	Community Corruption Public Policy	Anti-Competitive Behavior Compliance
PR	Social Performance: Product Responsibility	5	Customer Health & Safety Products & Service Labeling Marketing	Communications Customer Privacy Compliance

Source: The Global Reporting Initiative (GRI), 2011. Sustainability Reporting Guidelines, pp. 28–39. https://www .globalreporting.org/resourcelibrary/G3.1-Sustainability-Reporting-Guidelines.pdf. Reprinted with permission.

born out of necessity: colleges and universities need the specialized support of many experts to identify indicators and collect data on sustainability outcomes. Diverse knowledge, skills, and competences are required to audit colleges and universities, given that their complex operations are on a par with small cities. Every aspect of a institution's value chain (for example, purchasing, recycling, energy use, housing, curriculum, marketing, finance well-being) must be addressed as part of a sustainability audit.

Scholars, NGOs, and other stakeholders have worked collaboratively to identify the various sectors of relevant university activity for auditing sustainable development (Blackburn, 2007; Litten & Terkla, 2007). For example, in *The Sustainability Handbook,* Blackburn proposes three broad auditing sectors—Campus Operations Sector, University Curriculum, and Research. Litten and Terkla (2007) suggest four categories—environmental, financial, social, and academic. They identify an extensive list of indicators, with more than 100 indicators for the environmental category alone. NGO and government-developed sustainability audits include *EPA's 20 Questions for College and University Presidents, The Ecological Footprint Analysis of Colorado College, Campus Ecology Environmental Audit, C2E2 Environmental Management System Self-Assessment Checklist, U.K. HEPS Reporting for Sustainability Guidance for Higher Education Institutions,*

U.K. EcoCampus, Dutch Auditing Instrument for Sustainability in Higher Education, The Campus Sustainability Assessment Project, NJHEPS Campus Sustainability: Selected Indicators Snapshot and Guide, Good Company's Sustainability Pathways Toolkit, and the *USCB Campus Sustainability Assessment Protocol* (Blackburn, 2007).

The most ambitious initiative for tracking sustainability initiatives in U.S. and Canadian colleges and universities is an auditing framework developed by the Association for the Advancement of Sustainability in Higher Education (AASHE). AASHE is an association of higher education institutions and organizations that provides resources to support colleges and universities in their efforts to advance sustainability in governance, operations, curriculum development, and research (About AASHE, n.d.). Established in 2005 with fewer than two hundred organizational members, AASHE had reached one thousand members as of May 1, 2010.

AASHE is a member of the Higher Education Association Sustainability Consortium (HEASC), an informal network of associations in higher education committed to advancing sustainability (HEASC, n.d.). In response to a call by HEASC, AASHE developed a self-reporting framework that enables colleges and universities to gauge their relative progress toward sustainability. The framework—the Sustainability Tracking, Assessment & Rating System (STARS)—was released in 2010. It was developed as an initiative that can:

1. Provide a guide for advancing sustainability in all sectors of higher education, from education and research to operations and administration,
2. Enable meaningful comparisons over time and across institutions by establishing a common standard of measurement for sustainability in higher education,
3. Create incentives for continual improvement toward sustainability,
4. Facilitate information sharing about higher education sustainability practices and performance, and
5. Build a stronger, more diverse campus sustainability community. (STARS Technical Manual, 2012, p. 7)

STARS is designed to support the full spectrum of higher education institutions, from community colleges to research universities. It serves both those institutions that are already high-achieving and those that are taking first steps in implementing sustainability initiatives. Recognition takes the form of rating levels that are based on a minimum credit score, as shown in Table 16.2. Credits are meant to show progress toward achieving a specific sustainability outcome. Any institution that wants to participate in STARS but does not want their information to be released may participate as a STARS reporter. Contributors to the design of STARS believe that the act of participation itself "represents a commitment to sustainability that should be applauded" (Ratings and Credits, n.d.). Therefore STARS ratings are by design positive, with each level representing

TABLE 16.2   STARS RATINGS AND RECOGNITION SYSTEM

Recognition Level	Minimum Credits/Score
STARS Bronze	25
STARS Silver	45
STARS Gold	65
STARS Platinum	85
STARS Reporter	No scores are made public

Source: STARS Technical Manual, 2012, p. 11.

significant achievement. AASHE membership is not required for participation in STARS.

STARS credits include both quantitative indicators that are based on objective, measurable, and actionable criteria and qualitative indicators that are harder to define and measure. The credits are scrutinized using gatekeeper questions to determine (1) whether the performance led to improved environment, social and financial impacts (for example, accelerated transition to renewable energy systems), (2) the relevance and meaningfulness of the credit for diverse institutions (for example, being appropriate for most institution types), and (3) the appropriateness of the credit relative to performance (such as operation of a campus shuttle service). Information regarding STARS measures, metrics, indicators, credits, and rating system can be found in its online technical manual (STARS Technical Manual, 2012).

The STARS framework uses a two-tiered system. As shown in Table 16.3, Tier One credits "are worth one or more points each and are grouped into a subcategory (e.g., Curriculum) in a category (e.g., Education & Research)" (STARS Technical Manual, 2012, p. 9). Tier Two credits, worth .25 points, are important but tend either to have a smaller impact than Tier One credits—such as a bike-sharing program—or to represent benefits already captured by a Tier One credit—such as composting, which earns a Tier One credit on waste diversion. Tier One credits vary in the number of points allocated to a subcategory, with higher points representing a perceived greater contribution to improved economic, social, and environmental impacts or educational benefits (see STARS Technical Manual, 2012).

Information on calculating a STARS score using STARS 1.2 is explained in Appendix 16.2. The scores are based on credits earned in the three categories noted in Table 16.3: (1) Education and Research; (2) Planning, Administration, and Engagement; and (3) Operations. Each category represents 100 points. The score itself is an average of percentage points in these three categories plus any innovation credits earned for new practices not covered by STARS credits or that go beyond the criterion awarded by a specific STARS credit. Institutions can elect to continue using STARS 1.2 following release of STARS 2.0 in 2013.

TABLE 16.3 STARS 1.2 TABLE OF CREDITS

Credit Number	Credit Title	Possible Points	Credit Number	Credit Title	Possible Points
Category 1: Education & Research (ER)					
Co-Curricular Education (ER)					
ER 1	Student Sustainability Educators Program	5	ER 3	Sustainability in New Student Orientation*	2
ER 2	Student Sustainability Outreach Campaign	5	ER 4	Sustainability Materials & Publications	4
	Tier Two Credits	2			
Curriculum					
ER 5	Sustainability Course Identification	3	ER 10	Undergraduate Program in Sustainability*	4
ER 6	Sustainability-Focused Courses	10	ER 11	Graduate Program in Sustainability*	4
ER 7	Sustainability-Related Courses	10	ER 12	Sustainability Immersive Experience*	2
ER 8	Sustainability Courses by Dept.*	7	ER 13	Sustainability Literacy Assessment	2
ER 9	Sustainability Learning Outcomes*	10	ER 14	Incentives for Developing Sustainability Courses	3
Research					
ER 15	Sustainability Research Identification*	3	ER 18	Sustainability Research Incentives*	6
ER 16	Faculty Involved in Sustainability Research*	10	ER 19	Interdisciplinary Research in Tenure and Promotion*	2
ER 17	Departments Involved in Sustainability Research*	6		Total	100
Category 2: Operations (OP)					
Buildings					
OP 1	Building Operations & Maintenance	7	OP 3	Indoor Air Quality	2
OP 2	Building Design and Construction*	4			
Climate					
OP 4	GHG Emissions Inventory	2	OP 5	GHG Emissions Reduction	14
	Tier Two Credits	.5			
Dining Services					
OP 6	Food Purchasing*	6			
	Tier Two Credits	2.5			

(continued)

TABLE 16.3 STARS 1.2 TABLE OF CREDITS (continued)

Credit Number	Credit Title	Possible Points	Credit Number	Credit Title	Possible Points
Energy					
OP 7	Building Energy Consumption	8	OP 8	Renewable Energy	7
	Tier Two Credits	1.5			
Grounds					
OP 9	Integrated Pest Management*	2			
	Tier Two Credits	1.25			
Purchasing					
OP 10	Computer Purchasing	2	OP 12	Office Paper Purchasing	2
OP 11	Cleaning Product Purchasing	2	OP 13	Vendor Code of Conduct	1
	Tier Two Credits	.5			
Transportation					
OP 14	Campus Fleet	2	OP 16	Employee Commute Modal Split	3
OP 15	Student Commute Modal Split*	4			
	Tier Two Credits	3			
Waste					
OP 17	Waste Reduction	5	OP 20	Electronic Waste Recycling Program	1
OP 18	Waste Diversion	3	OP 21	Hazardous Waste Management	1
OP 19	Construction & Demolition Waste Diversion*	1			
	Tier Two Credits	1.5			
Water					
OP 22	Water Consumption	7	OP 23	Stormwater Management	2
	Tier Two Credits	1.25			
				Total	**100**

Category 3: Planning, Administration, and Engagement (PAE)

Coordination and Planning

Credit Number	Credit Title	Possible Points
PAE 1	Sustainability Coordination	3
PAE 2	Strategic Plan*	6
PAE 3	Physical Campus Plan*	4
PAE 4	Sustainability Plan	3
PAE 5	Climate Plan	2

Diversity and Affordability

PAE 6	Diversity & Equity Coordination	2	PAE 9	Support Programs for Future Faculty	4
PAE 7	Measuring Campus Diversity Culture	2	PAE 10	Affordability & Access Programs	3
PAE 8	Support Programs for Under-Represented Groups	2			
Tier Two Credits		.75			

Human Resources

PAE 11	Sustainable Compensation	8	PAE 14	Sustainability in New Employee Orientation	2
PAE 12	Employee Satisfaction Evaluation	2	PAE 15	Employee Sustainability Educators Program	5
PAE 13	Staff Professional Development in Sustainability	2			
Tier Two Credits		.75			

Investment

PAE 16	Committee Socially Responsible Investment*	2	PAE 18	Positive Sustainability Investments*	9
PAE 17	Shareholder Advocacy*	5			
Tier Two Credits		.75			

Public Engagement

PAE 19	Community Sustainability Partnerships	2	PAE 23	Community Service Hours	6
PAE 20	Inter-Campus Collaboration on Sustainability	2	PAE 24	Sustainability Policy Advocacy	4
PAE 21	Sustainability in Continuing Education*	7	PAE 25	Trademark Licensing*	4
PAE 22	Community Service Participation	6			
Tier Two Credits		.75			

Total					100

* Credit does not apply to all institutions.

Source: STARS Technical Manual 1.2 (2012), pp. 17–19. http://www.aashe.org/files/documents/STARS/stars_1.1_credit_checklist.pdf. https://stars.aashe.org. Reprinted with permission.

Frameworks and tracking systems enable colleges and universities to identify data needs, track internal performance, compare progress on sustainability efforts with that of other institutions, and report to stakeholders. The STARS reporting tool is especially useful to institutional researchers for this purpose, given that the indicators were developed specifically for colleges and universities, with input from industry experts. However, comparisons using STARS are limited to U.S. and Canadian colleges and universities that use the tracking system. Other broadly focused sustainability auditing frameworks and certification initiatives must be used to fill this gap.

Certification Initiatives

In addition to STARS and the GRI-type reporting systems, certification programs can be used to audit sustainability performance outcomes. For example, the U.S. Green Building Council oversees the Leadership in Energy and Environmental Design (LEED) certification program to verify measurable green building design and construction. The certification is now an internationally recognized green building certification system that provides third-party verification (Intro—What LEED is, n.d.). Similarly, for many years the International Organization for Standardization (ISO) has developed international management certification standards on diverse subjects, including environmental management (ISO standards, n.d.). ISO 14001 (ISO 14001:2004, n.d.) and ISO 26000 are of particular interest to colleges and universities working on sustainable development.

The LEED certification program for design and construction is voluntary. It can be applied to new construction, interior design, or significant retrofit or during any other lifecycle phase as a means to verify the use of sustainability principles in key performance areas (Intro—What LEED measures, n.d.). LEED points are awarded in the nine categories listed in Table 16.4: every

TABLE 16.4   EXAMPLE OF LEED POINT SYSTEM FOR COMMERCIAL INTERIORS

Category	Possible Points (100)
Sustainable Sites	21
Water Efficiency	11
Energy & Atmosphere	37
Materials & Resources	14
Indoor Environmental Quality	17
Bonus Points (10)	
Innovation in Design	6
Regional Priority	4

Source: Based on How to Achieve Certification (n.d.).

aspect of building performance, from CO_2 emissions reductions to improved indoor environmental quality to sensitivity concerning potential impacts, is captured in these performance areas.

LEED points are awarded on a 100-point scale, with an additional ten bonus credits available (How to achieve certification, n.d.). As shown in Table 16.4, LEED for Commercial Interiors weights the category for Energy and Atmosphere most heavily, at 37 possible points, and Water Efficiency least heavily, at 11 points; Innovation in Design and Regional Priority are bonus categories. Under the LEED Rating System 2009, projects can qualify for four levels of certification. For example, for LEED certification for Commercial Interiors, Certified would require 40+ points; Silver, 50+ points; Gold, 60+ points; and Platinum, 80+ points. The latest LEED manuals should be checked for up-to-date detailed requirements for the type of certification being sought. Information on how to proceed is available at http://www.usgbc.org/. (See Chapter 15 for more discussion on managing higher education facilities.)

ISO 14001 focuses on environmental management systems (EMS) that bring together people and processes for the purpose of managing environmental issues at an institution (ISO 14000 Essentials, n.d.). ISO 14001 identifies EMS requirements necessary to support an organization's ability to document and report on significant environmental issues. Among other things, organizations must show that their systems enable them to develop and implement policy, comply with legal requirements, and recognize important environmental factors. Environmental criteria are identified based on what the organization can control and/or influence. ISO does not state specific performance criteria; however, it does provide a means by which organizations can demonstrate conformity through self-declaration. It requires the use of stakeholders or third-parties for confirmation of results and certification of its environmental management system by an external organization. Additional information can be downloaded from the website (ISO 14001:2004, n.d.).

ISO 26000, also designated ISO SR (for ISO-Social Responsibility), was published in 2010. Its focus is social responsibility, but because it will not include requirements, the ISO has stated that it will "not be a certification standard" as defined by ISO 14001 and its other well-known manufacturing standards (ISO 9000). The purpose of ISO 26000 is instead to specify seven goals that assist and provide guidance to organizations in meeting their social responsibilities. These goals generally recognize the importance of complying with sustainability principles while respecting legal differences, engaging stakeholders, and reporting outcomes to enhance credibility. It calls for organizations to meet social responsibilities in a manner that is consistent with "existing documents, international treaties and conventions and exiting ISO standards" and without interfering with government's "authority to address the social responsibility of organizations" (About the Standard, n.d.).

External Uses of Sustainability Data

Although auditing systems are intended primarily for internal use, data collected and reported by colleges and universities in response to STARS-type initiatives are used by external parties for public disclosure of institutional performance on sustainability outcomes. The practice of ranking colleges and universities on these outcomes is relatively new, but it is likely to become a permanent fixture in higher education. Because of the media impact and potential implications for institutional reputation and branding, publicly available data, especially that used by ranking organizations, must be checked and rechecked for accuracy. Institutional researchers are well positioned to monitor the accuracy of rankings, to scrutinize the methodology, and to ensure the integrity of the data being used for this purpose.

Several major organizations already publish rankings based on college and university sustainability performance. For example, *The Princeton Review's Guide to 286 Green Colleges* (2010), published by The Princeton Review, Inc., in partnership with the U.S. Green Building Council, provides a qualitative and quantitative guide to a school's performance as an "environmentally-aware institution." The three criteria addressed by the ranking are: (1) whether the students have a campus quality of life that is both healthy and sustainable; (2) how well an institution is preparing its students for employment in the green energy economy of the twenty-first century, as well as for citizenship in a world now defined by environmental concerns and opportunities; and (3) the degree to which an institution's policies are environmentally responsible (*The Princeton Review's Guide*, 2010). *Princeton Review*'s sustainability survey questions are shown in Appendix 16.3.

The *College Sustainability Report Card* (n.d.) is a less inclusive but widely cited ranking published by the Sustainable Endowments Institute. Founded in 2005 as a project of Rockefeller Philanthropy Advisors, the Institute is a not-for-profit focused on increasing the sustainability of campus operations and endowment decisions in higher education (Sustainable Endowments Institute, n.d.). Data are gathered from publicly available sources and from four surveys that are sent to more than 300 colleges and universities. The surveys cover campus operations, dining services, endowment investment practices, and student activities. The institution's overall grade is based on nine equally weighted categories: administration, climate change and energy, food and recycling, green building, student involvement, transportation, endowment transparency, investment priorities, and shareholder engagement. Results and additional information on methodology and indicators are available at http://www.greenreportcard.org/.

The Bloomberg Businessweek: B-Schools: Social and Environmental Rankings is an example of a college-level ranking of business programs only. It is constructed using data from the Aspen Institute's biannual "Beyond Grey Pinstripes" research survey, which drew on approximately six hundred accredited full-time MBA programs to rank programs that integrate social and environmental steward-ship issues into the curriculum (Beyond Grey Pinstripes, n.d.). (As part of its Business and Society Program and the Aspen Institute Center for Business Education, the Institute itself used information collected through the Beyond Grey Pinstripes survey to publish *The Sustainable MBA: A Guide to Business Schools That Are Making a Difference*, 2009.) Beyond Grey Pinstripes collects data on coursework, faculty research, and institutional support. Points are allocated using four "raw score" metrics measuring: (1) availability of relevant courses (that is, the number of courses offered that contain social, environmental, or ethical content), (2) student exposure (that is, teaching hours cover-ing content and student enrollment in these courses), (3) relevant courses on for-profit impact (that is, the number of courses that demonstrate both relevance and address the intersection of social and environmental issues), and (4) faculty research (that is, the number of scholarly articles containing some environmental or ethical content being published in peer-reviewed busi-ness journals). The raw score metrics are statistically adjusted to produce a numerical value that represents how well a school or college does relative to other schools. The top one hundred schools are then ranked based on total points received. Information on methodology can be found at http://www .beyondgreypinstripes.org/about/methodology.cfm.

Ranking of institutional performance on sustainability by colleges and uni-versities has brought increasing attention to higher education's role in sustain-able development—but this has not been without controversy. Rankings and other assessments by NGOs such as the Sierra Club and magazines such as *Forbes* and *Newsweek* have blossomed since publication of the first assessment of sustainability in higher education by the National Wildlife Federation (NWF) in 2001 (Moltz, 2008, 2010). (In 2008, the NWF released a second study of 1,068 institutions in which schools with exemplary programs were identified [McIntosh, Gaalswyk, Keniry, & Eagan, 2008].) Response to the subsequent assessments and rankings has been both positive and negative, with critics questioning the reliability and validity of reported results. Criticisms concern, among other things, lack of uniform standards and metrics, lack of transpar-ency and accountability, and lack of third-party audits to support credibility of results (Moltz, 2010).

Governments, unlike the private sector, do not generally construct rank-ings. Instead, they focus on implementation of broadly based statutes that may directly or indirectly reflect government support of society's evolving sustain-ability values, such as clean water, workplace rights, and financial system integ-rity. For example, the European Commissioner for the Environment initiates and defines new environmental legislation and ensures that member states cor-rectly apply environmental mandates (European Commission—Environment, n.d.). Similarly, the U.S. Environmental Protection Agency (EPA) is charged with protecting human health and safeguarding the natural environment (About EPA, n.d.). Colleges and universities in most countries must comply with these environmental and social mandates, including required reporting on diversity and various other facets of workplace justice. Because institutional researchers frequently provide support for compliance activities, they are knowledgeable about data required for compliance reporting. This positions them to collaborate with other functions to incorporate this information when needed for sustainability audits and reports.

Sustainability initiatives in colleges and universities may also be supported by articulation of sustainability language in legislative mandates. For example, the U.S. Higher Education Opportunity Act of 2008 (HEOA) contains language that provides new grant opportunities in areas of sustainable development. Among other things, HEOA authorizes the Secretary of Education and the Environmental Protection Agency to award competitive grants to higher education and not-for-profit organizations to establish sustainability programs at colleges and universities (HEOA, 2008). The language provides for grants to develop higher education administrative and operations-based practices that test, model, and analyze principles of sustainability for the purpose of establishing multidisciplinary education, research, and outreach programs. Initiatives should address the environmental, social, and economic dimensions of sustainability and support student, faculty, and staff research and evaluation of sustainable practices. Institutional researchers can respond to government initiatives by monitoring new legislation, communicating the availability of new opportunities, and providing support for grant writing through collection, analysis, and reporting on data and relevant information. However, this requires that action plans be implemented to prepare for this task.

Preparing for Participation

At the institutional level, the role of institutional researchers in supporting sustainability auditing and reporting is still evolving. Institutional researchers have been preparing, sometimes unknowingly, for supporting these activities through compliance and other reporting responsibilities. In addition to government-mandated data submission, some colleges and universities are voluntarily providing data for the new elective Carnegie Foundation classification: Community Engagement. This classification describes "the collaboration between institutions of higher education and their larger communities . . . for the mutually beneficial exchange of knowledge and resources in a context of partnership and reciprocity" (Carnegie Foundation, n.d.). As with sustainability reporting, the required information includes data on curriculum and partnership activities that represent responsible citizenship on the part of the college or university.

Though institutional research is a major, logical, and centralized avenue for providing credible data on performance outcomes, understanding and knowledge of indicators for measuring performance on sustainability outcomes tends to be scattered across functional areas of the institution. The different functions collecting and managing sustainability data are and likely will continue to be decentralized and are, in some instances, heavily "siloed" with respect to their operations and missions. The challenge is to bring these functions together by working with other parties throughout the institution to form an auditing umbrella under which collecting, analyzing, and reporting sustainable development is perceived as a routine operation.

The question of how institutional researchers should structure their tasks to support sustainable development at their college or university is not easy to answer. However, the following four categories of activities should be considered:

1. *Strategic expansion of current data management role.* Institutional researchers can expand their current data management role to support sustainable development initiatives. This includes development of searchable sustainability databases, identification of appropriate sustainability indicators, and documentation of processes for supporting sustainability initiatives and reporting (Litten & Terkla, 2007). This will require identification of a sustainability framework in which to determine what relevant data are available, what data are needed, and who has access to the data.

2. *Action planning and stakeholder engagement.* Crafting an action plan requires identification of responsible parties, resource needs (people, technology, monetary), and timelines. Given the evolutionary character of the sustainability movement, updating of the plan should be ongoing. Most important, stakeholders from throughout the institution should be engaged in the process through formation of a dedicated working group. Those participating in the working group should be fully informed about useful sustainability resources and frameworks and should be part of the discussion about how the hundreds of potential sustainability indicators and metrics can be organized to create knowledge that is useful to their college or university.

3. *Environmental scanning for emerging sustainability issues.* Although institutional researchers can educate themselves about the current status regarding context, performance indicators, and reporting practices, the question of how to measure sustainability indicators is in a state of flux for all types of organizations and institutions found both inside and outside of higher education. Fortunately, there are widely available resources to support environmental scanning on sustainability initiatives and outcomes. In addition to published magazine and newspaper articles, specialized web portals give the public access to thousands of sustainability, corporate social responsibility, and citizenship reports posted by for-profit and not-for-profit organizations. These reports, available for download, can be used as models for development of metrics and best practices in reporting. For example, CorporateRegister.com, an independent, privately held, and self-funded organization, provides a global reference point for sustainability and corporate responsibility reports and resources. The

FIGURE 16.1 SUSTAINABILITY REPORTING PROCESS

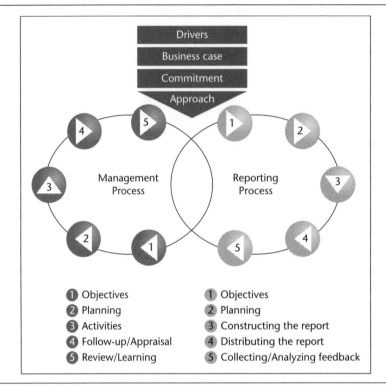

Source: World Business Council for Sustainable Development, Sustainable Development Reporting: Striking the Balance, 2002, P. 33. Reprinted with permission.

organization identifies best practices in responsibility reporting through its awards program. Though most reporting organizations represent the corporate sector, forty-five universities from multiple countries had, as of May 2010, submitted reports through this site (http://www.corporateregister.com).

4. *Strategic preparation for supporting the administration.* Institutional researchers can strategically prepare to support management and reporting processes through implementation of a sustainability reporting management initiative. In its "How to Report" guide, the World Business Council for Sustainable Development suggests a sustainability reporting process containing a management process circle and a reporting process circle; both require setting of objectives and planning (see Figure 16.1). The management process also requires identification of activities, follow-up and appraisal mechanisms, and reviews that feed back into learning. The reporting process aids in construction and distribution of the report, analysis of the data, and collection and analysis of feedback. Institutionalizing activities around these processes will enable institutional researchers to react more rapidly to requests for assistance from other college and university functions.

The activities just noted have potential benefits beyond the activities themselves. Litten and Terkla (2007) state that "participating in an institution's management for sustainable progress can carry IR to a new level of sophistication and service" (p. 105). They see institutional research as playing a key role in supporting sustainable development in higher education through "unprecedented types and levels of collaboration within an institution" (p. 105), noting that institutional researchers are uniquely positioned to build on this need for collaboration.

There is no denying that implementing a management model for sustainable development auditing and reporting will be challenging for many colleges and universities. There is growing evidence, however, that although the effort is voluntary, the public expects educational institutions to provide leadership in creating a more sustainable society, both for ourselves and future generations. Institutional researchers who are prepared and know about emerging sustainability concerns can play a critical role in the success of this higher education initiative.

References

About AASHE. (n.d.). Association for the Advancement of Sustainability in Higher Education. Retrieved from http://www.aashe.org/about

About EPA. (n.d.). Environmental Protection Agency. Retrieved from http://www.epa.gov/aboutepa/index.html

About GRI. (n.d.). Global Reporting Initiative. Retrieved from http://www.globalreporting.org/AboutGRI/

About ULSF. (n.d.). University Leaders for a Sustainable Future. Retrieved from http://www.ulsf.org/about.html/

About the standard. (n.d.). Social responsibility. International Organization for Standardization. Retrieved from http://isotc.iso.org/livelink/livelink/fetch/2000/2122/830949/3934883/3935096/07_gen_info/aboutStd.html

Agenda 21. Chapter 36. (1992). Earth Summit. Rio de Janeiro, Brazil. United Nations Educational, Scientific and Cultural Organization. Retrieved from http://portal.unesco.org/education/en/ev.php-URL_ID=34701&URL_DO=DO_TOPIC&URL_SECTION=201.html

Beyond Grey Pinstripes. (n.d.). The Aspen Institute Center for Business Education. Retrieved from http://www.beyondgreypinstripes.org/about/faq.cfm#1

Blackburn, W. R. (2007). *The sustainability handbook: The complete management guide to achieving social, economic and environmental responsibility.* Washington, DC: Environmental Law Institute, 751–764.

Brundtland Commission. (1987). *Our common future.* Report of The World Commission on Environment and Development. Oxford University Press, 43. Retrieved from http://www.un-documents.net/wced-ocf.htm

Carnegie Foundation. (n.d.). Classification description: Community engagement elective classification. The Carnegie Foundation for the Advancement of Teaching. Retrieved from http://classifications.carnegiefoundation.org/descriptions/community_engagement.php

The college sustainability report card. (n.d.). Sustainable Endowments Institute. Retrieved from http://www.greenreportcard.org

Edwards, A. R. (2005). *The sustainability revolution: Portrait of a paradigm shift*. Gabriola Island, BC, Canada: New Society Publishers.

European Commission—Environment. (n.d.). Retrieved from http://ec.europa.eu/dgs/environment/index_en.htm

G3 guidelines. (n.d.). Global Reporting Initiative. Retrieved from http://www.globalreporting.org/ReportingFramework/G3Guidelines/

HEASC. (n.d.). Higher Education Associations Sustainability Consortium. Retrieved from http://www2.aashe.org/heasc/

HEOA. (2008, August 14). Higher Education Opportunity Act of 2008. Part U—University Sustainability Programs. HEOA section 801, HEA section 881(a). Retrieved from http://www.nacua.org/documents/heoa.pdf

How to achieve certification. (n.d.). U.S. Green Building Council. Retrieved from http://www.usgbc.org/DisplayPage.aspx?CMSPageID=1991

Intro—What LEED is. (n.d.). U.S. Green Building Council. Retrieved from http://www.usgbc.org/DisplayPage.aspx?CMSPageID=1988

Intro—What LEED measures. (n.d.). U.S. Green Building Council. Retrieved from http://www.usgbc.org/DisplayPage.aspx?CMSPageID=1989

ISO 14000 essentials. (n.d.). International Organization for Standardization. Retrieved from http://www.iso.org/iso/iso_14000_essentials

ISO 14001:2004. (n.d.). International Organization for Standardization. Retrieved from http://www.iso.org/iso/iso_catalogue/catalogue_ics/catalogue_detail_ics.htm?csnumber531807

ISO standards. (n.d.). International Organization for Standardization. Retrieved from http://www.iso.org/iso/iso_catalogue.htm

Litten, L. H., & Terkla, D. G. (Eds.). (2007, Summer). Models and resources for advancing sustainable institutional and societal progress. In L. H. Litten & D. G. Terkla (Eds.), *Advancing sustainability in higher education* (pp. 107–115). New Directions for Institutional Research, no. 134. San Francisco: Jossey-Bass.

McIntosh, M., Gaalswyk, K., Keniry, L. J., & Eagan, D. J. (2008). Campus environment 2008: A national report card on sustainability in higher education. National Wildlife Federation.

McLaughlin, G. W., & Howard, R. D. (2004). *People, processes, and managing data* (2nd ed.). Tallahassee, FL: Association for Institutional Research.

Merkel, J., & Litten, L. H. (2007, Summer). The sustainability challenge. In L. H. Litten & D. G. Terkla (Eds.), *Advancing sustainability in higher education* (pp. 7–26). New Directions for Institutional Research, no. 134. San Francisco: Jossey-Bass.

Mission and History. (n.d.). American College and University Presidents' Climate Commitment. Retrieved from http://www.presidentsclimatecommitment.org/about/mission-history

Moltz, D. (2008). It's not easy being green. *Inside Higher Ed*. Retrieved from http://www.insidehighered.com/news/2008/09/04/green

Moltz, D. (2010). Call for better sustainability assessment. *Inside Higher Education*. Retrieved from http://www.insidehighered.com/news/2010/07/20/green

The Princeton Review's guide to 286 green colleges 2010–2011. (2010). Princeton Review, Inc. (in partnership with the U.S. Green Building Council).

Program Overview. (n.d.). *Sustainability Tracking, Assessment & Rating System* (STARS). Association for the Advancement of Sustainability in Higher Education. Retrieved from http://stars.aashe.org/pages/faqs/4101/?root_category=about

Ratings and Credits. (n.d). *Sustainability Tracking, Assessment & Rating System* (STARS). Association for the Advancement of Sustainability in Higher Education. Retrieved from http://stars.aashe.org/pages/faqs/4105/?root_category=about

Reporting Framework. (n.d.). Global Reporting Initiative. Retrieved from http://www
.globalreporting.org/ReportingFramework/G3Guidelines/

Reporting System. (n.d.). American College and University Presidents' Climate
Commitment. Retrieved from http://acupcc.aashe.org/data-views.php

Resources & Events. (n.d.). American College and University Presidents' Climate
Commitment. Retrieved from http://www.presidentsclimatecommitment.org/
resources

STARS Technical Manual (2012). Version 1.2. Association for the Advancement of
Sustainability in Higher Education. Retrieved from http://www.aashe.org/files/
documents/STARS/stars_1.2_technical_manual_final.pdf

Stockholm Declaration. (1972, June). Declaration of the United Nations Conference
on the Human Environment. Stockholm, Sweden. United Nations Environment
Programme. Retrieved from http://www.unep.org/Documents.Multilingual/Default
.asp?documentid=97&articleid=1503

Sustainability Assessment Questionnaire. (n.d.). Association of University Leaders for a
Sustainable Future. Retrieved from http://www.ulsf.org/programs_saq.html

Sustainable Endowments Institute. (n.d.). Retrieved from http://www.greenreportcard
.org/about/sustainable-endowments-institute

The Sustainable MBA: The 2010–2011 guide to business schools that are making a difference.
(2009, October 1). Business and Society Program. The Aspen Institute Center for
Business Education. Retrieved from http://www.aspeninstitute.org/publications/
sustainable-mba-making-difference

Talloires Declaration. (1990). Association of University Leaders for a Sustainable Future.
Retrieved from http://www.ulsf.org/programs_talloires.html

Tbilisi Declaration. (1978, April). Final report. The Tbilisi Declaration. (1977).
Intergovernmental Conference on Environmental Education. United
Nations Educational, Scientific and Cultural Organization/United Nations
Environment Programme. Retrieved from http://unesdoc.unesco.org/
images/0003/000327/032763eo.pdf

The Global Reporting Initiative (GRI). (2011). Sustainability Reporting Guidelines.
Retrieved from https://www.globalreporting.org/resourcelibrary/G3.1-Sustainability-
Reporting-Guidelines.pdf (pp. 28–39).

UNDESD. (2002, December 20). UN Resolution 57/254. 57th session. Agenda Item
87 a. 78th Plenary Meeting. United Nations Decade of Education for Sustainable
Development. Retrieved from http://www.un-documents.net/a57r254.htm

UNESCO. (n.d.) GHESP—Global Higher Education for Sustainability Partnership. UN
Educational, Scientific and Cultural Organization. Retrieved from http://portal
.unesco.org/education/en/ev.php-URL_ID=34701&URL_DO=DO_TOPIC&URL_
SECTION=201.html

Why Sign the Commitment? (n.d.). American College and University Presidents' Climate
Commitment. Retrieved from http://www.presidentsclimatecommitment.org/about/
commitment/why-sign

Appendix 16.1: The Talloires Declaration

We, the presidents, rectors, and vice chancellors of universities from all regions of the world are deeply concerned about the unprecedented scale and speed of environmental pollution and degradation, and the depletion of natural resources. Local, regional, and global air pollution; accumulation and distribution of toxic wastes; destruction and depletion of forests, soil, and water; depletion of the ozone layer and emission of "green house" gases threaten the survival of humans and thousands of other living species, the integrity of the earth and its biodiversity, the security of nations, and the heritage of future generations. These environmental changes are caused by inequitable and unsustainable production and consumption patterns that aggravate poverty in many regions of the world.

We believe that urgent actions are needed to address these fundamental problems and reverse the trends. Stabilization of human population, adoption of environmentally sound industrial and agricultural technologies, reforestation, and ecological restoration are crucial elements in creating an equitable and sustainable future for all humankind in harmony with nature. Universities have a major role in the education, research, policy formation, and information exchange necessary to make these goals possible.

The university heads must provide the leadership and support to mobilize internal and external resources so that their institutions respond to this urgent challenge. We, therefore, agree to take the following actions:

1. Use every opportunity to raise public, government, industry, foundation, and university awareness by publicly addressing the urgent need to move toward an environmentally sustainable future.
2. Encourage all universities to engage in education, research, policy formation, and information exchange on population, environment, and development to move toward a sustainable future.
3. Establish programs to produce expertise in environmental management, sustainable economic development, population, and related fields to ensure that all university graduates are environmentally literate and responsible citizens.
4. Create programs to develop the capability of university faculty to teach environmental literacy to all undergraduate, graduate, and professional school students.
5. Set an example of environmental responsibility by establishing programs of resource conservation, recycling, and waste reduction at the universities.
6. Encourage the involvement of government (at all levels), foundations, and industry in supporting university research, education, policy formation, and information exchange in environmentally sustainable development. Expand work with nongovernmental organizations to assist in finding solutions to environmental problems.

7. Convene school deans and environmental practitioners to develop research, policy, information exchange programs, and curricula for an environmentally sustainable future.

8. Establish partnerships with primary and secondary schools to help develop the capability of their faculty to teach about population, environment, and sustainable development issues.

9. Work with the UN Conference on Environmental and Development, the UN Environment Programme, and other national and international organizations to promote a worldwide university effort toward a sustainable future.

10. Establish a steering committee and a secretariat to continue this momentum and inform and support each other's efforts in carrying out this declaration.

Note: For names of signatories, see http://www.ulsf.org/programs_talloires.html, http://www.ulsf.org/talloires_declaration.html. Reprinted with permission.

Appendix 16.2: Calculating a STARS Score

STARS (Sustainability Tracking, Assessment & Rating System) scores are based on credits earned in three categories: (1) Education and Research, (2) Planning, Administration, and Engagement, and (3) Operations. The final score is

> the average of the percentage of applicable points earned in each of the three categories. For example, if an institution earned 20 percent of applicable points in the Education and Research category, 30 percent of applicable points in the Planning, Administration & Engagement category, and 40 percent in the Operations category, the institution's overall score would be 30 (the average of the three percentages).
>
> In addition to the credits in the three categories, institutions may earn up to 4 innovation credits for new and path-breaking practices and performances that are not covered by other STARS credits or that exceed the highest criterion of a current STARS credit. Innovation credits are not required to be specific to any category and are scored separately. Each earned innovation credit increases in an institution's overall score by one. In the previous example of an institution that achieved an overall score of 30, earning 2 innovation credits would result in a final score of 32. (http://www .aashe.org/files/documents/STARS/stars_1.2_technical_manual_final.pdf

Source: Scoring and Ratings (Pages 10-11). STARS Technical Manual. https://stars. aashe.org. Reprinted with permission.

Appendix 16.3: Survey Questions for the *Princeton Review Green Rating of Colleges*

1. The percentage of food expenditures that goes toward local, organic or otherwise environmentally preferable food

2. Whether the school offers programs including free bus passes, universal access transit passes, bike sharing/renting, car sharing, carpool parking, vanpooling or guaranteed rides home to encourage alternatives to single-passenger automobile use for students

3. Whether the school has a formal committee with participation from students that is devoted to advancing sustainability on campus

4. Whether new buildings are required to be LEED Silver certified

5. The school's overall waste diversion rate

6. Whether the school has an environmental studies major, minor or concentration

7. Whether the school has an "environmental literacy" requirement

8. Whether the school has produced a publicly available greenhouse gas emissions inventory and adopted a climate action plan consistent with 80 percent greenhouse gas reductions by 2050 targets

9. What percentage of the school's energy consumption, including heating/cooling and electrical, is derived from renewable sources (this definition included "green tags" but not nuclear or large scale hydropower)

10. Whether the school employs a dedicated full-time (or full-time equivalent) sustainability officer. (*Princeton Review Guide to 286 Green Colleges 2010–2011*, 2010)

PART THREE

BRIDGING INTERNAL AND EXTERNAL REQUIREMENTS FOR IR

Addressed in the chapters in Part Three are topics related to the building and management of data resources both external and internal to the campus. These data resources are typically the foundation of an institution's response to accountability demands from federal and state agencies, accrediting bodies, reputational publications, comparative studies, and internal analyses. The development, management, and use of these data sources have been a fundamental contribution of the institutional research profession to our data-based understanding and management of higher education. In this Part of the *Handbook*, we address accountability from the perspective of reporting mandates of the federal government and accrediting bodies nationally and regionally. Authors then discuss the development and use of data collected and stored nationally, at the state level, through collaborations between institutions, and at the campus level to support reporting mandates as well as campus management and planning.

At the national level, the Integrated Postsecondary Educational Data System (IPEDS) is the accountability mechanism through which the federal government collects data about institutions of higher education and their productivity. In the first chapter of this Part, Chapter 17, Carol Fuller, Cathy Lebo, and John Muffo describe the context for the government's investment in the development and use of mandated data collection through IPEDS and other governmental agencies, and the increasing internal pressure on campus leaders and decision makers to be accountable for the expenditure of resources and the resulting outcomes.

Recent demands from accrediting bodies, regional and professional, have been affecting and continue to affect the work of institutional research professionals on our campuses. In Chapter 18, Paula Krist, Elizabeth Jones, and Kimberly Thompson outline the primary demands being placed on our institutions and their programs by different types of accrediting agencies and the resulting expansion of information that is being asked of institutional research.

The topics discussed in the two chapters that follow reflect legal issues that must be acknowledged in the conduct of institutional research. In Chapter 19, Rachel Dykstra Boon discusses the legal, professional, and technical issues that the Federal Educational Records Privacy Act of 1974 (FERPA) and the Institutional Review Board (IRB) regulations demand be addressed when conducting research about students, faculty, and staff. Broadening this discussion, Andrew Luna, in Chapter 20, explores the notion of "proof" as defined in social science research and in the legal system. In the first case, research never proves anything, as all conclusions are conditional and based on probabilities. In the legal context, proof is based on the judgment of peers and precedent. How these two approaches can be reconciled is addressed in this chapter.

In Chapter 21, Gayle Fink and Chad Muntz describe the IPEDS databases, created and managed by the National Center for Education Statistics (NCES), and the tools that have been developed to support the access of these data by institutions and the public. In addition, they describe the national surveys conducted by NCES as well as the annual data collected by NSF to track research funding and expenditures.

Christine Keller, in Chapter 22, discusses the development of four systems of accountability that have been developed at the national level by higher education organizations. These voluntary data collection efforts and resulting data sources were developed in response to national questions about the transparency of costs and productivity of our colleges and universities,

and they provide easily accessible institutional level data to the public.

At the state level, Marsha Krotseng, in Chapter 23, describes institutional research that supports state-level higher education governance and coordination. The primary users and uses of institutional research at the state level are presented, with web references to many statewide institutional research offices, policy studies, and data collection strategies. In Chapter 24, Maryann Ruddock discusses recent efforts to develop statewide K–20 databases to be used for tracking student progress through all levels of education, providing data to assess the effectiveness of education at all levels and how they impact each other.

In Chapter 25, Julie Carpenter-Hubin, Rebecca Carr, and Rosemary Hayes discuss data exchanges and consortia that institutions have built to support analyses about specific types of institutions. The authors provide examples of a number of organizations that allow institutions to do comparative studies with participating institutions. In addition, they present a model that outlines, in a stepwise fashion, the creation and management of a useful data exchange.

In Chapter 26, the final chapter of this part, John Milam, John Porter, and John Rome discuss the development of institutional data and data structures to support accountability demands, planning, and decision support on the campus. Under the general headings of "business intelligence" and "academic analytics," they outline the collaboration needed between the campus institutional research function or office and others on campus, including those responsible for managing information technology and those operational units responsible for the initial collection of institutional data to build effective data systems to support planning, decision making, and reporting.

To summarize, in this part the reader is given an overview of the primary data resources that institutional research professionals use in responding to accountability mandates and in the creation of planning and decision support information at the campus, state, and national levels. In Part Four, tools and techniques that are used in the conduct of institutional research are presented and discussed in the context of supporting planning and decision making.

CHAPTER 17

CHALLENGES IN MEETING DEMANDS FOR ACCOUNTABILITY

Carol Fuller, Cathy Lebo, and John Muffo

In the United States, federal, state, and local governments and philanthropy have long provided funds to support some of the costs of higher education. This support continues to be based on a common understanding of the societal benefits contributed by colleges and universities—an educated citizenry, economic growth, social cohesion, scientific advances, innovation, and preservation of the cultural heritage, as well as direct service to local communities and regions (Carnegie Commission, 1973; Institute for Higher Education Policy, 1998; Baum, Ma, & Payea, 2010). By 1992, international competiveness in a global economy had been added as an important contribution by higher education to the nation's economic security (National Commission on Responsibilities for Financing Postsecondary Education, 1993).

Concerns about higher education's ability to continue to effectively provide these benefits have led to increased public scrutiny of the performance of colleges and universities. Burke (Burke & Associates, 2005) noted that "accountability for higher education has been a topic since the 1970s, but calls for accountability have become more intense [since 1990]" (p. xi). In recent years, a number of factors have led to increased demands for accountability. This chapter describes the pressures for accountability faced by colleges and universities, and the sources and types of accountability in higher education.

Our colleges and universities can expect heightened demands for accountability to continue. These may take the form of reports to external agencies or disclosures of information to students, employees, the public, and others. The scope of information requests will expand to new types of information and greater detail (for example, placement rates for certificate programs, announced in October 2010 as part of the program integrity regulations under Title IV of the Higher Education Act). Institutions may be required to provide information on very short notice and sometimes retroactively.

Institutional researchers need to be aware of developing issues so they can prepare for future changes in reporting and disclosure requirements, and so they can take advantage of opportunities to help shape new requirements; for example, review and comment on proposals issued by technical review panels for changes to the Integrated Postsecondary Education Data System (IPEDS) surveys (https://edsurveys.rti.org/IPEDS_TRP/Default.aspx). Institutional researchers must be prepared to navigate conflicting and confusing reporting requirements. They will spend more time monitoring, explaining (internally and externally), and addressing conflicting data and information. Institutional researchers can help to inform regulators, legislators, and policy analysts about existing sources of information, common standards for data collection, and institutional context. They will need to understand the historical, economic, and societal forces behind the requests for accountability information and the multiple audiences these requests serve. As the institutional brokers for most external data-based reporting, institutional research professionals are in a unique position to assume a leading role in informing and influencing discussions about the public purposes of higher education.

Increasing Demands for Accountability

Colleges and universities can expect continuing demands for accountability as the result of a number of concerns, events, and developments from within higher education and from the broader society.

Although a number of organizations and individuals have addressed the issues and challenges identified by the Commission on the Future of Higher Education (formed in 2005 by Margaret Spellings, the former secretary of education), the work of the Spellings Commission has perhaps received the most attention. An analysis published by the National Association of College and University Business Officers catalogued 1,363 online or paper articles and responses published from September 5, 2005 to September 7, 2007 (Ruben, Lewis, Sandmeyer, Russ, Smulowitz, & Immordino, 2008). (See Chapter 18 for a discussion of efforts in reaction to the Spellings Commission.)

The Commission was chartered to "consider how best to improve our system of higher education to ensure that our graduates are well prepared to meet our future workforce needs and are able to participate fully in the new global economy . . ." (http://www2.ed.gov/about/bdscomm/list/hiedfuture/about.html). The Commission's final report, "A Test of Leadership: Charting the Future of U.S. Higher Education" (U.S. Department of Education, 2006), highlighted a number of issues:

- Postsecondary education provides significant benefits for both the economic security and social mobility of individuals and for the future economic growth of the nation.

- Access to higher education is limited by inadequate preparation, lack of information about college opportunities, financial barriers, and poor alignment between high schools and colleges.
- Higher education institutions need to improve their efficiency and productivity to improve affordability.
- The financial aid system is "confusing, complex, inefficient, duplicative, and frequently does not direct aid to students who truly need it" (p. 3).
- The quality of student learning is "inadequate and, in some cases, declining" (p. 3). There are concerns about graduation rates, time-to-degree, core literacy skills, workplace skills, and lifelong learning.
- New pedagogies, curricula, and technologies are needed to improve learning.
- There is inadequate transparency and accountability for cost, price, and student outcomes.

In addition to the issues addressed by the Spellings Commission, concerns have been raised about the health and safety of students and staff at colleges and universities in response to high-profile incidents of violence and disease outbreaks that have posed serious threats to students, faculty and staff, and local communities. Concerns have also been raised about the behavior of employees (for example, conflicts of interest in research and student aid programs), and students (for example, copyright infringement). Rapid growth in the for-profit sector of postsecondary education has focused more attention on the financial and educational performance of all institutions.

These issues are heightened by developments external to the academy:

- Demographic changes have increased attention to how well postsecondary institutions meet the needs of older students, immigrant populations, and students from underrepresented racial and ethnic groups.
- Economic downturns lead to greater concerns about access and affordability, costs, and productivity. Adult participation in postsecondary education may increase significantly as individuals seek to obtain training for new jobs or to upgrade their skills. More students need financial assistance. State funding may decline and state and federal policy makers may seek more information about the return on the public investment in postsecondary education.
- Loss of trust and confidence in many types of institutions in the nation has led to calls for greater transparency and consumer protection.
- Technological changes, particularly improved communications technologies, have made it easier to produce and access information, leading to greater demands and expectations for information to be readily available.

Sources and Types of Accountability

The term *accountability* is frequently used in higher education contexts, but seldom defined. Minimally, it refers to the evaluation of information about an institution against a standard. The standards used may be qualitative and may not be explicitly stated (for example, judgments about "quality"). The information may be provided by the institution or obtained from other sources. Accountability may mean the demonstration, through reports or external audits, of compliance with regulatory requirements for processes or outcomes. For some measures, no satisfactory level of performance is defined, although institutions may be ranked from better to worse (for example, in graduation rates). Certain measures, such as class size, may have different standards depending on whether the goal is quality of instruction (effectiveness), or serving more students with a given level of resources (efficiency). Penalties may be imposed if an institution fails to comply with requirements or meet a specified standard. Rewards may be offered for achieving at or above a standard, or for improvement toward a goal.

The nature of accountability for institutions of higher education varies along five dimensions identified by Burke (Burke & Associates, 2005): To whom are they responsible? For what purpose? For whose benefit? By which means? With what consequences?

The answers to these questions are not always explicit or clear, and may shift over time.

To Whom?

Higher education institutions are accountable to many external and internal constituencies:

External Constituencies

- Local, state, and federal governments
- Local community
- General public
- Business community
- Market for higher education—prospective students and their families
- Programmatic and institutional accrediting agencies, disciplinary associations
- Higher education organizations that set standards for performance (for example, NCAA, AAUP)
- Foundations and philanthropic donors

Institutional/Internal Constituencies

- Governing boards and faith communities
- Alumni
- Students
- Employees

By Which Means?

The various accountability models emphasize different methods:

- Compliance with rules and regulations for processes or outcomes (sometimes called "bureaucratic control")
- Funding—direct control or incentives
- Information about institutional performance that is used internally for institutional improvement—accreditation, benchmarking
- Public information about institutional performance (for example, IPEDS)

With What Consequences?

Burke (Burke & Associates, 2005) identified the internal use of information for improvement as a "soft" consequence and resource gains or losses as "hard" consequences. Publicity falls in between. The expectation or realization of negative or positive publicity can have a significant impact, as institutions attempt to protect or enhance their reputations. Publicity can influence the market for students and employees, and internally it can affect employees, students, and governing boards. It can affect resources provided by donors, local communities, and government agencies.

Public information about institutional performance has several sources:

- Information released at the initiative of the institution
- Information released by the institution in compliance with regulatory requirements or in response to public pressure
- Information released by organizations or government agencies
- Information released by independent researchers and policy analysts
- Media—including guidebooks, rankings, news, and analyses

Institutional research offices face many internal and external requirements to directly provide public information. In addition, they must respond to many requests for information that will be made public by organizations or individuals. They also must monitor the publication of institutional information by other entities for accuracy and fairness.

For What?

Colleges and universities are responsible for their educational, research, and service functions. They also have a wide range of responsibilities for functions that they may share with other corporate entities, such as their responsibilities as employers, in building and maintaining facilities, for public accommodations, and for ensuring environmental protection and health and safety.

Internal Accountability

Discussions of accountability typically are focused on the relationship between an institution and an external entity (for example, a state or federal government agency). Internal accountability is focused on information used by institutional administrators and governing boards for institutional management and oversight. Internal and external accountability overlap—reports to external entities may also be used for internal purposes. A central internal issue is financial accountability—how has the institution used its resources? Program evaluation considers whether a program has achieved the goals it was intended to achieve in the ways it was intended to achieve them. Institutional researchers commonly combine financial and program performance data to create efficiency measures of various types. Studies of this kind might address questions such as the cost per student credit hour or per course (see Chapter 31); a thorough analysis would include overhead costs in addition to direct instructional costs. Other cost measures, such as square footage of space per student per credit hour per program, faculty and staff headcounts (HCs) and full-time equivalents (FTEs) and HC/FTE ratios by program, and so on, are also quite common and are used for internal as well as external purposes. Such data can be complex in their explanation and use, as there often seem to be idiosyncrasies. For instance, a small department may look expensive simply because it has a high proportion of senior faculty, but look less expensive in a year when one takes a leave of absence without pay. This is one of the reasons that these sorts of data often get misinterpreted when accessed directly by the public or even others in the academic community outside of institutional research.

There are a number of ways of evaluating performance internally and externally. One is by comparison—how do we stack up against our peers? It helps to have a designated peer group of some kind developed for comparison purposes, if only internally (see Chapter 36). It's even better if there is a peer group that is widely accepted both internally and externally; for example, athletic conferences. Good networking and much trust among colleagues are necessary to obtain the data to make comparisons across institutions if they are not mandated by external bodies. Data-sharing consortia provide opportunities for institutions to obtain comparative information (see Chapter 25). The National Center for Education Statistics provides several tools for obtaining comparative data from IPEDS (http://nces.ed.gov/ipeds/datacenter/) (see Chapter 21).

Another way to evaluate performance is by trend analysis—how are we doing now compared to the past few years? Are applications up or down? Is a higher or lower proportion of students completing the first developmental course? Sometimes three-year averages are better indicators of such measures due to the instability of single year measures. Yet another approach to accountability is measuring achievement of a target. For example, we said that we were going to reduce the cost of this course by 5 percent within a year; have we accomplished that goal?

State-Level Accountability for Institutional Performance

The discussion of accountability at the state level has been primarily focused on the relationship between state agencies and the public institutions in the state. The degree and nature of state oversight of the private for-profit and not-for-profit sectors of postsecondary education varies across the states (Zumeta, 2005). States regulate private institutions in their basic role as corporate entities, including, for example, consumer protection policies and local zoning or public safety regulations. Institutions are accountable for the use of state funds provided for financial aid for students in private institutions, direct aid to private institutions, and contracts with private institutions.

For public institutions, Burke (Burke & Associates, 2005) noted a "dramatic shift [in the 1990s] in the concept of accountability from complying with rules to producing results" (p. 216). Also, the focus shifted from academic concerns to state priorities. Burke described three primary approaches to institutional accountability used by states during the 1990s:

- Performance budgeting—performance is a factor in the allocation of resources
- Performance funding—distribution of funding is tied directly to performance indicators
- Performance reporting—relies on publicity for improving institutional performance

By 2003, performance reporting predominated. Performance may be measured by any or all of these data: improvement over time, comparisons with peer institutions, and comparisons with target levels or standards. Measures may be uniform, institutionally specific, or both.

The specific indicators used vary across states, reflecting the goals, needs, and context of each state. The 2002 report of a Western Interstate Commission for Higher Education forum, "The Changing Nature of Accountability," listed demographics, governance structures, legislative agendas, institutional and system initiatives, and economic conditions as factors leading to distinct state approaches (Western Interstate Commission for Higher Education, 2002). (For a discussion of state higher education planning and institutional research, see Chapter 23.)

Federal-Level Accountability

Higher education institutions are regulated by several federal agencies in regard to educational programs, research, employment, students and faculty, environmental protection, governance, and institutional operations such as radio stations and mailing permits (see the Campus Legal Information

Clearinghouse at http://counsel.cua.edu/). Institutional accountability at the federal level is accomplished in several ways and has several forms:

- State licensure and accreditation provide assurance of institutional integrity and acceptable educational quality
- Compliance with the terms of grants and contracts
- Compliance with federal laws
- Compliance with federal program eligibility and participation requirements, including audits, reports, and disclosures

The conditions for the awarding of grants and contracts or participating in federal programs include provisions directly relevant to the grant, contract, or program. However, federal funding also may be used to control institutional performance in completely unrelated areas. For instance, the Higher Education Act of 1965 (HEA) requirements for the Title IV student financial aid programs include provisions related to determining institutional integrity, fiscal stability, and educational quality, and provisions controlling the administration of the financial aid programs. The HEA requirements also include a number of provisions unrelated to the student aid programs, including many of the institutional reporting and disclosure requirements (for example, distribution of voter registration forms, disclosure of copyright infringement policies and sanctions, equity in athletics, and campus security).

Although the United States Constitution leaves education as a state responsibility, the federal government has taken on an ever increasing role in funding higher education in two main areas: federal student financial aid and funding of research. In terms of the research funding, the impact is limited primarily to the top 100 research universities that received 81 percent of the funds available in 2009, the most recent year for which data are available. The amounts are not small, with the highest ranked receiving nearly $1.6 billion in that year and the hundredth receiving over $100 million (Chronicle of Higher Education, 2011a). Of the different categories of student grant aid (institutional, state, federal, private, and so on), the federal portion is the largest and fastest growing (Chronicle of Higher Education, 2011b). The rapid increase in federal spending has heightened federal scrutiny of institutional performance.

Federal Institutional Disclosure and Reporting Requirements

All institutions that participate in the federal Title IV, HEA student financial aid programs are subject to the Title IV regulations administered by the U.S. Department of Education. Under the HEA, institutions must disclose certain information to current and prospective students, current and prospective employees, the general public, and others. (See National Postsecondary Education Cooperative, 2009, for more information.) The Higher Education Opportunity Act of 2008 (HEOA) provided a number of amendments to the

HEA (see a summary at http://ifap.ed.gov/dpcletters/GEN0812FP0810.html), including an increase in the number of institutional disclosure requirements to a total of forty—double the number previously required. In addition, the HEOA made a number of additions and revisions to the content of previously existing disclosure requirements (for more information, see the Association for Institutional Research, 2010). In addition to increased disclosures by institutions, the HEOA increased the amount and types of information that the Department of Education is required to publish about institutions—resulting in indirect institutional reporting mandates for institutions.

Compliance with the new or revised disclosure requirements has been challenging for institutions because of the number and diversity of topics, varying deadlines, and the distribution of responsibilities across many campus offices. Some of the requirements were retroactive—requiring data to be pulled from records that were not developed or maintained for that purpose. Many of the requirements were effective on the date of enactment of the HEOA. Institutions were expected to make a "good faith" effort to comply until final regulations were published (October 2009). As a result, data created to meet these disclosure requirements had to be developed without official or standardized guidance and may not be comparable across institutions or to the data produced following the publication of final official regulations.

In addition to greatly increasing the number and types of institutional disclosures, the HEOA includes a requirement for the National Center for Education Statistics (NCES) to post an extensive list of "consumer information" items to the College Navigator website and also to provide several types of information related to college prices and financial aid. The new disclosure requirements for NCES indirectly imposed new reporting requirements for institutions to provide to NCES the information needed for the NCES disclosures. Because of the deadlines imposed on NCES, many of these items had to be reported with very short notice and, in some cases, required historical data (Association for Institutional Research, 2008).

Federal Program Disclosure and Reporting Requirements

For educational programs to be eligible for funding under Title IV of the HEA, the programs must either lead to a degree or prepare students for "gainful employment in a recognized occupation." Final regulations include new disclosure and reporting requirements for institutions with students enrolled in Title IV–eligible nondegree programs that lead to gainful employment in a recognized occupation ("GE programs") (U.S. Department of Education, 2010). (See http://www.ifap.ed.gov/GainfulEmploymentInfo/index.html for complete information.)

Institutions must disclose information to prospective students for each GE program, including the Standard Occupational Classification (SOC) code of the occupations the program prepares students to enter, graduation rate, tuition and fees, costs for books and supplies and room and board (if applicable), job placement rate, and the median loan debt incurred by students who completed the program. Institutions must notify the Department of Education when they intend to add a new GE program, and they must report information to the Department of Education about the students who were enrolled in each GE program during each award year.

Conclusion

Burke (Burke & Associates, 2005) concluded that higher education does not need more accountability, but rather an integrated approach that coordinates accountability programs. This would require broad agreement on priorities and goals. The HEOA represents an approach wherein new or heightened concerns lead to disparate add-ons to institutional reporting requirements. Increased public expectations and demands for readily available information, and increasing reliance on public information to pressure institutions to change in particular ways, have resulted in myriad reporting and disclosure requests and mandates.

Responding to the demands for information has direct institutional costs and can divert resources from other objectives. Providing more and more information for prospective and current students can result in fewer funds available for student financial aid, student services, and educational programs, especially when institutions are continually reacting to new demands. Effective institutional management of information production and dissemination processes is and will continue to be essential to (1) minimizing both the costs associated with meeting accountability demands and the resulting disruptions to ongoing planning and decision support activities, and (2) maximizing internal benefits from organizational learning that should result from the generation and analysis of the required information.

References

Association for Institutional Research. (2008, August). AIR Alert # 36, New disclosure and IPEDS reporting requirements in the Higher Education Opportunity Act. Tallahassee, FL: Association for Institution Research. Retrieved from http://www.airweb.org/page.asp?page51601

Association for Institutional Research. (2010, March). Alert # 36, Update 2, Effective dates of disclosure requirements in the Higher Education Opportunity Act of 2008. Tallahassee, FL: Association for Institutional Research. Retrieved from http://www.airweb.org/page.asp?page52115

Baum, S., Ma, J., & Payea, K. (2010). Education pays 2010: The benefits of higher education for individuals and society. New York: College Board. Retrieved from http://trends.collegeboard.org)

Burke, J. C., & Associates. (2005). *Achieving accountability in higher education: Balancing public, academic, and market demands.* San Francisco: Jossey-Bass.

Carnegie Commission on Higher Education. (1973). *Who pays? Who benefits? Who should pay?* Hightstown, NJ: McGraw-Hill.

Chronicle of Higher Education. (2011a). A key research yardstick: The top 100 institutions in federal dollars for science, 2009. *Almanac of Higher Education 2011.* Retrieved from http://chronicle.com/article/The-Top-100-Colleges-in-Total/128216/

Chronicle of Higher Education. (2011b). Most aid to undergraduates has grown over time. *Almanac of Higher Education 2011.* Retrieved from http://chronicle.com/article/Most-Aid-to-Undergraduates-Has/128350

Higher Education Opportunity Act of 2008 (P.L. 110–315). (2008). Retrieved from http://frwebgate.access.gpo.gov/cgi-bin/getdoc.cgi?dbname=110_cong_public_laws&docid=f:publ315.110.pdf

Institute for Higher Education Policy. (1998, March). *Reaping the benefits: Defining the public and private value of going to college.* Washington, DC: Institute for Higher Education Policy.

National Commission on Responsibilities for Financing Postsecondary Education. (1993). *Making college affordable again.* Washington, DC: National Commission on Responsibilities for Financing Postsecondary Education.

National Postsecondary Education Cooperative. (2009, November). *Information required to be disclosed under the Higher Education Act of 1965: Suggestions for dissemination.* Washington, DC: National Postsecondary Education Cooperative. Retrieved from http://nces.ed.gov/pubsearch/pubsinfo.asp?pubid=2010831rev

Ruben, B. D., Lewis, L., Sandmeyer, L., Russ, T., Smulowitz, S., & Immordino, K. (2008). *Assessing the impact of the Spellings Commission.* Washington, DC: National Association of College and University Business Officers.

U.S. Department of Education. (2006). *A test of leadership: Charting the future of U.S. higher education.* Washington, DC: U.S. Department of Education. Retrieved from http://www2.ed.gov/about/bdscomm/list/hiedfuture/index.html

U.S. Department of Education. (2010, October 29). Retrieved from http://edocket.access.gpo.gov/2010/pdf/2010–26531.pdf

Western Interstate Commission for Higher Education. (2002). "The Changing Nature of Accountability." *Western Policy Exchanges.* Boulder, CO: Western Interstate Commission for Higher Education.

Zumeta, W. M. (2005). Accountability and the private sector: State and federal perspectives. In Burke, J. C., & Associates. *Achieving accountability in higher education: Balancing public, academic, and market demands.* San Francisco: Jossey-Bass.

CHAPTER 18

ACCREDITATION AND THE CHANGING ROLE OF THE INSTITUTIONAL RESEARCHER

Paula S. Krist, Elizabeth A. Jones, and Kimberly Thompson

What is accreditation, and why is it a major concern for colleges and universities? At the institutional level, accreditation means being recognized by an external agency that has developed standards to ensure that member institutions have the capacity, policies, and practices to provide quality academic programs. At the program level, accreditation is similar, but the standards are often more prescriptive than regional accreditors' expectations and sometimes require more evidence to document the quality of a specific academic program. In the United States, the Council for Higher Education Accreditation (CHEA) is the association that recognizes and monitors accrediting organizations. At present, CHEA reports approximately three thousand member degree-granting colleges and universities (Council for Higher Education Accreditation, 2006b). The goal of accreditation today is to ensure that education provided by institutions of higher education meets acceptable levels of quality assurance. Today, institutional accreditation is voluntary—but expected.

A Brief History of Accreditation

College and university accreditation began in the late 1800s as a way for schools that were "serious institutions of higher education" to differentiate themselves from institutions that called themselves colleges (Leef & Burris, 2002, p. 1). Established higher education institutions felt that voluntarily holding themselves to prescribed standards of quality (accreditation) would demonstrate that they represented educational quality. The Higher Education Act of 1952 limited federal financial aid only to students at accredited institutions (Leef & Burris, 2002). In effect, this legislation made accreditation compulsory. The

National Advisory Committee on Institutional Quality and Integrity (NACIQI) monitors the application of standards in accrediting processes for the Secretary of Education.

Today, virtually every institution of higher education is accredited. Some institutions are accredited by national agencies; more are accredited by the large regional accreditors. The main differences between regional and national accreditors are scope and purpose. National accreditation groups promote quality assurance at institutions with similar missions (such as biblical colleges) across the United States. Regional accreditors encompass institutions with varied missions within a specified geographic region of the United States.

Council for Higher Education Accreditation

The Council for Higher Education Accreditation defines its purposes as advocacy, service, and recognition. Accrediting bodies are expected to meet specific recognition standards. In many ways, CHEA's expectations of evidence for its recognized accrediting bodies are very similar to the expectations that the accrediting bodies have for the institutions or programs they accredit. They must evaluate themselves regularly, including an evaluation of their resources and implementation of the changes indicated by the self-study. They must be accountable to their constituents, including member institutions. They must employ "appropriate and fair practices in decision making" (Council for Higher Education Accreditation, 2006, p. 9). They must demonstrate that they regularly review their accreditation practices and make modifications as indicated.

Institutions of higher education want to be recognized by accreditors on CHEA's list. CHEA currently recognizes 23 institution-level accreditors for higher education institutions, including six regional accreditors. Approximately 50 program-level accrediting bodies are also recognized.

Some institutions receive accreditation from groups that are not recognized by CHEA. CHEA is the only nongovernmental higher education organization that examines and certifies the quality of regional, faith-based, private career and programmatic accrediting organizations (Council for Higher Education Accreditation, 2006). Because CHEA is known for consistent and thorough standards, institutions benefit by seeking and maintaining accreditation from an accreditor that is recognized by CHEA.

Institutional Research and Accreditation

Institutional researchers are vital to the success of an institution's accreditation efforts because they maintain and report the official data for their institutions. It is essential to any accrediting process to have accurate, timely data and to show that the data were translated into information that was used by constituents to make decisions. Those decisions may affect academic programs, administrative areas, and student support units.

Institutions vary in their organizational structure, and the number and types of staff who collect, analyze, and report data for accreditation purposes also differ. Depending on the organizational structure, institutional researchers may have a direct role in the design and development of assessment practices or they may serve in a very limited role within institutions using a more faculty-directed approach. In any case, institutional researchers create, analyze, and report on a variety of data elements that are used in conducting and writing self-study reports in connection with accreditation.

This chapter provides an overview of the most common levels of accreditation sought by institutions of higher education and explains ways in which institutional researchers may support each.

Regional Accreditation

By the late twentieth century and into the twenty-first century, accreditation by the six regional accreditors was regarded as the gold standard for postsecondary institutions in terms of quality assurance. These six are the Middle States Commission on Higher Education (MSCHE), New England Association of Schools and Colleges (NEASC), North Central Association Commission on Accreditation and School Improvement (NCA), Northwest Commission on Colleges and Universities (NWCCU), Southern Association of Schools and Colleges (SACS), and Western Association of Schools and Colleges (WASC). Today, most institutions of higher education in the United States are accredited by one of these six regional accrediting bodies. Some international institutions have obtained accreditation from U.S. regional accreditors; they are competing for students who otherwise might travel to the United States or Europe for their degrees. For example, MSCHE accredits many of the American University institutions abroad (such as those in Cairo, Beirut, Paris, Puerto Rico, Rome, and Sharjah).

Institutional Effectiveness and the Expectations of Regional Accreditors

Regional accreditors have specific expectations of the institution, its administration, its academic programs, and its student support services. To ensure that all institutions maintain standards regarding resources and programs, regional accrediting bodies developed public requirements that had to be met at a satisfactory level. For many years, if the requirements were met, an institution could earn and maintain accreditation. Accrediting bodies' expectations for evidence of educational quality have evolved over time in response to both concerns of the membership and federal legislation. Critics felt that either too much attention was given to educational inputs, and too little to educational outputs (that is, student outcomes), or there were no real consequences for institutions not meeting the standards for accreditation after initial accreditation (Wiley & Zaid, 1968; Leef & Burris, 2002). In the past few decades, accrediting organizations have taken a different approach, one that recognizes the individual identity and mission of each institution and focuses on student learning. SACS summarizes how institutional effectiveness is determined for regional accreditation: "The institution engages in ongoing, integrated, and institution-wide research-based planning and evaluation processes that (1) incorporate a systematic review of institutional mission, goals, and outcomes; (2) result in continuing improvement in institutional quality; and (3) demonstrate the institution is effectively accomplishing its mission" (Southern Association of Colleges and Schools Commission on Colleges, 2009, Core Requirement 2.5). Institutions are expected to set and assess outcomes that show evidence of the effectiveness of its educational programs (including student learning), administrative support service, academic support services, and research and community service, if the latter two are part of the institutional mission. The Middle States Commission on Higher Education (MSCHE) revised its standards in 2002 to include the expectation that an institution will conduct assessment that provides evidence of meeting each standard (Middle States Commission on Higher Education, 2005).

Institutions seeking accreditation or reaccreditation complete a self-study that includes an examination of essential elements of the institution's ability to support student learning at a recognized standard. Three elements of institutional effectiveness expected in an institution's self-study are capacity, faculty qualifications, and assessment of student learning. The self-study demonstrates a clear relationship between institutional mission and each program's mission, goals, and student learning outcomes. Each program and student support area is expected to develop and assess student learning outcomes, with the expectation of improving student achievement and the program. External peer reviewers conduct virtual or in-person reviews of the evidence presented in the institutional self-study, and this team makes recommendations to the accreditor that are considered when an institution is seeking initial or continued accreditation.

The next section describes the role of the institutional researcher in the context of the common elements of institutional effectiveness expected by the six regional accrediting bodies.

Institutional Research and Regional Accreditation

Capacity. WASC defines capacity as an institution's "resources, structures, and processes" and "infrastructure to support student learning outcomes assessment and program review" (Western Association of Schools and Colleges, 2008, p. 34). Capacity addresses the institution's infrastructure to support educational effectiveness. Resources include adequate faculty and other personnel, as well as classroom and lab space, student financial assistance, equipment, and technology. To show adequate resources overall, institutional financial records are required. Institutional researchers often oversee or collaborate on the institution's space and equipment inventory. They often have information regarding the technological infrastructure because that is reported to external agencies. Some institutional researchers deal with financial reporting and can address that aspect of capacity for accreditation. Because IR personnel are often responsible for IPEDS reporting, they are likely to have the most accurate longitudinal counts of faculty and staff in specific categories.

Faculty Qualifications. Faculty must have degrees in appropriate fields and at the appropriate level to teach students in the academic programs of the institution. Institutional researchers may be involved in assembling and maintaining centralized databases of faculty data. Institutional research offices report many faculty data elements to federal, state, and private organizations. Depending on the data management system, IR can expand existing databases to include information such as faculty degrees, research and publications. Institutional research can provide a centralized source of consistent faculty qualification information for all programs across the institution.

Student Learning Outcomes Assessment. Assessment of student learning outcomes for all academic programs is a key component of the accreditation review process, and institutional researchers may play many different roles. The Association of American Colleges and Universities (AAC&U) and the Council for Higher Education Accreditation (CHEA) have taken a strong position regarding institutions ensuring the setting and assessment of student learning outcomes in their new leadership statement (Association of American Colleges and Universities & Council for Higher Education Accreditation, 2008). Institutional researchers often provide official statistics and trend data to support program outcomes assessment for the self-studies required by a regional accreditor. In many institutions, institutional research personnel coordinate institutional-level assessment, including national standardized tests and surveys (for example, Collegiate Assessment of Academic Proficiency [CAAP], Measure of Academic Proficiency and Progress [MAPP], Cooperative Institutional Research Program Freshmen Survey [CIRP], National Survey of Student Engagement [NSSE]). This coordination involves administering, analyzing, and disseminating key results with faculty, administrators, and student support staff. Sometimes the institutional research office is also the assessment office and IR staff work with program faculty and student affairs staff to develop and assess student learning outcomes and to collect, analyze, and document evidence of student achievement. Because regional accreditors expect an institution-wide system for student learning outcomes assessment, institutional researchers may oversee the process and technology for collecting, managing, and reporting program-level student learning outcomes information. Institutional research personnel can develop useful alliances with faculty and student affairs staff as they help their colleagues develop and implement student learning outcomes assessment plans. They also help others understand the important role of student learning outcomes assessment in institution-level accreditation.

Institutions of higher education that offer degree-granting programs online and at more than one campus must include those programs within the self-study and show that they are comparable to those taught in a more traditional model or at the main campus. When institutions create new programs, make major changes to existing programs, or modify program delivery, all of the regional accrediting bodies require a document detailing this "substantive change." Institutional researchers may work as part of the institutional team that develops the substantive change documentation.

Online and For-Profit Institutions and Regional Accreditation

Regional accreditation is an important endorsement for colleges and universities. Institutions that offer online programs and alternative methods of course delivery exclusively find regional accreditation useful, if not necessary, to be considered by prospective students. All of the regional accrediting bodies accredit some fully online degree granting institutions. These institutions must meet the same standards for institutional effectiveness required of more traditional colleges and universities. The same is true in the case of for-profit degree granting institutions. Some of the larger for-profit schools have sought and received regional accreditation, including Capella University, Art Institute of Atlanta, Art Institute of Pittsburgh, University of Phoenix, DeVry University, Strayer University, Miami International University of Art and Design, Kaplan University, Walden University, and American InterContinental University. In addition to regional accreditors, there are four accrediting organizations for online universities that accredit all degrees, in all subject areas, in an entire university. They are the Board of Online Universities Accreditation (BOUA), the Universal Council for Online Education Accreditation (UCOEA), the International Accreditation Agency for Online Universities (IAAOU), and the World Online Education Accrediting Commission (WOEAC). (See Appendix 18.1 for the websites of accrediting agencies included in this chapter.)

Institutional research personnel provide much support and often assume leadership roles for the regional accreditation of an institution. However, institutional research offices are relatively new to online and for-profit institutions, and many have not established one. This is likely to change for those online institutions that seek or have regional accreditation, because regional accreditation is very data intensive.

State Accreditation

In addition to recognizing regional and national accrediting agencies, the U.S. secretary of education also recognizes some state agencies that approve public postsecondary vocational education programs and nurse education. These state agencies have met recognition requirements that include criteria similar to the regional and national accrediting agencies recognized by the secretary. For example, each must include self-analysis by institutions requesting accreditation, site visits conducted by visiting teams, and regular reevaluation of the institutions or programs that it has approved.

There are four state agencies recognized for the approval of public postsecondary vocational education programs: New York State Board of Regents; Oklahoma Board of Career and Technology Education; Pennsylvania State Board of Vocational Education; and Puerto Rico State Agency for the Approval of Public Postsecondary Vocational, Technical Institutions and Programs. There are six state agencies recognized by the secretary of education for approval of schools of nursing: Kansas State Board of Nursing; Maryland Board of Nursing; Missouri State Board of Nursing; Montana State Board of Nursing; New York State Board of Regents, State Education Department, Office of the Professions (Nursing Education); and North Dakota Board of Nursing. The Nurse Training Act of 1964 provides authority for recognition of nursing programs, as amended (42 U.S.C. 298b[6]), and detailed criteria for recognition are published in the Federal Register. Accredited schools of nursing are required to submit a comprehensive annual report to the accrediting agency, including current data on such items as number of admissions and graduations and the performance of students on state board examinations for the past five years. Schools of nursing are also required to submit data on progress toward achievement of their stated objectives in nursing education.

The role of the institutional researcher at institutions accredited by one of the state accrediting agencies is similar to the role that would apply to regional or national accrediting agencies recognized by the secretary of education. All recognized accrediting agencies have, as their primary concern, ensuring the quality of the education being offered. Institutions must be able to demonstrate, using a variety of measures, effectiveness as it relates to student learning outcomes (among other criteria).

States grant authority to award degrees to institutions operating in their jurisdictions. Degree authorization is different from accreditation in that degree authorization refers to the legality of an award (that is, a diploma), whereas accreditation concerns itself with the quality of the education received. States typically require institutions to obtain and maintain accreditation by an accrediting agency recognized by the U.S. Department of Education. In this way, states can assume the quality of the education leading to the degree or formal award.

The role of the institutional researcher in state authorization is likely limited, as there are rarely particular data requirements for maintaining state approval to award degrees. Because quality is demonstrated via the national or regional accreditation process, normally no other data or reporting requirements would be expected at the state level. One exception to this might be the case of an institution making initial application to operate in a particular state. Institutional researchers should be certain that they are aware of any state-specific requirements for data or reporting as they relate to their legal authority to operate and award degrees in the state.

Some states also certify particular professional programs, such as nursing and education. Such certifications are state-specific, and institutional researchers should be certain that they are familiar with the particular requirements for the state in which they are located. Typical reporting requirements include data on enrollment and degrees awarded, and they frequently include data on licensure exam pass/fail rates for students graduating from the institution in particular professional programs. Institutional researchers can usually find information on state accreditation, authorization, and certification and/or approval of professional programs on the websites of their state department of higher education.

Specialized or Programmatic Accreditation

Specialized, professional, or programmatic accreditation is a specific type of accreditation status given for freestanding schools, departments, programs, schools, or colleges within a college or university. This type of accreditation focuses on formal evaluations of the quality of particular dimensions of the department, program, school, or college's specific professional preparation areas of study. For example, programmatic accreditation is a statement about the quality of academic programs in certain fields, such as education, health professions, medicine, business, law, engineering, and other professional fields of study. Some professions are also regulated and dependent on a state or national licensing board that may require college graduates to pass certain standardized exams and to complete educational programs that are appropriately accredited by specialized programmatic accrediting organizations.

A number of benefits are associated with specialized program assessment. Accreditation can provide various stakeholders (including parents, students, employers, and policy makers) with certification that a program meets or exceeds stated public standards associated with quality educational programs. Accreditation ensures that there is some uniformity of expectations associated with strong educational practices and standards. Accreditation provides students with a concrete way to identify quality programs and employers often give priority to hiring graduates from accredited programs. In addition, researchers found that accreditation helps to ensure greater program competiveness, "increased bargaining leverage for universities resources, and faculty recruitment advantages" (Roller, Andrews, & Bovee, 2003, p. 199). The accreditation process itself helps program faculty better understand how their programs can be improved and helps them to be "more committed to the proper resources and delivery requirements for quality education" in professional preparation programs (Alstete, 2004, p. 24).

Accreditation for professional preparation programs originally was often focused on a smaller set of large doctoral and research universities. In colleges or schools of business, for example, the American Association of Collegiate Schools of Business (AACSB), founded in 1916, was viewed by academicians and employers as the major quality assurance for business schools (Hardin & Stocks, 1995). For many years, AACSB standards were feasible only for top-tier business programs at research-oriented universities (Tullis & Camey, 2007, p. 47). In the early 1990s, AACSB changed its orientation and adopted an approach to make their accreditation mission-driven. In 2003, they further revised their standards by focusing on assessment of learning outcomes as defined by the business programs. In 1988, a second accrediting organization, the Association of Collegiate Schools of Business and Programs (ACBSP), began accrediting business programs and business schools. This organization focuses on being mission driven and has been more open and accessible to regional state and small private affiliated schools that are more likely to have a primary emphasis on teaching (Tullis & Camey, 2007, p. 48). In addition, this organization accredits business programs in community colleges.

Many professional program accreditation standards have shifted from examining inputs to assessing outcomes and providing constructive help to numerous professional preparation faculty members as they seek accreditation. The majority of specialized accreditors articulate a specific set of standards that they expect accredited specialized programs (including baccalaureate, master's, and doctoral degree programs) to reach in order to become accredited. Accreditors have many standards; in this section we review the three major areas of the curriculum and student learning, faculty qualifications, and resources.

Reviewing the Curriculum and Providing Evidence of Student Learning

Accreditors expect programs to demonstrate that their graduates have achieved the knowledge, skills, and abilities considered necessary for entry-level professional positions regardless of the delivery mode of the instruction the programs may provide (Council for Higher Education Accreditation, 2002, p. 2). Specialized programmatic accrediting organizations typically express the types of knowledge, skills, and abilities that program graduates need for entry into their chosen profession. This point is a major difference from regional accreditation. Numerous professional preparation program faculty have designed competency-based curriculum and competency standards as the major mechanism to ensure quality; this enables these programs to apply the same standards to both site-based and distance learning (Council for Higher Education Accreditation, 2002).

AACSB (2012, p. 62) requires that accredited business programs have core learning goals for the general knowledge and skills to be achieved by their students including communication abilities, ethical understanding and reasoning abilities, analytical skills, use of information technology, dynamics of the global economy, multicultural and diversity understanding, and reflective thinking skills (American Association of Collegiate Schools of Business, 2012, p. 71). They do not require specific courses, but in the case of AACSB and other professional accrediting organizations, they expect students will participate in learning experiences designed to address specific important skills and abilities often associated with liberal learning. Although these courses are often part of the general education curriculum, the professional program accreditors expect that the curriculum in the major will continue to help students develop these types of skills and abilities. Most professional program accreditors then expect that the faculty will articulate goals for student learning in these types of liberal learning areas. In addition, most professional program accreditors expect that specific specialized knowledge and skills will be developed that relate directly to the majors. For example, AACSB also requires that the curriculum address management-specific skills that business students should gain from performing "management tasks from the business portion of their degree requirements" (American Association of Collegiate Schools of Business, 2012, p. 63). Business students are expected to achieve learning in such disciplines as accounting, management science, marketing, human resources, and operations management. Course hours, content of the curriculum, and structure of business programs are very consistent regardless of the type of university or college (Tullis & Camey, 2007, p. 48), because the business accrediting organizations have very similar accreditation requirements, so there is little difference among programs.

Institutional researchers can help faculty in the professional fields design and implement appropriate assessment plans so that accrediting organizations gain useful information that college students have reached the necessary standards. Faculty should also gain useful information for their own internal purposes as well. Institutional researchers can work with program faculty to clearly articulate learning goals or competencies and help faculty identify a variety of direct and indirect assessments to gauge student learning. For example, often faculty members want to develop an alumni survey. In professional preparation programs, graduates can better evaluate their own learning when they apply it to their full-time professional positions. Alumni surveys often seek to gauge the skills and competencies that graduates have gained from their educational programs. Institutional researchers can help design a quality survey—typically an online instrument—and also assist with interpreting, analyzing, and reporting the results. Institutional researchers' expertise in helping others understand the results is crucial so that program faculty can use the findings to identify improvements to strengthen their programs. AACSB refers to assessment as "assurance of learning" when faculty provide concrete evidence of student learning so that accreditors know with confidence that students have attained specific learning goals.

Accrediting organizations expect to review real examples of student work, especially from course-embedded assessments when they conduct an on-site review at the college or university. Program faculty members usually have numerous examples of student work that can serve as evidence of student performance in tests or in projects completed in their coursework. However, a major challenge is keeping track of multiple assessments and the results of administering them. Institutional researchers can help faculty members develop databases that organize assessment information so that it can be retrieved on a timely basis, as it is needed. Such a comprehensive system helps program faculty better address the assessment expectations required by the specialized programmatic accreditors. Smaller programs may find developing a comprehensive system to be unreasonable, given limited resources. For example, faculty at Bellevue University wanted a web-based system but found too many challenges in designing their own, so they purchased a commercial web-based system and found that it made their assessment simpler and more manageable (Banta, Jones, & Black, 2009, p. 130).

Evaluating Qualifications of Faculty Members

Program accreditors also carefully evaluate the qualifications of faculty members. For example, in both business-accrediting organizations (AACSB and ACBSP), nearly all full-time faculty must hold doctoral degrees in their teaching fields. A faculty member teaching in the marketing major needs to have a doctoral degree in marketing rather than sociology or higher education administration. Accreditors expect faculty members to be specifically trained in their teaching field and productive in producing published work. AACSB requires documentation of the "intellectual contributions" that faculty members have made. Institutional researchers can help schools or colleges to identify and implement systems that keep track of these contributions, such as the number of peer-reviewed journal articles, research monographs, books, chapters in books, or peer-reviewed paper presentations.

Evaluating a Variety of Resources

Another major area that program accreditors review is the allocation of resources. For example, AACSB wants a thorough analysis of the costs and resources allocated to support specific initiatives. Institutional researchers can assist with the determination of whether realistic financial resources are in place and planned to sustain and improve specific activities. In terms of supporting student learning experiences, resources such as the classrooms, offices, laboratories, and computer equipment are evaluated to ensure that they are adequate to "support high quality operations" (American Association of Collegiate Schools of Business,

2012, p. 29). Technology support for online learning or classroom simulations is reviewed. Finally, researchers examine support for students in terms of advising and placement services and for faculty activities such as professional development and attendance at professional conferences. Institutional researchers can help faculty members evaluate the quality of their advising processes and student support services to determine whether these operations are sufficient to support students' needs. They can also evaluate the quality of instructional technology that is available and identify the strengths of these resources and areas that can be improved. The results from such formal evaluations can provide meaningful information that can be used to address accreditation requirements as well as provide important results that faculty can use for internal purposes.

Accreditation for professional programs at colleges and universities is a very demanding process, dictated by specific standards set by external professional accrediting organizations. Ideally, institutional researchers can form close partnerships with professional preparation program faculty to address these external standards. Institutional researchers can design high-quality assessments and evaluations to help faculty better understand what is working well and which areas need targeted improvements.

Accreditation, Accountability, and the Educational Landscape

Despite the oversight of national, regional, and programmatic accreditors by CHEA and HEAC, some members of federal government agencies remain mistrustful of them and have called for one national-level accreditor for colleges and universities. Since the Spellings Commission Report (U.S. Department of Education, 2006), external agencies have focused on the need for transparency and accountability across institutions of higher education. The American Association of State Colleges and Universities (AASCU) and the Association of Public and Land-grant Universities (APLU) developed the Voluntary System of Accountability (VSA) that uses a few standard measures to describe postsecondary institutions such as the Collegiate Assessment of Academic Proficiency (CAAP) from ACT, the Measure of Academic Proficiency and Progress (MAPP) from the Educational Testing Service (ETS), and the Collegiate Learning Assessment (CLA) from the Council for Aid to Education (Banta, 2008). Participating colleges and universities are required to complete the College Portrait, which provides data from standardized tests of generic skills and surveys as well as institutional data (Banta, 2007). Such common measures allow potential and current students, their parents, and the general public to compare specific institutions (Banta, 2008).

To expand data that can be compared across institutions beyond standardized tests, the AAC&U's Liberal Education and America's Promise (LEAP) initiative sponsored the Valid Assessment of Learning in Undergraduate Education (VALUE) Project, which employed rigorous methodology to create a set of scoring rubrics for the assessment of 15 essential institutional student learning outcomes (Rhodes, 2010). These rubrics are designed to collect standardized assessment data from authentic, course-based assignments and from student support offices, with the expectation that these data will permit a more in-depth look at undergraduate education across institutions.

The national call for institutional accountability is affecting the role of the institutional researcher. Institutions are examining the organizational structure and the number of staff who are involved in accreditation data collection, analysis, and reporting. Because assessment has become a prominent feature for all accrediting entities, institutional researchers may have a direct role in the design and development of assessment practices or a supportive role in a more faculty-driven process. In any case, institutional researchers create, analyze, and report on a variety of data elements that are used in conducting self-study and writing reports in connection with accreditation.

Within the institution, institutional researchers can coordinate data used in individual accreditation studies and may serve to coordinate all of the accreditation activities that take place when the institution has multiple accrediting agencies. These coordination services reduce redundancy and facilitate one effort that serves multiple accreditation purposes. The institutional researcher should always be a member of the leadership team coordinating accreditation at any level for an institution of higher education.

References

Alstete, J. W. (2004). Accreditation matters: Achieving academic recognition and renewal. ASHE Higher Education Report, *30*(4). San Francisco: Jossey-Bass.

American Association of Collegiate Schools of Business. (2012). Eligibility procedures and accreditation standards for business accreditation. Tampa, FL: American Association of Collegiate Schools of Business.

Association of American Colleges and Universities & Council for Higher Education Accreditation. (2008). *New leadership for student learning and accountability: A statement of principles, commitments to action.* Washington, DC: Association of American Colleges and Universities & Council for Higher Education Accreditation.

Banta, T. W. (2007). The search for the perfect test continues. *Assessment Update, 19*(6), 3–5.

Banta, T. W. (2008). Trying to clothe the emperor. *Assessment Update, 20*(2), 3–4, 15.

Banta, T. W., Jones, E. A., & Black, K. E. (2009). *Designing effective assessment: Principles and profiles of good practice.* San Francisco: Jossey-Bass.

Council for Higher Education Accreditation. (2002). *Specialized accreditation and assuring quality in distance learning.* Washington, DC: Council for Higher Education Accreditation.

Council for Higher Education Accreditation. (2006a). *CHEA at a glance.* Retrieved from http://www.chea.org

Council for Higher Education Accreditation. (2006b). *Recognition of accrediting organizations: Policies and procedures.* Washington, DC: Council for Higher Education Accreditation.

Hardin, J. R., & Stocks, M. H. (1995). The effect of AACSB accreditation on the recruitment of entry-level accountants. *Issues in Accounting Education, 10*(1), 83–90.

Leef, G. C., & Burris, R. D. (2002). *Can college accreditation live up to its promise?* Washington, DC: American Council of Trustees and Alumni.

Middle States Commission on Higher Education. (2005). *Assessing student learning and institutional effectiveness: Understanding Middle States expectations.* Philadelphia, PA: Middle States Commission on Higher Education.

Rhodes, T. L. (2010). *Assessing outcomes and improving achievement: Tips and tools for using rubrics.* Washington, DC: Association of American Colleges and Universities.

Roller, R. H., Andrews, B. K., & Bovee, S. L. (2003). Specialized accreditation of business schools: A comparison of alternative costs, benefits, and motivations. *Journal of Education for Business, 78*(4), 197–204.

Southern Association of Colleges and Schools Commission on Colleges. (2009). *The principles of accreditation: Foundations for quality enhancement.* Atlanta, GA: Southern Association of Colleges and Schools Commission on Colleges.

Tullis, K. J., & Camey, J. P. (2007). Strategic implications of specialized business school accreditation: End of the line for some business education programs? *Journal of Education for Business, 83*(1), 45–51.

U.S. Department of Education. (2006). A test of leadership: Charting the future of U.S. higher education: A report of the commission appointed by Secretary of Education Margaret Spellings. Jessup, MD: ED Pubs, Education Publications Center, U.S. Department of Education.

Western Association of Schools and Colleges. (2008). *Handbook of accreditation.* Alameda, CA: Western Association of Schools and Colleges.

Wiley, M. G., & Zaid, M. N. (1968). The growth and transformation of educational accrediting agencies: An exploratory study in social control of institutions. *Sociology of Education, 41*(1), 36–56.

Appendix 18.1: Accrediting Agencies' Websites

Association of American Colleges and Universities (AAC&U): http://www.aacu.org

Board of Online Universities Accreditation (BOUA): http://www.boua.org

Higher Education Accreditation Commission (HEAC): http://www.heac.org

International Accreditation Agency for Online Universities (IAAOU): http://www.iaaou.org

Middle States Commission on Higher Education (MSCHE): http://www.msche.org

New England Association of Schools and Colleges (NEASC): http://www.neasc.org

North Central Association Commission on Accreditation and School Improvement (NCA): http://www.northcentralassociation.org

Northwest Commission on Colleges and Universities (NWCCU): http://www.nwccu.org

Southern Association of Schools and Colleges (SACS): http://www.sacscoc.org

The State Higher Education Executive Officers (SHEEO): http://www.sheeo.org/

The U.S. Department of Education Database of Accredited Postsecondary Institutions and Programs: http://www.ope.ed.gov/accreditation/

Universal Council for Online Education Accreditation (UCOEA): http://www.ucoea.org

Western Association of Schools and Colleges (WASC): http://www.wasc.org

World Online Education Accrediting Commission (WOEAC): http://www.woeac.org

CHAPTER 19

REGULATED ETHICS

Institutional Research Compliance with IRBs and FERPA

Rachel Dykstra Boon

Ethical behavior should result from a personal commitment to engage in ethical practice and an attempt to act always in a manner that assures integrity. All members of AIR should pledge to maintain their own competence by continually evaluating their research for scientific accuracy, by conducting themselves in accord with the ethical standards expressed in this Code, and by remembering that their ultimate goal is to contribute positively to the field of postsecondary education.

—PREAMBLE TO THE AIR CODE OF ETHICS, 2001

The Association for Institutional Research initially created a Code of Ethics for its members in 1992 and updated it in 2001. The purpose of the Code, as noted in its preamble, was to provide guidance in instances of "ethical uncertainty" and to serve as a training guide for those new to the profession. Institutional researchers can also obtain a great deal of guidance on ethical conduct from two key areas of federal regulation: human subject research and student educational record privacy laws. Each of these areas viewed independently can seem amorphous and bound with overly onerous hurdles for compliance; however, the consistency with which the AIR Code of Ethics aligns with both of them indicates that a base level of ethical behavior appropriate to the profession is represented in these regulations. Compliance with human subjects and the Family Education Rights and Privacy Act (commonly called "FERPA") regulations can best be considered as not just persisting through layers of federal red tape, but as ethical best practice for the profession of institutional research.

Human subject research is governed by the federal government with a simple goal: ensuring the ethical treatment of all participants in research studies. At most institutions, human subject research oversight is accomplished through an Institutional Review Board (IRB). The critical and detailed eye they cast on the ethics and justification for any study involving human subjects makes IRBs a much maligned body on campus, particularly among social and behavioral researchers, in whose studies the risks often seem much less threatening (such as recall of unpleasant experiences) than the more obvious physical risks (such as death, injury, or delay of alternative treatment) inherent in much biomedical research. Criticisms of federal involvement in research oversight note that (1) although the objective of protecting participants is appropriate, it may not be best carried out through a government body (Hamilton, 2005; Ribeiro, 2006), or (2) the oversight provided is inappropriately vague and complicated at times resulting in delays and uneven application (Ashcroft & Krause, 2007; Infectious Diseases Society of America, 2009).

To better understand why IR, much of which is classified as social and behavioral research, oftentimes falls under the purview of IRBs, consider the relationship between a student and the institution. The "institution" includes the faculty who teach and assess students, assigning them grades for coursework and from whom students are likely to request recommendation letters or other professional guidance. The "institution" also includes administrators who will make decisions in cases in which student conduct is under review and who will finally certify degrees at the point of graduation. Student vulnerability, or at least a student's perceived sense of vulnerability, to the institution when it conducts research should be fairly obvious at this point. IR also involves faculty and staff in some projects, and the risks to those individuals are equally relevant, as the institution also serves as their employer and the source of their livelihood.

Research aside, institutions collect a great deal of data on students, faculty, and staff that are necessary for operational purposes. In this realm, student vulnerabilities are protected by FERPA. Information covered includes everything from home address to grades, course schedules, and even notes taken by advisors during one-on-one meetings. Due to the operational necessity, institutional researchers are generally free to use these student records to examine trends, outcomes, or other specially designed studies for internal use. Expansion beyond such internal usage must be done with careful consideration of FERPA implications. Such expansion includes provision of private student record data to contracted third parties, sharing of identifiable student information with constituents on other parts of campus in the course of a project, and any other disclosure of identifiable information to a party other than the student him- or herself.

There is overlap between FERPA and human subjects guidelines in as much as they both protect the use of private student information. IRBs expand on this to examine the treatment of students in any interventions or interactions, as well as covering interactions with any other constituents being studied (that is, faculty, staff, alumni, prospective students, community members). In the rest of this chapter the background of IRBs and FERPA will be detailed to provide additional understanding of why they are an important element of IR. As well, guidance and examples of how to effectively work with these regulations to maintain institutional compliance and best ethical practice are provided.

Institutional Review Board

Standards and ethical guidance for human subject research in the United States have been in place since as early as the 1930s, but only since the 1970s has Congress become involved in setting regulations. IRB review has been required for human subject research funded by federal agencies since the National Research Act was passed in 1974. The National Research Act also authorized the creation of the National Commission for the Protection of Human Subjects in Biomedical and Behavioral Research. This Commission issued a set of guidelines for human subject research in the Belmont report in 1979 which forms the basis on which IRB considerations of research are made (Kennedy, 2005). Today IRBs and human subject research are regulated by the Office of Human Research Protections (OHRP), under the auspices of the U.S. Department of Health and Human Services (HHS). HHS grants funds for research extensively across the postsecondary education sector, and it will provide IRB review of studies it funds for unaffiliated researchers or those whose institutions are unable to do so.

To keep the IRB reviews of funded research at the institutional level an organization can obtain a Federal-Wide Assurance (FWA) with OHRP. Part of the assurance indicates that all human subject research undertaken by researchers at the institution must be reviewed, even if it is not federally funded. This is an important reason why IR professionals should make a habit of submitting studies for review. FWAs can benefit an institution whose researchers often obtain federal funding for research or collaborate with peers at other institutions, and the loss of FWA due to noncompliance could be very detrimental to an institution's overall research portfolio and standing.

Standards for Review

Biomedical research and social and behavioral research are reviewed with the same set of principles in mind, a frustration to some social and behavioral scientists (Hamilton, 2005; Ashcroft & Krause, 2007; Ribeiro, 2007). These principles, as found in the Belmont Report (U.S. Department of Health, Education, and Welfare, 1979), have important applications, however, to any research involving human subjects. They are:

   I. Respect for persons
  II. Beneficence
 III. Justice

Principle one, "respect for persons," applies specifically to the treatment of all people as autonomous agents and to provision of special protection for those with diminished autonomy. In other words, all people who are able should be permitted to fully decide about their own participation in a study with an appropriate amount of information provided to make such a decision. Those with diminished capacity to make their own decisions (such as children, adults with mental impairments, and prisoners) must be afforded additional protection to ensure that their diminished self-determination is not being abused. In most cases institutional research does not engage in research with these protected classes, but there could be instances in which prisoners or those with mental disabilities are engaged in an educational program being examined, or more likely, a study of prospective students still under the age of eighteen. Some ambiguity exists about whether other classes of people are also vulnerable and require special protections. There is support both within the Belmont Report and in other circles for treating some individuals as "economically" or "socially" vulnerable populations (U.S. Department of Health, Education, and Welfare, 1979; Grady, 2009). Though it is somewhat more difficult to establish at times, there is reason to consider that studies focused on participants who are exclusively racial or ethnic minorities, undocumented immigrants, or of low-income status should be reviewed with exceptional sensitivity to the principle of "respect for persons" and individual autonomy.

A brief return to the AIR Code of Ethics will be instructive here. Section III (d) focuses on "Special considerations for data collection" and notes, "The institutional researcher shall ensure that all subjects are informed of their right of refusal and of the degree of confidentiality with which the material that they provide will be handled, including where appropriate, the implications of any freedom of information statute. Any limits to confidentiality should be made clear" (Association for Institutional Research, 2001).

In this passage the emphasis on informing subjects of their right to refusal and degree of confidentiality is what ensures that respect for persons is present. The Code clearly reinforces the ethical stance that is regulated by the federal government. The primary mode of complying with this guideline in research is through informed consent, almost always documented prior to the initiation of participant involvement in the study. Many samples of informed consent documents can be found on IRB websites. A checklist of elements generally required in these documents is on the NIH website (http://www.nia.nih.gov/researchinformation/cttoolbox/).

Another example of applying "respect for persons" to IR projects is those projects in which personally identifiable information about a student is used, although a specific interaction with students is not employed. For example, a study of grade inflation might seek access to student grades and assorted demographic information. If student identifiers (such as ID number, SSN, and name) are part of that information, it is human subject research requiring protection. It is best practice in these cases to have the data pulled and stripped of identifiers by someone who has approved access but is not participating in analysis of the data. In this way the risks of data security concerns are mitigated and the study likely qualifies as exempt because there is no way to tie data to individuals.

"Beneficence" is an obligation described in principle two as having two rules: "(1) do not harm and (2) maximize possible benefits and minimize possible harm" (U.S. Department of Health, Education, and Welfare, 1979). Maximization of benefits is typically accomplished in IR through the results of a study leading to improved institutional operations or through a more general contribution to the body of research or policy analysis under study. The minimization of possible harm is accomplished through careful study design and attention to the confidentiality and security of data gathered. Again, guidance from the Code of Ethics, Section III (d) reinforces this point: "The institutional researcher shall, at the design stage of any project, thoroughly explore the degree of invasion of privacy and the risks of breach of confidentiality that are involved in the project, weigh them against potential benefits, and make therefrom a recommendation as to whether the project should be executed, and under what conditions" (Association for Institutional Research, 2001).

Note that the ethical guidance is not that invasion of privacy must be avoided and that there are no risks to breaches of confidentiality. Risks of this nature are almost never entirely avoidable, short of not engaging in the research at all. Rather, the risks should be minimized, and in its review the IRB will assess the ways in which risks have been minimized, leaving it to the researcher to justify the presence of any remaining risk in the face of the potential benefits.

As in the example regarding a grade inflation study, removing identification from the data is one means to minimize risk. A different study, in which an IR office provides analysis of faculty or staff salary disparities by gender and department, must account for identifiability in results. Small departments may have only one male or female; in such a case, seeking ways to combine disciplines or withhold data in some cells will be the best way to minimize possible harm. However, it is important to also consider that a study of this nature may uncover major disparities, so a good study will include a plan for disseminating results to appropriate decision makers and the larger body of knowledge on this issue.

The final principle, "justice," provides the basis on which the benefits and burdens of the research should be distributed. It often serves as the root for concerns about population selection in studies: Was selection random, thus likely to benefit all? Was it a specified population (such as athletes) to study a topic relevant just to that group (perhaps leadership skills gained in competition)? Was it a specified population (such as athletes) to study a topic from which all students could benefit (perhaps the effectiveness of a certain pedagogy on general education learning outcomes)? Institutional researchers must therefore be cognizant of the breadth of any research study to ensure that participant selection and burden is appropriately distributed.

When Should IR Projects Be Submitted for IRB Review?

The first task in determining whether an IR study must be submitted for IRB review is to answer the question, is this research? In 45 CFR 46.102(d), the federal government defines research as a "systematic investigation, including development, testing, and evaluation, designed to develop or contribute to generalizable knowledge. Activities which meet this definition constitute research for the purposes of this policy, whether or not they are supported under a program which is considered research for other purposes." At times, IR seeks simply to do an internal program evaluation using surveys of participants in which the objective is not to provide commentary on this type of program outside the boundaries of the institution (that is, not contributing to generalizable knowledge), but to give the director of a division some data to inform operational decision making. Such projects do not necessarily qualify for IRB review, even when they involve interactions with students, faculty, or staff. This is not to say that the ethical standards found in human subjects regulations and in the AIR Code of Ethics do not apply. To the contrary, ethical standards of the practice of IR as stated in the Code of Ethics or any other professional code are meant to guide day-to-day activities and not to be situationally specific in the manner of human subjects regulations.

Before answering the question "Is this research?" one might also ask one more question: If the intent of the study is not to get "generalizable knowledge" but the study is nonetheless scientifically designed and run, how would one handle any particularly noteworthy results? In answering a hypothetical question of this nature, one might still find that the purpose is entirely internal and focused on evaluating programs only at one's own institution; thus the activity is not research. On the other hand, if noteworthy results might spark a desire to submit a paper to a journal or present the findings at a conference as a contribution to the body of knowledge about such programs, then IRB submission is a good idea. IRB approval cannot be made after the fact, and the potential desire to use data collected from people in the course of the study is probably reason enough to pursue treating it as a research project from the start.

Back to the initial question (is this research?): if the response was Yes, then one must next consider whether the study engages human participants. The designation of "human" might seem to be a label easily applied. According to the Code of Federal Regulations (CFR) governing IRBs, a human subject is defined as

> a living individual about whom an investigator (whether professional or student) conducting research obtains
>
> (1) Data through intervention or interaction with the individual, or
> (2) Identifiable private information. (45 CFR 46.102(f)(1),(2))

Institutional researchers often engage in data-gathering via surveys. Sometimes the surveys are conducted under contract with an external organization, and some surveys are developed and administered and the results analyzed entirely internally. A survey qualifies as obtaining "data through . . . interaction with the individual," thus meeting a key qualifier for IRB review. Other common IR methods that involve interactions with individuals include focus groups and interviews.

Some IR projects do not involve interacting with persons but instead use identifiable private information. As noted earlier, when used for operational purposes this is often not qualified as "research" in the sense in which IRBs are concerned. However, when identifiable private information is used in research in which there is even minimal risk that the subjects could be compromised, the project requires IRB review. Recall that the principle of "beneficence" includes the obligation to minimize possible harm. The IRB reviewer will review a project with no human interactions except the use of identifiable private information with particular attention to data security, confidentiality of identity in reporting of the study, and credentials and role of anyone with access to the study data. In essence, the IRB will require the IR professional who submitted the proposal to document information that is consistent with the AIR Code of Ethics statement in III(d)(2) on standards for data collection: "Where appropriate, the institutional researcher shall adopt a written description of any specific steps beyond the regular guidelines within the institutional research office that are necessary during a specific assignment to ensure the protection of aspects of privacy and confidentiality that may be at specific risk" (Association for Institutional Research, 2001).

Exempt, Expedited, or Full Board Review—Who Makes the Call?

The final question to answer prior to preparing an IRB proposal is in the category of the submission-exempt, expedited, or full board review. An *exempt* designation is an indication that the principal investigator or person submitting the study believes it is not one that requires official IRB review or approval. Of the three categories, this one is most likely to be handled differently based on each institution's norms of practice. In general, determination of exempt status should not be made by the investigator him- or herself, as the conflict of interest and potential lack of training on important IRB issues might lead to a wrong determination. Examples of studies that might qualify for exempt status, but should be submitted include the following:

A. Surveys with anonymous respondents
B. Studies using student data stripped of identifiers
C. Interviews or focus groups with no audio or video recording and no identifiers used in field notes or reports

Expedited review is the category most commonly used in IR studies that are not exempt from review. In expedited studies, it is important that risk of harm (physical, psychological, personal standing, or otherwise) is no more than minimal and that protected classes of people are not participants in the study. Sometimes a submission that is believed to be exempt might be rerouted by the IRB as expedited if a reviewer senses harm or identifiability is at a higher level than that perceived by the person submitting the proposal. An expedited review generally has a reasonably quick turnaround—typically between five days and three weeks—though there is no official standard, and institutions will vary.

The third type of submission is for a *full board review*. Studies of this nature are uncommon in institutional research in higher education, as they generally involve protected classes of individuals not typically part of college and university settings. However, some institutions do offer educational opportunities to nearby inmate populations, or perhaps offer literacy programs to community members in which vulnerable adults may enroll. In such instances or in those in which risk to the participants is more than minimal, a full board review will be required. The preparation for a submission for full board review is not typically greater than that for expedited review, but the review itself may take a bit longer, as it requires a meeting of a quorum of IRB members. IRBs must have at least five members, including a nonscientist, a community member, and a scientist. IRBs are encouraged to have members that represent the disciplinary, racial or ethnic, and gender diversity of the organization. Depending on the institution, that group may meet weekly, monthly, or even less often; thus planning ahead is critical for such studies.

In any type of IRB submission, it is common to have a response from the reviewers that requires at least modest revisions to the study's procedures or materials. Novice and experienced researchers encounter this, so it is important not to let the request for modifications be a deterrent to submitting for review in the first place. IRB reviewers are trained to catch things that are easily missed by researchers but can improve the protection of the subjects involved. That is the most important objective to attain.

Projects Contracted with Outside Entities

In response to calls for accountability and competitiveness, present-day IR has come to rely increasingly on data and instruments that permit peer, regional, or national comparisons. Generally this is done through a contract or agreement with a third party that will administer and analyze the data and provide results and return the raw data to partner institutions after having processed it. Some of the most well-known examples of such organizations are the Center for Postsecondary Research at Indiana University (NSSE, CSEQ, CSXQ, BCSSE, LSSSE, and FSSE) and the Higher Education Research Institute at UCLA (CIRP Freshmen Survey, YFCY, HERI Faculty Survey, College Senior Survey). Other chapters in this book talk more extensively about the utility and critical aspects of instruments offered by these entities, but as they pertain to the ethical conduct of research and IRB guidelines, there are three key aspects to consider.

First, the organizations that gather this data and analyze the results are generally pursuing an active research agenda of their own with it. Although they happily provide assistance at the individual campus level in ways that can contribute to improving postsecondary education, these organizations also want to contribute to the national and sometimes the international knowledge base in their areas of expertise. Because their staffs are indeed the principal investigators with these projects, they will often have obtained IRB approval at their home institutions or an affiliate as appropriate. Most such studies will have required an expedited review because they include personally identifiable information on participants. The IRB approval likely covers the data collection process as administered by them; however, they may advise, or in some cases require, that each institution also obtain IRB approval on its own campus because its students, faculty, or staff are involved. If so, many of the materials required for submission may be supplied by the third-party organization, and these should be used.

Second, once IRB approval is granted by either the host or home institution, it is important to strictly adhere to the guidelines of administration that are provided. Because of technology permitting day-by-day tracking of response rates, it can be tempting to make adjustments to recruitment of individuals to participate in the survey, but unless such adjustments are part of the initial approval, they should be avoided. Sometimes flexibility is built into the research protocol that makes such real-time adjustments acceptable, but the key is to be familiar with the process that was approved by the IRB and stick to it to remain in compliance.

Finally, when working with a third-party provider on research involving human subjects, IR should ensure that the institution uses the data obtained through the process. A critical factor to consider in any human subject research is the degree to which this is necessary. Any time that an intervention or interaction with humans takes place as a part of a research process, there is risk involved (even if extremely low), so unnecessary exposure to risk of any level should be avoided. Additionally, at an institution that already engages its students in other survey or data collection enterprises, an IR office should carefully weigh the risk to the institution of oversurveying. The need for data to provide accountability and assessment is important, but when it comes to interactive data collection efforts, focus on collecting only data that will be used.

Assessment

The past decade has seen a marked shift in the attention paid to assessment of educational outcomes at universities. Though there are some functional and structural differences between institutional research and assessment, many institutions rely on IR offices to provide a great deal of support for assessment activities. Determining whether or not assessment activities qualify as research can be confusing at times, but a good rule of thumb is to treat most activities much the same as other IR projects.

In deciding whether an assessment activity qualifies as research, consider again the federal definition of research in 45 CFR 46 and note especially the second clause in the definition. Once again, it states that research is a "systematic investigation, including development, testing, and evaluation, *designed to develop or contribute to generalizable knowledge*. Activities which meet this definition constitute research for the purposes of this policy, whether or not they are supported under a program which is considered research for other purposes." (45 CFR 46.102[d]) (emphasis added). An assessment activity can fit the federal definition and thus necessitate IRB review even if the individual conducting it would not think of it as research. A couple of examples of assessment activities regularly undertaken will illustrate the point.

Classroom-Based Assessment of Pedagogy. Faculty and institutions tuned into the scholarship of teaching and learning often engage in examinations of personal or institutional pedagogical styles. At my institution, examinations of this sort have sometimes entailed a change in pedagogy from one semester to the next and a review of student performance on the same classroom examination methods used in both terms. A good teacher at any level will constantly assess his or her performance in order to improve it. Engaging in this type of activity does not inherently meet the federal definition of research. Faculty members who plan such pedagogical experiments with the intent of determining the effectiveness of different teaching methods, and who may also wish to translate it into papers or presentations within their disciplines, *are* engaging in a systematic investigation. Though some disciplines may not recognize this as research, it does fit the federal definition and therefore requires an IRB review.

Classroom-Based Assessments of Learning Outcomes. Other assessment activities focus on obtaining data on student learning of specific outcomes. When these are embedded in the classroom as expectations for students enrolled in the course, it may seem unnecessary to involve the IRB. If a campus has made a systematic determination of how it will gather this information to assess, say, a writing outcome, it would quite likely benefit from some level of IRB review. Some electronic portfolio systems permit campus-wide use of rubrics to collect data on writing assignments; thus identifiable student data become part of broad, systematic efforts to assess learning. Under an expedited review, this would likely mean the project would require informed consent for students, which can be complicated to obtain although beneficial to the process. It is possible that an IRB would approve a study like this that requested waiving informed consent, but in either case submission for review is advisable.

Assessments External to the Classroom. As noted earlier, use of instruments from outside entities is common in institutional research. The same is true for assessment. The Collegiate Learning Assessment (CLA), MAPP, and CAPP are all examples. As was noted, IRB approval may have been obtained by the host organization, or it may be required of IR staff at their home institution. It is best practice to work closely with the outside organization in these instances.

If assessments of learning outcomes at the institution are designed internally and intended to occur outside the classroom, it will generally be best to ask whether there is any reason not to submit for IRB review. As public use and scrutiny of these data are likely and seems to have increased in recent years, the protection provided by having obtained IRB approval can be reassuring to IR and assessment practitioners.

Family Education Records Privacy Act

The Family Education Records Privacy Act of 1974 (FERPA) governs the release of and access to student educational records maintained by an educational institution. The regulations distinguish between directory type information, which has fewer protections, and other private student data. Acceptable directory information is defined as follows:

Name

Identification number (other than social security number)

Address

Phone number

Email address

Photograph

Date and place of birth

Grade level

Enrollment status (undergraduate or graduate; full-time or part-time)

Participation in officially recognized activities or sports

Weight and height of athletic team members

Degrees

Honors and awards received

Most recent school attended

Students are permitted to block public disclosure of all or part of this information through the appropriate university office. There are instances in which institutions may disclose information without written student permission; examples relevant to the practice of institutional research are described in the following section.

Regulations in FERPA (found in 34 CFR part 99) apply to any educational institution that receives federal funding from programs administered by the Department of Education, so nearly every college and university in the United States must comply with the standards it sets. In addition, it defines a student as any person enrolled at the institution currently or in the past, including those in distance education programs who never set foot on the physical campus.

As with IRB and human subjects guidelines, the FERPA guidelines align well with elements found in the AIR Code of Ethics. Section III.c., Release of Confidential Information, states, "The institutional researcher shall permit no release of information about individual persons that has been guaranteed as confidential, to any person inside or outside the institution except in those circumstances in which not to do so would result in clear danger to the subject of the confidential material or to others; or unless directed by competent authority in conformity with a decree of a court of law" (Association for Institutional Research, 2001).

Annual Disclosure of FERPA Rights to Students

All educational institutions are responsible for making an annual disclosure regarding FERPA rights to currently enrolled students. The source of the disclosure will typically be the office of the registrar or a similar office. Elements mandated for inclusion in the disclosure include notice of the posting of directory information, unless students officially request such information be withheld, as well as the process for withholding such information.

School Officials

Generally speaking, official student records are procured and maintained by offices other than an office of institutional research. The offices of the registrar, financial aid, admissions, and student life have some, college/school units have others, and eventually alumni and development hold still other records. IR professionals generally obtain the data under the FERPA provision that allows access to "other school officials within the institution determined by the institution to have a legitimate educational interest" (Hicks et al., 2006). The functions IR offices perform for institutions constitute legitimate educational interest, so these personnel, including student workers in an IR office, can reasonably access much of a student's private information in the process of performing their job functions. As stated in the AIR Code of Ethics, however, unnecessary release of confidential data to any person, even if inside the institution, does not meet an expected level of ethical practice and IR should carefully protect such data.

State and Local Reporting

Though resistance to the creation of a national individual unit record database persists, many states have been collecting unit record data for years. The IR office may be responsible for providing these data to the state or local entity, and it is acceptable to do so. Guidance provided by the Department of Education based on the 2008 update of FERPA indicated that disclosures of personally identifiable information without consent of students to state or local authorities are permitted under law when the purpose is to perform an "audit, evaluation or compliance or enforcement activity" (Federal Register, 2008). Clarifications note that this can include disclosures of information to state boards of higher education that may have an oversight function for an institution and conduct evaluations and research studies for this purpose (34 CFR 99.35). No written agreement is required for reporting private information for this purpose, and the disclosure does not need to be recorded in a student's record.

Third Party Entities

Aside from state or local government entities operating by statute, there are times when other entities external to the institution request student data. When the data are aggregate, there are no FERPA concerns. If data requested is identifiable private student information needed to conduct a study or service on behalf of the institution, FERPA permits a release of the data without student permission. The entity conducting the research is considered an authorized representative of the institution. Organizations and surveys mentioned earlier in regard to IRB implications are relevant here. For example, institutions participating in the CLA must provide some directory information on the students who take the CLA, as well as their ACT or SAT scores at time of admission—information that is clearly private. This disclosure is permissible because the institution could reasonably state it is paying CLA officials to do a function it would otherwise do itself.

The primary restriction of FERPA in this case is that these third parties cannot then redisclose personally identifiable information on students, and "information secured must be destroyed when no longer needed for their projects" (Hicks et al., 2006). The American Association of Collegiate Registrars and Admissions Officers recommends obtaining this assurance in writing with any third party recipient of student data. Several other elements should also be included in agreements with third parties that access data for educational research purposes. See Appendix 19.1 for a more comprehensive listing of what to include in an agreement to share personally identifiable data.

Conclusion

One of the most interesting things about the federal regulations for protection of human subjects through IRBs and protection of student records information through FERPA is their codification of the ethical standards consistent with those that IR professionals have set for themselves in the AIR Code of Ethics (Association for Institutional Research, 2001) (see Chapter 3). The only extraordinary measure in complying with these regulated ethics is ensuring that the appropriate paperwork and documentation is in place. Guidance from the federal government on how to maintain compliance is regularly updated, and the laws themselves go under review and are revised periodically. In fact, IRB regulations were undergoing review and public comment as this chapter was being written, with proposed changes anticipated in 2012. Implications for the type of work done in IR could be significant, and each campus-level IRB is likely to revise its own policies in the wake of changes to federal regulation. IR professionals should work with appropriate offices on their campuses to ensure due diligence in meeting the spirit of both of these laws.

References

Ashcroft, M. H., & Krause, J. A. (2007). Social and behavioral researchers' experiences with their IRBs. *Ethics and Behaviors, 17*(7), 1–17.

Association for Institutional Research. (2001). Code of ethics for institutional research. Tallahassee, FL: Association for Institutional Research.

Federal Register. (2008, December 9). Department of Education, Family Educational Rights and Privacy, Final Rule, *73*(237).

Grady, C. (2009, Spring). Vulnerability in research: Individuals with limited financial and/or social resources. *Journal of Law, Medicine and Ethics,* 19–27.

Hamilton, A. (2005). The development and operation of IRBs: Medical regulations and social science. *Journal of Applied Communication Research, 33*(3), 189–203.

Hicks, D. J., et al. (Eds.). (2006). FERPA Guide. Washington, DC: American Association of Collegiate Registrars and Admissions Officers.

Infectious Diseases Society of America. (2009). Grinding to a halt: The effects of the increasing regulatory burden on research and quality improvement efforts. *Clinical Infectious Diseases,* 49, 328–325.

Kennedy, J. M. (2005). Institutional researchers and institutional review boards. In P. D. Umbach (Ed.), *Survey research emerging issues* (pp. 17–31). New Directions for Institutional Research, no. 127. San Francisco: Jossey-Bass.

Ribeiro, G. L. (2007). IRBs are the tip of the iceberg: State regulation, academic freedom, and methodological issues. *American Ethnologist, 33*(4), 529–531.

U.S. Department of Health, Education, and Welfare. (1979, April 18). The Belmont report: Ethical principles and guidelines for the conduct of human subjects of research. Washington, DC: The National Commission for the Protection of Human Subjects in Biomedical and Behavioral Research.

Appendix 19.1: FERPA Concerns to Address in Agreements with Third Parties for Disclosure of Identifiable Data for Educational Research

1. Statute 34 CFR 99.31(a)(6)(ii)(C) requires a written agreement with a third party to which personally identifiable student record information will be disclosed must include the following:
   a. Purpose of the study
   b. Scope of the study
   c. Duration of the study
   d. Information to be disclosed
2. Statute 34 CFR 99.31(a)(6) states that the organization receiving the data must destroy or return to the educational institution all identifiable data when no longer needed for the purposes of the study. The time period for this action must be specified in the written agreement.
3. Statute 34 CFR 99.31(a)(6)(ii)(A) requires that studies must be conducted in a manner that does not permit personal identification of parents or students by anyone other than representatives of the organization that have legitimate interest in the information (in other words, if cell counts are so small that individuals can be identifiable to someone without access to the data, it should not be reported). This provision is not required as part of the written agreement, but it is advisable.
4. Statute 34 CFR 99.31(a)(6) also requires that the disclosure of identifiable information to individuals within the organization be limited to those with whom there is a legitimate interest in the information. Again, this provision is not required as part of the written agreement, but it is advisable.
5. FERPA does not prohibit these agencies from redisclosing data that has been properly "de-identified" to other independent researchers, so when entering agreements with third parties, it is advisable to clarify this point in the written agreement.
6. FERPA holds institutions responsible for ensuring through the written agreement that the organization conducting the study has appropriate controls in place to protect the personally identifiable information being provided to them.

CHAPTER 20

DATA, DISCRIMINATION, AND THE LAW

Andrew L. Luna

The institutional research function frequently finds itself designated as the institutional official source of data. One of the primary databases maintained by many institutional research offices involves faculty and faculty activity. Many aspects of using these data are discussed in chapters on measuring and evaluating faculty workload (Chapter 31) and analyzing equity in faculty compensation (Chapter 32). These two faculty aspects, critical to all higher education institutions, have also been where institutional research and case law may well have come into contact. When an institution becomes involved in a discrimination lawsuit, many things happen—not the least of these is a realization that the courts and the institutional research function have different frames of reference and, frequently, different language. What may be considered "right" may not be considered legal, or statistical evidence worthy of a national, peer-reviewed publication may not be compelling enough for the court.

This chapter highlights some of the key differences between the science of statistics and the practice of law when the two are combined to address a social and legal issue such as discrimination. The chapter focuses on discrimination, but much of what it discusses is also appropriate for other legal issues, such as disabilities, admissions, athletics, and the many other rules, regulations, and laws that surround institutions of higher education.

Our Environment and Culture

The United States has become a litigious society, with IR and higher education having to answer the clarion call to respond to many legal issues, including discrimination, harassment, and reasonable accommodations. Since 1972, when Title VII of the 1964 Civil Rights Act was extended to cover both public and private educational institutions, numerous lawsuits have arisen from the halls of academe. Although these court decisions have helped administrators more effectively align institutional policy within the confines of the law so that lawsuits might be minimized, lawsuits still occur quite frequently in higher education.

Furthermore, as more cases address the issue of discrimination, the courts increasingly face two distinctive problems. First, discrimination claims are more complex for faculty, staff, and students to prove and for institutions to defend against, due to the subjective nature of academic higher education (Barbezat, 2002; Kaplin & Lee, 1995). Second, the use of statistics, particularly regression analysis, is often difficult for jurists and jurors alike because both have to struggle with the probative value (that is, having the effect of proving) of statistical results to the case at hand (Lempert, 1985).

There is a rich literature on the topic of discrimination and other legal issues in higher education. As one might expect, most of the literature is based on analytical methodologies. Luna (2006) extends the analytical discussions by including a review of case law and how court decisions have defined the statistical methodologies that are recognized as a significant part of these cases. When one becomes involved in supporting legal discussions with data analysis, it is important to gain an understanding of the relevant case law and appreciate the impact of case law on policy. Discussions reporting the results of IR analyses and data should also include relevant legal decisions. Most discrimination law is based on federal law. There are also many state laws that deal with discrimination. There are also court case decisions. How courts interpret the law governs, to some extent, how institutions may work within it (Simpson & Rosenthal, 1982).

The Role of Statistics

It is difficult for those lawyers who may not be familiar with them to understand statistics and what role statistics can actually play in establishing or refuting a prima facie case of discrimination. For instance, statistical analysis has become a central means of attempting to prove or disprove discrimination in a wide variety of cases. However, classical statistical inference can neither prove the cause of a disparity nor identify all of the possible factors that caused the disparity (Paetzold & Willborn, 2001). Statistics provides only information on the likelihood of a particular outcome.

It has become increasingly important for IR to study the nature and extent of certain legal problems—such as faculty salary discrimination, salary compression, hiring practices, and accessibility issues—and to use these studies to supply information to administrators and policy makers to either rectify a problem that may exist or to provide compelling legal evidence if a discrimination issue is taken to court (Lee and Liu, 1999). Again, Chapters 31 and 32 give a great deal of more detailed analytical information about how statistics can inform the discussion of faculty activity and salary. However, a well-crafted piece of research that replicates well-known methodologies published in respected journals may not pass the basic rules of evidence or may not be what the courts have articulated they want.

To clarify this, this chapter identifies some inherent differences between the statistics of IR and the law, underscores the difficulty of combining the two in cases involving higher education issues, and then addresses how the two can and should be mutually supportive of each other. When these two divergent disciplines are forced to merge, and when statistical evidence is introduced, conflicts often arise from misunderstandings on how lawyers and statisticians see the world. One of the key components to bridging this gap between statistics and law may be regular discussions between the compliance function, the institutional legal function, and the institutional research office. Traditionally, IR offices deal with data, statistical applications, and policy issues—often in a seamless environment. A well-developed IR office should be able to stay informed of new or updated laws, recent court decisions, and the latest statistical tests and research. This level of awareness, supported by compliance and legal staff, needs to be matched with increased awareness of what data are available and how to analyze and interpret this data. What follows is a discussion of laws of discrimination, recent court decisions, and statistical tests recognized by the courts, which should help the IR office build its knowledge of the differences and similarities surrounding statistics and the law.

Laws of Discrimination

Understanding case law and how statistical evidence applies to it may be an important step in preventing salary discrimination lawsuits on campus (Simpson & Rosenthal, 1982). Information gained from case law may allow administrators, institutional researchers, and faculty to more effectively plan and conduct gender salary equity studies on their campuses, using the results to help account for any unexplained salary variations, and may allow the institution to properly remedy any possible salary disparities in the context of current legal jurisprudence. An understanding of case law will also aid in preparing a more legally sound statistical model if a salary dispute goes to court.

Background

Most lawsuits involving colleges and universities concern discrimination in some way. Essentially, there are two basic models of discrimination: one focuses on the intentions of the decision makers, the other on the criteria decision makers use (Paetzold & Willborn, 2001). Although harassment and reasonable accommodation are somewhat different from these two models, they were derived from them. Because this chapter is focused on discrimination law, it is necessary to understand the relevant laws and how they affect higher education.

There are two statutes on which claims of discrimination in employment are filed: the Equal Pay Act and Title VII of the 1964 Civil Rights Act. Currently faculty members use both statutes to dispute pay disparities in higher education. It is important to understand that there are only two ways in which a federal law may change: through legislative act or the interpretation of the court dealing with a particular point of law in a case. The legislature created both the Equal Pay Act and the Civil Rights Act of 1964. Over the years, however, the courts have made various changes to the law through their function of interpretation (Wren and Wren, 1986).

Equal Pay Act

When a male and a female employee perform job functions that are substantially equal but they receive different salaries, the Equal Pay Act is often used to decide whether discrimination exists. The statute prohibits employers from paying unequal wages to people working in jobs that "require equal skill, effort, and responsibility and which are performed under similar working conditions, except where such payment is made pursuant to (i) a seniority system, (ii) a merit system, (iii) a system which measures earnings by quantity or quality of production, or (iv) a differential based on any other factor other than sex" (29 U.S.C. sec. 206(d)(1)).

The U.S. Supreme Court has established a two-step process for evaluating an Equal Pay Act claim. First, the plaintiff must prove a violation by showing that the skill, efforts, and responsibility required in performance of the jobs are substantially equal. Once the plaintiff makes a prima facie case, the employer then has the opportunity to show that the pay differential was due to one of the four affirmative defenses just listed (*County of Washington v. Gunter*, 1981).

Title VII of the Civil Rights Act of 1964

When the job structure at a business or institution is substantially segregated by sex, race, or ethnicity, and workers of any *suspect class* (a presumptively unconstitutional distinction made between individuals on the basis of race, national origin, alienage, or religious affiliation, in a statute, ordinance, regulation, or policy) are paid less than other workers who perform the work that is of comparable value or worth to their employer, the lower-paid worker may file a claim under Title VII. This statute is considered the most comprehensive and therefore has been the most frequently used of the federal employment discrimination laws. In 1972, the statute was extended to cover public and private educational institutions, and today it is the most used discrimination statute within higher education.

Title VII essentially has two parts. The first stipulates that it shall be unlawful for an employer "to fail or refuse to hire or to discharge any individual, or otherwise to discriminate against any individual with respect to his compensation, terms, conditions, or privileges or employment, because of such individual's race, color, religion, sex, or national origin." The next section makes it unlawful for an employer "to limit, segregate, or classify his employees or applicants for employment in any way which would deprive or tend to deprive any individual of employment opportunities or otherwise adversely affect his status as an employee because of such individual's race, color, religion, sex, or national origin" (42 U.S.C sec. 2000e-2[h]). The major exception to this statute is a bona-fide occupational qualification (BFOQ) that is necessary to the normal operation of a business or enterprise. For example, gender could be a BFOQ in an all-male residence hall, and religion could be a BFOQ at a religiously affiliated college or university. Two legal models are used in defining and establishing a Title VII case.

Disparate impact. The disparate impact model concerns employment practices that are "fair in form but discriminatory in operation" (*Griggs v. Duke Power Co.*, 1971, p. 424). The employer does not need to have any intent to discriminate; rather, some presumably neutral policy of the employer has a discriminatory effect on the claimants or the class of person they represent (Kaplin & Lee, 1995). In its unanimous opinion in *Griggs*, the U.S. Supreme Court created a two-step process for establishing a prima facie case under the disparate impact model. The court prohibited employment practices that (1) operate to exclude or otherwise discriminate against employees or prospective employees on grounds of race, color, religion, sex, or national origin and (2) are unrelated to job performance or not justified by business necessity. Under this model, both requirements must be met before Title VII is violated.

Disparate treatment. The disparate treatment model involves intentional discrimination with a discriminatory motive, and under a class action suit the evidence must establish a pattern, practice, or custom of discrimination (*Barnett v. Grant*, 1975). The U.S. Supreme Court established a three-step process for evaluating a disparate treatment claim. First, the plaintiffs bear the burden of establishing a prima facie case of discrimination by a preponderance of the evidence (*McDonnell Douglas Corp. v. Green*, 1973; *Texas Department of Community Affairs v. Burdine*, 1981). Second, once they have done so, the burden shifts to the defendant to articulate some legitimate, nondiscriminatory reason for the challenged employment practice (*McDonnell Douglas Corp. v. Green,* 1973). In cases where the plaintiff has relied on statistical evidence to establish a prima facie case of discrimination, the defendants may also attempt to undermine the plaintiff's prima facie case by attacking the validity of that statistical evidence or introducing statistical evidence of their own showing that the challenged practice did not result in disparate treatment (*Berger v. Iron Workers Reinforced Rodmen Local 201*, 1988; *International Brotherhood of Teamsters v. U.S.,* 1977). Third, if the defendants meet this burden of proof, the plaintiffs must then show either that the defendants' statistical proof is inadequate or that the defendants' explanation for the challenged practice is merely a pretext for discrimination (*Zahorik v. Cornell University*, 1984).

The Structure of the Courts

Within the U.S. judicial system are several levels of courts, each performing a specific function. The federal courts, where most salary equity cases are tried, have three levels: the district or trial court, the intermediate appellate or circuit court, and the final appellate or U.S. Supreme Court. There are 84 district courts and 13 circuit courts of appeals. District courts cover a specific geographical area in a particular state that is based on that area's population. With the exception of the District of Columbia and federal circuit (the only court that has its jurisdiction based wholly on subject matter rather than geographic location), each circuit court of appeals encompasses several states. Within each of the first two judicial levels, the courts act independently of each other. In other words, for example, the decisions and interpretations by the U.S. Court of Appeals for the Fourth Circuit in one case may contradict the decisions and interpretations of the U.S. Court of Appeals for the Second Circuit in a similar case.

The trial or lower court's responsibility is to collect evidence from both parties, determine how that evidence relates to the law, and make a decision based on the court's conclusions of the evidence and interpretation of the law. The job of the appellate court is to ensure that the trial court applied the relevant and appropriate points of law to the evidence provided. Very rarely do appellate courts reevaluate or redetermine findings of facts made at the trial level (Wren & Wren, 1986).

Case Precedents

At this point, it is important to distinguish between case precedents that are *mandatory* and those that are *persuasive*. Mandatory precedent cases are those from the highest court in that particular jurisdiction. Because many discrimination cases involve federal law, the U.S. Supreme Court is the highest court in the federal jurisdiction. Persuasive cases come from lower federal courts and are used as guidance to other cases (Wren & Wren, 1986). For example, district court decisions, as well as other appellate court decisions, are persuasive only to another appellate court. Appellate court decisions, however, are mandatory in the circuit they reside, and cases decided by the U.S. Supreme Court create mandatory precedent that each district and appellate court must follow. If, however, there are inconsistent decisions coming from the federal appellate courts, the U.S. Supreme Court may be compelled to make a decision on one of these cases so that a mandatory precedent can be established. Therefore appellate court decisions are considered the law of the land for all who reside within that circuit's jurisdiction, and U.S. Supreme Court decisions are considered the law of the land for the entire country.

What Is Fair Versus What Is Legal

Before a discrimination issue has the chance to leave the halls of academe and go to court, it is wise for the administration to investigate all allegations and redress any inequities, if apparent, no matter how significant the financial burden on the institution (Boudreau & others, 1997). Furthermore, Braskamp, Muffo, and Langston (1978) argue that any fair review of discrimination issues requires a clear definition of the policies on campus and how these policies are related to professional experiences, scholarly achievements, instructional effectiveness, and service. During this type of analysis, however, the use of basic human judgment and what may or may not be fair often weighs in heavily on both administrators and faculty (Moore, 1993).

The View from the Institution

On one side of the human equation process are history and the argument that many studies have shown compelling evidence, and courts have agreed that there is discrimination among particular classes of people (Barbezat, 2002). On the other side of the equation is the argument that the judgment of whether inequities exist should be answered by the distinct fields of law, economics, and statistics (Moore, 1993).

In some instances, legal decisions on discrimination may not correlate with what faculty or administrators believe to be justifiable arguments based on institutional mission and culture, human capital theories, or statistical studies. In some cases, court decisions have even redefined well-established statistical measures and practices. Furthermore, some legal scholars have argued that the methods of proving discrimination through statistical models are based on faulty statistical and factual assumptions and misconceived interpretations of the meaning of statistical evidence (Browne, 1993). This often-strong dichotomy of reasoning between legal scholars and statistical and economical scientists is a strong argument as to why discrimination disputes should be settled within the institution and not wind up in court. Essentially, when the courts review quantitative evidence on a discrimination issue, it is not to develop a general theory of human behavior but to decide which evidence is legally stronger in order to settle a dispute (Simpson & Rosenthal, 1982).

When court decisions are rendered, many have been questioned as to how fair or just they are, and discrimination cases are not immune to this type of inquiry. Although an institution may be compelled to follow a particular court decision concerning discrimination, such a decision should not automatically prevent administrators from further investigating the fairness of its employment structure or move beyond the law in their quest for a more equitable structure. It should also be noted, however, that statistics are only part of the court's analysis of a case. Law, the experience of the jurists, and intuition all serve as guides in the resolution of a case (Baldus & Cole, 1980).

Statistics and the Courts

Although in theory, statistics and the legal system are almost dichotomous, in practice the courts have nonetheless acknowledged the use of statistics in discrimination cases. In 1973, the U.S. Supreme Court established the basic analytical framework for providing an individual case of intentional discrimination, or disparate treatment, under Title VII. The Court stated that the plaintiff could prove unlawful discrimination, and once the showing has been made, an employer must articulate a legitimate, nondiscriminatory reason in order to avoid liability (*McDonnell Douglas Corp. v. Green*, 1973). This decision induced plaintiffs and defendants alike to use statistics as part of their probative evidence. Soon after its decision, courts were obligated to recognize an increase of statistical evidence in discrimination cases. In *Hazelwood School District v. U.S.* (1977), the Court clarified the use of statistics in Title VII cases by stating that the government could establish a prima facie case of race discrimination by the use of statistics. The U.S. Supreme Court's decision in *International Brotherhood of Teamsters v. U.S.* (1977) further confirmed the use of statistics in discrimination cases when it held that statistics are probative of discrimination, especially when they are combined with anecdotal evidence. As we will later see, courts have had to rely solely on anecdotal evidence when the statistical models used become either too complex or too esoteric.

Federal Rules of Evidence

In addition to what the courts have said, the Federal Rules of Evidence define as relevant all "evidence having any tendency to make the existence of any fact that is of consequence to the determination of the action more probable or less probable than it would be without the evidence" (Federal Rules of Evidence, 401, 2001). Moreover, these rules indicate two grounds by which statistical evidence may be excluded if it fails to be statistically significant. The first, Rule 703 (Federal Rules of Evidence, 703, 2001), provides that the evidence must be "of a type reasonably relied upon by in the particular field in forming opinions or inferences upon the subject." Second, Rule 403 (Federal Rules of Evidence, 403, 2001) states that all relevant evidence may be excluded if its probative value is substantially outweighed by its tendency to waste time, confuse the issues, or mislead the jury. As Toutkoushian and Hoffman (2002) stated, there is a wide range of statistical methods for measuring wage disparity, each with varying levels of complexity and difficulty. Although the authors stress that the type of model used is based in part on how the research results will be used, it is also clear that the courts may find that the simpler single-equation model satisfies Rule 403 more than the multiple-equation methods will. However, this assumption has yet to be directly tested.

Since 1977, when the U.S. Supreme Court became more receptive to the use of statistics, lower federal courts have struggled with the significance and probative value of statistics in discrimination cases, as well as with their admissibility in general. This result of the struggle for jurists to understand statistics has been courts from different jurisdictions simultaneously interpreting statistics differently. As the U.S. Supreme Court hears more cases involving statistical methodologies, a narrower definition and scope of the role of statistics and their interpretation will clearly result.

The Logical Dilemma Between Law and Statistics

Due to the perception that the science of statistics and the practice of law are, for the most part, incongruent, scholars believe that the two contradict each other and caution should be used when applying the two in analysis.

A Difference in Establishing What Is Truth

When statistical evidence is introduced, conflicts arise due to the gaps between statistical and legal reasoning. These differences, which arise from the significant way in which statisticians and lawyers differ in their view of the world, are defined by Paetzold and Willborn (2001) as follows.

The language of statistics is uncertainty, while the language of law is certainty. In other words, classical statistical evidence should only reject or fail to reject a null hypothesis rather than prove it. The language of statistics describes the probability of occurrence under an appropriate set of assumptions. Statistical tests can support only that something either happened or did not happen by chance. In contrast, the preponderance of evidence in a court of law is used to "prove" someone's guilt or innocence no matter what the actual truth may be. This language can cause confusion because courts may refer to their decisions as proof, but in reality they are not proving guilt or innocence; rather, they are drawing conclusions based on the preponderance and persuasiveness of the evidence, in much the same way that traditional hypothesis testing does not prove or disprove a null hypothesis.

Statistical methodologies and the philosophy of statistics are mainly based on deductive reasoning, whereas the practice of law is mainly based on inductive reasoning. Deductive reasoning is the process by which someone makes conclusions based on previously known facts—for instance, all oranges are fruit, and all fruit grows on trees, and therefore all oranges grow on trees. Contrary to deductive reasoning, inductive reasoning is the process of arriving at a conclusion based on a set of observations. For example, all observers have testified that every flame they've ever encountered is hot, so all flame is hot; kicking a ball made it go up in the air, ten times out of ten, so all balls that are kicked go up in the air. Inductive reasoning, however, may not be a valid method of proof. Just because someone observes a number of situations in which a pattern exists does not mean that the pattern is true for all occasions.

Lawyers use data only they need to prove a case, whereas the practice of statistics requires the use of all pertinent data, and any anomalies should be identified. Whereas the vast majority of attorneys live by their profession's ethical codes, they are still (and should be) biased to their clients whom they are representing. This bias is antithetical to the ethical codes of statisticians, who are required to use whatever data are needed to complete the analysis.

The statistician may view evidence inconclusively, whereas the lawyer is obligated to view evidence decisively. In law, what is considered proof follows a well-defined standard based on the preponderance of evidence or facts at hand. In statistics, the nature of truth is always probabilistic. In law, the standard of proof is subjective and depends on the nature of the case. Here the attorney is interested in submitting as much evidence as he or she is allowed to submit to prove or refute a case. In statistics, the scientist has to be concerned with the fact that all occurrences have variability and error and should be reported that way.

Statistical language may confuse jurists, whereas legal language may confuse statisticians. It is no secret that both attorneys and statisticians use terminology that does not easily transfer to the other's discipline. Statistical jargon confounds attorneys, and legal jargon baffles statisticians. Caught in the middle are jurors, who are equally confused and frustrated by both.

On the face of it, attorneys have rules and laws they must obey, and the preference they show to their clients is clearly demonstrated in the evidence they present. Although attorneys who use research in court cases may not intentionally bias statistical results, partiality to a particular statistical finding may still be implied (Simpson & Rosenthal, 1982). For instance, according to Hunt (1979), "Almost never do you see a researcher who appears as an independent witness, quite unbiased. You almost always see a witness appearing either for the FTC [Federal Trade Commission] or for the industry. You can almost predict what is going to be concluded by the witness for the FTC. And you can almost predict what will be concluded by the witness for industry. That says that research in this setting is not after full truth and it is not dispassionate in nature" (p. 152).

There can be different definitions of key terms. Although statistical evidence is valuable, it can also be misleading because of the difference between the legal definition of *discrimination* and the statistical translation underlying statistical inference. According to Paetzold and Willborn (2001), whenever statistical evidence is used, three types of models contribute to the inferential process: the legal model, which determines how evidence can be used in court; the situational model, which focuses on either the intentions of the employer or the actual criteria employers used in the employment process, or both; and the statistical model, which consists of the formal rules and methodologies that guide the scientific process.

The Nature of Research

Because of the nature of research, statistical evidence cannot prove that discrimination actually exists. It can show only that a probability may exist whereby an institutional standard of employment is beyond the boundaries of chance occurrence. Therefore, when the statistical model indicates a potential deviation from the norm, it is up to the lawyers to incorporate the intentions and the outcomes of the process in the inferential process to determine whether it is more likely than not that discrimination occurred (Paetzold & Willborn, 2001). When this happens, the objective nature of statistics may be overwhelmed by the rules of evidence, attorney-client bias, or circumstantial evidence.

To show how the reasoning of statistical inference may be contradictory to the practice of law, consider the measurement of height and Sir Francis Galton. Galton, cousin to Charles Darwin, first used the term *regression* to support his theory that taller fathers tended to have shorter sons, and shorter fathers tended to have taller sons. In other words, the height of fathers' sons tended to regress toward the mean. Using a regression analysis in this manner would create a statistical inference to the height of a son based in part on the height of the father or mother, or both.

Suppose that a woman gives birth to a child. She is five feet four inches tall, and her husband is five feet seven inches tall. Let us further suppose that according to a statistical table that was determined after running a point-in-time regression model of thousands of parents, the fully grown son's height would fall within five feet five inches and six feet one inch if it is to be within acceptable standards of random variation. If the son's actual height is significantly over or under this range, it becomes a significant deviation from normal. According to statistical reasoning, this variation could be attributed to a special cause or causes, it could signal an outlier with no apparent specific cause, or there could be enough error in the model to induce the researcher to falsely reject the null hypothesis.

If this height variation were submitted as evidence in court, the legal, situational, and statistical models described by Paetzold and Willborn (2001) would be scrutinized to establish a prima facie case against the mother, indicating that her husband was not the father of her son. The burden of proof would then fall on the mother to show beyond a reasonable doubt that her husband was in fact the actual father. In this case, the attorney for the mother might incorporate statistical evidence consisting of a longitudinal regression analysis that may refute the claim. Unless her evidence is significantly compelling, the woman might be found guilty of promiscuity simply because her legally forced burden to prove her husband was the real father may be beyond the capabilities of statistical inference. This example may *sound* extraordinary, but that may not actually be the case.

Conclusions Differ for Different Cases in Different Courts

Many courts have recognized that excluding chance as a factor is not the same as determining the occurrence of impermissible discrimination; other courts, however, do not understand the difference and are not so careful. In *Palmer v. George P. Shultz* (1987, p. 90), the court stated, "Nor can statistics determine, if chance is an unlikely explanation, whether the more probable cause was intentional discrimination or a legitimate nondiscriminatory factor in the selection process." In *Maddox v. Claytor* (1985, p. 1552), the court concurred, stating that "it is important to stress that a disparity translating into a large number of standard deviations does not automatically point to discrimination as the cause."

Contrary to these decisions, in *Payne v. Travenol Lab.* (1982, p. 820), the court stated, "Absent explanation, standard deviation of greater than three generally signals discrimination." In *Ivy v. Meridian Coca-Cola Bottling Co.* (1986, p. 157), the court decided in part that "a fluctuation of two or three standard deviations indicates that the result is caused by discriminatory intent rather than chance." Likewise, in *Rivera v. City of Wichita Falls* (1982, p. 532), the court stated that "standard deviation analysis quantifies the likelihood of a benign explanation for an observed discrepancy."

The Use of Data in Discrimination Cases

IR offices manage most of the data that are used in discrimination cases. Although these personnel and other administrative records were not originally collected for the purpose of addressing actual or potential allegations of discrimination, they are used for investigating such concerns. The challenge for institutional researchers is to organize those records in a manner that can address specific legal issues regarding possible differences in the experiences of employees or applicants based on race, sex, or other classes protected under Title VII or other EEO laws (Christenson, Maher, & Mueller, 2008).

However, rather than wait to use these data until an actual discrimination action is presented to the institution, it is wise to use the data at hand to conduct self-critical analyses that identify institutional risk with respect to maintaining equity in their personnel practices and workforce. If analyses are conducted on a regular basis, the institution will have a much higher-quality database and can act in a timely manner to detect potential issues and/or correct any problems before they have the chance of become litigious crises. Although institutions face a risk because the information generated may be considered discoverable in legal proceedings, they are also at risk if they fail to adequately evaluate the potential for discrimination in their employment decisions.

Conclusion

Statistical hypothesis testing determines whether the deviation of a variable is within the realm of chance occurrence or there is a significant probability that the deviation is beyond the boundaries of chance. Although this testing is different from and more empirical than the legal standard of weighing a verdict on the preponderance of the evidence, there are still challenges in using statistical evidence as proof of the existence or absence of discrimination. Just because there may be a disproportionately and significantly higher rate of members of one class of people getting jobs, promotions, raises, and so on over another group of qualified candidates does not automatically mean that an institution is acting in a discriminatory way.

It is also very likely that in any case there will be statisticians for both sides and their results will be differentially supporting the argument of the side they are supporting.

Evidence from a plaintiff that is considered statistically significant forcibly narrows the opportunity for the defendant to show chance as the cause for the disparity. The defendant then has to prove, beyond a reasonable doubt, either that there is no disparity or that the apparent disparity is not caused by illegal discrimination.

Although there are no clear-cut answers to these questions, it is clear that a greater understanding of the relationship between statistics and the law should be sought and that institutional research practitioners may be best suited to effectively blend these divergent philosophies into a more useful and coherent resource.

A good starting point is to address the issues discussed in the section on the different views of what the truth is. This involves conversations at the institutional level between institutional research and the key participants, such as the lawyers and those who manage risk and compliance. A second important step is to ensure that there is a single official source of institutional data in the areas most at risk. These of course include demographic characteristics and institutional outcomes such as tenure decisions, salary, and faculty activity. Many of these data are also found in the Affirmative Action Plan of those institutions that have such a plan. The third important step is for those who do institutional research to become familiar with the methodologies that have been used in lawsuits, the outcomes of those lawsuits, and the cases that apply to the specific location of the institution. A final step is to ensure that IR is keeping the senior administration informed every step of the way.

References

Baldus, D., & Cole, J. (1980). *Statistical proof of discrimination*. New York: McGraw-Hill.

Barbezat, D. (2002). History of pay equity studies. In R. Toutkoushian (Ed.), *Conducting salary-equity studies: Alternative approaches to research* (pp. 9–39). New Directions for Institutional Research, no. 115. San Francisco: Jossey-Bass.

Barnett v. Grant, 518 F.2d 54 (1975).

Berger v. Iron Workers Reinforced Rodmen Local 201, 269 U.S. app. D.C. 67 (1988).

Boudreau, N., & others. (1997). Should faculty rank be included as a predictor variable in studies of gender equity in university faculty salaries? *Research in Higher Education, 38*(3), 297–312.

Braskamp, L., Muffo, J., & Langston, I. (1978). Determining salary equity: Politics, procedures, and problems. *Journal of Higher Education, 49*, 231–246.

Browne, K. (1993). Statistical proof of discrimination: Beyond "damned lies." *Washington Law Review, 68,* 477–558.

Christenson, B. A., Maher, K. M., & Mueller, L. M. (2008). Organization and maintenance of data in employment discrimination litigation. In A. L. Luna (Ed.), *Legal applications of data for institutional research* (pp. 47–66). New Directions for Institutional Research, no. 138. San Francisco: Jossey-Bass.

County of Washington v. Gunter, 452 U.S. 161 (1981).

Federal Rules of Evidence, 401 (2001).

Federal Rules of Evidence, 403 (2001).

Federal Rules of Evidence, 703 (2001).

Griggs v. Duke Power Company, 401 U.S. 424 (1971).

Hazelwood School District v. U.S., 433 U.S. 399 (1977).

Hunt, H. (1979). The ethics of research in the common interest. In N. Ackerman (Ed.), Panel summary. In *Proceedings of the American Council of Consumer Interests Conference.* Milwaukee.

International Brotherhood of Teamsters v. U.S., 431 U.S. 324 (1977).

Ivy v. Meridian Coca-Cola Bottling Co., 641 F. Supp. 157 (1986).

Kaplin, W., & Lee, B. (1995). *Law in higher education.* San Francisco: Jossey-Bass.

Lee, J., & Liu, C. (1999). Measuring discrimination in the workplace: Strategies for lawyers and policymakers. *University of Chicago Law School Roundtable, 6,* 195–234.

Lempert, R. (1985). Symposium on law and economics: Statistics in the courtroom. *Columbia Law Review, 85,* 1098–1116.

Luna, A. L. (2006). Faculty salary equity cases: Combining statistics with the law. *Journal of Higher Education, 77*(2), 193–224.

Maddox v. Claytor, 764 F.2d 1539 (1985).

McDonnell Douglas Corp. v. Green, 411 U.S. 792 (1973).

Moore, N. (1993). Faculty salary equity: Issues in model selection. *Research in Higher Education, 34,* 107–125.

Paetzold, R., & Willborn, S. (2001). *The statistics of discrimination: Using statistical evidence in discrimination cases.* Colorado Springs: Shepard's/McGraw-Hill.

Palmer v. George P. Shultz, 815 F.2d 84 (1987).

Payne v. Travenol Lab., Inc., 673 F.2d 798 (1982).

Rivera v. City of Wichita Falls, 655 F.2d 531 (1982).

Simpson, W., & Rosenthal, W. (1982). The role of the institutional researcher in a sex discrimination suit. *Research in Higher Education, 16,* 3–26.

Texas Department of Community Affairs v. Burdine, 450 U.S. 248 (1981).

Toutkoushian, R., & Hoffman, E. (2002). Alternatives for measuring the unexplained wage gap. In R. Toutkoushian (Ed.), *Conducting salary-equity studies: Alternative approaches to research* (pp. 71–90). New Directions for Institutional Research, no. 115. San Francisco: Jossey-Bass.

Wren, C., & Wren, J. (1986). *The legal research manual: A game plan for legal research and analysis* (2nd ed.) Madison, WI: Adams & Ambrose.

Zahorik v. Cornell University, 729 F.2d 85 (1984).

CHAPTER 21

FEDERAL HIGHER EDUCATION REPORTING DATABASES AND TOOLS

Gayle M. Fink and Chad Muntz

Since late in the decade of the 1980s, three forces have come together to allow the public and institutions greater access to data about postsecondary education. These forces are (1) greater demands for accountability from higher education and its public funding sources, (2) demands that the funding and processes of higher education become more transparent, and (3) the development of technology to provide access to and usability of complex national data sets. The increasing cost of higher education is causing many—including public officials, the general public, students, and parents—to question whether there is a viable "return on investment" when participating in postsecondary education. Cries for greater transparency are heard from federal and state legislatures, accrediting bodies, and parents, to justify the increased cost of attending higher education as well as the support needed from public funding agencies.

Not only are colleges and universities being held to greater degrees of accountability, but federal and state agencies also are being required to demonstrate accountability and transparency to their constituents. This chapter focuses on how the U.S. Department of Education and the National Science Foundation (n.d.) are using technology to deliver free datasets and information to public and private constituencies. The websites noted in this chapter were successfully accessed in February 2012. Please note that they are subject to change as data access tools and analytical capabilities evolve.

U.S. Department of Education

Most postsecondary institutions are required, as a condition of federal student financial aid, to report a wealth of information to the U.S. Department of Education. A majority of this reporting is to the Institute of Education Sciences

(IES), whose mission is to provide rigorous evidence on which to propose federal education policy. This is accomplished through the work of its four centers—Evaluation, Research, Statistics, and Special Education Research. The Statistics Center is named the National Center for Education Statistics (NCES), and it is the primary federal entity for collecting and analyzing data related to education throughout the United States and its territories (http://nces.ed.gov).

NCES fulfills a congressional mandate to collect, collate, analyze, and report complete statistics on the condition of American education; conduct and publish reports; and review and report on education activities internationally. The Postsecondary, Adult, and Career Education Division (PACE) within NCES collects universe data on postsecondary institutions; conducts sample surveys on student financial aid and student access, persistence, completion, and outcomes of postsecondary education; and collects data on the education and training that youth and adults need to prepare for work. In addition, PACE has responsibility within NCES for responding to the congressional mandate to collect and report data on career and technical education for high school students, college students, and adults. The most recognized reports published by PACE are the Digest of Education Statistics, Projections of Education Statistics, and The Condition of Education. These three reports cover a broad range of K–12 and postsecondary education issues as well as respond to congressional directives.

In addition to Congress, NCES and PACE provide information to a number of constituencies, which use comparison information to support national, state, and local decision making. These groups include:

- Federal agencies—to study the supply of trained manpower produced by colleges
- State education agencies—to produce comparison statistics within and among states
- State and local officials—to examine issues of staffing and financing public education
- Educational organizations and individual postsecondary institutions—to examine data for lobbying, planning, and research
- The news media—to inform the public about matters such as college enrollment and expenditures per student and student success
- Business organizations—to forecast the demand for their products
- The general public—to make informed decisions about choosing a college and its associated cost and to make intelligent decisions concerning educational issues (National Center for Education Statistics, n.d.; Martin Conley & Fink, 2009)

NCES Datasets

Before discussing the primary dataset used by postsecondary institutions—the Integrated Postsecondary Education Data System (IPEDS) (n.d.)—it is important to recognize that NCES also conducts an extensive survey research program that concentrates on following groups of students and faculty over time. In contrast to IPEDS, which focuses on institutional-level aggregated information, the sample surveys focus on collective student and faculty experiences. These sample surveys provide a wealth of information on student education expectations, how students finance college, postsecondary completion, and the transition to work. Faculty are asked questions regarding their background, instructional responsibilities, scholarly activity, job satisfaction, and compensation. (Appendix 21.1 presents a brief summary of all the NCES sample surveys.)

These sample surveys are helpful to institutional researchers, as they provide national information on a number of topics related to students and faculty. National-level information may provide a prospective to campus issues: for example, do low-income students at my institution tend to borrow more than students at comparable institutions? In addition, these sample survey instruments are helpful when developing internal institutional surveys. One can incorporate questions into internal surveys and when compiling the internal analysis, provide added richness by comparing a specific institution's data to national-level data.

PACE sample surveys are accessed through a tool called the DataLab. This interface enables users to create tables quickly using QuickStats or compiling a complex analysis in the Data Analysis System (DAS). There is also a library of existing tables from federal reports (Condition of Education, for example) for use by researchers. To navigate to these sample surveys, access the NCES website (http://nces.ed.gov) and choose the "Surveys & Programs" tab on the main menu bar.

The Integrated Postsecondary Data System

The IPEDS surveys are the heart of postsecondary education data reporting to the federal government. The completion of all IPEDS surveys is mandatory for institutions that participate in any federal student financial aid program. IPEDS supports reporting requirements from other federal requirements: the Carl D. Perkins Vocational Education Act (career and technical education), Title VI of the Civil Rights Act of 1964 and subsequent amendments (race or ethnicity and gender of students and staff), the Student Right-to-Know Act (completion rates), and the Higher Education Opportunity Act of 2008 (providing consumer information about postsecondary institutions) (http://nces.ed .gov/ipeds).

More than 6,700 institutions complete IPEDS surveys each year. These include research universities, state colleges and universities, private religious and liberal arts colleges, for-profit institutions, community and technical colleges, and non-degree-granting institutions such as career schools (beauty, truck driving, technical professions, and the like).

IPEDS presently has nine component surveys collecting hundreds of data elements reflecting institutional-level characteristics. These nine surveys can be grouped under three headings: general information (one survey), institutional resource information (two surveys), and surveys about students (six surveys). Appendix 21.2 presents a complete description of each of the nine surveys. An understanding of the data collected in these nine surveys is necessary for the efficient use of the data extraction tools described as follows.

IPEDS Data Tools

There are three primary tools that institutional researchers use to extract IPEDS information—College Navigator, the Executive Peer Tool, and the Data Center. A description of these tools follows. In addition, a seldom-used but excellent resource is the IPEDS Tables Library. The Tables Library summarizes data that has been released in NCES reports and/or related to current issues of interest typically rolled up at the national, regional, and segmental levels. For example, the Tables Library is an excellent source to find national graduation rate data by segment. The tables in the Library can be downloaded into Excel for further analysis or to use in internal reports. All of the IPEDS tools and the Tables Library can be accessed through the IPEDS website.

College Navigator. College Navigator (http://nces.ed.gov/collegenaviga tor/) was mandated by Congress as a free information tool to help students, parents, high school counselors, and others access information about post-secondary institutions in the United States and other jurisdictions. The primary dataset that populates the tool is IPEDS. However, College Navigator includes other useful information from the U.S. Department of Education; the Office of Postsecondary Education (OPE) provides data on varsity athletic teams, accreditation, and campus security, and the Federal Student Aid (FSA) office provides data related to student loan default rates. Each of these non-IPEDS sites has datasets that can be easily searched and provide for data downloads. The OPE and FSA website links are within College Navigator.

In College Navigator, institutional data are divided into eleven distinct categories. IPEDS is the source for the following categories: general information, tuition, fees and estimated student expenses, financial aid, enrollment, admissions, retention and graduation rates, and academic programs. The information provided on varsity sports teams, accreditation, campus security, and federal loans originates from other offices in the Department of Education.

The search engine features built into College Navigator include an option that is not in the other IPEDS data tools—the ability to search for institutions within 5 to 250 miles of a zip code. This information is helpful when compiling competitor program marketing data. Once the user has selected a set of institutions, there is the capability to download basic directory information to Excel or CSV file. The download includes the institution's IPEDS ID, which can be copied into the other IPEDS tools as a peer group.

College Navigator provides institutional researchers with a quick way to get a snapshot of basic information about a set of institutions (comparisons can be built for up to four institutions at a time). It also provides an access point to other DOE tools. Because College Navigator was built as a consumer information tool, it has limited usefulness for institutional researchers. The primary tool used by institutional research professionals is the IPEDS Data Center, which provides current and historical IPEDS data useful for institutional comparisons.

Executive Peer Tool. The Executive Peer Tool (ExPT) (http://nces.ed.gov/ipeds/datacenter/) was developed to provide decision makers with an easy tool to build comparisons between a focus institution and a group of peer institutions, using all of the data available in the printed IPEDS Data Feedback Report (DFR), described shortly. ExPT is located in the NCES Data Center—the primary web-based tool designed to enable a user to easily retrieve summary data on a group of postsecondary institutions of the user's choice. To access ExPT, the user must enter the Data Center and select ExPT and DRF from the menu on the left side of the page.

A working knowledge of the ExPT is a potentially important tool for institutional researchers. Every fall, NCES sends to each IPEDS participating institution's chief executive officer their institution's DFR. The DFR is intended to give institutions a context for examining the data they submitted to IPEDS. NCES's goal is to produce a report that is useful to institutional executives and to improve the quality and comparability of IPEDS data.

The DFR contains selected indicators from IPEDS data elements for the most recent collection cycle. The 2011 DFR included fifteen figures presenting multiple data elements that compare an institution's value with a comparison group's median value. Data are presented on admissions, enrollment, cost of attendance, financial aid, retention and graduation rates, degrees awarded, faculty and staff, faculty salaries, and finance. The DFR can be accessed directly through the Executive Peer Tool (ExPT) (http://nces.ed.gov/ipedspas/expt/).

Designed to accompany the IPEDS Data Feedback Reports, ExPT provides straightforward access to a limited number of institutional-level IPEDS data and calculated values. It includes these capabilities:

- Recreate the DFR using different comparison groups
- Download institution-level data
- Create and download a Statistical Analysis Report showing statistics, tables, and graphs for the selected variables
- Create and save a custom comparison group that may be used again in the ExPT or other IPEDS Data Tools

- Download a focus institution's IPEDS DFRs for several recent years
- Download the most recent printed IPEDS DFRs for comparison group institutions
- Download a data file of ExPT variables for the focus and comparison group institutions

The ExPT provides institutional researchers with a starting place for developing institutional effectiveness indicators. Most regional accrediting agencies require institutions to demonstrate that they are meeting their mission or vision and strategic goals. Evidence includes an ongoing, systematic approach to evaluation that includes measures of internal goal attainment as well as external comparisons (other institutions, within state, region, nationally). However, only the most recent year is accessible. To obtain historical data, the user must access the IPEDS Data Center.

Data Center. As mentioned earlier, the Data Center (http://nces.ed.gov/ipeds/datacenter/) is the workhorse of the IPEDS tools—a one-stop shop for IPEDS data back to 1980 in some cases. Even though the Data Center is fairly straightforward, new users should expect to spend a fair amount of time becoming familiar with the tool. Training is offered through both NCES and AIR at national, regional and affiliated group conferences. In addition, there are IPEDS trainers who are available to help one understand how to use the Data Center. A listing of the IPEDS trainers and training sessions are on the AIR website (http://www.airweb.org/?page=819).

The Data Center allows users to retrieve IPEDS data using functions listed on the main menu. These include: "Look Up an Institution," "Compare Individual Institutions," "Rank Institutions on One Variable," "View Trend for One Variable," "Create Group Statistics," "Generate Pre-Defined Reports," "Download Survey Data Files," and "Download Custom Data Files."

Generally, the Data Center is used to extract current and longitudinal data about an institution or a comparison group of institutions. When choosing "Compare Individual Institutions," the user first selects a focus institution and then identifies a list of comparison institutions by name/IPEDS ID, by groups using predefined variables, by variables identified by the user, or by uploading a previously saved comparison group. Once the comparison group is defined, the user selects the variables to include in a data file or report.

At this point, knowledge of IPEDS data elements is essential for efficient use of the Data Center. If the user does not have a working knowledge of the IPEDS variables collected in each survey, the user can go to the IPEDS website and access currently collected items in the "Data Provider Center" or, for historical surveys, access the "IPEDS Resource Center" from the home page and select "Survey Instrument Library." Another resource tool in the Resource Center is the Classification of Instructional Programs (CIP) link (http://nces.ed.gov/ipeds/cipcode/Default.aspx?y=55). CIP is a classification scheme for programs of study used in the IPEDS Completions survey, allowing programmatic comparisons across institutions. The Completions Survey collects "degrees awarded" data by program and can be used to determine which institutional academic offerings are useful in developing market analyses.

The user must keep in mind that certain data are collected every other year and in the off year the data is optional. Additionally, variables are added, deleted, or changed over time. Variables also represent different points in time. For example, there is fall snapshot data (Institutional Characteristics, Fall Enrollment, Human Resources), annual data (Completions, 12-Month Enrollment, Finance, Student Financial Aid), and data over a time frame (Graduation Rates, Graduation Rate 200). Frequently Used/Derived Variables items include data elements from ExPT. It is advisable to spend time before entering the Data Center to map out the data elements and the number of years needed to complete the assignment and to identify the IPEDS survey where the needed variables can be found.

Once the user has selected the years and variables for comparison, variable-level data by institutional output is provided on the screen or in a downloadable format. Once the comparison group of institutions is set, the user can download an IPEDS Institutional Identifier or .uid file from the Data Center to store and upload again in a subsequent session. If the user is updating variables annually, it is useful to download the variables in a Master Variable List or .mvl file. This will allow the user to upload the variables after the next collection cycle, update the years, and download the new data fairly quickly.

There is more functionality in the Data Center than described here. For example, the Data Center allows for rank and trend reports for a single variable and predefined reports on price, admissions applicant, admit and yield rates, enrollment trends, graduation rates, and student financial aid, to name a few. The user can even download entire survey data files or create custom data files. New users or those familiar with the IPEDS are encouraged to attend NCES/ AIR training sessions to become more familiar with this tool and its uses.

Collaboration with Institutional Research Community

In addition to responding to congressional mandates, NCES strives to provide users with tools that are timely and relevant. The agency's connection to the institutional research community is through the National Postsecondary Education Cooperative (NPEC) (http://nces.ed.gov/npec/index.asp). NPEC was established by NCES in 1995 as a voluntary organization that encompasses all sectors of the postsecondary education community, including federal agencies, postsecondary institutions, associations, and other organizations with a major interest in postsecondary education data collection. NPEC's mission is to promote the quality, comparability, and utility of postsecondary data and information that support policy development at the federal, state, and institution levels. The NPEC IPEDS R&D panel does this by developing a research and development agenda for IPEDS, identifying topics that will help improve the quality, comparability, and utility of IPEDS data for the postsecondary education community, consumers, and policy makers, as well as providing expertise to NCES on related IPEDS R&D projects. A listing of recent and ongoing projects as well as membership is on the NPEC website.

AIR also uses Association members to link with governmental and other agencies and the media that collect, analyze, disseminate, and use postsecondary data through the Higher Education Data Policy Committee (HEDPC) (n.d.), a standing committee of the Association. HEDPC is charged with (1) developing and operating a program to identify important higher education data policy issues and providing the AIR board of directors with guidance on the issues; (2) with the concurrence of the board of directors, taking action to provide the AIR and IR point of view to operational agencies and organizations; and (3) keeping the membership informed on the status of relevant higher education issues through various media. The committee also creates and coordinates the operation and reporting of ad hoc task forces to advise relevant agencies and organizations responsible for state, national, and international higher education issues. HEDPC communicates with AIR members through AIR Alerts and through the electronic AIR monthly e-newsletter (http://www.airweb.org/).

National Science Foundation and the National Institute for Health Datasets

The National Science Foundation (NSF) and the National Institutes of Health (NIH) annually grant billions of dollars to university researchers to fund scientific research projects. In return, higher education institutions provide relevant data for the purpose of tracking trends in science and engineering research expenditures, research facilities, education of scientists and engineers, and the science and engineering labor market. These data are collected by the Division of Science Resource Statistics (SRS) through annual, biannual, and ad hoc surveys. The findings are later reported in a variety of publications, and the raw data are made available through online tools and downloads. Currently, information about the surveys can be found at http://www.nsf.gov/statistics/survey.cfm.

Surveys

The NSF collects a variety of surveys, occasionally in partnership with NIH, on a scheduled or ad hoc basis. The surveys are completed within an institution by individuals, institutional research offices, academic departments, or academic business offices (for example, controller, accounting, research administration). Additionally, other surveys are completed by nonacademic stakeholders including the general public, companies, as well as non-profit, state, and federal agencies.

There are four surveys with which the NSF collects data from individuals. The first is the *National Survey of Recent College Graduates* (NSCRCG), completed annually by a sample of individuals with bachelor's or master's degrees in science and engineering programs who have recently transitioned as students into the workforce. Second is possibly the most well known survey, the *Survey of Earned Doctorate* (SED), an annual census survey of all recent doctorial recipients. Third, every two years doctoral recipients may be sampled to participate in a longitudinal study called the *Survey of Doctorate Recipients* (SDR). Fourth, biennially, individuals with a bachelor's or higher degree may be sampled to participate in a longitudinal study called the *National Survey of College Graduates* (NSCG). Through these surveys, data are collected about educational or workforce-related activities in the science and engineering fields.

Research institutions may be requested to complete three NSF/NIH surveys internally. The annual *Graduate Students and Post Docs in Science & Engineering Survey* (GSS; formerly known as the *Graduate Student Survey*), which requests graduate, post-doc, and nonfaculty researcher headcount, demographic, and financial support data at the academic program level, is likely completed by the institutional research office. Another annual survey completed by academic institutions, the *Research and Development Expenditures at Universities and Colleges Survey (R&D)*, tracks annual institutional expenditures by academic field and source of funding. A third, congressionally mandated biennial survey is called the *Survey of Science and Engineering Research Facilities*; it may require coordination with a variety of campus offices to provide data about the allocation, repair/renovation, construction, condition, and funding source for research space. In combination, these surveys inform the NSF/NIH, government agencies, academia, and higher education affiliated agencies about funding priorities to support research programs in higher education.

Federal and state government agencies, industry, and the general public provide data for the six additional surveys. The *Federal Science & Engineering Support to Universities, Colleges, and Non-Profit Institutions Survey* is congressionally mandated and, in conjunction with the *Survey of Research & Development Expenditures at Federally Funded Research & Development Centers*, is completed by nineteen federal government agencies. Thirty government agencies complete the *Survey of Federal Funds for Research & Development*. Similarly, state agencies complete the *Survey of State Funds for Research & Development*. The *Business Research and Development and Innovation Survey* (BRDIS; formerly, *The Survey of Industrial Research & Development*) is completed by public companies and collects R&D expenditures and output as well as workforce data. Finally, the general public regularly provides attitudinal data about science and technology in the *Survey of Public Attitudes Towards and Understanding of Science & Technology*. All together, the data collected through these surveys further a national understanding about the research and development in the sciences, serve for international comparison, and inform decision makers for strategic purposes.

The NSF conducts other studies on an ad hoc basis as resources are available and the need for information is evident. Currently, the NSF has three inactive surveys. Similar to companies, higher education, and government agencies, non-profit organizations may be required to provide data about research and development in the *Survey of Research & Development Funding and Performance by Non-Profit Organizations*. Occasionally, academic institutions are sampled to provide data for *the Survey of Academic Research Instruments and Instrumentation Needs*. Finally, the NSF has general *Higher Education Surveys* of which the survey instrument will change depending on data requirement needs at the time. Appendix 21.3 presents a complete listing of all the NSF surveys and although dated, Milam (2003) provides additional reference information.

NSF Data Access

The NSF survey data are available to all science and engineering stakeholders to support planning and decision making. Summary data are available in a variety of formats through publications, online data tools, and data downloads. Data are available in public-use preformatted tables, public use data files, and restricted-use data files that require a license agreement to protect confidentiality and prevent misuse.

Data available publically online can be accessed using one of three web tools. WebCASPAR (Integrated Science and Engineering Resource Data System; https://webcaspar.nsf.gov/) makes data available from a variety of the NSF surveys as well as selected data from other sources such as the National Center for Education Statistics (NCES). IRIS (Industrial Research & Development System; http://www.nsf.gov/statistics/iris/) is a comprehensive collection of the NSF Industrial Research & Developmental data. SESTAT (Scientists and Engineers Statistical Data System; http://www.nsf.gov/statistics/sestat/) contains data from NSF surveys about employment, demographics, and education of scientists. All of these tools provide the option to download data tables into a variety of formats and also offer researchers tutorials and help sections to facilitate use.

Restricted-use datasets are available with strict adherence to a data license agreement between the user and NSF. One advantage of requesting access to custom, restricted-use datasets is the opportunity to match the data against other NSF surveys as well as selected NCES datasets to create a more comprehensive data file. Users are advised to plan ample time for a research project if a license agreement involves a review of the research proposal or research findings. In addition, there are external agencies, like the National Opinion Research Center (NORC; n.d.; http://www.norc.org/sed/survey+of+earned+doctorates .htm), that also provide custom data tables of select NSF surveys—in this case, the *Survey of Earned Doctorate* (SED). Finally, institutional researchers may contact other campus business officers hoping for opportunities to inquire about purchasing the campus data—for example, the SED campus data are available to the graduate dean for purchase.

In summary, the NSF, in partnership with NIH, actively conducts numerous surveys about students in science and engineering fields, funding, and public opinion. These data are not only required for congressionally mandated accountability but also serve institutions by providing data for national comparisons. Public aggregate survey data are available online for the most recent years and may be needed by institutional researchers for internal data requests to inform campus decision makers.

Conclusions

Surveys and other data collection efforts conducted by the National Center for Education Statistics and the National Science Foundation have generated voluminous amounts of data to address accountability and transparency demands at state and federal levels. These federal databases provide key data to evaluate attributes and productivity at one institution relative to other institutions.

For example, if a research institution was interested in the primary graduate student financial support profiles in chemistry, researchers could find comparative data in the NSF Graduate Students and Post Docs in Science and Engineering Survey. These data would be useful to a graduate dean or program chair, who could understand the strategic use of source funds needed to create competitive assistantships that attract students to the program. Specifically, if research assistantships are used more commonly, then teaching assistantships may be less competitive. However, such a shift in mechanisms of support may require the institution to increase federal fund sources that create research assistantships and new institutional sources for adjunct hires to replace teaching assistants.

Competitor enrollment management information is readily available through the NCES Data Center. Comparing institutional profile information (such as admissions criteria, test scores, and financial aid) of those institutions that enroll freshmen who also were accepted by the researchers' own admissions office not only informs of contenders for your students but also provides an indication of the financial aid packages of first-time freshmen.

Tools developed over the past decade not only have made these data available but also provide great flexibility for downloading and analyzing the data. Familiarity with these national data sources and tools provides institutional researchers with the ability to access national data and generate issue-specific, national comparisons for institutional decision makers and stakeholders.

References

AIR Higher Education Data Policy Committee. (n.d.). Retrieved from http://www.airweb.org

Integrated Postsecondary Education Data System. (n.d.). Retrieved from http://nces.ed.gov/ipeds

Martin Conley, V., & Fink, G. (2009). Using national datasets for institutional research. Association for Institutional Research Foundations Institute.

Milam, J. H. (2003). Using national datasets in postsecondary education research. In W. E. Knight (Ed.), *The primer for institutional research* (pp. 123–149). Tallahassee, FL: Association for Institutional Research.

National Center for Education Statistics. (n.d.). Retrieved from http://nces.ed.gov

National Opinion Research Center. (n.d.). Retrieved from http://www.norc.org/

National Science Foundation. (n.d.). Retrieved from http://www.nsf.gov/statistics/survey.cfm

National Science Foundation. (n.d.). Retrieved from http://www.nsf.gov/statistics/database.cfm

APPENDIX 21.1   NCES SAMPLE SURVEYS

Name	Description
Baccalaureate and Beyond—B&B	B&B studies follow students who complete their baccalaureate degrees. Initially, students in the NPSAS surveys are identified as being in their last year of undergraduate studies. Students are asked questions about their future employment and education expectations, as well as about their undergraduate education. In later follow-ups, students are asked questions about their job search activities, education, and employment experiences after graduation. Individuals who had shown an interest in becoming teachers are asked additional questions about their pursuit of teaching and, if teaching, about their current teaching position.
Beginning Postsecondary Students Longitudinal Study—BPS	BPS studies follow students who first begin their postsecondary education. Initially, students in the NPSAS surveys are identified as being first-time beginners of undergraduate studies. These students are asked questions about their experiences during and transitions through postsecondary education and into the labor force, as well as family formation. Transfers, persisters, stopouts/dropouts, and vocational completers are among those included in the studies.
Career/Technical Education Statistics—CTES	The 2006 Carl D. Perkins Career and Technical Education Improvement Act mandates that "as a regular part of its assessments, the National Center for Education Statistics shall collect and report information on career and technical education for a nationally representative sample of students." To meet this requirement, NCES uses the Career/Technical Education Statistics (CTES) system. The CTES system relies on existing and special-purpose NCES surveys to provide data on career/technical education from students, faculty, and schools at the secondary and postsecondary levels, as well as on adults seeking work-related education and training.
High School and Beyond—HS&B	The HS&B describes the activities of seniors and sophomores as they progressed through high school, postsecondary education, and into the workplace. The data span 1980 through 1992 and include parent, teacher, high school transcripts, student financial aid records, and postsecondary transcripts in addition to student questionnaires and interviews.
National Postsecondary Student Aid Study—NPSAS	The NPSAS is a comprehensive study that examines how students and their families pay for postsecondary education. It includes nationally representative samples of undergraduate, graduate, and first-professional students; and students attending public and private less-than-two-year institutions, community colleges, four-year colleges, and major universities. Both students who do and do not receive financial aid participate in NPSAS. Comprehensive student interviews and administrative records, with exceptional detail concerning student financial aid, are available for academic years 1986–87, 1989–90, 1992–93, 1995–96, 1999–2000, and 2003–04.
National Study of Postsecondary Faculty—NSOPF	The National Study of Postsecondary Faculty (NSOPF) was developed in response to a continuing need for data on faculty and instructional staff. NSOPF includes a nationally representative sample of full- and part-time faculty and instructional staff at public and private not-for-profit two- and four-year institutions in the United States. The NSOPF was designed to provide data about faculty and instructional staff to postsecondary education researchers, planners, and policy makers.

APPENDIX 21.2   IPEDS SURVEYS

Name	Description
General Information	
Institutional Characteristics (IC)	*Directory information*: Name and address, institutional control, levels of awards, calendar system, system affiliation, athletic association
	Admissions information: Applied, accepted, enrolled, standardized test scores, admissions considerations, special learning opportunities
	Price/student charges: undergraduate and graduate application fee; full-time and per credit hour tuition (in-district, in-state, out-of-state); room and board charges; first-time, full-time cost of attendance
	Estimated fall headcount: by level and full- or part-time
Institutional Resources	
Finance (F)	*Revenue and expenditures*: Accounting method, statement of net assets, operating and nonoperating revenue by source (tuition and fees, governmental operating contracts, auxiliary services, other services), expenditures by functional area (instruction, research, public service, academic support, student services, institutional support, operation and plant maintenance, scholarships or fellowships, auxiliary, independent operations), scholarships and fellowships by source, endowment assets, debt and assets
Human Resources (HR)	*Employees* by employment status, primary functional area, tenure status, salaries of full-time instructional faculty by tenure status and contract length, full-time instructional faculty fringe benefits, full-time faculty race and gender by rank, salary intervals of primary functional areas by race and gender, new faculty hire information
Students	
Completions (C)	*Number of awards* by level, Classification of Instructional Program (CIP) code, race and gender, second degrees collected
12-month Enrollment (E-12)	Unduplicated student counts for an entire twelve-month period by level, race/ethnicity and gender, credit hours/contact hours for an entire twelve-month period, FTE by level
Fall Enrollment (EF)	*Fall enrollment* by level (including first-time and transfer in for undergraduate students), race or ethnicity and gender; for selected programs (even years), by age (odd years), by residence of first-time first-year (even years)
	Retention rates: Fall-to-fall retention by initial attendance status, first-time degree or certificate-seeking undergraduate students
Graduation Rates (GRS)	Number of students entering first-time, full-time degree-seeking in a fall term by race and gender and the completion rates of those students within 150 percent of normal time by race or gender, number transferred to other institutions
Student Financial Aid (SFA)	*Financial aid information* for all undergraduates by source (federal, state, institution, private) and type (Pell Grants, grants or scholarships, and loans) and for first-time, full-time undergraduates by various groupings
GRS 200 (GR200)	*Number of completers* within 200 percent of normal time

APPENDIX 21.3 NSF SURVEYS

Survey	Type	Respondent	Frequency	Data	Data
National Survey of Recent College Graduates (NSCRCG)	Sample	Recent baccalaureate and master's recipients	Annual	General demographic, primary employment and satisfaction; occupational information and training; educational history; financial support and debt	SESTAT; http://www.nsf.gov/statistics/sestat/
Survey of Earned Doctorate (SED)	Census	Recent Ph.D. recipients	Annual	General demographic, primary and secondary employment; occupational information and training; educational history; post-doctoral study/research; graduate financial support and total debt	WEBCASPAR; https://webcaspar.nsf.gov/
Survey of Doctorate Recipients (SDR)	Sample; longitudinal	College graduates	Biennial	General demographic; educational history; primary employment status and satisfaction; postdoctoral status	SESTAT; http://www.nsf.gov/statistics/sestat/
National Survey of College Graduates (NSCG)	Sample; longitudinal	Ph.D. recipients	Biennial	General demographic; academic employment; educational history; primary employment status and satisfaction; publication and patent activities; work-related training	SESTAT; http://www.nsf.gov/statistics/sestat/
Graduate Students and Post Docs in Science & Engineering Survey (GSS)	Population	Academic research institution	Annual	General demographic for graduate students, post-doctoral appointees, and nonfaculty researchers; enrollment status; primary source of support; primary mechanism of support; educational attainment; institutional	WEBCASPAR; https://webcaspar.nsf.gov/
Research and Development Expenditures at Universities and Colleges Survey (R&D)	Population	Academic research institution	Annual	R&D expenditures by source, R&D expenditures by character of work, R&D expenditures passed through to subrecipients, R&D expenditures received as a subrecipient, total and federally funded R&D expenditures by S&E field, total and federally funded R&D expenditures by non-S&E field, total and federally funded R&D equipment expenditures by S&E field, federally funded expenditures by S&E field and federal agency, academic institution/FFRDC, institutional characteristics, FFRDC characteristics	WEBCASPAR; https://webcaspar.nsf.gov/

Survey	Type	Respondent	Frequency	Description	URL
Survey of Science and Engineering Research Facilities	Population	Academic research institution	Biennial	Amount and type of science and engineering research space; condition of research facilities; current expenditures for projects to construct and repair/renovate research facilities; planned construction and repair/renovation of research facilities; research animal facilities; source of funds for construction and repair/renovation of research facilities; information technology: bandwidth and networking; IT infrastructure	http://www.nsf.gov/statistics/facilities/
Federal Science & Engineering Support to Universities, Colleges, and Non-Profit Institutions Survey	Population	Federal agencies	Annual	R&D; fellowships, traineeships, and training grants (FTTGs); R&D plant; facilities and equipment for instruction in science and engineering; general support for science and engineering; other activities related to science and engineering; academic institution; federal agency; obligations; performer; R&D plant; institutional characteristics	WEBCASPAR; https://webcaspar.nsf.gov/
Survey R&D Expenditures at Federally Funded R&D Center	Population	Federal agencies	Annual	R&D expenditures by source of funds; R&D expenditures by character of work (basic research, applied research, or development)	www.nsf.gov/statistics/ffrdc/
Business Research and Development and Innovation Survey (BRDIS)	TBD	Public companies	TBD	Replaces the Survey of Industrial Research & Development. Survey to address (1) a company's domestic and worldwide R&D relationships, including R&D agreements, R&D "outsourcing," and R&D paid for by others; (2) the strategic purpose of a company's worldwide R&D activities and their technology applications; and (3) patenting, licensing, and technology transfer activities, and companies' innovative activities	IRIS; http://www.nsf.gov/statistics/iris/
Survey of Public Attitudes Towards and Understanding of Science & Technology	Sample	Public opinion	Annual	How information about S&T is obtained; interest in science-related issues; visits to informal science institutions; S&T knowledge; attitudes toward science-related issues	http://www.nsf.gov/statistics/seind10/

(Continued)

APPENDIX 21.3   NSF SURVEYS (Continued)

Survey	Type	Respondent	Frequency	Data	Data
Survey of Research & Development Funding and Performance by Non-Profit Organizations	Population	Non-profits	Inactive	Non-profit organization, non-profit performer of R&D, expenditures for intramural R&D, character of work, fields of science and engineering, sources of funds, type of nonprofit R&D performer, extramural funding of R&D at other institutions, non-profit funder of R&D, types of non-profit funders of R&D, funds provided for medical and nonmedical R&D and R&D capital, R&D funds provided to types of recipients	http://www.nsf .gov/statistics/ question.cfm
Survey of Academic Research Instruments and Instrumentation Needs	Population	Academic research institution	Inactive	Adequacy of research equipment; instrumentation needs; maintenance/repair expenditures, provision, and purchase price of academic research equipment; type and use of academic equipment	Publications only: http://www.nsf .gov/statistics/ nsf96324/
General Higher Education Surveys	Varies	Academic research institution	Ad hoc	Topic dependent	WEBCASPAR; https:// webcaspar.nsf .gov/

CHAPTER 22

COLLECTIVE RESPONSES TO A NEW ERA OF ACCOUNTABILITY IN HIGHER EDUCATION

Christine M. Keller

The beginning of the new century was marked by increasing demands for accountability and transparency from institutions of higher education across all sectors—public and private, two-year and four-year. College and universities were under increasing pressure to provide more outcomes-based evidence of the value of their educational offerings. The calls for accountability and transparency originated from many different sources—legislators at the state and federal levels, policy makers, accreditors, students, families, the public, and higher education leaders themselves.

The demands for more explicit demonstrations of institutional and student performance were the result of a complex and interrelated set of factors that included shifts in state funding models, economic constraints, changing demographics, labor market expectations, and public perceptions of the necessity and value of higher education. The calls for accountability and transparency became more vocal and focused during the George W. Bush administration and with the formation of the Commission on the Future of Higher Education in September 2005 by then Secretary of Education Margaret Spellings. The final report of the Commission (commonly referred to as the Spellings Commission), released in 2006, was quite critical of higher education institution policies and practices, maintaining that the "lack of useful data and accountability hinders policymakers and the public from making informed decisions and prevents higher education from demonstrating its contribution

Note: The following individuals provided background information for this chapter: for the University and College Accountability Network, Wendy Weiler of the National Association of Independent Colleges and Universities; for Transparency by Design, Kimberly Pearce from Capella University and Cali Morrison of WCET; for the Voluntary Framework of Accountability, Bernadette Farrelly and Kent Phillippe of the American Association of Community Colleges.

to the public good" (U.S. Department of Education, 2006, p. 4). The report's conclusion was accompanied by the inference that the failure of higher education to voluntarily create a more comprehensive accountability reporting model could lead to the federal government's imposing its own accountability standards and metrics on institutions.

In response to all of these concerns, postsecondary institutions began to develop common, voluntary standards of accountability and public disclosure. This chapter focuses on four collective responses to accountability demands that were organized by groups of similar institutions. It should be noted that some institutions elected not to join community efforts but to respond on their own, within state systems, or as part of other consortia. The accountability responses discussed in this chapter include the following four initiatives (websites for all appear in the resource list at the end of the chapter):

- *University College Accountability Network (U-CAN)* is sponsored by the National Association of Independent Colleges and Universities (NAICU). As of summer 2011, U-CAN included over eight hundred independent college and university participants.
- *Voluntary System of Accountability (VSA)/College Portrait* is jointly sponsored by the Association of Public and Land-grant Universities (APLU) and the American Association of State Colleges and Universities (AASCU). As of summer 2011, the VSA included 320 public colleges and universities.
- *Transparency by Design (TbD)* is collectively sponsored by a group of online adult-serving institutions and WCET, a division of the Western Interstate Commission for Higher Education. As of summer 2011, TbD included eighteen institutions.
- *Voluntary Framework of Accountability (VFA)* is collectively sponsored by the American Association of Community Colleges (AACC), the Association of Community College Trustees (ACCT), and the College Board. As of summer 2011, forty pilot sites had tested the proposed accountability measures to determine the clarity of the technical definition and the usability of each metric. The results of pilot testing are informing the finalized version of the VFA's stage one technical manual, which was released in early fall 2011 as the second phase of this multiphase initiative came to a close.

Overview of Initiatives

This section describes each of the four accountability initiatives, including the development process, data elements, current status, and future plans. The initiatives are reviewed in the order in which they were created: U-CAN, VSA, TbD, and VFA.

University and College Accountability Network (U-CAN)

The University and College Accountability Network or U-CAN is designed to provide web-based, consumer-friendly information on independent colleges and universities in a common format to assist prospective students and families in their college search. U-CAN is sponsored by the National Association of Independent Colleges and Universities (NAICU). The primary goal of the U-CAN initiative is to help consumers sort through and identify the colleges and universities that best reflect the potential student's individual priorities, goals, and college criteria and then to direct the user to the relevant institution websites. Institutional participation in the U-CAN initiative is voluntary and is limited to independent (private, not-for-profit) institutions; however, institutions do not have to be a member of NAICU to participate.

The U-CAN initiative began in spring 2007 when the NAICU board of directors approved the development of a reporting template and website to address the needs of consumers, institutions, and policy makers. Individual data elements were selected based on the results from student and family focus groups who were asked to identify information important to them in their search for a college. Other key consumer considerations included the need to keep the information pointed and concise, easy to understand through visual representations, and formatted to allow for comparisons across institutions.

From the institutional perspective, it was important that the initiative did not increase the data collection burden for institutions through the addition of new data elements and that it allowed institutions to underscore their distinctiveness through narrative blocks and links to institution web pages. Policy makers needed the U-CAN template to be responsive to calls for comparable and transparent information and to contain data elements characterized as important by the Spellings Commission and discussions surrounding the reauthorization of the Higher Education Act. After gathering input from consumers, institution members, and policy makers, NAICU launched the U-CAN website in fall 2007 with nearly six hundred independent college and university participants.

Data Elements. Each U-CAN profile provides key statistical data complemented by narrative descriptions and subject-specific links to relevant campus web pages. The information is divided into six sections: (1) Institution, (2) Students, (3) Graduates, (4) Financial, (5) Faculty, and (6) Campus Life. The individual data elements in the six sections cover admissions, enrollment, academics, student demographics, graduation rates, most common fields of study, transfer credit policies, accreditation, faculty information, class size, tuition and fee trends, price of attendance, financial aid, campus housing, student life, campus safety, average loans at graduation, undergraduate class-size breakdown, and net tuition. Participating institutions may decide which of the data elements to publish on their institutional profile.

In addition to the data elements, each U-CAN profile displays twenty-five different links to an institution's website and a brief narrative description of the institution. The web links are grouped into the following categories: What Makes Us Special; Life After College; Academics; Transfer of Credit; Accreditation; Student Housing; Campus Setting; Student Life; and Campus Safety. The information is displayed through a variety of formats such as bar charts, graphs, and text descriptions. Help text defines terms such as *net price, graduation rate,* and *retention* and clarifies the dates of information presented. Together, the quantitative and qualitative information is intended to give consumers an opportunity to see what sets each college or university apart in mission, academics, programming, costs, and student life.

The U-CAN profiles are compiled and accessed through a central website that includes seventeen different search criteria, such as location, institution size, student enrollment, graduation and retention rates, and tuition and fee ranges. In addition, individual U-CAN profiles can be downloaded and printed.

Current Status and Future Plans for the Initiative. With over eight hundred independent colleges and universities participating from forty-five states, the U-CAN initiative has helped build consumer awareness of the range of institution options available to prospective students. The U-CAN reporting template and website offers several advantages for users:

- The central website gives consumers access to meaningful, comparable information that will empower their educational decision making and addresses their most urgent questions and concerns.
- The visual representation of data makes information less intimidating and more accessible and understandable.
- The dynamic search criteria allows for a quicker, more concise consumer search of institutions that meet their criteria; a standard template allows for comparability; and the presence of web links and text boxes allows an institution to simultaneously bring to the fore its unique mission, personality, and distinctiveness, as well as allow the consumer to easily perform a deeper search on those topics or institutions that are of special interest to them.

NAICU focuses significant time and energy on outreach to promote the U-CAN website through such avenues as radio media tours, social media (Wikipedia, Facebook, YouTube, Google keyword advertising), traditional press outreach, and partnerships with key groups such as the National Association of College Admission Counselors. The public reception for the U-CAN website has been positive, as evidenced by national and regional media coverage as well as endorsements by college counselor columns and blogs. U-CAN was also named as one of the top ten college search sites by CBSMoneywatch.com. Since its inception in fall 2007, the U-CAN website has attracted 1.3 million visits and 2.1 million page views.

From the institutional perspective, the U-CAN website aids in admissions efforts, reaches an international audience, and drives consumers to institution websites. U-CAN profiles also include information identified by policy makers as important for institutional accountability, as Congress and the U.S. Department of Education have called for comparable, concise, relevant, and easily accessible information to help the public better evaluate and choose colleges.

NAICU supports the U-CAN website with no external sponsorship or funding to minimize undue influence over its content; the website was created specifically to address the information needs of prospective students and their families during their college search. NAICU continues to solicit feedback from U-CAN users through a variety of mechanisms, including an ongoing user survey on the U-CAN website that invites users to provide feedback and critiques. Feedback is also gathered through outreach to high school guidance counselors and students. NAICU responds to the feedback through annual updates of the website. For example, increased search capabilities were added so a more concise list of institutions could be produced that meets more of users' institutional criteria. NAICU plans to continue encouraging institution participation and reaching out through traditional and social media to increase consumer awareness and usage.

Voluntary System of Accountability (VSA)

The Voluntary System of Accountability (VSA) is an initiative by public four-year universities to supply understandable and comparable information on the undergraduate student experience to important stakeholders (particularly students and families) through a common web report—the *College Portrait*. The VSA and *College Portrait* serve as a college search tool for consumers and an accountability report for colleges and universities, with three primary goals:

- Provide a streamlined college search tool for prospective students, families, and high school counselors
- Provide a mechanism for public institutions to demonstrate transparency and accountability
- Support institutions in the measurement and reporting of student learning outcomes through original research and by providing a forum for collaboration and exchange

The VSA *College Portrait* was created in 2007 by the Association of Public and Land-grant Universities (APLU) and the American Association of State Colleges and Universities (AASCU), working in collaboration with their members. Development and start-up funding for the VSA was provided by the Lumina Foundation as well as in-kind contributions from APLU, AASCU, and the public universities directly involved in its development.

Seven task forces of eighty higher education leaders—presidents, provosts, student affairs officers, institutional researchers, and assessment professionals—from seventy public colleges and universities selected the data elements and created the structure of the *College Portrait*. The task force members were guided by the framework outlined in three discussion papers, input from student and family focus groups, higher education research, and feedback from the higher education community and state and federal policy makers. (For more information on the VSA development process, see http://www.voluntarysystem.org/index.cfm?page=background.) The VSA *College Portrait* template was approved and recommended by the APLU and AASCU boards in November of 2007, and over two hundred early adopters were displaying their *College Portrait*s by mid-2008.

As with the U-CAN initiative, participation in the VSA is voluntary. However, unlike U-CAN institutions, VSA institutions commit to posting all required data elements according to a timeline that ranges from three months to four years from initial sign-up. Participation in the VSA is limited to public institutions that are members of either APLU or AASCU.

Data Elements. The VSA *College Portrait* presents a variety of data elements grouped into three broad sections—student/family (consumer) information, student experience/engagement data, and student learning outcomes. Individual data elements are drawn from the Common Data Set (CDS); the Integrated Postsecondary Education Data System (IPEDS); the National Student Clearinghouse StudentTracker; one of four student surveys (National Survey of Student Engagement—NSSE; College Senior Survey—CSS; College Student Experiences Questionnaire—CSEQ; or the University of California Undergraduate Experience Survey—UCUES); and one of three learning outcomes assessments (Collegiate Assessment of Academic Proficiency—CAAP; Collegiate Learning Assessment—CLA; or ETS Proficiency Profile). By using established sources, definitions, and practices, the VSA developers sought to make the information displayed in the *College Portrait* more transparent and comparable and minimize the workload for participating institutions.

To supplement the standard data elements, VSA participants have multiple opportunities to more fully describe the special characteristics of their institutions through text boxes, links, and graphics. The *College Portrait* was carefully constructed to balance the desire for common information with the desire to accurately portray the diversity of U.S. public universities.

In addition to the more commonly reported consumer information (such as student characteristics, degree programs, cost of attendance) the *College Portrait* presents several unique elements of value to prospective students, families, and policy makers: the Success and Progress Rate, the College Affordability Estimator, student experiences on campus, and student learning outcomes.

- *Success and Progress Rate.* A key data element in the VSA is the Success and Progress Rate—a student progress indicator that uses data available through the National Student Clearinghouse (NSC), whose data system represents 92 percent of the postsecondary enrollments and nearly 80 percent of the degrees granted in the United States. The comprehensive nature of the NSC data enables visitors to track students who remain enrolled or graduate from their original institution as well as students who transfer to another institution and are enrolled or graduate from the transfer institution. Enrollment and completion are tracked for both first-time, full-time students and full-time transfer students. The VSA Success and Progress Rate provides a more complete picture of student progress through higher education, as the majority of students attend more than one institution before they graduate (Adelman, 2006).

- *VSA College Affordability Estimator.* Another important element in the *College Portrait* is a net price estimator that allows a prospective student to enter a subset of family and income information and receive an estimate of what her or his net cost will be at a particular institution. The tool is designed to provide an estimate of out-of-pocket costs so that students, particularly low-income students, will not forgo college because they mistakenly believe the cost of attending is much higher than it actually is. The VSA College Affordability Estimator also meets the Higher Education Opportunity Act (HEOA) requirement that a net price estimator be available for all postsecondary institutions.

- *Student Experiences on Campus.* VSA institutions provide prospective students with a snapshot of student life on campus through the selected responses from one of four student engagement surveys. Survey responses are grouped into six categories of experiences positively correlated with student learning and student success: group learning, active learning, experiences with diverse groups of people and ideas, student satisfaction, institutional commitment to student learning and success, and student interaction with faculty and staff (Astin, 1992; Pascarella & Terenzini, 2005). The common categories also allow *College Portrait* users to compare responses across surveys and institutions.

- *Student Learning Outcomes.* Measuring and reporting of core learning outcomes are key components of the *College Portrait* and responsive to the calls from federal commissions, members of Congress, employers, and the academy itself to better assess what universities contribute to the core learning of students earning a bachelor's degree. The results from one of the three tests are reported as learning gains, using comparable methodologies and reporting. The *College Portrait* also reports evidence of how institutions evaluate student learning locally, including links to institution-specific outcomes data such as program assessments and professional licensure exams.

Current Status and Future Plans for the Initiative. With 320 public college and university participants, the VSA *College Portraits* represent over half of public four-year institutions in the U.S. and 65 percent of student enrollments—nearly 4.5 million students. With the widespread adoption of the VSA by public universities, prospective students, families, government officials, policy makers, and the public at large have easy access to a broad array of relevant information on public colleges and universities presented in an understandable and comparable format.

The *College Portrait* website has received positive reviews from counselors for its straightforward presentation of data, the lack of commercial sponsorship, the variety of information offered, and the simple fact that it is free to students. Each month over forty thousand unique visitors access the *College Portrait* website. The *College Portrait* is intended to be not a static report, but a dynamic collection of information. To this end, a VSA Oversight Board was created to help guide the future direction of the VSA project as well as to consider and act on feedback from institutional and public users to augment or adjust the *College Portrait* content and display.

In addition to providing a college search tool, the VSA project has served as a catalyst for further research in the area of student learning outcomes. In the fall of 2007, APLU and AASCU, in collaboration with the Association of American Colleges and Universities (AAC&U), secured a $2.4 million FIPSE grant to study three complementary approaches for measuring student learning outcomes: (1) a test validity study of the three outcomes measures that are options for VSA universities; (2) development of rubrics to identify, from student portfolios, the cognitive outcomes arising from the university experience; and (3) development and field testing of an instrument to measure changes in student preparation for success in the workplace and success in civic engagement. The research was concluded in late 2009.

Of particular relevance to the VSA were the results from the test validity study. The study demonstrated the three learning outcomes tests used as part of the VSA provide highly correlated results. These findings allow VSA institutions to select the instrument that best fits the circumstances at their particular institution, with increased confidence in the technical and measurement abilities of the three options (see http://www.voluntarysystem.org/docs/reports/ TVSReport_Final.pdf).

To help institutions work through the challenges of measuring and reporting student learning outcomes, the VSA offered a series of free workshops on effective test administration practices in the summer of 2009 and on the application of test results for institutional decision making and improvement in summer 2010. Participants were able to learn more about the testing instruments and their administration and application, examine national research on student learning and development, and hear examples of assessment strategies on campuses. The workshops also provided a forum to exchange ideas and make connections among VSA institutions. Both sets of workshops were funded through a grant from the Lumina Foundation, involving over four hundred participants from two hundred institutions. Beginning in summer 2011, a webinar series was introduced as a resource for VSA participating institutions.

Although a variety of national publications and websites compile information about higher education institutions, the *College Portrait* was created to provide information beyond simple demographic characteristics and institution descriptions—more complex information about student experience and learning outcomes—the kind of information that stakeholders desire but that institutions have been reluctant to report publicly. The VSA developers believe the initiative has started a new conversation about U.S. higher education that can result in better consumer decisions and more focused policy discussions about the benefits that public colleges and universities offer their constituencies.

Transparency by Design (TbD)

The mission of the Transparency by Design (TbD) initiative is to increase the number of adult learners who successfully complete some level of higher education (such as certificates, associate degrees, bachelor's degrees, and graduate degrees). TbD works to achieve this goal through its *College Choices for Adults* website, which provides students with data on academic program learning outcomes and results, student and alumni satisfaction with academic outcomes, and other consumer information on distance higher education.

TbD began in 2006 as an action project of the *Presidents' Forum*—a collaboration of presidents from regionally accredited, adult-serving institutions, and programs delivered through distance education (see http://presidentsforum.excelsior.edu/). As a first step, the presidents developed a set of common principles that are founded on best practices in distance higher education and address the unique needs of adult learners. All TbD institutional members have pledged to uphold a set of *Principles of Good Practice for Higher Educational Institutions Serving Adults at a Distance,* which include measures and benchmarks in the following eight areas: (1) institution mission, goals, and objectives; (2) accountability to stakeholders; (3) responsiveness; (4) curriculum development, revision, and delivery; (5) interaction and student engagement; (6) faculty qualifications, training, and evaluation; (7) student evaluation and learning outcomes assessment; and (8) institutional integrity and disclosure. The presidents also established reporting expectations and worked with pilot institutions to build common data definitions.

In 2008, the TbD institutions partnered with WCET (www.wcet.info)—a cooperative network focusing on the role of technology in higher education—to provide third-party quality assurance of the data. The project also received a multiyear grant from the Lumina Foundation to build the initial website and administer the initiative. The *College Choices for Adults* website was launched in 2009 with twelve institutions and over thirty programs.

Unlike the other accountability initiatives, participation in TbD is not limited to one particular sector or type of institution. Any regionally accredited, adult-serving institution that offers at least some programs at a distance or online can join—public, private not-for-profit, private for-profit, two-year, or four-year institutions. While U-CAN and the VSA report data primarily at the institution level, TbD institutions provide data at the institution level and data for at least two distance/online programs.

Data Elements. At the institutional level, the *College Choices for Adults* website includes information on each institution's mission, accreditation, degree or certificate programs, enrollment, student demographics, student engagement and satisfaction, and alumni outcomes by degree level. To lessen the burden on participating institutions, TbD uses IPEDS definitions for the institutional information and student demographics. Student engagement results are reported from senior level students and can be taken from the National Survey of Student Engagement (NSSE), the Community College Survey of Student Engagement (CCSSE), or the Priorities Survey for Online Learners (PSOL). Alumni outcomes are reported from a common set of four questions that TbD participants embed in their current alumni surveys.

To display its profile on the *College Choices* website, an institution must include information on at least two programs that have some distance element (for example, fully online, hybrid, or some other form of distance education). The choice of which programs to display is determined by each institution; however, the institution must report at least three data points: (1) program learning outcomes, (2) how the learning outcomes will be measured, and (3) the results of the measurements of student learning. Each institution sets its own learning outcomes for programs and how those outcomes will be measured. TbD does not require participating institutions to select from a list of standardized outcomes or measurement instruments. However, institutions must report the results from direct assessments of student learning—using either internally development metrics, such as e-portfolio rubrics, or external exams or assessments, such as licensure exams or standardized commercial tests. Indirect measures such as satisfaction surveys cannot be used in this section. TbD participants update their institutional data on an annual basis each April. The update cycle for programs data is typically every one to two years.

Current Status and Future Plans for the Initiative. The Transparency by Design project is an unprecedented collaboration among institutions that provide adult distance education, reaching across higher education sectors and institution types. The developers believe that the collaboration and common reporting have contributed to greater clarity in determining learning outcomes for distance education programs and selecting appropriate metrics for measuring student success—in particular, the need for an evidence-based formative assessment system. The initiative has also fostered experimentation with different assessment approaches for distance education programs and highlighted the need for additional assessment resources and infrastructure on many of the participant campuses.

The TbD initiative currently includes 18 member institutions and one associate member. To ensure the success and sustainability of the initiative, an executive committee supervises and guides the future direction of TbD, including the potential inclusion of new data elements, expansion of reporting options, and recruitment of additional institution members.

Voluntary Framework of Accountability (VFA)

The Voluntary Framework of Accountability (VFA) is a system being developed for community colleges to measure outcomes and processes and to demonstrate greater public accountability. The VFA will provide opportunities for community colleges to benchmark their student progress and completion data against peers and to provide stakeholders with critical information. The VFA is sponsored by the American Association of Community Colleges (AACC) in collaboration with the Association of Community College Trustees (ACCT) and the College Board.

As with other higher education sectors, policy makers, legislators, researchers, commissions, and the public are stressing the need for community colleges to focus on institutional accountability and, in particular, increase the success rates for all students. Because students enter a community college for a variety of reasons—among them upgrading job skills, fulfilling lower-division courses for transfer to a four-year institution, and personal enrichment—the VFA responds to the need for appropriate measures specific to the community college sector. The current lack of commonly accepted performance measures often limits community college leaders' ability to gauge performance and improve outcomes, fulfill external demands for accountability, and demonstrate institutional contributions to the educational needs of the communities they serve.

The VFA's primary goal is to give institutions a useful set of measures to benchmark their data against peers and to give stakeholders critical information on institutional performance. Compared with the other accountability initiatives, the VFA focuses less on developing a college search tool or providing a consumer information source, as prospective community college students typically stay within their local district to attend college.

The VFA project is being conducted in multiple phases. Phase I, completed in 2009, consisted of background research on accountability measures already in use at community colleges across a sample of ten states, as well as a review of current research on accountability frameworks to assess the need for a common accountability framework. These efforts were supported by the Lumina Foundation and resulted in two reports that outlined the next steps for the initiative. (See Appendix 22.1 for links to individual reports.)

The second phase of VFA development began in fall 2009 and is scheduled to be completed in fall 2011. During Phase II, four working groups made up of thirty-seven community college leaders are defining measures and developing a strategic plan for participation within the overall framework. A VFA steering committee will review the work of the groups and assist in making the final decisions about the composition and promotion of the VFA. The objectives for Phase II are to:

- Analyze current college and state data collection efforts.
- Define accountability metrics and progress benchmarks.
- Develop workforce, economic, and community development measures.
- Create a blueprint for data collection, analysis, and dissemination.
- Implement and test the VFA measures at pilot sites.
- Develop a plan to promote community college participation and engagement for broad acceptance and widespread use of the VFA measures.

Phase III of VFA development will be the national implementation of the measures established in Phase II.

Data Elements. A critical aspect of Phase II of the VFA development process is the identification, development, and pilot testing of potential measures that provide transparent outcomes to internal and external stakeholders and enable community college leaders to benchmark their performance against appropriate peer groups. More specifically, the VFA aims to create measures of accountability to show institutional effectiveness related to (1) student learning outcomes; (2) student persistence, transition, and completion rates; (3) meeting of the developmental education needs of underprepared incoming students; and (4) contributions to meeting local workforce, economic, and community development needs. From the pilot sites, the VFA working groups will be able to determine the utility and burden of calculating each measure. The pilot sites will also evaluate the metric's usefulness as a benchmarking tool.

As with the other accountability initiatives, the VFA developers intend to evaluate and adopt existing measures whenever possible. Given the diversity of community colleges in terms of programs, students, resources, and operating systems, as well as differences in data collection and analysis capability and focus, the VFA may consider a range of potential measurements for a specific area. For example, to evaluate the performance of community colleges in preparing students for the workforce, there may be a choice of potential measures, such as state wage data records, surveys of employers of recent graduates, skills certificates awarded, and licensure examinations passed.

Current Status and Future Plans for the Initiative. The VFA initiative seeks to determine how best to measure community college effectiveness in ways that are appropriate and sensitive to the missions of these institutions, while also being relevant and rigorous in addressing the legitimate concerns of stakeholders interested in the performance of community colleges. The VFA initiative will also provide a foundation for college leaders to perform any additional analysis to improve institutional outcomes.

Conclusions

The demands on institutions of higher education that were present at the time of the Spellings Commission and served as a catalyst for the development of the accountability initiatives described in this chapter continue to increase in scope and intensity for several reasons. Recent attention has focused on the need for an educated workforce to benefit individuals, society, and U.S. global competitiveness. At the same time, the proportion of young working adults in the United States with postsecondary education has declined relative to other countries (Organization for Economic Cooperation and Development, 2009). These factors compelled President Barack Obama (2009) and his administration to establish a goal for the United States to "lead the world in higher education degree attainment" by 2020. Other organizations and foundations have endorsed and built on President Obama's goal, including the Lumina Foundation, the Gates Foundation, the State Higher Education Executive Officers, and the College Board.

The recession that began in the middle of the 2008 academic year has led to state budget gaps and sharp cuts in state support for public institutions as well as declines in investment earnings for private institutions. According to some estimates, higher education may see a permanent reduction of roughly 10 percent of its revenue base (Desrochers, Lenihan, & Wellman, 2010). Due in large part to decreasing revenues from outside sources, published college prices continue to rise more rapidly than the prices of other goods and services, particularly at public four-year institutions (Trends in College Pricing, 2009). When the costs are higher, the stakes for selecting the "best fit" college goes up for prospective students and their families—particularly for students who are first generation or lower income or come from underrepresented groups that are less familiar with higher education language and practices. Thus the increasing need for postsecondary education, coupled with the increasing share of costs borne by consumers, leads to an understandable skepticism and a demand for more evidence of the value and outcomes associated with the individual and public investments.

Given the current economic, social, and political environment, the accountability and transparency initiatives described in this chapter remain relevant and provide tangible evidence of the willingness of higher education institutions to respond to the needs of their internal and external audiences.

References

Adelman, C. (2006). *The toolbox revisited: Paths to degree completion from high school through college.* Washington, DC: U.S. Department of Education.

Astin, A. W. (1992). *What matters in college? Four critical years revisited.* San Francisco: Jossey-Bass.

Desrochers, D. M., Lenihan, C. M., & Wellman, J. V. (2010). Trends in college spending: 1998–2008. A report of the Delta Cost Project.

Obama, B. (2009, February 24)). *Making College More Affordable*. Retrieved from http://www.whitehouse.gov/issues/education/higher-education

Organization for Economic Cooperation and Development. (2009). Education at a glance 2009: OECD indicators. Retrieved from www.oecd.org/edu/eag2009

Pascarella, E. T., & Terenzini, P. T. (2005). *How college affects students* (vol. 2): *A third decade of research.* San Francisco: Jossey-Bass.

Trends in College Pricing. (2009). College board trends in higher education series. Retrieved from http://www.collegeboard.com/trends

U.S. Department of Education. (2006). *A test of leadership: Charting the future of U.S. higher education.* Washington, DC: U.S. Department of Education.

Appendix 22.1: Initiative Websites, Resources, and Reports

TbD

Transparency by Design (TbD): http://www.wcet.info/2.0/index
.php?q=TransparencybyDesign
College Choices for Adults: http://www.collegechoicesforadults.org/
President's Forum: http://presidentsforum.excelsior.edu/

U-CAN

University and College Accountability Network (U-CAN): http://ucan-network.org/

VFA

Voluntary Framework of Accountability (VFA): http://www.aacc.nche.edu/Resources/
aaccprograms/vfa/Pages/default.aspx
Performance Accountability Systems for Community Colleges: Lessons from 10 States
(CCRC): http://ccrc.tc.columbia.edu/Collection.asp?cid=9
Principles and Plans: A Voluntary Framework of Accountability (VFA) for Community
Colleges (AACC): http://www.aacc.nche.edu/About/Governance/Documents/
vfa_1208.pdf

VSA

Voluntary System of Accountability (VSA): http://voluntarysystem.org/
College Portrait: http://www.collegeportraits.org/
Improving Student Learning in Higher Education Through Better Accountability and
Assessment, NASULGC discussion paper, April 2006: http://voluntarysystem.org/
docs/background/DiscussionPaper1_April06.pdf
Elements of Accountability for Public Universities and Colleges, NASULGC Discussion
Paper, July 2006: http://voluntarysystem.org/docs/background/DiscussionPaper2_
July06.pdf
Toward a Voluntary System of Accountability Program (VSA) for Public Universities and
Colleges, NASULGC Discussion Paper, August 2006: http://voluntarysystem.org/docs/
background/DiscussionPaper3_Aug06.pdf

CHAPTER 23

SYSTEM- AND STATE-LEVEL DATA COLLECTION ISSUES AND PRACTICES

Marsha V. Krotseng

Individuals who occupy key information management roles in higher education must be able to provide information with a solid "understanding of the institution and its environment, the issues and decisions that are most vital and the preferences of decision makers about how information is presented" (Keller, 1993, p. 15). Close cooperation between decision makers and information experts is essential. Information managers must be responsive, flexible, and knowledgeable.

Attributes associated with highly effective institutional researchers—a keen understanding of higher education's internal and external environments, comprehension of the most crucial issues and decisions, and appreciation for decision makers' preferences for receiving information—hold true to an even greater degree for those who are affiliated with multi-campus systems and state-level coordinating agencies. At the system and state levels, principal decision makers who rely on accurate, consistent, and timely information include the system or agency head (or both), the governing board for the system, a state coordinating board (if the system governing board does not also serve that role), campus presidents, the governor, and legislators. The environment and issues are often complex, demanding objective analyses and timely, accurate, relevant reports that inform higher education policy for a system or an entire state and that sometimes find their way into state legislation.

The System and State Environment

Governing and coordinating board decision-making environments are shaped by the expectations and goals that policy makers hold for higher education in their state. The board implements policies and actions based on these expectations as it carries out its statutory role and mission. The institutional research office, in turn, translates data into information to guide the board's policy development and strategic initiatives. These intersecting roles characterize the multidimensional environment that defines the work of system- and state-level institutional researchers.

Show Me the Data

Now more than ever, state political leaders are demanding accountability of their public postsecondary institutions. In its 2006 report, *Transforming Higher Education: National Imperative—State Responsibility,* the National Conference of State Legislatures' Blue Ribbon Commission on Higher Education urged legislators to define clear goals for higher education and "hold institutions accountable for their performance and their results. Make sure your state has a system of collecting the data you will need to evaluate performance" (p. 7). The report also advises legislators, "You cannot begin to articulate meaningful goals for your state higher education system if you lack reliable information about current and future students. Locate and study demographic data to analyze how your state and your students are changing" (p. 6). In 2010, National Governors Association (NGA) Chair Chris Gregoire placed college completion and productivity in the national spotlight through the "Complete to Compete" initiative. One product of that effort, *From Information to Action: Revamping Higher Education Accountability Systems* (Reindl & Reyna, 2011), conveys the need for states to do "a better job of measuring the performance of our higher education systems. Governors need to know how well our colleges and universities are doing at moving students to and through certificates and degrees if we're going to make smart investments with our limited dollars and gauge the return on those investments" (p. ii).

Hearing this continuous refrain of "Show me the data," heads of higher education systems and coordinating agencies are diligently working to achieve greater transparency in reporting. In this context, system/state institutional researchers play the vital role of ensuring that decision makers have valid, meaningful, consistent, and timely information as a solid basis for critical policy recommendations and as a demonstration of accountability and stewardship to the public. This chapter offers a general overview of the role and function of postsecondary governing and coordinating boards, addresses expectations for institutional research in this environment, cites existing reports and documents to illustrate specific topics and concerns of greatest interest to state higher education and political leaders, and discusses presentation format as a major factor influencing how decision makers value and use the analyses they receive.

Role of Governing and Coordinating Boards

Twenty-six U.S. states have one or more multi-campus governing boards. Such boards establish policies and procedures governing the actions of all the institutions under their control. The mission, composition, and authority of these entities are defined by state code and, in some cases, by the state constitution. In addition to the policy-setting function, they are responsible for developing the system budget and submitting the budget request on behalf of all system institutions. Other responsibilities typically performed by a governing board include academic program review, appointment and evaluation of the system and campus CEOs, administration of a uniform classification system for personnel, strategic planning, facilities master planning, and approval of capital projects. In Hawaii, Montana, Nevada, North Dakota, and Rhode Island, a single statewide board governs all public postsecondary campuses in the state, including research universities, comprehensive regional institutions, and community colleges. Two or more multi-campus governing boards exist in states such as California (the University of California System, California State University System, and California Community Colleges System), Maine (the University of Maine System and Community College System of Maine), New York (the State University of New York and City University of New York), and Texas (the University of Texas System, Texas A&M University System, Texas State University System, University of Houston System, University of North Texas, and the Texas Tech University System). (The Education Commission of the States [n.d.] offers further examples of governing board states in the comprehensive database of Postsecondary Governance Structures on its website.)

The purpose and expectations of a state system are clearly illustrated in the following mission statement of the University of Maine System:

> The University of Maine System Board of Trustees, in consultation with the Chancellor, is the governing and planning body of the University System responsible for developing and maintaining a cohesive structure of public higher education in the State of Maine. As such, the Board has final authority over all matters within its jurisdiction, including all educational, public service, and research policies, as well as all personnel and financial policies. The Board provides leadership on higher education policy within the System and the State, is committed to strengthening the unique characteristics of each University's mission, and advocates aggressively for adequate resources to support the System and its universities. (University of Maine System, n.d.)

In many states with multiple postsecondary governance structures, there are coordinating boards to develop a unified statewide agenda or plan for postsecondary education and to provide higher education public policy recommendations to the state governor and legislature. In some cases, these responsibilities involve both public and independent higher education. Examples of the 29 states with higher education coordinating agencies are Alabama, Colorado, Connecticut, Indiana, Kentucky, Missouri, Ohio, Virginia, and Washington. (Additional states with a coordinating board structure also are identified in the Education Commission of the States [n.d.] database. Note that both higher education coordinating boards and multi-campus governing boards coexist in some states.)

As one illustration, the state *Code of Virginia* (n.d., §23–9.3) specifies that the purpose of its coordinating board, the State Council of Higher Education for Virginia, is "to promote the development and operation of an educationally and economically sound, vigorous, progressive, and coordinated system of higher education in the Commonwealth of Virginia."

Incorporating greater detail, *West Virginia State Code* (n.d., §18B-1–1a) charges its two state-level coordinating boards (the Council for Community and Technical College Education and the Higher Education Policy Commission) with serving the state in the following ways:

(A) By developing a public policy agenda for various aspects of higher education that is aligned with state goals and objectives and the role and responsibilities of each coordinating board;

(B) By ensuring that institutional missions and goals are aligned with relevant parts of the public policy agenda and that institutions maximize the resources available to them to fulfill their missions and make reasonable progress toward meeting established state goals;

(C) By evaluating and reporting on progress in implementing the public policy agenda;

(D) By promoting system efficiencies through collaboration and cooperation across institutions and through focusing institutional missions as appropriate; and

(E) By conducting research, collecting data and providing objective recommendations to aid elected state officials in making policy decisions.

Institutional Research for Governing and Coordinating Boards

The system/state institutional research office provides information and analyses that assist the governing or coordinating board and its CEO (president, chancellor, commissioner, or executive director) in carrying out its defined responsibilities and informing the development of system and state higher education policy. Insight into the primary roles and expectations of institutional research offices in this environment can be found in their mission statements. For example, the institutional research team for the University of Massachusetts System is expected to serve as "an information resource for the President's Office, the University Board of Trustees, the UMass campuses, and external constituencies. Institutional Research works closely with the five UMass campuses to collect, analyze and distribute data that supports system-wide planning and decision-making, policy development, and evaluation" (University of Massachusetts System, n.d.).

Similarly, the mission of Institutional Studies and Policy Analysis for the University of Texas System is "to provide management information and analyses in support of the strategic objectives and institutional improvement efforts of the University of Texas System. Responsibilities of the office include providing an integrated approach to institutional research, conducting policy analyses, maintaining a repository of management information, and disseminating information for use by decision-makers" (University of Texas System, n.d.).

For the Administrative Offices of the Connecticut Community Colleges, the Office of Planning, Research and Assessment is expected "to provide leadership and direction in all areas of college administration regarding assessment, strategic planning, policy analysis and development, research, legislative and regulatory analysis, and program management" (Connecticut Community Colleges, n.d.).

As demonstrated by these statements, institutional researchers who serve system governing boards lead the collection and analysis of data from the campuses; generation of management information to be used by the system head, board, and institutions for planning, decision making, and evaluation or improvement; distribution of system information to internal and external constituents; and development of reports that inform state higher education policy makers, including the governor and legislature. In addition, the mission statement for the Office of Planning and Policy Analysis for the University of Maine System highlights the important connections of that office " . . . with state and federal governmental agencies, professional associations, and other external groups" (University of Maine System Office of Planning and Policy Analysis, n.d.). This role takes on special significance at a time when the federal government has placed heightened emphasis on completion of a postsecondary credential or degree to reposition the United States as the nation with the highest proportion of college graduates by 2020 (Hebel & Selingo, 2009).

With regard to coordinating agencies, the Research and Data portal of the Missouri Department of Higher Education (MDHE) emphasizes collection and analysis of data as "a vital component in the MDHE's continuing effort to improve the condition of postsecondary education in Missouri. Data are collected at the student and aggregate levels using a variety of survey instruments, and are disseminated in a number of reports published by the department" (Missouri Department of Higher Education, n.d.). Within the Arkansas Department of Higher Education, the Research and Planning office is charged with providing " . . . information about student performance and institutional activity at the state's colleges and universities" to the state's top-level higher education decision makers (Arkansas Department of Higher Education, n.d.).

The following sections illustrate how system/state-level institutional researchers bring meaning and value to data from multiple campuses through the contexts of strategic planning and decision making, accountability, effectiveness, and policy analysis and development. As the NGA publication *From Information to Action* clearly points out, these expected outcomes require that the system or state board have sufficient capacity for data collection and analysis (Reindl & Reyna, 2011). While different environments may prioritize certain functions above others, institutional research offices that most effectively serve governing or coordinating boards demonstrate solid technical expertise in data collection, integrity, warehousing, extraction or mining, analysis, interpretation, and presentation; survey research design and administration (both locally developed and national instruments such as the National Survey of Student Engagement); research methodology and statistics; use of national and regional data sources; planning; policy; communication; and meeting facilitation.

Vital Issues and Decisions

Institutional researchers contribute to their governing or coordinating board's understanding of vital issues and decisions that must be addressed by providing data and expertise in strategic planning, producing accountability reports, and undertaking special research or policy studies relating to a specific topic. The examples that follow highlight how these distinct, but interconnected, roles translate into good practice in a number of states.

Strategic Planning

As the office mission statement of the Connecticut Community Colleges, cited earlier, clearly defines, one of the key responsibilities of a system- or state-level board is adoption of a strategic plan for the system or a strategic higher education policy agenda for the state, or both. According to *The Leadership Dynamic in Public College and University Systems*, overseeing the development of a strategic plan is among the primary responsibilities of the board and system head (National Association of System Heads, American Association of State Colleges and Universities, & Association of Governing Boards of Universities and Colleges, 2009, p. 12). This includes creating an implementation plan for achieving system-wide goals and establishing benchmarks for the assessment of progress. System- and state-level strategic planning efforts have gained wider visibility since 2005 as board members and states have begun to insist on clear accountability and the identification of measurable goals.

Requirements for a strategic plan may be specified in state statute and further clarified in board policy. For instance, *North Dakota Century Code* (n.d., 15–10–14.2) includes the following provision for its governing board: "The state board of higher education shall adopt a strategic planning process and develop a strategic plan to define and prioritize university system goals and objectives. The board shall provide an annual performance and accountability report regarding performance and progress toward the goals outlined in the university system's strategic plan and accountability measures."

In West Virginia, the legislature has enumerated ten goals for public higher education in State Code (§18B-1–1a) and expects its state-level higher education coordinating bodies for the four-year institutions and community colleges to develop "a public policy agenda for various aspects of higher education that is aligned with state goals and objectives and the role and responsibilities of each coordinating board" (*West Virginia State Code*, n.d.).

A sound strategic plan or public policy agenda must be grounded in accurate, consistent, and current data if it is to chart the future course for public higher education. Good data and analysis are integral components of the planning process and represent important contributions that institutional researchers can offer. Meaningful strategic goals and measurable objectives are informed by trends in data over a period of recent years as well as by future projections. As goals and related objectives are developed around specific issues (for example, achieving a higher level of educational attainment in the state), they will be informed by data that focus on the following questions: What future do we envision for our higher education system or state? (*What level of educational attainment is desired?*); What is our current situation relative to that target? (*What is the state's current level of educational attainment based on U.S. Census data?*); What course must we take to reach the target? (*Based on the data and best practices, what strategies will raise educational attainment?*); What resources will be required to succeed? (*What human and financial resources are needed to reach that level of attainment?*); and How will we know if we are on track to reach the target? (*What are the most valid measures of progress, and what intermediate levels are desired?*)

The Kentucky Council on Postsecondary Education (n.d.) developed a five-year public agenda for postsecondary and adult education in 2005. This plan emphasized accountability, degree completion, and affordability and was organized around a set of key questions: (1) Are more Kentuckians ready for postsecondary education? (2) Is Kentucky postsecondary education affordable for its citizens? (3) Do more Kentuckians have certificates and degrees? (4) Are college graduates prepared for life and work in Kentucky? and (5) Are Kentucky's people, communities, and economy benefiting? (Kentucky Council on Postsecondary Education, n.d.). Each question, reflecting a strategic goal, was linked to a number of key indicators used to assess progress. For example, key indicators associated with the first question include: the average ACT score of Kentucky's graduating high school seniors, students scoring 3 or higher on Advanced Placement examinations, the percentage of Kentucky high school graduates requiring developmental education in college, and the number of GED graduates in Kentucky. Trend data covering a series of multiple years are displayed on the Council's website in easy-to-interpret graphs or tables, which include an arrow indicating how that measure is progressing.

Involvement of both internal and external stakeholders is essential to the development of the strategic plan. As SUNY Chancellor Nancy Zimpher affirms in a statement to the general public on the system's website: "What's most exciting about this plan ["The Power of SUNY"] is that we could not have done it without you. From Buffalo to Long Island . . . and even online, New Yorkers participated in the comprehensive process that brings this plan to life" (State University of New York, n.d.). Such a process presents an exceptional opportunity for system- or state-level institutional researchers to engage with numerous constituent groups, both within and outside of higher education, in an effort to understand their perspectives and weave their comments into the final document. North Dakota has been recognized for its Higher Education Roundtable, which brings members of the State Board of Higher Education together with state legislators, along with leaders from the private sector, K–12 education, and other state agencies to arrive at a shared agenda for public higher education (Lane, 2008). The North Dakota University System's strategic plan, approved in December 2009, reflects the convergence of common themes that were expressed in a series of meetings with internal and external stakeholders, including the Roundtable, the State Board of Higher Education, legislative committees, business and industry leaders, campus representatives, and the chancellor's cabinet, which consists of the system's presidents and chancellor's senior staff.

The goals that emerge through a comprehensive strategic planning process represent the most critical higher education issues facing the system and state; when properly implemented, these inform decisions, including budgeting and resource allocation. System/state strategic goals often address the broad issues of quality, cost, and access—commonly referenced as higher education's "iron triangle" (Immerwahr, Johnson, & Gasbarra, 2008). These join the following related themes, which recur as goals across the contemporary postsecondary planning documents of many states and systems: student success, graduating more students, meeting the needs of a changing student population, preparation for college, maintaining affordability, state economic development, excellence in academics, leadership in science and technology, innovation or entrepreneurial thinking, meeting state needs for an educated workforce, global competitiveness, effective and efficient stewardship, and accountability.

Stewardship and Accountability

While the strategic plan guides the system toward a longer-term vision, system officials require ongoing internal reports, both for insight into each constituent campus's current contributions to the overall vision and to ensure that the campuses and the system as a whole remain on track. Typical information required by the system head and governing board includes a variety of reports about students, faculty, and staff; tuition comparisons; salary comparisons; and research activities. Data generally are presented for the system as a whole and also, in many cases, by institution. Such reports offer five- or ten-year trends and display percentage changes over time. Student analyses focus on enrollment numbers (headcount, FTE, resident/nonresident, county/metropolitan area of residence, full-time/part-time, gender, race/ethnicity, age, major, freshman characteristics, and transfer), credit hour enrollment, degrees conferred, financial aid recipients, student transfer among institutions, and retention and graduation rates. In addition, results from satisfaction surveys or data from the National Survey of Student Engagement/Community College Survey of Student Engagement often are summarized for the board's information. Reports focused on faculty generally indicate their numbers by rank, highest degree, tenure status, full-time/part-time status, and demographic characteristics. Other analyses portray total numbers of personnel by occupational category, full-time/part-time status, and demographic characteristics.

Documents such as these should be readily available for all systems. Several examples include the comprehensive University of Texas System *Facts & Trends* (n.d.); current enrollment and academic year reports of the Washington State Board for Community and Technical Colleges (n.d.); and student and faculty reports for the University System of Georgia (USG), including access to the "USG by the Numbers" portal (University System of Georgia, n.d.). Another notable feature of the USG website is the inclusion of file structures, data dictionaries, and documentation for reference by campus institutional researchers. This is a critical component of system-level work that ensures the accuracy and consistency of data reported across multiple and diverse institutions. The University of North Carolina System publishes an annual *Statistical Abstract*, and its website enables visitors to search for facts and figures on academics, enrollment, degrees conferred, facilities inventory, tuition and fees, and research (University of North Carolina System, n.d.).

Institutional research staff for state coordinating boards prepare similar reports, as illustrated by the mission of the Policy, Planning, and Research Division of the Tennessee Higher Education Commission, which includes "collecting and analyzing institutional data" and serving as "a clearinghouse for . . . census data related to education in Tennessee" (Tennessee Higher Education Commission, n.d.). The Division's responsibilities include preparation of the *Tennessee Higher Education Fact Book*. Admissions and enrollment data, degrees awarded, financial aid, and retention and graduation rates for Virginia's public colleges and universities are compiled and published on the Web by the State Council of Higher Education for Virginia (n.d.), and the South Carolina Commission on Higher Education (n.d.) reports enrollment, completions, course and credit hour data, facilities, faculty, and SAT scores. The annual statistical profile of Ohio institutions provides trend data relating to enrollment, student preparation and academic progress, degrees awarded, time and credits to degree, post-graduation employment outcomes, tuition, financial aid, and costs and expenditures per student (Ohio Board of Regents, n.d.). Independent institutions are included in some states' reports. Public, independent, and for-profit or career schools are profiled in *A Factual Look at Higher Education in Nebraska,* which fulfills, in part, the statutory requirement that Nebraska's Coordinating Commission for Postsecondary Education annually report data submitted by the state's institutions to the Integrated Postsecondary Education Data System (IPEDS) (Nebraska Coordinating Commission for Postsecondary Education, n.d.). This document presents a statewide analysis, summarizing the data in ten-year trend charts.

Beyond these basic analyses, institutional researchers at the system/state level play an integral role in preparing performance or accountability measures reports that are essential to both internal and external stakeholders. Statewide higher education report cards first emerged during the 1980s and early 1990s as state lawmakers sought greater accountability from their public higher education systems and institutions. Colorado, New Mexico, South Carolina, Tennessee, and West Virginia were among the early states that required presentation of an annual "report card" to the state legislature (Mercer, 1993). Since that time, state statutes creating higher education accountability reports (and, in some cases, even establishing the specific measures) have become commonplace. A good example is *North Dakota Century Code* (n.d., 15–10–14.2), which requires the system's governing board to "provide an annual performance and accountability report," with mandatory accountability measures detailed in legislation. North Dakota's *Accountability Measures Report* is organized according to five key themes: Economic Development, Education Excellence, Flexible and Responsive System, Accessibility, and Funding, each of which is associated with a number of accountability measures. Education Excellence, for example, is evidenced by graduation and retention rates, performance on national examinations, first-time pass rates on licensure examinations, and student and alumni satisfaction. All measures are shown in aggregate form for the system as a whole or, where appropriate (as in tuition comparisons), for the various institutional sectors (research universities, four-year regional universities, and community colleges). Data relating to individual institutions are not included in this report; rather, they are compiled and shared with each president for internal management. The document is produced in hard copy format for presentation to the State Board of Higher Education and the state legislature and also can be accessed on the system's website (North Dakota University System, 2011).

The *Annual Indicators Report* produced by the University of Massachusetts System (n.d.) offers another excellent illustration. This document highlights measures in the five primary areas of Academic Quality, Student Success and Satisfaction, Access and Affordability, Service to the Commonwealth, and Financial Health. Encompassed within these areas are nine strategic priorities of the University: Improve the student learning experience, strengthen research and development, renew faculty, continue a focus on diversity and positive climate, maintain and improve access and affordability, develop leadership role in public service, increase endowment, improve administrative and IT services, and develop first-rate infrastructure. Some indicators (especially those relating to Access and Affordability, Service to the Commonwealth, and Financial Health) are presented in aggregate form for the overall system.

The report also includes data for each institution and is available on the system's website.

These two documents, like their counterparts in other states, display the data using a combination of graphs, data tables, and brief narrative in order to provide the reader with clear, concise, and meaningful information that can be readily understood. Trends are conveyed through longitudinal data reflecting changes over the past five to ten years. Comparative data representing national, regional, or peer averages lend valuable context to the system data.

The Minnesota State Colleges and Universities (MnSCU) system posts an accountability dashboard designed for the board of trustees, policy makers, and other stakeholders on its website (Minnesota State Colleges and Universities System, n.d.). Dials on the dashboard's main page display color-coded performance categories ("exceeds expectations," "meets expectations," or "needs attention") for ten categories identified by the board as representing the outcomes most critical to achieving the directions of its strategic plan. These measures include: percent change in enrollment, net tuition and fees as a percentage of median income, licensure exam pass rate, persistence and completion rate, high-quality learning, student engagement, partnerships, related employment of graduates, innovation, and facilities condition index. Performance categories are assigned to the system as a whole, to all colleges as a group, to all universities as a group, and to individual institutions. Detailed data and graphs underlie and support the performance level that is shown relative to an established threshold.

Although state coordinating boards are not charged with direct governance of institutions, policy makers also expect them to demonstrate accountability across the various institutions and systems within a state. Accountability is among the statutory responsibilities of the State Council of Higher Education for Virginia (SCHEV), which "shall develop and revise from time to time . . . objective measures of educational-related performance and institutional performance benchmarks for such objective measures." (*Code of Virginia*, n.d., §23–9.6:1.01). SCHEV's *Assessment of Institutional Performance* (n.d.) provides campus-specific data for defined performance standards such as in-state enrollment, underrepresented enrollment, degree awards, retention rate, and total transfers, displaying the institution's actual performance compared to an established target. Green ("target achieved"), yellow ("threshold achieved"), or red ("threshold not achieved") indicators signal the extent of progress for each institution.

The Indiana Commission for Higher Education adopted a set of strategic initiatives based on recommendations from an extensive study, *Reaching Higher: Strategic Directions for Higher Education in Indiana* (2007). That document concluded, "[N]o single sector of public investment is more important for shaping Indiana's future than its system of postsecondary education . . . The plan aims to ensure that the state's investment in postsecondary education is maximized to its fullest potential" (p. 19). Progress toward the state's goals is measured using the key indicators of college completion, affordability, preparation, community colleges, research, and accountability. Performance is monitored at two levels: with a state-level benchmark in comparison with other states and nations, and at the institutional level. Indiana's *Higher Education Dashboard* addresses the indicators with data, graphs, and arrows indicating progress.

In addition to indicators cited earlier, the University of Missouri System's comprehensive set of accountability indicators, *Measuring Success* (n.d.), includes externally funded research, outreach programs, continuing education, commercialization of knowledge, and technology transfer reflecting its land-grant and research missions. After an initial three-year reporting period, green ("met or exceeded target"), yellow ("making progress"), and red ("no progress") "stoplights" were incorporated into the document as a quick visual reference.

The Nebraska Higher Education Progress Report (Nebraska Coordinating Commission for Postsecondary Education, 2010) provides the Nebraska legislature with comparative statistics to monitor and assess progress toward achieving three key priorities for Nebraska's postsecondary education system: increasing the number of students who enter postsecondary education in Nebraska; increasing the percentage of students who enroll and successfully complete a degree; and reducing, eliminating, and reversing the net migration from the state of Nebraskans with high levels of educational attainment. Graphs, trend data, and narrative are used to highlight performance on a variety of indicators for all higher education sectors, including independent and for-profit institutions.

Whether serving multiple campuses within a single system or multiple institutions and systems across a state, the institutional researcher encounters similar responsibilities and challenges. It is an exciting opportunity to work with a group of diverse campuses, each having its own focus, culture, and environment. In addition to the strong technical and analytical abilities required of all institutional researchers, individuals working at the system or state level must possess a broad higher education perspective, including sensitivity to the unique issues pertinent to various institutional types, along with well-honed communication, interpersonal, and political skills. System- and state-level institutional researchers must coordinate with representatives of numerous campuses who at times may offer differing opinions on crucial data definition or reporting issues. The ability to achieve consensus and keep the campus representatives focused and moving forward in concert is vital to the mission of the governing or coordinating board.

Institutional researchers serving governing and coordinating boards also must constantly strive to create and maintain positive relationships with their institutions. Boards and legislative committees frequently make time-sensitive requests of a central office that, in turn, require communication with the campuses to collect or verify data. Rather than demanding immediate compliance, the savvy system/state institutional researcher will understand that his or her request has inserted a new obligation into existing campus priorities and will work with institutional personnel to complete the task as quickly as possible. In turn, researchers on the campuses should understand and respect that their system/state counterparts are endeavoring to respond to an important constituent and provide the requested information in a timely manner. It is important that the practice of expecting a quick turn-around be reserved for genuinely urgent situations and not become routine operating procedure. Mutual respect and cooperation of both parties is critical, because the success of a multi-campus system is intertwined with the success of its institutions.

Special Research and Policy Studies

The reports referenced earlier are generated on at least an annual basis and more frequently in the case of semester enrollment figures. However, governing and coordinating board staffs also are called on to produce a wide range of special research and policy studies to inform decisions of the board and of the governor and legislature. For example, research on dual credit enrollment has been undertaken by the Oregon University System (n.d.) and the Washington State Board for Community and Technical Colleges (n.d.), among others. Both the Washington Higher Education Coordinating Board (n.d.) and the State Council of Higher Education for Virginia (n.d.) have published detailed cost studies, the latter focusing on average nonresident student tuition and mandatory Educational and General fees as a percentage of the average cost of education. Systems and states also rely on enrollment projections to assist in strategic planning and budgeting as exemplified by Oregon and Virginia. (Oregon University System Enrollment Projections, n.d.; State Council of Higher Education for Virginia Enrollment Projections, n.d.). Other special topics include transfer and articulation, student placement and success in developmental or learning support courses, distance or online instruction, faculty salaries, and diversity.

Common to many states are high school feedback reports, which "are generated by colleges to inform high schools about their students' college readiness by describing their graduates' performance in college (typically their first-year performance)" (Walsh, 2009). Walsh's survey of state higher education executive officers found that some states publish high school feedback reports for all schools, while in others, postsecondary institutions provide feedback reports regarding "entering first-year students from specific high schools." The University System of Georgia, Indiana Commission for Higher Education, Kentucky Council on Postsecondary Education, and Ohio Board of Regents are among the system- and state-level agencies that have created feedback reports by school (and also for districts and the state) that indicate how well students are making the transition from high school to college, giving special attention to such measures of preparation and college success as enrollment in remedial or developmental courses, retention, progression, and graduation.

To encourage conversations about students' preparation for college, the Minnesota legislature requires the University of Minnesota and the Minnesota State Colleges and Universities to report data on recent public high school graduates enrolled in developmental courses. This *Getting Prepared* report includes state and high school summary data on the number and percentage of graduates taking at least one developmental course in college and is transmitted to the Minnesota Department of Education and the superintendents of all Minnesota school districts (Minnesota State Colleges and Universities and University of Minnesota, n.d.). Each superintendent also receives an individualized summary report on graduates from the district who have enrolled in developmental courses, so that schools have access to the data for improvement.

The publication *State Reporting on Developmental Education: Analysis of Findings* (Fulton, 2010) provides an excellent summary of over fifty state and higher education system reports on developmental education. The appendix offers a rich resource for researchers, listing reports from thirty states along with their website locations. The analysis identifies three main categories of data published in these reports: participation of students in developmental education, success of developmental education students, and cost of developmental education. The majority of these system and state studies focus on recent high school graduates (although some are based on total enrollment or first-time students) and on developmental course pass rates. While the study concludes that the sheer number of reports indicates "the importance that states and postsecondary systems place on collecting and publishing remedial [developmental] education data," it also observes, "the data need to be more consistent, comparable and consumable" within and across states (p. 7). It suggests that ideally, postsecondary systems and states should collect and report on developmental course pass rates, retention/persistence rates (to a second year), college-level course pass rates (typically related to developmental courses), graduation rates (certificate or degree), and transfer rates (to a four-year institution).

The North Dakota University System produces a follow-up report on graduates of its eleven institutions that indicates the number and percentage who are employed in the state, pursuing additional education in the state, or both, one year after graduation. State legislators take special note of these data because of their interest in retaining public college and university graduates to meet the state's workforce needs. This document is available both in hard copy and on the system's website (North Dakota University System, 2012).

In 2005, the Washington State Board for Community and Technical Colleges published "Building Pathways to Success for Low-Skill Adult Students: Lessons for Community College Policy and Practice from a Longitudinal Student Tracking Study" (Washington State Board for Community and Technical Colleges, 2005). This study tracked the progress over five years of a cohort of the system's students age 25 and older who entered with at most a high school diploma. It concludes that "attending college for at least one year and earning a credential provides a substantial boost in earnings for adults with a high school diploma or less who enter higher education through a community college" (p. 5). Following this methodology, the Community College Research Center (CCRC) of Teachers College, Columbia University, developed an easy-to-follow template and list of data elements required to replicate the model and determine the number of students who attain this threshold or "tipping point" of at least two semesters and a credential. The CCRC's "A Short Guide to 'Tipping Point' Analyses of Community College Student Labor Market Outcomes" (Jenkins, 2008) is a valuable research tool. The data demonstrate the importance of achieving certain milestones and can empower system staff to implement processes or programs aimed at increasing the number of students who successfully reach the tipping point.

Preferences of Decision Makers

No matter how thorough and detailed, the most rigorous analysis or insightful information may remain less than fully utilized or undervalued if the conclusions are not clearly outlined for the specific decision maker(s). The intended audience is paramount. The CEO and board or commission members are the initial beneficiaries of institutional research expertise at the system or state level. They not only use the research and analyses for internal decision making but must convey a solid understanding of that information to the governor, legislators, media, and public. With only limited time and energy to devote to any single issue, the system head and other policy makers prefer concise summaries of data, with bullet points highlighting the most important findings, interpretations, and policy implications. In crafting such statements, it is important to consider and be sensitive to the diverse perspectives of the higher education and political leaders who will read the work. Well-designed graphs or dashboards also are powerful communication tools. The key is to present sound information in a succinct, precise, and understandable format that does not overwhelm the recipient with detail.

Although it originally referenced higher education leadership, the following advice by Mortimer (1992) applies equally for all policymakers, "Documents and reports prepared for administrators [should] not be dominated by excessive treatments of methodology. Given the administrative reality that there is never enough time to complete everything that needs to be done, recognize that administrators will read summaries and read *at*, rather than *digest*, extensive amounts of analytical work" (p. 83). The framework, methodology, and other background can be available as supplementary material for those interested in gaining a deeper understanding of the issue.

Conclusion

Members of governing and coordinating boards "need comprehensible, comprehensive information about the institution [or system] that enables them to carry out their fiduciary responsibilities. But they also need such information to help direct their attention to . . . strategic decisions. It's difficult to keep focused on the wider issues of governance without appropriate information, and it's tempting to focus on nitpicking detail, if that's all you're informed about" (Winston, 1994, quoted in Krotseng, 2000, pp. 1–2). Thus, the system/state-level institutional researcher must always keep the broad context in mind even while fully immersed in the data. The researcher must engage in skillful listening, paying close attention to the question(s) being asked. Rigorous and objective research methodology must combine with open, clear, and honest communication and the skill to address especially sensitive or controversial issues. Those who are most effective cultivate an in-depth knowledge of the relevant internal and external environments, of critical issues facing the state and system, and of key decision makers' preferred reporting styles.

Given the multiple stakeholders with input into the decision-making process of a higher education governing or coordinating board—the board members themselves, system or commission CEO, campus personnel, and executive and legislative branches—the ability to view and address information from various perspectives is essential. Institutional researchers at system and state levels hold a significant responsibility because of the potential of their analyses to impact statewide higher education policy. Coupled with this responsibility, however, is the extraordinary opportunity to make a tangible difference through data-informed decision making.

References

Arkansas Department of Higher Education. (n.d.). Retrieved from http://www.adhe.edu/divisions/researchandplanning/Pages/researchandplanning.aspx

Code of Virginia. (n.d.). Retrieved from http://leg1.state.va.us/cgi-bin/legp504.exe?000+cod+TOC

Connecticut Community Colleges. (n.d.). Retrieved from http://www.commnet.edu/planning/

Education Commission of the States Postsecondary Governance Structures Database. (n.d.). Retrieved from http://www.ecs.org/html/educationIssues/Governance/GovPSDB_intro.asp

Fulton, M. (2010). *State reporting on developmental education: Analysis of findings.* Denver: Education Commission of the States. Retrieved from http://www.ecs.org/clearinghouse/85/27/8527.pdf

Hebel, S., & Selingo, J. J. (2009, March 6). Obama's higher-education goal is ambitious but achievable, leaders say. *Chronicle of Higher Education, 55*(26), A21.

Immerwahr, J., Johnson, J., & Gasbarra, P. (2008). *The iron triangle: College presidents talk about costs, access, and quality.* San Jose, CA: National Center for Public Policy in Higher Education.

Indiana Commission for Higher Education. (2007). *Reaching higher: Strategic directions for higher education in Indiana*. Indianapolis: Indiana Commission for Higher Education.

Jenkins, D. (2008). A short guide to "tipping point" analyses of community college student labor market outcomes (CCRC Research Tools No. 3). New York: Community College Research Center, Teachers College, Columbia University. Retrieved from http://ccrc.tc.columbia.edu/Publication.asp?UID=600

Keller, G. T. (1993). Strategic planning and management in a competitive environment. In R H. Glover & M. V. Krotseng (Eds.), *Developing executive information systems for higher education* (pp. 9–16). New Directions for Institutional Research, no. 77. San Francisco: Jossey-Bass.

Kentucky Council on Postsecondary Education. (n.d.). Retrieved from http://cpe.ky.gov/planning/strategic/

Krotseng, M. V. (2000, May). *Meeting the information needs of governing boards and legislators.* Paper presented at the annual SHEEO/NCES Network Conference, Washington, DC.

Lane, J. E. (2008). *Sustaining a public agenda for higher education: A case study of the North Dakota Higher Education Roundtable*. Boulder, CO: Western Interstate Commission for Higher Education.

Mercer, J. (1993, September 1). States' practice of grading public colleges' performance gets an F from critics. *Chronicle of Higher Education, 40*(2), A39.

Minnesota State Colleges and Universities System. (n.d.). Retrieved from http://www.mnscu.edu/board/accountability/index.html

Minnesota State Colleges and Universities and University of Minnesota. (n.d.). *Getting prepared*. Retrieved from http://www.mnscu.edu/media/publications

Missouri Department of Higher Education. (n.d.). *Measuring success*. Retrieved from http://www.dhe.mo.gov/data

Mortimer, K. P. (1992). Confessions of a researcher turned policymaker. In J. I. Gill & L. Saunders (Eds.), *Developing effective policy analysis in higher education* (pp. 75–84). New Directions for Institutional Research, no. 76. San Francisco: Jossey-Bass.

National Association of System Heads, American Association of State Colleges and Universities, & Association of Governing Boards of Universities and Colleges. (2009). *The leadership dynamic in public college and university systems*. Washington, DC: AGB Press.

National Conference of State Legislatures. (2006). *Transforming higher education: National imperative—state responsibility*. Denver: National Conference of State Legislatures.

Nebraska Coordinating Commission for Postsecondary Education. (2010). *Nebraska higher education progress report*. Lincoln: Coordinating Commission for Postsecondary Education. Retrieved from http://www.ccpe.state.ne.us/publicdoc/ccpe/Reports/progressReport/2010/default.asp

Nebraska Coordinating Commission for Postsecondary Education. (n.d.). Retrieved from http://www.ccpe.state.ne.us/publicdoc/ccpe/Reports/FactLook/default.asp

North Dakota Century Code. (n.d.). Retrieved from http://www.legis.nd.gov/information/statutes/cent-code.html

North Dakota University System. (2011). *2011 Accountability Measures Report*. Retrieved from http://www.ndus.edu/information

North Dakota University System (2012). *Follow-up report*. Retrieved from http://www.ndus.edu/information

Ohio Board of Regents. (n.d.). Retrieved from http://regents.ohio.gov/perfrpt/statistical_profiles.php

Oregon University System. (n.d.). Retrieved from http://www.ous.edu/

Oregon University System Enrollment Projections. (n.d.). Retrieved from http://www.ous.edu/dept/ir/enroll/future

Reindl, T., & Reyna, R. (2011). *From information to action: Revamping higher education accountability systems*. Washington, DC: NGA Center for Best Practices.

South Carolina Commission on Higher Education. (n.d.). Retrieved from http://www.che.sc.gov/New_Web/Rep&Pubs/DataRepts.htm

State Council of Higher Education for Virginia. (2008, July 7–8). Full cost report. In *Agenda book*, 67–73. Retrieved from http://docs.google.com/viewer?a=v&q=cache:_2BnIUW8POAJ:www.schev.edu/SCHEV/AgendaBooks/2008July/AgendaBook0708.pdf+agenda+book+july+2008&hl=en&gl=us&pid=bl&srcid=ADGEESiZ2QI5N_aZFvCHNXaz1_wpMisPnbUdbfAJQRrppQEOjkzlLucRa0F3UR5EGJrxLWtDtIVSKv1YKWmtL5FdrHjTSR8Omu_9pC6gFGHiCVe73wDTUvyoqCMXrf62tvIVzGP1iH8M&sig=AHIEtbRRYrnQJiM46uFh9aQMyhFiCzSRTQ

State Council of Higher Education for Virginia. (n.d.). Retrieved from http://research.schev.edu/

State Council of Higher Education for Virginia *Assessment of Institutional Performance*. (n.d.). Retrieved from http://research.schev.edu/topicpages.asp?t=7

State Council of Higher Education for Virginia Enrollment Projections. (n.d.). Retrieved from http://research.schev.edu/topicpages.asp?t=8

State University of New York. (n.d.). Retrieved from http://www.suny.edu/powerOfSuny

Tennessee Higher Education Commission. (n.d.). Retrieved from http://www.tn.gov/thec/Divisions/PPR/PPR.html

University of Maine System. (n.d.). Retrieved from http://www.maine.edu/system/policy_manual/policy_section301.1.php

University of Maine System Office of Planning and Policy Analysis. (n.d.). Retrieved from http://www.maine.edu/system/ppa/ppa.php?section=10

University of Massachusetts System. (n.d.). Retrieved from http://www.massachusetts.edu/aasair/irindex.html

University of Massachusetts System. (n.d.). *Annual Indicators Report*. Retrieved from http://www.massachusetts.edu/ir/irannualpublications.html

University of Missouri System, Measuring Success. (n.d.). Retrieved from http://www.umsystem.edu/ums/about/accountabilitymeasures

University of North Carolina System. (n.d.). Retrieved from http://www.northcarolina.edu/web/facts.php

University System of Georgia. (n.d.). Retrieved from http://www.usg.edu/research/

University of Texas System. (n.d.). Retrieved from http://www.utsystem.edu/isp/

University of Texas System. (n.d.). *Facts & Trends*. Retrieved from http://www.utsystem.edu/isp/factstrends.htm

Walsh, E. J. (2009). P-16 Policy alignment in the states: Findings from a 50-state survey. In *States, schools, and colleges: Policies to improve student readiness for college and strengthen coordination between schools and colleges*. San Jose, CA: National Center for Public Policy in Higher Education. Retrieved from http://www.highereducation.org/reports/ssc/index.shtml

Washington Higher Education Coordinating Board. (n.d.). Retrieved from http://www.hecb.wa.gov/PublicationsLibrary/PolicyResearch

Washington State Board for Community and Technical Colleges. (2005). *Building pathways to success for low-skill adult students: Lessons for community college policy and practice from a longitudinal student tracking study*. (Research Report No. 06–2). Retrieved from http://www.sbctc.ctc.edu/docs/education/ford_bridges/bldg_pathways_to_success_for_low-skilled_adult_stdts.pdf

Washington State Board for Community and Technical Colleges. (n.d.). Retrieved from http://www.sbctc.ctc.edu/college/d_index.aspx

West Virginia State Code. (n.d.). Retrieved from http://www.legis.state.wv.us/WVCODE/Code.cfm?chap=18b&art=1

CHAPTER 24

DEVELOPING K–20+ STATE DATABASES

Maryann S. Ruddock

Institutional researchers and others are currently working on ways to track students through their entire educational experience in order to make informed decisions relating to the management and funding of education. The work on these statewide student longitudinal databases reflects the fluidity around the standards and protocols on how to design and use these systems. This chapter discusses what these statewide longitudinal databases look like and the issues surrounding their design, implementation, and use at the time of the writing. Federal and state decisions will influence the future of statewide longitudinal databases. How institutional researchers can help in the development and use of student longitudinal databases is also discussed.

Educating our citizens to lead productive lives benefits our nation—economically, politically, and socially. The education process spans K–12 education, postsecondary education, and workforce education. By looking at students' progress across these educational levels longitudinally, we can determine where to place resources to improve a student's chance of becoming a productive citizen. K–20+ student longitudinal databases provide a structure for collecting, processing, and reporting the data and information needed by legislators, administrators, researchers, teachers, students, and parents for making informed decisions relating to the management and funding of education. These databases also give institutional researchers access to an important data source for creating planning and decision support at their institutions.

Evolution of K–20+ Education in the United States

Education in the United States and globally has had to change over the past 100 years to accommodate changes in how we live and work. The notion of K–20+ education is the latest in these accommodations. In the early 1900s, universal public education went through only the primary grades (1–6), because most of the workforce worked on farms or in other labor-intensive jobs not requiring more education. When manufacturing took over from agriculture as the primary workforce occupation, a high school (K–12) education was necessary to meet the demands of these positions. With the current move from the Industrial Age to an Information Age, the workplace now demands at least two years of college (K–14), and in many cases, a bachelor's degree (K–16). History is repeating itself, with colleges and universities now taking on the role that high schools played in the 1930s and 1940s in educating the primary component of our workforce (Van de Water & Krueger, 2002).

K–20+ Data Systems

This section describes the types of questions a K–20+ student longitudinal database can answer, along with a discussion of the stakeholders involved in these databases. The design and functionality of the database depend on who is using the data and for what purposes.

A robust K–20+ longitudinal database can support a number of important program and process evaluations across all levels of education. For K–12 education, the right longitudinal data make it possible to (1) evaluate the effectiveness of schools and programs in improving student achievement, (2) identify consistently high-performing schools so that educators can learn about promising practices, (3) intervene in a timely way to help students who are struggling, and (4) determine how well schools are preparing students to complete high school and enroll in postsecondary education (MPR Associates/National Center for Educational Achievement, 2005). For higher education, longitudinal databases allow us to trace the enrollment patterns of students (often referred to as "swirling"), determine the time to degree by program, and provide insights about where to place resources. For the workforce, longitudinal databases allow us to determine which programs best prepare our workers, how training should best be conducted, and the current and potential supply available to meet demands for various jobs.

K–20+ longitudinal databases allow researchers and practitioners to focus on student transitions: from secondary to postsecondary education, from the workforce to postsecondary education, and from all education levels into employment and careers. With the proper data, studies can be developed to answer questions about the impact of courses students take, the credits and credentials they earn, their persistence in postsecondary education, and their in-school and out-of-school employment. These systems help in answering key questions about performance, progress toward continuous improvement, and ultimately about student success in both the academic realm and the workforce.

There are many stakeholders who will have access to these K–20+ databases or the results of research based on these data. Increased access and use of data will also lead to increased data quality (Data Quality Campaign, 2009a). When data were used just for compliance purposes, there was no feedback loop from a higher education institution back to high schools or a specific high school about the performance of their students. With a K–20+ database system in place, data can flow both ways, with many stakeholders able to examine them closely and make policy decisions from an informed perspective. Ultimately, this will lead to enhanced data quality and use.

The stakeholders involved in the development and use of K–20+ student longitudinal databases help determine the process for their development, data collection and storage, and access protocols. The Data Quality Campaign (2009a) lists the following key stakeholders for K–20+ longitudinal databases: governors, state legislators, chief state school officers, school board members, district and school administrators, early learning administrators, postsecondary and K–12 educators, state higher education executives, parents, students, and advocacy/improvement/research organizations.

Those building the database must be aware of who will be using it and how they will be using it. Different stakeholders need to see data in different ways. The design of a statewide K–20+ database should allow for the various stakeholders (a parent, a teacher, a policy maker, and so on) to use a single database for answering all of their questions. However, how a parent accesses and uses the data will be much different from how policy makers or researchers access and use the data. This has implications for collection, storage, and access protocols. It is efficient and cost-effective to design and implement a database that contains aggregate data and that would fulfill most of the needs for students, parents, and policy makers. However, most researchers would require data at the student unit level. To meet the needs of both of these sets of users, the database would have to be designed so that different types of data and reports can be extracted.

Elements of K–20+ Databases: An Overview

Statewide student longitudinal databases are receiving attention across the nation with the impetus being both cost-effective and efficient ways to gather and report data for decision making. K–20+ data systems are comprehensive longitudinal data systems. Comprehensive refers to the connecting of administrative student datasets from different educational entities and business foci. Longitudinal refers to connecting data about individual students over time, across educational systems, and their work. The majority of the data we have now on students is cross-sectional, or "snapshot" data. There is a record, as of a given point in time, of each student's status (demographic variables, grades, GPA, test scores, and so on). Cross-sectional data are good for determining how groups of students are doing at that point in time and can be used for determining achievement gaps among groups of students. What cross-sectional data do not give us is a record of how a given student is doing over time. Longitudinal data allow for assessing individual student and group progress. Many institutional researchers have had to create "work-arounds" for nonexistent longitudinal data consisting of multiple runs against cross-sectional data. One example of this deals with student flow, wherein snapshot data are pulled periodically throughout the year and then used to create a tracking system. A statewide student longitudinal database would provide easy access to longitudinal data.

Three specific ongoing efforts are discussed here, to compare and contrast thinking about what should go into a statewide student longitudinal database. Table 24.1 identifies the elements of these three efforts.

The Data Quality Campaign (DQC) is a national, collaborative effort created to encourage and support state policy makers to increase the availability and use of high-quality education data to improve student achievement. Their goals are to: (1) build longitudinal data systems with end users in mind, (2) create toolkits for education stakeholders that demonstrate the power of longitudinal data, (3) advocate for continued investments in state data systems, and (4) generate opportunities for states to learn from one another (Data Quality Campaign, 2006).

In a collaborative effort by the 14 managing partners of the DQC (which include Achieve, Inc.; The Education Trust; NCHEMS; and the National Center for Educational Accountability), they were able to identify 10 elements that are essential in a longitudinal data system. The elements (organized to match SHEEO's categories, as identified by Ewell and L'Orange, 2009) are:

Student Data—Statewide student identifier; student-level enrollment data; information on untested students

Course/Test Data—Student-level SAT, ACT, and Advanced Placement Exam data; student-level test data; student-level course completion (transcript) data; student-level graduation and dropout data

Operational Characteristics—Statewide teacher identifier with a student-teacher match; ability to match student-level P–12 and higher education data

Governance Data—A state audit system

In annual reports, the DCQ looks at how the states are using these essential elements to improve student achievement. Data are presented by state and by data element (Data Quality Campaign, 2010a).

In 2007, the U.S. Congress passed the America Creating Opportunities to Meaningfully Promote Excellence in Technology, Education, and Science (COMPETES) Act. This act was aimed at ensuring the nation's competitive

TABLE 24.1 NATIONAL PERSPECTIVES ON ELEMENTS OF STATEWIDE LONGITUDINAL DATABASES

Data Quality Campaign's 10 Essential Elements of a State Longitudinal Data System, K–12	American Creating Opportunities to Meaningfully Promote Excellence in Technology, Education, and Science (COMPETES) Act of 2007	SHEEO The Ideal Postsecondary Data System: 15 Essential Characteristics and Required Functionality
Statewide student identifier	A unique identifier for every student that does not permit a student to be individually identified (except as permitted by federal and state law)	A unique statewide student identifier Privacy protection for all individually identifiable student records A single state-level student unit record (SUR) system for all public institutions
Student-level enrollment data	The school enrollment history, demographic characteristics, and program participation record of every student	Student-level enrollment, degree completion, and demographic data for all public colleges and universities Student-level financial aid data
Student-level test data	Students' scores on tests required by the Elementary and Secondary Education Act	Student-level data on assessed academic achievement
Information on untested students	Information on students who are not tested, by grade and subject area	
Statewide teacher identifier with a teacher-student match	A way to identify teachers and to match teachers to their students	
Student-level course completion (transcript) data	Information from students' transcripts, specifically courses taken and grades earned	Student-level course/transcript-level data
Student-level SAT, ACT, and Advanced Placement Exam data	Students' scores on tests measuring whether they are ready for college	
Student-level graduation and dropout data	Information on when a student enrolls, transfers, drops out, or graduates from a school	Student-level persistence and graduation data Student-level transfer data
Ability to match student-level P–12 and higher education data		The ability to match student records with data on K–12 educational activity
	Data on students' success in college, including whether they enrolled in remedial courses Data on whether K–12 students are prepared to succeed in college	Student-level (1) remediation data and (2) developmental education participation and success data
		The ability to match student records with data on employment The inclusion of independent and for-profit institutions of higher education
A state data audit system	A system of auditing data for quality, validity, and reliability	A data audit system assessing data quality, validity, and reliability Alignment with broader state goals, demonstrated usability, and sustainability

position in the world through improvements to math and science education and a strong commitment to research. Title VI/Part III/Subtitle D/Section 6401 of that act (Alignment of Secondary School Graduation Requirements with the Demands of 21st Century Postsecondary Endeavors and Support of P–16 Education Data Systems) lays out 12 elements required for funding of P–16 education data systems.

The elements (organized to match the State Higher Education Executive Officers [SHEEO] categories as identified by Ewell and L'Orange, 2009) are:

Student Data—A unique identifier for every student that does not permit a student to be individually identified (except as permitted by federal and state law); the school enrollment history, demographic characteristics, and program participation record of every student; information on students who are not tested, by grade and subject area; information on when a student enrolls, transfers, drops out, or graduates from a school

Course/Test Data—Students' scores on tests required by the Elementary and Secondary Education Act; information from students' transcripts, specifically courses taken and grades earned; students' scores on tests measuring whether they are ready for college; data on students' success in college, including whether they enrolled in remedial courses; data on whether K–12 students are prepared to succeed in college

Operational Characteristics—A way to identify teachers and to match teachers to their students

Governance Data—A system of auditing data for quality, validity, and reliability

The federal government financially supports work done on educational longitudinal databases. Funding that states might receive to support (or leverage) the effective use of longitudinal data to improve student outcomes is published annually. A summary of these opportunities is published by the Data Quality Campaign (2011).

The organization of State Higher Education Executive Officers (SHEEO) has produced a description of the ideal state postsecondary data system (Ewell and L'Orange, 2009). Although targeted at postsecondary institutions, these characteristics include linkages to K–12 and employment data. The 15 essential characteristics are:

Student Data—A unique statewide student identifier; student-level enrollment, degree completion, and demographic data for all public colleges and universities; student-level financial aid data; student-level persistence and graduation data; student-level transfer data

Course/Test Data—Student-level data on assessed academic achievement; student-level course/transcript data; student-level remediation data; and developmental education participation and success data

Operational Characteristics—Privacy protection for all individually identifiable student records, a single state-level student unit record (SUR) system for all public institutions, the ability to match student records with data on K–12 educational activity, the ability to match student records with data on employment, the inclusion of independent and for-profit institutions of higher education

Governance Data—A data audit system assessing data quality, validity, and reliability; alignment with broader state goals; and demonstrated usability and sustainability

SHEEO has a continuing interest in statewide databases and ensuring student achievement. The organization has worked with the Council of Chief State School Officers to develop model data standards for K–12 and postsecondary education (State Higher Education Executive Officers, 2010) and convened a meeting on defining alignment and achieving college readiness (State Higher Education Executive Officers, 2011), among other endeavors.

These are but three examples of a broad area of work in the creation of student longitudinal databases in states across the country. These efforts not only serve as a guideline to designing K–20+ databases but also inform institutional researchers of how they can provide support in the design and implementation of K–20+ databases. Institutional researchers can also help identify potential pitfalls, different data definitions, timing of the data, and how to operationally define the measures needed to answer questions concerning postsecondary data.

Design and Implementation: Data In

As with any database, data need to be collected and stored in such a way that they can be accessed to answer a number of questions. At a very basic level, we are dealing with putting data into a database system and then getting the data out. In this section we discuss the design or "data in" aspects of the database; a discussion of the retrieval or "data out" aspects follows.

A statewide K–20+ longitudinal database can help answer the question: "On which pressure points should the state focus to improve student achievement and smooth transitions from early learning to K–12 to postsecondary education?" It can also answer questions such as "Which leads to better success in college mathematics, taking Algebra I in eighth grade or ninth grade?" But to enable users to answer these, the database must be carefully and thoughtfully designed and implemented. The successful design of a longitudinal data system ensures there is buy-in by principal participants and stakeholders, that data definitions are clear and agreed on, and that data security and individual privacy are ensured. The integrity of the data that is built into a statewide student longitudinal database will determine both the usefulness and the use of the database.

Student Unit Record Data

Data reported at the student unit record level consists of the same information reported on each student; that is, the student is the unit of analysis. This allows for the collection of detailed data that permits comparisons across institutions as well as within institutions, which is important, given the high degree of mobility of students today. A majority of states today have some form of unit-record reporting across all levels of education (Data Quality Campaign, 2009–2010). The federal government has conducted feasibility studies concerning the reporting of unit record data for the IPEDS system reporting (Cunningham and Milam, 2005). However, at the time this chapter was written it did not appear that unit record reporting will be done at the national level to support IPEDS.

However, the federal government (U.S. Department of Education, 2010) does collect unit record data on financial aid recipients. From the private sector, the National Student Clearinghouse (n.d.) also uses student unit records for verification of institutional enrollment and degrees awarded for each student. These are the only two national-level student data collections that collect student-level data at this time.

Unique Identifier

One of the greatest barriers to building student longitudinal files is the inability to track an individual student across educational and workforce sectors. What unique identifier do you use? Social security number? University ID? A unique student identifier (USI) is a necessity for tracking purposes. There must be a way to link information about an individual student from numerous databases. Student privacy and FERPA issues come into play with the determination of which identifier to use. (See Chapter 19 concerning FERPA/IRB.)

The linkage between the USI and the student's identity is the key factor. According to the Fordham Center on Law and Information Policy (2009), "when an institution successfully creates a non-personally identifiable USI that is used specifically for reporting information from the local educational agency to the state, that data reporting qualifies as a permitted disclosure of 'anonymized' data; all other personally identifiable information is withheld" (p. 32). Ott and DesJardins (2009) describe best practices surrounding data security and confidentiality as well as the overall management of SUR data. They conclude that it is important for policy makers, administrators, and constituents to grasp that the overarching purpose of state unit record data is to improve a state's ability to understand and administer their P through 20 programs, not to meet federal reporting requirements.

The USI is a two-edged sword. It allows for tracking of individual students, which allows for better data and the ability to make better decisions. According to L'Orange (2008), data alone do not improve performance, but good data systems are a valuable tool for improving policy making. The downside of the USI is the concern with the possibility of identity theft (if the SSN is used) and the limitations of data sharing due to FERPA considerations. However, the bottom line is that there must be a way to link student information from multiple databases.

Data Definitions

K–12 and higher education have historically been treated as, and acted as, separate systems. This disjointedness has led to the development of independent data collection and reporting mechanisms between the two entities. Combining these systems, or even creating a new one, is often difficult because, although they may use the same words (*enrolled student, faculty, time to degree, student identifier*, and so on), they are often speaking two different languages.

Work is currently being conducted by the Postsecondary Electronic Standards Council (PESC) to adopt common data standards for a key subset of K–12 (that is, demographics, program participation, and course information) and K–12 to postsecondary education transition variables (Postsecondary Electronic Standards Council, 2010). PESC is developing standards for data definitions and code sets, technical specifications, and the relationships that exist between data elements.

Database Design

This chapter is not intended as a manual for designing longitudinal databases; rather, it discusses the issues an institutional researcher would deal with in implementing and using longitudinal databases. Only a small amount of time will be spent on database structure. At a very basic level, structure can be thought of in terms of how data are connected. In a series of meetings of state, system, and institutional representatives, SHEEO panels (State Higher Education Executive Officers, 2009) discussed state-level postsecondary data systems. They concluded that there can be alternatives to the single master database or warehouse, which is the model most stakeholders have for statewide longitudinal databases. Instead of having a single database, a functional alignment between existing databases may serve the state better. They conclude that states should focus on interoperability of systems (both within and between states), allowing collaboration between systems and thereby making the data even more useful (p. 1).

In terms of storing the student identifier, database structure can be conceptualized as dual or unified (Fordham Center on Law and Information Policy, 2009). In a dual database system, student identifier information is stored in one file and another separate database stores the detailed longitudinal data about the student. The unified database system contains both the identifier and the longitudinal data in a single database. Where and how the student identifier is stored has implications for FERPA compliance (see Fordham Center on Law and Information Policy, pp. 31–43 for a full discussion of these issues).

Design and Implementation: Data Out

Once the data have been collected and verified, the question becomes one of how the information can be accessed. Data access depends on how the data are stored. Most data are stored in a "warehouse" that is accessed by students, parents, institutions, and others. This is where the user "touches" the data and information in the longitudinal data system. The design of a shared data system, a single data warehouse, a distributive system providing conduits to original data, or some combined approach is a technical issue and is beyond the scope of this chapter. Its operation, however, is an issue that concerns the data providers, project directors, and key stakeholders.

Because the "warehouse" will be a central repository of data to be used by various stakeholders, access to the data and information is determined by the sophistication of the users and what information they need. This access can be discussed in terms of levels, ranging from predefined reports for general use through access to student-level data for the most sophisticated of researchers. Various stakeholders have access to different levels of the data—need determines level of access. The data user also determines control over the access to the data. The Data Quality Campaign (2010b) has published examples of portals and reports. Table 24.2 presents an example of the types of access and levels of control for various stakeholders.

Standard Reports

Predefined reports contain the aggregate information most often asked for; these are produced on a periodic basis. Institutional researchers are vital in helping to define these types of reports. One way to manage the data in these reports is to organize them around themes. Some themes suggested by MPR and Associates for the State of Texas (MPR Associates, 2010) are preparation for college and career, transitions after high school, adult transitions, completions, and employment outcomes.

TABLE 24.2   ROLE AND SOPHISTICATION OF STAKEHOLDERS AS DETERMINANTS OF DATA ACCESS

| Stakeholders | Types of Access (Control) | | |
	None	Controlled Access	Review Board
Students	Standard Reports		
Parents	Standard Reports		
Teachers	Standard Reports	Aggregate Data	Student-Level Data
Administrators	Standard Reports	Aggregate Data	Student-Level Data
Researchers		Aggregate Data	Student-Level Data

Other examples of reports that are descriptive include: "If your child had a SAT score between X and Y, how likely is she to succeed in a two-year institution?" and "How likely are children who received free or reduced lunches to go on to college?" There are no limitations to the access of these types of standardized reports; they consist of public information and require no special permission to be accessed.

Aggregate Data

Reporting data in aggregate form is a useful way to describe a specific population of students. Summarized or aggregate data—such as high school to college enrollment, graduates that enrolled in the first fall and the number of them that persisted in higher education the second fall, by high school—helps the institution understand the students they are enrolling. These are aggregate data, but they still tell a story of student persistence. Other types of aggregate data that help institutional researchers understand students are, for example, test scores by types of student, movement by race and gender through different levels of education, and number of students progressing from elementary to middle school. Data on shifts in the populations and demands by different populations may be of interest to administrators. Researchers use aggregate data in order to do policy or management studies at the state and institutional levels. There may be some control over access to these data, such as restricting data to the school districts and colleges being reported on, but for the most part aggregate data are public data.

Student-Level Data

The most sophisticated level of user will want direct access to the database in order to answer specific research questions. But with direct access, data privacy issues must be addressed. Access will need to be controlled, most likely through an oversight advisory board for all uses of unit record information in the database. Periodic formal reports will be needed to document all requests for access to the database and the decision of the advisory board. The database developers will also need to adopt risk assessment/audit processes for all data resources containing individually identifiable data; models for this include the Texas Education Resource Center (University of Texas at Austin, 2010) and the Florida Education Data Warehouse (Florida Department of Education, 2010).

Student-level data may be used for diagnostic reports on individual students, such as (1) early warning system reports that provide information on whether individual students are at risk and in need of extra assistance; (2) readiness reports to identify whether and to what extent each elementary, middle, and high school student is on track for college and career readiness by high school graduation; and (3) predictive reports on individual students that analyze past performance to see whether students are likely to reach a performance goal (Data Quality Campaign, 2009a).

Current Context

One current aspiration for states is a complete K–20+ database that allows access by various stakeholders to data and information at the student level on all aspects of a student's educational career, from preschool to graduate school and the workforce. The reality is that states are still working to achieve this goal. Typically, the states have bits and pieces of what might someday become a statewide comprehensive K–20+ database. But given that we are currently being asked to provide more and better data and information for decision making, it is essential that we make the most of what we now have.

SHEEO has published *Strong Foundations: The State of State Postsecondary Data Systems* (Garcia & L'Orange, 2010), in which they found (among other findings) that:

- Demographic, postsecondary enrollment, and completions data are the most common types of data in SUR systems.
- The social security number is the primary identification number used as the postsecondary internal primary key and in the matching process with other agencies or entities.
- A high proportion of states generate retention, transfer, and remediation reports with the SUR data collected.
- Course type, course title, course grade, and high school GPA provide more information about the population of students entering college than do admissions and/or placement exam scores alone.
- Hours worked, wages earned, and U.S. Census or U.S. Department of Labor employment codes/titles all serve to highlight higher education's return on investment.

En Route to Seamless Statewide Education Data Systems: Addressing Five Cross-Cutting Concerns (Conger, 2008) reports on a workshop sponsored by SHEEO as a forum for states to engage in peer-to-peer learning. The workshop identified the following five core processes that are key to successfully implementing longitudinal data initiatives:

- Identifying shared benefits as a foundation for cooperative work across sectors
- Reconciling technical differences between independently created data systems
- Ensuring student privacy while sharing data to foster improvement
- Designing a data system to enable effective use by key constituencies
- Planning for long-term sustainability of state longitudinal data systems

The discussion of these processes serves as a framework to help states get started and to address specific issues commonly encountered.

Even though a particular state may not have a fully developed K–20+ database system, there are incremental steps the institutional researcher can take to maximize what currently exists, as well as promoting the development of a K–20+ database. Two steps that can be taken now are learning what information is currently available and developing cooperative agreements with schools.

Many state higher education offices have undertaken efforts to collect data to track students moving between higher education institutions in the state, as well as from public K–12 schools. For example, the Texas Higher Education Coordinating Board (THECB) has hosted Data Fellows workshops in which they bring together data users from K–12, community colleges, and four-year institutions by city to learn about what data are currently available about their students. Topics included high school to college links (such as college applications submitted; Free Application for Federal Student Aid [FAFSA] submission rates; dual credit courses high school graduates enrolled and persisting by diploma type, district and region) and success of high school graduates in higher education and beyond (such as college persistence in two-year and four-year institutions, income by type of college degree and work location, financial aid and loan debt). Researchers met their local counterparts from other levels of education, data collected by the THECB were distributed, and data fellows had an opportunity to design research queries using current, live data. This required the support of the state agency (and grant money), but it is a model for learning about what data exist at different levels of the educational community.

Pfeiffer, Klein, and Levesque (2009) published a brief describing what can be done now with American Recovery and Reinvestment Act (ARRA) Student Longitudinal Data Systems (SLDS) Grant Program (2010). The brief describes opportunities that can assist states in designing, developing, and implementing statewide education longitudinal data systems. A pertinent aspect of this brief is its description of projects that could be done now with ARRA funding that build on current practices and data.

Institutional researchers can be instrumental in forging the links between K–12 and higher education. Basically, a K–12 school district wants to know how well their students do in college and the workforce, and a college wants to know the preparation of the students it accepts. Through a memorandum of understanding (MOU) between the school district and university, information can be exchanged. To be legally operative, a MOU must (1) identify the contracting parties, (2) spell out the subject matter of the agreement and its objectives, (3) summarize the essential terms of the agreement, and (4) be signed by the contracting parties (Business Dictionary, 2010). An example of these issues can be found in the MOU between the Maryland State Department of Education and a number of other Maryland state agencies (Data Quality Campaign, 2009b).

Promoting the Development and Use of K–20+ Databases

What can institutional researchers do to promote the development and use of K–20+ databases? Probably the most efficient avenue for input into the development and use of K–20+ databases is through local or state associations for institutional research. These organizations are structured to represent the interests of data users and producers at all levels of higher education. For example, the chair of the Texas Association for Institutional Research Data Advisory Committee was asked to be on the Texas Special Commission on Data-Driven Education Policy, which initiated initial discussions about the design and development of a statewide K–20+ database for the state of Texas (MPR Associates, 2010).

Many of the questions institutional researchers routinely address at the campus level are relevant across all levels of education. Student preparedness is an issue on campus (admissions to exit criteria to graduate follow-up) that can be expanded across sectors, as is student flow related to transitions. Educators at all levels are concerned with what works. Institutional researchers are often asked to study such issues as the impact of differences in styles of teaching, the effectiveness of study groups and other aids, early interventions, and other issues related to student learning. Experience gained from conducting these types of studies gives institutional researchers insights valuable to the design and implementation of statewide databases.

Conclusion

Interest in K–20+ statewide longitudinal data systems has grown nationally over the past five to six years, with these projects being promoted by ARRA, the Gates Foundation, the Data Quality Campaign, SHEEO, and others. It is the author's belief that these systems will exist in every state within the next ten years. This belief is founded on the large number of people with a vested interest in this area and the amount of funding being made available for the development of these systems by both the federal government and various foundations. As a result, the field is in flux; thus this chapter reflects only where we are at the time of its writing. Economic issues will influence who will be major players in the development of the various state K–20 databases.

Perhaps with foundations providing major funding, nongovernmental agencies will become influential drivers in this area. As with all initiatives that are relatively new and therefore in flux, only time will tell the final outcome; but good data are always needed for efficient and effective decision making, which is the final goal. Current design and implementation issues that will need to be resolved include the use of unique identifiers, data definitions, technical aspects of database design, protocols governing access to data, and cooperation among the different educational strata in each state. It behooves institutional researchers on campuses to become involved, as the creation of these databases will certainly have an impact on our capacity to answer questions about the effectiveness of our institutions, as well as how we report data to our states, IPEDS, and other federal agencies.

References

American Recovery and Reinvestment Act (ARRA) State Longitudinal Data Systems (SLDS) Grant Program. (2010). Retrieved from http://nces.ed.gov/programs/slds/

Business Dictionary. (2010). Retrieved from http://www.businessdictionary.com/definition/memorandum-of-understanding-MOU.html

Conger, S. B. (2008). *En route to seamless statewide education data systems: Addressing five cross-cutting concerns.* State Higher Education Executive Officers. Retrieved from http://www.sheeo.org/Seamless_Data.pdf

Cunningham, A. F., & Milam, J. (2005). *Feasibility of a student unit record system within the Integrates Postsecondary Education Data System* (NCES 2005–160). U.S. Department of Education, National Center for Education Statistics, Washington, DC: U.S. Government Printing Office. Retrieved from http://www.sheeo.org/Seamless_Data.pdf

Data Quality Campaign. (2006). *Creating a longitudinal data system: Using data to improve student success.* Retrieved from www.DataQualityCampaign.org

Data Quality Campaign. (2009a). *The next step: Using longitudinal data systems to improve student success.* Retrieved from www.DataQualityCampaign.org

Data Quality Campaign. (2009b). *Memorandum of understanding on data sharing by and among the Governor's Office for Children, the Department of Health and Mental Hygiene, the Department of Human Resources, the Department of Juvenile Services, and the Maryland State Department of Education.* Retrieved from http://www.dataqualitycampaign.org/files/Dashboard_MOU_draft_08–21–09_clean_.pdf

Data Quality Campaign. (2009–2010). *2009–2010 National Survey Results: Essential elements.* Retrieved from http://www.dataqualitycampaign.org/survey

Data Quality Campaign. (2010a). *Data for action 2010: DQC's state analysis.* Retrieved from http://www.dataqualitycampaign.org/

Data Quality Campaign. (2010b). *What does role-based access look like? Examples from states.* Retrieved from http://www.dataqualitycampaign.org/files/portals_examples.pdf

Data Quality Campaign. (2011). *Federal funding opportunities for supporting the use of longitudinal data: Fiscal year 2011.* Retrieved from http://www.dataqualitycampaign.org/files/FY%202011%20analysis.pdf

Ewell, P., & L'Orange, H. (2009). *State postsecondary data system: 15 essential characteristics and required functionality.* State Higher Education Executive Officers. Retrieved from http://www.sheeo.org/datamgmt/unit%20record/ideal_data_system.pdf

Florida Department of Education. (2010). *Florida education data warehouse.* Retrieved from http://www.fldoehub.org/Research/Pages/default.aspx

Fordham Center on Law and Information Policy. (2009). *Children's educational records and privacy: A study of elementary and secondary school state reporting systems.* Retrieved from http://law.fordham.edu/center-on-law-and-information-policy/14769.htm

Garcia, T. I., & L'Orange, H. (2010). *Strong foundations: The state of state postsecondary data systems.* State Higher Education Executive Officers. Retrieved from http://www.sheeo.org/pcn/Uploads/StrongFoundations_Full.pdf

L'Orange, H. (2008). *Unit record data systems: A state perspective.* State Higher Education Executive Officers. Retrieved from http://www.sheeo.org/datamgmt/unit%20record/Unit%20Record%20Data%20Systems%20-%20A%20State%20Persepctive.pdf

MPR Associates. (2010). *Texas data-driven policy-making study: Enhancing Texas data to support college and career success: Summary report.* Unpublished manuscript.

MPR Associates/National Center for Educational Achievement. (2005). *Judging student achievement: Why getting the right data matters.* Retrieved from http://www .dataqualitycampaign.org/files/Tools-Judging_Student_Achievement.pdf

National Student Clearinghouse. (n.d.). Retrieved from http://www .studentclearinghouse.org/

Ott, M., & DesJardins, S. (2009). *Protection and accessibility of state student unit record data systems at the postsecondary level.* State Higher Education Executive Officers. Retrieved from http://www.sheeo.org/pubs/SUR_Final_Report-20091118.pdf

Pfeiffer, J., Klein, S., & Levesque, K. (2009). *Leveraging ARRA funding for developing comprehensive state longitudinal data systems.* MPR Associates. Retrieved from http://www. mprinc.com/products/pdf/SLDS_ARRA_Vision_Paper.pdf

Postsecondary Electronic Standards Council. (2010). *Common data standards initiative.* Retrieved from http://www.commondatastandards.org/aboutcds.html

State Higher Education Executive Officers. (2009). *Recommendations for state postsecondary data systems: A report from state experts.* Retrieved from http://www.sheeo.org/network/ State%20Data%20System%20Advisory%20Panel%20Report%20-%2011-23-09.pdf

State Higher Education Executive Officers. (2010). *Common education data standards.* Retrieved from http://www.sheeo.org/pcn/PCN/Topic.aspx?id=1030

State Higher Education Executive Officers. (2011). Defining alignment and achieving college readiness: The roles of higher education organizations and leaders in common core state standards and assessment. Meeting held May 9–10, 2011. Retrieved from http://www.sheeo.org/pcn/Topic.aspx?id=1040

United States Congress. (2007). *America Creating Opportunities to Meaningfully Promote Excellence in Technology, Education, and Science (COMPETES) Act.* Retrieved from http:// www.govtrack.us/congress/bill.xpd?bill=h110–2272

U. S. Department of Education. (2010). *Federal student aid.* Retrieved from http:// studentaid.ed.gov/PORTALSWebApp/students/english/index.jsp

University of Texas at Austin. (2010). *Texas Education Research Center.* Retrieved from http://www.utaustinerc.org/

Van de Water, G., & Krueger, C. (2002, June). *P-16 Education.* ERIC Digest 159, June 2002. Retrieved from http://eric.uoregon.edu/publications/digests/digest159.html

CHAPTER 25

DATA EXCHANGE CONSORTIA

Characteristics, Current Examples, and Developing a New Exchange

Julie Carpenter-Hubin, Rebecca Carr, and Rosemary Hayes

Over the past several decades, colleges and universities have developed sophisticated data systems and become adept at using data to support and inform decision making. Higher education is a fundamentally collaborative enterprise, and as technology has made it ever easier to produce data in formats amenable to interinstitutional analyses, institutions have developed data exchanges as one means of sharing information and producing comparative data. Higher education data exchanges provide opportunities for the voluntary sharing of data among similar organizations in order to better understand their own practices and performance. These comparative data allow institutions to consider performance in the broader context of generational shifts, economic climate, and domestic and international political environments.

Higher education institutions of all sizes and types share data in many ways that fall outside the definition of a data exchange. All institutions participating in federal financial aid programs provide data to the federal government, through the National Center for Education Statistics' Integrated Postsecondary Education Data System (IPEDS). These data are made available to the public and are an important source of information for higher education institutions. Many institutions supply data to state governing boards, which then make the data, in full or summarized form, available to contributors. Publishers collect data from institutions, and some conduct opinion surveys about the quality of institutions, creating new data. This information is shared back with institutions through publications, generally provided free of charge or at reduced rates to data contributors. In recent years, business consulting groups have turned their attention to higher education and facilitated data sharing among some colleges and universities. Units within colleges and universities provide data to their associations; for example, human resources departments provide data to the College and University Personnel Association (CUPA), and libraries share data through the Association of Research Libraries (ARL).

Characteristics of Data Exchanges

The preceding examples of data sharing demonstrate many of the ways valuable information about higher education is made available for use by colleges and universities. Direct exchanges of data between groups of institutions in a consortium are another very important method of data sharing. In their 1996 article "Data-Sharing Models," Susan Shaman and Daniel Shapiro described different data-sharing paradigms using eleven process attributes or dimensions. Four of these dimensions can be used to clearly distinguish data exchange consortia from other types of data-sharing activities.

Primacy of Purpose: Primary Versus Incidental

This dimension examines the principal activity or purpose of the organization that facilitates data sharing. For many organizations that collect and share data with colleges and universities, this function is not their raison d'être. Publishers, for example, have a primary goal of selling magazines; consultants' goals are to sell their expertise. Associations such as ARL and CUPA provide leadership to their professions, and data collections in large part support and inform their missions. Data exchange consortia, on the other hand, exist first and foremost to facilitate the sharing of data among members.

Control of Process: Internal Versus External

Decisions about the data to be collected, the schedule for the collection, and data definitions are either made internally by members of the data-sharing group or imposed by an external body. The *control of process* dimension is very much related to *primacy of purpose*. Because data exchanges are created for the express purpose of data sharing between institutions, consortia members retain control of the process. They may delegate decisions about the process to a governing body of the organization or to staff they have retained, but control remains within the organization itself. This internal control distinguishes data exchange consortia from federal, state, and system-level data sharing, wherein participating institutions may advise about process, but are not decision makers.

Membership Criterion: Invitational Versus Mandatory

Membership in data exchange consortia is voluntary rather than mandatory, which also differentiates data exchange consortia from federal, state, and system-level data sharing. Membership in consortia may be by invitation, open to those institutions that fit certain criteria, or open to all institutions with a shared interest. In this way, membership criteria distinguish not only between data-sharing consortia and other data-sharing models, but also among consortia.

Number of Partners: Bilateral Versus Multilateral

Whereas individuals within a consortium may share information on a bilateral, ad hoc basis, data exchange consortia are multilateral. Such organized exchanges with multiple partners provide richer datasets and better comparative information for participants.

In addition to the characteristics that distinguish the data exchange as a unique structure, a number of characteristics further differentiate between data exchanges. The following five dimensions from Shaman and Shapiro's (1996) typology apply equally to data exchange consortia and other types of data-sharing organizations: *formality of arrangements* (formal versus informal), *regularity of activity* (regular versus occasional), *scope of information* (multitopical versus specific focus), *heterogeneity of participants* (heterogeneous versus homogeneous), and *openness* (anonymity versus public identification). Each of these is useful for understanding differences among consortia.

With technological advances, an appropriately updated description for the dimension *provision of analysis* (data analyzed versus simple tabulation) would be *provision of data* (direct access versus analytic reports). Data provision ranges from those exchanges that make data directly accessible from a data warehouse to those that summarize data from multiple institutions on spreadsheets and make those available to consortium members as PDF files.

Given that Shaman and Shapiro proposed their typology in 1996, it is not surprising that their *media* dimension distinguished between paper and electronic exchanges. Happily, that comparison is no longer relevant. The move away from paper has expanded the amount of data shared and given the data much greater utility.

Data exchange consortia share data as their primary purpose, define and control their own processes, and have nonmandatory membership. Beyond these shared characteristics, data exchange consortia conduct their activities in ways that suit the unique needs of their membership. One of the principal benefits of membership in a data exchange is the network of colleagues available for advice and guidance in all higher education data-related matters.

Examples of Data Exchange Consortia

There is no better way to understand the various combinations of data exchange attributes than to take closer look at a variety of data exchange consortia and how they share data. The following section provides descriptions of a number of higher education data exchange consortia.

Association of American Universities Data Exchange

The core function of the Association of American Universities Data Exchange (AAUDE) is the exchange of data or information of common interest, including (1) the scheduled collection of exchange items as defined by the membership, (2) the sharing of results of ad hoc inquiries and special studies, and (3) the promotion of communication and collegiality among the membership.

AAUDE began somewhat serendipitously at the 1973 AIR Forum when five IR directors met informally to discuss creating a faculty load and salary study. Since its informal beginning with such a specific focus, AAUDE—whose membership is limited to institutions that are members of the Association of American Universities (AAU)—has grown in both membership and the scope of data exchanged.

AAUDE exchanges more than 30 sets of data that are both public (such as IPEDS, NSF) and AAUDE-specific topics. An email discussion list provides the capability for informal and ad hoc data collections. Data are exchanged on the basis of mutual confidentiality and the honor system, with the expectation that those who do not provide data will not use them. Member institutions use the data to conduct comparative analyses on a variety of subjects, such as faculty and administrator salaries, tuition and fees, and doctoral time to degree. Ad hoc queries help institutional researchers to conduct special comparative studies on any aspect of higher education.

Though the organization has a director and data warehouse analyst—funded by a flat membership fee—with partial FTEs, the bulk of the work is done by volunteer effort. Each exchange item has a caretaker who oversees revision of the instructions, data collection, auditing, and compilation. The resulting data are stored in a restricted-access data warehouse. More information is available at http://www.aaude.org.

Consortium for Student Retention Data Exchange

The Consortium for Student Retention Data Exchange (CSRDE)—founded in 1994 and housed at the University of Oklahoma—is dedicated to helping institutions achieve student success through sharing data, knowledge, and innovation. CSRDE has grown to serve more than 660 member institutions. Two-year and four-year institutions are eligible to apply for one of three levels of membership.

One of CSRDE's most visible activities is the collection of extensive retention and graduation rate data. Member institutions submit data electronically using Excel spreadsheets. The Consortium office handles the data collection, data auditing, internal consistency checking, and analysis, formatting, and reporting to member institutions.

In return for providing data, members receive a comprehensive report with retention and graduation benchmarks, and a customized peer report. These data cannot be acquired from any other source, including IPEDS.

In addition to the data collection efforts, the consortium also facilitates networking and sharing of best practices related to student retention and success through the annual National Symposium on Student Retention and the monthly CSRDE Webinar Series. More information is available at http://csrde .ou.edu.

The Higher Education Data Sharing Consortium

The Higher Education Data Sharing Consortium (HEDS) was established in 1983, originally funded by a grant from Educom, with a focus on technology. By 1990, the emphasis had shifted to data sharing.

HEDS is a consortium of more than 125 private colleges and universities. Membership requires approval and is restricted to non-profit, accredited institutions that meet established criteria. The membership fee is determined by institutional enrollment, with larger schools paying a higher fee.

Member institutions share data on dozens of topics, including admissions, early applications and deposits, endowment, finance, financial aid, graduation rates, and tuition and fees, among others. The datasets are both public (for example, IPEDS, NSF) and collected by other agencies (for example, AAUP, HERI, NACUBO, NSSE), as well as HEDS-developed topics.

A five-member staff is responsible for data collection, data auditing, analysis, and preparing or distributing reports for member institutions. Data are available from a series of standard reports and through a data warehouse. Access to a specific set of data access is available only to institutions that provide that data.

In addition to the standard reports and data access, the Consortium holds an annual meeting for their community of engaged members and hosts electronic discussion lists. More information is available at http://www.e-heds.org.

National Community College Benchmark Project

As a response to pressure for accountability and peer comparisons, Johnson County Community College in Kansas worked with ten other U.S. colleges to create the National Community College Benchmark Project (NCCBP). The stated purpose of the organization is to "provide a national data collection and reporting process that enables community colleges to compare student outcomes and performance indicators to those of peer institutions" (Juhnke, 2006, p. 68).

Reporting processes and a collection of benchmark measures were implemented in 2004. The benchmarks cover such topics as student performance, satisfaction and engagement, career preparation, access and participation, human resources, and organizational performance.

Any U.S. community college is eligible to join. Over 200 community colleges from across the United States participated in 2009. For a flat fee, subscribers receive a standard report that compares their institution to those of all other respondents as well as unlimited access to subscription-year data. Use of the information is subject to confidentiality and data use restrictions. More information is available at http://www.nccbp.org.

The National Study of Instructional Costs & Productivity

Originally funded by a grant from FIPSE, the Office of Institutional Research at the University of Delaware started the National Study of Instructional Costs & Productivity (the Delaware Study) in 1992. The study has become the tool of choice for comparative analysis of discipline-level faculty teaching loads, direct instructional costs, and separately budgeted scholarly activity.

Participation in the Delaware Study is available to four-year degree-granting institutions. Nearly 200 institutions participated in the 2010 exchange; over five hundred institutions have been part of the study since its inception. Like CSRDE, the Delaware Study functions like a contracted service that provides data not available from other sources. Comparisons are provided on measures such as cost per student credit hour, student-to-faculty ratio, staffing patterns, and faculty instructional productivity. More information is available at http://www.udel.edu/IR/cost for the Delaware Study and http://www.udel.edu/IR/focs for the Faculty Activity Study. (See Chapter 31 for a detailed description of these data collections.)

The National Study of Community College Instructional Costs & Productivity

The National Study of Community College Instructional Costs & Productivity (the Kansas Study) was modeled after the Delaware Study to meet the needs of community colleges. Like its four-year counterpart, the Kansas Study provides data to compare instructional costs at the discipline level.

The study is free of charge for participants. Participation requires data submission for at least ten academic disciplines and a signed agreement about confidentiality and data use. Seventy community colleges participated in the 2009 collection. More information is available at http://www.kansasstudy.org. (See also Chapter 31 in this volume.)

Polytechnic Data Sharing for Higher Educational Research

Polytechnic Data Sharing for Higher Educational Research (PolyDASHER) was established in 2008 by the University of Wisconsin-Stout to meet the increasing demand for benchmarking and comparison data in both accreditation and decision making.

PolyDASHER is available to any polytechnic institution at no cost, provided they submit data annually and agree to the privacy and security restrictions of the exchange. Currently, eight institutions participate in the exchange.

PolyDASHER collects data on a range of topics that include enrollment, graduation and retention rates, incoming freshmen, faculty characteristics, tuition rates, degrees conferred, placement, and financial aid. Using their Common Data Set and institutional fact book, users enter the data elements directly into an online collection tool. In addition, institutions can upload electronic documents for file sharing and specifically select national survey results (for example, NSSE, HERI, ACT Student Opinion Survey). These files are then available for other institutions to download and review.

To obtain data, users log in to the PolyDASHER website, where they can customize their peer network and download data from their fully customizable online query tool. Data can be downloaded, viewed, or emailed. All uploaded files are available to other members. More information is available at http://www.polydasher.org.

Southern University Group Data Exchange

The Southern University Group Data Exchange (SUG) was founded in the 1960s to provide a data exchange and information network for the flagship public research and land-grant universities in the region of the Southern Regional Education Board. Participation is limited to those institutions (http://www.sair.org/about_sair/SAIR_Essentials/Brief_History_SAIR/Brief_History_of_SAIR.html).

The primary exchange item for SUG is a fall summary form that contains data on enrollment headcount and FTE, enrollment by race/ethnicity, salary increases for faculty and staff, a narrative section to describe significant events or situations, and peer group universities. The information is collected annually in spreadsheets and made available in PDFs on the organization's website.

Other data collections are coordinated by member institutions on specific topics such as salaries of department heads and chairs, administrative salaries, and library staff salaries. In addition, the organization also makes use of exchanges by other organizations (for example, CSRDE, Delaware Study, and Oklahoma State Faculty Salary Survey) and has an email discussion list for ad hoc queries.

The organization meets twice a year in conjunction with other conferences, and members communicate and exchange information throughout the year about topics of interest. There is no fee to participate, and all work is done by members on a volunteer basis. Content from their website (http://www.sugweb.org) is available to members only.

University 15 Data Exchange

The University 15 Data Exchange (U15DE; formerly known as the Group of 13 Data Exchange or G13DE) is a consortium founded in 2000 to provide comparative analyses and benchmarking data for decision support for the University 15. The purpose of the latter group, commonly referred to as the "U15," is to advance the cause of fifteen research-intensive Canadian universities in the development of national research and academic policies. When established, the U15DE was modeled after AAUDE because two institutions are members of both the U15 and the AAU.

The exchange draws information from publicly available data sources (such as Statistics Canada, AUTM), datasets developed specifically by the U15DE (such as departmental profiles, graduate student financial support), datasets that have been purchased or contracted, and ad hoc projects initiated by individual institutions.

The data exchange comprises IR directors (or associate/assistant directors) as main representatives plus at least one alternate at each institution. The U15DE is formalized by a constitution and protocols and led by a full-time coordinator.

The organization, which also serves as a community for dialogue about matters related to higher education, relies on a variety of means for their work including an annual meeting. The organization's website (http://www.data-exchange.ca) is intended for members only.

Creating a Data Exchange

As with the creation of any organization, the process of creating a data exchange requires planning and careful consideration. The following section of this chapter will discuss the five phases of the Data Exchange Lifecycle: Problem Identification, Stakeholder Identification, Development, Implementation, and Review.

The Data Exchange Lifecycle shown in Figure 25.1 is intended to model a cyclical developmental process for building a framework on which the data exchange can be created, grow, and remain responsive to its members. An organization can function effectively only as long as it meets the needs of its members (Trainer, 1996). Thus organizers of a new data exchange should begin their efforts with the understanding that the goals and processes of the exchange must be periodically reviewed and improved on if the new organization will be one of any lasting duration.

FIGURE 25.1   THE DATA EXCHANGE LIFECYCLE

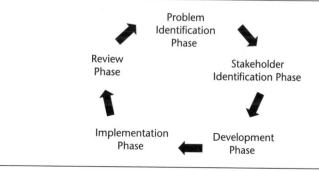

Problem Identification Phase

The most critical task for organizers of a new data exchange is the problem identification phase, during which the reason for forming the data exchange is crystallized. Hackett (1996) refers to this process as defining the opportunity. There are three components to the problem identification phase: identification of the information gap, uncovering the underlying causes for the gap, and evaluating the capacity of potential data exchange members to successfully address the problem through data sharing. Data exchanges are often developed in response to an observed information gap. These data may be needed to benchmark institutional performance on an issue such as undergraduate retention or to identify improvement gaps and monitor the progress of interventions intended to address those gaps (Sapp, 1996). The imperative to get data becomes stronger as institutions become aware of the implications or the costs (Trainer, 1996) associated with not having adequate information. Although the recognition of an information gap may begin with the inability to meet a request for information from a college or university executive, ultimately the scope of the problem can be understood through conversations with other colleagues. Professional meetings and conferences provide an excellent opportunity to gauge the collective will to address the information gap.

Interactions with colleagues are also essential for answering two other important questions. First, what are the underlying reasons for the apparent inaccessibility of the data? Second, is there a capacity to address the gap through cooperative data sharing? Information gaps may be caused by a lack of capacity, data inaccessibility, or the logistical difficulties involved in collecting the data. Obviously, if data are available but have not been shared for lack of a mechanism to do so, this increases the potential for building a successful data exchange. In some cases, data may be accessible, but there may be policy or legal limitations that prohibit its being shared.

The proponents of the new data exchange need to determine whether the obstacles to sharing data can be removed. In the case of institutions that are interested in the topic, a well-crafted participation agreement that outlines rules may be sufficient to gain their participation. Limitations due to budget cuts and workload constraints may temporarily limit an institution's ability to participate; however, where there is interest, efforts should be made to find ways for the institution to remain involved and engaged until the budget crisis passes. If the proponents discover major obstacles that prevent large numbers of target participants from providing data, the project could be tabled; or they could scale back and, together with a small group of colleagues from data-enabled institutions, conduct proof of concept studies and present the results at professional conferences. Taking time to educate colleagues about the issue and the benefits of forming a data exchange may pay off in the future.

The problem identification phase helps clarify the overriding purpose of the new data exchange, though there will most likely be shifts as more institutions participate. However, to be most effective the new data exchange should have a fairly tight focus and mission (Achtemeier & Simpson, 2005). If the preliminary investigation indicates that there are no major impediments to collecting the data needed to address the information gap, the proponents can begin to explore expanding the network of stakeholders.

Stakeholder Identification Phase

A data exchange is a community effort. Before moving forward it is essential to get a sense of how important the problem is to colleagues at other institutions. The colleagues, who share the problem, as well as the capacity and willingness to address it through a data exchange, will be fellow stakeholders.

The general recommendation however, is to begin small by targeting institutions within a defined peer group and build a solid core of participation (Trainer, 1996; Sapp, 1996), even if the long-term goal is to open participation in the exchange to a more diverse group of institutions. By taking advantage of existing contacts among peer institutions, proponents of the new data exchange can concentrate efforts on discussing the issues. Additionally, the ability to make peer comparisons using exchanged data is an important draw for membership (Hayes, 2003). A new data exchange built on an established group of similar institutions has a distinct advantage over an exchange whose initial membership is open to a diverse group of institutions. Peer institutions are typically identified as institutions that share a set of characteristics, although in some cases administrators will also use the term *peer institution* for institutions with characteristics they aspire to achieve (Sapp, 1996). The Consortium for Student Retention Data Exchange (CSRDE) serves as an example of a data-sharing organization that began with a core of peer institutions and then grew. CSRDE began by sharing retention and graduation data among a group of regional and institutional peers and has gradually expanded to include over 650 colleges and universities with very diverse institutional characteristics.

Exchange proponents should attempt to identify other groups or organizations that are working on the same issue or that have developed a related data collection tool. Where possible, partnering with these institutions and groups can save time and expand the base of interested institutions. Initiating discussions at meetings with peer institutions and conducting presentations at professional meetings can help provide insight into the extent to which other institutions share the problem and are interested in the proposed solution (Hackett, 1996).

Development Phase

There are three essential areas that need to be developed in the development phase of data exchange: (1) data elements and collection instruments, (2) data collection and reporting processes, and (3) the membership agreement. Prototypes of key survey instruments, membership agreements, administration and governance policies, and budgets and fees should be subjected to testing and review by the founding institutions. This involvement does two important things. First, it helps cement buy-in and ownership in the new data exchange. Second, by exposing the survey instruments, membership agreements, and other important items to the scrutiny of peers, those developing the exchange can catch design flaws early. Identifying and addressing design flaws early in the process will save the fledgling data exchange time and money and ensure robust membership enrollment.

To maximize the usefulness of data collected through the data exchange, one must maximize the participation of the members and the quality of the data. In the problem identification phase, the data needed to address the information gap was identified. It cannot be assumed that all participants understand or will agree to what needs to be reported in the data collection process. During the development phase, the data elements and data collection process must be identified and defined carefully to ensure the validity of the data, especially when used for comparative benchmarking (Sapp, 1996; Achtemeier & Simpson, 2005). In addition to collecting data on a specific issue, consideration should also be given to include collection of institutional and student body characteristics that might aid in selecting peer institutions for comparative benchmarking.

Where possible, developers should build on definitions and data elements collected in other federal, state, or agency-based surveys (Trainer, 1996). For example, if full-time equivalencies (FTE) are of interest, developers can see whether the IPEDS definitions for FTE could be used. There are a number of advantages to this approach. First, the participants will be able to use a concept and definitions with which they are already familiar. Second, there will very likely already be report methodologies in place that could be repurposed for the new data exchange's survey. Third, there will be considerable time savings for those tasked with working on the data definitions.

The watchwords for a useful data collection instrument are *consistent*, *easy*, and *efficient*. So, when designing the survey instrument, strike a balance between the ease of completing the survey and the efficiency of extracting the data so that it can be analyzed and compiled. Whenever possible, give participants the option of providing survey data in a choice of formats, such as an Excel file or a comma delimited format. Be aware, however, that as the number of data submission methods increases, so does the time required by the coordinating institution to compile the data for use by the membership, especially as the consortium grows.

After defining data elements and providing clear directions for using the survey instrument, the next step is to identify a routine process for cleansing and editing the data and documenting the status of the data once it has been reviewed. The extent to which this should be done will depend in large measure on the needs of the membership, particularly with respect to how the data will be used. Data submissions should be reviewed for completeness.

If possible, developers should build mechanisms into the electronic survey instruments that can detect logical errors, internal consistency problems, and data entry errors and give participants visual cues to alert them to potential problems. Giving participants an opportunity to correct common errors and document anomalies before the data leaves their offices will improve data quality and increase the efficiency of the coordinating office. If additional quality checking is desired, processes can be developed to subject submitted data to computerized error detections applications. Follow-up communications with colleagues and documentation will be needed whenever questions about data completeness, consistency, or possible errors arise.

In a manner similar to that of developing survey instruments, consideration must be given to how data will be reported back to the membership. One of the chief benefits to data exchange members is receiving timely access to data (Hayes, 2003). Developers should determine the amount of analysis and summarization needed before the data are reported back to the participants. Some will value the ability to generate reports online; others may prefer highly formatted printed reports. Member needs and available resources should be the guide in these decisions.

Although voluntary, data exchanges rely on the commitment of their members to cooperatively share data. To be effective, the data exchange needs a clear set of ground rules (Trainer, 1996) or organizing principles of membership. A membership agreement makes clear the cooperative nature of the exchange and the responsibilities of its membership. The formality of the membership agreement will depend on the needs of the originating members. However, it is recommended that the agreements be written, even if just in the form of written minutes, to document the conditions of membership that were developed and approved by the founding members.

One time-honored rule in a data exchange is that an institution must contribute data in order to receive data (Hackett, 1996; Sapp, 1996; Trainer, 1996); this is sometimes referred to as "don't give, don't get." Hackett refers to the work done by a member institution to compile and submit data as "sweat equity." Limiting access to those institutions that contributed data is a way of recognizing the value of a member's contribution and also serves as a powerful incentive for institutions to contribute data.

Trust is the glue that holds a data exchange together. Why would institutions that may be competing with each other for students or grant funding be willing to share data that, in some cases, depicts them in an unfavorable light? Effective data exchanges can overcome this concern because the expectations are made explicit regarding the appropriate use of data. Membership agreements typically require member institutions to agree that data received through the data exchange will be used for internal planning purposes only and that it will not be published without appropriate written permission. Making clear in the membership agreement what constitutes appropriate use of data will help build trust and cooperation among participants.

Each member institution should formally identify an institutional contact who must ensure that their college or university will abide by the conditions of membership. This individual makes certain that data are contributed to the exchange and responds to questions concerning their data. In some situations the primary contact identifies other staff members who can answer specific questions during the data collection process.

Finally, as part of the development phase, developers must consider the level of administrative support needed to operate the exchange activities. Ultimately, the answer will depend on the goals of the exchange and the needs of its membership. Some exchanges can operate by rotating responsibility for coordinating the data-sharing project among willing member institutions. Exchanges whose goal is to have national data collection processes, with extensive data auditing, major data repositories, and a variety of automated reporting options, obviously are more resource intensive. These types of exchanges most likely will include paying a membership fee and contributing data as conditions of membership. Hackett (1996) makes the point that institutions often balk about paying membership fees to participate in a data-sharing exchange. What they may not be considering, according to Hackett, is the inherent cost of poor decisions made in the absence of good information. The efficiencies realized through the centralized data collection and distribution processes of a data exchange are difficult for an individual institution to replicate. More often, exchanges grow and evolve in response to the changing needs of its membership.

Implementation Phase

With these foundational elements in place, developers can invite colleagues at target institutions to join the effort. In addition to sharing the purposes and processes of the new data exchange, developers should provide a production calendar that specifies the dates when surveys are distributed and collected, as well as when compiled data will be available. Get the word out about the new data exchange through meeting presentations, conferences, and requesting that colleagues that have an email discussion list send out a notice about the exchange. Manage expectations by letting new participants know that this will be the first major implementation of the data collection and that input will be sought to improve the process at the end of the first cycle.

It is essential for the development of the data exchange that new members grasp the value of participation in the exchange by seeing their work turned into useful information early in the life of the new exchange (Hackett, 1996).

Review Phase

As Trainer (1996) points out, data exchanges, like other organizations, continue only if they meet the needs of their customers. It is essential for the growth of the data exchange that feedback from the participants be collected, discussed, and considered so that they have a sense of ownership and an expectation that their concerns will be heard. Even if the initial participation in the data exchange cycle is small, the feedback received from participants will be extremely important. Opportunities for improvement can be identified by implementing the newly developed instruments and procedures. The process for review of the mission, membership, and methods of the data exchange should be established. Routine processes for reviewing the work of the data exchange and implementing improvements will strengthen the organization and the commitment of its members.

A thriving, well-functioning organization does not happen by chance. Data exchanges bring institutions that may be competing for students, faculty, and resources together to form a partnership. Data exchanges tap into the true spirit of higher education by expanding knowledge through cooperation (Proulx, 2007). Participating institutions are supported in this cooperative endeavor through a well-crafted framework that ensures the quality of the data shared and makes explicit the requirements for being a member in good standing. The data exchange lifecycle models the process used for building that framework and supporting the ongoing evolution of the data exchange.

References

Achtemeier, S., & Simpson, R. (2005). Practical consideration when using benchmarking for accountability in higher education. *Innovative Higher Education, 30*(2). doi:10.10007/s10700–005–5014–3

Hackett, E. R. (1996, Spring). Creating a cost-effective data exchange. In Trainer, J. (Ed.), *Inter-institutional data exchange: When to do it, what to look for, and how to make it work*. New Directions in Institutional Research, no. 89. San Francisco: Jossey-Bass.

Hayes, R. (2003, May). *Shaping policy and informing practice through data sharing*. Paper presented at Association for Institutional Research, 43rd Forum in Tampa, Florida.

Juhnke, R. (2006). The National Community College Benchmark Project. In J. A. Seybert (Ed.), *Benchmarking: An essential tool for assessment, accountability, and improvement* (pp 67–72). New Directions for Community Colleges, no. 134. San Francisco: Jossey-Bass.

Proulx, R. (2007). Higher education ranking and league tables: Lessons learned from benchmarking. *Higher Education in Europe, 32*(1). doi:10.1080/03797720701618898

Sapp, M. (1996, Spring). Benefits and potential problems associated with effective data-sharing consortia. In Trainer, J. (Ed.), *Inter-institutional data exchange: When to do it, what to look for, and how to make it work*. New Directions in Institutional Research, no. 89. San Francisco: Jossey-Bass.

Shaman, S., & Shapiro, D. (1996, Spring). Data-sharing models. In Trainer, J. (Ed.), *Inter-institutional data exchange: When to do it, what to look for, and how to make it work*. New Directions in Institutional Research, no. 89. San Francisco: Jossey-Bass.

Trainer, J. (1996, Spring). To share and share alike: The basic ground rules for inter-institutional data sharing. In Trainer, J. (Ed.), *Inter-institutional data exchange: When to do it, what to look for, and how to make it work*. New Directions in Institutional Research, no. 89. San Francisco: Jossey-Bass.

CHAPTER 26

BUSINESS INTELLIGENCE AND ANALYTICS

The IR Vision for Data Administration, Reporting, Data Marts, and Data Warehousing

John Milam, John Porter, and John Rome

The many topics, tools, and techniques for institutional research (IR) presented in this volume typically involve the use of data. Different types of data are presented in terms of how they may be collected, analyzed, and reported for some purpose. This requires that the data be obtained, stored, analyzed, and shared.

This process of working with data is often learned based on the need to know, professional development, and mentoring. Historically this approach has worked fairly well, due to sheer effort and good will, but it no longer works because of the "exaflood" of data that is coming toward us. The amounts of data will double every two years for the next decade (Fishman, 2010; Gilder & Swanson, 2008). This phenomenon has "far outstripped our ability to reform or replace the business, legal, and cultural practices that defined our relationship to information in the era before data superabundance" (Yanosky, 2009, p. 12).

New strategies for documenting, storing, and using data require that technologies such as data warehousing be aggressively implemented and expanded and that knowledge management (KM) practices such as business intelligence (BI) and analytics be embraced (Milam, 2001). These strategies require clean, accurate, and meaningful data that are possible only if there is effective data administration. As a result, IR professionals must be active and informed about the principles and standards of data administration and understand the concepts of analytics.

As BI and academic analytics solutions are put in place, frequently it is the IR professional who is most knowledgeable about and prepared to address the legacy and shadow systems of data that exist. It is imperative that institutions have the benefit of IR expertise. To provide this, IR staff must become cofacilitators and cocreators of data solutions. This chapter is designed to help lay out such a strategy.

First we review the status of BI and analytics, because these create many of the demands for managed data. The chapter then provides an introduction to the topics of data administration, data management, and the use of managed data. Solid data administration is critical to ensuring quality data. The complexity of understanding and documenting data requires different roles, functions, and processes to be in place; these are discussed next. The work of managing data involves assessing the constraints and benefits of different data models and designs, such as the use of dimensions, from the perspective of both operational, transaction systems and reporting needs. Data management also addresses issues of security; access; processes for extracting, transforming, and loading data; and data integrity. Under the aegis of using managed data, an expanding range of query and reporting tools, data applications, data marts, and data warehouses provide the systems and technologies for BI and analytics. Finally, we present a vision of what BI and analytics mean in the context of institutional research, with examples gleaned from the authors' experience with institutions and state and federal agencies.

Business Intelligence and Analytics

While there are strong parallels to the work of IR, the concepts of BI and analytics provide emerging technologies for, and new insights into, the analysis and presentation of data. The BI vision encompasses a wide range of tools and approaches to leveraging disparate and complex data that have the potential to transform the dialogue about managing higher education. It is imperative that IR professionals understand how these changes will affect perceptions and expectations of their work.

Business Intelligence

Long before databases and data management, the idea of BI was put forward by Luhn (1958) in the *IBM Journal of Research and Development*. Luhn envisioned that data processing machines would be used to automatically abstract and encode documents and tie them to profiles of interest for organizational "action points." Less appreciated at the time, BI was eclipsed by the corporate focus on database technology and development.

Most often, BI involves the use of technologies for analysis, with "inferences and knowledge discovered by applying algorithmic analysis to acquired information" (March & Hevner, 2007, p. 1031). The authors cite Drucker's four types of information about organizations—*foundation, productivity, competence,* and *resource allocation.* Tools such as the data warehouse make this information understandable and adaptable, and they incorporate "experience-based organizational knowledge" (p. 1035). BI includes "tools an organization uses to gain a greater understanding of operations, markets, and competition" (Bhatnagar, 2009, p. 33).

Online analytical processing (OLAP) functions are used in BI tools to provide "rapid, interactive and easy ad hoc exploration and analysis of data with a multidimensional user interface" (Bedard, Merrett, & Han, 2001, p. 61). First termed in 1993 by Codd (Inmon, 2003), OLAP includes drilling up and down on different levels of aggregation using cubes, as well as the ability to filter, slice, dice, and pivot on data. OLAP is what makes customized reporting possible within a single application, giving infinite possibilities that are not feasible with traditional print reports.

Although BI is a key tool for IR, it encompasses much more than traditional support, with emerging technologies such as digital dashboards and visualization, as well as specialized software applications such as customer relations management (CRM). (See Fayerman, 2002; Luan & Serban, 2002 for discussion of CRM in higher education.) BI includes the development of online data applications, data marts, and data warehouses that provide capabilities far beyond the requirements of mandated federal and state reporting (Phillips, 2010; Swoyer, 2010). BI lets users make sense of transaction-level data extracted from operating systems that were not designed to meet many of a manager's decision-making needs. BI also includes support for environmental scanning, benchmarking, collaboration, and other strategic tools such as KPIs and dashboards. (See Chapter 35 on strategic tools for more discussion of the use of KPIs and dashboards.)

Analytics

BI is "a set of technologies and processes that use data to understand and analyze business performance" (Davenport & Harris, 2007, p. 7). BI includes all three aspects—accessing, reporting, and analyzing the data. Analytics is the "extensive use of data, statistical and quantitative analysis, explanatory and predictive models, and fact-based management to drive decisions and actions" (p. 7). From standard, ad hoc reporting that defines a problem and explains what happened, BI emerges into the language of analytics, which explores questions such as "Why is this happening?" "What will happen next?" and "What's the best that can happen?" (p. 8).

The power of analytics is demonstrated in the success of internet companies such as Google, eBay, and Amazon. These dot-coms "recognize that by continuously analyzing e-content, they can gain intelligence about customers' experience and engagement, products, collections management, channels, partners, target markets, competitors, and much more" (Bhatnagar, 2009, p. 32). There is great potential in the use of analytics to understand enrollment behavior, productivity, and costs, particularly with newly available data about learning management systems (LMSs) such as Blackboard, and learning objects. Much of this type of analytics has been developed for the IR field. (For more information on analytics and data mining, see Chapters 27 and 28. For more information on supporting senior university executives, see Chapter 8.) A fuller discussion of the role of analytics in corporations is given in *Competing on Analytics* (Davenport & Harris, 2007).

Analytics introduces many challenges for institutional researchers because of limitations in technology and the idiosyncratic differences in vendor solutions. At some level of analysis, most technologies lack the flexibility to replicate the policies and practices of the institution. This is especially true when viewing data longitudinally. For example, many institutional researchers apply unique algorithms when calculating official FTE. Replicating all of the calculations in a BI solution may be impossible or may require careful planning on the part of the institutional researcher and IT professional to ensure that the data structures needed for an accurate result are available. Even then, there will be a limit to the level of drill down available to the customer, and the institutional researcher will be required to invest additional effort in maintaining the unique data structures over time. Multiply this many times over, and institutional researchers quickly learn that BI solutions do not reduce workload but rather change its focus.

Data Administration

Operational, administrative information systems are quite complex; they can have multiple modules of processes, thousands of tables with hundreds of data elements each, millions of transactions, and measurements for every transaction. A glimpse into the complexity of these data structures was presented in the 1971 National Center for Higher Education Management Systems (NCHEMS) Data Element Dictionary. Subsequent versions were provided by the Consortium for Higher Education Software Services (CHESS) with its Data Definitions for Colleges and Universities (Thomas, 2004a). What has changed is the complexity of the tables, relationship of entities and attributes, update protocols, and business rules of our current Enterprise Resource Planning (ERP) systems.

The first step in preparing for the exaflood of data is to understand the standard data elements required and report structures needed from each system. These data and reporting requirements include, but are not limited to, curriculum, student, course, human resource (HR), room inventory, space, finance, research, equipment, workforce, noncredit, events management, alumni, and LMS. Also see the chapters on federal databases (Chapter 21) and data exchanges (Chapter 25) in this handbook.

The process of integrating the processes and technology required to produce data is often referred to as data administration. There are several classic descriptions of data administration. Saupe explains that "Data administration is the function that attempts to insure that the data captured from the operational data systems are meaningful" (1990, p. 5).

According to Bernbom (1999), data administration's focus is on the quality of information, working to make sure that data are authentic, authoritative, accurate, shared, intelligible, and secure. The institution-wide view of the data administrator crosses the different transaction-based administrative information systems to look at campus-wide practices and policies. Bernbom also provides a checklist for assessing data management practices, with questions about standards, policies, and procedures for purposes such as reducing or eliminating data redundancy, common definitions for data items, and issues of quality, access, and security.

A recent EDUCAUSE study examines practices in data quality, including whether each major data element has: (1) a system of record, (2) a single definition, (3) been coded and stored consistently across systems, (4) had any value changes propagated across all official systems, and (5) had these changes also made across any shadow systems. It is noted that data quality processes should be in place at the point of capture or origin, be automated to validate data across systems, and document and review all identified quality issues (Yanosky, 2009).

Data administration is part of a continuum of information support functions, along with information planning, standards administration, operational system management support, administrative services, end user support, and technical development (McLaughlin, Howard, Balkan, & Blythe, 1998). If these roles and processes are not formalized and in place, IR end users are "essentially stuck with what data they could get," with "great amounts of time being spent by decision makers quarreling among whose data were 'correct'" (Levy, 2008, p. 34). IR then encounters numerous "inconsistencies between data systems" and difficulty reconciling reports (Saupe, 1990).

These roles and functions mirror, on a larger scale, the issues that are faced in conducting any type of data analysis project (McLaughlin & Howard, 2001). How are the data defined, coded, and stored? How have the rules changed over time? How have the data been extracted, cleansed, standardized, or normalized for use in reporting? How may they be accessed and extracted for different purposes? What is the level of data integrity? What questions do they answer?

Many of the data quality tasks fall under a custodian role, which needs to: (1) "identify critical and key university elements and codes"; (2) "define and document data elements and related codes"; and (3) "measure and verify data and code quality and integrity" (McLaughlin, Howard, Balkan, & Blythe, 1998, p. 42). Yanosky explains that "data should be 'owned' by the people who know it best and have the best incentives to care for it and keep it secure" (2009, p. 7). "Owned" means that custodians feel responsible for data quality—they do not actually "own" the data any more than the comptroller owns tuition dollars. These senior individuals often manage the data stewards who perform the daily tasks of handling the data.

A broker often mediates between the data managers and the data users or customers. The data broker or IR professional "obtains data from various data sources and transforms them into information" (McLaughlin et al., 1998, p. 42). Milam (2005) describes this knowledge management role in IR as the "infomediary." The infomediary "creates or manages systems to connect employees with the knowledge they need" and keeps a "finger on the pulse of the knowledge flowing around the organization" (Costello, 2000, p. 33).

One of the key processes of data administration is the documentation of data about data, or metadata. Three kinds of metadata include (1) process, with statistics about report and system usage; (2) technical, with data element names, descriptions, security, and source information; and (3) business, the rules used to build data items over time, documentation about reports, and training materials (Phillips, 2010). Addressing concerns over global student mobility, there is now movement toward international data interoperability standards for student information systems. Along with the work of the Postsecondary Electronic Standards Council (PESC) and the Common Education Data Standards (CEDS) initiative of the National Center for Education Statistics (NCES), IR must help institutions incorporate these changes in standards for their "impact on the ability to recruit students" and to maintain competitive advantage (Lowendahl, 2010, p. 12).

In application, data administration presents several challenges to institutional researchers, given the IR professional's enterprise view of the data. Coordination with data stewards requires a fair amount of diplomacy and is critical to ensure that the various instances of the data are maintained in the BI environment. For example, "full-time" often means something different academically than when reporting or estimating tuition revenues. Data administration has to preserve both of these views over time, as well as support any needed drill downs. Other data administration challenges often overlooked by institutional researchers have to do with the impact of business rules, some of which may not be fully reflected in data repositories. Sometimes business rules change frozen data, unless all instances of the data are frozen, which often is not practical. The institutional researcher cannot resolve all of these issues, but they must be understood and documented in BI and considered in data administration.

After considering the need to provide BI and analytics, we examined the role of data administration. Now we look at some of the specifics of managing data. This includes designing the data flow, balancing security and access, and creating the data repository or warehouse.

Managing the Data

Managing the data starts from a design concept of balancing effectiveness and efficiency. The implementation of the design concept calls for a balance of access and security. Once these characteristics are considered, it is appropriate to look at how the data will be brought into a repository and how that repository will be developed and managed. This must be done with processes that ensure adequate data integrity.

Design and Efficiency

Design of a data process depends on its purpose. Transaction systems document information about one student, faculty member, expenditure, or class at a time and store the data in a relational data model that is designed to minimize redundancy. They report on the status of the process and the status of any given individual in the process. These systems are very rigid and formalized, with procedures for entering and processing data (Saunders, 1979). Most of these operational systems are now based on a table-type, relational data model, replacing previous sequential data systems that were based on a model of hieratical, indexed, sequentially accessed data. The relational data model, based on a normalized form and the relationships between different tables of information, has existed for more than forty years. Data models are based on a visualization of the dependencies between different objects or types of data in order to avoid inconsistencies and unnecessary relationships (Boehnlein & Ende, 1999). Although efficiency is enhanced for storage, the retrieval of large amounts of data with this model can be very inefficient (Phillips, 2010; Bedard et al., 2001). When data are denormalized and value labels for categorical variables are stored alongside continuous or numeric data, it is easier for the novice data user to do reporting. However, problems arise as one moves from table to table and labels and coding schemes change.

As a result, data warehousing has moved toward the use of the dimensional data model. This is at the heart of Kimball's (2008) *Data Warehouse Lifecycle Toolkit*. The dimensional data model is a "retrieval oriented data storage method" (Phillips, 2010, p. 4). It is "oriented toward measuring a process, rather than collecting data about a process" (p. 8). Facts are measured according to different attributes or dimensions. The combinations of facts and dimensions are called "stars," based on Edelstein's star join model. "Each conformed dimension can be used as needed in the stars associated with any given functional area, such as student records and class records. Conformed dimensions reduce redundancy, reduce ambiguity and allow data from multiple stars to be combined [joined] and reported together" (p. 9). Dimensions may have multiple levels of aggregated data, with the grain as the lowest level. Using cubes, it is possible to roll up or drill down on different dimensions of data (Gray et al., 1997). Conformed dimensions are reusable across applications. Other multidimensional models are the Snowflake Schema and the Fact Constellation (Bedard et al., 2001; Boehnlein & Ende, 1999).

Based on the work of Kimball, nine decision points for dimensional modeling should be considered when building a data model: (1) what process is being modeled? (2) grain of each fact table; (3) dimensions, how facts will be analyzed; (4) facts, precalculated and derived; (5) attributes of dimensions, described in business terms; (6) tracking changes; (7) aggregation and other models; (8) historical duration; and (9) data load urgency (Fish & Stark, 2009).

Functional tables are another approach that is much simpler for the end user. Single tables of data are delivered as a solution that requires no merges or joins by users, bringing together data from disparate systems in a manner similar to a view. Functional tables are comparable to a single worksheet in a spreadsheet, yet the technology behind them allows for refreshing the underlying dimensions, attributes, and values based on the snapshot of data. See Brooks (2005) and Hammons (2006) for their work at the University of Missouri–Rolla.

Fortunately, models for data warehouse applications in each topical area already exist, with descriptions of conformed dimensions for higher education. When needed, new structures are developed by identifying (1) business measures, (2) dimensions and dimension hierarchies, and (3) integrity constraints along the hierarchies (Boehnlein & Ende, 1999).

Each data model and design has its place, relative to the use of traditional, transaction-based systems and the development of data storage and warehousing. For a small IR office that is still doing the most basic of BI tasks—such as publishing factbooks, preparing federal and state reports, and responding to ad hoc requests—functional tables may be a reasonable and accommodating solution, albeit one that more sophisticated offices might tire of. There is no one single design needed for all types of organizations. Rather, the development of technology for sharing data must serve the management style, IT complexity, resources, and academic infrastructure.

Access/Security

IR may be tasked, alongside the information technology (IT) function and the registrar, with ensuring compliance with federal and state laws such as FERPA, FOIA, Education Services Reform Act of 2002 (ESRA), the Confidential Information Protection and Statistical Efficiency Act (CIPSEA), the Health Insurance Portability and Accountability Act (HIPAA), and the Computer Security Act of 1987. IR staff are acutely aware of the issues involved in collecting and sharing individually identifiable data. However, transaction-based systems for admissions, registration, financial aid, finance, and payroll still must include social security numbers and other internal identifiers if they are used for tax, Title IV aid, and immigration reporting; sex offender registries; and state police tracking.

Sophisticated technologies, protocols, and procedures are in place to prevent identify theft and to safeguard the use of these individually identifiable data. Extracts for data warehousing often use an assigned, internal identifier or one that is encrypted. Internal identifiers are promulgated across systems, and their integrity must be maintained for BI use, with lookup tables of changes over time. As is demonstrated by the requirements of obtaining data through the National Student Clearinghouse, much can be done in matching and merging records without the direct use of SSN (Romano & Wisniewski, 2005).

Typically there are fears about lost or stolen data. Some would argue that breaches are rare. As explained in The Data Warehouse Institute's *Best of BI 2009*, "Data security is another constraint but one that is largely illusory" (Eckerson & Russom, 2010, p. 34). Several components of security include "single sign-on," with access based on the roles of the individual user; the use of virtual private networks (VPN) to encrypt all communication; and multiple levels of security (database, file, row/record level, network, and personal computer) (Rome, 2003). This discussion, which can quickly become very technical and complicated, is beyond the scope of this handbook. Every data structure does need to have someone responsible for data security. Each institution should have policies on security and the responsible use of data. Sophisticated social engineering schemes are in place to penetrate security, and these require ongoing training for awareness and prevention.

Levels of access and security clearance are given to users based on business needs, reporting relationships, and account-level rights. Frost, Wang, and Dalrymple (1999) describe a general view for security, which does *not* include personally identifiable data, and a complete view, which gives access to all of the data in a system. Casual users and power users have different access needs. Different data have different levels of sensitivity. The goal, though, is to provide access to those with a legitimate business need for the data. Most IR functions seem to need access to the major databases at their institutions if they are to provide reports and use BI and analytics to support decision making.

In BI, reports developed by institutional researchers for their institution are frequently made accessible through the institution's security system. This means the IR professional needs to develop reports for internal and external use according to an overall plan, because reports tend to be delivered not individually but in groups. Otherwise, delivering reports in BI becomes overly complex and difficult to maintain.

Extract, Transform, Load

With the development of a design that balances efficiency and effectiveness and the creation of a process that balances access and security, the next step is to accumulate the data. This often creates a critical task for IR in obtaining data from different sources. Obtaining these data needs to involve rules for "cleansing, enhancement, restructuring, integration, and aggregation" of the source data (Guan, Nunez, & Welsh, 2002, p. 172).

There should be a primary "information resource dictionary" with a "customer-driven data architecture" that supports structured query language (SQL); is compatible with transaction systems and can be ported to the data warehouse; identifies common and frequently used variables across different systems; and documents metadata, including a description of each data element and where it exists, along with how it is referenced, validated, stored, and used in reporting (McLaughlin et al., 1998). Data dictionaries are now being documented with online tools such as wikis (Thomas, 2004b) and Google Docs. Data repositories need (1) inflow, "consolidating data from legacy systems"; (2) upflow—the "combining, summarizing, and aggregating of data into subject areas"; (3) downflow—the "process of archiving the data"; and (4) outflow, "where data becomes available to the customer" (McLaughlin et al., 1998, pp. 52–53).

Data structures in the relational model are defined in terms of how the entities and their attributes are related to each other. The entity relationships (ERs) in different systems are documented with diagramming tools and provide the content of data definitions (Porter & Rome, 1995). The extraction and merging of data are also very dependent on timing. It is critical for IR to understand the concept of census dates with static data values versus live operational data; the concept is explained by Clagett and Huntington (1990) and Borden, Burton, Keucher, & Vossburg-Conaway (1996). The process for capturing or extracting data from administrative information systems is identified formally as *extract, transform, and load* (ETL). The difficulty of ETL is often underestimated (Inmon, 2003).

It is important to recognize the difference between data used for operational support and data reporting for decision making. Davis, Imhoff, and White (2009) discuss the concept of "operational BI," which is used more directly in support of specific business processes—like registration, helping make them faster, and creating a "closed-loop decision-making environment." Operational systems have many reports that may be used for different levels of internal decisions, such as the monitoring and use of wait lists. Although IR staff may be brought into day-to-day operations, they also have a different function, and they would be well advised to understand when operational versus reporting data are needed and the requirements for data administration within each instance. Census files for official reporting usually receive a high level of scrutiny, data cleansing, and data integrity checks. It is critical to anticipate how the data will be used and to know the results of key reports before they are submitted to regulatory bodies.

Data Integrity

According to Gose (1989, p. 1), data integrity "concerns the error-free (noncorrupted) or error-prone (corrupted) integrity of data." Sometimes this is relatively straightforward. Saunders (1979), for example, describes a typical use of an HR extract prepared by the payroll office for analysis of faculty salaries. The custodian of the data looks at them from the perspective of the system's function: getting people paid. Built-in audit checks ensure that the salaries are correct. However, there may be no such checks for data pulled from other, related tables, such as biographical information about terminal degrees. Unfortunately, sometimes there is little incentive for someone to maintain the integrity of a data element when it does not directly affect the process that person is working on (Valcik & Stigdon, 2008). Fishbone diagrams are a useful technique for documenting breakdowns in data integrity, provided in the total quality management literature on process improvement. (See Chapter 37 for more discussion of ways to support process quality.)

There are many sources of data integrity problems. As explained by Gose (1989), these include "changes in institutional policies, new meaning associated with a datum, user experimentation with the system, purging/consolidation of corrupted data, referential integrity, inadequate analysis and testing of software, running obsolete versions of a program, restructuring set relationships on a database, and the trade-off between editing and performance" (p. 2). Problems in referential integrity occur when changes to a lookup table of values do not get propagated fully throughout the system, resulting in invalid or outdated codes. It is necessary to understand the use of primary keys for distinct records and foreign keys to link records with references to other tables. "Rampant data duplication" and the lack of data element continuity are discussed by Nakabo-Ssewanyana (1999). Issues are also encountered when extracts from different data structures are combined (Levy, 2008; Valcik & Stigdon, 2008).

The level of organizational reporting possible between two systems or silos of data may not be identical, so different levels of aggregation may be needed. IR users need to create crosswalks or mappings for different purposes; see Milam (2006) for a discussion of taxonomies. Sometimes different levels of aggregation must be used as imperfect lenses on the data.

Using Managed Data

After a discussion of opportunities for using BI and analytics, we examined data administration as a way to support them. A balance of efficiency and effectiveness and access and security are needed for sufficient integrity for both reporting and management decision making. In this section, we discuss using these data.

Reporting, Topical Data Applications, and Data Marts

The design of IR reports is discussed by Sanders and Filkins (2009) in terms of purpose, audience, structure, format, and use of technology for delivery. This discussion is also part of their chapter in this handbook (Chapter 33).

Much of the process for publishing reports changed with the emergence of the World Wide Web in 1993. As explained by Massa, "From a single page of results, as in an executive summary, down to the source data itself, the information can be published and interlinked within itself, allowing the reader to drill up or down between levels of aggregation of the data as desired" (2003, p. 120). As mentioned, this "presentation component" is often called BI, representing "different levels of services from simple reporting to roll-up and drill-down functionality to true ad hoc query capability" (Guan et al., 2002, p. 172). The IR task of delivering data involves the need to "match format to analytical sophistication and learning preferences of recipients" (Clagett & Huntington, 1990, p. 23). The evolution of web-based reporting in IR is described by Massa (2003), Milam (1999), and others.

The advent of the Internet ushered in an era of static HTML and then dynamic, data-driven reports to meet the growing demand for customization. Online data applications continue to evolve—with different database packages, scripting and programming languages, and middleware products that communicate between the two—along with the constraints of web servers and operating systems. The user usually just needs a browser, with reports that are designed to be "as intuitive as possible, so that no training at all would be required" (Maxwell, 2008, p. 41). Numerous tools are available. When selecting tools, it is important that they be easy to use, support connectivity with the databases and middleware being used, cross databases and platforms, export results in multiple formats, support ad hoc and static queries, web-enabled, and affordable (Rome, 2003).

Data marts are stand-alone data structures built for a specific problem or application (Rome, 2003). They are often "initial efforts" at distributing data for BI. Data marts can be built more quickly and at lower cost, but can duplicate the effort of a warehouse. Some of the responsibilities for extracting and cleansing the data for a data mart are the same as for a warehouse, though there is sometimes greater knowledge of the specific data types involved and how they can inform management (Borden, Massa, & Milam, 2001). Data marts are usually "independent of other data stores, and serve specific, localized needs, such as providing data for a particular application or business unit" (Ariyachandra & Watson, 2008, p. 146). Data are stored in the way that best supports how they are used.

Data Warehousing

Because the use of data often involves their integration from many functional areas, the individual data mart is not able to meet evolving institutional needs. The next step, therefore, is to integrate data across functional data areas into a warehouse. The definition of a data warehouse has been standardized on Inmon's (1996) description as "a subject-oriented, integrated, non-volatile, and time-variant collection of data used to support management's decisions" (p. 33). It is integrated, with data from different systems; subject-oriented to answer a variety of questions organized by topic; time-variant, representing different points in time based on periodic extracts, not tied to current transactions; and non-volatile, in that data are never deleted, but expanded upon (Guan et al., 2002; Rome, 2009).

Kimball (1996, p. 310) explains the data warehouse as "a copy of transaction data specifically structured for query and analysis" and Kelly (1996, p. 55) as "a single, integrated store of corporate data which provides the infrastructural basis for informational applications in the enterprise." Rome's definition expands upon this as "an integrated repository of enterprise-generated, departmentally captured, and/or externally acquired data used to facilitate data access, reporting, and tactical/strategic decision-making" (2003, p. 3).

Legacy systems built for processing transactions are the original source of current, detailed data, using a normalized structure. In comparison, the warehouse is built for analysis and decision support using current and historical, read-only data that are aggregated into summary form with a denormalized structure (Bedard et al., 2001). The key challenge is that a warehouse needs to be "designed for change," evolving with new data, definitions, and tools (March & Hevner, 2007). A variety of specialized tools are necessary for a warehouse, including data modeling, ETL, database, and reporting/BI. A variety of roles are also necessary as part of a data warehouse team, including manager, sponsor, technical architect, database administrator, business analyst, data transformation analyst/programmer, BI analyst, and trainer (Rome, 2003).

Thomas, Lorenz, Schaefer, Sullivan, & Wright (2009) provide an IR perspective on expectations for the data warehouse with presentations about "What I Get/Wish I Could Get from the Warehouse: The View from Institutional Research." The data warehouse should provide IR with:

1. Snapshot data
2. Clean data, subjected to edit rules and procedures and carefully constructed with rules for translating problem records
3. Carefully constructed data, with value-added variables for executive reporting
4. Carefully documented and disseminated data, designed to reduce user confusion, especially when there are multiple definitions, and with a BI front-end that directs users to the most helpful data
5. Workload reduction, giving users self-service for simple reporting tasks
6. Access to data, not just reports with analytic statistics
7. Data structured to support a spectrum of reports and analytics
8. Data integrated with the rest of the warehouse to support validation of reports and answer questions that bridge functional areas
9. Effective collaboration with IR on definitions, testing, priorities, data modeling, and prototyping reports
10. An appropriate role for IR to play in developing and managing BI and the warehouse

Kimball's methodology for building and deploying a data warehouse documents these steps: (1) project definition; (2) identifying requirements; (3) system design, data modeling, implementation, and application development; (4) reporting system deployment; and (5) reporting system maintenance, assessment, and improvement (Phillips, 2010). When applied to higher education, this process has special challenges. Some standards are difficult to enforce. Federal, state, and accreditation oversight is greater, with an increasing burden for mandated reporting. Decision making involves consensus building with faculty, staff, and other stakeholders. The complexity of institutions like universities is daunting, with a large customer set and payroll, along with other income sources, a number of accounts, and fixed assets.

Wierschem, McBroom, and McMillen (2003) present a methodology for developing a data warehouse that is based on the system development life cycle (SDLC) of analysis, design, and implementation. Analysis involves understanding what currently exists: demands and requirements, needs and feasibility. Design examines optimal software and hardware technology and how the warehouse will break free of the limits of the legacy systems. Discussion of operations—such as updates, servers, reporting tools, query tools, and interfaces—are addressed as part of design. Implementation makes analysis and design into a working system.

The evolution of a data warehouse may be understood using The Data Warehouse Institute's Maturity Model, which has six stages: prenatal (production reporting), infant (spreadmarts), child (data marts), teenager (data warehouses), adult (enterprise DW), and sage (analytic services). As of April 2009, Cornell and Arizona State University rated themselves teenagers, with ASU on its eighteenth birthday; Rensselaer Polytechnic Institute saw itself as an adult, and Indiana University as a "tween" (Wilhelm, Rome, Singleton, & Start, 2009).

Another scale is provided by an EDUCAUSE study: (1) transaction system only; (2) operational data store or single mart, no ETL; (3) operational data store or single mart with ETL and reporting tools; (4) data warehouse or multiple marts, with no ETL, OLAP, or dashboards; (5) data warehouse or multiple marts, with ETL, no OLAP or dashboards; and (6) enterprise-wide, data warehouse or marts with ETL, reporting tools, dashboards, and/or alerts (Goldstein, 2005).

Lessons from a successful data warehouse implementation at Arizona State University are described by Porter and Rome (1995). These include recommendations to: (1) "develop an enterprise strategy," (2) "identify a project champion," (3) "avoid cost justification," (4) "be ready for technology shortfalls," (5) "make users aware of costs up front," (6) "find ways to capture metadata," (7) "build integrity and integration," (8) "let the warehouse fill operational gaps," (9) "invest in training," and (10) "make sure a support structure is in place" (p. 47). A decade later, Rome (2003, p. 32) explains more lessons learned, including: (1) secure a budget, (2) have a historical data plan, (3) "build in integrity and integration," (4) "remember that data quality is not as good as you think," (5) capture useful metadata, (6) "be aware that customers will want more granular data with more frequent loads," (7) "support all tools but standardize on one," (8) "make customers happy," and (9) "invest in end-user support."

Business Intelligence and Analytics in the Context of Institutional Research

BI and analytics are not new to IR. However, as these tools are used increasingly by other offices and functions to address the exaflood of data, newcomers do not have the time or inclination to understand the contribution of IR's role and knowledge base. It is important that the work of IR is leveraged so that organizations build on existing capacity, use resources wisely, and meet critical information needs. That said, what has IR learned over the years about using BI and analytics that is important for newcomers to BI and analytics to know?

First, there are key report structures and displays used to monitor progress and goals, and these do not need to be created from scratch simply because of a change in tools and perspective. Whether they be simple performance measures used for peer comparison or tabular lists of data displayed in groups of rows and columns, there are standards for effective presentation of census and operational data that should be used. There are many models for static, dynamic, and print publications; factbooks; dashboards; and data applications suited to different audiences, institutional missions, and technology. There is no substitute for understanding the key ways to collect, analyze, and present data by type or for being able to negotiate the problems in mapping data from different sources.

BI vendors with data mart, data warehouse, interactive BI, and dashboard products usually provide a list of tables to be extracted and loaded from operational systems, demonstrate how these may be used to create an underlying data structure with meaningful tables and reporting dimensions for each silo of data, and then provide sample displays of standardized reports and graphs. The list of tables, variables, dimensions, report structures, graphical displays, and topical dashboards is well evolved for each transaction system. One can find extensive guidance about the levels of aggregation that are of interest to managers, along with ways to drill down on the data to meaningful details. In planning for BI and analytics, the availability and maturity level of these features need to be assessed.

If starting from scratch, the history of failed and unappreciated attempts at comparable reports and dashboards by IR is very useful. For example, there are many efforts at daily enrollment monitoring reports and the comparison of key measures of new students and transfers to targets and projections. Previous effective use of project champions, team partnerships, and ways to prevent scope creep are also important to understand. If an effort has been under way for some time, what are the roadblocks and milestones? Are the table structures too complex, the reports redundant? How are different types of users using the reports? How has the user community grown and changed? Many factbook displays and common reports are developed to anticipate ad hoc requests. After a while they appear routine and less interesting, but they are still needed. Is there an evaluation of the BI initiative with satisfaction ratings by customers, comments about process problems, and a plan for change management?

In reviewing the authors' experience with BI and analytics, we looked at lessons learned from work with Arizona State University (ASU), the State University of New York (SUNY) system, George Mason University (GMU), and the U.S. Department of Education's NCES.

ASU was an early adopter, implementing a student warehouse in 1992–93. IR has been integral in its development, acceptance, and usage. A recent ERP implementation led to the replacement of the homegrown warehouse with a purchased solution that was integrated with the new ERP. One lesson from this upgrade is that packaged warehouses are really "starter kits" that require significant expansion and enrichment after installation.

Today, ASU's ERP data warehouse is mission critical to the institution: operationally, tactically, and strategically. ASU no longer has information silos. However, although BI and analytics have been instrumental to success, there is still a tendency to duplicate reports and queries. Also, the complexity of the data structures, dimensional models, and ETL presents a challenge to effectively utilize these tools.

BI and analytics have great potential to benefit IR at the state and system level as well. The SUNY system uses data warehousing, BI, and analytics for its student longitudinal systems. The technology helps facilitate the development of information as it is received, stored, and migrated into the data warehouse.

Like other state unit record systems, the SUNY system collects files of data via the Web, enforcing various business rules. Records with data errors must be corrected before a submission is locked. BI and analytics are used by system staff to review the reasonableness and completeness of data before they are accepted for migration into the central data repository. There is a matching process to identify new records and assign unique student IDs. Once migrated into SUNY's repository, data are loaded into data warehouse stars. When loading the stars, various derivations are applied to make them useful. Dashboards are used to communicate information in the submission process, benchmark key performance metrics, and help campuses improve source data over time. (For further discussion of data management in state agencies, see Chapter 23.)

A homegrown data warehouse was launched by George Mason University's IR office in 1995 using ColdFusion and SQL Server, with aggregate reports with drill down capability on cubes and dimensions of student enrollment, course, human resources, finance, space, and induced course load matrix (ICLM) data. Some of these applications are still in place today. They have allowed managers to view data in standardized but customizable, reports for their areas of responsibility, using census snapshots, daily and monthly extracts, and trend displays. Although more official data warehouse initiatives have eclipsed this effort, the goals are different and the utility of the original report structures has not changed, for two reasons: (1) they were created to be relevant and timely to the typical, ongoing work of individuals and their specific roles, providing data not available elsewhere; and (2) the data come from the IR office and are therefore more clean, reliable, and consistent with other official reports.

In developing online BI applications for NCES over the course of a decade, tools were designed to accommodate various levels of sophistication with the intricacies of IPEDS and working with data generally. Some of the applications dynamically generate graphs and PDF publications, allowing for a high level of customization. Others handle complex merges, recodes, and transformations from multiple years of multirecord data and qualifying variables behind the scenes so that simple tables of data, syntax programs, and documentation are provided to users for analysis.

This is analogous to the ETL process for taking complex tables from a transaction system and creating meaningful dimensions that are then presented to users with the seemingly simple and intuitive display of a digital dashboard. As applications evolve over time and are subsumed under other development efforts, it is worthwhile to note their changes in features and purpose, as well as the success that comes with continuous improvement and actively addressing customer needs and interests.

These institutional, state system, and federal examples provide just a glimpse into what is possible with BI and analytics. They also hint at the competing visions and constraints that face IT and IR as they work together to create applications and serve as trusted stewards of the data.

Additional Resources

Given the brevity of this chapter, we recommend that the reader seek out a comprehensive book on the topic, such as Kimball and Ross's (2010) *The Kimball Group Reader*. Those interested in data administration and data warehousing may want to participate in the Higher Education Data Warehouse Forum (HEDW) (http://www.hedw.org); and EDUCAUSE (http://www.educause .edu). The associations AIR and Society for College and University Planning (SCUP) have related tracks and sessions at their national and regional meetings. There are also numerous BI and analytics resources under the umbrella of each vendor's formal and informal user groups.

References

Ariyachandra, T., & Watson, H. J. (2008). Which data warehouse architecture is best? *Communications of the ACM, 51*(10), 146–147.

Bedard, Y., Merrett, T., & Han, J. (2001). Fundamentals of spatial data warehousing for geographic knowledge discovery. In H. J. Miller and J. Han (Eds.), *Geographic data mining and knowledge discovery* (pp. 53–73). London: Taylor and Francis.

Bernbom, G. (1999). Institution-wide information management and its assessment. In J. Pettit and L. Litten (Eds.), *A new era of alumni research: Improving institutional performance and better serving alumni* (pp. 72–83). New Directions for Institutional Research, no. 109. San Francisco: Jossey-Bass.

Bhatnagar, A. (2009, November/December). Web analytics for business intelligence. *Online*, pp. 32–35.

Boehnlein, M., & Ende, A. U. (1999). Deriving initial data warehouse structure from the conceptual data models of the underlying operational information systems. Paper presented at DOLAP 1999 conference in Kansas City, MO.

Borden, V.M.H., Burton, K. L., Keucher, S. L., & Vossburg-Conaway, F. (1996). Setting a census date to optimize enrollment, retention, and tuition revenue projects. *AIR Professional File*, no. 62.

Borden, V.M.H., Massa, T., & Milam, J. (2001). Technology and tools for institutional research. In R. D. Howard (Ed.), *Institutional research: Decision support in higher education* (pp. 195–222). Resources for Institutional Research. Tallahassee, FL: Association for Institutional Research.

Brooks, A. (2005). The data warehouse: A transitional bridge between Legacy and PeopleSoft. PowerPoint presentation at CUMREC 2005 Conference in Keystone, CO.

Clagett, C. A., & Huntington, R. B. (1990). *The institutional research practitioner: A guidebook to effective performance.* Silver Spring, MD: Red Inc. Publications.

Costello, D. (2000). For knowledge, look within: Businesses are discovering the value of internal infomediaries. *Knowledge Management, 3*(9), 33, 39–41.

Davenport, T. H., & Harris, J. G. (2007). *Competing on analytics: The new science of winning.* Cambridge: Harvard Business School Press.

Davis, J. R., Imhoff, C., & White, C. (2009). Operational business intelligence: The state of the art. *Business Intelligence Research.* Retrieved from http://www.b-eye-network.com/files/Operational%20BI%20Research%20Report.pdf

Eckerson, W., & Russom, P. (2010). Can BI and DW teams find benefits in recession? Or, the data mart and the pendulum. *TDWI's Best of BI, 7.*

Fayerman, M. (2002). Customer relationship management. In A. M. Serban and J. Laun (Eds.), *Knowledge management: Building a competitive advantage in higher education* (pp. 57–67). New Directions for Institutional Research, no. 113. San Francisco: Jossey-Bass.

Fish, O., & Stark, J. (2009, April). Dimensional modeling workshop. PowerPoint presentation at Higher Education Data Warehousing Forum conference in Bloomington, IN.

Fishman, J. (2010, February 24). Professors find ways to keep heads above "exaflood" of data. *Chronicle of Higher Education*, Wired Campus.

Frost, J., Wang, M., & Dalrymple, M. (1999). A new focus for institutional researchers: Developing and using a student decision support system. *AIR Professional File*, no. 73.

Gilder, G., & Swanson, B. (2008). *The impact of video and rich media on the Internet: A "zettabyte" by 2015?* Seattle: Discovery Institute.

Goldstein, P. J. (2005). Academic analytics: The uses of management information and technology in higher education. EDUCAUSE Center for Applied Research.

Gose, F. J. (1989). Data integrity: Why aren't the data accurate? *AIR Professional File*, no. 33.

Gray, J., et al. (1997). Data cube: A relational aggregation operator generalizing group-by, cross-tab, and sub-totals. *Data Mining and Knowledge Discovery, 1*, 29–53.

Guan, J., Nunez, W., & Welsh, J. F. (2002). Institutional strategy and information support: The role of data warehousing in higher education. *Campus-Wide Information Systems, 19*(5), 168–174.

Hammons, J. (2006). Data warehousing: A proven solution to sustaining a vibrant business. PowerPoint presentation at EDUCAUSE 2006 conference in Dallas, TX. Retrieved from http://www.educause.edu/Resources/DataWarehousingAProvenSolution/156192

Inmon, W. H. (1996). *Building the data warehouse* (2nd ed.). New York: Wiley.

Inmon, W. H. (2003). The story so far. *Computerworld, 37*(15), 26.

Kelly, S. (1996). *Data warehousing*. New York: Wiley.

Kimball, R. (1996). *The data warehouse toolkit: Practical techniques for building dimensional data warehouses*. New York: Wiley.

Kimball, R., et al. (2008). *Data warehouse lifecycle toolkit*. Indianapolis: Wiley.

Kimball, R., & Ross, M. (2010). *The Kimball Group Reader: Relentlessly practical tools for data warehousing and business intelligence*. Indianapolis: Wiley.

Levy, G. D. (2008). A beginner's guide to integrating human resources faculty data and cost data. In N. A. Valcik (Ed.), *Using financial and personnel data in a changing world for institutional research* (pp. 25–47). New Directions for Institutional Research, no. 140. San Francisco: Jossey-Bass.

Lowendahl, J.-M. (2010). *Hype cycle for education, 2010*. Stamford, CT: Gartner.

Luan, J., & Serban, A. (2002). Technologies, products, and models supporting knowledge management. In A. M. Serban and J. Laun (Eds.), *Knowledge management: Building a competitive advantage in higher education* (pp. 85–104). New Directions for Institutional Research, no. 113. San Francisco: Jossey-Bass.

Luhn, H. P. (1958). A business intelligence system. *IBM Journal of Research and Development, 2*(4), 314–319.

March, S. T., & Hevner, A. R. (2007). Integrated decision support systems: A data warehousing perspective. *Decision Support Systems, 43*, 1031–1043.

Massa, T. (2003). Using the Web for institutional research. In William E. Knight (Ed.), *The primer for institutional research*. Resources for Institutional Research, no. 14. Tallahassee, FL: Association for Institutional Research.

Maxwell, C. J. (2008). Building and operating a web-based reporting system: A case study. In T. T. Ishitani (Ed.), *Alternative perspectives in institutional planning* (pp. 41–56). New Directions for Institutional Research, no. 137. San Francisco: Jossey-Bass.

McLaughlin, G. W., & Howard, R. D. (2001). Theory, practice, and ethics of institutional research. In R. D. Howard (Ed.), *Institutional research: Decision support in higher education* (pp. 163–194). Resources for Institutional Research. Tallahassee, FL: Association for Institutional Research.

McLaughlin, G. W., Howard, R. D., Balkan, L. A., & Blythe, E. W. (1998). *People, processes, and managing data*. Resources for Institutional Research, no. 11. Tallahassee, FL: Association for Institutional Research.

Milam, J. (1999). Using the Internet for institutional research and planning. ASHE Reader on Institutional Research, Association for the Study of Higher Education.

Milam, J. (2001). Knowledge management for higher education. In ERIC Digest. ED 464 520. Washington, DC: ERIC Clearinghouse on Higher Education. Retrieved from http://www.ericdigests.org/2003–1/higher.htm

Milam, J. (2005). Organizational learning through knowledge workers and infomediaries. In A. Kezar, *Higher education as a learning organization: Promising concepts and approaches* (pp. 61–73). New Directions for Higher Education, no. 131. San Francisco: Jossey-Bass.

Milam, J. (2006). Ontologies in higher education.. In A. S. Metcalfe (Ed.), *Knowledge management and higher education: A critical analysis* (pp. 34–61). Hershey, PA: Information Science Publishing.

Nakabo-Ssewanyana, Sarah. (1999). Statistical data: The underestimated tool for higher education management. *Higher Education, 37*, 259–279.

Phillips, J. (2010). Reporting solutions. Higher Education User Group Product Advisory Group—Reporting Solutions. White paper. Retrieved from http://www.heug.org/p/do/sd/sid=10238&type=0 (login required)

Porter, J. D., & Rome, J. J. (1995, Winter). Lessons from a successful data warehouse implementation. *CAUSE/EFFECT*, pp. 43–50.

Romano, R. M., & Wisniewski, M. (2005). Tracking community college transfers using National Student Clearinghouse data. *AIR Professional File*, no. 94. Tallahassee, FL: Association for Institutional Research.

Rome, J. (2003). *Development of data warehouse.* Washington, DC: NACUBO.

Rome, J. (2009). Designing dashboards to die for. PowerPoint presentation at Higher Education Data Warehousing Forum, Bloomington, IN.

Sanders, L., & Filkins, J. (2009). *Effective reporting* (2nd ed.). Tallahassee, FL: Association for Institutional Research.

Saunders, L. E. (1979). Dealing with information systems: The institutional researcher's problems and prospects. *AIR Professional File*, no. 2. Tallahassee, FL: Association for Institutional Research.

Saupe, J. L. (1990). *The functions of institutional research* (2nd ed.). Tallahassee, FL: Association for Institutional Research.

Swoyer, S. (2010). BI's value put to the test. *TDWI's Best of BI*, 7, 5–9.

Thomas, C. R. (2004a). *CHESS data definitions for colleges and universities.* Boulder, CO: National Center for Higher Education Management Systems.

Thomas, C. R. (2004b). Data warehouse efforts and metadata foundations. EDUCAUSE. Retrieved from http://www.educause.edu/Resources/DataWarehouseEffortsand Metadat/159178

Thomas, E., Lorenz, L., Schaefer, E., Sullivan, L., & Wright, D. (2009, April). What I get/wish I could get from the warehouse: The view from institutional research. PowerPoint presentation at Higher Education Data Warehousing Forum conference in Bloomington, IN.

Valcik, N. A., & Stigdon, A. D. (2008). Using personnel and financial data for reporting purposes: What are the challenges to using such data accurately? In N. A. Valcik (Ed.), *Using financial and personnel data in a changing world for institutional research*, (pp. 13–24). New Directions for Institutional Research, no. 140. San Francisco: Jossey-Bass.

Wierschem, D., McBroom, R., & McMillen, J. (2003). Methodology for developing an institutional data warehouse. *AIR Professional File*, no. 88.

Wilhelm, J., Rome, J., Singleton, J., & Start, J. (2009, April). Building for analytics: Critical success factors. PowerPoint presentation at Higher Education Data Warehousing Forum conference in Bloomington, IN.

Yanosky, R. (2009). Institutional data management in higher education. EDUCAUSE Center for Applied Research, p. 12. Retrieved from http://net.educause.edu/ir/library/pdf/ers0908/rs/ers0908w.pdf

INSTITUTIONAL RESEARCH TOOLS AND TECHNIQUES

Institutional research has grown and developed primarily as an analytical administrative function of the institution and the scholarly activity of research, as represented by its name. The core of these capabilities comes from an ability to use a broad range of tools and techniques in its practice. The first section of Part Four is composed of seven chapters that include social science research techniques that form a basis of our traditional research skills. They include analytic techniques, used primarily to study two key components of our institutions—students and faculty—and a report on the results of our analytical studies.

The second section of Part Four addresses the institutional elements of our discipline, with five chapters specifically focused on managing our institutions and the IR office. The first three of these chapters (34, 35, and 36) relate to traditional management tools; the final two relate to the improvement of the effectiveness of our institutions and our institutional research offices.

Chapters 27 and 28 deal with analyzing data. In Chapter 27, Gerald McLaughlin, Richard Howard, and Daniel Jones-White provide a basic overview of analytic research techniques. These include basic hypothesis testing, descriptive statistics, univariate and multivariate analyses, and modeling of outcomes. The qualitative techniques reviewed include six approaches to collecting and analyzing data. There is also a review of mixed methods.

In Chapter 28, Jing Luan, Thulasi Kumar, Sutee Sujitparapitaya, and Tom Bohannon set the context for data mining. They then demonstrate the use of three advanced techniques, presented as case studies: (1) cluster analysis, (2) decision tree, and (3) artificial neural nets. Although these techniques are relatively new, recent developments in technology and databases make them increasingly relevant to our work. The authors conclude with recommendations for using data mining.

The next two chapters are the core of how we collect much of the data that we use in our studies of students, faculty, and staff. In Chapter 29, Sean Simone, Corbin Campbell, and Daniel Newhart present the basic aspects of research inquiry. For those doing a survey, they describe the key steps: developing research questions, creating the survey questions, creating and testing the instrument, and interpreting the results. They also discuss conducting focus group interviews and unobtrusive measures.

In Chapter 30, Julie Noble and Richard Sawyer discuss instruments currently available to support decision making about students, as well as key issues in the use of these instruments. This includes the traditional tests for academic performance and the alternative of noncognitive measurement. They discuss instruments to support decisions in the movement of students through colleges. They also identify an extensive list of websites containing an extremely broad range of instruments, with a discussion of their use.

The focus of the next two chapters is the methodologies measuring key aspects of faculty: their activities and their salaries. In Chapter 31, Heather Kelly, Jeffrey Seybert, Patrick Rossol, and Allison Walters discuss the major resources available for studying faculty activities, which include federal surveys, national surveys, and data sharing consortia. They describe databases for four-year institutions and community colleges, with examples of how these data might be used.

Salaries are one of the prime means of rewarding faculty. In Chapter 32, Robert Toutkoushian and Dennis Kramer review the purposes and methodologies of faculty equity studies. They discuss conducting external and internal studies and the current state of modeling salaries. The chapter also includes a discussion of unresolved issues, such as the use of rank as

an explanatory variable, how to measure productivity, and compression.

The final chapter in this section on traditional research covers the reporting of results. In Chapter 33, Liz Sanders and Joe Filkins show how effective reporting is the key to delivering informative results. They review tabular alternatives and the use of visual displays, including dashboards, and discuss the reporting of qualitative data. Finally, they comment on communicating results. A list of practices that should be avoided is part of their discussion.

As previously noted, the authors of the final five chapters in Part Four discuss the means by which institutional research can support the management of our institutions—tools and techniques for viewing and supporting the institutional aspect of our profession. These techniques span the various institutional functions discussed in Parts Two and Three. The authors discuss the decisions informed by the data and information frequently created by tools described in the first section of Part Four.

In Chapters 34 and 35, Jan Lyddon, Bruce McComb, and Patrick Mizak lay out a roadmap for supporting strategic decision making. Chapter 34 contains tools for evaluating an institution's situation and for developing and evaluating strategies to be successful in that context. Knowledge of the environment must be integrated with the institution's mission and its resources. This chapter also lays out the steps for benchmarking and setting benchmarks.

The success of strategy depends on implementation and monitoring. In Chapter 35, the authors discuss executing strategy metrics that form key performance indicators. These indicators need to represent a balanced view of the institution's strategic issues. The use of these KPIs in scorecards and dashboards is demonstrated, with examples that show how these tools work together with strategy maps.

Setting goals and objectives for KPIs often requires the use of an appropriate group of other institutions to make comparisons about quality and productivity. In Chapter 36, Glenn James describes the steps in this process. This discussion includes identifying the different types of institutional groups that a college or university might find useful and exploring how the comparison group might be used. Also described are the methodologies that can be used for forming these groups.

In the final two chapters, 37 and 38, specific methodologies for organizational improvement are discussed. As such, they bridge back to the chapters in Part One concerning the practice of IR in organizational learning (Chapter 6) and change management (Chapter 7).

In Chapter 37, Jonathan Fife and Stephen Spangehl discuss the concepts that underpin improving institutional effectiveness and quality. They illustrate specific processes that can improve quality in closed organizational systems. They also describe the available tools for identifying where to start and demonstrating that progress is being made. They stress the importance of having the appropriate organizational culture to achieve improvement.

The focus of the final chapter is on IR use of tools to improve the effectiveness of our offices. In Chapter 38, Sharron Ronco, Sandra Archer, and Patricia Ryan reflect on how IR can improve its own effectiveness and efficiency, asking: What does IR do? Are we doing the right things? Are we doing things right? They examine ways in which the staff in an institutional research office can evaluate themselves and their work. Options include doing a self-study, getting customer feedback, and obtaining external feedback.

Chapter 38 was specifically selected as the final chapter in this *Handbook* to emphasize that we must apply continued evaluation and improvement to ourselves and our responsibilities as well as to other activities on our campuses and in the higher education environment. We began, in the first chapter of this volume, with a discussion of the growth and evolution of the profession's history. In this final chapter, we conclude with a reminder of the need to apply our professional knowledge and analytical skills introspectively to continually improve the capabilities and effectiveness of our profession.

CHAPTER 27

ANALYTIC APPROACHES TO CREATING PLANNING AND DECISION SUPPORT INFORMATION

Gerald McLaughlin, Richard Howard, and Daniel Jones-White

Best and Kahn (1998) describe research as "the systematic and objective analysis and recording of controlled observations that may lead to the development of generalizations, principles, or theories, resulting in prediction and possibly ultimate control of events" (p. 18). This classic definition of research reflects the purpose for which quantitative methods of producing information were developed.

During the past two decades arguments have been raised about the relevance of traditional empirical research as related to understanding the feelings and behaviors of people. These arguments have posited that the use of experimental designs creates an artificial situation or environment and results in artificial reactions or behaviors on the part of the research subjects. These arguments have suggested that qualitative methods—that is, methods that study the individual holistically, rather than by controlling all aspects but one of the phenomena being studied—are the only way to understand *truth*.

These two approaches to creating knowledge are guided by two paradigms, *positivist* and *constructivist* (or *naturalist*). Developing a thorough discussion, comparing and contrasting these two paradigms and their implications for the conduct of research, is beyond the scope of this chapter; we refer the reader to Guba (1991) and Gliner and Morgan (2000) for descriptions and comparisons of the two paradigms. However, there are several philosophical questions that reflect important differences in how one thinks about reality and as such how one attempts to create knowledge (Howard and Borland, 1999). These differences are summarized in Table 27.1.

TABLE 27.1   KEY QUESTIONS: CONSTRUCTIVIST VERSUS POSITIVIST

Question	Constructivist	Positivist
"What is truth?"	Truth is relative to a point in time, the place observed, and perceptions of the researcher.	Truth is orderly and lawful, and predictable, with cause-and-effect relationships, and allows us to predict behavior.
"What is studied?"	Human beings are studied as holistically individuals within natural systems.	Studying defined variables and selected individuals allows researchers to generalize to groups.
"What is the role of the researcher?"	The researcher is the primary instrument for all steps that typically influence observations in the research.	The researcher designs the research as a neutral party and objectively interprets the data.
"What can be accomplished?"	Descriptive results are possible, with sufficient key detail to generalize to other situations.	Statistically conclusive interpretations are possible, with assignable risk of mistakes.

These two perspectives have tended toward different methodologies: the positivist has favored quantitative approaches, and the constructivist has tended to favor qualitative approaches. Both approaches have analytical methodologies that can be of value in the conduct of institutional research. In the following section, we discuss some of the main techniques for both quantitative and qualitative approaches and also briefly touch on mixed methods, a strategy for using a combination of qualitative and quantitative tools.

Quantitative Approaches and Methods

Quantitative analytics involve the purposeful use of numbers to convey meaning. This use has discernible steps and identifiable characteristics. It also involves the measurement of variables.

Types of Measurement

The level of measurement available to the researcher greatly influences the choice of appropriate analyses. The four basic levels of measurement scales are

Nominal: Objects are assigned to a category or set of categories based on their attributes.

Ordinal: Objects are assigned to a metric that can be used to rank order the objects.

Interval: Objects are assigned to a scale with equal units of measurement.

Ratio: Objects are assigned to a scale that has equal intervals as well as a true or absolute zero.

Often the scales are referred to in the sequence shown in this list, because statistics that can be applied to a given scale can also be applied to scales with more restrictive assumptions. In other words, if a statistic can be applied to ordinal data, it can also be applied to interval and ratio data. Interval and ratio data can be ranked and then the ordinal statistic can be applied. The reverse is typically not true, and a statistic that requires an interval scale cannot be produced if the scale is ordinal or nominal (Stevens, 1946).

Nonparametric statistics can use nominal and ordinal scales, and they can also be used on the interval and ratio scales. Nonparametric statistics don't make assumptions about the distribution of the measures on which they are calculated. Parametric statistics generally cannot be used with nominal and ordinal data. Typically, assumptions are made about the distribution of measures, and the assumption is that the measure is normally distributed.

Using Analytics

There are several primary steps in the use of analytics. The first is to determine the general purpose of the activity: is it to describe something, or is it to infer something? If the purpose is to describe an event or series of events or to describe a set of attributes or to describe a sample, then a *descriptive* methodology is used. Typical examples are measures of central tendency and dispersion. Primary measures of central tendency are the mean, median, and mode. The mean requires an interval scale, the median requires an ordinal scale with rank ordering, and the mode requires a nominal scale with categories. Descriptive statistics can also include measures of dispersion. Here again the allowable statistics will depend on the scale of measurement. An interval scale allows one to compute various dispersion measures, such as the standard deviation and the interquartile range. An ordinal scale in which items are ranked allows one to discuss the rank difference between objects. Dispersion for a nominal scale would be represented by the percentage of objects in a given category. Descriptive statistics can also include measures of association, such as the various correlations and cross-tabulation or contingency tables.

If one wants to generalize a descriptive statistic to a population, one must make an inference about the likelihood that the statistic occurred by chance. There are two basic types of inference: experimental and individual differences. In the experimental situation, one is looking to make statements about causality. This typically requires specific approaches, such as randomized treatments on random samples. It can also include quasi-experimental approaches, in which random assignment has not occurred but one wants to make causal inferences based on the analytics (Shadish, Cook, & Leviton, 1991). When there is an interest in looking at the likelihood that various groups were drawn from specific populations or that specific associations exist in underlying populations, one can make inferences based on distributions of various statistics. If no distribution is assumed, as is frequently found when using ordinal and nominal scales, this involves nonparametric statistics. If a distribution is assumed and there is an interval or ratio scale, this typically results in various parametric statistics, including Bayesian statistics, wherein the estimate is based on some prior belief about the likelihood that various events will occur.

If the general approach is to look at individual differences, then groups can be compared on specific characteristics, or the relationship between variables can be investigated. This leads to general types of statistics, such as correlation and multiple regressions with inferences to a population. It does not lead to statements about cause and effect. If the variables also occur at different points in time, then the associational approach will allow for making inferences about future events.

Specific Types of Techniques

There are several analytical strategies traditionally employed in analyzing data in an institutional research office. These generally have both a descriptive methodology and an inferential methodology. These include probability of occurrence, comparisons, associations, and several types of modeling, detailed in subsequent sections.

Probability of Occurrence. Many of our analyses are based on the probability of an event occurring. What is the likelihood that a student will graduate? In this case, if nothing else is known, the probability is determined by the historical proportion of similar students who have graduated. What is the likelihood that a student will graduate and will get a job? This becomes a more complicated issue because there are two events. If the events are independent, the probability is the multiplication of the two probabilities. If the two events are not independent—which, for this question, one would expect to be the case—conditional probabilities will need to be used. Probabilities can also be used to infer the degree to which outcomes reflect some underlying probability: did the proportion of students responding to the survey reflect the proportion in the population of students surveyed? This use of probability enables us to make inferences.

The calculation of the probability of occurrence frequently involves the use of permutations and combinations. Permutations are the number of different ways events can be combined where sequence is important. Combinations are ways that objects can be combined when sequence is not relevant (for more on this, see http://www.themathpage.com/aprecalc/permutations-combinations.htm).

In the case in which events are not independent, then the methodology involves conditional probabilities. Bayes' rule then applies, because there is prior knowledge, and this prior knowledge improves the accuracy of estimates. Bayesian statistics were developed around the concept of using prior knowledge, and they result in a different set of formulas for the use of classical statistics, which do not assume prior knowledge (Congdon, 2001).

Comparisons. Institutional research frequently uses techniques that compare a sample to an underlying characteristic or compare two or more samples to determine if they are different (Coughlin, 2005). The variable on which the samples are compared is called the independent variable. When the characteristic for comparison, known as the dependent variable, is measured on an interval or ratio scale and there is a sample of twenty or more observations, such comparisons are normally done using a parametric technique such as the t-test or the analysis of variance (ANOVA). When these requirements are not met, nonparametric techniques like the Kruskal-Wallis one-way analysis of variance by ranks can be used. (This and other nonparametric techniques are described by Howard, McLaughlin, and McLaughlin, 2005).

In hypothesis testing for a mean or two means, researchers must decide whether to use a one-tail or a two-tail test. In the one-tail test, also known as a directional hypothesis, the null hypothesis is rejected only if the critical value of the statistic falls in the appropriate tail of the distribution. In the two-tail test, the null hypothesis can be rejected in either direction. Directional hypotheses require less of a value of the statistic for a given probability, because the entire rejection region is on one side of the distribution. If the standard deviation of the measure is known, the Z-test is used. This is equivalent to a t-test with an infinite number of observations. Another option is to identify a set of confidence limits wherein researchers can say with a certain confidence that similar samples will contain a population parameter between an upper and a lower limit.

The analysis of variance (ANOVA) is used when there are more than two categories or groups of observations for the independent variable. In addition, ANOVA works for situations in which there are multiple independent variables. For example, if one wanted to compare freshmen and sophomores on a survey item, one could use a t-test. On the other hand, if one wanted to compare the responses of freshmen and sophomores and also consider their major as a science or nonscience major, then one would use ANOVA. ANOVA considers the importance of the independent variables and also the importance of their interaction. The main effects and interaction effects will be associated with degrees of freedom and variance components. They are tested against an error term with its degrees of freedom, and the result is compared to a probability distribution known as the F-distribution (Lind, Marchal, & Wathen, 2010).

If an independent variable has more than two groups in the ANOVA and it is desirable to make statements about differences between group means, then a procedure must be used that adjusts the likelihood of differences occurring by chance for the fact that more than one difference is being tested. This procedure, typically referred to as pairwise comparisons, tells the researcher where significant differences between group means exist when there are more than two groups. (For further discussion of using ANOVA in institutional research, see Ploutz-Snyder, 2005.)

Just as in the situation in which more than two categories create multiple pairs of comparisons and require adjustments before making statistical statements, if groups are compared on multiple variables, then it is inappropriate to do multiple ANOVAs when each has a single dependent variable. The appropriate methodology is known as multivariate analysis of variance (MANOVA). As with the single variable ANOVA, when one is concerned about the need to adjust groups for an associated characteristic, one can use a multivariate analysis of covariance (MANCOVA) (Dillon & Goldstein, 1984).

Associations. Comparisons allow us to discuss the likelihood that differences occur by chance; there are also statistics to represent the strength of association between characteristics. Many of these techniques are types of correlations, the most traditional being the Pearson product-moment correlation. Measures of association differ from comparisons in that traditionally there is not an independent or dependent variable and associations are co-occurrences rather than directional.

The traditional correlation is a measure of the covariation of two characteristics and is standardized for their individual variation—the covariance divided by the product of the standard deviations for the two variables. The square of the linear correlation can be interpreted as the percentage of variance that can be explained in one variable by knowing the other variable. In order for the correlation coefficient to represent the true association between two variables, each variable must be either interval or ratio and also continuous, and their relationship must be linear. If the relationship is other than linear, such as log-linear, transformations should be made before calculating the correlation coefficient and interpreting the results.

If the variables are ordinal, then there are several variations of rank-order correlations. Perhaps the most common are Spearman's rank-order correlation and Kendall's tau. The issue with rank-order correlations is how to handle situations in which various ranks are tied and corrections for these statistics are available (Howard, McLaughlin, & McLaughlin, 2005). There are also numerous measures of association for various special cases.

Modeling: Regression Analysis for Models with Continuous Dependent Variables. Regression models extend association by showing how one variable would estimate the value of another. Regression analysis has been used to analyze a variety of research questions of interest to institutional researchers, including identifying factors associated with faculty salaries (Toutkoushian, 1998), assessments of faculty quality (Broder & Dorfman, 1994), and academic honesty (McCabe, Feghali, & Abdallah, 2008). Multiple regression models extend our ability to find the degree to which multiple variables jointly explain a dependent variable.

Inputs for a regression include one or more independent variables and the dependent variable—which is continuous—that is being modeled. Outputs include regression weights, which are multiplied by the associated variable to estimate the dependent variable, and which can be tested for statistical significance from zero. Outputs also include measures of the relative importance of the independent variables in the form of standardized regression weights or beta coefficients. The output also includes an overall measure of the proportion of variance in the dependent variable, explained by the combination of the independent variables, R^2.

If multiple regression is to be interpreted in some sense of being a "best" description of the relationships of the variables, then the variables need to be measured at least on an interval scale. Furthermore, the relationship between the variables should be linear and adequately described by additive terms (Myers, 1990). If the relationship between the variables is not linear, then appropriate transformations, such as the square root or logarithm, should be employed (Barbezat & Hughes, 2005; Umbach, 2007).

If there is extremely high similarity between two or more independent variables then the resulting statistics will be very unstable. This is known as multicollinearity. A primary indication of this problem can be seen when the error variance of the regression weights, or variance inflation factors, are larger than ten. There are techniques such as ridge regression that reduce the impact of multicollinearity (Myers, 1990).

If there is an overly large number of independent variables, the solution is often to use one of the stepwise methodologies, in which variables are either entered because they make a significant marginal contribution to the R^2 or are deleted because they fail to make such a contribution.

There are two important considerations when looking at variables and specific observations. First, decisions need to be made about how to handle missing data. These options basically involve estimating the data that are missing, deleting an observation that has any missing data, or deleting the observation for only the variable where data are missing. The other consideration involves "outliers"—points that are substantially separated from the rest of the observations. These outlier points can overly influence the regression equation and may require either adjustment or exclusion from the analysis (Myers, 1990).

Two recent developments in linear modeling have developed into their own methodology: structural equation modeling (SEM) and hierarchical linear modeling (HLM). SEM is appropriate in situations in which there is interest in estimating the total effect of a variable as it acts both directly and indirectly (through other independent variables) on the dependent variable (Kaplan, 2000; Coughlin, 2005). HLM is used when there are multiple observations on one variable nested within another variable; for example, modeling student performance when students are nested within classes and classes are nested within faculty. HLM techniques are purported to better fit the underlying structure inherent in most educational data (Bryk & Raudenbush, 1992; Raudenbush & Bryk, 1986; Porter, 2005) and have been used to model student engagement (Hu & Kuh, 2002), persistence to degree attainment (Oseguera & Rhee, 2009), and job satisfaction (Seifert & Umbach, 2008).

Modeling: Regression Models with Categorical Dependent Variables. In higher education, there are frequently situations in which the dependent variable represents a categorical rather than a continuous variable. For example, if one were attempting to develop a model predicting whether or not a faculty member is tenured (Perna, 2001), whether or not a student responds to a survey (Porter & Umbach, 2006a), or whether or not an alumnus volunteers for his alma mater (Weerts & Ronca, 2008), the resulting dependent variable would reflect the dichotomous categories associated with membership or exclusion from the category of interest. When the dependent variable has only two categories, then the logistic regression model can be used to predict the log odds ratio, which can be used to calculate a predicted probability that an individual will be in one of the two categories. The problem with using ordinary regression is that with probabilities close to zero or one, it is possible to predict that a person has a negative probability of graduating or has a probability of greater than one. The challenge for logistic regression is interpreting the regression weights; it involves working with the log of an odds ratio, and this tends to be difficult to explain to others.

When the dependent variable of interest includes more than two categories of interest that are unordered, multinomial logit models may be appropriate to estimate the underlying data generating process. Although less common in the institutional research setting than the binary logit model, applications of the multinomial logit model have been used to explore the factors related to the choice to reenroll, stop out, or drop out of college (Stratton, O'Toole, & Wetzel, 2008); the decision to go to college (Engberg & Wolniak, 2010); multi-institutional graduation outcomes (Jones-White, Radcliffe, Huesman, & Kellogg, 2010); tenure and promotion outcomes (Perna, 2005); and choice of college major (Porter & Umbach, 2006b).

The resulting outcomes from logistic and multinomial logistic regression are probabilities of membership. In addition to the approximate R^2 metrics that are available, one can look at the number of observations that are correctly classified. This involves setting a probability separating the predicted successes from the predicted failures. Although many people set this cut point at 0.5, there is also a methodology called ROC curves whereby one looks at the true positives and false positives based on a sliding cut point (for more, see http://www.medcalc.be/manual/roc.php).

Modeling: Structural Analyses and Latent Variables. One of the challenges facing institutional researchers is to develop a parsimonious discussion of various topics by inferring underlying structures of groups or implied variables. In term of groups, see Chapter 28 on data mining for a discussion of cluster analysis. In terms of underlying but not observed variables, the basic technique is factor analysis. Some other available techniques that deal with specific aspects of the multidimensional space represented by the original set of items are multidimensional scaling, structural equation modeling, cluster analysis, discriminate analysis, latent structure analysis, and canonical correlation (Coughlin, 2005).

Factor analysis is a mathematical process of sequentially identifying solutions to the equations that can be developed by the interrelationships of a set of items. One initial decision involves what is used in the diagonal of the interrelationship matrix. For correlations, the use of 1.0 in the diagonal results in principal components analysis. If there is some estimate of the amount of variance the item has in common with the other items, communalities can be used. Another decision is how many factors to extract. In confirmatory factor analysis, in which one is trying to best model a theoretical structural model, the number of factors is set by the theory. For example, in their study of charitable giving, Weerts, Cabrera, and Sanford (2010) identify two distinct dimensions of alumni support suggested by the literature: political advocacy and volunteerism. They then use confirmatory factor analysis to assess whether the data support this supposition. Confirmatory factor analysis has been employed in a number of studies, exploring issues such as student learning and student learning outcomes (Pike & Killian, 2001), institutional commitment (Nora & Cabrera, 1993), and faculty departure (Rosser, 2004).

In exploratory factor analysis, in which the number of factors is not specified, the identification of the number of factors is based on rules of judgment. A popular rule from Catell is the scree test, in which, using the sequence of eigenvalues,, one looks for a large drop after a small drop and then a group of small drops (Cattell, 1966). Another method is to look for Thurstone's simple structure. In this case every important item has a coefficient, known as a factor loading, that is substantial on one and only one factor, and every factor has several substantial loadings. This is often considered after the rotation of the factors that have been extracted.

Rotation, as just mentioned, is a typical second step in factor analysis. After extraction, the first factor (or *eigenvector*) typically has a large proportion of the highest loadings, and this proportion of variance decreases to the last eigenvector retained. These solutions are typically hard to interpret, so the factors are rotated to interpret them. The rotation can retain the condition of right angles between all pairs of factors, known as an orthogonal rotation. If the factors can be correlated, it is known as an oblique rotation. There are several criteria for both types of rotations. The most popular orthogonal rotation is the varimax rotation, wherein the criterion is to maximize the variance of the loadings on individual factors. This tends to produce a range of high and low weights on each factor and aids in interpretation. One popular oblique rotation is a promax rotation, wherein the cube of the original loadings becomes the target matrix and then the procedure is iterated until the loadings converge.

Returning to considering the number of factors, if after rotation a factor has only one substantial loading, it's likely that too many factors have been extracted. If important items load on multiple factors, then probably too few factors have been extracted.

Objects can also be located in a reduced space using discriminate analysis. In this case linear combinations of variables, called discriminate functions, are computed to best classify individuals into different groups for which group membership is known before the analysis is done. This is often a part of the use of classification analysis. It represents a methodology that combines the aims of MANOVA and factor analysis. If the groups are not significantly different, as found by MANOVA, then it is less likely to be possible to appropriately classify objects into the correct group (Borden, 2005).

Modeling: Event History Analysis.

Modeling: Event History Analysis. Institutional researchers may sometimes be interested in research questions that pertain to the timing or duration of an event; for example, understanding how long it takes students to graduate from college or determining the length of time required to reach the rank of full professor. In such cases, the dependent variable measures the duration of time, which may be measured in hours, days, months, or years. The semicontinuous nature of the dependent variable makes it tempting to apply ordinary least squares regression to the study of the dependent variable, because "duration data must be positive, it is often the case that the response variable will exhibit considerable asymmetry, particularly if some observations have exceptionally long duration times" (Box-Steffensmeier & Jones, 2004, p. 16). To better analyze these data, researchers have turned to a class of approaches frequently referred to as "event history analysis," although the terms *survival analysis* and *duration modeling* are also used, reflecting the application of these models within disciplines such as medicine and engineering (Kiefer, 1988).

One problem frequently encountered in the application of event history analysis is the issue of censoring, which typically occurs when an observation's event history is incomplete. This may occur when a subject's event history extends beyond the study period or if a subject exits the study before an opportunity for the event to occur. Consequently, in event history analysis the structure of duration data is extremely important (Kiefer, 1988; Steele, 2005). It is suggested that the minimum requirements include recording both the starting and stopping times for each observation, as well as the event state at the end of the recorded duration span (Cleves, Gould, Gutierrez, & Marchenko, 2008). Other complications likely to be encountered include time varying covariates, competing risks, overdispersion and unobserved heterogeneity, and multiple event occurrences (Hutchison, 1988).

Because event history analysis incorporates various methodological techniques, it is helpful to distinguish between different classes of duration models. When the dependent variable of interest measures duration continuously—meaning that the occurrence of an event can transpire at any time—researchers suggest that the Cox proportional hazard model is appropriate (Box-Steffensmeier & Jones, 2004). For example, exploring policy outcomes for forty-two states, Hearn, McClendon, and Mokher (2008) use the Cox proportional hazard model to identify the factors related to the year in which a state adopted a student unit record system. In cases in which data for continuous processes are captured in discrete increments, researchers use event history models for discrete time processes (DesJardins, Ahlburg, & McCall, 1999).

Qualitative Approaches and Methods

With the acceptance of qualitative research as a viable approach to creating knowledge, unique methodologies have evolved to address specific situations. Creswell (1998) identified six "traditions" or general approaches to conducting qualitative research. Each of these approaches (summarized as follows) seeks to answer a unique type of question about human beings.

- Historical research is focused on understanding the past.
- Biographical research is the study of the life of one person.
- Phenomenology is focused on the meaning of a human experience and the construction of meaning within a selective group of participants.
- Grounded theory seeks to develop a model or theory where none exists.
- Ethnography is focused on describing and interpreting one culture to another culture.
- Case study is focused on developing an in-depth analysis of a single organization, system, family, event, etc. or multiple cases wherein all of the possible internal and external relationships are considered: describing all possible relationships within the "big picture" or system.

A seventh qualitative approach or methodology is action research where the intent is to study an "immediate application, not on the development of a theory or on generalization of applications" (Best & Kahn, 1998, p. 21). Although action research often is thought of as an approach taken to solve classroom problems, it may also be applied to the study of processes and outcomes at the organizational or university level. The practice of institutional research is, in many instances, a form of action research.

Often, institutional researchers can use qualitative approaches in the creation of planning and decision support information. These approaches are useful in generating information to help understand *why* a particular behavior or situation is observed.

Data collection and analysis in general are the same for each of the approaches. Best and Kahn (1998) describe the following types of data typically collected in qualitative studies.

Data Sources

Observations can provide detailed notation of behaviors and events and the contexts surrounding them. Patton (1990) indicates five conditions that should be considered with the observations. First, the researcher may be anyone from a full participant to a complete outsider. Second, the observations may be done in a covert manner with all, some, or none of the subjects aware of the observation. Third, the subjects can be given complete explanations, partial explanations, no explanation, or false explanations. The fourth condition is the length of the observation. Fifth is the breadth of the focus of the observations, from very broad (an entire school or system) to very narrow (reactions to a specific curricular intervention).

A second source of data is interviews. The purpose of interviews is to collect data about an individual's experience and knowledge, opinions, beliefs, and feelings, as well as demographic data (Best & Kahn, 1998). There are four types of protocols that can be used to conduct interviews:

a. Informal interviews (interview protocol evolves from the discussion)
b. Guided approach (topics and issues are defined, interviewer defines the order and approach to the interview)
c. Standardized open-ended (structured protocol)
d. Closed, fixed response (multiple choice)

Documents can be reviewed; they often can provide a great deal of context for a study, such as the history, various policy statements, minutes from meetings, and other archival data.

A final type of data reflect basic descriptive statistics about the person or subjects. These statistics give a context for interpreting the results of the qualitative study.

Analysis

As described earlier, in qualitative research the researcher not only designs the study but typically is also the primary instrument for data collection and analysis. As such, researchers must be aware that they could and often do influence all aspects of the research. Trustworthiness is at risk. As such, the research design must include structure that increases levels of certainty about relative truth and decreases subjectivity ("unreliable, biased, or probably biased") while increasing objectivity ("reliable factual, confirmable, or confirmed") (Lincoln & Guba, 1985).

The analysis of qualitative data is an iterative, continuous process that begins with the first data collected and continues until all data are collected and conclusions developed about what the data have to say. Howard and Borland (1999) presented a conceptual model that illustrates the qualitative research process and in particular the data analysis process. In this model, processes to limit two sources of error are illustrated. The first is *factual error*. This source of error occurs when the researcher misrepresents the subject's comments or responses to questions. The technique, member checking, simply asks the research subject to verify that the recorded narrative data is what the subject said. The second source of error is *interpretation error*. In this case, the research misinterprets the data and draws an inaccurate conclusion. To reduce this source of error, peer reviewers or auditors start with the researcher's data and validate the logic that led to the researcher's conclusion.

Qualitative research is well suited for the development of two types of information. It can be used to develop theories and models to be tested using quantitative approaches—the first step in the scientific method. Qualitative approaches can also be used to explore the meaning that humans attach to quantitatively derived and tested conclusions, which is the third step in the scientific method.

However, qualitative research is limited in terms of inferential power or generalizability. The researcher should not generalize the findings to a population or other context. Generalizing the results of qualitative research is the responsibility of the consumer of the research. As such, the reporting of qualitative research requires a thorough description of the context in which the research was conducted. (See Chapter 33 for more discussion of reporting qualitative data.) The consumer needs enough information about the research, the research participants, and the context in which the research was conducted to determine whether the findings are applicable enough to be useful in understanding his or her particular situation.

Mixed Methods Approaches and Methods

Building on the notions just discussed, paradigms and methodologies should not be thought of as synonyms, nor does the belief in one world view or paradigm demand the use of a particular methodological approach. As is always the case, the appropriate method and form of data collection are dependent on the question to be answered by the research. If the intent is to develop a theory or hypothesis, then specific individuals may be selected to study, and both quantitative and qualitative methodologies can be used to create the desired information. If the intent is to discover and/or describe a trend within a population or to study an attribute of a population, then a representative sample is selected and the trend or attribute is studied, quantitatively or qualitatively, and the results are generalized to the population. From this perspective, the key issue is how the people to be studied are selected—randomly from a defined population or purposefully to reflect a specific characteristic (Howard & Borland, 2007).

The two paradigms and respective research methodologies can be thought of as the extremes of a "research continuum," with the positivist at one end and the constructivist at the other. Borland (2001) suggests that "The relationship between qualitative and quantitative research should not be considered in terms of a mutually exclusive dichotomy but rather as a continuum of complementary paradigms within systematic scientific inquiry that, when used in concert, produce complete or useful knowledge" (p. 5). This concept of approaching research is termed *mixed methods research* by Johnson and Onwuegbuzie (2004). They suggest that this approach to creating knowledge may be thought of as a third research paradigm that bridges the "schism between quantitative and qualitative research" (p. 15). Creswell (2005) further discusses mixed methods research as a worldview or paradigm in which the pragmatists believe in "what works" for a particular problem and believe that the researcher should use whatever methods are necessary to understand the problem.

It seems that this is a particularly attractive philosophy for those practicing institutional research. One reason is that the theoretical intent of systematic scientific inquiry, which transcends particular research paradigms and methodologies, is to ultimately address all possible "what," "why," and "so what" questions. In a practical sense, the institutional research professional's work is both limited and delimited. She or he is constrained by limited resources of time and money as well as a specific institutional context that is bounded by organizational structures, processes, and values. The real task of the institutional research professional is to develop alternatives or answers to questions of decision makers, regardless of the restrictions positivist or constructivist paradigms might impose.

Creswell (2005) defines mixed methods research design as a "procedure for collecting, analyzing, and 'mixing' both quantitative and qualitative data in a single study to understand a research problem" (p. 510). Although the use of mixed methods has been around since the early 1930s, it is only within the past couple of decades that it has become an accepted form of research. In this text, Creswell also describes the evolution of mixed methods research over the past eighty years, providing a rationale for why it is only relatively lately that mixed methods have become an accepted approach to conducting research. An ASHE Reader (Howard, Kennedy-Philips, & Watt, 2010) discusses the theoretical foundations and conduct of mixed methods research.

Resources and the Role of Assumptions

This overview was intended to provide a review of the fundamental aspects of the analyses of qualitative and quantitative data. As anyone practicing institutional research will quickly agree, the ability to analyze these types of data is critical to the development of planning and decision support information. However, it is beyond the scope and intent of this chapter to provide a "textbook" covering all aspects of these analytical techniques. Most of the techniques discussed in this chapter (we've touched on their assumptions, formulas, and theoretical bases) are covered in detail in introductory and mid-level statistics and qualitative data analysis courses. And although the practice of institutional research does not always require the use of advanced statistics or research methodologies, there are instances when their use is appropriate, if not mandated. There are a number of textbooks, handbooks, and monograph series that provide an overview of the calculation data collection and use of data analysis techniques.

Quantitative Analysis

For quantitative analysis, the SAGE series on quantitative applications in the social sciences gives numerous focused monographs on specific methodologies. For those interested in more advanced methodology, there are books related to specific disciplines, such as the *SAGE Handbook of Quantitative Methodology for the Social Sciences* (Kaplan, 2004) and the Wiley series on statistics. *Applied Regression Analysis* (Draper & Smith, 1998) and *Classical and Modern Regression with Applications* (Myers, 1990) are good basic references for regression. *The Handbook of Parametric and Nonparametric Statistical Procedures* (Sheskin, 2011) is an excellent starting point for looking at a very broad range of techniques and the role of assumptions for each of them, for both parametric and nonparametric statistics.

Qualitative Analysis

The preceding discussion of qualitative methodology provides a basic overview of the issues and methods that may be applied in the collection and analysis of qualitative data. Over the past two decades this field has seen significant growth and development. Citing the vast amount of available literature that addresses various qualitative applications, methodologies, and theories is beyond the scope of this chapter.

The foundation reference for qualitative research is *The SAGE Handbook of Qualitative Research*, by Norman K. Denzin and Yvonna S. Lincoln (2005). Good basic texts in this area include *An Introduction to Qualitative Research* (Flick, 2006), and *Qualitative Research Practice* (Gobo, Gubrium, & Silverman, 2007). *Designing Qualitative Research* (Marshall & Rossman, 2006) and *The Practice of Qualitative Research* (Hesse-Biber & Leavy, 2010) put qualitative analysis into a research context.

Assumptions

All of the analytic methodologies discussed in this chapter create data reduction based on assumptions. We offer here a brief discussion of the assumptions in some of the techniques. For example, although muticollinearity was mentioned for linear regression, regression also assumes normally distributed scores with adequate variation, independence of the error terms, error terms that have a normal distribution and an average of zero, error variance that is not a function of the scores, and linearity of the relationship. Some of these assumptions, such as the assumption of linearity just noted, can be statistically tested against a null hypothesis of chance. Others, such as response bias in a survey, are not easily tested. Some techniques, such as the nonparametric techniques, require fewer assumptions. Bootstrapping or simulations also tend to have less restrictive assumptions. Almost all assumptions are violated to some degree. Many assumptions, along with tests of the likelihood the assumptions are being met, are discussed in the various articles and books cited in this chapter.

The question is: How damaging to the conclusions is the violation of an assumption? As with the beauty of a rose, this discussion can get very vigorous. At the scholarly level it has produced discussions between those who use Bayesian statistics, those who use classical Pearson statistics, and those who empirically explore the data. It has formed discipline specific analytics such as Biometrics, Psychometrics, and Econometrics to name a few. Even at the technique level there are different groups formed around different assumptions such as the two major approaches to Item Response Theory. Although there are some strategies to ameliorate the violation of assumptions, satisfying many of the assumptions required by methodologies will never be resolved. The challenge is to use the analytic technique that best represents understandable reality as a result of its use.

References

Barbezat, D. A., & Hughes, D. A. (2005). Salary structure effects and gender pay gap in academia. *Research in Higher Education, 46*(6), 621–640.

Best, J. W., & Kahn, J. V. (1998). *Research in education* (8th ed.). Boston, MA: Allyn and Bacon.

Borden, V. M. (2005). Identifying and analyzing group differences. In M. A. Coughlin (Ed.), *Intermediate/advanced statistics in institutional research* (pp. 132–168). *Resources in Institutional Research, 16.* Tallahassee, FL: Association for Institutional Research.

Borland, K. W. (2001). Qualitative and quantitative research: A complementary balance. In R. D. Howard & K. W. Borland, Jr. (Eds.), *Balancing qualitative and quantitative information for effective decision support* (pp. 5–13). New Directions for Institutional Research, no. 112. San Francisco: Jossey-Bass.

Box-Steffensmeier, J., & Jones, B. S. (2004). *Event history modeling: A guide for social scientists.* New York: Cambridge University Press.

Broder, J. M., & Dorfman, J. H. (1994). Determinants of teaching quality: What's important to students? *Research in Higher Education, 35*(2), 235–249.

Bryk, A. S., & Raudenbush, S. W. (1992). *Hierarchical linear modeling: Applications and data analysis methods.* Thousand Oaks, CA: SAGE.

Cattell, R. B. (1966). The scree test for the number of factors. *Multivariate Behavioral Research, 1*(2), 245–276.

Cleves, M., Gould, W., Gutierrez, R., & Marchenko, Y. (2008). *An introduction to survival analysis using stata* (2nd ed.). College Station, TX: Stata Press.

Congdon, P. (2001). *Baysian statistical modeling.* New York: Wiley.

Coughlin, M. (Ed.). (2005). Applications of intermediate/advanced statistics in institutional research, *Resources in Institutional Research, 16.* Tallahassee, FL: Association for Institutional Research.

Creswell, J. W. (1998). *Qualitative inquiry and research design: Choosing among five traditions.* Thousand Oaks, CA: SAGE.

Creswell, J. W. (2005). *Educational research: Planning, conducting, and evaluating quantitative and qualitative research* (2nd ed.). Upper Saddle River, NJ: Pearson.

Denzin, N. K., & Lincoln, Y. S. (2005). *The SAGE handbook of qualitative research.* Thousand Oaks, CA: SAGE.

DesJardins, S. L., Ahlburg, D. A., & McCall, B. P. (1999). An event history of model of student departure. *Economics of Education Review, 18*(3), 375–390.

Dillon, W. R., & Goldstein, M. (1984). *Multivariate analysis methods and applications.* New York: Wiley.

Draper, N. R., & Smith, H. (1998). *Applied regression analysis* (3rd ed.). New York: Wiley Interscience Publications.

Engberg, M. E., & Wolniak, G. C. (2010). Examining the effects of high school contexts on postsecondary enrollment. *Research in Higher Education, 51*(2), 132–153.

Flick, U. (2006). *An introduction to qualitative research.* Thousand Oaks, CA: SAGE.

Gliner, J. A., & Morgan, G. A. (2000). *Research methods in applied settings: An integrated approach to design and analysis.* Mahwah, NJ: Erlbaum.

Gobo, G., Gubrium, J. F., & Silverman, D. (2007). *Qualitative research practice.* Thousand Oaks, CA: SAGE.

Guba, E. G. (1991). The alternative paradigm dialogue. In E. G. Guba (Ed.), *The paradigm dialog* (pp. 17–30). Thousand Oaks, CA: SAGE.

Hearn, J. C., McClendon, M. K., & Mokher, C. G. (2008). Accounting for student success: An empirical analysis of the origins and spread of state student unit-record systems. *Research in Higher Education, 49,* 665–683.

Hesse-Biber, S. N., & Leavy, P. (2010). *The practice of qualitative research.* Thousand Oaks, CA: SAGE.

Howard, R. D., & Borland, K. W. (1999). Qualitative and quantitative research in institutional research: Complementary or competitive paradigms and methodologies? Paper presented at the Association for Institutional Research Forum, Seattle, WA.

Howard, R. D., & Borland, K. W. (2007). The role of mixed method approaches in institutional research. In R. D. Howard (Ed.), *Using mixed methods in institutional research* (pp. 2–8). Tallahassee, FL: Association for Institutional Research.

Howard, R. D., Kennedy-Philips, L., & Watt, C. (Eds.). (2010). *Qualitative & quantitative research: A mixed methods approach in higher education* (3rd ed.). ASHE Reader Series. Boston, MA: Pearson Learning Solutions.

Howard, R. D., McLaughlin, G. W., & McLaughlin, J. S. (2005). Nonparametric statistics: Applications in institutional research. In M. A. Coughlin (Ed.), *Intermediate/advanced statistics in institutional research* (pp. 1–50). *Resources in Institutional Research, 16.* Tallahassee, FL: Association for Institutional Research.

Hu, S., & Kuh, G. D. (2002). Being (dis)engaged in educationally purposeful activities: The student and institutional characteristics. *Research in Higher Education, 43*(5), 555–575.

Hutchison, D. (1988). Event history and survival analysis in the social sciences, II: Advanced applications and recent developments. *Quality & Quantity, 22*(2), 255–278.

Johnson, R. B., & Onwuegbuzie, A. J. (2004). Mixed methods research: A research paradigm whose time has come. *Educational Researcher, 33*(7), 14–26.

Jones-White, D. R., Radcliffe, P. M., Huesman, R. L., & Kellogg, J. P. (2010). Redefining student success: Applying different multinomial regression techniques for the study of student graduation across institutions of higher education. *Research in Higher Education, 51*(2), 154–174.

Kaplan, D. (2000). Structural equation modeling: Foundations and extensions. *Advanced quantitative techniques in the social sciences series: Vol. 10.* Thousand Oaks, CA: SAGE.

Kaplan, D. (Ed.). (2004). *The SAGE handbook of quantitative methodology for the social sciences.* Thousand Oaks, CA: SAGE.

Kiefer, N. M. (1988). Economic duration data and hazard functions. *Journal of Economic Literature, 26*(2), 646–679.

Lincoln, Y. S., & Guba, E. G. (1985). *Natural inquiry.* Thousand Oaks, CA: SAGE.

Lind, D. A., Marchal, W. G., & Wathen, S. A. (2010). *Basic statistics for business and economics.* New York: McGraw-Hill.

Marshall, C., & Rossman, G. B. (2006). *Designing qualitative research.* Thousand Oaks, CA: SAGE.

McCabe, D., Feghali, T., & Abdallah, H. (2008). Academic dishonesty in the Middle East: Individual and contextual factors. *Research in Higher Education, 49*(3), 451–467.

Myers, R. H. (1990). *Classical and modern regression with applications* (2nd ed.). Boston, MA: PWS-KENT Publishing.

Nora, A., & Cabrera, A. F. (1993). The construct validity of institutional commitment: A confirmatory factor analysis. *Research in Higher Education,* 34(2), 243–262.

Oseguera, L., & Rhee, B. S. (2009). The influence of institutional retention climates on student persistence to degree completion: A multilevel approach. *Research in Higher Education, 50*(6), 546–549.

Patton, M. Q. (1990). *Qualitative evaluation and research methods* (2nd ed.). Thousand Oaks, CA: SAGE.

Perna, L. W. (2001). Sex and race differences in faculty tenure and promotion. *Research in Higher Education, 42*(5), 541–567.

Perna, L. W. (2005). Sex differences in faculty tenure and promotion: The contribution of family ties. *Research in Higher Education, 46*(3), 277–307.

Pike, G. R., & Killian, T. S. (2001). Reported gains in student learning: Do academic disciplines make a difference? *Research in Higher Education, 42*(4), 429–454.

Ploutz-Snyder, R. J. (2005). Analysis of variance applications in institutional research. In Coughlin, M. (Ed.), *Applications of intermediate/advanced statistics in institutional research. Resources in Institutional Research, 16.* Tallahassee, FL: Association for Institutional Research.

Porter, S. R. (2005). What can multilevel models add to institutional research? In Coughlin, M. A. (Ed.), *Intermediate/advanced statistics in institutional research* (pp. 1110–1131. Resources in Institutional Research 16. Tallahassee, FL: Association for Institutional Research.

Porter, S. R., & Umbach, P. D. (2006a). Student survey response rates across institutions: Why do they vary? *Research in Higher Education, 47*(2), 229–247.

Porter, S. R., & Umbach, P. D. (2006b). College major choice: An analysis of student-environment fit. *Research in Higher Education, 46*(7), 429–449.

Raudenbush, S., & Bryk, A. S. (1986). A hierarchical model for studying school effects. *Sociology of Education, 59*(1), 1–17.

Rosser, V. J. (2004). Faculty members' intentions to leave: A national study on their worklife and satisfaction. *Research in Higher Education, 45*(3), 285–309.

Seifert, T. A., & Umbach, P. D. (2008). The effects of faculty demographic characteristics and disciplinary context on dimensions of job satisfaction. *Research in Higher Education, 49*(4), 357–381.

Shadish, W. R., Cook, T. D., & Leviton, L. C. (Eds.). (1991). *Foundations of program evaluation: Theories of practice.* New York: SAGE.

Sheskin, D. J. (2011). *The handbook of parametric and non-parametric statistical procedures* (5th ed.). New York: Chapman and Hall/CRC.

Steele, F. (2005). Event history analysis: A National Centre for Research Methods briefing paper. *NCRM Methods Review Papers.* Retrieved from http://eprints.ncrm.ac.uk/88/1/MethodsReviewPaperNCRM-004.pdf

Stevens, S. S. (1946). On the theory of scales and measurement. *Science, 103,* 677–680.

Stratton, L. S., O'Toole, D. M., & Wetzel, J. N. (2008). A multinomial logit model of college stopout and dropout behavior. *Economics of Education Review, 27,* 319–331.

Toutkoushian, R. T. (1998). Using regression analysis to determine if faculty salaries are overly compressed. *Research in Higher Education, 39*(1), 87–100.

Umbach, P. D. (2007). Gender equity in the academic labor market: An analysis of academic disciplines. *Research in Higher Education, 48*(2), 169–192.

Weerts, D. J., Cabrera, A. F., & Sanford, T. (2010). Beyond giving: Political advocacy and volunteer behaviors of public university alumni. *Research in Higher Education, 51*(4), 346–365.

Weerts, D. J., & Ronca, J. M. (2008). Characteristics of alumni donors who volunteer at their alma mater. *Research in Higher Education, 49*(3), 274–292.

CHAPTER 28

EXPLORING AND MINING DATA

Jing Luan, Thulasi Kumar, Sutee Sujitparapitaya, and
Tom Bohannon

This chapter provides a brief introduction to data mining: its key concepts, as well as three case studies covering cluster analysis, decision tree, and finally neural network modeling. These cases, from institutional research projects at various institutions, include examples of how to present results for each methodology. Also, from these three cases and based on the application of data mining to various institutional research projects, we provide a set of recommendations for practitioners in institutional research, including the use of several models to validate findings—namely algorithmic bias analysis and the practice of testing models on training datasets prior to confirming results on validation datasets.

The Scope and Nature of Exploratory Methods

"Data mining" is really a misnomer. It should be—and indeed was, for a while—called "knowledge discovery in databases (KDD)." Data mining or KDD is meant for uncovering hidden patterns in large databases for which traditional tools or methods are of limited use. In higher education, once the data have accumulated for more than three to five semesters, the database is a mile deep and a mile wide. Without scalable tools and multiple models of data mining, it is impossible to fully understand and exploit all the patterns, trends, and factors in the database.

Data mining analyzes data with two general approaches: unsupervised and supervised. To understand hidden patterns in a vast database, the researcher starts with the unsupervised approach. In this case, the researcher conducts a variety of visualization, association, and clustering activities. If it is a small and manageable dataset, or an online analytical processing (OLAP) cube that is built for reporting, the researcher may rely on only tables and charts to gain understanding. This approach is highly exploratory. Unsupervised techniques include Kohonen nets, generalized rule induction, K-means, and sequence detection algorithms. Supervised data mining, on the other hand, refers to techniques deployed when the researcher has prior knowledge of the patterns in the database and is looking for predictive outcomes. The researcher then develops several models for predictive outcomes in search of an optimal one. The search for the best predictive model is also exploratory. Among the most popular supervised techniques are artificial neural nets, classification and regression technique, C5.0, and rule induction.

Data mining is different from traditional statistical methods not only in its ability to interface and query large databases, but also in some fundamental approaches to data. First, it strongly emphasizes the use of data visualization. Data are fundamentally an abstract way of describing one's analog world, whereas graphics are a more direct way. There is a latent and potent relationship between data and graphics. Probably the best example to illustrate this symbiotic relationship is Charles Joseph Minard's famous statistical graphing of the progress of Napoleon's army in its retreat from Moscow (Minard, 1869/2009). One can use formulas to study the world around us as well as using statistical graphics.

When examining the supervised approach closely, one will notice that there is less emphasis on assumptions about data; that is, Gaussian distribution, variable interaction (multicollinearity), and establishing hypotheses. Instead, the predictive models rely mostly on empirical accuracy validations by running the models on one dataset followed by running the same models on another. This is a key data mining principal.

John Tukey was one of the first who foresaw the value of explorative data analysis. His work laid the foundation for modern data mining to share a similar philosophical root with exploratory data analysis. In his landmark 1962 article "The Future of Data Analysis," Tukey documented his shift in thinking from a statistical point of view to a data analysis point of view—that is, from fixating inferences from the particular to the general to fully recognizing the specificity within the data themselves and a lessened interest in generalization.

Differences Between Hypothesis Testing and Exploratory Methods

In a clinical trial for a new medication or a study for the effectiveness of a new teaching method, the researcher will design the study by first splitting the subjects into two randomly assigned groups. One group receives the medication or the new teaching method; the other receives nothing new. Neither the researcher nor the subjects know which group is the control and which group is experimental. The researcher declares that the results will be the same for both groups unless proven otherwise. This is a typical example of hypothesis-based research. Yet only in rare situations would data mining be applied for control/experimental studies in which group means and test of significances are the measurements. Data mining, being exploratory, does not need to have a hypothesis.

A hypothesis often lends a "magic touch" to research inquiries because it furnishes a tangible and straightforward criterion: level of significance—a threshold for assessing the defensibility or sustainability of a hypothesis based on a sample. It is a convenient rule-of-thumb index but is often used as the only gatekeeper that safeguards the legitimacy of inference from a sample to a population.

Luan and Zhao stated, in their co-edited article "Data Mining in Action: Case Studies of Enrollment Management" (2006), that hypothesis testing does not have specific meaning for data mining because data mining does not start from a theory or hypothesis. Because data mining can handle a large amount of data, often the whole population is its study universe. Therefore the significance level used in statistics for the purpose of estimating the accuracy of inference loses its relevance.

In addition, being statistically significant often does not relate directly to the practical usage or value of findings. In statistics, the selection of significance level, based on which the hypothesis will be rejected as invalid, is arbitrary. Most studies in statistical research choose the conventional significance level (such as a p value of less than .05 or .01) regardless of the nature of the research and subjects in the study. Statistical significance does not automatically imply practical significance. This is especially the case in large datasets, in which statistical significance is easily obtained when there are minute changes in cases. Further, although hypothesis testing is the cardinal rule in statistical reasoning and long cherished in the research community, there are practical difficulties and ethical concerns about maintaining test-control groups in a higher education setting. Researchers in higher education often do not have the luxury of conducting a clinical-trial type of analysis. Random assignment is traditionally not available. Thus hypothesis testing in its strictest sense becomes severely limited.

Because of its attention to case-level specificity, data mining is advantageous in providing individual and granular findings by producing scores for individual subjects or cases. This is more desirable in institutional research work such as understanding and predicting enrollment versus yield, persistence versus dropout, alumni donations, and GPAs, to name a few. In the ensuing sections of this chapter, readers will notice that hypothesis testing has not been used in any of the case studies.

The rest of the chapter contains three case studies: cluster analysis, decision tree, and neural networks. The sequence of the content is arranged as such because data mining typically starts with unsupervised modeling, such as cluster analysis, before progressing to supervised modeling. These studies are highly illustrative of data mining studies in higher education. At the end of each case, we provide implications for institutional research. Due to chapter length limitation, less commonly used modeling techniques are not discussed. Many of the various techniques are discussed in Nisbet, Elder, and Miner (2009). The chapter concludes with five recommendations to institutional researchers based on the best practices and lessons learned in data mining.

Cluster Analysis

Cluster analysis is an exploratory data analysis tool used to sort cases (people, things, events, and so on) into groups, or clusters, so that the degree of association is stronger among members of the same cluster and weaker among members of different clusters (Wishart, 2010). Cluster analysis helps to understand natural grouping in the data as well as the relationship among the important variables.

In many of today's institutional research applications, cluster analysis can be used to preprocess the data to identify which variables are important to distinguish or characterize different groups of students. Explanatory and predictive models that differentiate these groups, focusing on the more relevant variables, can then be built. As cluster analysis is based on distances, the variables are typically interval or ordinal, although dichotomous variables can be used to represent categories of nominal measures. In addition, any items that use the Likert scale are considered a close approximation of interval scale and are widely used for cluster analysis.

Cluster analysis techniques are gaining popularity in institutional research due to the myriad of variables used in describing student experiences, satisfaction, and engagement. Students exhibiting similar characteristics can be grouped together. Students within the group exhibit more or less similar characteristics and are closer to students within the group than to the students in other groups or clusters. Identifying the natural groupings enables the institutional researchers to focus on specific groups of students and important variables for further detailed analysis. In data mining, clustering is often considered as one of the first steps in the entire data mining project.

Considering the wide range of data and information collected in today's institutional research studies and surveys, cluster analysis is often employed to identify distinct groups within the survey respondents. (For more information on surveys, see Chapter 30 on published tests and Chapter 29 on surveys.) However, as an exploratory method, cluster analysis provides an understanding of group (cluster) characteristics, but not the definite solutions. As students within the cluster may still exhibit somewhat different behaviors on certain attributes, several solutions need to be explored before employing some intervention strategies. Also, cluster analysis is often followed by graphing, charting, cross tabulation, and descriptive analysis to better understand the group behavior.

Thanks to increasing computing power, numerous cluster analysis algorithms are available. Some of the most popular cluster algorithms include K-means clustering, hierarchical clustering, and Kohonen self-organizing maps

(Kohonen, 2001). K-means is the simplest and easiest to understand and to implement. In a typical K-means clustering, the researcher selects K, the initial number of clusters and forms clusters. Frequently several attempts are made before finding the right number of clusters for the dataset. Typically three to seven clusters are investigated, with five being the most preferred. Because the clusters are preselected and are small in relation to the number of records, K-means often executes faster than other cluster algorithms.

The letter "K" in K-means indicates the number of clusters selected for analysis; the "means" represents the centroid or the mean values of the observation in a cluster. In the initial phase, the K-means algorithm searches for the well spaced specified number of observations (K). These are used as initial clusters, and all observations are assigned to one of the selected number of clusters, using the least distance to the alternative centroids. The most widely used distance function is the Euclidean distance, which represents the straight line between two points. If the variables are considered equally important, they need to be measured on a similar scale or otherwise have comparable dispersion. At the completion of the process of assigning observations to individual clusters, the researcher recalculates the mean values or the centroid using all observations assigned to that cluster. The newly calculated cluster mean or centroid is used to reassign all observations, and the process is repeated until the optimum cluster solution is reached.

The following provides an example of the K-means clustering technique to understand student engagement using the data from the National Survey of Student Engagement (NSSE).

Cluster Analysis Example: Student Engagement Typologies

Since the introduction of the NSSE, many colleges and universities have used it to understand student engagement in educationally purposeful activities. A higher level of student engagement has positive effects on student learning and often leads to student retention (Pike & Kuh, 2005). However, understanding student engagement with more than 80 variables and developing strategies to enhance student engagement is difficult. To simplify the understanding of the student engagement, NSSE provides each institution with a set of five benchmarks using 42 key items from the survey: (1) level of academic challenge, (2) active and collaborative learning, (3) student faculty interaction, (4) enriching educational experiences, and (5) supportive campus environment. Collectively, these represent the active learning environment, opportunities to collaborate, and interactions with faculty and staff, as well as learning experiences beyond the traditional classroom. The individual items used in the construction of the benchmarks were created with a blend of theory and empirical analysis conducted by the NSSE researchers and reflects the multidimensional nature of student engagement at all levels (http://nsse.iub.edu/2009_Institutional_Report/benchmark_construction.cfm). Furthermore, each of the variables used in the construction of the benchmarks is standardized on a scale of 0 to 100, before calculating the mean of all variables for the benchmark value. Because the cluster analysis presented in this chapter used the data from the five benchmarks, instead of using the 42 variables that the benchmarks comprise, no further standardization of the variables was necessary.

Also, the NSSE argues that the students exhibit more varying levels of engagement within the institution than across institutions (Pike & Kuh, 2005). However, students' engagement is influenced by the individual student behavior and the institutional characteristics (Luan, Zhao, & Hayek, 2009). Therefore the institutional level of student engagement typologies is fundamental in understanding the various levels of students' engagement.

The following K-means clustering analysis uses the data from the five benchmarks of effective educational practices from the 2008 survey of 441 senior students at a Midwestern research university.

Clustering with K-Means Method

Clustering using K-means is ideal, especially when the researcher is confronted with several variables of importance in data analysis. It is not uncommon to input 30 or more variables into the cluster analysis. Which variables to input and how many records are needed depends entirely on the domain knowledge of the institutional researcher. However, the number of observations or records should be sufficient to capture the variations in the student engagement. In a purely exploratory analysis, clusters can be performed on a dataset with as little as a few hundred records.

K-means analysis using the five benchmarks of effective educational practices produced five distinct clusters of students. One criterion for the quality of the cluster analysis is measured by its silhouette, an index measuring the cohesion and separation. The silhouette value for a point is how similar that point is to points in its own cluster compared to points in other clusters, and ranges from −1 to +1 (http://www.mathworks.com/access/helpdesk/help/toolbox/stats/silhouette.html). For the five-cluster model, the silhouette was 0.3, indicating that the model was fair. If the silhouette value is poor, the researcher can modify the properties of the K-means clustering node to improve the quality of the clusters (Kaufman & Rousseeuw, 1990). Students in each of the five clusters exhibited widely varying degrees of engagement and were more similar to other students in the same cluster than those students outside the cluster. Table 28.1 shows the cluster means for five benchmarks of effective educational practices for the five clusters identified by the K-means analysis.

Figure 28.1 shows the scatter plot of the means for the five clusters using the drop line method. A drop line chart helps to develop a more descriptive way of identifying and naming the clusters—such as Academically Engaged or Highly Engaged—than the generic cluster names (Cluster 1, Cluster 2, and so on) provided by the K-means analysis. It does require, however, that the

TABLE 28.1   CLUSTER MEANS OF STUDENT ENGAGEMENT TYPOLOGY

Cluster Description	No. of Students	Level of Academic Challenge (ACa)	Active and Collaborative Learning (ACL)	Student-Faculty Interaction (SFI)	Enriching Educational Experiences (EEE)	Supportive Campus Environment (SCE)
Withdrawn and Alienated	100	39.1	35.2	25.6	26.5	43.2
Highly Engaged	71	68.4	67.3	75.7	52.2	70.1
Academically Engaged	101	59.1	49.8	28.4	37	45.8
Highly Homogeneous	88	55.6	52.5	57.5	51.4	52.5
Less Engaged and More Fragmented	81	54.6	49.6	41.9	37.8	67.1

FIGURE 28.1   DROP LINE OF CLUSTER MEANS

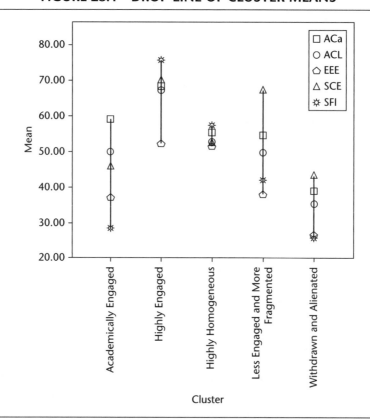

institutional researcher have a familiarity with the variables and primary concepts in the research area as well as with the methodology.

The following section shows how an institutional researcher could present these results to administrators. We briefly describe some of the major characteristics of the students in each of the five clusters. We then show how the clusters differ on individual items of interest. It is important to remember that the individual students in each of the clusters may still exhibit somewhat varying levels of engagement on certain variables.

The students are each identified as belonging to one of the following five groups:

- *Withdrawn and Alienated:* Students in this group exhibit low levels of student engagement and prefer to stay aloof from faculty and other students.
- *Highly Engaged:* Students in this group are intensively involved in academic efforts and educationally enriching experiences, both inside and outside the classroom.
- *Academically Engaged:* Students in this group are typically involved in academically challenging efforts, but in a less collaborative way. These students tend to be solo learners, with less interaction with faculty, and to participate less in diverse learning opportunities.
- *Highly Homogeneous:* Students in this group are highly centric in their behavior and exhibit similar characteristics across the five benchmarks of effective educational practices.
- *Less Engaged and More Fragmented:* These students are less engaged in academically challenging and collaborative learning opportunities and take a somewhat middle-of-the-road approach to diverse learning opportunities. These students are similar to those in the Withdrawn and Alienated category, although to a lesser extent.

In addition to describing the general characteristics of groups, it is often helpful to look at group differences in terms of key items. The following describes some of the key differences in student engagement in individual clusters based on several of the selected items from the NSSE instrument. These items were selected because they represent important issues to colleges.

It is a well-known fact that academic advising plays a major role in retaining at-risk students and also helps students to better navigate their college education. Figure 28.2 shows that the students in the Highly Engaged and Homogeneous groups indicate that the overall quality of academic advising that they received during the course of their education is "good" to "excellent." On the other hand, more than 50 percent of the students in the Withdrawn and Alienated category feel that the quality of academic advising they received during the course of their education is "poor" or "fair."

Figure 28.3 illustrates an interesting relationship between "educational experiences" and "return to the same institution." Those in either the Withdrawn and Alienated or the Academically Engaged groups who rated their educational experiences to be "poor" or "fair" do not plan to return to the same school.

FIGURE 28.2 ACADEMIC ADVISEMENT

Value △	Proportion	%	Count
Academically Engaged		22.9	101
Highly Engaged		16.1	71
Highly Homogeneous		19.95	88
Less Engaged and More Fragmented		18.37	81
Withdrawn and Alienated		22.68	100

advise

☐ $null$ ■ 1 (Poor)   ■ 2 (Fair)   ■ 3 (Good)   ☐ 4 (Excellent)

FIGURE 28.3 EDUCATIONAL EXPERIENCES: INFLUENCE ON RETURN TO THE SAME INSTITUTION

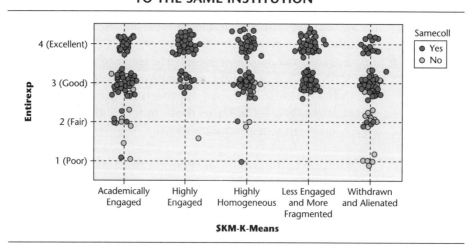

Applications for Institutional Research

The application of exploratory methods such as K-means for survey data involving large numbers of variables clearly indicates that the IR professional should actively employ these techniques for institutional data analysis to understand the nature of the data before further using inferential techniques. If groups do not differ on specific items, these items would be less important for further investigation. The analysis clearly indicates that the educational experiences that are beyond the classroom—such as interaction with faculty and other students, membership in fraternities and sororities, staying on campus, and good academic advisement—are fundamental to student learning and retention even in the senior year.

Decision Trees

Often institutional research involves situations in which it is not appropriate to assume linear and additive relationships between variables. In addition, many of the situations do not produce data that fit the normal parametric assumptions. Decision trees split larger groups of objects into smaller multiple subgroups, based on rules that use the independent variables that best explain the dependent variable. They do not include parametric assumptions or assumptions of linear and additive relationships. These splits continue until there is not sufficient improvement in the ability to explain the dependent variable, or the size of the group drops below some minimum specified size.

Most people understand decision trees intuitively and find them to be easily applicable to real-life problems. Because decision tree induction is a nonparametric approach, it does not require any prior assumptions regarding the type of probability distributions satisfied by the class and other attributes. Decision tree induction is the supervised learning of a decision tree structure that predicts or classifies future observations based on a set of decision rules. Data are first divided into two sets: a training set and a testing set. Rules developed in the training set are applied to the testing set as a form of validation. Creating a decision tree takes several steps: (1) a subset of attributes is chosen from the training dataset; (2) this subset is then used by the algorithm to create a decision tree; (3) the remaining instances are used to test the accuracy of the constructed tree; and (4) this procedure continues until a tree that adequately classifies members of the testing set has been assembled. Instances that do not contribute to the accuracy of the tree are ignored (Tan, Steinbach, & Kumar, 2006). The Decision Tree methodology can yield very useful information about the data and can be used to reduce the data to relevant fields before training another learning technique, such as a neural net.

Two different algorithms for performing rule inductions are C5.0 and classification and regression tree (C&R tree). The C5.0 algorithm works by splitting a dataset based on the attribute that provides the maximum information gain. Each subgroup defined by the first split is then split again, usually based on a different field, and the process is repeated until the subgroups cannot be split any further. Finally, the lowest-level splits are reexamined, and those that do not contribute significantly to the value of the model are removed, or "pruned." It works only when the outcome variable is a categorical measure.

The rule induction C5.0 provides two types of output: a decision tree and a rule set. A decision tree is a straightforward classification technique. Each terminal node describes a particular subgroup of the training data, and each case in the training data belongs to exactly one terminal node in the tree. A rule set is derived from decision trees and, in a way, represents a simplified version of the information found in the decision tree. The main difference is that with a rule set, more than one rule may apply for any particular instance, or no rules at all may apply based on the weighted votes (Dunham, 2003).

Unlike C5.0, the C&R tree can accommodate output measures that have numeric ranges as well as categorical attributes (Dunham, 2003). Another difference is that the C&R tree always performs binary splits on the data regardless of whether attributes are categorical or numeric. The C&R tree starts by examining the predictors to find the best split, measured by the reduction in an impurity index that results from the split. It is noted that an impurity index was used to measure the impurity or heterogeneity of the input (Breiman, Friedman, Olshen, & Stone, 1984; Shmueli, Patel, & Bruce, 2007). The split defines two subgroups, each of which is subsequently split into two more subgroups, and so on, until one of the stopping criteria is triggered.

Decision Tree Example: First-Year Student Retention Analysis

Research studies have shown that the most vulnerable stage for student retention at all institutions of higher education, including highly selective colleges and universities, is the first year of college (Learning Slope, 1991). Because the seeds of leaving university tend to be planted early, it is important for institutions to identify these students early in their academic careers and tailor institutional support and intervention programs to improve the retention outcomes.

The following modeling describes an approach to examine critical predictors influencing the decisions of first-time freshmen on completion of their first year. Three questions formed the basis for this study: (1) Are certain profiles typical of those first-time freshmen who are more likely to reenroll? (2) Do the noncognitive data collected on the CIRP Freshman Survey enhance our ability to predict retention? (3) If the reenrollment pattern can be identified and predictive models established, how well can future reenrollment be predicted?

Data Selection and Exploration

The fall 2008 population of first-time freshmen who completed the CIRP Freshman Survey (n = 1,304) at a large urban university was used. These freshman records included CIRP Freshman Survey results, self-report student profile information, and university-specific information such as placement tests scores and enrollment data. Of these freshmen, a total of 1,044 (80 percent) reenrolled in the following fall. Thus the outcome attribute—the freshman's decision—has two options: reenrolled at the beginning of their second year or stopped out. Table 28.2 presents descriptions of the twenty-six predictors that were used in this analysis, grouped into five categories.

Before data mining can begin, the quality of the data must be assessed. This involves both checking for blank or missing information and understanding the range and distribution of value within each attribute. Figure 28.4 shows the Type node that was used to investigate the integrity of data. The Data Audit output option can be used to examine missing values or blanks in a data

TABLE 28.2   PREDICTORS INCLUDED IN THIS RESEARCH MODEL

Variable	Description
Preparation for University Study	
1. High School GPA	High school grade point average
2. High School API	High school's Academic Performance Index (API) Score
3. Private High School	Coded 1 if student graduated from private high school
4. Remedial English	Coded 1 if student failed English Placement Test (EPT)
5. Remedial Math	Coded 1 if student failed Entry Level Math (ELM)
6. Remedial Math and English	Coded 1 if student failed both English and Math
7. Admission Basis	Coded 1 if student met all the regular admission criteria
8. SAT Composite Scores	SAT composite (converted) scores; conversion is used if only available ACT composite
9. Eligibility Index	Eligibility Index (combination of test scores and high school GPA)
Academic Outcomes and Enrollment Behaviors	
10. Undeclared Major	Coded 1 if student had undeclared major during first semester
11. STEM Major	Coded 1 if student declared one of STEM major during first semester
12. BUS Major	Coded 1 if student declared one of business major during first semester
13. Orientation	Coded 1 if student had undeclared major during first semester
Student Demographics	
14. Age	Age at time of matriculation (in year)
15. Gender	Coded 1 if female
16. CA Residency	Coded 1 if California state resident based on tuition status
17. Underrepresented Minority	Coded 1 if student's ethnicity was black, Latino, or Native American—IPEDS
18. Living on Campus	Coded 1 if lives on campus
Financial Aid	
19. Low-Income Family	Code 1 if below poverty line (based on family size and annual family contribution)
20. Parent Income	Annual parent income
21. Received Financial Aid	Code 1 if student received financial aid
22. Applied for Financial Aid, No Aid Received	Code 1 if student applied for financial aid, but aid was not received
23. Not Applied for Aid	Code 1 if student did not apply for financial aid
24. First-Generation Students	Code 1 if parent's (both father and mother) highest education is high school or less
CIRP Freshman Survey: Construct Parameters	
25. Academic Self-Concept	Personal beliefs regarding abilities and confidence in academic environment
26. Social Self-Concept	Personal beliefs regarding abilities and confidence in social situations

FIGURE 28.4   TYPE NODE AND DATA AUDIT OUTPUT

Type Node: Missing Column

Data Audit Output: Examining Missing Value Types

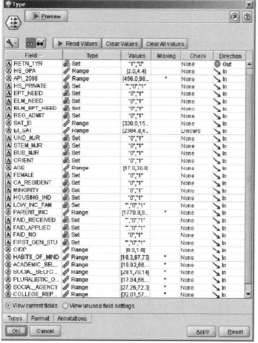

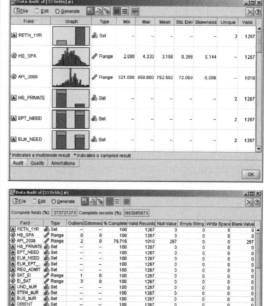

stream that allow a better understanding of the attributes themselves and completeness of data. These and the following analysis uses SPS Clementine (now referred to as SPSS Modeler) and use the terms from that software (http://www.spss.com/software/modeling/).

The C&R tree handles missing values better than many of the other techniques by using the substitute (surrogate) predictor field whose split is most strongly associated with that of the original predictor to direct a case with a missing value to one of the split groups during the tree-building process. It is noted, however, that most of the other techniques do not deal with blanks explicitly, and the presence of blanks in a dataset will increase the complexity of the data and modeling process.

In this study, student records were randomly separated into two subsamples for the training and testing stages of model building. By using one sample (50 percent) to generate the model and a separate sample (50 percent) to test it, the researcher can gain a good indication of how well the model will generalize to larger datasets that are similar to the current data.

Model Building

The C5.0 and C&R tree were chosen to handle this binary (categorical) outcome. It is noted that these algorithms use nonstatistical measures for selecting a predictor. An information (or entropy) measure is used for C5.0 and an impurity (or dispersion) measure is used for the C&R tree. As decision trees grow large and bushy, the lowest-level rules do not always generalize well to the testing dataset and may have rules that apply to tiny groups of data. Therefore lower-level splits often are discarded or pruned by setting model specifications for number of level and/or minimum group size.

Developing rules for returning and nonreturning students. Figure 28.5 displays the C&R tree rules that define the model. To identify the "stopped-outs" group (0), attention should be given to the records whose values align with one of the following conditions:

- Condition 1: Eligibility Index (EI_SAT) <= 3,297, High School API (API_2008) <= 803, Academic Self-Concept <= 53.63, Applied for Financial Aid (FAID_APPLIED), and Social Self-Concept <= 40.24

or

- Condition 2: Eligibility Index (EI_SAT) <= 3,297, High School API (API_2008) <= 803, Academic Self-Concept > 53.63

FIGURE 28.5   RULES WITH INSTANCE AND CONFIDENCE FIGURES AND LIST OF VARIABLES IMPORTANCE

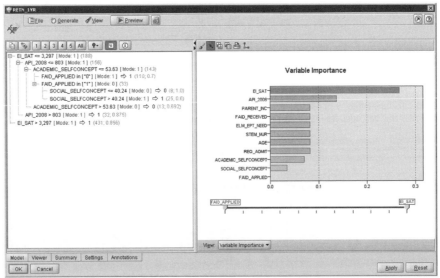

Note: The Rules with Instance and Confidence Figures appear in the left pane; the List of Variables Importance appears in the right pane.

Line 6 and Line 8 in the left pane of Figure 28.5 indicate that eight and thirteen students met Conditions 1 and 2, respectively. The confidence figures for this set of individuals are 1.0 and 0.692 and represent the proportion of records in this set that are correctly classified (predicted to leave and actually having left the institution). The Tree Alternative format to present the results is also available in the Tree View.

It is noted that Figure 28.5 shows only a selected set of important predictors that had a strong relationship to the outcome attribute. However, the C&R tree normally provides other relatively important predictors in the Variable Importance chart. Because the values are "relative," they do not relate to model accuracy. In practice, these attributes are useful for preliminary screening—particularly when dealing with large datasets with large numbers of predictors—and more useful in fine-tuning the model.

To avoid drawing conclusions on one test, it is important to understand the rule and determine the highest predictive accuracy from multiple models. Figure 28.6 shows the prediction results that are based on the probability of correct and wrong predictions between the C5.0 ($C-RETN) and the C&R tree ($R-RETN). The probability of correct "dropped-out" prediction from these

FIGURE 28.6   ANALYSIS OUTPUT OF C5.0 AND C&R TREE

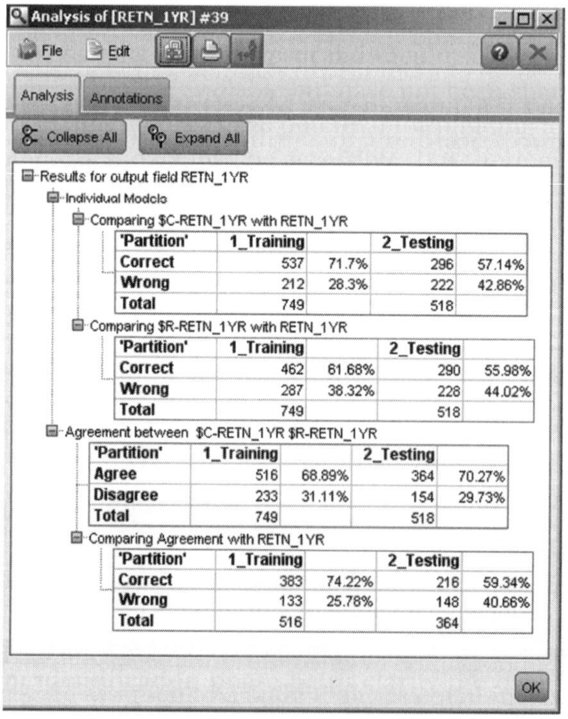

Analysis of [RETN_1YR] #39

File   Edit

Analysis   Annotations

Collapse All   Expand All

Results for output field RETN_1YR
Individual Models
Comparing $C-RETN_1YR with RETN_1YR

'Partition'	1_Training		2_Testing	
Correct	537	71.7%	296	57.14%
Wrong	212	28.3%	222	42.86%
Total	749		518	

Comparing $R-RETN_1YR with RETN_1YR

'Partition'	1_Training		2_Testing	
Correct	462	61.68%	290	55.98%
Wrong	287	38.32%	228	44.02%
Total	749		518	

Agreement between $C-RETN_1YR $R-RETN_1YR

'Partition'	1_Training		2_Testing	
Agree	516	68.89%	364	70.27%
Disagree	233	31.11%	154	29.73%
Total	749		518	

Comparing Agreement with RETN_1YR

'Partition'	1_Training		2_Testing	
Correct	383	74.22%	216	59.34%
Wrong	133	25.78%	148	40.66%
Total	516		364	

OK

models was about 71.7 percent for C5.0 and 61.68 percent for the C&R tree, supported by results from the corresponding testing groups of 57.14 percent and 55.98 percent, respectively. Thus the C5.0 model performed the best in this study. With the training sample results, the C5.0 model predicted about 77.3 percent of the "dropped-out" category correctly and 62.9 percent of the reenrollment correctly. The C&R tree model, on the other hand, predicted only about 68.1 percent of the "dropped-out" category correctly and 57.2 percent of the reenrollment correctly. Therefore results with the testing sample for C5.0 model compare favorably, which suggests that this model will perform well with new data.

As a result of these analyses, the answer to all three research questions was "yes." First, the predictors for first-year retention can be developed to identify the profiles of reenrolled students. Moreover, the noncognitive variables collected on the CIRP Freshman Survey were statistically significant predictors of retention. Finally, the probability of correct or wrong prediction describes how well predicted values from a generated model fit the actual values. Figure 28.6 indicates that the C5.0 achieved about 71.7 percent predictive accuracy.

Applications for Institutional Research

This study suggested that the level of complexity of the data and the outcome predicted may largely determine the selection of a particular analytical tool. The data mining algorithm worked notably well with a larger dataset with many fields and provided appropriate predictive outcomes at the individual level. The results were actionable and practical. Therefore the impact of this study centers on identifying additional students who are at risk to allow for effective intervention. Tables comparing actual outcomes with anticipated outcomes are useful in explaining the results and also for gaining statistical confidence of the methodology.

It is also important that institutions consider using the appropriate predictive models in combination with other interventions to improve student retention and graduation. This study focused on a snapshot of leavers, but this needs to be accompanied by targeted studies of individual student cohorts. Improving retention rates must be a multifaceted endeavor.

Artificial Neural Networks

On occasion the institutional researcher is faced with a very complex set of data with many variables, likely nonlinear and non-additive interactions, limited input from existing theories, and a large number of observations. In data analysis, artificial neural networks (ANN) are a class of flexible nonlinear models used for supervised classification or prediction problems. The models trained by ANN are parametric models, in contrast to decision tree models, which are nonparametric models. The advantage of ANN models is their ability to model very complex relationships between the target variable and predictors. Yet because of the ascribed analogy to neurophysiology, they are usually perceived to be more glamorous and complex than other (statistical) prediction models. They are also more difficult to explain to others.

The basic building blocks of an artificial neural network are called *hidden units*. Hidden units are modeled after the neuron. Each hidden unit receives a linear combination of input variables. The coefficients are called the weights rather than parameters. An activation function transforms linear combinations and then outputs them to another unit that can then use them as inputs.

Multilayer Perceptron Architecture

An artificial neural network is a flexible framework for specifying a variety of models. The most widely used type of neural network in data analysis is the multilayer perceptron (MLP): a feed-forward network composed of an input layer, hidden layers composed of hidden units, and an output layer. There are many other ANN architectures; due to limited space, our discussion will be limited to MLP. Figure 28.7 graphically illustrates an MLP with one input layer, one hidden layer, and one output layer. Note that there may be a different number of hidden units in hidden layers and there can be any number of hidden layers. For a more detailed discussion of ANN, the reader is referred to Bishop (2006).

FIGURE 28.7   EXAMPLE OF AN MLP

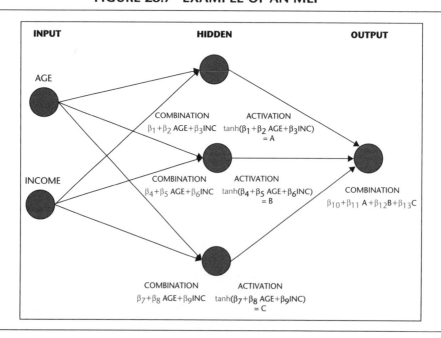

The hidden layers are composed of hidden units. Each hidden unit outputs a nonlinear function of a linear combination of its inputs—the *activation function*.

The output layer has units corresponding to the target. With multiple target variables or multiclass (>2) targets, there are multiple output units. The network diagram is a representation of an underlying statistical model. The unknown parameters (weights and biases) correspond to the connections between the units.

Each hidden unit outputs a nonlinear transformation of a linear combination of their inputs. The linear combination is the net input. The nonlinear transformation is the activation function. The activation functions used with MLPs are sigmoidal curves (surfaces).

A hidden layer can be thought of as a new space that is usually lower-dimensional and a nonlinear combination of the previous layer. The output from the hidden units is linearly combined to form the input of the next layer. The combination of nonlinear surfaces gives MLPs their modeling flexibility.

An output activation function is used to transform the output into a suitable scale for the expected value of the target. In statistics, this function is called the inverse *link function*. For binary targets, the logistic function is suitable because it constrains the output to be between zero and one (the expected value of a binary target is the posterior probability). The logistic function is sometimes used as the activation function for the hidden units as well. This sometimes gives the false impression that the link function and the activation function are related. The choice of output activation function depends only on the measurement scale of the target.

Figure 28.7 illustrates these concepts with a very simple example consisting of only two inputs: one hidden layer with three hidden units, and one output layer. The hyperbolic tangent function is used as the activation function in this example. This ANN allows the data miner to model very complex nonlinear relationships between the target variable and the predictors. If the relationship between the target variable and predictors were linear, then using logistic regression would be a reasonable choice to model the relationship, assuming the target was categorical.

Rules and general guidelines for determining the number of hidden layers and the number of units within a hidden layer are given by Nisbet, Elder, and Miner (2009). In general, they state that as the complexity of the relationship between the target and predictors increases, the number of units in the hidden layers should increase. They also state that the number of hidden units should be no more than one-fifth to one-tenth the number of training cases. Increasing the number of hidden layers or number of hidden units could lead to overfitting the model, so care must be taken in selecting the number of hidden layers and units.

Example: Using Neural Networks as a Part of Overall Analysis

As noted earlier, institutions use predictive models to identify those students who are at risk of not returning for the following semester. Neural network modeling was used to train a model to predict which of those new freshmen who entered in fall 2008 and reenrolled in spring 2009 would not reenroll for fall 2009. In data mining, this is the group of students that is to be scored by the model; it is often called the scoring dataset. This group of students is referred to as Freshmen2008.

The model was trained or built on those new freshmen who entered in the fall of 2007 and reenrolled in spring 2008. The target, or dependent, variable was coded "1" if the student did not enroll in the fall of 2008 and "0" if the student enrolled. This group of students is referred to as Freshmen2007. The model that is trained will predict the probability that a student in the Freshmen2008 dataset will not enroll in the fall of 2009, which is the probability that a student is at risk. The variables used to build this model are defined in Table 28.3, and SAS Enterprise Miner will be used to train the model on Freshmen2007 and score Freshmen2008.

As shown in Figure 28.8, the Data Partition Node follows the Freshmen2007 modeling dataset node; the split is 70 percent for training and

TABLE 28.3   PREDICTORS SELECTED FOR NEURAL NETWORK MODEL

		Wald	
Effect	DF	Chi-Square	Pr>ChiSq
Att_hrs_fall	1	0.6423	0.4229
Att_hrs_spr	1	0.4995	0.4797
Dorm_rate	1	18.4396	<.0001
Extra_curr	1	1.2603	0.2616
Fall_GPA	1	37.7362	<.0001
GENDER	1	1.5609	0.2115
IMP_Avg_Income	1	2.0443	0.1528
IMP_Distance	1	0.9674	0.3253
IMP_HIGH_SCHOOL_PERCENTILE	1	7.0116	0.0081
IMP_Hs_rate	1	96.0923	<.0001
IMP_Major_rate	1	0.2605	0.6098
Instate	1	3.4950	0.0616
M_Avg_income	1	1.9436	0.1633
M_Distance	1	0.9591	0.3274
M_HIGH_SCHOOL_PERCENTILE	1	3.3987	0.0652
M_Hs_rate	1	14.4479	0.0001
M_Major_rate	1	1.2067	0.2720
Need_pct_rate	1	7.8872	0.0050
Perc_hrs_comp_fall	1	10.6305	0.0011
SAT	1	6.0054	0.0143
Transcrip	1	63.3874	<.0001

FIGURE 28.8 FLOW PROCESS FOR NEURAL NETWORK ANALYSIS

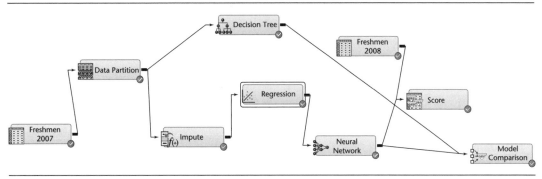

30 percent for validation. Next is the Impute Node, in which missing values are imputed for both categorical and interval variables by the tree method. To compare predictive results by multiple models, namely Algorithmic Bias Analysis, a Decision Tree Node is connected to the Data Partition Node and a Regression Node is connected to the Impute Node. The Regression Node is used to select those variables that are most important and they are passed to the Neural Network Node; the variables selected are shown in Table 28.3. Those variables starting with Imp or M were created by the Impute Node. The Neural Network Node is run with one hidden layer and three hidden units, which is the default for SAS Enterprise Miner. Several other combinations were tried, but the default setting yielded the best results in terms of average square error on the validation dataset. A Model Comparison Node was added to compare the decision tree model and the regression model, with results showing that the neural network model performed better. Both the misclassification rate of .08 and the average square error of .06, which are measures of model fit, indicate that the neural network model has fit our data very well, better than the decision tree model. The predictive power of the model is shown to be very strong by examining the ROC curve in Figure 28.9 and noting that the ROC index is .9 on the validation dataset and .08 for the decision tree. The ROC index is the area under the curve; an index greater than .7 is considered good, thus an index of .9 is excellent. Thus the neural network model is chosen over the decision tree model.

Our next task is to score or predict those students in Freshmen2008 that are most likely not to return in fall 2009. This is accomplished in Enterprise Miner by using the Scoring Node and connecting the Freshmen2008 dataset to the Scoring Node. Enterprise Miner builds a new dataset that shows the probability of a student not returning in the fall semester, based on the attributes of that student. Those students with probabilities greater than a chosen cutoff are flagged for intervention; this cutoff may be based on resources available or

FIGURE 28.9   ROC CURVES FOR DECISION TREE AND NEURAL NETWORK MODELS

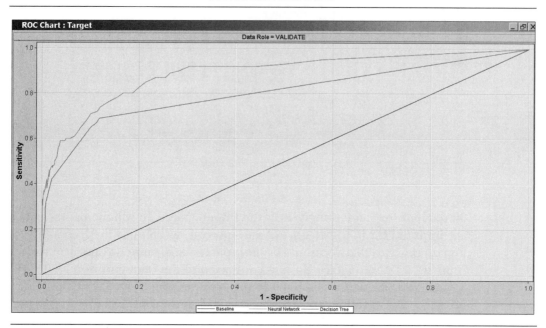

could be based on historical data. In this case, when a cutoff of .5 was used, 54 out of 3,013 students were selected for intervention; that is, 54 of the probabilities produced by the neural network model were greater than or equal to .5.

Applications for Institutional Research

This example illustrates the use of predictive modeling in institutional research and in particular the use of neural networks for predictive modeling. These techniques and modeling tools can be applied to other problems commonly addressed by institutional research, such as identifying students most likely to enroll, identifying students most likely to default on a student loan, and other modeling type problems. (See Chapter 13 for more discussion on student success in retention and graduation.) As can be seen, neural networks are among the more sophisticated data methodologies, and they can also be among the most powerful, particularly for complex situations. As with decision trees, two-way tables that provide the frequencies of correct classifications can be extremely useful. Also as with decision trees, there are rules that are used to compute the probability of group membership. These rules can be extremely complex, so the best way to predict an outcome is to form an analytical methodology that does the prediction and produces the predicted probability as an attribute of the individual.

Conclusions

One among a host of recent technology innovations, data mining is making changes to the entire makeup of our skills and comfort zones in information analysis. Not only does it introduce an array of new concepts, methods, and phrases, but it also departs from the well-established traditional hypothesis-based statistical techniques. Data mining is a new type of exploratory and predictive data analysis whose purpose is to delineate systematic relations between variables when there are no (or no complete) a priori expectations as to the nature of those relations. Based on the use of data mining in various institutional research situations, we have begun to identify some basic guidelines, which we now present along with some basic recommendations.

Recommendation 1: Conduct unsupervised modeling prior to supervised modeling

Rationale: This chapter began with cluster analysis, a form of unsupervised data modeling activity for the purpose of understanding data. The cluster analysis example helped researchers zero in on the subsets of populations of students that are clearly similar in certain aspects, thereby increasing the accuracy of predictions of predictive modeling later down the road. Unsupervised data mining also includes visualization and multidimensional data tables. Many potential problems—such as ill-fitting data, dirty data, noise, and poorly defined variables—can be identified and resolved in this process as well.

Recommendation 2: Validate outcomes through replication

Rationale: We recommend that researchers build models on a test dataset and validate the findings using a holdout dataset through replication. In studies whose findings are not replicated using a holdout sample, there is no way to judge how biased the sample may have been—and therefore how valid the findings could be. Guttman (1985) pointed out that "the idea of accepting or rejecting a null hypothesis on the basis of a single experiment . . . is antithetical to science" (pp. 4–5). But despite its importance, the replication of studies based on replication is rare in social science practices.

Recommendation 3: Adopt algorithmic bias analysis

Rationale: We recommend that institutional researchers adopt the use of multiple algorithms to compare results. This also implies the use of a training dataset and at least one validation dataset for conducting algorithmic bias analysis. We have been arguing against the practice of scholars examining and reporting the results based on one statistical test. In many cases at least two or more statistical tests are needed to make sure the results are free from the bias of the test itself. It is a documented fact that results may vary—and at times vary dramatically—from test to test. To rely on results from one test (algorithm) alone to draw conclusions that affect the decisions made by an institution or even larger organizational body is unscientific. The resulting impact on the lives of students demands that we give serious consideration to stopping that practice.

Recommendation 4: Explore the power of real-time database scoring

Rationale: We recommend that data mining models, once finalized, be deployed over live data warehouses to score the data in real time. Most data mining activities, as indicated by published articles and the case studies reported in this chapter, have stopped before the last—yet most useful—step: live scoring. This happens largely because the data warehouse technology currently avails itself only as a one-way street, meaning that the researchers can obtain the data for analysis but are unable to write back. Being able to deploy a data mining model over a live database—in much the same way as any number of applications that interface with Banner, SAP, PeopleSoft, or Datatel—would provide the greatest business advantage. The expression "knowledge discovery in databases" is meant to describe the task of scoring the data using a data mining model in a live database so that decision makers can obtain results in real time.

Recommendation 5: Present results that communicate to your users

Rationale: We recommend that users of data mining provide the results in fairly direct numerical and graphical visualizations. Where it is appropriate to discuss technical details, we suggest providing a technical appendix. We also recommend including a justification in the results for using data mining by explaining how the data cannot be appropriately analyzed by older forms of analysis or how data mining produces more value in interpretation than the older forms of analysis.

References

Bishop, C. (2006). *Pattern recognition and machine learning.* New York: Springer Science.

Breiman, L., Friedman, J., Olshen, R., & Stone, C. (1984). *Classification and regression trees.* Belmont, CA: Wadsworth International Group.

Dunham, M. H. (2003). *Data mining: Introductory and advanced topics* (pp. 100–103). Upper Saddle River, NJ: Pearson Education.

Guttman, L. (1985). The illogic of statistical inference for cumulative science. *Applied Stochastic Models and Data Analysis, 1,* 3–10.

Kaufman, L., & Rousseeuw, P. J. (1990). *Finding groups in data: An introduction to cluster analysis.* Hoboken, NJ: Wiley.

Kohonen, T. (2001). *Self-organizing maps.* New York: Springer Series in Information Sciences.

Learning Slope. (1991). *Policy perspectives.* Philadelphia: Institute for Research in Higher Education.

Luan, J., & Zhao, C. M. (Eds.). (2006). *Data mining in action: Cases studies of enrollment management.* New Directions for Institutional Research, no 131. San Francisco: Jossey-Bass.

Luan, J., Zhao, C. M., & Hayek, J. (2009, February). Using a data mining approach to develop a student engagement-based institutional typology. IR Applications. Retrieved from http://www.airweb.org/images/irapps18.pdf

Minard, C. J. (1869/2009). National Survey of Student Engagement. *Assessment for improvement: Tracking student engagement overtime-annual results 2009.* Bloomington: Indiana University Center for Postsecondary Research. Retrieved from http://www.edwardtufte.com/tufte/posters

Nisbet, R., Elder, J., & Miner, G. (2009). *Handbook of statistical analysis and data mining applications.* Burlington, MA: Elsevier.

Pike, G. R., & Kuh, G. D. (2005). A typology of student engagement for American colleges and universities. *Research in Higher Education, 46*(2), 185–209.

SAS Institute. (2010). SAS Enterprise Miner. Cary, NC: SAS Institute.

Shmueli, G., Patel, N. R., & Bruce, P. (2007). *Data mining for business intelligence: Concepts, techniques, and applications in Microsoft Office Excel with XLMiner.* Hoboken, NJ: Wiley-Interscience.

Tan, P., Steinbach, M., & Kumar, V. (2006). *Introduction to data mining.* (pp. 150–172). New York: Addison-Wesley.

Tukey, J. W. (1962). The future of data analysis. *Annals of Mathematical Statistics, 33,* 1–67.

Wishart, D. (2010). What is cluster analysis? Retrieved from http://www.clustan.com/what_is cluster analysis.html

CHAPTER 29

MEASURING OPINION AND BEHAVIOR

Sean Simone, Corbin M. Campbell, and Daniel W. Newhart

The purpose of this chapter is to summarize and synthesize the literature on the predominant methods used by institutional researchers
to measure opinion and behavior. This chapter illustrates the steps required to
prepare for a research inquiry and discusses three techniques used to measure
opinion and behavior: survey studies using questionnaires, focus groups, and
unobtrusive measures.

Preparation for a Research Inquiry

This section of the chapter details four steps institutional researchers should
consider when preparing for a research inquiry: choosing a method, defining
a purpose, developing research questions, and creating a timeline.

Step 1: Choose a Method

The methods discussed in this chapter can address many of the research questions that arise in institutional research. Survey methods are most appropriate
when research questions are narrowly tailored and when one is interested in
understanding the opinion and behavior of a large group of individuals. Survey
researchers are interested in breadth; they seek to generalize the findings or
a specific construct from a smaller sample to a larger population. In situations
in which institutional researchers are more interested in exploring the depth

This chapter is intended to promote the exchange of ideas among researchers and policy makers.
The views expressed in this chapter represent the opinions of the authors alone and do not
necessarily represent the positions or policies of the National Center for Education Statistics, the
Institute for Education Sciences, or the U.S. Department of Education.

of an issue, survey methods are not as appropriate unless used as a follow-up to a qualitative study (such as with focus groups, described shortly). Additionally, if there is no theory to guide the development of a survey instrument, institutional researchers should consider another method.

Focus groups, on the other hand, are best used when the purpose of the assessment is to "learn about the perceptions, beliefs, or opinions of the students or others who use campus facilities, services or programs" (Schuh & Upcraft, 2001, p. 42) and exploring the depth of a topic is important. One should not use a focus group if the intent is the acquisition of statistical data or the goal is to save time and money (Schuh & Upcraft, 2001). If one is concerned with issues that might be contentious, one could consider the one-on-one structured or unstructured interview as a qualitative data collection procedure rather than a focus group involving many people. One might also consider these types of methods if the researcher would like to go into greater depth regarding a phenomenon than a group setting would allow.

Step 2: Define the Purpose of the Study

After choosing the most appropriate method, the institutional researcher should define a clear purpose for the study by developing research questions. By this point the researcher has already asked questions such as "What do you want to know?" "Who wants to know it?" and "For what purpose will the results be used?" When it is time to plan the survey instrument or focus group protocol, there are additional questions to consider. Table 29.1 displays questions that would guide institutional researchers through the development of survey items or focus group protocol.

The results should provide actionable recommendations to address a policy issue and influence decisions. Any questions or items that either detract from a study's ability to inform decisions or are unrelated to the research questions (developed in the next step) should be discarded.

Step 3: Develop Research Questions

Once institutional researchers are confident that they have defined the purpose of the study, subsequent decisions will be informed by the research questions. The development of research questions should be preceded by a literature review. The literature will help in defining concepts, articulating theory, and assessing relationships among variables. Drawing from the literature and the objectives from the study, the analyst should develop a list of what is known about the issues, what is not known, and what is known but untested for the population of interest. With this information, the institutional researcher should develop clear, specific, and practical research questions for initial internal use. The actual research questions for the study are developed depending on the research tradition; these are described later in the chapter.

TABLE 29.1   QUESTIONS AN INSTITUTIONAL RESEARCHER SHOULD ADDRESS WHEN DESIGNING A STUDY

Topic Area	Questions
Preparation	How will the results be used? What are the objectives of your study? What are the critical questions to be answered? What information do you need to answer the questions? What concepts need to be defined? What have others done on this topic? Do you really need a survey or focus group; can data be obtained through other means? How will you analyze and report the data? (Suskie, 1996, pp. 3–6)
Audience	Who will see the data? Who will see the formalized results? Who will want to see the results, but might not have access? Who will the results affect?
Sample	Who will participate in the study? What do they know about the topic? What are their assumptions? What might be sensitive topics for this population? Where are they developmentally—and how might that affect how they perceive questions?
Logistics	When will the survey or focus group be administered and analyzed—and how does the timeline relate to your population and audience? Where will the survey or focus group be administered? How might the environment affect the outcome? Is the study cross-sectional or longitudinal? (Creswell, 2008)
Analysis Plan	What variables or attributes might you use to cut or code the data? Will you be doing a cross-sectional or longitudinal analysis?

Source: Adapted from Creswell, 2008; Fowler, 2002, 2009; Suskie, 1996; Upcraft and Schuh, 1996.

Step 4: Create a Timeline

The final step in planning the research study is to develop a timeline using specific date targets for each stage of the study. For surveys, all communications (whether it be email, U.S. mail, or telephone conversation) should be written out in advance, and dates should be set for each communication, with launch and close dates for the survey. For the focus group study, researchers should also set dates for moderator training, communications, and the focus group. In addition, time targets should be mapped out in the focus group protocol.

Surveys and Questionnaires

The preceding section described the general method for conducting a research inquiry. Many of these research inquiries involve the development and use of surveys and questionnaires. The following section discusses the steps in this development in more detail.

Designing a Survey Study

Designing a survey study to gain factual responses that measure opinion and behavior can be challenging. This section outlines the process for developing clear questionnaire items, and creating the survey instrument.

Developing Research Questions. Research questions for a survey study should be narrow enough that the question can be answered using quantitative methods, but broad enough to address a practical policy issue. Consider these examples:

1. To what extent does institutional diversity influence student success?
2. To what extent does involvement in diversity training influence a student's ability to work on a team in X course?
3. To what extent does [X gateway course or diversity intervention] influence a student's tolerance or acceptance of diversity?

The first question is too broad. Because "diversity" and "student success" are not defined, the research question will generate too many questionnaire items to be practical. The second question is too narrow. Although the question is specific enough to generate questionnaire items, it will not inform institutional decisions and does not have any implications, except with regard to the specific intervention. The third question strikes a balance between being narrow enough to develop a measure and broad enough to have policy implications at the institution. When possible, the analyst should share the proposed questions with a group of reviewers to refine and narrow the focus. Suskie (1996) wisely advises that there is no point in including research questions or survey questionnaire items over which leaders have no control in changing.

Mapping Survey Topics onto the Research Questions. Research questions often have several facets that the analyst may want to investigate. Creating a map that links the various facets of the research question—the audience, survey logistics, analysis plan, and potential additional research questions—will ensure that (1) the topic or research question is well-developed and defined and (2) the collected data will be relevant to the topic of interest. Here is an example:

Research Question 1: How challenging is the academic experience for freshmen at State University?

Developing the Items. The objective of item development is to develop reliable and valid measures of a construct that connects to the study's research questions. A survey question is reliable if all of the following apply:

1. The questions mean the same thing to every respondent.
2. The possible responses mean the same thing to every respondent.
3. In a given situation with the same conditions, the same respondent would always select the same answer (Fowler, 2002, 2009).

A survey question is valid if it accurately measures the intended construct. There are four common problems with the validity of survey questions: "1) They do not understand the question. 2) They do not know the answer. 3) They cannot recall it, though they do know it. 4) They do not want to report the answer in the interview context" (Fowler, 2009, p. 105). A fifth common concern for validity might be that respondents cannot accurately report an answer due to incorrect self-perceptions (for example, self-reported learning outcomes).

Although it is nearly (if not completely impossible) to eliminate all forms of error associated with questionnaire items, it is possible to increase their reliability and validity. Table 29.2 displays eight tips for doing so.

Selecting Response Scales. Response scales are important in determining the reliability and validity of questionnaire items. The type of response scale also often determines the types of analyses that can be conducted on the data. One initial decision for determining the type of response scale is whether the response will be "closed" (that is, the survey provides options from which the respondents select) or "open" (that is, the respondents provide their own free-form responses) (Saris & Gallhofer, 2007). Open questions are often useful if there is no existing literature on the topic from which to develop possible responses or if little is known about how the specific sample will respond. Even when these conditions exist, it is often impractical to use open responses in a large-scale survey because of the time and expense required for coding and analyzing free responses. (For more information about coding and analyzing free responses, see Chapter 33.) If the survey has many open response questions, institutional researchers should consider a focus group method as an alternative to the survey.

Ideally, in closed response items, response options will perfectly match respondents' experiences, attitudes, or behaviors (Saris and Gallhofer, 2007). In practice, item developers attempt to cover a broad range of possible experiences in a limited number of response options. There are four types of closed response options (Fowler, 2002, 2009): nominal, ordinal, interval, and ratio, ranging from unordered to ordered categories. Table 29.3 provides examples for how each of these response scales are used in questionnaire items.

To ensure that the response options include all the best answers for a given population, institutional researchers should use literature on the topic, previous survey results from the population, and the general knowledge of the population. Also consider the analysis plan when choosing response options. Generally, the higher the order of response options (that is, ratio is best), the

TABLE 29.2 BEST PRACTICES FOR DEVELOPING QUESTIONNAIRE ITEMS, WITH EXAMPLES

Tip	Example	Problem with the Question(s)	For more information see:
Avoid double-barreled or "multiple" questions Use wording that has significance either universally or for the respondents.	How many hours per week do you read or study outside of class? How many hours per week do you spend studying for your general education courses?	Is the objective of the survey item to measure reading or studying? Do all respondents know what "general education courses" are? One common trap in survey development is using jargon that is common use for those who developed the survey but may be foreign to the respondents. This is especially true if the developers and the respondents are of different generations or cultures.	Fowler, 2002; Iarossi, 2006 Fowler, 2002
Avoid ambiguous terms. When they are necessary, there are two options: define the construct for them or allow them to define the construct for you.	Do you agree or disagree with the following statement: I work hard in my coursework at State University.	This example allows respondents to answer the question based on their own perception of what "hard work" means. The item measures the perception of working hard. A better option would define the ambiguous term: Do you agree or disagree with the following statement: I work hard (that is, spend more than twenty hours per week) in my coursework at State University.	Fowler, 2002; Iarossi, 2006
Avoid questions that measure perceptions, not necessarily fact. Meaning, the response could be valid (true to the respondent's perception of the answer) and reliable (the respondent and all other respondents who have that same perception would choose the same answer), yet not indicative of the real underlying construct.	How would you rate your ability to develop a research question?	In this case, the answer might be indicative of how skilled the respondent is at creating research questions, the respondent's self-confidence about creating research questions, or some combination of the two.	
Do what you can to enhance recall. More significant and more recent events are more likely to be recalled. Therefore, when asking respondents to recall information from the past, consider the following strategies: Add an introduction, asking the respondents to think about context: details can trigger memory.	How would you rate the advisors at the academic support center?	This question is not specific enough to enhance recall. A revised question prompts the respondent to recall a specific experience:	Fowler, 1998

(continued)

TABLE 29.2 BEST PRACTICES FOR DEVELOPING QUESTIONNAIRE ITEMS, WITH EXAMPLES (*Continued*)

Tip	Example	Problem with the Question(s)	For more information see:
Make the questions longer, to get respondents to spend more time thinking about them. Ask multiple questions about the same event, to improve the likelihood of recall.		Think about the last time you visited the academic support center in the student union. How would you rate the academic advisor that you spoke with there?	Fowler, 1998, 2002
Take deliberate measures to reduce social desirability. Social desirability is a phenomenon wherein respondents report their behavior or attitudes as closer to the societal norms than their actual behavior or attitudes. Social desirability is particularly likely for items that are personal or deal with controversial topics. Respondents choose more socially desirable responses for three reasons: (1) they want to make themselves look good; (2) they actually perceive themselves as better than they are; or (3) they feel threatened by the question.	Do you have a problem with alcohol (such as drinking every day)?	Some suggestions for reducing social desirability (Fowler, 1998, 2002): • Avoid language that infers that the researcher is being judgmental. Stress the importance of accuracy. • Ensure confidentiality or anonymity, if possible. • Make sure that the question and topic are appropriate for your specific respondents. • Place the items later in the survey, after some more general and less invasive questions (Fowler, 2002). • To address social desirability, a revised question could state: All responses are confidential. The accuracy of your responses is very important to this survey. How many days per week do you drink an 8-ounce alcoholic beverage? 0 days / 1–2 days / 3–4 days / 5–6 days / 7 days	
Avoid language that is "leading." Leading questions cause respondents to respond in a certain way.	What is your attitude about making a difference in our environment by recycling?	This question leads respondents to believe that they should recycle, which would likely influence their responses.	Iarossi, 2006
Ask multiple questions about the same survey objective/topic. Asking multiple questions to measure the same construct has been linked to improved reliability and validity.	Do you agree or disagree with the following statement: I am satisfied with State University.	Creating scales or factors based on multiple items that tap the same construct can reduce measurement error (see section on Factor Analysis). Additional questions can help to increase precision: Do you agree or disagree with the following statements? I am satisfied with State University. I would recommend State University to a friend. If I had to do it all over again, I would enroll at State University. My general attitude toward State University is positive.	Fowler, 2002

TABLE 29.3   RESPONSE SCALES

Response Scale	Description	Example
Nominal	Unordered categories of responses; dichotomous: special case of nominal with two categories only	Red, blue, purple, orange
Ordinal	Ordered responses that do not necessarily have the same distance between each response option	Strongly Agree, Agree, Disagree, Strongly Disagree (there is an order, but the distance between first and second is not necessarily the same as the distance between third and fourth)
Interval	Ordered responses with equal intervals between responses, but without a meaningful zero	Fahrenheit temperature
Ratio	Ordered responses with equal intervals between responses, with a meaningful zero and meaningful ratios between responses	*How many hours do you work?* Response indicates the number of hours.

Source: Adapted from Fowler, 2002, 2009.

more flexibility an institutional researcher has in analyzing the data. Ratio-level data can be collapsed into categories, but categories cannot be expanded into ratios. If choosing to use response categories, they should be limited to five to seven options to strike a balance between the variability of responses required for analysis and the avoidance of possible cognitive overload for respondents (Groves, Fowler, Couper, Lepkowski, Singer, & Tourangeau, 2004). On a practical note, having the same response scales for multiple items can reduce the space needed or the time burden placed on respondents.

Creating the Survey Instrument. After the questionnaire items have been developed, each question should be evaluated for inclusion and placed in the appropriate objective in the survey design map (see Table 29.4). The following questions help determine where to place the item on the survey design map:

- What, specifically, do you want to know from each item?
- How does each item contribute to the larger purpose of your survey?
- What role does it serve?

The final step is checking to ensure that the item is constructed appropriately for the objective, audience, sample, and logistics—this is the last item to check before survey layout.

- Does each item map onto an appropriate objective?
- Is there at least one associated item for each objective (and for each variable within each objective)?
- Is each item appropriate based on the audience, respondents, logistics, and analysis plan?

TABLE 29.4 SURVEY DESIGN MAP

Research Question/ Subtopic	Audience Considerations	Sample Considerations (assumptions, knowledge, sensitive topics, and so on)	Logistical Considerations	Analysis Plan
Quantity of work: How much work are freshmen students doing in their coursework?	Provost and college deans are interested in this topic due to concern that students do not feel challenged academically.	Freshmen's perception of work might be relative to their high school experience. Respondents' experience will be based on their specific coursework.	Survey is administered eight weeks into the first semester. Will they have had mid-terms by this point?	Cut by college, race, gender. Cut by whether or not they had taken a mid-term at this point.
Quality of work: What types of work are students doing in their coursework?	Provost and college deans are interested in this topic due to concern that students do not feel challenged academically.	Consider that freshmen courses tend to be larger— what implications does this have on activities like discussions?	At eight weeks into the fall semester, will respondents know what kinds of work their courses demand?	Cut by college, race, gender. Cut by whether or not they had taken a mid-term at this point.

Note: For additional examples of how to map your research objectives, see Fowler, 1998.

Ordering and Layout of the Instrument. After an analyst decides which questionnaire items to include, the next step is to order the items. Generally, the first few items in a survey should be easy to answer and quick and should pose no personal or controversial topics (Fowler, 2002, 2009; Iarossi, 2006). The items should flow from topic to topic without abrupt changes (Iarossi, 2006). The most important or personal items of the survey should be placed in the middle of the questionnaire. Researchers should be cautious about where they place controversial and personal items or items that may evoke extreme emotions and thus alter the responses for items that follow.

The final items in your survey also deserve special consideration, especially if the survey is long. Long surveys place a greater burden on the respondents. Often there will be lower response rates to the last items in long surveys (Iarossi, 2006). As a result, it is inadvisable for the most central items to appear late in the survey. In contrast, there is little evidence that length of survey affects overall response rate (Iarossi, 2006). Make sure to time your pilot survey and assess whether the survey length is appropriate for your particular population (Fowler, 2002, 2009). Iarossi (2006) provides the following recommendations for laying out a survey:

- Generally, simpler is better.
- There should be ample space between the items.

- Each survey should contain an identification number on each page.
- Branching or filter questions can reduce the burden on respondents; however, the layout for branching must be simple and clear.
- Instructions should be distinguished from items (for example, by using boxes or a larger, bold font).

Obtaining Feedback. Prior to fielding a completed questionnaire, the researcher should obtain feedback to ensure that items are interpreted as they were intended. A poorly designed questionnaire yields substandard data. Obtaining feedback ensures that items will not be discarded during analysis because of misinterpretations, poor skip patterns, or confusing instructions. This section focuses on four feedback mechanisms that can be used to improve the questionnaire:

Cognitive interviews. This technique is designed to help analysts understand how respondents think through their responses to survey items. It is useful in survey research for identifying misinterpretation of items, confusing instructions, or answers not present in a response set. Jobe and Mingay (1989) recommend a number of techniques for conducting cognitive interviews including, but not limited to:

- Think-alouds—Respondents describe how they came to answer a question either concurrently or retrospectively.
- Paraphrasing—Respondents repeat a question using their own words.
- Focus interview—An unstructured discussion of the survey topics.
- Probes—Follow-up questions to gain more information about the respondent's strategy for answering the question.

Expert interviews. The goal of expert interviews is to improve the questionnaire instrument by eliciting feedback from experts who are knowledgeable with the topic area covered in the survey. In addition to providing feedback on the interpretation of questions and instructions, experts can provide feedback on the theory behind the questionnaire item and/or provide recommendations for adding items from other surveys.

Expert reviews. Expert reviews focus on survey or market researchers instead of experts with experience in the topic area. IR analysts use survey experts (often found within the college or university academic departments) to further refine and improve the clarity of questionnaires.

Pilot studies. The final step in improving the questionnaire is by conducting a pilot study—that is, a practice implementation of the questionnaire instrument. Pilot studies can range from very small and limited to large and comprehensive. Pilot studies are valuable in providing real data for understanding the viability of questionnaire items, the clarity of instructions, or the viability of skip patterns.

After making corrections to the survey instrument based on feedback from these processes, it is advisable to conduct a final check of the questionnaire using IR or student staff to ensure that paper forms scan properly (for paper and pencil administration), the web forms capture data (for electronic administration), or the revisions are not in themselves confusing. After the vetting process, the questionnaire is ready to be administered in the field.

Sampling Procedures: Populations and Sampling

The next step in the process is to define the population and select a sample from that population. A population is defined based on the research question. For example, if one is interested in understanding how new students adapt to a diverse environment, the population is incoming students. Once a population is clearly defined, then an analyst can select the sample from that set of persons. Table 29.5 presents four of the less complex sampling methods: simple random sampling (SRS), stratified sampling, stratified sampling with disproportionate selection probabilities, and convenience sampling. For other more complex sampling design methods (for example, clustered, two-stage clustered, multistage) see Groves et al. (2004).

Determining an adequate sample size depends on an analyst's tolerance for sampling error. Prior to sampling the population, the researcher needs to make decisions about the desired confidence level (typically 95 percent) and the desired sampling error (or level of precision). The lower the sampling error and higher the confidence interval, the larger the sample required. The formula for estimating a sample size in a simple random sample using these parameters is shown in Figure 29.1 (see Cochran, 1963).

Interpreting Survey Data

After data collection, data cleaning, and data coding are complete, an institutional researcher needs to take a number of steps in order to properly interpret survey data. Primarily, the researcher needs to scrutinize the response rate for the survey and determine whether the survey is representative of the population. Suskie (1996) notes that survey researchers recommend obtaining a response rate between 70 and 80 percent. Although obtaining a high response rate is desirable, high-quality responses are more important than the quantity of responses (Suskie, 1996). In fact, with the increased use of web surveys directed toward students, it is not uncommon for institutional researchers to receive response rates below 35 percent. The National Center for Education Statistics (2002) *Statistical Standards* recommends conducting an analysis of the magnitude of nonresponse bias when unit or item responses fall below 85 percent. To assess nonresponse bias, institutional researchers can use statistical tests to compare the characteristics of the sample with the characteristics of a population of students using institutional data, compare descriptive statistics between the population and sample, and compare respondents to a particular survey question with other respondents to the survey.

TABLE 29.5 TYPES OF SAMPLING PROCEDURES

Sampling Procedure	Description	Representative of the Population?	Statistical Adjustments Required
Simple Random Sampling (SRS)	Simple random sampling is the gold standard in survey research; most basic statistical hypothesis tests presume that samples are random. Simple random sampling presumes that all members of the population have an equal probability of being selected to take a survey. Obtaining a simple random sample can be impractical when researchers do not have complete access to the population or when subgroups in the sample do not respond to the survey.	Yes	No adjustments are required if the survey is conducted properly.
Stratified Sampling	To obtain a stratified sample, an analyst can divide the sample into subgroups called stratum (such as race or ethnicity, class standing, age groups). The analyst then uses simple random sampling procedures within each stratum to obtain an overall sample. The advantage to selecting a stratified sample rather than a simple random sample is in precision; known variability is removed from the sample, increasing the likelihood of hypothesis tests to uncover differences among respondents.	Typically no. If the response rates are different by stratum, then adjustments are required.	The sample should be weighted for unit nonresponse. Assuming there are enough respondents per stratum, the stratum with low response rates should be given increased weight, whereas the stratum with high response rates should be given lower weight.
Stratified Sampling with Disproportionate Sampling Probabilities	Sometimes stratified samples require adjustment to ensure that all subgroups are represented in a survey study. For example, institutional researchers will find that stratifying by race can be problematic because of the low number of some racial/ethnic groups. Employing a stratified sample with disproportionate selection probabilities is the most appropriate technique if it is required to compare racial groups. In this sampling design, participants in each stratum have a different probability of being selected.	No	The sample should be weighted for disproportionate sampling probabilities. Respondents in a stratum with a higher probability of selection should be weighted lower than the rest of the sample.
Convenience Sampling	The sampling designs described above can be expensive, because institutional researchers do not have access to the entire population of potential respondents at once. Institutional researchers do have access to students during regular intervals through an institution's administrative processes (such as admissions, registration, financial aid, and student enrollment in gateway courses).	No	If the analyst can use one of these processes to obtain a large proportion of respondents through a census or a response rate above 80 percent, the analyst may conduct an analysis of nonresponse, which would assist in making judgments about the representativeness of the sample to the population.

Source: Adapted from Groves et al., 2004, and Suskie, 1996.

FIGURE 29.1 EQUATIONS FOR DETERMINING THE SIZE OF A SAMPLE

$$n' = \frac{z^2 \times p \times (1-p)}{e^2} \quad n = \frac{n'}{1 + \left(\frac{n'}{N}\right)}$$

n' – sample size required for the projected variance of a s^2 (which is $P \times (1-P)$) irrespective population size

p – the anticipated proportion of an attribute or variable of interest in the study (the most conservative estimate being 0.5 where responses are equally distributed above and below the mean (maximum variability)).

z – the z-score associated with the desired confidence level, cut off at the tails of the distribution (a 95% confidence interval is associated with a z-score of ±1.96).

e – the desired sampling error, a range of 5% (or ± 2.5%) is 0.05.

n – corrected sample size adjusted for the size of the population (the finite population correction (*fpc*))

N – size of the population of interest

Assessing Reliability and Validity. In the measurement of human behavior and attitudes, there is always error. As indicated by Groves et al. (2004), error can be caused by (1) problems with measurement or (2) problems with the representation of the sample. With regard to measurement, error can come from construct validity, measurement error, or errors in data processing. With regard to the representativeness of the sample, error can result from coverage error (e.g., misrepresentation of the target population), sampling error, or nonresponse error. Yet, as we have mentioned throughout the section on survey design, there are several ways to reduce error. After the survey is administered and data are collected, there are four ways to determine how valid your survey is in measuring the desired constructs:

- Analyze the data to see whether expected relationships with predictors hold true.
- Compare to other items intended to measure similar constructs using a similar sample.
- Compare answers against records.
- Measure consistency of responses across time.

After completing these steps, survey data are ready for more rigorous statistical analysis (for more on this, see Chapter 27).

Focus Groups in Institutional Research Settings

Focus groups offer a way to determine not only the "why" and "how" behind a phenomena, but also the unique way in which participants react to one another as a function of the participant responses. A researcher could capture not only suggestions for the improvement of a program but also how other students in the focus group might react to other participants' suggestions (Trosset, 2007).

Focus Group Sampling

After determining whether a focus group is appropriate for the study, a focus group organizer might wonder about the question of sampling. The purpose of qualitative methods is to gather in-depth information about a particular phenomenon, not to generalize. Lincoln and Guba (1986) argue that qualitative methods are concerned with what is called "transferability" or the idea that the findings from the research study are comparable to contexts outside the research study. However, the important key to transferability is a thorough description of the research setting in the research reports (Lincoln & Guba, 1986). One would not want to transfer findings from a large, Research I university to a community college without an adequate description of the study context and setting. One of these key elements would be a description of the sampling design.

According to Merriam (1998), there are three types of sampling in qualitative data collection procedures: *purposive sampling, maximum variation sampling,* and *network sampling* (sometimes called snowball or chain sampling). One would use *purposive sampling* when the goal of the study is to collect data from people who are particularly well informed about the situation the research question is focused on (Merriam, 1998). Purposive sampling should seek information-rich cases—those cases that will inform the study greatly (Patton, 2002). Researchers pursuing purposive sampling should also seek critical cases—those cases that are very important in answering the research question (Munhall, 2001). Purposive sampling is the sampling procedure most often relied on in focus group data collection (Miles & Huberman, 1984).

In the second sampling procedure often used in focus groups, *maximum variation sampling,* the researcher seeks out a group of participants who did not know much about the subject of the research, to find out why they are uninformed about some phenomena. For example, one might conduct a focus group which explores student's lack of knowledge of services on campus provided by a student affairs division by bringing together students who have been identified as not using the university services through a service utilization survey.

The third sampling procedure used in constructing a focus group is called *network sampling.* Some focus groups use this type of sampling, though it is not recommended unless the topic is very specific. This type of sampling could be helpful in identifying people who may have been overlooked in the study and might know a great deal (Schuh & Upcraft, 2001).

Scholars (Carnaghi, 1992; Morgan, 1998) state that ideally a focus group should number no more than seven to ten people. The number of participants should also make sense given the depth of the topic. A smaller group of participants is desirable to explore topics that are complex, contentious, or both; a larger group may be warranted for topics that participants may not know much about.

Developing a Focus Group Study

The next task in planning a focus group study is to construct the focus group protocol; that is, the questions to be asked during the data collection phase. The protocol and its format are contingent on the research question, and should relate back to this question in order to keep the focus group study relevant to the topic. There are two types of focus group protocol: unstructured (or informal) and structured (or standardized) (Schuh & Upcraft, 2001). Schuh and Upcraft state that the structured focus group protocol is useful if the researcher is trying to gain a lot of information from participants and is interested in keeping the group on a specific topic. If a researcher is interested in collecting information about a topic that participants do not know too much about, a more unstructured protocol might be explored in the focus group to allow for exploration into the research topic.

When talking about protocol construction, Schuh and Upcraft (2001) provide some examples of structured and unstructured focus group protocol questions. Some structured protocol question examples are "What major did you choose? Why did you select this major?" or "What would you say to a prospective first-year student about academics at the college?" (p. 49). Unstructured focus group questions examples are "When you think of academics at the college, what pops into your mind?" or "As you reflect on your academics, what might have been disappointing to you?" (p. 49). Schuh and Upcraft provide a list of possible parameters that would apply to both structured and unstructured questions:

- The questions should be clear (no acronyms or institutional research jargon).
- Ask questions which are open-ended (and can be answered with more than a yes or no).
- Ask one question at a time, and make sure the order in which you ask the questions makes sense.
- Avoid leading questions, such as "How has our new learning program helped you in your academics?"

Developing Focus Group Moderators

The researcher interested in collecting useful qualitative data from the focus group should be concerned with recruiting a competent moderator—someone who is trained to listen to the participants, rather than someone who interjects his or her own opinions. A moderator should be able to hear all voices, not just the positive ones, and should not respond to criticism or lack of knowledge until the end of the focus group. A good moderator should be able to use effective probes and reinforcers (Goldenkoff, 2004) to draw out more rich data from the participants. These probes and reinforcers should be as neutral as possible; for example, following a comment with an approving "That's an absolutely excellent comment, Sam" could be perceived as leading the conversation a certain way, even toward what is perceived as a socially desirable response. Additionally, the moderator should have a neutral role relative to the focus group participants. For example, supervisors should not conduct focus groups of their employees.

Perhaps as important as the moderator is the assistant moderator (Goldenkoff, 2004) or scribe—the person who is there to take notes as the focus group occurs. Though some might think that a recording device could be used instead of an assistant moderator, both are recommended. Some researchers who use focus groups recommend that the assistant moderator take notes in case the device fails, or take notes on observations that the recorder cannot capture. For instance, did the mood of the group seem to change as a result of a participant's comment? An assistant moderator could note that the body language of the group changed, or perhaps that some of the participants did not talk after a particular comment.

Conducting the Focus Group

In a focus group setting, a moderator should take time to introduce him- or herself at the beginning of a focus group, along with the assistant moderator. In this introduction, the moderator should discuss the following:

- The affiliation the study is under (for example, a university institutional research office)
- A voluntary participation statement, indicating that any participant who feels uncomfortable at any time may leave the study without penalty
- A confidentiality statement, especially if the focus group is being recorded
- How the data will be used
- The importance of just one person speaking at a time, as the note taker would have a difficult time taking notes with multiple people talking, and/ or the recording device might not pick up multiple voices speaking at once

If the university or college Institutional Review Board (IRB) has reviewed the study, this is an appropriate time to state this approval as well (one should also do this in recruitment contacts, if applicable). During the focus group, the assistant moderator should take notes unobtrusively. Time should be scheduled at the end of the session, to discuss any specific questions that need clarification. This final step helps with validation later in the study in the form of member checking.

Analyzing Focus Group Data

Just as it is for advanced data procedures in quantitative data analysis, advanced training is also required for an in-depth analysis of qualitative data (Harper & Kuh, 2007). Harper and Kuh state: "The best data emerge from systematic, thoughtful, and rigorous procedures for which methodological regulations have been written" (p. 10). However, it may be that most institutional research offices do not have people who are trained in qualitative methods. As Goldenkoff (2004) states, the depth of an analysis of qualitative data from a focus group may be a function of the resources available to the researcher. Goldenkoff also states that "when quick decisions are needed (whether to move ahead on a proposed program, for example) or when the results of the focus groups are self-evident, a brief summary and analysis would suffice" (p. 359). This type of rudimentary data analysis could be compared to running descriptive statistics on survey data. However, if the research question is more complex or the project is much more ambitious in its scope, one should seek a more in-depth, rigorous analysis of the qualitative data. There is some additional discussion of analyzing data from focus groups in Chapter 33.

Steps to Help the Data Analysis Process. Krueger (1998) recommends that immediately after a focus group session, researchers hold a debriefing session with the moderator and assistant moderator and include the following questions:

1. What are the most important themes or ideas discussed (in the focus group)?
2. How did these differ from what we expected?
3. What points need to be included in the report?
4. What quotes should be remembered and possibly included in the report? and
5. Should we do anything differently for the next focus group?" (Krueger, 1998, cited in Schuh and Upcraft, 2001, p. 55)

Taking the time to work through these initial questions will help the researcher who is writing the report make sense of the data along with those who have experienced the focus group from the data collection side. The step also helps ensure some forms of validity, as discussed in the next section.

Analysis and Coding. To have data to analyze, one must transcribe the data. A researcher, depending on time constraints, could write very detailed notes or directly transcribe the recording. As mentioned previously, a key component of this transcription is being able to hear the voices of the participants, and the recording device experiment discussed should help gain a clear transcription. Transcriptions, once checked by those involved in the study, can then be used for the coding process of qualitative data analysis. Most people who use focus groups use a transcript that captures the focus group verbatim and use content analysis as a data analysis tool (Goldenkoff, 2004). Content analysis, though a very involved procedure, is discussed accessibly in Krippendorf (2004). (For more discussion of qualitative data analysis, see Chapter 27.)

Validity. Validity is an important issue in qualitative data collection and research. Caudle (2004) mentions certain steps that may help establish validity in a focus group study. The threats to validity in qualitative studies that she mentions are incomplete data, misinterpretation of data, discounting of data, and failure to document the chain of evidence. She gives a number of practical, easily applied steps to help counter these threats to validity. For example, Caudle recommends quick transcription of the data (in this case, from the focus groups) to protect against incomplete data. She suggests comparing the findings that emerge with other available research on the topic, making a critical examination of the relationships between data and the connections the researcher makes, and using consistent, thorough coding practices to protect against misinterpretation of the data. She recommends, if the resources are available, having the coding analyst recode the data and then another analyst code the same data to "increase coding accuracy" (p. 430). To protect against discounting the data, she recommends looking at those cases that do not fit the emerging data patterns, which she calls "negative case analysis" (p. 430). Finally, to help avoid the risk of not documenting the evidence well enough, she recommends looking at the debrief report (as suggested earlier by Krueger, 1998) and preparing documentation of the data analysis procedures as if it might be checked by an external party. As a side effect, this helps researchers in other contexts determine whether the findings from the focus study are transferable to their contexts.

Interpretation of the Data

The interpretation of qualitative data from the focus group emerges after the coding process is complete. After the forms of validity checking have been completed, researchers can use the initial debrief report, along with the codes from the transcriptions and emerging themes, to transfer the data into findings from the focus group study. Researchers should keep their audience in mind when writing, but the idea is that the work that one has been doing through the data collection and analysis process will feed directly into the final report. Though it is tempting to use every quote directly and present the findings this way, Patton (2002) recommends that researchers focus on what is essential to the point, by providing enough context, evidence, and detail to make the point convincingly. Finally, in any qualitative study one should make sure that those involved in the data collection and analysis complete the final report or at least edit it; this helps ensure that those close to the data have had a chance to make sure there was nothing missing in the presentation of the results. As Berg (2004) reminds us, findings differ from results in that findings lend themselves to being descriptive only, whereas results are the product of an in-depth analysis.

Unobtrusive Measures

Unobtrusive measurement techniques were developed as a data collection strategy to address social desirability bias (also known as "measurement reactivity" or the "Hawthorne effect") resulting from the change of behavior caused by an awareness of being measured (Marrelli, 2007). Webb, Campbell, Schwartz, and Sechrest (1966) pioneered a new data collection method whereby subjects are unaware of the data collection; for example:

- Comparing the wear from foot traffic on floor tiles in front of particular museum exhibits to measure the relative popularity of the different exhibits
- Reviewing newspaper and magazine articles to measure social attitudes
- Using observation techniques in the field (Marrelli, 2007)

This section reviews the unobtrusive measures available to institutional researchers for measuring opinion and behavior.

Secondary Data Analysis

The first technique available to institutional researchers is secondary data analysis. Many colleges and universities operate large data systems to track registration, coursework, billing, house assignments, admissions, and faculty workload. These data systems track student behavior without the risk of social desirability bias. Institutional researchers can use this transactional data to measure factors that contribute to student persistence, academic performance, and course popularity. Data systems also contain data that allow institutional researchers to measure how student characteristics are correlated with a variety of academic performance variables. College and university data systems can also be used to measure the effectiveness of business practices, including the efficiency of filling courses, the popularity of dining hall options, the success of book rental programs, and the ratio of revenues to costs for operations.

Observation of Established Institutional Practices and Procedures

Another unobtrusive method available to institutional researchers is tracking student contact through institutional practices and procedures. This method involves the observation or tracking (using available technology) of student behaviors at the university; for example:

- The frequency of checking out library books
- The frequency of registering for courses online versus in person
- The number of contacts in student services offices (career center, counseling center, legal affairs, residence life, and so on)
- The number of times students change their course schedule, to assess decision making

Content/Archival Analysis

Content or archival analysis uses documents to evaluate a research question to measure opinion and behavior (Marrelli, 2007). Colleges and universities produce a vast number of documents available for study. Institutional researchers can take advantage of records (via the institution's archivist) for historic analysis of institutional policy or the general social behavior of the student population in the past. Institutional researchers can also take advantage of students' work products to evaluate learning outcomes for courses or programs.

The Ethics of Secondary Analysis

Although unobtrusive measures can address social desirability bias in research, this technique is fraught with ethical issues. By definition, researchers do not gain the consent of the student or subject to conduct the research, so institutional researchers should use extreme caution when using unobtrusive methods. It is safer to evaluate organizational processes or the aggregate behavior of the student body rather than the behavior of an individual student. Unobtrusive methods, however, can be especially useful to supplement data from survey or focus group studies as a validation technique. Supplementing data in this way has the advantage of student consent. (For more discussion of IRB and FERPA, see Chapter 19.)

Conclusion

This chapter presented three methods for measuring opinion and behavior: survey questionnaires, focus groups, and unobtrusive measures. Although other methods are available to measure opinion and behavior (such as structured interviews, unstructured interviews, and polling), these three are more widely used in institutional research.

References

Berg, B. L. (2004). *Qualitative research methods for the social sciences*. Boston, MA: Allyn & Bacon.

Carnaghi, J. E. (1992). Focus groups: Teachable and educational moments for all involved. In F. K. Stage & Associates (Eds.), *Diverse methods for research and assessment of college students*. Washington, DC: American College Personnel Association.

Caudle, S. L. (2004). Qualitative data analysis. In J. S. Wholey, H. P. Hatry, & K. E. Newcomer (Eds.), *Handbook of practical program evaluation*. San Francisco: Jossey-Bass.

Cochran, W. G. (1963). *Sampling techniques* (2nd ed.). New York: Wiley.

Creswell, J. W. (2008). *Research design: Qualitative, quantitative, and mixed methods approaches*. Thousand Oaks, CA: SAGE.

Fowler, F. J. (1998). *Improving survey questions: Design and evaluation*. Thousand Oaks, CA: SAGE.

Fowler, F. J. (2002). *Survey research methods* (3rd ed.). Thousand Oaks, CA: SAGE.

Fowler, F. J. (2009). *Survey research methods* (4th ed.). Thousand Oaks, CA: SAGE.

Goldenkoff, R. (2004). Using focus groups. In J. S. Wholey, H. P. Hatry, & K. E. Newcomer (Eds.), *Handbook of practical program evaluation*. San Francisco: Jossey-Bass.

Groves, R. M., Fowler, F. J., Couper, M. P., Lepkowski, J. M., Singer, E., & Tourangeau, R. (2004). *Survey methodology*. Hoboken, NJ: Wiley.

Harper, S. R., & Kuh, G. D. (2007). Myths and misconceptions about using qualitative methods in assessment. In S. R. Harper & S. D. Museus (Eds.), *Using qualitative methods in institutional assessment*. New Directions for Institutional Research. San Francisco: Jossey-Bass.

Iarossi, G. (2006). *The power of survey design: A user's guide for managing surveys, interpreting results, and influencing respondents*. World Bank Publications.

Jobe, J. B., & Mingay, D. J. (1989). News from NCHS: Cognitive research improves questionnaires. *American Journal of Public Health, 79*(8).

Krippendorf, K. (2004). *Content analysis: An introduction to its methodology*. Thousand Oaks, CA: SAGE.

Krueger, R. A. (1998). *Analyzing and reporting focus group results*. Thousand Oaks, CA: SAGE.

Lincoln, Y. S., & Guba, E. G. (1986). But is it rigorous? Trustworthiness and authenticity in naturalistic evaluation. In D. Williams (Ed.), *Naturalistic evaluation*. New Directions for Program Evaluation, no. 30. San Francisco: Jossey-Bass.

Marrelli, A. F. (2007). Unobtrusive measures. *Performance Improvement 46*(9), p. 43–47.

Merriam, S. B. (1998). *Qualitative research and case study applications in education*. San Francisco: Jossey-Bass.

Miles, M. B., & Huberman, A. M. (1984). *Qualitative data analysis: A source book of new methods*. Thousand Oaks, CA: SAGE.

Morgan, D. L. (1998). *The focus group guidebook*. Thousand Oaks, CA: SAGE.

Munhall, P. L. (2001). *Nursing research: A qualitative perspective*. London, UK: Jones and Bartlett.

National Center for Education Statistics (2002). Statistical standards. Retrieved from http://nces.ed.gov/statprog/2002/std4_4.asp

Patton, M. Q. (2002). *Qualitative research and evaluation methods*. Thousand Oaks, CA: SAGE.

Saris, W. E., & Gallhofer, I. N. (2007). *Design, evaluation, and analysis of questionnaires for survey research*. Hoboken, NJ: Wiley-Interscience.

Schuh, J. H., Upcraft, M. L., & Associates (2001). *Assessment practice in student affairs*. San Francisco: Jossey-Bass.

Suskie, L. A. (1996). *Questionnaire survey research: What works* (2nd ed.). Tallahassee, FL: Association for Institutional Research.

Trosset, C. (2007). Qualitative research methods for institutional research. In R. D. Howard (Ed.), *Using mixed methods in institutional research*. Tallahassee, FL: Association for Institutional Research.

Upcraft, M. L., & Schuh, J. H. (1996). *Assessment in student affairs: A guide for practitioners*. San Francisco: Jossey-Bass.

Webb, E. J., Campbell, D. T., Schwartz, R. D., & Sechrest, L. (1966). *Unobtrusive measures: Nonreactive research in the social sciences*. Skokie, IL: Rand McNally.

CHAPTER 30

INSTITUTIONAL RESEARCH WITH PUBLISHED INSTRUMENTS

Julie Noble and Richard Sawyer

Data from published instruments are a valuable resource for institutional researchers. These instruments provide data on students' background characteristics, educational plans, and career goals, as well as on their cognitive skills. In this chapter, we describe admission and course placement tests, as well as instruments that measure students' psychosocial characteristics (such as motivation and social engagement). We first briefly describe the published instruments and then summarize how data from them can be used to conduct and inform institutional research. The chapter concludes with a discussion about the role of institutional researchers in acquiring data from published instruments and in evaluating results of research based on these data.

The instruments described in this chapter are registered trademarks of ACT, Inc.; the College Board; ETS (the Educational Testing Service); the Graduate Management Admissions Council; the Law School Admissions Council; Noel-Levitz; H&H Publishing Company; Multi-Health Systems, Inc.; and the Association of American Medical Colleges (AAMC). Information about these instruments used in this chapter was obtained from publicly available documents and personal correspondence with members of these organizations. The organizations were not involved in the production of this chapter and have not endorsed it.

Published Instruments: Overview of Cognitive Tests

Tables 30.1 through 30.5 provide an overview of published instruments discussed in this chapter. A table of web resources that provide additional details about instrument components, data sources for postsecondary institutions, norms, validity evidence, and relevant manuals and guides is available on the Association for Institutional Research website (www.airweb.org/redirects/pages/IRChapter30.aspx). Readers can also refer to the Buros *Mental Measurements Yearbook* for more detailed information about these and other published instruments (for online reviews see http://www.ovid.com/site/catalog/DataBase/120.jsp).

Undergraduate Admission Tests

Table 30.1 describes the four primary published test batteries used in college undergraduate admission. They are the ACT, the SAT, the SAT Subject Tests, and the Test of English as a Second Language/Test of Written English (TOEFL/TWE). In addition to the test components, the ACT, the SAT, and the SAT Subject Tests include extensive noncognitive information about students, such as background characteristics; high school coursework, grades, GPA, and/or class rank; planned major; needs for help; high school activities; intended activities in college; postsecondary plans and institutional preferences; and institutional choices (the institutions to which students send their scores). The ACT also includes self-reported grades for high school courses, students' career interests (UNIACT Interest Inventory; ACT, 2009b), and the order in which they ranked their institutional choices. The testing agencies provide all of the noncognitive information in students' electronic test records.

Student test records. Institutions can obtain students' ACT, SAT, and SAT Subject Test records in several ways. Ideally (from the perspective of institutions), students direct the testing agencies to send their scores and other information to particular institutions that they identify. The testing agencies then send official results either by paper or electronically. Some institutions allow students to submit unofficial score reports (copied from high school transcripts) when they apply for admission, but require official reports prior to enrollment or purchase them from the testing agencies. The testing agencies require institutions to obtain written permission from their enrolled students. Other institutions administer admission tests themselves to their admitted or enrolled students who do not already have official score reports.

Norms. Testing agencies provide various types of normative (that is, benchmarking) information for their tests. The testing agencies calculate user norms for the ACT, the SAT, and the SAT Subject Tests for particular high school graduating class cohorts; they are available for all tested students (national), by state, and for various other student groups. For the TOEFL/TWE tests, the Educational Testing Service (ETS) provides a yearly report online that includes reference norms for different populations of entering students (ETS, 2010d). (See Chapter 34 about using benchmarking and Chapter 36 about forming comparison groups.)

TABLE 30.1   UNDERGRADUATE ADMISSION TESTS

Test name	Publisher	Cognitive skills measured	Intended uses	Background characteristics	HS experiences/ accomplishments	HS coursework	HS course grades	HS GPA	HS rank	Career interests	Planned major/ career	Needs for help	Post-HS plans	Postsecondary preferences	Postsecondary institutional choices	Comments
1. ACT	ACT	English Mathematics Reading Science Composite Writing Combined English /Writing	Undergraduate admission Course placement	×	×	×	×	×	×	×	×	×	×	×	×	Paper and pencil admin. Writing test is optional. Combined English/ Writing score not included in Composite. Choice order of institutions provided.
2. SAT	College Board	Critical Reading Mathematics Writing Total	Undergraduate admission Course placement	×	×	×		×	×		×	×	×	×	×	Paper and pencil admin. Writing test is required. Choice order of institutions not provided.
3. SAT Subject Tests	College Board	Knowledge and skills taught in twenty college-preparatory subjects	Undergraduate admission Course placement	×	×	×		×			×	×	×	×	×	Paper and pencil admin. Students take all tests separately.
4. TOEFL/ TWE	ETS	Reading Skills Listening Skills Writing Skills Speaking Skills Total	Undergraduate and graduate admission	×												Internet delivery; paper and pencil option.

Other information collected on registration form

Graduate/Professional School Admission Tests

Table 30.2 presents information about published graduate and professional school admission tests, including the Graduate Record Exam (GRE) General Test (ETS, 2010b), the GRE Subject Tests (ETS, 2010c), the Graduate Management Admission Test (GMAT; Graduate Management Admission Council [GMAC], 2010), the Law School Admission Test (LSAT; Law School Admission Council [LSAC], 2010), and the Medical College Admission Test (MCAT; Association of American Medical Colleges [AAMC], 2010). In addition to the test components, these tests collect a limited amount of noncognitive data. The GRE collects the most extensive information, but the information is not included in students' test records. The GRE results for an applicant may include the ETS Personal Potential Index (PPI), for which evaluators selected by the applicant rate the student on his or her knowledge and creativity, communication skills, teamwork, resilience, planning and organization, and ethics and integrity. However, PPI reports are provided to institutions as individual text and graph reports; they are not provided as standard data files (ETS, 2010a).

Student test records. As with undergraduate admission tests, students who take the GRE, MCAT, LSAT, or GMAT can identify institutions, professional application services, or third-party vendors to which they want their results sent. The testing agencies send the results as paper score reports, on CD-ROM, or via the Internet. Institutions can also obtain applicants' electronic GRE records directly from ETS, but they must first be formally approved by ETS as a GRE score user (ETS, 2009).

Norms. ETS provides normative information, based on multiple years of examinees, for both the GRE General Test and the Subject Tests. MCAT norms are based on students taking the test in a given year; for further information, readers should contact AAMC. LSAT and GMAT norms are based on three years of student test results. For web locations of normative information for these tests, visit the Association for Institutional Research website, www.airweb. org/redirects/pages/IRChapter30.aspx.

Course Placement Tests

Institutions also use published instruments for placement in standard first-year courses, developmental courses, English as a second language (ESL) courses, and honors or advanced courses. These tests can be used alone, in combination with other published instruments, or in combination with locally developed tests.

Among the tests intended primarily for making course placement decisions, the most widely used are ACCUPLACER, ASSET, and COMPASS, shown in Table 30.3. The ACT and the SAT are also used in course placement, in addition to admission. ACCUPLACER and COMPASS also provide tests for placing students with limited English proficiency in appropriate ESL courses, shown in Table 30.4. Each of these tests includes a short section on background information

TABLE 30.2 GRADUATE/PROFESSIONAL SCHOOL ADMISSION TESTS

Test name	Publisher	Cognitive skills measured	Intended uses	Other information collected on registration or other form									Comments
				Background characteristics	College experiences/ Accomplishments	College coursework	College program / major	College GPA	Career interests	Post-undergraduate degree plans	Institutional preferences	Institutional choices	
1. Graduate Record Exam (GRE) General Test	ETS	Analytical Writing Verbal Reasoning Quantitative Reasoning	Admission to master's and Ph.D. programs	×		×	×	×		×		×	Internet delivery; paper and pencil option in some locations.
2. Graduate Record Exam (GRE) Subject Tests	ETS	Knowledge and skills taught in eight undergraduate programs	Admission to master's and Ph.D. programs	×		×				×		×	
3. Medical College Admission Test (MCAT)	Association of American Medical Colleges	Physical Sciences Verbal Reasoning Writing Sample Biological Sciences	Admission to medical schools	×		×				×			Internet delivery.
4. Graduate Management Admission Test (GMAT)	Graduate Management Admission Council	Analytical Writing Assessment Quantitative Section Verbal Section	Admission to graduate business programs and schools	×								×	Internet delivery. Information collected on Appointment Scheduling Form.
5. Law School Admission Test (LSAT)	Law School Admission Council	Reading Comprehension Analytical Reasoning Logical Reasoning Writing sample	Admission to law schools	×									Paper and pencil administration.

TABLE 30.3   UNDERGRADUATE COURSE PLACEMENT TESTS

Test name	Publisher	Cognitive skills measured	Other information collected												Comments
			Background characteristics	HS experiences/accomplishments	HS & post-HS coursework	HS course grades	HS GPA	HS rank	Career interests	Planned major or career	Needs for help	Post-HS plans	Reason for attending this institution	Transfer plans	
5. ACCUPLACER	College Board	Sentence Skills Reading Comprehension Arithmetic Elementary Algebra College Level Math Written Essay Computer Skills Placement	Bkgrd. Quest.		Bkgrd. Quest.										Internet delivery (ACCUPLACER); paper and pencil option (COMPANION).
6. ASSET	ACT	Writing Skills Numerical Skills Reading Skills Elementary Algebra Intermediate Algebra College Algebra Geometry	Educ. Plng. Form	Educ. Plng. Form	Educ. Plng. Form	Educ. Plng. Form	Educ. Plng. Form			Educ. Plng. Form	Needs Ass.	Educ. Plng. Form			Paper and pencil administration.
7. COMPASS	ACT	Reading Writing Skills Writing Essay (e-Write) College Algebra Geometry Trigonometry	Educ. Plng. Form	Educ. Plng. Form	Educ. Plng. Form	Educ. Plng. Form	Educ. Plng. Form			Educ. Plng. Form	Educ. Plng. Form	Educ. Plng. Form			Internet delivery; local CBT option.

TABLE 30.4   UNDERGRADUATE ESL COURSE PLACEMENT TESTS

Test name	Publisher	Cognitive skills measured	Other information collected												Comments
			Background characteristics	HS experiences/ accomplishments	HS & post-HS coursework	HS course grades	HS GPA	HS rank	Career interests	Planned major/career	Needs for help	Post-HS plans	Reason for attending this institution	Transfer plans	
5. ACCUPLACER ESL	College Board	ESL Reading Skills ESL Sentence Meaning ESL Language Use ESL Listening WritePlacer ESL	Bkgrd. Quest.												Internet delivery.
6. COMPASS/ ESL	ACT	Listening Reading Grammar/Usage Essay	Educ. Plng. Form	Educ. Plng. Form	Educ. Plng. Form	Educ. Plng. Form	Educ. Plng. Form			Educ. Plng. Form	Educ. Plng. Form	Educ. Plng. Form			Internet delivery; local CBT option.

and high school coursework; some also include additional planning and need for help information. Institutions can choose the non-test information collected on all of these tests except ASSET.

Student test records. Because ACCUPLACER, COMPASS, and their ESL counterparts are administered on the Internet, they are scored on the testing agencies' central servers. Institutions can, however, download electronic records for their students at any time. ASSET results are scored locally (self- or machine-scored), so records are available immediately after the test administration. ASSET/ACT/COMPASS concordances are available on the ACT website (ACT, 2010d).

Norms. State and national normative information are available from ACT for ASSET, COMPASS, and COMPASS ESL. For ACCUPLACER, local norms are provided at the time of testing; further information about national and state norms is available on a secure website, with access requiring a user ID and password.

Undergraduate Honors Placement and Credit by Exam

Institutions can use Advanced Placement (AP) scores to grant course credit and/or to exempt students from taking a college course comparable to the AP course they have taken (College Board, 2010b). College-Level Examination Program (CLEP) tests allow students to obtain credit for course content that

TABLE 30.5   UNDERGRADUATE HONORS TESTS AND CREDIT-BY-EXAMINATION

Test name	Publisher	Cognitive skills measured	Comments
5. Advanced Placement Program (AP)	College Board	Knowledge of material taught in thirty college-level courses.	• Offered in conjunction with AP courses taught in high school. • Paper and pencil administration in May at participating schools. • Basic background characteristics collected on registration form.
6. College-Level Examination Program (CLEP)	College Board	Knowledge of material taught in thirty-three college-level courses in: • Composition and Literature • Foreign Languages • History and Soc. Sciences • Science and Mathematics • Business	• Internet delivery; paper and pencil option. • Basic background characteristics collected on registration form.

they have already mastered (College Board, 2010d). Both testing programs collect background information on tested students. The College Board encourages institutions to establish their own policies related to the use of results from these tests for course placement and/or awarding course credit.

Student score reports and norms. Institutions can obtain electronic (Internet or CD) or transcript AP or CLEP score reports for their score senders. The College Board web site provides normative comparisons for AP tests at state and national levels. CLEP provides only local institutional norms.

Published Instruments: Overview of Noncognitive Measures

Recent research emphasizes the importance of noncognitive or psychosocial factors in studying students' success in college. Robbins, Lauver, Le, Langley, Davis, and Carlstrom (2004) and Le, Casillas, Robbins, and Langley (2005) found that, of the various measures considered, specific psychosocial and behavioral attributes within defined motivational, self-regulation, and social engagement constructs were most predictive of postsecondary success. Subsequent research found that measures based on these constructs were stronger predictors of retention to the sophomore year than admission test scores, but that test scores were stronger predictors of first-year GPA (Robbins, Allen, Casillas, Peterson, & Le, 2006).

Institutions can use noncognitive measures to identify and advise students who are at risk of academic failure or dropping out. There are several published, nationally available noncognitive instruments designed for this purpose, and we summarize them in Table 30.6. The Non-Cognitive Questionnaire (NCQ; Sedlacek, 1991) is included in this group of instruments, although it is not a published, static questionnaire. This instrument has been revised and used for a variety of research and institutional purposes (see Sedlacek, 1991, 1993; Fuertes & Sedlacek, 1994). It can be downloaded by institutional researchers and modified as needed for local research. Links to additional resources for these instruments can be obtained from the Association for Institutional Research website (www.airweb.org/redirects/pages/IRChapter30 .aspx). Other instruments are still being developed, such as Schmitt and others' Situational Judgment Inventory and biodata measure (Oswald, Schmitt, Kim, Ramsay, & Gillespie, 2004; Schmitt et al., 2007; Sternberg & the Rainbow Project Collaborators, 2005).

Several authors have recommended that noncognitive measures not be used for high-stakes decision making. The primary problem in using them for high-stakes decision making is that they are self-report inventories and are therefore susceptible to coaching. Other problems with high-stakes use include lesser reliability and predictive validity relative to standardized tests or HS GPA (Geisinger, 2006; Lievens & Sackett, 2007; Thomas, Kuncel, & Credé, 2007; Tomsho, 2009).

TABLE 30.6   PSYCHOSOCIAL INSTRUMENTS

Instrument name	Publisher	Constructs measured	Intended uses	Comments

5. BarOn Emotional Quotient Inventory (EQ-i: HEd)	Multi-Health Systems, Inc.	• Intrapersonal
		  Self-Regard
		• Emotional Self-Awareness
		  Assertiveness
		  Independence
		  Self-Actualization
		• Interpersonal
		  Empathy
		  Social Responsibility
		  Interpersonal Relationships
		  Stress Management
		  Stress Tolerance
		  Impulse Control
		  Adaptability
		  Reality Testing
		  Flexibility
		  Problem Solving
		  General Mood
		  Optimism
		  Happiness
		  Validity
		  Positive Impression
		  Inconsistency Index
			Identify students at risk of dropping out	• Paper-and-pencil administration and internet delivery.
				• Student and counselor reports available immediately after administration.
				• Student Comprehensive, Student Summary, and Counselor Reports are available.
				• Norms based on individuals who have taken the Inventory; contact publisher for additional information on norms.

6. College Student Inventory (short and long forms)	Noel-Levitz	• Academic Motivation • Social Motivation • General Coping • Receptivity to Support Services • Initial Impression	Identify students who are most likely to persist	• Paper-and-pencil administration and Internet delivery. • Coordinator, Advisor/Counselor, Student, and aggregate Summary and Planning Reports are provided. • Results for all scales are based on national norms. • Contact publisher for detailed information about norms, scoring, and other technical documentation.

Instrument	Author/Publisher	Constructs/Scales	Uses	Notes
7. Learning and Study Strategies Inventory (LASSI)	H&H Publishing Company	• Information Processing • Selecting Main Ideas • Test Strategies • Attitude • Motivation • Anxiety • Concentration • Time Management • Self-Testing • Study Aids	• Help students improve learning and study strategies • Identify areas for educational intervention; evaluate intervention programs	• Paper-and-pencil administration and Internet delivery. • National norms are provided; see website for technical documentation.
8. Non-Cognitive Questionnaire (NCQ)	William Sedlacek	• Positive Self-Concept or Confidence • Realistic Self-Appraisal • Understands and Deals with Racism • Prefers Long-Range Goals to Short-Term or Immediate Needs • Availability of Strong Support Person • Successful Leadership Experience • Demonstrated Community Service • Knowledge Acquired in a Field	• College admissions and advising, particularly for nontraditional students	• Instrument downloadable from website. • See Sedlacek website for additional information.
9. ENGAGE College (formerly the Student Readiness Inventory, or SRI)	ACT	• Academic Discipline • Academic Self-Confidence • Commitment to College • Communication Skills • Determination • Goal Striving • Social Activity • Social Connection • Steadiness • Study Skills	• Identify students at risk for academic failure or for dropping out	• Paper-and-pencil administration and Internet delivery. • Paper and electronic student and advisor reports, a roster of student records, and an aggregate institutional demographic report are provided. • National percentiles are provided. • See the ENGAGE website for additional information.

Institutional Research with Published Instruments

Enrollment management encompasses activities such as marketing, recruitment, net revenue management, admission, financial aid, course placement, advising, identifying high-risk students, and retention. Research is an important component of all these efforts, and published instruments can inform the research. In this section, we focus specifically on research related to recruitment, admission, course placement, and identification of high-risk students. Much of this discussion, though generally focused on undergraduate students, also applies to research on graduate students and programs.

Recruitment

Many institutions strive to maintain or increase enrollment through various recruitment strategies, including market research. Undergraduate admission test records provide a rich variety of data on students' background characteristics, interests, goals, and institutional preferences (see Table 30.1) that can help institutions identify students who are a good match with the institution's mission and who might consider enrolling. Because students specify the institutions to which they want their score reports sent, admission test data also act as a key information link between institutions and prospective students.

Market Research. ACT and the College Board offer undergraduate market research services that describe market segments defined by students' location, academic skills, background characteristics, and preferences for institutional characteristics (ACT, 2010f; College Board, 2010e). Using software developed by the testing agencies, institutions can create statistical summaries of market segments according to criteria that make sense to them. The statistical summaries include student characteristics in the test record, as well as market yield, as determined by students' actual enrollment. Because this kind of market research depends on data of all tested students, individual institutions must work through the testing agencies to do it.

High School Outreach. Many two-year institutions administer course placement tests in local high schools (ACT, 2010c) to give students who might later enroll in a particular institution an early indication of their academic skills. Underprepared students can improve their skills while still enrolled in high school; more academically advanced students can enroll in dual credit courses. Moreover, an institution can establish relationships with students that could increase the likelihood that they will enroll in the future. An institution can also easily determine the enrollment yield from its outreach programs.

Score Senders and Prospects. A student who has taken an admission test is either a score sender (sent a score report to an institution) or a non–score sender (did not send a score report to an institution). Testing agencies provide software for use with score-sender data to facilitate typical querying and reporting needs (ACT, 2010b; College Board, 2010c). An institution can also purchase contact information on non–score senders who have characteristics desired by the institution and might be enticed to apply for admission (ACT, 2010g; College Board, 2010g). Institutions then communicate with the prospects to make them aware of the institutions' interest in them.

Student Group Profiles. Comparing groups of students at different points in the admission process is a simple way to make inferences about the types of students who find an institution attractive (namely, through data mining; see Chapter 28). For example, an institution could compare score senders versus applicants, applicants versus admitted students, and admitted students versus enrolled students. Both ACT and the College Board offer services to expedite this kind of research (ACT, 2010b; College Board, 2010e). The testing agencies can also do competitor analyses comparing the students at a client institution with students at the clients' competitors.

Predictive Modeling. A more powerful tool for identifying potential enrollees is to estimate the probability that an individual score sender will enroll at a particular institution or at a certain type of institution (such as out of state). With a predictive model, institutions can shape recruitment efforts according to score senders' estimated probability of enrollment. The usefulness of this strategy, however, depends on the expected *net gain* in enrollment associated with recruitment efforts (the difference in enrollment rate with or without the recruitment efforts). In principle, an institution could focus its recruitment efforts on the probability range associated with the highest net gain. For example, an institution might achieve a greater net gain by focusing its recruitment efforts on students with a moderately high probability of enrollment (with the assumption that high-probability students will likely enroll even without the recruitment efforts). A more sophisticated approach would apply different recruitment strategies to students in different probability ranges.

Some institutions choose to do their own predictive modeling, using predictor variables they know to be useful for them. ACT (2010i), Noel-Levitz (2010), and other organizations offer predictive modeling services using student characteristics known from previous research to predict enrollment. One can also develop predictive models for non–score sender prospects and for general inquirers (who might not have taken an admission test). Institutions can use the predictions for non–score sender prospects to decide how many and which individuals to contact. Institutions can use the predictions for general inquirers to decide how best to respond to their inquiries. (See Chapter 13 for further discussion of enrollment management.)

Admission

Institutions with traditional, selective, or highly selective admissions consider their applicants' academic knowledge and skills, among other characteristics, in making admission decisions. To do this, institutions typically rely on high school coursework, high school grades, and admission test scores (Breland, Maxey, Gernand, Cumming, & Trapani, 2002). Institutions use high school coursework to verify that students have had the opportunity to acquire the knowledge and skills they will need to succeed in college. High school grades are indicators of how much knowledge and skills students have acquired in their courses.

Institutions use admission test scores for diverse reasons. Test scores improve institutions' capability to measure students' readiness for college work, beyond that provided by high school coursework and grades. Further, test scores are standardized objective measures: they mean the same for all applicants, regardless of the high school they attend and the high school courses they take. Admission tests are not, however, designed specifically for use as diagnostic tests. They also do not measure proficiency at minimum competency levels, as many states' K–12 assessments do.

Validity Research. Both ACT and the College Board offer free research services to document the predictive validity of their tests at individual institutions (ACT, 2010h; College Board, 2010a). These research services provide estimates of the correlations of first-year college GPA with test scores, with high school grades, and with test scores and high school grades jointly. These studies typically find that high school GPA is more strongly correlated with first-year college GPA than test scores are, but that test scores have incremental predictive validity (Kobrin, Patterson, Shaw, Mattern, & Barbuti, 2008; ACT, 1999; ACT, 2008).

In studying the relationship between first-year GPA and test scores, institutional researchers should also consider using refinements of the simple linear model. Potentially important refinements include interaction effects (Sawyer, 2010), nonlinear relationships (Robbins et al., 2006), and random effects associated with nesting of students within different units, such as high schools or colleges (Sawyer, 2008, 2010).

Limitations of Correlations. An institution makes admission decisions about its applicants; thus, the effectiveness of test scores and high school GPA in making admission decisions pertains to the applicant population. An institution cannot calculate correlations using data for its entire applicant population, however, because academic outcome data are not available for students who are denied admission or who otherwise do not enroll. Typically, the enrolled student population has a restricted range of high school GPA and test scores compared with the applicant population. One can make adjustments for this restriction of range effect (see, for example, Lord & Novick, 1968). The practical effect of the adjustments is to increase the magnitude of correlations estimated from enrolled students.

Data loss in calculating correlations with first-year GPA also results from enrolled students who do not complete the first year and therefore do not have a first-year GPA. One approach to this problem is to use students' GPA when they leave the institution, if they have a GPA. Another approach is to sort GPA into "successful" and "unsuccessful" categories and to consider withdrawal from the institution as an unsuccessful outcome. One can then model the relationship between preenrollment measures and the success dichotomy with logistic regression (Hosmer & Lemeshow, 2000).

Correlations and other typical regression statistics are indicators of the overall strength of the linear relationship between first-year GPA and the predictor variables. However, these statistics do not directly address the *usefulness* of test scores and high school grades in achieving an institution's goals in admission. Two typical goals of institutions are

- Maximizing academic success among enrolled students
- Accurately identifying those applicants who could be academically successful if they attended the institution, and enrolling as many of them as possible

These goals seem similar, but they are not identical. The first goal is related to the proportion of applicants who would *succeed* academically if they enrolled—the *success rate*. The second goal is related to the proportion of applicants whom an institution *correctly identifies* as likely to succeed or likely to fail—the *accuracy rate*. Given certain assumptions, correlation coefficients are mathematically related to success rates and accuracy rates, but they do not indicate usefulness as directly as success rates and accuracy rates do. Of course, in making admission decisions institutions also have other goals that are not directly related to academic success.

Highly selective institutions can easily pursue the first goal because they typically have many more academically qualified applicants than they can admit. Less academically qualified students tend not to apply to these institutions (or send their admission test scores) to begin with; these potential applicants in effect select themselves out of the applicant pools (Astin, 1991; Hossler & Kalsbeek, 2009; Sawyer, 2007a). As a result, variance in the predictors is restricted at highly selective institutions, and predictive correlations are typically lower for those institutions than for less selective institutions.

All institutions would ideally like to maximize academic success among their enrolled students. However, publicly supported institutions, regional institutions, and other institutions that are moderately selective also consider the second goal to be important. These institutions' mission is to educate a broad portion of the population, not just the most academically able. A principal goal in their admission decision making is to distinguish accurately between applicants who are likely to be successful from those who are not likely to be successful. This goal is more difficult to achieve than the first, because it depends not only on maximizing academic success among enrolled students, but also on making sure that the applicants who are denied admission are the ones who would have had little chance of succeeding if they had enrolled.

Noble and Sawyer (2004) studied accuracy rates by defining success in terms of different levels of first-year GPA. They found that high school GPA is more effective than ACT scores in accurately identifying successful students when success is defined as completing the first year of college with a 2.0 (C) or higher GPA. When success is defined as completing the first year of college with a high level of success (such as 3.50 or higher GPA), however, high school GPA is much less accurate than ACT scores.

Course Placement

The primary goal of course placement is to match students with coursework that is appropriate to their academic preparation and interests. Like admission, course placement can be viewed as a selection decision; unlike admission, however, course placement pertains to the population of enrolled students rather than to applicants. At two-year institutions, course placement decisions usually involve determining whether a student should enroll in a standard college-level course (typically credit bearing) or in a developmental course (typically not credit bearing). Many two-year institutions have more than one level of developmental course to which placement decisions apply. Four-year institutions also offer developmental courses, although some states prevent their public four-year institutions from doing so.

Course placement can also pertain to advanced courses. Use of CLEP and AP tests, described earlier in this chapter, implies a kind of course placement, in the sense that some students are not required to enroll in certain lower-level courses.

Similarly, establishing course equivalence across institutions or across modes of delivery (dual credit or dual enrollment programs for high school students) is a third type of course placement. Institutions and systems need to determine that transfer students, or entering students with college credits obtained in high school, are prepared to succeed in subsequent coursework—in essence, that these students have the same knowledge and skills as students taking similar coursework on the local campus. Although there is a great deal of interest in dual credit or dual enrollment programs, especially those offered by two-year colleges, there is a strong need for research to demonstrate that students and institutions benefit from these programs. Examples of research on this topic are Karp, Calcagno, Hughes, Jeong, and Bailey (2008), Kim (2006), and Peterson (2003).

Cutoff Scores. Many institutions make course placement decisions using cutoff scores (minimum scores that students must have to enroll in particular courses). Both ACT and College Board provide institutions with recommendations for initial cutoff scores, as well as national norms, proficiency descriptions, and other tools that institutions can use to adapt initial cutoff scores to local conditions. Both testing agencies also provide institutions with local norms and validity research services that institutions can use to refine their cutoff scores after they have accumulated sufficient local data.

Although decision rules based on cutoff scores are easy to understand and convenient to apply, more sophisticated placement procedures might yield more accurate placement and more effective use of resources. For example, students whose placement test scores are near the cutoff could meet with an academic adviser, who could obtain information about characteristics that are important for academic success but not measured by the placement test. Examples of these other characteristics are personal responsibilities (hours worked on a job, care for dependents) and psychosocial characteristics (motivation, self-discipline, connection to the institution), such as those measured by the noncognitive instruments described earlier in this chapter.

Validity Research. Two of the principal academic goals in making course placement decisions are to maximize academic success among students placed in the higher-level course and to identify accurately students who are placed in either the lower-level or higher-level course. The first goal is related to the success rate in the higher-level course; the second is related to the accuracy rate (the estimated percentage of students for whom an accurate course placement decision is made). The second goal is relevant because no one wants students to take a lower-level course if they could have succeeded in the higher-level course.

Both ACT and the College Board offer institutional research services to document the local predictive validity of their course placement tests (ACT, 2010e; College Board, 2010a). These research services report conditional probabilities of success, success rates and/or accuracy rates, as well as correlation coefficients. Institutions can use these statistics to establish or adjust their cutoff scores.

Effectiveness of Developmental Instruction. Institutions with course placement systems also need to study the benefits of developmental or remedial courses. Most research has found that students who take developmental courses are not as successful academically as students who do not take developmental courses (see, for example, Adelman, 1999). This may result from other characteristics—in addition to being academically underprepared—that negatively affect students who take developmental courses. Even if a developmental course improves students' academic knowledge and skills, the students might disproportionately have other characteristics (such as care for dependents, low income, psychosocial characteristics) that hold them back.

Instead of studying developmental students' absolute rate of success, an institution can study the "value added" by a developmental course; that is, whether students who take a developmental course are subsequently more successful than they would have been if they had not taken the developmental course. This goal is less ambitious, but more realistic than bringing the long-term academic success of students in developmental courses up to that of other students.

One can do value-added research using observational longitudinal data for students who, for whatever reasons, took particular courses. It is not practically feasible to study this issue in an ideal manner with random assignment of students to courses. Perkhounkova, Noble, and Sawyer (2005) found that the value added by taking a developmental course depends on a student's grade in the course: students who earn an A or B in a developmental course are more successful in subsequent higher-level courses, and are less likely to drop out, than they would have been if they had not taken the developmental course. In contrast, there is typically no benefit to taking a developmental course if students do not earn at least a B.

An institution can also study the effectiveness of a developmental course by post-testing students at the end of the course. With a paper-and-pencil placement test, the institution would need to use an equated alternate form. Two relevant statistics are the average score gain and the percentage of students who meet the cutoff for placement in the higher-level course. With pre-post research designs, however, measurement error is compounded; researchers can estimate expected gains due to measurement error alone as a baseline to compare against actual gains (Sawyer & Schiel, 2000).

Identifying At-Risk Students

Students can be at risk in college for academic failure and/or for dropping out. Researchers can use information from the published instruments described here to identify students in either or both categories, especially when persistence through the beginning of the second year is of interest. Both cognitive test scores and noncognitive variables can be useful for this purpose.

Academic Risk. Preenrollment measures, as well as those obtained at college entry, are important for predicting academic risk because they are available at the beginning of students' collegiate experience. They can be used to identify students who are at risk of academic failure during their first semester of college. Moreover, data obtained from published instruments are standardized, and do not require that they be interpreted in context, as do high school GPAs or rank, or undergraduate GPAs for students enrolling in graduate school.

The most accepted measures for identifying students at academic risk are measures of students' preparation for college coursework: admission test scores, high school GPA or class rank, high school coursework, course placement test scores, and so forth (links to validity information may be obtained from the Association for Institutional Research website, www.airweb.org/redirects/pages/IRChapter30.aspx). Comparable measures are available for graduate school and professional programs. Psychosocial variables have also been found to have incremental value in predicting college GPA (see, for example, Robbins et al., 2004; Robbins et al., 2006; Schmitt et al., 2007; and see the following retention discussion).

Retention. Most early college retention models rely on academic measures such as high school GPA and/or admission test scores; some use other test record data (see, for example, Perkhounkova, Noble, & McLaughlin, 2006), but most do not. Newer strategies emphasize the overlap between predictors of enrollment at a particular institution and predictors of a student's likelihood of persisting in college. Consistent with theories on retention or persistence (Tinto, 1993; Bean, 1980), research has shown relationships between fit indexes from ACT's predictive modeling service (campus-specific, institutional type, mobility, and selectivity indexes), career fit indices (such as interest-major congruence; see, for example, Tracey & Robbins, 2006), and students' likely persistence to the second year of college. Students' choice set for enrollment is also predictive of retention (see, for example, Radcliffe, Huesman, & Kellogg, 2007; Cruce, 2008). All of these indices are based on variables from students' ACT test records.

Retention is also influenced by behavioral and psychosocial factors, including clarity of career goals, uncertainty as to college major, academic challenge, transition problems, expectations, engagement, and institutional integration (Johnson, Priest, Atwell, Wang, Ding, & Ehasz, 2006). Research has also shown that psychosocial variables are stronger predictors of retention than admission test scores, but that admission test scores have incremental predictive power (Allen, Robbins, Casillas, & Oh, 2008; Allen, Robbins, & Sawyer, 2010; Robbins et al., 2006; Schmitt et al., 2007).

Traditional statistics—such as R, R^2 or pseudo-R^2—do not directly inform institutions as to their usefulness in identifying at-risk students, or the extent to which they improve identification of at-risk students (Sawyer, 2007a). One way to document the usefulness of a variable for identifying at-risk students is shown by example in Figure 30.1. An institution with five hundred enrolled students ranks them according to their risk predicted from an instrument. Starting with the highest-risk students, the institution flags a certain number of the students for intervention (shown on the horizontal axis). The vertical axis denotes the expected number of students who drop out, among those who are flagged for intervention. The lower dashed line shows the expected number of unsuccessful students one would capture by random selection. The top dashed curve shows the number of unsuccessful students one could hypothetically identify with perfect selection. (The example assumes that there are fifty unsuccessful students.) The solid curve shows the expected number of unsuccessful students identified by the instrument. If the instrument is effective in identifying at-risk students, the solid curve should be closer to the top line than to the bottom line. (See Chapter 13 for additional discussion of enrollment management.)

Other Uses of Published Instruments in Institutional Research

As noted earlier for course placement, identifying at-risk students is only the first step. An institution must also determine whether its interventions with at-risk students are effective.

FIGURE 30.1 EFFECTIVENESS OF AN INSTRUMENT FOR IDENTIFYING AT-RISK STUDENTS

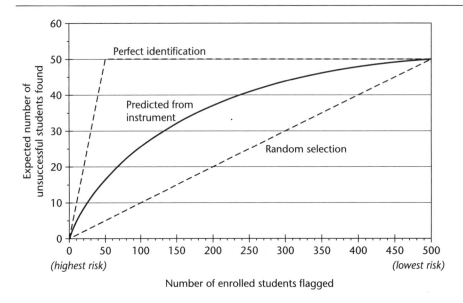

Evaluating intervention programs. Using published instruments for evaluating interventions depends on the purpose of the interventions and on whether and how students are selected. In most situations, it is important to include measures of prior academic achievement in the research. Because they are standardized measures, published admission or course placement test scores are useful covariates. High school rank or high school GPA are also useful, but they may be problematic due to variation among high schools.

Published instruments are often used in conjunction with published or locally developed questionnaires in program evaluation research (see, for example, Miller, Tyree, Riegler, & Herreid, 2010). Questionnaire information may be more relevant to the intervention or program than information obtained from published instruments. (See Chapter 29 for further discussion on the use of questionnaires in institutional research.)

Advantages and Limitations of Using Published Instruments in IR

The preceding sections have discussed a broad range of published instruments that are available for many of the tasks involved in managing enrollment and the academic process. There are, however, both advantages and disadvantages to using these published instruments.

Advantages of Using Published Instruments

Access to information collected by published instruments provides several advantages to institutional researchers. First, published instruments are standardized in content; what they measure and how they measure it are fixed. Moreover, their uses for typical institutional research purposes have been validated; what they measure is directly or indirectly related to college success. Published instruments, particularly cognitive tests, are also standardized in administration and in scoring. Cognitive tests are completed under fixed time limits and under conditions that inhibit sharing of information among students. Further, scores are typically equated so that they can be interpreted the same way over different forms and over time. Testing agencies document any content and/or format changes that occur, and they usually provide some means of converting information from old formats to new formats, and vice versa.

A second advantage of published instruments is that they can be used to collect information about students prior to or very early in their college careers. Substantial research suggests that success in the first year of college is very important in predicting later success. Institutions therefore need measures obtained before or just after enrollment to predict success in the first year.

Undergraduate college admission and course placement tests are also cost efficient: not only are they are relatively inexpensive, but institutions also can use them to address a variety of research questions ranging from recruitment to retention research to evaluating programs and predicting degree completion.

The advantages of published instruments can also be limitations, however. Information is collected on these instruments in one way and in one format, at a specific time in students' lives. For some research, such data may not be relevant or appropriate. For example, researchers often study the relationship of preenrollment measures with later college outcomes, such as timely program completion and cumulative GPA. Although it is important to investigate long-term success, to do this effectively one should also take into account the mediating effects of variables occurring *during* a student's enrollment. A prime example of a mediating variable is first-year GPA: students who are unsuccessful during the first year are less likely to succeed in the long term, thereby preempting much of the direct effects of preenrollment measures. A study of long-term success based only on preenrollment measures will therefore miss important variables related to long-term success. Furthermore, omitting post-enrollment variables could result in misleading estimates of the relationships of preenrollment measures.

Concerns in Using Data from Published Instruments

Some of the concerns about using published instruments involve the degree to which they validly measure constructs of concern, the extent of missing data, and the appropriateness of comparing scores among institutions. There are, however, several concerns specific to the use of data from published instruments.

Access to complete undergraduate admission test results is particularly critical for institutional researchers. Institutions with open or liberal admission policies, including most two-year colleges, do not require ACT or SAT scores for admission. Some of the more selective institutions allow students to apply to colleges using unofficial test scores (obtained from high school transcripts) to expedite the application process. About 40 percent of students enroll in college with unofficial test scores; they do not submit an official test record, either as part of the application process or after they have been accepted to the institution (ACT, 2009a). Some institutions obtain the test records from the testing agencies after students have enrolled. The testing agencies require these institutions to obtain written permission from their non–score sender enrolled students. As a result, many institutions do not have ACT and/or SAT records for their students, and most institutions that use the tests in admission have access only to students' test scores, and not to the background and noncognitive data collected by the tests. Institutions are therefore unable to use much of the information provided in students' test records for institutional research.

A further consideration in data access and use pertains to admission test scores. Students have the option of sending results from particular test administrations, or even those for particular test components across administrations, to an institution. For example, ACT uses students' scores from their most recent test administration in its research, but the NCAA allows students to combine scores across test administrations (see http://www.act.org/aap/infosys/scores .html). Researchers need to know their institutions' policies related to the scores of multiple-tested students and how to use and interpret the scores, given the institution's policies.

The cognitive data available from course placement tests are likely to be less comprehensive than the data available from admission tests. Most institutions exempt their students from taking course placement tests if their scores on college admission or K–12 state assessments are high enough. Moreover, some students take course placement tests in only one or two subject areas, rather than in all subject areas. Finally, within a subject area (such as mathematics), student might have a score on only one or two of a series of tests (such as elementary algebra and intermediate algebra) rather than on all the tests.

Additionally, test scores may not be appropriate for admission or course placement for students who have had intervening coursework or training or who tested more than a couple of years before enrolling. Out-of-date scores might not represent what students know and are able to do when they enrolled. Institutions should contact the testing agencies or visit their websites to determine the best approaches for using such scores.

Data comparability is of concern for institutions that use multiple instruments for admission and course placement. Concordance tables allow users to convert scores from one test to another (see, for example, ACT Composite to SAT Total or vice versa, ASSET/ACT/COMPASS, etc.; ACT, 2010a; 2010d; College Board, 2010f). However, these tables are limited in the tests that they relate. Moreover, concordant scores must be interpreted in light of the differences in tests' contents, purposes, and reliabilities (ACT, 2010j). A student's actual score could differ from the concordant score. The practical effect of this difference, in terms of admission decisions, is greatest for students who are on the borderline of being granted or denied admission. Where sufficient data exist, conducting parallel analyses using actual scores is preferable to using concordant scores, especially for predictive validity studies (Sawyer, 2007b).

Role of the Institutional Researcher

Institutional researchers and directors of assessment on larger campuses are well placed to provide guidance to faculty and administrators on the appropriate uses and interpretations of published test information. In particular, in politically charged discussions related to college admission or course placement criteria, or program and/or institutional evaluation, institutional researchers can provide empirical evidence about the validity and usefulness of local versus published instruments and can help faculty and decision makers understand the costs and benefits, as well as the limitations, of using either.

An important role of institutional researchers is to provide local evidence of the validity of uses and interpretations of published instruments at their institutions. Although testing agencies provide global validity evidence and preliminary cutoff scores, the appropriateness of this information for local students depends on the extent to which the local student population is comparable to that used to develop the global recommendations. To the extent that these populations differ, students who are actually ready for college could be either denied admission or placed into lower-level courses, or students who are not academically well prepared could be placed incorrectly in courses too difficult for them.

IR offices also have a role in resolving issues related to obtaining and storing data from published instruments, including access and use policies and data comparability and benchmarking. As mentioned earlier, to the extent that institutions do not require students to submit official admission test records or do not purchase or acquire these records in other ways, these data will have limited utility. Similarly, some institutions may not allow for storage of students' complete test records on university data systems. IR staff may wish to revisit the data elements that are stored from students' test records to determine whether important information is not currently being loaded into their system.

FERPA policies on data access and use often restrict the sharing of data on and between some campuses; institutions frequently differ in their interpretation of FERPA policies (Dougherty, 2008). There are permitted ways to share such data, however. Testing agencies are allowed to obtain data from institutions for research purposes, and institutions can obtain norms and conduct research in collaboration with testing agencies. Aggregate summaries can also be developed across collaborating institutions for benchmarking purposes (see, for example, Consortium for Student Retention Data Exchange [CSRDE]). Institutional researchers are encouraged to explore these options to enhance the use of information provided by published instruments at their institutions.

References

ACT. (1999). *Prediction research summary tables.* Iowa City, IA: ACT.

ACT. (2008). *Updated validity statistics for ACT Prediction Service.* Iowa City, IA: ACT.

ACT. (2009a). *National Class Profile Report.* Iowa City, IA: ACT.

ACT. (2009b). *ACT Interest Inventory technical manual.* Iowa City, IA: ACT.

ACT. (2010a). *ACT-SAT concordance.* Iowa City, IA: ACT. Retrieved from http://www.act.org/aap/concordance/

ACT. (2010b). *AIM: ACT Information Manager.* Iowa City, IA: ACT. Retrieved from http://www.act.org/aim/index.html

ACT. (2010c). *COMPASS guide to successful high school outreach.* Iowa City, IA: ACT. Retrieved from http://www.act.org/compass/pdf/HS_OutreachGuide.pdf

ACT. (2010d). *Concordant ACT, COMPASS, and ASSET scores.* Iowa City, IA: ACT. Retrieved from http://www.act.org/compass/pdf/Concordance.pdf

ACT. (2010e). *Course Placement Service.* Iowa City, IA: ACT. Retrieved from http://www.act.org/research/services/crsplace/index.html

ACT. (2010f). *Enrollment Information Service.* Iowa City, IA: ACT. Retrieved from http://www.act.org/eis/index.html

ACT. (2010g). *Enrollment Opportunity Service.* Iowa City, IA: ACT. Retrieved from http://www.act.org/eos/index.html

ACT. (2010h). *Prediction Service.* Iowa City, IA: ACT. Retrieved from http://www.act.org/research/services/predict/index.html

ACT. (2010i). *Predictive Modeling Service.* Iowa City, IA: ACT. Retrieved from http://www.act.org/predictmodel/index.html

ACT. (2010j). *Understanding concordance.* Iowa City, IA: ACT. Retrieved from http://www.act.org/aap/concordance/understand.html

Adelman, C. (1999). *Answers in the toolbox.* Washington, DC: NCES.

Allen, J., Robbins, S., Casillas, A., & Oh, I.-S. (2008). Third-year college retention and transfer: Effects of academic performance, motivation, and social connectedness. *Research in Higher Education, 49,* 647–664.

Allen, J., Robbins, S., & Sawyer, R. (2010). Can measuring psychosocial factors promote college success? *Applied Measurement in Education, 23,* 1–22.

Association of American Medical Colleges (2010). *Medical College Admission Test (MCAT).* Retrieved from http://www.aamc.org/students/mcat/start.htm

Astin, A. (1991). *Assessment for excellence.* New York: American Council on Education/MacMillan Series on Higher Education.

Bean, J. (1980). Dropouts and turnover: The synthesis and test of a casual model of student attrition. *Research in Higher Education, 12,* 155–187.

Breland, H., Maxey, J., Gernand, R., Cumming, T. and Trapani, C. (2002). *Trends in college admission 2000: A report of a national survey of undergraduate admission policies, practices, and procedures.* Retrieved from http://airweb.org/trends.html

College Board. (2010a). *Admitted Class Evaluation Service* (ACES). Retrieved from http://professionals.collegeboard.com/higher-ed/validity/aces/study

College Board. (2010b). *Advanced Placement Program* (AP). Retrieved from http://professionals.collegeboard.com/higher-ed/placement/ap

College Board. (2010c). *Basic Profile Service.* Retrieved from http://professionals .collegeboard.com/testing/sat-reasoning/scores/cb-seniors-higher-ed

College Board. (2010d). *CLEP®.* Retrieved from http://professionals.collegeboard.com/ higher-ed/placement/clep

College Board. (2010e). *Enrollment Planning Service* (EPS). Retrieved from http:// professionals.collegeboard.com/higher-ed/recruitment/eps

College Board, (2010f). *SAT-ACT concordance tables.* Retrieved from http://professionals .collegeboard.com/data-reports-research/sat/sat-act

College Board. (2010g). *Student Search Service* (SSS). Retrieved from http://professionals .collegeboard.com/higher-ed/recruitment/sss

Cruce, T. M. (2008). *The effects of institutional attributed on the initial choice of college: An analysis of stated and revealed preferences.* Paper presented at the Annual Forum of the Association for Institutional Research in Seattle.

Dougherty, C. (2008). Getting FERPA right: Encouraging data use while protecting student privacy. In M. Kanstoroom & E. C. Osberg (Eds.), *A byte at the apple: Rethinking education data for the post-NCLB era* (pp. 38–68). Washington, DC: Thomas B. Fordham Institute Press.

ETS. (2009). *GRE Guide to the use of scores 2009–2010.* Retrieved from http://www.ets .org/Media/Tests/GRE/pdf/gre_0910_guide.pdf

ETS. (2010a). *About the ETS Personal Potential Index.* Retrieved from http://www.ets .org/ppi/schools/about/

ETS. (2010b). *Graduate Record Exam (GRE) General Test.* Retrieved from http://www .ets.org/gre/general/about/index.html

ETS. (2010c). *Graduate Record Exam (GRE) Subject Tests.* Retrieved from http://www .ets.org/gre/institutions/about/subject/index.html

ETS. (2010d). *TOEFL test and score data summary for TOEFL internet-based and paper-based tests: January–December 2009 test data.* Retrieved from http://www.ets.org/Media/Tests/ TOEFL/pdf/test_score_data_summary_2009.pdf

Fuertes, J. N., & Sedlacek, W. E. (1994). *Using noncognitive variables to predict the grades and retention of Hispanic students.* Retrieved from http://williamsedlacek.info/publications/ articles/using994.html

Geisinger, K. F. (2006, August 13). Non-cognitive measures and academic success. In A. E. Schmidt (Chair), *Use of noncognitive measures for guidance and selection.* Symposium conducted at the American Psychological Association Convention, New Orleans.

Graduate Management Admission Council. (2010). *Graduate Management Admission Test* (GMAT). Retrieved from http://www.mba.com/mba/thegmat

Hossler, D., & Kalsbeek, D. H. (2009). Admissions testing and institutional admissions processes: The search for transparency and fairness. *College & University, 84*(4), 2–11.

Hosmer, D. W., & Lemeshow, S. (2000). *Applied logistic regression* (2nd ed.). New York: Wiley.

Johnson, S. K., Priest, D., Atwell, R. H., Wang, M., Ding, W., & Ehasz, M. (2006). *A winning duo for retention: Data mining and academic advising.* Paper presented at the 2006 National Symposium on Student Retention in Albuquerque.

Karp, M. M., Calcagno, J. C., Hughes, K. L., Jeong, D. W., & Bailey, T. (2008, February). *Dual enrollment students in Florida and New York City: Postsecondary outcomes.* Community College Research Center Brief. Retrieved from http://ccrc.tc.columbia .edu/Publication.asp?UID=578

Kim, J. (2006). *The impact of dual credit and articulated credit on college readiness and total credit hours in four selected community colleges.* Retrieved from http://occrl .ed.uiuc.edu/Publications/graduate_research/index_print.htm

Kobrin, J. L., Patterson, B. F., Shaw, E. J., Mattern, K. D., & Barbuti, S. M. (2008). *Validity of the SAT for predicting first-year college grade point average.* (Research Report #2008–5). New York: College Board.

Law School Admission Council. (2010). *Law School Admission Test.* Retrieved from http://www.lsac.org/LSAT/about-the-lsat.asp

Le, H., Casillas, A., Robbins, S., & Langley, R. (2005). Motivational and skills, social, and self-management predictors of college outcomes: Constructing the Student Readiness Inventory. *Educational and Psychological Measurement, 65,* 482–508.

Lievens, F., & Sackett, P. R. (2007). Situational judgment tests in high stakes settings: Issues and strategies with generating alternate forms. *Journal of Applied Psychology, 92,* 1043–1055.

Lord, F. M., & Novick, M. L. (1968). *Statistical theories of mental test scores.* Reading, MA: Addison-Wesley.

Miller, T. E., Tyree, T., Riegler, K. K., & Herreid, C. (2010). The use of a model that predicts individual student attrition to intervene with those who are most at risk. *College & University, 84*(3), 13–19.

Noble, J., & Sawyer, R. L. (2004). Is high school GPA better than admissions test scores for predicting academic success in college? *College & University, 79,* 4, 17–22.

Noel-Levitz, Inc. (2010). *ForecastPlus for recruitment.* Retrieved from https://www.noellevitz.com/Our+Services/Recruitment/ForecastPlus

Oswald, F., Schmitt, N., Kim, B., Ramsay, L., & Gillespie, M. (2004). Developing a biodata measure and situational judgment inventory as predictors of college student performance. *Journal of Applied Psychology, 89,* 187–207.

Perkhounkova, Y., Noble, J. P., & McLaughlin, G. W. (2006). Factors related to persistence of freshmen, freshman transfers, and nonfreshman transfer students. AIR Professional File No. 99.

Perkhounkova, Y., Noble, J. P., & Sawyer, R. (2005). Modeling the effectiveness of developmental instruction. (ACT Research Report #2005–2). Iowa City, IA: ACT.

Peterson, K. (2003). *Overcoming senior slump: The community college role.* Los Angeles, CA: ERIC Clearinghouse for Community Colleges. (ERIC Document Reproduction Service No. ED 477 830).

Radcliffe, P. M., Huesman, R. L., & Kellogg, J. P. (2007). *Modeling the incidence and timing of student attrition: A survival analysis approach to retention analysis.* Paper presented at the Annual Forum of the Association for Institutional Research in Kansas City.

Robbins, S., Allen, J., Casillas, A., Peterson, C., & Le, H. (2006). Unraveling the differential effects of motivational and skills, social, and self-management measures from traditional predictors of college outcomes. *Journal of Educational Psychology, 98,* 598–616.

Robbins, S., Lauver, K., Le, H., Langley, R., Davis, D., & Carlstrom, A. (2004). Do psychosocial and study skill factors predict college outcomes? A meta-analysis. *Psychological Bulletin, 130,* 261–288.

Sawyer, R. L. (2007a). Indicators of usefulness of test scores. *Applied Measurement in Education, 20*(3), 255–271.

Sawyer, R. L. (2007b). Some further thoughts on concordance. In N. Dorans & P. W. Holland (Eds.), *Linking and aligning scores and scales.* New York: Springer Science+Business Media.

Sawyer, R. L. (2008). *Benefits of additional high school course work and improved course performance in preparing students for college.* (ACT Research Report No. 2008–1). Iowa City, IA: ACT.

Sawyer, R. L. (2010). *Usefulness of high school average and ACT scores in making college admission decisions.* (ACT Research Report No. 2010–2). Iowa City, IA: ACT.

Sawyer, R. L., & Schiel, J. (2000). Posttesting students to assess the effectiveness of remedial instruction in college. (ACT Research Report #2000–7). Iowa City, IA: ACT.

Schmitt, N., Oswald, F. L., Kim, B. H., Imus, A., Drzakowski, S., Friede, A., & Shivpuri, S. (2007). The use of background and ability profiles to predict college student outcomes. *Journal of Applied Psychology, 92,* 165–178.

Sedlacek, W. E. (1991). *Using noncognitive variables in advising nontraditional students.* Retrieved from http://williamsedlacek.info/publications/articles/using391.html

Sedlacek, W. E. (1993). *Issues in advancing diversity through assessment.* Retrieved from http://williamsedlacek.info/publications/articles/issues593.html

Sternberg, R. J., & the Rainbow Project Collaborators (2005). Augmenting the SAT through assessments of analytical, practical, and creative skills. In W. Camara & E. Kimmel (Eds.), *Choosing students: Higher education admission tools for the 21st century.* Mahwah, NJ: Erlbaum.

Thomas, L. L., Kuncel, N. R., & Credé, M. (2007). Noncognitive variables in college admissions: The case of the Non-Cognitive Questionnaire. *Educational and Psychological Measurement, 67,* 635–657.

Tinto, V. (1993). *Leaving college: Rethinking the causes and cures of student attrition.* Chicago: University of Chicago Press.

Tomsho, R. (2009, August 20). Adding personality to the college admissions mix. *Wall Street Journal.*

Tracey, T.J.G., & Robbins, S. B. (2006). The interest-major congruence and college success relation: A longitudinal study. *Journal of Vocational Behavior, 69,* 64–89.

CHAPTER 31

MEASURING AND EVALUATING
FACULTY WORKLOAD

Heather A. Kelly, Jeffrey A. Seybert, Patrick M. Rossol,
and Allison M. Walters

After visiting campuses across the country in the late 1980s, Ernest Boyer (1990) came to the conclusion that undergraduate education and faculty time would become topics of interest to both internal and external constituencies. Over two decades later, this has become a reality in the form of an accountability movement that is taking a close look at faculty productivity. When conversations center around faculty productivity, faculty workload is typically at the forefront of people's minds. One of the first questions asked is, "How much do faculty teach?" However, few colleges and universities actually know how faculty spend their time, primarily because it is difficult to demonstrate the output and product of faculty activity (Middaugh & Isaacs, 2003). Faculty workload needs to be described in a manner that is easily understood inside and outside of higher education.

Higher education experiences pressures from both internal and external constituencies to demonstrate faculty productivity. These constituencies want to know the return on their investment in full-time, tenured, and tenure track faculty (Palmer, 1998). Congress and state legislatures are concerned about instructional costs and are demanding greater accountability from colleges and universities. This is apparent in activities such as the U.S. Department of Education's Higher Education Opportunity Act. In addition, a number of state legislatures have mandated that higher education institutions use faculty performance indicators (Hebel, 1999a; Hebel, 1999b; Lovell, 2000; Schmidt, 1996; Wilson, 1997).

One of the primary roles of institutional researchers is to provide the appropriate resources and tools to higher education administrators to manage and plan effectively. It is suggested that, "given the central role of the faculty and their involvement with students in and outside the classroom, it is critical to understand faculty work in order to assess institutional effectiveness" (Middaugh, Kelly, & Walters, 2008, p. 41). It is imperative that institutional researchers understand and communicate the complete picture of faculty workload, which encompasses teaching, scholarship, and service. The extent to which faculty engage in these three activities is directly related to an institution's mission. Boyer (1990) states, "The work of the professor becomes consequential only as it is understood by others" (p. 23). For this reason, credible conversations regarding faculty workload need to include measuring and evaluating faculty inputs as well as outputs. Colleges and universities must have the tools and resources to describe what faculty members do. This chapter provides the resources to help researchers paint that complete picture of faculty workload.

Current Data Sources

It is important to use multiple means when measuring and evaluating faculty workload, due to the limitations of an individual data source and the applicability of this source to unique institutions. That being said, external data sources can help inform conversations regarding faculty workload. Offices of institutional research will find scholarly databases as well as their own internal databases helpful. Two examples of scholarly databases include the Institute for Scientific Information's (ISI) U.S. University Science Indicators database and Academic Analytics.

The National Research Council examines data on faculty scholarly output by reviewing the U.S. University Science Indicators database. This database summarizes publication and citation statistics for many of the major universities throughout the United States (Middaugh, 2001).

Academic Analytics has created the Faculty Scholarly Productivity (FSP) Index and Database, which measures faculty scholarly productivity based on book and journal publications, journal article citations, federally funded research grants, and honorific awards. Although Academic Analytics promotes the FSP Index and Database as a ranking tool, Lawrence Martin, dean of the graduate school at Stony Brook and founder of Academic Analytics, has stated that "the index's real value lies in its raw data" (Wasley, 2007, p. A10). The real value in both of these data sources is that they allow for comparative benchmarking.

Internal data sources can also help inform conversations regarding faculty workload. Two examples of internal data sources are data enterprise warehouses and the annual faculty appraisal process.

Surveys and Research Studies. Three specific survey and research studies focusing on faculty workload are the Joint Commission on Accountability Reporting (JCAR), the National Center for Education Statistics' National Study of Postsecondary Faculty (NSOPF), and the Higher Education Research

Institute (HERI) Faculty Survey. JCAR focuses on faculty activity and how it influences institutional outcomes. JCAR not only measures the percentage of time spent on teaching, scholarship, and service, but also describes faculty activity in terms of output measures. JCAR attempts to define teaching, scholarship, and service (Middaugh, 2001).

NSOPF is a federally mandated reporting effort that describes faculty activity in terms of percentages of time. NSOPF focuses on instructional faculty and staff characteristics, percentage time spent on teaching, research, and administrative activities, time spent in the classroom and student contact hours, publications and presentations, and compensation. According to fall 2003 NSOPF data, full-time faculty at four-year institutions report that they work approximately 54 hours per week (Cataldi, Bradburn, Fahimi, & Zimbler, 2005).

The perception outside academe is that faculty have one primary responsibility: to teach students. This is further compounded by the NSOPF data. Fall 2003 NSOPF data indicate that full-time instructional faculty and staff at four-year institutions report they spend more than half (58 percent) of their time on teaching activities, which includes approximately nine hours per week in the classroom (Cataldi, Bradburn, Fahimi, & Zimbler, 2005).

In fall 2003, full-time instructional faculty and staff at four-year institutions reported spending 22 percent of their time on research activities and 21 percent of their time on administrative and other activities (Cataldi, Bradburn, Fahimi, & Zimbler, 2005). The data reported through the 2004 NSOPF survey reveal that faculty members are currently spending most of their time on teaching, followed by research and administrative and other activities combined. The NSOPF data may be viewed as an accurate reflection of faculty responsibilities in order of priority: teaching, research, and service.

Over the years, NSOPF data have been used by researchers to inform those interested in issues related to faculty in higher education. Both faculty and administrators would find it worthwhile to review the wide variety of research studies based on NSOPF data. A research topic might include analyzing faculty workload as it relates to the research productivity of tenured and tenure track faculty (Porter & Umbach, 2001). The NSOPF data can be used to take a close look at faculty turnover and answer questions about the difference between the intentions of full-time tenured and nontenured faculty to leave their institution, as well as to better understand how this affects institutional policy and practice related to personnel and finances (Zhou & Volkwein, 2004). Furthermore, NSOPF data can be used to monitor the changing landscape in higher education. For example, Sallee and Tierney (2011) analyzed NSOPF data related to faculty in schools of education to explore how the composition (time and tenure status) and the responsibilities of these faculty have changed over a decade.

Faculty at community colleges are predominantly part-time (Leslie & Gappa, 2002; Eagan, 2007). For this reason, Leslie & Gappa (2002) used NSOPF data to understand "who [part-time community college faculty] are, what they do, and how they differ from their full-time colleagues" (p. 59). Mamiseishvili

(2010) analyzed NSOPF data related to foreign-born community college faculty to explore how the composition, job satisfaction, and perceptions of these faculty differ from their U.S.–born colleagues. The goal of this analysis is to use the findings to attract and retain foreign-born community college faculty by providing appropriate resources and support. Eagan (2007) analyzed NSOPF data related to part-time community college faculty to explore how the composition and attitudes and beliefs of these faculty have changed over time and how these findings compare to full-time community college faculty.

It is understood in higher education that faculty play a key role helping colleges and universities fulfill their missions. For this reason, it is very important to understand faculty work-life issues, and this is the very reason the Cooperative Institutional Research Program (CIRP) at HERI initiated a faculty survey in 1978. In 1989–90, CIRP began to administer the survey on a triennial basis. As of this writing, the most recent HERI Faculty Survey results are available for the 2007–2008 administration. A total of 22,562 full-time college and university faculty representing 372 four-year institutions responded to the survey. "Faculty" are "defined as any full-time employee of an accredited four-year college or university who spends at least part of his or her time teaching undergraduates" (DeAngelo, Hurtado, Pryor, Kelly, Santos, & Korn, 2009, p. 1). The HERI Faculty Survey results typically include community colleges, but due to low participation these were not included in the 2007–2008 results.

The 2007–2008 HERI Faculty Survey norms describe full-time undergraduate faculty by type of institution (all four-year universities, four-year colleges), control (public, private, non-specified, Catholic, other religion), and rank (all ranks combined, full professor, associate professor, assistant professor, lecturer, instructor, no response) for all faculty, men, and women. The results of the 2007–2008 HERI Faculty Survey detail faculty activity, type and level of engagement, and productivity. Specific examples related to faculty workload from the 2007–2008 HERI Faculty Survey results include time spent on teaching, research, and service, as well as working with and engaging undergraduates on research projects.

The HERI Faculty Survey finds that, overall, faculty spend most of their time preparing for class, followed by teaching, research, and finally, committee work. The survey finds that more than half of overall faculty have worked with undergraduates on a research project in the last two years (DeAngelo et al., 2009). The survey also finds that only more than half (approximately 58 percent) are satisfied with their teaching load (DeAngelo et al., 2009).

Institutions use results of the HERI Faculty Survey to inform discussions about pedagogy and understand faculty perceptions on institutional policies, the planning process, and overall job satisfaction. The results of the Survey are also used to improve faculty professional development programs and support the evidence-based accreditation self-study process. One of the greatest benefits of the HERI Faculty Survey is the ability to access normative benchmark data, which can facilitate informed decision making (Higher Education Research Institute, n.d.).

The University of Central Oklahoma (UCO) has participated in the HERI Faculty Survey three times since 2008 and uses the results to "make program improvements and ultimately improve student learning" (Gentry, 2008, p. 1). The UCO Office of Assessment took a close look at their institutional results and developed a report that highlights items considered academically significant among the comparison groups. UCO asked two important questions: "What have we learned?" and "What are we going to do about it?" (Gentry, 2008, p. 6). It is important to note that UCO has closed the communication feedback loop by sharing the HERI Faculty Survey results with various working groups as well as campus decision makers, so they have the opportunity to hear and consider the faculty voice on their campus.

The notion that faculty have three primary responsibilities—teaching, scholarly activity, and service—has been confirmed over time through the administration of both the NSOPF and the HERI Faculty Survey. The survey and research studies just cited focus primarily on the allocation of faculty time. In addition to taking a close look at the allocation of faculty time, it is also very important to understand the allocation of personnel and fiscal resources.

Understanding Faculty Workload and Costs Through Data-Sharing Consortiums

If one is going to analyze and interpret the faculty workload at an institution, this can be done through internal comparisons. It can also be done through external comparisons. The following sections describe the major databases and how they can be used.

The National Study of Instructional Costs and Productivity

The National Study of Instructional Costs and Productivity (also referred to as the Delaware Study) (http://www.udel.edu/IR/cost) is a national benchmarking study examining faculty workload and instructional expenditures at four-year institutions. Originally supported by a grant from TIAA-CREF in 1995 and the recipient of a grant from the U.S. Department of Education Fund for Improvement of Postsecondary Education (FIPSE) from 1996 to 1999 (Middaugh & Isaacs, 2005a), the study has become a tool of choice for examining teaching load by faculty type and instructional and externally funded expenditures, all at the discipline level of analysis. This benchmarking study is widely regarded as a valuable aid to institutional decision making in higher education. For example, the Delaware Study enables researchers to answer questions such as: How much do our faculty teach compared to the national norm? What proportion of our undergraduates are taught by regular faculty? Is it more expensive to deliver a student credit hour at our institution compared to others? How do our separately funded research and service expenditures compare to national benchmarks or our current and aspirational peers?

The Delaware Study's first national data collection took place in 1992 with 86 participating institutions (Middaugh, 2001; Middaugh & Isaacs, 2003; Middaugh & Isaacs, 2005a). Since then over 500 institutions have participated in the Delaware Study, with approximately 200 institutions participating annually. Both public and private four-year institutions participate, spanning the research, doctoral, masters, and baccalaureate Carnegie classifications. State system offices, such as those at the University of North Carolina system and University of Missouri system, use the Delaware Study results annually to examine their public institutions' cost and productivity data. In addition, groups such as the American Association of Universities Data Exchange (AAUDE) and the Southern University Group (SUG) Data Exchange use their institutional members' Delaware Study data for comparisons within their data-sharing consortium.

Delaware Study Data Elements. The Delaware Study data collection consists of fall teaching load data by faculty type distributed as student credit hours and organized class sections by level of course (that is, lower and upper division undergraduate and graduate levels). This teaching activity data is detailed over four distinct faculty categories. Tenured and tenure eligible faculty are examined, along with what are referred to as "other regular faculty"—those faculty on recurring contracts who are hired primarily to teach with no expectations of scholarship or service and with no possibility of academic tenure. The teaching activity of supplemental faculty (such as adjunct faculty and administrators teaching courses) and graduate teaching assistants is also examined. Additionally, academic and fiscal year data are collected: student credit hours by undergraduate and graduate level, and direct expenditure data reported within the three functional areas of instruction, research, and public service. Institutional participants submit these data elements for their institutions' academic disciplines, coded with the appropriate Classification of Instructional Program (CIP) code. Average degrees awarded in the discipline are also collected. The 2010 Delaware Study departmental data collection form is presented in Figure 31.1.

Delaware Study Results and Benchmarks. With approximately 200 four-year institutions participating annually, the Delaware Study benchmarks offer a robust set of normative values for data comparisons. National benchmarks are produced annually in three distinct arrays: Carnegie classification, highest degree awarded in the discipline, and undergraduate/graduate program mix. Disciplinary data are aggregated to the four-digit (such as 26.02) and two-digit CIP codes (such as 26.00) and categorized appropriately for each set of the benchmarks. The results of the Delaware Study display fall teaching load data (student credit hours, organized class sections, and full-time equivalent [FTE] students taught) within faculty category. Results are provided for the academic and fiscal year, with summaries of direct instructional costs

FIGURE 31.1   2010 DELAWARE STUDY DATA COLLECTION FORM

2010 National Study of Instructional Costs and Productivity

(Office use only)

Institution:

Department/Discipline:

Associated CIP Identifier: CIP Verified?

Please indicate the **average** number of degrees awarded in this discipline at each degree level over the period from 2006–07 through 2008–09. If a degree level is not offered, leave as zero. If data are not available, please enter 'm' in the boxes.

Bachelor's:
Master's:
Doctorate:
Professional:

Place an 'X' in the box below if this discipline is non-degree granting.

A. INSTRUCTIONAL COURSELOAD: FALL SEMESTER, 2009

Please complete the following matrix, displaying student credit hours and organized class sections taught, by type of faculty, and by level of instruction. Be sure to consult definitions before proceeding. Do not input data in shaded cells except for those mentioned in the important note below that pertains to (G) and (J).

| Classification | FTE Faculty | | | Student Credit Hours | | | | | | | | | Organized Class Sections | | | | |
	(A) Total	(B) Sep. Budg.	(c) Instruc-tional	(D) Lower Div. OC*	(E) Upper Div. OC*	(F) Undergrad Indv. Instruct.	(G) Total Undergrad SCH	(H) Grad OC*	(I) Graduate Indv. Instruct.	(J) Total Graduate SCH	(K) Total Student Credit Hours	(L) Lab/Dsc/ Rec. Sections	(M) Lower Div.	(N) Upper Div.	(O) Graduate	(P) Total
Regular faculty: - Tenured/Tenure Eligible																
- Other Regular Faculty																
Supplemental Faculty		NA														
Teaching Assistants: - Credit Bearing Courses		NA														
- Non-Credit Bearing Activity		NA		NA	NA	NA	NA	NA	NA	NA	NA					
TOTAL																

*OC = Organized Class   NA = Not applicable

In the box to the right, indicate the number of individualized instruction student credit hours from the total that are devoted to supervised doctoral dissertation.

Mark with 'X' the box that indicates your academic calendar
Semester: Quarter:

Reminder: Use Fall 2009 semester data as of your official census date.

Important note: If you cannot differentiate between "Organized Class" and "Individualized Instruction" student credit hours, assign all credit hours to the appropriate "Organized Class" column. Similarly, if you cannot differentiate between "Lower Division" and "Upper Division" undergraduate student credit hours, report all those hours under "Total Undergraduate SCH."

B. COST DATA: ACADEMIC AND FISCAL YEAR 2009–10

1. Total student credit hours generated during Academic Year 2009-10, that were supported by the department/discipline instructional budget. (NOTE: Semester calendar institutions will typically report fall and spring student credit hours; quarter calendar institutions will report fall, winter, and spring student credit hours.)

A. Undergraduate
B. Graduate

2. Total direct expenditures for instruction in Fiscal Year 2009–10

A. Salaries   *Are the benefits included in the number reported for salaries(Y/N)?*
B. Benefits   *If the dollar value is NOT available, what percent of salary do benefits constitute at your inst.*
C. Other than personnel expenditures.
D. Total (including benefits if it was calculated)

0
0

3. Total direct expenditures for separately budgeted research activities in Fiscal Year 2009–10

4. Total direct expenditures for separately budgeted public service activities in Fiscal Year 2009–10

© 2010 University of Delaware. The National Study of Instructional Costs and Productivity was initially developed under a grant from the Fund for the Improvement of Postsecondary Education (FIPSE).

per student credit hour and per FTE student taught. Direct expenditures for research and public service per FTE tenured and tenure track faculty are also provided. Participating institutions gain access to the Delaware Study's secure website, where they can download their own institutional results along with the national benchmarks. The website also allows participants access to query the dataset and complete customized peer group analyses while keeping individual institutional results unidentifiable.

Recent Enhancement to Methodology. From its inception, the Delaware Study has collected data from both semester and quarter calendar institutions. To equate the calculation of an annual FTE student, the following convention is applied: an FTE student taught for semester academic calendar institutions is equivalent to 30 undergraduate student credit hours or 18 graduate student credit hours; that for quarter academic calendar institutions is 45 undergraduate or 27 graduate student credit hours. Over time, anecdotal evidence from quarter calendar institutions pointed to another Delaware Study data element in need of adjustment. Studying the academic and fiscal year result "direct instructional expenditure per student credit hour" revealed that an adjustment was required to ensure comparability between semester and quarter calendar institutions (dividing quarter calendar institutions' academic year student credit hours by 1.5) (Walters, 2009). This is necessary because quarter calendar institutions operate with three major terms in an academic year, whereas semester calendar institutions have two. This additional adjustment to the academic and fiscal year data calculations was first incorporated into the 2008 Delaware Study results and has proved effective in ensuring comparable data between semester and quarter calendar institutions.

Using the Delaware Study. Participation in the Delaware Study affords an institution a valuable array of productivity and cost indicators for each reported discipline. Delaware Study institutions find that these data add value to the academic program review process and answer questions about their departmental teaching activity and costs of instruction, research, and public service activities. They particularly underscore the usefulness of the benchmark data to situate their institutional activities in alignment with and compared to the national trends in teaching loads, productivity, and cost of instruction.

At the University of Delaware, the provost, deans, and chairs use Delaware Study data within activities of academic program review and departmental planning. Specifically, they are interested in six data elements from the Delaware Study, which focus on tenured and tenure track faculty productivity as well as total teaching activity for all faculty within the discipline, instructional cost, and separately budgeted research and service expenditures. The data elements are:

- Undergraduate student credit hours taught per FTE tenured and tenure track faculty
- Total student credit hours taught per FTE tenured and tenure track faculty
- Total class sections taught per FTE tenured and tenure track faculty
- Total student credit hours taught per FTE faculty, all categories combined
- Total direct instructional expense per student credit hour taught
- Total separately budgeted research and service expenditures per FTE tenured and tenure track faculty

These six indicators are typically displayed in a single-sheet departmental profile in which five years of University of Delaware data are compared to benchmark data for Carnegie research institutions. Viewing the data in this way allows for the examination of teaching activities in context with instructional cost and research and service expenditures. For example, where the total student credit hours taught by tenured and tenure track faculty (Figure 31.2) were less than the national benchmark from 2001 through 2005, this was not a surprise in light of the department's focus on diverting their teaching to the "other regular faculty" category of faculty. In fact, the decrease in tenured and tenure track teaching was purposeful: to give these faculty the release time they would need to increase their research activity, a goal of the department during this time. This offset to their teaching is visible to administrators in the variable displaying the steady increase of research and public service expenditures over the national average. The addition of new tenured and tenure track faculty, along with the heavy weight of the added salaries, is evident given the increase of direct instructional expenditures per student credit hour, which were also in excess of the national average.

The University of Delaware does not use the data to reward or penalize departments, but as an additional tool in evaluating program quality and fit with the overall institutional mission. The Delaware Study serves as a rich data resource for institutions to assess fiscal and human resource allocations at the academic unit level, while the benchmarks situate institutional disciplines in the national context.

FIGURE 31.2   TOTAL STUDENT CREDIT HOURS TAUGHT PER FTE TENURED AND TENURE TRACK FACULTY FOR A SCIENCE DEPARTMENT

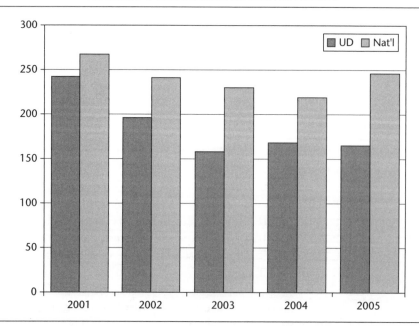

The Kansas Study of Community College Instructional Costs and Productivity

Prior to the implementation of the Kansas Study of Community College Instructional Costs and Productivity (Kansas Study) in 2004, there were no national data sharing or data reporting consortia dedicated solely to community colleges. The Kansas Study was conceived as a two-year college analog to the widely used Delaware Study for four-year colleges and universities. In 2002, the Office of Institutional Research at Johnson County (Kansas) Community College applied for, and was awarded, an approximately $280,000 grant from FIPSE to support the design and initial implementation of a national instructional load or cost data collection or reporting initiative for the nation's two-year colleges. The design phase of the project was guided by a national advisory committee composed of leading community college institutional researchers, chief academic and business officers, and representatives of national community college policy organizations.

The Study collects and reports community college faculty workload (that is, the proportion of credit hours taught by full- and part-time faculty), as well as the cost per credit hour of that instruction, at the discipline level of analysis. Since its inception in 2004, nearly 200 two-year colleges across the country have participated in the Kansas Study, making the resulting dataset the most comprehensive collection of community college instructional cost and productivity data to date.

Kansas Study Data Elements. Participating institutions, usually the director of institutional research or an IR analyst, provide individual discipline-level data to the Study. After the enrollment process is completed, the participants are granted access, through the Kansas Study website (http://www.KansasStudy. org), to the web-based institutional demographic profile and Study data entry functionalities, as well as to the online documentation. The Kansas Study disciplines are closely tied to CIP codes, which facilitate data entry independent of an individual institution's disciplines. The demographic profile collects institutional characteristics, which may be used to construct peer comparison groups in the Study's peer analysis tool. As noted earlier, the Study collects and reports data by discipline for credit courses (that is, those eligible for Title IV funding). The data collection template has two parts: Part A, which collects fall semester instructional workload data by faculty type, and Part B, which collects fiscal year instructional cost data (specifically, salaries and benefits for faculty, support staff, and direct administrators). Participants complete either Part A or Part B or (preferably) both for each discipline for which they wish to report data.

The participant-only section of the study website can be accessed using an assigned login and password. It provides access to (1) tables of annual national aggregate results, (2) individual institutional-level reports, and (3) the peer analysis tool. Using this peer analysis tool, participants may create lists of peer groups, by discipline, by either searching and selecting from the list of participating colleges or using the institutional demographic variables to construct a group of institutions similar to their own. Kansas Study subscribers can then access the peer groups' individual reported values. Because all the institution's names are masked, the confidentiality of the data is ensured.

Kansas Study Results and Benchmarks. Study results are provided to participating institutions in a series of national norms tables. These tables contain data only for those disciplines for which data were provided by five or more participating colleges. An example of a partial national norms table is provided in Table 31.1. Although the national aggregate reports display data for all disciplines for which data were provided by participants, subscribing colleges also receive customized reports for their individual institution that mirror the national norms tables and compare their individual institution's data to those national norms.

Kansas Study staff and others have performed additional analyses using Study data. Seybert and Rossol (2010) reported the ten most expensive disciplines in community colleges nationwide in terms of cost-per-credit-hour (Dental Hygiene, Medical Laboratory Technician, Respiratory Care, Occupational Therapy Assistant, Surgical Technology, Liberal Studies, Nursing, Journalism, Physical Therapy Assistant, and Electronics Equipment Repair) (Table 31.2), and the least expensive (Anthropology, Real Estate, Sociology, Psychology, History, Economics, Philosophy, Nutrition and Wellness, Political Science, and Communications) (Table 31.3). In addition, they found that the major instructional cost driver in community colleges was who delivers that instruction (full- versus part-time faculty) rather than what type of instruction is delivered (discipline).

Using the Kansas Study. Kansas Study data have been shown to be valuable to support accountability initiatives, planning, and decision making in both state

TABLE 31.1 KANSAS STUDY: PERCENT STUDENT CREDIT HOURS TAUGHT BY FACULTY TYPE AND ACADEMIC DISCIPLINE, NATIONAL REFINED MEANS, FALL 2002

Academic Discipline	Number of Institutions Reporting	National Refined Means Percent Student Credit Hours Taught by		
		Full-Time Faculty	Part-Time Faculty	Full-Time Employees
Biological Sciences–Life Sciences	42	69	30	0
Business Administration and Management, General	40	59	40	0
Computer and Information Sciences, General	41	55	43	0
Mathematics (excluding developmental)	44	67	32	0
Psychology	42	55	43	1

TABLE 31.2   KANSAS STUDY: INSTRUCTIONAL COST PER STUDENT CREDIT HOUR—MOST EXPENSIVE DISCIPLINES

Academic Discipline	Instructional Costs	N
Dental Hygienist	$484	10
Occupational Therapist Assistant	$309	8
Medical Assistant	$300	12
Clinical-Medical Laboratory Technician	$262	9
Respiratory Care	$254	9
Physical Therapist Assistant	$253	13
Nursing	$240	50
Liberal Arts and Sciences–Liberal Studies	$235	6
Dental Assistant	$232	12
Licensed Practical Nurse	$217	16

TABLE 31.3   KANSAS STUDY: INSTRUCTIONAL COST PER STUDENT CREDIT HOUR—LEAST EXPENSIVE DISCIPLINES

Academic Discipline	Instructional Costs	N
Anthropology	$50	16
Psychology	$58	47
History	$58	42
Life Skills, Basic Skills	$59	5
Humanities	$60	16
Social Sciences	$60	10
Real Estate	$61	8
Sociology	$62	35
Philosophy and Religion	$62	28
Political Science	$64	31

system and individual institutional settings. For example, all thirteen community colleges in Tennessee have participated in the Study since its inception. The Tennessee Board of Regents has incorporated Study data in the state's performance funding program for its community colleges. Specifically, "for its 2005–2010 performance funding cycle, one of eleven standards that Tennessee community colleges had to meet was devoted exclusively to the collection and use of Kansas Study data" (Malo & Weed, 2006, p. 19). At the institutional level, Nashville State Technical Community College has used Study data to realign faculty positions, as an important component of its program review process, and to document several core requirements of its Southern Association of Colleges and Schools (SACS) reaccreditation process.

In addition, Northeast State Technical Community College (NSTCC) used Kansas Study data to identify programs for review based on the finding of where costs per credit hour were highest among Study participants. Kansas Study data were also instrumental in decisions to shift vacant full-time faculty positions from departments in which the proportion of adjunct faculty was significantly lower than the Study median to those in which the percentage of adjuncts was notably higher than the Study median. Finally, NSTCC used Kansas Study data to (1) support the college's compliance with SACS accreditation requirements to demonstrate that the college engaged in ongoing planning and evaluation processes resulting in continuous improvement, (2) show that it employs an adequate number of full-time faculty, and (3) show that it maintains a sound financial base and financial stability (Malo & Weed, 2006).

In summary, the Kansas Study has provided a heretofore unavailable and important data resource for information on faculty workload and instructional costs by discipline at community colleges, on a national basis.

The National Community College Benchmark Project

The National Community College Benchmark Project (NCCBP) measures a wide array of over 150 two-year college input and output indicators, encompassing student learning outcomes, access, workforce development, faculty or staff, human resources, and finance variables at the institutional level. This broad scope assists project participants in evaluating and benchmarking faculty workload and instructional costs in a broader context.

In 2002–2003, the Community College Benchmark Task Force, a group of institutional research representatives from large, prominent community colleges and the League for Innovation in the Community College responded to the rapidly growing demand for accountability in higher education by designing and implementing an approach to benchmarking community college outcomes. Over the years, the NCCBP has become self-sustaining and grown into the largest national community college data collection or sharing consortium in the United States, with over 350 participating community colleges since its inception. Among these are the state systems in Colorado, Florida, Hawaii, Indiana (Ivy Tech), Kentucky, New York, Pennsylvania, Tennessee, and Wyoming. In addition, several large community college districts have also participated, including Austin, Alamo (all Texas), Chicago (Illinois), Collin County, Dallas, El Paso (all Texas), Kansas City (Missouri), Maricopa (Arizona), Miami Dade (Florida), Portland (Oregon), and St. Louis (Missouri). In 2011, a record number of 280 two-year institutions enrolled.

NCCBP Data Elements. NCCBP data are collected at the institutional level. In terms of data related to faculty workload and instructional cost, NCCBP participants submit the following data elements:

- Total FTE faculty (differentiated by full-time or part-time faculty status)
- FTE students

- Total student credit hours taught (differentiated by full-time or part-time faculty status)
- Total credit sections taught (differentiated by full-time or part-time faculty status)
- Total direct credit instructional expenditures
- Total fiscal year (FY) student credit hours

The data collection process begins annually in January and ends in July. Until 2010, the principal data collection instrument was a Microsoft Excel workbook, including definitions of data elements, instructions, and data-entry forms on separate worksheets. Beginning in 2011, all participating institutions began entering their data directly on the new NCCBP website (http://www.NCCBP.org), which allows automatic calculation of all Benchmark Project benchmarks. This leads to a faster analytic turnaround time; thus participants receive Benchmark Project reports much earlier in the year.

The NCCBP data collection process automatically checks for missing and inconsistent data. Participating institutions are required to address all data entry errors before they can proceed to the next validation step: the outlier check. At this stage in the data verification process, institutions' benchmark values are compared with means of values reported by all participants. Participants are then prompted to confirm the accuracy of any outlier data—that is, +/− two standard deviations from the mean. Updated benchmark values then become bases for the annual reports.

NCCBP Results and Benchmarks. In the case of faculty workload and instructional cost, the NCCBP reports the following benchmarks: student/faculty ratio; percentage of credit hours by type of faculty (full-time versus part-time); percentage of sections by type of faculty (full-time versus part-time); cost per credit hour; and cost per FTE student.

NCCBP subscribers have access to three benchmarking functionalities: (1) national and system aggregate data reports, (2) the peer comparison tool, and (3) the best practices report.

1. The national aggregate reports illustrate percentile ranks of the participating college on each of the 150-plus benchmarks. The reports also provide the 10th, 25th, 50th (median), 75th, and 90th percentile for each benchmark in the entire national dataset. Institutions receive individual system aggregate reports if an intact college system or district has enrolled in the Benchmark Project. Some participating colleges use selected NCCBP benchmarks as key performance indicators (KPIs), which arise from their institution's mission statement and can be used to track institutional progress quantitatively over time.

2. The NCCBP's peer comparison tool lets subscribers select comparable institutions in one of two ways: directly from the list of Benchmark Project

participants or on the basis of institutional demographics such as the size of the unrestricted operating budget, IPEDS enrollment size, minority student population, and the like. Participants can then select individual benchmarks to compare with those of their peer group. To maintain individual college data confidentiality, this functionality requires the participant to select at least five peer institutions. Individual institutional identities are then masked and the participant can access peer data knowing that the filtered dataset contains results of only the selected peer group.

3. For each NCCBP benchmark the best practices report identifies all institutions that scored above the 80th percentile (or in some cases below the 20th percentile). The participating institutions can then contact "best practice" colleges to determine the educational programs, initiatives, and innovations that underlie their achievement on a given benchmark.

Using the NCCBP. NCCBP benchmarks have provided the basis for strategic planning and quality improvement efforts at community colleges across the nation. Participants use aggregate results and peer comparisons to inform local quality improvement initiatives and accreditation requirements (for example, peer comparison requirements in the North Central Association of Colleges and Schools [NCA] Higher Learning Commission's Academic Quality Improvement Program [AQIP]). Des Moines Area Community College used NCCBP data to address the AQIP accreditation criteria and respond to mandated questions in their AQIP Systems Portfolio (Linduska & Emmerson, 2011). Similarly, Ouachita Technical College integrated NCCBP data into its Achieving the Dream initiative to support and sustain its culture of inquiry, evidence, and accountability (Prince, 2011). NCCBP benchmarks have also been incorporated into performance processes such as the Tennessee Higher Education System performance funding model, and they play an important role as part of strategic planning processes in multicollege systems. Participants use comparative data provided by the NCCBP for institutional program reviews and assessment initiatives and discussions of issues such as course retention and success rates and program completions (Juhnke, 2006). Other colleges, including North Arkansas College and North Central Texas College, have incorporated NCCBP benchmarks into their institutional scorecards and executive dashboards to provide a quick performance overview to executives and boards of trustees (Hadlock, Seybert, & Nutt, 2011).

The NCCBP serves as a higher education transparency and accountability instrument that provides community college institutional researchers with the necessary peer comparison tools to effectively pursue targeted quality-improvement processes, prepare accreditation reports, and provide the executive leadership of participating institutions with systematic and regularly provided quantitative indicators, leading the way to enhanced institutional effectiveness.

Understanding Faculty Productivity

Although the Delaware Study is extremely effective in describing faculty workload and associated costs, these data do not capture the full range of faculty work. In reality, there are other non-classroom faculty activities involving student research, scholarly activity, and departmental service in which faculty spend their time to positively influence their students, departments, and institutions. These certainly will affect teaching loads and productivity and should be acknowledged when examining these data at both departmental and national levels. The primary purpose of the Selected Measures of Out-of-Classroom Faculty Activity Study is to supplement faculty workload data and provide contextual information related to nonclassroom faculty activities at four-year institutions.

Selected Measures of Out-of-Classroom Faculty Activity Study

With the assistance of a grant from FIPSE in 2001 and the work of a national Advisory Committee, the Delaware Study expanded to address out-of-classroom demands on faculty time in order to describe output measures and the products of faculty activity. The expanded Delaware Study is known as the Faculty Activity Study. The first full data collection cycle took place in spring 2003; four subsequent data collections have taken place.

The Faculty Activity Study attempts to address the shortcomings of faculty workload studies previously discussed. For instance, the Faculty Activity Study focuses on faculty activity that takes place outside the classroom and includes some qualitative measures. These measures include the number of refereed versus nonrefereed publications, juried shows, commissioned performances, competitive exhibitions, grants, contracts and fellowships formally awarded, formal presentations, and leadership positions. The data analyses for the Faculty Activity Study are descriptive, not inferential. Although this may not be ideal, descriptive analyses will enhance the ability of participating schools to understand what their faculty do outside the classroom and the associated outcomes. Middaugh and Isaacs (2005a, p. 80) suggest specifically:

- It will provide some measure of quantification of out-of-classroom faculty activity as a context for examining the standard teaching load and instructional cost benchmarks generated annually by the Delaware Study.
- The type of activities reported by faculty should help to underscore the different institutional missions of schools participating in the Delaware Study. Research and doctoral university faculty might be expected to engage in traditional measures of scholarship—publishing, research, and public service—whereas comprehensive and baccalaureate institutional faculty might be involved with more activity directly engaging students

(such as academic advising, supervision of interns, and undergraduate research).

- The data collected should help to underscore the different types of scholarship and other activities in which faculty engage across the disciplines. For example, fine and performing arts faculty do not publish; they perform. In addition, the volume of sponsored research and service activity in the sciences, engineering, and agricultural sciences might be expected to be significantly larger than in the humanities.

Faculty Activity Study Data Elements. The Faculty Activity Study surveys faculty about the demands on their out-of-classroom time. The data collection summary form currently consists of forty-two variables (Figure 31.3) relating to teaching, scholarship, and service, as well as the number of FTE tenured faculty in the discipline, the number of FTE tenure track faculty in the discipline, and the number of FTE faculty included in the data collected. The current methodology for the Faculty Activity Study is as follows: a Summary Form is distributed to department chairs at participating institutions, along with a Faculty Checklist that mirrors the Summary Form in content. To ensure that each item on the Summary Form is clear and self-explanatory, Data Definitions and a Sample Departmental Walk-Through have been developed and are intended to facilitate the data collection process. The Faculty Activity Study data collection instruments, as well as two briefing papers can be found at http://www.udel.edu/IR/focs/.

Faculty Activity Study Results and Benchmarks. Once data verification and analyses are complete, national benchmarks for measures of out-of-classroom faculty activity at the discipline level of analysis by Carnegie classification and highest degree offered are produced. Refined means are not calculated, due to the small number of participating institutions and the large variance. The national benchmarks include the minimum, maximum, mean, and median values. The large variance for the majority of the variables in each Carnegie classification makes the median a better statistic to describe the central tendency for the sample. We will now take a close look at the median results for faculty activity related to service for a science department (Figure 31.4).

With respect to teaching, baccalaureate institutions do not show any evidence of graduate research or graduate advisees. It is no surprise that, with regard to activities related to scholarship, there is an upward trend from baccalaureate to research institutions for external grant proposals and external grants awarded. Looking at professional service, all institutions—regardless of Carnegie classification—focus on institutional service (Middaugh, Kelly, & Walters, 2008).

Although all four-year faculty engage in the three functions of teaching, scholarship, and service, the emphasis on each depends on the type of institution where the faculty member is employed. The Faculty Activity Study results provide evidence that in addition to time spent in the classroom teaching

FIGURE 31.3 FACULTY ACTIVITY STUDY SUMMARY FORM

Delaware Study of Instructional Costs and Productivity

Selected Measures of Out-of-Classroom Faculty Activity: Summary Form

Institution: _____ FICE Code: _____

Discipline: _____ CIP Code: _____

Degrees Offered in Discipline (check all that apply): _____ Bachelor's _____ Master's_____ Doctorate_____ Professional

This study focuses on the discipline level of analysis. Please carefully consult the data definitions accompanying this data collection form before reporting information. All data should be reported for the most recent _12-month faculty evaluation period_ as defined in instructions. Please denote any not-applicable data as 'na' and any data element that is truly zero as '0'.

DISCIPLINE-SPECIFIC STATISTICS

A. Total full-time equivalent (FTE) tenured faculty   _____

B. Total FTE tenure-track faculty   _____

C. Total FTE tenured and tenure-track faculty on which your responses below will be based.   _____

ACTIVITIES RELATED TO TEACHING

1. Total number of separate course preparations.   _____

2. Number of *existing* courses where faculty have redesigned the pedagogy or curriculum under the auspices of a grant or course-release time.   _____

3. Number of new courses which faculty have created and have been approved for delivery. _____

4. Number of courses indicated in the previous items which are delivered fully or primarily online.   _____

5. Unduplicated headcount of *undergraduate* academic advisees *formally assigned* to faculty. _____

6. Unduplicated headcount of *graduate* academic advisees *formally assigned* to faculty.   _____

7. Number of thesis/dissertation committees where faculty served as chairperson.   _____

8. Number of thesis/dissertation committees where faculty served in a non-chairing role.   _____

9. Number of undergraduate senior theses (e.g., senior portfolio project, recital, art show, other capstone experience) that faculty have supervised.   _____

10. Total number of students taught individually in independent or directed studies (e.g., one-on-one student-faculty interaction for credit toward satisfying a degree requirement).   _____

11. Number of undergraduate students <u>formally</u> engaged in research with a faculty mentor.   _____

12. Number of graduate students <u>formally</u> engaged in research with a faculty mentor.   _____

13. Number of clinical students (e.g., student nurses), practicum students (e.g., student teachers), internship students, and students in cooperative and service learning education programs who are formally assigned to faculty.   _____

14. Number of students (undergraduate and graduate) who have co-authored a journal article or book chapter with a faculty mentor.   _____

15. Number of students (undergraduate and graduate) who have co-presented a paper at a state, regional, national, and international professional meeting with a faculty mentor.   _____

16. Number of assessment projects or separate assignments for purpose of program evaluation (as distinct from individual courses) faculty have undertaken.   _____

17. Number of institution-sanctioned professional development activities related to teaching efforts (e.g., attending conferences on General Education, participating in workshops on undergraduate research, participating in workshops offered by Center for Teaching Effectiveness).   _____

(continued)

FIGURE 31.3   FACULTY ACTIVITY STUDY SUMMARY FORM (*Continued*)

Delaware Study of Instructional Costs and Productivity

Selected Measures of Out-of-Classroom Faculty Activity: Summary Form

Institution: _____ FICE Code: _____

Discipline: _____ CIP Code: _____

ACTIVITIES RELATED TO SCHOLARSHIP

18. Number of print or electronic *refereed* journal articles, book chapters, reviews,
    and creative works published by faculty.   _____

19. Number of print or electronic *non-refereed* journal articles, book chapters, reviews,
    and creative works published by faculty.   _____

20. Number of single-author or joint-author books or monographs written by faculty and
    published by an academic or commercial press.   _____

21. Number of manuscripts (e.g. journal articles, books) *submitted* to publishers.   _____

22. Number of books, collections, and monographs *edited* by faculty.   _____

23. Number of pre-publication books, journal articles, and chapters *reviewed* by faculty.   _____

24. Number of grant proposals reviewed by faculty related to field of expertise.   _____

25. Number of editorial positions held by faculty.   _____

26. Number of juried shows, commissioned performances, creative readings, and
    competitive exhibitions by faculty.   _____

27. Number of non-juried shows, performances, creative readings, and exhibitions by faculty. _____

28. Number of digital programs or applications (e.g., software development,
    web-based learning modules) designed by faculty related to field of expertise.   _____

29. Number of provisional or issued patents based on faculty products.   _____

30. Number of faculty works in proqress (e.g., journal articles, paintings, musical compositions). _____

31. Number of formal presentations made by faculty at state, regional, national,
    and international professional meetings.   _____

32. Number of external and internal qrant, contract, and scholarly fellowship
    proposals submitted by faculty.   _____

33. Number of *new* external grants, contracts, and scholarly fellowships formally
    awarded to faculty or to the institutior on behalf of faculty.   _____

34. Total dollar value of the *new* externally funded grants, contracts, and scholarly
    fellowships reported in Item 33.   _____

35. Number of *new* internal grants and contracts formally awarded to faculty.   _____

36. Total dollar value of the *new* internal grants and contracts reported in Item 35.   _____

37. Number of continuing external and internal grants, contracts, and scholarly fellowships. _____

38. Number of institution-sanctioned professional development activities related to
    scholarship (e.g., participating in a grant writing workshop, attending a training session
    to learn a new research tool or software application, enrolling in a statistics course).   _____

ACTIVITIES RELATED TO SERVICE

39. Number of faculty activities related to institutional service (e.g., faculty governance,
    faculty committees, peer mentoring, academic programs in residences, recruiting efforts,
    student activity advisor, other student activity involvement).   _____

40. Number of faculty extension and outreach activities related to field of expertise
    (e.g., civic service, K-12 service, community workshops, invited talks to
    community groups, seminars, lectures, demonstrations).   _____

41. Number of faculty activities related to recognized or visible service to profession (e.g., service
    on a regional or national committee, service on a self-study visitation team for another
    institution, serving as an invited or volunteer juror for a show, performance, or exhibition). _____

42. Number of leadership positions in a professional association held by faculty
    (e.g., elected officer, committee chairperson, conference chair).   _____

Thank You!
http://www.udel.edu/IR/focs/

FIGURE 31.4   OUT-OF-CLASSROOM FACULTY ACTIVITY RELATED TO SERVICE FOR A SCIENCE DEPARTMENT

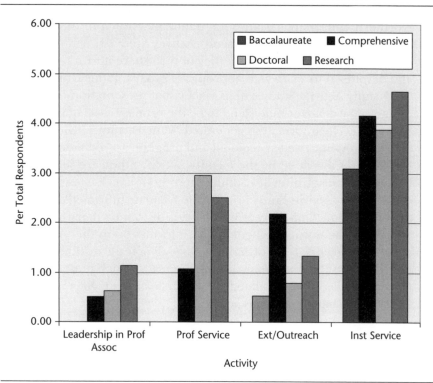

students, faculty engage in numerous activities related to departmental and institutional missions. These activities include, but are not limited to, curriculum redesign, academic advising, thesis and dissertation supervision, academic scholarship, and service to the institution, community, and profession. It is clear that the results of how faculty spend their time are a reflection of institutional mission. In addition, regardless of Carnegie classification, it is evident that faculty do not focus on any one activity area and are engaged in activities related to teaching, scholarship, and service.

Using the Faculty Activity Study. The Faculty Activity Study helps quantify what faculty *actually* do outside of the classroom by type of institution. For this reason, the Faculty Activity Study can be used as a management tool to assess the extent to which a college or university is fulfilling its overall institutional and departmental missions (Middaugh, Kelly, & Walters, 2008). This is possible due to the Faculty Activity Study's ability to provide information that will enhance discussions about what faculty actually do, how much they do, and the associated products.

Four institutions that have participated in the Faculty Activity Study were featured in a briefing paper that highlights exemplary practices related to data collection and using the Study results (Middaugh & Isaacs, 2005b). Ohio Northern University has an open data collection and information-sharing approach. The results of the Faculty Activity Study are shared with deans and chairs via a visual presentation; they in turn share it with faculty. Reports are also developed to share with appropriate groups. Rider University also shares the Faculty Activity Study results via a visual presentation to the presidential cabinet. The deans at Rider tend to be the primary users of the Faculty Activity Study data. The information generated by the Faculty Activity Study is used for program review as well as regional and program accreditation. The normative benchmarks provided by the Faculty Activity Study are seen as the greatest benefit for Rider University. Southeastern Louisiana University uses the results of the Faculty Activity Study primarily to facilitate informed decision making at their institution. University of West Florida distributes departmental summaries along with the normative benchmark information to the provost, deans, and department chairs. It is worth noting that all of these institutions have the support of their senior academic leadership team, which underscores the importance of collecting data related to out-of-classroom faculty activity and having the ability to benchmark this activity.

Using Faculty Workload Data

The purpose of the various survey and research studies, as well as the data-sharing consortiums described in this chapter, is to improve the quality of information about faculty workload that administrators and faculty receive. The data described here will provide information to make knowledgeable decisions and answer accountability questions related to what faculty do, how much they do, how well they do it, and the associated products and costs. These survey and research studies and data-sharing consortiums should be viewed as resources to facilitate effective management in higher education and to encourage more efficient use of resources.

Conclusions

The profile of institutional research offices will continue to increase along with the ability to describe the complete picture of faculty workload so it is easily understood by those internal and external to higher education. That complete picture of faculty workload needs to be clear and transparent. With financial resources becoming more limited and demands for accountability becoming more widespread, higher education will not be immune to data requests related to faculty workload. When the time comes to answer such data requests, a response will no longer be optional; it will be required. Higher education must be prepared to provide multiple means to answer these requests, and institutional research offices will play a key role.

References

Boyer, E. L. (1990). *Scholarship reconsidered: Priorities of the professoriate.* Princeton, NJ: The Carnegie Foundation for the Advancement of Teaching.

Cataldi, E. F., Bradburn, E. M., Fahimi, M., & Zimbler, L. (2005). *2004 National Study of Postsecondary Faculty (NSOPF:04): Background characteristics, work activities, and compensation of instructional faculty and staff: Fall 2003* (NCES Publication No. NCES 2006–176). U.S. Department of Education. Washington, DC: National Center for Education Statistics. Retrieved from http://nces.ed.gov/pubsearch/pubsinfo. asp?pubid=2006176

DeAngelo, L., Hurtado, S., Pryor, J. H., Kelly, K. R., Santos, J. L., & Korn, W. S. (2009). *The American college teacher: National norms for the 2007–2008 HERI faculty survey.* Los Angeles: Higher Education Research Institute, UCLA.

Eagan, K. (2007). A national picture of part-time community college faculty: Changing trends in demographics and employment characteristics. In R. L. Wagoner (Ed.), *The current landscape and changing perspectives of part-time faculty* (pp. 5–14). New Directions for Community Colleges, no. 140. San Francisco: Jossey-Bass.

Gentry, C. (2008). *University of Central Oklahoma Faculty Survey 2008.* Retrieved from http://www.uco.edu/academic-affairs/assessment/files/docs/uco-surveys-reports/faculty-survey08.pdf

Hadlock, E., Seybert, J. A., & Nutt, L. A. (2011, February). *Identifying key performance indicators: The foundation of an institutional dashboard.* Paper presented at the annual League for Innovation in the Community College Conference, San Diego, CA.

Hebel, S. (1999a, May 28). Virginia Board wants to link state aid for colleges to their performance in key areas. *Chronicle of Higher Education*, p. A33.

Hebel, S. (1999b, October 29). A new governors' approach rankles colleges in Colorado. *Chronicle of Higher Education*, p. A44.

Higher Education Research Institute. (n.d.). HERI Faculty Survey. Retrieved from http://www.heri.ucla.edu/facoverview.php

Juhnke, R. (2006). The National Community College Benchmark Project. In J. A. Seybert (Ed.), *Benchmarking: An essential tool for assessment, improvement, and accountability* (pp. 67–72). New Directions for Community Colleges, no. 134. San Francisco: Jossey-Bass.

Leslie, D. W., & Gappa, J. M. (2002). Part-time faculty: Competent and committed. In C. L. Outcalt (Ed.), *Community college faculty: Characteristics, practices, and challenges* (pp. 59–67). New Directions for Community Colleges, no. 118. San Francisco: Jossey-Bass.

Linduska, K. J., & Emmerson, J. E. (2011, June). *Benchmarking data and AQIP accreditation.* Paper presented at the annual National Higher Education Benchmarking Conference, Overland Park, KS.

Lovell, C. D. (2000). Past and present pressures and issues of higher education: State perspectives. In J. Losco & B. L. Fife (Eds.), *Higher education in transition: The challenges of the new millennium* (pp. 109–132). Westport, CT: Bergin & Garvey.

Malo, G. E., & Weed, E. J. (2006). Uses of Kansas Study data at state system and institutional levels. In J.A. Seybert (Ed.), *Benchmarking: An essential tool for assessment, improvement, and accountability* (pp. 15–24). New Directions for Community Colleges, no. 134. San Francisco: Jossey-Bass.

Mamiseishvili, K. (2010). Characteristics, job satisfaction, and workplace perceptions of foreign-born faculty at public 2-year institutions. *Community College Review, 39*(1), 26–45.

Middaugh, M. F. (2001). *Understanding faculty productivity: Standards and benchmarks for colleges and universities.* San Francisco: Jossey-Bass.

Middaugh, M. F., & Isaacs, H. K. (2003). Describing faculty activity and productivity for multiple audiences. In W. E. Knight (Ed.), *The primer for institutional research* (pp. 24–47). Tallahassee, FL: Association for Institutional Research.

Middaugh, M. F., & Isaacs, H. K. (2005a). Benchmarking departmental activity via a consortial approach: The Delaware Study. In J. E. Groccia & J. E. Miller (Eds.), *On becoming a productive university: Strategies for reducing costs and increasing quality in higher education* (pp. 70–83). Bolton, MA: Anker Publishing.

Middaugh, M. F., & Isaacs, H. K. (2005b). *A study of exemplary practices in collection of data on out-of-of-classroom faculty activity: Part II A briefing paper from the Delaware Study of Instructional Costs and Productivity.* Newark: University of Delaware, Office of Institutional Research and Planning.

Middaugh, M. F., Kelly, H. A., & Walters, A. M. (2008). The role of institutional research in understanding and describing faculty work. In D. G. Terkla (Ed.), *Institutional research: More than just data* (pp. 41–56). New Directions for Higher Education, no. 141. San Francisco: Jossey-Bass.

Palmer, J. (1998, September). Enhancing faculty productivity: A state perspective. *Education Commission of the States Policy Paper.*

Porter, S. R., & Umbach, P. D. (2001). Analyzing faculty workload data using multilevel modeling. *Research in Higher Education, 42*(2), 171–196.

Prince, J. (2011, June). *Use of NCCBP data for evidence-based decision making.* Paper presented at the annual National Higher Education Benchmarking Conference, Overland Park, KS.

Sallee, M. W., & Tierney, W. G. (2011). The transformation of the professors of education. *Journal of the Professoriate, 4*(1), 1–38.

Schmidt, P. (1996, May 24). Earning appropriations: States link spending on colleges to progress in meeting specific goals. *Chronicle of Higher Education,* pp. A23–A24.

Seybert, J. A., & Rossol, P. M. (2010). What drives instructional costs in community colleges: Data from the Kansas Study of instructional costs and productivity. *Planning for Higher Education,* 38–44.

Walters, A. M. (2009). Comparing apples to oranges: An evaluation of quarter calendar data in the Delaware Study of Instructional Costs and Productivity (Doctoral dissertation, University of Delaware). Retrieved from Dissertations & Theses @ University of Delaware. (Publication No. AAT 3360265).

Wasley, P. (2007, November 16). Faculty-productivity index offers surprises. *Chronicle of Higher Education,* p. A10.

Wilson, R. (1997, February 28). Faculty leaders in New York and California unite on productivity issues. *Chronicle of Higher Education,* p. A12.

Zhou, Y., & Volkwein, J. F. (2004). Examining the influences on faculty departure intentions: A comparison of tenures versus non-tenured faculty at research universities using NSOPF-99. *Research in Higher Education, 45*(2), 139–176.

CHAPTER 32

ANALYZING EQUITY IN FACULTY COMPENSATION

Robert K. Toutkoushian and Dennis A. Kramer II

It should not be surprising to learn that colleges and universities give significant attention to issues involving faculty and staff. The production of knowledge in higher education is a very personnel-intensive process, and a quick glance at most any institution's budget will reveal that the vast majority of expenditures are spent on faculty and staff. Institutions of higher education rely on faculty to teach students, conduct research, and engage in service activities within their communities, states, and nations, along with their professional associations. Accordingly, finding and retaining high-quality faculty is of the utmost importance to colleges and universities. In addition, there are numerous other personnel employed by institutions of higher education—administrators, academic-professionals, and support and clerical staff—all of whom are essential to helping their institutions achieve their goals and objectives.

Although in academia most attention is given to an individual's paid salary, it is important to remember that a university employee's compensation includes not only the individual's base salary, but also fringe benefits such as health care and retirement. Labor economists would be quick to point out that colleges and universities, much like any other labor market, compete with each other as well as with employers in nonacademic labor markets for faculty and staff; thus a primary factor in the attraction and retention of high-quality faculty and staff is the manner in which they are compensated in salary and benefits (Toutkoushian, 2003, 2006).

Institutions often rely on their institutional research offices to provide the administration with data and information on the status of compensation for their employees. The types of analyses performed by institutional researchers can be grouped into external and internal salary equity studies. In a study of external salary equity, one frequently asked question is, are the current salaries paid to faculty and staff fair relative to comparable institutions? To conduct this type of investigation requires the institutional research office to determine what a "comparable" institution is, find accurate data on salaries, and select a level of aggregation of faculty by rank and/or department. In contrast, internal salary equity studies ask the institutional research office to determine whether faculty and staff are treated equitability within the institution relative to each other with regard to gender, race, and age. The design of an internal salary equity study is significantly different from that of an external salary equity study, and both inquiries can provide powerful information to administrators. Although issues of equity in compensation apply to all university employees, most of the work typically done focuses on faculty, because salary data for nonfaculty employees are difficult to obtain and compare. More information on conducting salary equity studies for nonfaculty employees can be found in Brozovsky and McLaughlin (1995), Curran and Bach (1996), Ferber and Westmiller (1976), Gordon and Morton (1976), Stanley and Adams (1994), and Toutkoushian (2000).

In this chapter we explore the ways in which institutional research offices can contribute to external and internal salary equity analyses of faculty. Although our chapter focuses on faculty, the same general principles and issues apply to conducting salary equity studies for all university employees. We discuss the purposes behind external and internal salary equity studies, show how an external salary equity study can be conducted, and explain how internal salary equity studies are performed. Finally, we discuss several important issues that an institutional research office should keep in mind as they conduct salary equity studies.

Purposes of Salary Equity Studies

Again, salary studies conducted by institutional research offices can be classified as either external or internal. External salary equity studies are performed routinely within institutional research offices and are often incorporated into an office's annual reporting in their factbook. Internal salary equity studies, on the other hand, typically are done on only an occasional basis. Both external and internal salary equity studies are very important to an institution, albeit for different reasons. The methodologies used to conduct each type of study also differ extensively, with external salary equity studies relying on descriptive statistics and internal salary equity studies using multivariate statistics.

External Salary Equity Studies. In an external salary equity study, the institutional researcher seeks to determine how equitable faculty salaries at the institution are relative to what faculty earn at other institutions. External salary equity provides useful information because the relative salary paid by an institution is a crucial factor in being able to recruit and hire new faculty, as well as preventing high-achieving and productive faculty members from choosing the alternative of moving to either another institution or another profession where salaries are higher.

The institutional researcher must first determine the level of aggregation for the analysis. The most obvious way to conduct an external salary equity study is to compare the average salary for all faculty members at the institution with the average salary for all faculty members at designated, or "peer" institutions. However, another approach would be to group faculty according to rank (that is, compare the average salaries for full professors at Institution A to those at other institutions). Grouping faculty by rank provides a more precise comparison of relative faculty salaries because the rank distribution of faculty across institutions can influence their overall average salaries. The analysis could also be done by disaggregating faculty by academic field or discipline. The advantage of disaggregating by field is the removal of field-specific influences in salary from the average salary of all faculty members at an institution. This is important because of the wide variation in faculty salaries by academic discipline, due in part to different salaries in nonacademic labor markets.

The second issue to be addressed in external salary equity studies is which specific institutions should be used as a comparison group. The normal practice is for an institution to use its official set of peer institutions as the comparison group, because these institutions are thought to be similar to the institution in question and the group will likely be acceptable to administrators and other stakeholders. However, in some situations an argument can be made for choosing a different set of institutions if one or more peer institutions do not generally compete with the institution for faculty. Identifying institutional competitors for faculty can be difficult due to a variety of complexities (for example, competitors for faculty in economics versus those in history).

A third issue to be considered is directly related to the data sources used to obtain salary information. There are two main sources that can be used to find average faculty salaries by institution. The National Center for Education Statistics (NCES) collects data from all colleges and universities (including two-year, four-year, and for-profit institutions) on average faculty salaries. This information is obtained through the annual Integrated Postsecondary Education Data System (IPEDS) Faculty Salary Survey. The NCES data are publicly accessible through their searchable website. In this way, researchers can easily retrieve data on average faculty salaries for a designated set of institutions and compare the averages to make inferences about salary equity. Because the IPEDS Faculty Salary Survey also asks for average salary by rank, similar analyses can be conducted for faculty at the assistant, associate, and full professor ranks. Another good source of aggregated faculty compensation data is the American Association of University Professors (AAUP). The AAUP surveys not only obtain data on average faculty salaries by rank and gender but also collect information on total fringe benefits and percentage salary increases for "continuing faculty"—faculty employed in the prior year. The raw data for all institutions is reported in the AAUP's March/April edition of *Academe*.

Finally, if the researcher is interested in doing department-level comparisons of salary equity (an analysis across institutions by field), one source of information is in the annual survey conducted by the Office of Institutional Research at Oklahoma State University. This report shows the average, high, and low salary by rank and six-digit Classification of Instructional Program (CIP) code for institutions that participate in the survey. Institutional researchers can use this report to compare the average salaries by discipline at their college or university to the averages and ranges shown in the report. However, the number of participating institutions who report salary data for specific CIP codes is limited, and one must purchase the report from Oklahoma State University. The College and University Professional Association (CUPA) also collects data on faculty salaries by field through their annual faculty survey. Participating institutions can obtain average salaries by field as defined by CIP codes for other participating institutions. Similar to the limitations of the Oklahoma State University faculty compensation survey, the CUPA data includes only participating institutions and reports statistics only in aggregate form for the chosen comparator group, and the results cannot be obtained when there are fewer than five institutions in a specific category.

Most studies of external salary equity rely on descriptive statistics. Typically, an institutional researcher creates a table showing how the average salary for faculty at his or her institution compares to the averages for their peer institutions. Although the median is probably a better measure of central tendency for this purpose, the mean is often presented as well because it is readily available within the IPEDS and AAUP surveys. Table 32.1 provides an example of how the average salary for faculty at the University of Georgia compared to the median and mean salaries at their designated peer institutions in 2006. The set of peers shown in the table was selected by the University of Georgia. Note that in 2006, the University of Georgia ranked twelfth out of 17 institutions in terms of their overall average salary. Their average faculty salary across all ranks ($80,086) was $2,399 below the median for their designated peer group ($82,485) and almost $12,000 below the top institutions within their peer group. Regardless of the average salary measure used, University of Georgia average faculty salaries are below the average for their official peer institutions.

Similarly, it is possible to do the same type of comparison separately by rank. Table 32.2 provides an example of this for the same set of institutions shown in Table 32.1. These data show that the University of Georgia is far less competitive with its peers in compensation for the highest-ranked faculty members (full professor) than for faculty at the assistant professor level. Campus administrators could use this information to reexamine their salary structure for faculty if their institutional priorities become the competitive attraction and retention of more senior scholars. This information would be lost if the

TABLE 32.1 COMPARISON OF AVERAGE FACULTY SALARIES FOR THE UNIVERSITY OF GEORGIA AND ITS PEERS, 2006

Institution	State	Average Faculty Salary
Georgia Institute of Technology–Main Campus	GA	$94,432
University of Maryland–College Park	MD	$94,181
University of California–Davis	CA	$91,003
University of Iowa	IA	$85,300
Arizona State University at the Tempe Campus	AZ	$84,198
Virginia Polytechnic Institute and State University	VA	$84,111
Michigan State University	MI	$83,941
Indiana University–Bloomington	IN	$83,356
University of Colorado at Boulder	CO	$81,614
Texas A&M University	TX	$81,177
North Carolina State University at Raleigh	NC	$80,649
University of Georgia (UGA)	**GA**	**$80,086**
University of Kansas Main Campus	KS	$79,912
University of Nebraska at Lincoln	NE	$76,792
Iowa State University	IA	$73,977
University of Missouri–Columbia	MO	$68,800
University of Oregon	OR	$66,025
Median Salary for UGA Peers		**$82,485**
Comparison of UGA to Median		**–$2,399**
Mean Salary for UGA Peers		**$81,842**
Comparison of UGA to Mean		**–$1,756**

TABLE 32.2 COMPARISON OF AVERAGE FACULTY SALARIES BY RANK FOR THE UNIVERSITY OF GEORGIA AND ITS PEERS, 2006

Institution	Full Professors	Associate Professors	Assistant Professors
Georgia Institute of Technology–Main Campus	$123,913	$85,914	$72,481
University of Maryland–College Park	$121,106	$84,234	$77,395
Arizona State University at the Tempe Campus	$113,701	$76,385	$67,820
University of California–Davis	$111,216	$74,976	$68,404
Virginia Polytechnic Institute and State Univ.	$110,788	$79,257	$65,754
Michigan State University	$110,233	$79,158	$61,834
University of Iowa	$109,838	$75,355	$65,799
Indiana University–Bloomington	$109,048	$75,055	$66,006
Texas A&M University	$108,972	$76,330	$67,395
University of Colorado at Boulder	$106,724	$77,995	$67,504
North Carolina State University at Raleigh	$103,886	$77,433	$66,264
University of Kansas Main Campus	$103,663	$71,701	$62,626
University of Missouri–Columbia	$100,589	$68,521	$56,596
University of Georgia (UGA)	**$99,879**	**$71,027**	**$64,966**
Iowa State University	$99,661	$73,385	$64,528
University of Nebraska at Lincoln	$98,547	$69,880	$61,008
University of Oregon	$88,476	$62,110	$59,825
Median Salary for UGA Peers	**$109,010**	**$75,843**	**$65,903**
Comparison of UGA to Median	**–$9,133**	**–$4,816**	**–$937**

institutional research office simply reported salary comparisons for all ranks combined for the institution and their peers.

It may also be useful for the institutional researcher to provide information to administrators on the change over time in the relative position of faculty salaries at their college or university. To do this, one would simply repeat the average salary comparison for an earlier point in time. Care must be taken, however, to ensure that the same set of peers is used in both time periods. Table 32.3 illustrates how the salary positions for fifteen four-year public institutions in the state of Georgia have changed relative to their officially designated peer groups from 2001 to 2006. The first comparison column shows how the average faculty salary at the University of Georgia compares to the median of the average salaries for their peers in 2001, and the analysis is repeated in the middle comparative column for the year 2006. The final column highlights how the relative positions have changed over this five-year interval. It can be seen from this table that by 2006 all but one institution in the study was below the median for their peer group, and that all but two institutions lost ground relative to their peers. Because all of the institutions in this table are four-year public colleges and universities, they rely heavily on the state for financial support to supplement faculty compensation. Therefore, the results might suggest to administrators that the reduction in competitiveness of these institutions over this time period is related to state funding.

Finally, the institutional researcher can use the data on average salary comparisons to estimate the magnitude of salary advantage or deficiency relative

TABLE 32.3   CHANGE IN RELATIVE SALARY POSITIONS FOR PUBLIC INSTITUTIONS IN THE UNIVERSITY SYSTEM OF GEORGIA WITH DESIGNATED PEERS, 2001–2006

Institution	Percent Above Median: 2001	Percent Above Median: 2006	Change: 2001 to 2006
Abraham Baldwin Agricultural College	3.3%	−12.2%	−15.5%
Augusta State University	−5.4%	−3.4%	2.0%
Bainbridge College	11.9%	−2.5%	−14.4%
Columbus State University	1.5%	−8.1%	−9.6%
Dalton State College	0.5%	−7.3%	−7.8%
Georgia College and State University	−2.5%	−8.1%	−5.6%
Georgia Institute of Technology	15.5%	0.1%	−15.4%
Georgia Perimeter College	−4.9%	−3.8%	1.1%
Georgia Southern University	−6.0%	−6.5%	−0.6%
Kennesaw State University	−11.8%	−18.4%	−6.7%
Medical College of Georgia	−3.6%	−5.4%	−1.8%
Middle Georgia College	5.7%	−5.4%	−11.0%
North Georgia College & State U	−3.7%	−7.7%	−4.0%
University of Georgia	−1.2%	−2.9%	−1.7%
Valdosta State University	0.6%	−7.5%	−8.1%

Notes: The table includes only four-year public institutions in Georgia that submitted designated peer institutions to the National Center for Education Statistics. Average salary deficiencies are defined as the percentage difference between the mean salary for each institution and the median of the average salaries for their designated peer institutions.

to a specific goal. For example, one could calculate the difference in dollars or percentages between an institution's average faculty salary and, say, the median average salary for their peer group. Other targets, such as the 75th percentile, could also be used for this purpose. This will help administrators determine how much it might cost to increase faculty salaries and reach certain goals. In Table 32.4, we show how an institutional researcher could use the salary deficiencies for the fifteen Georgia institutions in Table 32.3 to estimate the funding increase that would be needed to bring faculty salaries up to the medians for their peer groups. The necessary salary increases shown in the fourth

TABLE 32.4 COST OF RAISING AVERAGE FACULTY SALARIES FOR SELECTED PUBLIC INSTITUTIONS IN GEORGIA TO THE MEDIAN FOR PEERS, 2006

Institution	Average Salary	Median Salary for Peers	Amount Above/ Below Median	Salary Increase	Benefit Increase	Total
Abraham Baldwin Agricultural College	$41,896	$47,717	($5,821)	$547,174	$180,567	$727,741
Augusta State University	$56,301	$58,292	($1,991)	$437,910	$144,510	$582,420
Bainbridge College	$42,349	$43,455	($1,106)	$80,738	$26,644	$107,382
Columbus State University	$52,825	$57,483	($4,658)	$1,141,088	$376,559	$1,517,646
Georgia College and State University	$54,723	$59,556	($4,833)	$1,333,770	$440,144	$1,773,914
Georgia Institute of Technology	$94,432	$94,357	$76	$0	$0	$0
Georgia Perimeter College	$46,139	$47,946	($1,807)	$833,027	$274,899	$1,107,926
Georgia Southern University	$58,132	$62,202	($4,070)	$2,739,110	$903,906	$3,643,016
Kennesaw State University	$57,183	$70,093	($12,910)	$7,655,630	$2,526,358	$10,181,988
Medical College of Georgia	$68,821	$72,718	($3,897)	$705,267	$232,738	$938,004
Middle Georgia College	$42,596	$45,009	($2,413)	$193,000	$63,690	$256,690
North Georgia College & State Univ.	$51,973	$56,301	($4,328)	$792,024	$261,368	$1,053,392
University of Georgia	$80,086	$82,485	($2,399)	$4,162,265	$1,373,547	$5,535,812
Valdosta State University	$53,852	$58,225	($4,373)	$1,915,374	$632,073	$2,547,447

Notes: Median salary for peers is defined as the 50th percentile of the average salaries across all ranks for faculty at peer institutions. The sets of peers used for each institution were supplied by the institutions to the National Center for Education Statistics. Projected salary increases were obtained by multiplying the amount below the median by the number of full-time faculty at each institution. Projected benefit increases were estimated as 33 percent of salary.

column of figures are obtained by multiplying the average salary deficiencies in the third column by the number of full-time faculty at the institution. Similarly, the benefit increase is estimated as one-third of the salary increase (assuming that benefits are about one-third the size of the salary pool). This type of information can be invaluable for faculty, administrators, and state legislators in crafting policies to help make their institutions more competitive.

Internal Salary Equity Studies. Often an institutional research office is asked to perform an internal salary equity study in response to a complaint filed by one or more faculty members on the basis of unfair treatment. The most frequent cause of concern regarding salary equity in academia is the possible existence of pay disparity between comparable male and female faculty; however, similar questions are raised about possible pay disparities by race or ethnicity and age. If not addressed by an institution, such complaints may lead to litigation and result in significant financial cost to the institution. Beyond legal concerns associated with salary inequity, this topic is important because institutions are conscious of the need to treat all employees in a fair and equitable manner if they hope to attract and retain them.

The natural starting point for an internal salary equity study is to compare the average salaries for designated groups of faculty. The difference in average salaries between two groups such as male (m) and female (f) faculty is referred to as the *total wage gap*:

$$(1) \quad \text{Total Wage Gap} = \bar{Y}_m - \bar{Y}_f$$

where $\bar{Y}_m$ = average salary for male faculty and $\bar{Y}_f$ = average salary for female faculty. As noted earlier, average salaries for male and female faculty can be found in the IPEDS Faculty Salary Survey and the AAUP's annual survey. Table 32.5 shows how the average faculty salaries compare for males and females at different ranks and types of institutions. It can be seen that, on average, male faculty earn about 24 percent more than female faculty, and the total wage gaps are larger at more research-oriented institutions (28 percent at doctoral institutions versus 11 percent at baccalaureate institutions) and at higher ranks (13 percent for full professors versus 7 percent for assistant professors).

It is important to note, however, that average salary comparisons have limited value when assessing actual internal equity. Faculty salaries can be affected by a set of personal- and work-related factors (denoted X) such as professional experience, academic field of study, level of education, and productivity, in addition to gender and race. Average salaries for males and females may therefore differ for legitimate reasons, and if these reasons are correlated with the factor of interest, such as gender, then some portion of the average salary difference between the two groups might reflect these reasons and not gender bias. As a result, the total wage gap shown in equation (1) could be due to differences in nondiscriminatory characteristics ("explained wage gap"), and the remaining difference is referred to as the unexplained wage gap:

TABLE 32.5   SELECTED COMPARISONS OF AVERAGE FACULTY SALARIES BY GENDER, 2008–2009

Category	Male	Female	Difference in Dollars	Difference as % of Female Salary
All Institutions, All Ranks	$86,170	$69,622	$16,548	24%
Doctoral Institutions, All Ranks	$97,889	$76,539	$21,350	28%
Master's Institutions, All Ranks	$73,365	$64,547	$8,818	14%
Baccalaureate Institutions, All Ranks	$70,488	$63,352	$7,136	11%
All Institutions, Full Professors	$112,235	$98,942	$13,293	13%
All Institutions, Associate Professors	$78,259	$73,088	$5,171	7%
All Institutions, Assistant Professors	$65,997	$61,533	$4,464	7%

Source: American Association of University Professors, *Academe*, March/April 2009, Table 31.5.

(2)   Total Wage Gap = Explained Wage Gap + Unexplained Wage Gap

The most common starting place for measuring the explained and unexplained wage gaps is to specify an equation expressing a faculty member's salary (Y) as a function of a set of factors X as in:

$$(3) \quad Y_i = \alpha + X_i\beta + u_i$$

where α = intercept of the regression line, β = set of slope coefficients for the regression line, and u = random error term. It is standard practice to use the natural logarithm of salary as the dependent variable in equation (3) because of the compounding nature of salaries over time. For example, if salaries increase at relatively constant percentage increments, then using the log of salary as the dependent variable will lead to a better fit of the regression model. For ease of explanation in this chapter, we will use only actual salary as the dependent variable. However, the methods and issues that we discuss here can all be applied in situations in which the natural log of salary represents the dependent variable. The coefficients β show the impact of each factor in X on faculty salary, holding constant the effects of all of the other variables in the model. These coefficients are typically estimated by applying multiple regression analysis to individual-level data on faculty. The difference between a faculty member's actual and predicted salary gives a measure of the extent to which someone is paid more or less than would be predicted.

Many studies have shown that faculty salaries are affected by factors such as their years of academic experience, educational attainment, and research productivity (Barbezat, 2002; Ehrenberg, 2004; Perna, 2001; Ransom & Megdal, 1993). It also tends to be the case that these variables are correlated with gender because, on average, male faculty members are older than female faculty members. Similarly, there tends to be a higher proportion of male faculty members in higher paying fields such as engineering, finance, and hard science disciplines, whereas female faculty are more often found in lower-paying fields in the humanities, education, and liberal arts (Nettles, Perna, Bradburn, & Zimbler, 2000).

There are two basic statistical approaches that institutional researchers can use to measure the unexplained wage gap between two groups of faculty: single- and multiple-equation methods. In each case, the goal is to obtain a more reliable measure of the unexplained wage gap between two groups of faculty after taking into account the effects of other explanatory variables on a faculty member's salary. To perform these studies, the researcher must first identify the variables that they want to include as controls in their model and then acquire data on the attributes of individual faculty members that are needed to generate these variables. There are numerous studies that institutional researchers can use to guide them in the choice of variables to use in an internal salary equity study, including Barbezat (2002), Ferber and Loeb (2002), McLaughlin and Howard (2003), and Moore (1993).

Once decisions are made about the variables to use in the salary model, the institutional researcher is in a position to acquire data on individual faculty. Typically, the data are found in an institution's human resource legacy system, which usually contains the following types of data on individual faculty members: date of hire, salary, date of birth, length of appointment (nine- or twelve-month), gender, race or ethnicity, highest degree, academic rank, department and college affiliation, dates of promotion and job changes at the institution, and whether the faculty member also holds an administrative position. These data can be used to construct variables such as years of seniority and others that should be included in the set X shown in equation (3).

Decisions about which faculty to include in the study also represent an essential part of the analysis. Because part-time and nontenure-eligible (for example, adjunct faculty) faculty are compensated in substantially different ways from tenure-eligible faculty, most internal salary equity studies restrict the dataset to full-time, tenure-eligible faculty. Similarly, it is common practice to omit other groups of faculty in clinical fields (such as medicine) from internal salary equity studies if it is known that they are paid in unusual ways relative to traditional academic faculty. When in doubt, however, it is advisable to obtain all human resources data on all faculty members at the institution because it is easier to omit retrieved data than it is to add data at a later stage of the analysis. Studies by Moore (1993), Knight (2003), Colbeck (2002), Haignere (2002), McLaughlin and Howard (2003), and Toutkoushian (2002) each provide insight into the "nuts and bolts" of conducting salary equity studies and using human resource data to build a model.

It also should be remembered that because human resource legacy systems are designed for reporting and payroll functions and not research purposes, they will rarely contain data on other relevant factors such as research productivity, teaching evaluations, professional awards, and work experience prior to being hired by their current institution. Therefore the institutional researcher must decide either to collect additional data on prior experience or productivity or to construct a model with the available human resource data.

Single-Equation Method. The simplest way to measure the unexplained wage gap is to add a dummy (dichotomous) variable for gender to the salary model:

$$(4) \quad Y_i = \alpha + X_i \beta + G \gamma + u_i$$

where all variables are defined as before, G is a dummy variable equal to 1 for a female faculty member and 0 for a male faculty member (or vice versa), and $\gamma =$ the estimated pay difference between male and female salaries, controlling for the variables in X. The parameter γ can be thought of as the unexplained wage gap in equation (2). This method is appealing to researchers for several reasons. First, it is relatively simple to implement and can be done in most any statistical software package. Second, the results of the model allow the researcher to directly test whether the pay difference between male and female faculty is statistically significant. This is done by dividing the estimated coefficient by its standard error and comparing the resulting t-ratio to the critical t-ratio. Finally, the results from the model are easy to interpret because by construction every female faculty is under- or overpaid by the same amount, represented by the coefficient γ.

For these reasons, the vast majority of internal salary equity studies rely on the single-equation method (for more discussion, see Toutkoushian & Hoffman, 2002). Large-scale studies usually rely on data from various iterations of the National Study of Postsecondary Faculty (NSOPF), conducted by the National Center for Education Statistics. Ransom and Megdal (1993) along with Barbezat (2002) have compiled summaries of the findings from selected internal equity studies using institutional- and national-level data. They have shown that even after controlling for a range of relevant personal and work characteristics, in most cases female faculty earn significantly less compensation than comparable male faculty. Based on the studies reviewed, most institution-specific studies included variables for a faculty member's years of experience, highest degree earned, and academic department or field. It is generally less common to control for a faculty member's rank and/or research productivity.

Table 32.6 provides an illustration of how the single-equation method could be implemented at an institution. In this example, there are 432 faculty members at an institution. The analyst specifies three models to explain faculty salaries. In the first model, the only independent variable used is a dummy variable for gender. In Model 2, the analyst also controls for academic rank by adding two dummy variables for the academic ranks of full and associate professor. Finally, in the third model the analyst controls for gender, rank, and the number of times each faculty member was cited in the year in question (traditionally as a measure of research productivity). The last three rows in the table contain the total wage gap, explained wage gap, and the unexplained wage gap for each model. In each case, the unexplained wage gap is equal to the coefficient on the variable of gender. The total wage gap is equal to the average salary difference between male and female faculty ($10,992.78). Finally, the explained wage gap is calculated as the total wage gap minus the unexplained wage gap.

TABLE 32.6   ILLUSTRATION OF SINGLE-EQUATION METHOD FOR MEASURING THE UNEXPLAINED WAGE GAP

Variable	Single-Equation Regression Model		
Regression Results	Model 1: Gender	Model 2: Gender and Rank	Model 3: Gender, Rank, and Citations
Gender (1=male)	10992.78** (1756.31)	3354.54* (1545.20)	2833.15* (1493.83)
Full Professor	—	22832.22** (1783.23)	21839.05** (1729.48)
Associate Professor	—	7991.61** (1815.38)	7876.64** (1751.87)
Citations	—	—	181.10** (31.69)
Intercept	45841.14** (1566.10)	37651.18** (1681.56)	36945.67** (1627.31)
R-Squared	0.08	0.38	0.43
Total Wage Gap Decomposition			
Total Wage Gap	$10,992.78	$10,992.78	$10,992.78
Explained Wage Gap	$0.00 [0%]	$7,638.24 [69%]	$8,159.63 [74%]
Unexplained Wage Gap	$10,992.78 [100%]	$3,354.54 [31%]	$2,833.15 [26%]

Notes: Dependent variable for all models is the annual base salary for faculty members. Standard errors are shown in parentheses below each coefficient. Values in square brackets denote the shares of the total wage gap that are either explained or unexplained by the nongender variables in the regression model.

** $p < .01$, * $p < .05$ (two-tailed tests). Full professor = 1 if rank is full professor, 0 otherwise. Associate professor = 1 if rank is associate professor, 0 otherwise. Assistant professor is used as the reference category for rank. Citations = number of times a faculty member's research was cited in the year of the study.

In Model 1, there is a large and statistically significant pay difference between male and female faculty. The unexplained wage gap is equal to the total wage gap in this model because no other control variables are included in the model. The unexplained wage gap falls by 69 percent, however, after controlling for academic rank (Model 2). Similarly, controlling for rank and number of citations reduces the unexplained wage gap by 74 percent. In each case, however, the unexplained wage gap is still statistically significant at the 5 percent level. The analyst would need to explore the sensitivity of this finding to adding control variables for factors such as field, experience, and educational attainment before drawing final conclusions about the relative pay status of males and females at the institution. Decisions would also have to be made about the appropriateness of controlling for faculty rank, because inequitable treatment in promotion would lead to lower estimates of pay disparity when rank is included in the salary model (covered shortly).

Despite the popularity of the single-equation method, it has limitations. The single-equation method restricts all variables to having the same effect on salaries for both male and female faculty. Accordingly, the results would not allow the institutional researcher to determine whether unexplained pay differences between the two groups are due to, say, male faculty receiving larger salary increases than female faculty each year, or having a higher salary premium in certain departments. Second, the single-equation method restricts each female faculty member to having the same level of pay disparity, when it is quite possible that some female faculty members are more severely underpaid than others. Multiple-equation methods such as those developed by Oaxaca (1973), Blinder (1973), Reimers (1983), Cotton (1988), Neumark (1988), and others have since been introduced to address these issues in internal salary equity studies.

Multiple-Equation Methods. A more complicated, but potentially more valuable, way of conducting an internal salary equity study is to use a multiple-equation method. Multiple-equation methods decompose the total wage gap shown in equation (2) into the explained and unexplained portions as follows:

$$(5) \quad \bar{Y}_m - \bar{Y}_f = (\bar{X}_m - \bar{X}_f)\,b_n + [(b_m - b_n)\,\bar{X}_m + (b_n - b_f)\bar{X}_f]$$

where b_n = "no-discrimination" wage structure that would exist in the absence of discrimination. Accordingly, the quantity $(\bar{X}_m - \bar{X}_f)\,b_n$ represents the explained wage gap, which is the average difference in attributes between male and female faculty multiplied by the no-discrimination wage structure. The remaining quantity $(b_m - b_n)\,\bar{X}_m + (b_n - b_f)\,\bar{X}_f$ is the unexplained wage gap. An important advantage of multiple-equation methods is that the estimated level of pay disparity can now vary across individuals. The reader is referred to Toutkoushian and Hoffman (2002) for more details on these issues.

One of the main drawbacks to the multiple-equation methods is that they are more difficult to use. Not only does the researcher need to estimate separate salary models for males and females, but the results require manipulation to obtain the unexplained wage gap. The researcher also has to make a decision about what to use for the no-discrimination wage structure. It has been shown in other studies (Neumark, 1988; Oaxaca & Ransom, 1994; Perna, 2003) that the no-discrimination wage structure can affect the unexplained wage gap between male and female faculty, as well as the specific amounts by which individual faculty members are underpaid. Although there is no single "best" choice for the no-discrimination wage structure, it is most common for researchers to use the coefficients from either the male equation or the female equation as the no-discrimination wage structure.

Table 32.7 shows a hypothetical example of how the multiple-equation methods might be applied to an internal salary equity study. In this example, the average salary for male faculty ($86,000) exceeds the average salary for female faculty ($70,000) by $16,000. This quantity is the total wage gap.

TABLE 32.7 ILLUSTRATION OF TOTAL WAGE GAP DECOMPOSITION USING MULTIPLE-EQUATION METHODS

Category	Male Faculty	Female Faculty	Difference
Average Salary ($\overline{Y}$)	$86,000	$70,000	$16,000
Average Years of Experience ($\overline{X}$)	20	16	4
Intercept (α)	$20,000	$20,000	$0
Slope (β)	$3,300	$3,125	$175

Explained Gap Using Male Slope = (20–16)*($3,300) = $13,200
Unexplained Gap Using Male Slope = ($3,300–$3,125)*16 = $2,800
Percentage Salary Adjustment for Female Faculty = ($2,800/$70,000) = +4.0%
Explained Gap Using Female Slope = (20–16)*($3,125) = $12,500
Unexplained Gap Using Female Slope = ($3,300–$3,125)*20 = $3,500
Percentage Salary Adjustment for Female Faculty = ($3,500/$70,000) = +5.0%

Notes: The illustration assumes that the estimated salary equation for male faculty is $\hat{Y}$ = 20,000 + 3,300*X and that the estimated salary equation for female faculty is $\hat{Y}$ = 20,000 + 3,125*X.

For simplicity, we assume that the salary model includes only one variable (X = years of experience) and that the beta coefficients for male and female faculty for this variable are $3,300 and $3,125 respectively. We also assume, based on known demographics, that male faculty members average twenty years of experience and female faculty members average sixteen years of experience.

The table shows how the total wage gap between male and female faculty can be decomposed, and how the choice of no-discrimination wage structure can affect the final results. First, we assume that the male beta coefficient is the "no-discrimination" coefficient. This means that in the absence of discrimination, all faculty members should receive $3,300 for each year of experience. Accordingly, the explained wage gap would be $(\overline{X}_m - \overline{X}_f)\beta_n$ = $13,200 and the unexplained wage gap is $(\beta_m - \beta_f)*\overline{X}_f$ = $2,800. The interpretation is that on average, female faculty members are underpaid by $2,800 (or 4 percent of their average salary). In contrast, if we assumed that the female beta coefficient was used as the no-discrimination coefficient, the explained wage gap would be smaller ($12,500) and the unexplained wage gap would be larger ($3,500 or 5 percent of average female salary). In both instances, however, the total wage gap ($16,000) is the sum of the explained and unexplained wage gaps.

Current Issues in Salary Studies

The information just presented forms the basis for most inquiries that an institutional research office would need to do to help assess external and internal salary equity for faculty. As in most any area of inquiry, however, there are current issues that are also important to understand. We briefly discuss several of these issues in this section.

Controlling for Rank in Internal Salary Equity Studies

From the equations just shown, it can be seen that the choice of control variables X to include in the salary model can be critical. There is a substantial amount of debate in the field regarding whether the salary model should include control variables for a faculty member's current academic rank (Becker & Toutkoushian, 2003; Strathman, 2000). The proponents of using faculty rank within an analysis argue that (1) salary is very often explicitly tied to rank (as faculty receive salary increases when promoted), and (2) rank is a universal measure of a faculty member's productivity, which is theoretically related to salary. Given that there is a larger proportion of high-ranking male faculty members compared to female faculty members (Becker & Toutkoushian, 2003), controlling for rank usually leads to a reduction in the unexplained pay gap between genders. However, if the uneven rank distribution of faculty by gender is due in part to discrimination, then adding a control variable for rank to the salary model will unfairly penalize women and make them appear to be less underpaid than is true.

We recommend that analysts take one of two basic approaches to this problem. The first is to conduct a statistical test to examine any evidence of gender bias in rank. This can be done by estimating a logistic regression model in which a dichotomous variable for rank is used as the dependent variable. It is possible to determine from this model whether female faculty members with characteristics similar to those of male faculty members are more or less likely to hold higher ranks. If the evidence concludes a gender bias in rank, then an argument could be made for omitting the controls for rank in the salary model and vice versa. The second approach to the problem is to estimate two salary models—one with rank and the other without rank—and report the results in both forms. This allows the researcher to determine how sensitive the findings are to academic rank.

Faculty Productivity

Most observers of academe would agree that faculty productivity in research, teaching, and service is, or should be, tied to higher compensation. Despite this acceptance, institution-specific studies of internal salary equity often do not include direct measures of faculty productivity in their statistical models, because legacy systems in human resources are unable to capture and/or contain information on productivity measures. This omission also presents problems for analysts, because if faculty productivity is correlated with gender, then the estimated effect of gender on salary may be biased.

There are several options that could be considered by institutional researchers who want to add productivity information to their analyses. If curriculum vitae are available for all faculty at the institution, one could manually count publications, teaching awards, and other factors that relate to productivity and use this information in the internal salary equity study. The challenges in doing so are: (1) curriculum vitae on all faculty at an institution are rarely accessible; (2) there are no guarantees that the data are complete, accurate, or up-to-date; (3) decisions have to be made about what to count as measures of productivity and how to standardize across fields; and (4) a substantial amount of time and resources are likely needed to do this work.

The institution may have information in other places on other factors that are at least tangentially related to faculty productivity. For example, a college or university may compile a list of all professors who are members of the National Academy of Sciences or who have won university-wide teaching awards or secured external funding for research from large organizations such as the National Science Foundation. Although these are not perfect measures of faculty productivity, their use can help to reduce any potential bias in the unexplained wage gap due to omitted productivity variables. Bibliometric methods can also be used to obtain data on the publications or citations of individual faculty members. Many universities now provide access to the Web of Science, which allows individuals to conduct searches for publications by individuals and observe the number of citations per faculty publication. There is a rather sizable literature on the use of bibliometric methods in education research (see, for example, Budd, 1988; Budd & Magnuson, 2010; Toutkoushian, 1994b), and analysts need to be aware of the limitations of these measures when used. Nonetheless, this is a promising area of research for addressing the omitted variable bias in internal equity studies.

How Best to Remove Salary Inequities

Institutional research offices can be helpful to administrators by determining not only equity among faculty compensation, but also by providing recommendations on how to correct salary deficiencies if found. Studies have shown that there are a number of different ways to measure the precise amount by which individuals are underpaid (Becker & Goodman, 1991; Toutkoushian, 1994a; Becker & Toutkoushian, 1995; Gaylord & McLaughlin, 1991; Haignere, 2002; Oaxaca & Ransom, 2003; Snyder, Hyer, & McLaughlin, 1993). This is worthy of attention because the resulting cost to an institution of making salary adjustments can vary significantly depending on whether across-the-board or individualized salary adjustments are made.

Legal Considerations

Institutional researchers should also be aware that there are potentially serious legal considerations to take into account when deciding whether and how to conduct an internal salary equity study. In some instances, these studies are initiated in response to a legal claim by one or more faculty of inequitable treatment in pay. The methods used to conduct the study and the findings from the study would therefore be subject to significant scrutiny by parties involved in the lawsuit. Even studies that are performed by an IR office for internal purposes may invite lawsuits if they reveal significant pay differences between male and female faculty members. In both instances, the results of the study may be viewed as biased by certain individuals on campus because the IR office is part of the administrative structure at the institution. Recommendations to make individualized salary adjustments are likely to invite close scrutiny from faculty, particularly those who are set to receive lower increments than others. At the University of Minnesota and Northern Arizona University, for example, faculty members have brought forth legal action over the manner in which salary increments were awarded. Eckes and Toutkoushian (2006) compared the cost and legal implications of using alternative methods to remove salary inequities and showed that across-the-board adjustments based on the single-equation approach can offer financial and legal advantages to institutions. These factors have led a number of institutions to turn to external consultants to conduct their internal salary equity studies.

Salary Equity by Race/Ethnicity

Concerns regarding possible pay discrimination have been directed not only toward gender but also race or ethnicity. As noted by Barbezat (2002), relatively few internal salary equity studies have been conducted on race or ethnicity, because at many institutions there are not enough minority faculty members to reliably estimate the unexplained wage gap between them and other faculty. This problem is particularly relevant for multiple-equation methods. For this reason, most internal salary equity studies of pay differences by race rely on national data from the NSOPF surveys (Toutkoushian, 1998a). When an institution-specific study is performed, perhaps the best that can be done in many circumstances is to use a single-equation method and aggregate all minority faculty (for example, black, Hispanic) into a single category. It should be recognized, however, that the resulting dummy variable will still likely have little variation, and as a result, the standard error on the coefficient will be large and the calculated t-ratio will be small. This approach will also mask any individual group differences. Thus studies of salary equity by race/ethnicity are difficult to conduct. (See Chapter 20 for more discussion of the legal aspects of discrimination.)

Salary Compression

Institutional research offices are occasionally asked to investigate whether faculty salaries are either overly compressed or are becoming more compressed over time. Salary compression means that new faculty members are receiving salaries closer to, or exceeding, the salaries of more senior faculty. There is debate as to whether a narrowing of salary differences by experience level reflects unfair treatment of more senior faculty, changes in the salaries paid in external markets, or rising qualifications of new faculty (Snyder, McLaughlin, & Montgomery, 1992; Toutkoushian, 1998b). The most commonly used approach for examining salary compression is to compare the average salaries for faculty at different ranks (including newly hired faculty) and track the ratios over time (Blum, 1989; Dworkin, 1990; Heller, 1987; Snyder, McLaughlin, & Montgomery, 1992). Toutkoushian (1998b) developed a five-step procedure that uses multiple regression analysis to examine salary compression. This is accomplished by comparing the actual salaries for recently hired faculty with their predicted salaries generated by a salary model estimated over more senior faculty.

Salary Equity for Nonfaculty

Colleges and universities employ substantial numbers of individuals who are not faculty members. It is therefore natural to ask whether an institution provides equitable salaries to these individuals. The lack of publicly available data on salaries for many types of university employees makes it difficult to assess external salary equity in academia. It is possible, however, to conduct an internal salary equity study in a manner similar to that shown for faculty. For example, nonfaculty could be categorized based on job title and where they are employed by the institution. This is more challenging than for faculty because (1) there are numerous job titles for nonfaculty employees in most institutions, (2) the jobs performed by individuals at an institution can differ substantially within a given job category, and (3) there may be some job titles held by only a few individuals—or even just one. Perhaps the greatest challenge is that because nonfaculty employees are performing substantially different jobs, it is next to impossible to obtain a comparable measure of their productivity or other key measures to conduct the appropriate model to assess pay equity.

Conclusions

In this chapter, we provided the reader with an overview of internal and external studies for salary equity, including the sources of information that can be used and the methods employed to assess equity. One common theme among these studies is that the results can be very sensitive to the particular way the institutional researcher conceptualizes and articulates the method. External salary equity, for example, depends crucially on the set of institutions that are used for comparison. Although an institution's official peer group may be the most expedient to use for this purpose, institutional researchers need to also ask whether it serves as the right set to use for determining whether faculty are compensated fairly across institutions. Another issue to address is whether faculty salaries across institutions may vary due to geographical differences in the cost of living. In particular, institutions in California and the New England states have higher cost-of-living indexes and need to compensate faculty members more in order to compete in the local labor markets. The findings from internal salary equity studies are also very sensitive to the set of control variables used in the analysis, decisions about who to include in the dataset, and the method used to measure the unexplained wage gap.

There may also be times when it is preferable for an institution to find an outside group to conduct an external or internal salary equity study. When concerns about salary equity are raised by faculty at an institution, the results of an internally generated study may be received with skepticism regardless of the quality of the analysis or absence of bias. Given the possibility of large financial judgments against an institution, sometimes an institution must consider whether the study is best conducted by the institutional research office at the institution or by another entity. Finally, the social benefits associated with equitable compensation provide an additional justification for routine analyses of compensation among the various groups within higher education. Using the tools provides in this chapter, institutional researchers can conduct both within and between comparisons that will inform institutional policy and practices. The legal issues involved in salary equity are discussed in more detail in Chapter 20. Measures that may be useful in the various models are discussed in Chapter 10.

References

Barbezat, D. (2002). History of pay equity studies. In R. Toutkoushian (Ed.), *Conducting salary-equity studies: Alternative approaches to research* (pp. 9–39). New Directions for Institutional Research, no. 115. San Francisco: Jossey-Bass.

Becker, W., & Goodman, R. (1991). The semilogarithmic earnings equation and its use in assessing salary discrimination in academe. *Economics of Education Review, 10*, 323–332.

Becker, W., & Toutkoushian, R. (1995). The measurement and cost of removing unexplained gender differences in faculty salaries. *Economics of Education Review, 14*, 209–220.

Becker, W., & Toutkoushian, R. (2003). Measuring gender bias in the salaries of tenured faculty members. In R. Toutkoushian (Ed.), *Unresolved issues in conducting salary-equity studies* (pp. 5–20). New Directions for Institutional Research, no. 117. San Francisco: Jossey-Bass.

Blinder, A. (1973). Wage discrimination: Reduced form and structural estimates. *Journal of Human Resources, 8*, 436–455.

Blum, D. (1989). Colleges worry that newly hired professors earn higher salaries than faculty veterans. *Chronicle of Higher Education, 36*, A1, 21.

Brozovsky, P., & McLaughlin, G. (1995). Issues in studying administrative faculty salary equity. Paper presented at the annual meetings of the Association for Institutional Research, Boston, MA.

Budd, J. (1988). A bibliometric analysis of higher education literature. *Review of Higher Education, 28,* 180–203.

Budd, J., & Magnuson, L. (2010). Higher education literature revisited. Citation patterns examined. *Research in Higher Education, 51,* 294–314.

Colbeck, C. (Ed.). (2002). *Evaluating faculty performance.* New Directions for Institutional Research, no. 114. San Francisco: Jossey-Bass.

Cotton, J. (1988). On the decomposition of wage differentials. *Review of Economics and Statistics, 70,* 236–243.

Curran, F., & Bach, N. (1996). The University of Vermont: An equity study of full-time staff pay. Working paper, Office of Institutional Studies, University of Vermont.

Dworkin, A. (1990). The salary structure of sociology departments. *American Sociologist, 21,* 48–59.

Eckes, S., & Toutkoushian, R. (2006). Legal issues and statistical approaches to reverse pay discrimination in higher education. *Research in Higher Education, 47,* 957–984.

Ehrenberg, R. (2004). Prospects in the academic labor market for economists. *Journal of Economic Perspectives, 18,* 227–238.

Ferber, M., & Loeb, J. (2002). Issues in conducting an institutional salary-equity study. In R. Toutkoushian (Ed.), *Conducting salary-equity studies: Alternative approaches to research* (pp. 41–70). New Directions for Institutional Research, no. 115. San Francisco: Jossey-Bass.

Ferber, M., & Westmiller, A. (1976). Sex and race differences in nonacademic wages on a university campus. *Journal of Human Resources, 11,* 366–373.

Gaylord, C., & McLaughlin, G. (1991). Adjusting observations to make residuals of a subgroup sum to zero. VAS Chapter, American Statistical Association, Blacksburg, VA.

Gordon, N., & Morton, T. (1976). The staff salary structure of a large urban university. *Journal of Human Resources, 11,* 374–382.

Haignere, L. (2002). *Paychecks: A guide to conducting salary-equity studies for higher education.* Washington, DC: American Association of University Professors.

Heller, S. (1987). Faculty pay up 5.9 pct. to $35,470; best raise in 15 years, AAUP says. *Chronicle of Higher Education, 33,* 1, 16.

Knight, W. (Ed.). (2003). *Primer for institutional research.* Resources in Institutional Research, no. 14. Tallahassee, FL: Association for Institutional Research.

McLaughlin, G., & Howard, R. (2003). Faculty salary analyses. In W. Knight (Ed.), *The primer for institutional research* (pp. 48–78). Tallahassee, FL: Association for Institutional Research.

Moore, N. (1993). Faculty salary equity: Issues in regression model selection. *Research in Higher Education, 34,* 107–126.

Nettles, M., Perna, L., Bradburn, E., & Zimbler, L. (2000). *Salary, promotion, and tenure status of minority and women faculty in U.S. colleges and universities.* Washington, DC: National Center for Education Statistics.

Neumark, D. (1988). Employers' discriminatory behavior and the estimation of wage discrimination. *Journal of Human Resources, 23,* 279–297.

Oaxaca, R. (1973). Male-female wage differentials in urban labor markets. *International Economic Review, 14,* 693–709.

Oaxaca, R., & Ransom, M. (1994). On discrimination and the decomposition of wage differentials. *Journal of Econometrics, 61,* 5–21.

Oaxaca, R., & Ransom, M. (2003). Using econometric models for intrafirm equity salary adjustments. *Journal of Economic Inequality, 1,* 221–249.

Perna, L. (2001). Sex differences in faculty salaries: A cohort analysis. *Review of Higher Education, 24,* 283–307.

Perna, L. (2003). Studying faculty salary equity: A review of theoretical and methodological approaches. In J. C. Smart & A. Bayer (Eds.), *Higher education: Handbook of theory and research* (vol. 18, pp. 323–388). Dordrecht, Netherlands: Kluwer Academic Publishers.

Ransom, M., & Megdal, S. (1993). Sex differences in the academic labor market in the affirmative action era. *Economics of Education Review, 12,* 21–43.

Reimers, C. (1983). Labor market discrimination against Hispanic and black men. *Review of Economics and Statistics, 65,* 570–579.

Snyder, J., Hyer, P., & McLaughlin, G. (1993). Faculty salary equity: Issues and options. Paper presented at the 1993 AIR Forum, Chicago, IL.

Snyder, J., McLaughlin, G., & Montgomery, J. (1992). Diagnosing and dealing with salary compression. *Research in Higher Education, 33,* 113–124.

Stanley, E., & Adams, J. (1994). Analyzing administrative costs and structures. *Research in Higher Education, 35,* 125–140.

Strathman, J. (2000). Consistent estimation of faculty rank effects in academic salary models. *Research in Higher Education, 41,* 237–250.

Toutkoushian, R. (1994a). Issues in choosing a strategy for achieving salary equity. *Research in Higher Education, 35,* 415–428.

Toutkoushian, R. (1994b). Using citations to measure sex discrimination in faculty salaries. *Review of Higher Education, 18,* 61–82.

Toutkoushian, R. (1998a). Racial and marital status differences in faculty pay. *Journal of Higher Education, 69,* 513–541.

Toutkoushian, R. (1998b). Using regression analysis to determine if faculty salaries are overly compressed. *Research in Higher Education, 39,* 87–100.

Toutkoushian, R. (2000). Addressing gender equity in nonfaculty salaries. *Research in Higher Education, 41,* 417–442.

Toutkoushian, R. (2002). *Conducting salary equity studies.* New Directions for Institutional Research, No. 115. San Francisco: Jossey-Bass.

Toutkoushian, R. (2003). What can labor economics tell us about the earnings and employment prospects for faculty? In J. Smart (Ed.), *Higher education: Handbook of theory and research* (vol. XVIII, pp. 263–321). Dordrecht, Netherlands: Kluwer Academic Publishers.

Toutkoushian, R. (2006). Economic contributions to institutional research on faculty. In R. Toutkoushian & M. Paulsen (Eds.), *Applying economics to institutional research* (pp. 75–93). New Directions for Institutional Research, no. 132. San Francisco: Jossey-Bass.

Toutkoushian, R., & Hoffman, E. (2002). Alternatives for measuring the unexplained wage gap. In R. Toutkoushian (Ed.), *Conducting salary-equity studies: Alternative approaches to research* (pp. 71–89). New Directions for Institutional Research, no. 115. San Francisco: Jossey-Bass.

CHAPTER 33

EFFECTIVE REPORTING

Liz Sanders and Joe Filkins

The primary role of the institutional researcher is to provide information that supports institutional planning, policy formation, and decision making (Saupe, 1990). Now, take a stroll down the hall to your vice president's office and take a look at her desk. You will likely see stacks of reports containing valuable pieces of information that could contribute to discussions about policies and decisions on campus. Quite probably, some of your very own reports are in these stacks already. Are these reports being used to inform the decisions? If not, how can we ensure that we are successful in advancing our research through this already cluttered decision-support environment?

Weiss (1980) suggests that policy makers use research less to arrive at decisions than to orient themselves to problems. The information that is used has bubbled up, or percolated, into university discourse and become part of the stock of knowledge shared in informed discussion. In this way, information shapes decisions and the context in which decisions are made. For a researcher's work to be a part of this process, that work must first reach its intended readers and deliver a message perceived to be both relevant and important in a format that is understandable, inviting, accurate, and memorable. An effective report is one that has cut through the noise, connected with the reader, and successfully contributed to informed discussions. In this chapter, we discuss how to prepare an effective report with content, tables, and graphics that connect with the reader to become part of the stock of knowledge for informed discussion.

Preparing for Effective Reporting

Effective reporting is more than just knowing how to format and write a report. It is a process that can involve a number of people and steps. Before any data are collected, any SPSS analysis is executed, or any pie chart is generated, it is important to organize the research project by asking several questions.

Client and Audience

Let's say you walk into the office one Monday morning and the voicemail light on your phone is blinking. Upon listening to the message, you discover that the president of the university is gathering information for an annual planning retreat to better understand student engagement and has asked you to prepare a report. Knowing both the client who requested the report and the intended audiences helps you appropriately frame the research questions and determine how to most effectively answer them.

Who Might Read the Report: Different Audiences?

Your client is the one with the greatest vested interest in the outcomes of the study and is also the most ardent user of the results. However, it is very unlikely that the retreat members are the only people at your institution who will be interested in the results of your study. Bers and Seybert (1999) identify other individuals who might comprise the audience for your report, including the university administration (president, provost, deans, vice-presidents), trustees or regents, faculty and staff, experts in the field of study, and prospective students and their parents.

More often than not, the audience for any particular report will be some combination of these individuals, as well as others inside and outside of your institution who might happen upon your report. This fact makes the preparation of any report a difficult undertaking, as one must attend to the level of complexity in the report, finding a balance between practice versus theory, tables and numbers versus charts and graphs, quantitative versus qualitative analyses, and so on. In addition, once your report has been written, it becomes part of the institutional knowledge upon which administrators may draw in the future. As a result, your report may have unintended as well as intended uses.

The Research Checklist

As we stated earlier, before the researcher begins conducting her analyses and generating her reports, it is important to organize the research project by asking several questions. We call this list of questions the *research checklist:*

- *Who is the client of the research?* The client is the individual (or office, committee, task force, and so on) who commissioned the research and resulting report.
- *What information is the client requesting?* Although the client's question will seem clear enough on the surface to provide the researcher with the necessary direction, it is important, however, to clarify any issues about the analysis prior to beginning.

- *Why is the client asking for this report, and what is its intended use?* It is important to know why the client is requesting this information, in order to (1) make sure the analysis is as complete as possible and (1) produce a report with the greatest likelihood of being used in discussion and decision making.
- *What information does the client really need?* One of the greatest challenges is to prepare a report that answers the client's questions, because often the client does not know what she really wants (until she sees the report she has requested and then realizes it is not responding to her questions).
- *With whom will the client share the report?* A good rule of thumb for the institutional researcher is to prepare any piece of information as if it will be shared with the president of the institution. This approach minimizes the confusion that quick, informal analyses can cause with incomplete data definitions, unclear labels, and missing data sources.
- *When is the research needed?* It is important to clarify at the outset when the client needs the report and when the client plans to share the findings.
- *How is the report best prepared?* This question relates primarily to the style in which the report is produced, and the answer is influenced by the institutional culture, the intended audiences, and the style of the IR office.
- *How is the report best delivered?* As a rule of thumb, a multipronged proactive approach may be most effective: push information out to the client via an executive summary (which can be oral or written) and pull readers in to your website to view new materials via direct links to reports.

Armed with an understanding of the institutional culture and the answers to the previous questions, the researcher will have a sufficient amount of information to begin the analysis.

What Other Information Gets Conveyed in the Reporting Process?

Have you ever been to a research presentation where the presenter is obviously unprepared? Have you ever read a report that was riddled with spelling errors? What was your reaction? Much more is communicated to the audience than just the data during the reporting process. You are representing the people with whom you work—and even the university, if the research is being presented to an outside group.

Bers and Seybert (1999) suggest asking the following questions:

- What does the audience *need* to know?
- What does the audience *want* to know?
- What do I want to tell them?
- What decisions might the audience make in light of this report?
- With whom might the audience share this report?
- Who else might be interested in this subject?

Different Types of Quantitative Information

The challenge just outlined is to better understand both the context for the research (using the research checklist) as well as the audience. Now we examine the types of information that IR offices prepare, on a continuum from data to information to insights, so as to better understand who the primary users are of each type of content and when each type is most appropriate.

Access to Data

At the left end of the reporting continuum are the raw data. Some institutional researchers provide access to raw data that can be used by others on campus, depending on the culture of the institution and the research skills of others. We share data to manage internal resources and to build a network of informed and capable users outside the IR office who can share in providing university decision support. Typically, information users who are statistically or technically savvy benefit from access to data and the tools for data analysis and manipulation. These tools are valuable not just to those outside the IR office; they also enable the researcher to answer questions more quickly and to be more efficient and effective.

We would like to point out two considerations here. First, although data sets can be shared either directly as raw data or via a variety of tools, these data must be shared only with appropriate security measures in place. Inadequate security of the data can result in the inappropriate use or misreporting of statistics, as the IR professional loses control over how the data are handled. Second, sharing data decentralizes data access and may lead to misunderstandings about what the data actually reflect. Although we IR professionals may provide detailed descriptions and footnotes on the specifics of the data, these can easily be overlooked in a quick ad hoc analysis by a novice user. Each IR office must evaluate the available financial and human resources and campus culture in determining which solutions are best.

Access to Information

Further along the continuum is access to information—what we consider one step beyond access to raw data. A set of tables that is part of an enrollment report is a good example of information. We share such tables to provide a breadth of information that is already distilled into meaningful pieces for a wide variety of end users. Information is most useful for engaged and interested end users. Although they do not have to be researchers to find the trends, they do still need to uncover the meaningful pieces of information, and this is the double-edged value of numerical reports.

Access to Insights

At the right end of the continuum is the category of insights. We share insights by telling the story of the data and highlighting the key findings. The reader does not need to manipulate a data set or scan several pages of survey tables to learn the most important findings—these findings are served up in the executive summary and appropriate sections of the report. Sharing insights allows institutional researchers to demonstrate their analytical value in synthesizing large amounts of data into relevant, useful insights about trends and relationships.

No IR office can meet all the users' needs all the time, but a balanced strategy of (1) providing access to data for power users in an on-demand tool platform, (2) supplying information tables for broad consumption to all program directors, and (3) sharing insights on important strategic efforts with the executive leadership may enable the IR office to manage the information needs of its community of users more effectively and efficiently.

Reports

Although as researchers we may be more enthusiastic about immersing ourselves in data and analysis, the additional work of putting our thoughts in writing, describing what we did to an audience that is not so quantitatively inclined, and building enthusiasm for our findings is probably the most important task we perform in our jobs.

Preparing a report need not be an onerous task. Perhaps it is perceived as such because people believe that, when writing, it must be perfect the first time; it must be inspired and spontaneous; it must proceed quickly. Writing a report or preparing a presentation is not difficult, though it does not proceed quickly (that is, it is an iterative process). We should start the process by outlining the report, then prepare iterative drafts for review by colleagues, engage a copyeditor for editing, and always use a proofreader for a final review.

What Goes Into a Report?

Ultimately, the content of the report is dependent upon its purpose. Bers and Seybert (1999) outline five specific purposes for reports:

- *Provide historical context.* For example, a report of retention rates for the past 10 years provides not only the current performance, but a historical record of the past rates.
- *Support current planning and decision-making discussions.* An analysis of the impact of early academic probation on likelihood of graduation may support decisions about first-year support programs.

- *Build good will or put the institution in a favorable light.* A report on the performance of students from particular feeder high schools may be used to demonstrate the university's commitment to its partner high schools and build good will.
- *Communicate information.* For example, the primary purpose of a fall enrollment report may be to communicate information about students enrolled and revenue generated.
- *Meet external reporting requirements.* Reports may be generated throughout the year to document such information as university enrollment, degrees awarded, and online coursework in order to comply with federal and state reporting guidelines, or partnership agreements.

Regardless of the purpose, however, there are several strategies you can follow when drafting reports that will make them ultimately more effective.

- Make sure your information is sufficient, relevant, timely, and consistent. Taken all together, these four parameters help to ensure that your information is usable. When preparing your report, answer the appropriate research questions and provide information that relates to the questions or issues at hand. Report information in the same way, with the same numbers. Deliver your report in sufficient time for the data to be useful when decisions are involved.
- Know your audience. Don't assume that your audience knows the intricacies of your data and analytics, or what your statistical procedures mean.
- Distill important findings for the reader. To get your points across, think about distributing one-page briefs, refer readers to full reports for more information, summarize the key findings of the narrative, and be concise.
- Practice effective writing skills. Always be mindful of the importance of an engaged audience. Consider presenting reports in a Q&A (question and answer) format. Include anecdotes and quotes to enliven the report.

Types of Reports

Here we outline several report types, ordered from most to least demanding in terms of written detail and length.

- *Narrative or full reports* are largely inclusive documents that provide detailed descriptions of the purpose for doing the research, methods employed, findings, and implications. For such reports, the importance of having an executive summary comes to the fore.
- *Report memos* usually focus on a narrow topic and are developed for a small audience with a specific interest in the topic.
- *Top-line reports* are usually part of a comprehensive research report, summarizing the key findings in a short document for top management. Written

for senior management, these reports are jargon-free and action-oriented by nature.

- *Bulleted reports* replace prose with brevity and are popular since they can be generated relatively quickly, particularly in comparison to a narrative or a report memo.
- *Web reports* and visual analytics involve dynamic tables and charts in a Web environment with a series of menus and options that allow the user to drill deeper into the data.
- *Dashboards* measure performance using easy-to-understand graphics to show the status of current activity. Dashboards are most useful for those data elements that need regular monitoring.
- *Presentations* are reports presented orally and visually, rather than in writing.
- *Ad hoc requests* require time to evaluate. Although tracking these requests can seem time-consuming or overly bureaucratic, it is time well spent. Often these requests come on a regular cycle, perhaps annual or quarterly, so they can be anticipated and standardized, leading to better-quality reporting and more responsive customer service. Also, similar types of ad hoc requests can be consolidated into one and scheduled as a regular activity.

Components of Reports

Most reports will contain some combination of the following components, depending on the audience, topic, and type of report (Bers & Seybert, 1999).

- *Meaningful title.* The title often convinces the reader to read the report, so use something that will capture the reader's attention. Sometimes, the title page will also include key words and phrases that can be used by database search engines.
- *Executive summary.* This provides a brief overview of the main findings of the report; it can serve as a stand-alone piece and also as part of the larger report. Never underestimate the value of a good executive summary—it is often the only part that the decision maker reads.
- *Table of contents.* This should give a clear indication of the contents of each section of the report or information presented in each table.
- *Introduction and purpose.* This describes why the study was performed.
- *Methodology.* You need to explain how you conducted the research, whether by administering a survey or scanning the environment. If the methodology gets technical and/or complex, you can append the details in a technical appendix, with a brief overview of the methodology included in the main body of the report.
- *Findings.* The findings—which, along with conclusions, are the heart of the report—are presented in narrative, tabular, or graphic form.
- *Summary, conclusions, implications, recommendations.* Some clients will want you to provide only the findings and conclusions, allowing the members of the committee to make their own interpretations as part of the group discussion.

- *References.* This is essential in a report that includes background literature. These can appear in a separate section at the rear of the report or be integrated into the text as footnotes.
- *Glossary.* In a report in which the use of jargon and/or acronyms is unavoidable, a glossary can be a useful reference for the reader.
- *Appendices, exhibits, attachments.* Large data tables, special graphics or charts, technical matter, and other such materials should be placed at the rear of the report as clearly labeled appendices.

Delivering a Good Presentation

All those who have made presentations, whether formal stand-up presentations with handouts or informal discussion-type presentations, know that presenting the findings of an analysis is a different experience for both the institutional researcher and the audience member than sharing findings in a written report. In a presentation, compared to a narrative, you do not have the opportunity to go into as great a level of detail, so you must rely more heavily on visual aids such as graphs to make your point, and you control the pace at which your information is consumed by the audience.

Communications experts Grice and Skinner (Allyn & Bacon Public Speaking, n.d.) note that we enjoy listening to speakers who are energetic, vigorous, exciting, inspiring, spirited, and stimulating. Keep in mind that although the presentation may not be fresh to you, the audience is hearing it for the first time. Good presenters have an appropriate physical appearance, effectively maintain eye contact with their audience, speak in a way that can be understood, and use effective body language and move around during the presentation.

Anxiety is what impedes presenters most in giving highly effective presentations. It has been our experience that few institutional researchers are trained presenters, and even those who are comfortable giving presentations to small groups of colleagues may be intimidated by presentations to larger groups in unfamiliar settings. One strategy to resolve this is to have a class on public speaking delivered by members of the college's public speaking or theatre faculty. There are also a variety of resources online that can help researchers improve their public speaking skills and gain confidence in front of an audience, such as the Allyn & Bacon Public Speaking website (http://wps.ablongman.com/ab_public_speaking_2/) and the Toastmasters International website (http://www.toastmasters.org/tips .asp). One basic piece of advice is practice, practice, practice!

The Role of the Presenter and the Presentation Software

The role of the presenter is to connect with the audience, direct and hold their attention throughout the presentation, and help them to understand the material so they will be most likely to remember it (Kosslyn, 2007). The presenter may prepare visual aids to show to the audience. There has been a great deal of debate about the value of presentation software like Microsoft PowerPoint, the depth of which is outside the scope of this chapter (Atkinson, 2008; Kosslyn, 2007; Tufte, 2001, 2006). Remember that whether preparing paper handouts or PowerPoint presentation slides, these visual aids play a supporting role to the presenter.

Designing Quantitative Data for Tables

As we progress in the writing of our report, we realize that the presentation of data in narrative form is becoming tedious, and a table or graph may be more effective. A *table* is a structure for organizing and displaying data, where those data are encoded as text or numbers (Few, 2004). It is preferable to use a table over a graph when any of the following is true:

- The report will be used to look up or compare individual values.
- Precise values are required.
- The quantitative information to be communicated involves more than one unit of measure (that is, the data can be put in multiple columns easily).

Designing Effective Tables

Table design can be more art than science, although there are guidelines regarding spacing of columns and rows, fonts, decimals, and so on. Remember, the primary distinguishing characteristic of a table is that it organizes data into rows and columns. A table's support components are the non-data "ink" objects that highlight or organize the data components, as well as the ways by which we can delineate these rows and columns from each other.

When designing your own tables, we recommend that you use white space alone—whenever the space allows—rather than grid lines to delineate columns and rows. When you can't use white space, use *subtle* fill colors (no bright reds or hot pinks!). When you can't use subtle fill colors, use rules, but we strongly advise against using grids. Here are additional guidelines:

- Minimize what Tufte terms "chart junk" and any extra attractions (such as clip art) that are not relevant to the story you are trying to tell.
- Avoid text orientations other than horizontal, left to right.
- Sort data in a meaningful way.
- Left-justify text; right-justify numbers and align decimal points.
- Center nonnumeric data.
- Always use commas in whole numbers.

- Do not exceed the required level of precision. There is no need to have six digits after the decimal!
- Express months as two-digit or three-letter entries.
- Select a legible font, in terms of both size and type, and be consistent.
- Use bold, italics, and coloring for emphasis.
- Repeat the header row on tables with multiple pages of data.

Following these guidelines results in the development of attractive tables that your readers will find easy to follow and comprehend. This increases the likelihood that the information presented in the table (and the story you are telling in the overall report) will be better retained for later reference.

Static Tables and Dynamic Data Table Tools

The types of tables considered up to this point are what we call static tables—think of the tables printed on a sheet of paper. The reader cannot change the cell entries herself. For most reports you will prepare, static tables will be the modus operandi. However, technological developments have enabled us to provide *dynamic* tables for our clients. Dynamic tables appear in a web environment, and a series of pull-down menus allows the user to change the contents of the cells depending on the conditions he places on the data.

Today, the institutional researcher has many alternatives for creating dynamic tables, which can be placed on the Internet or as desktop tools, both accessing a centrally located database. These tool alternatives include the following:

- Microsoft Excel offers a pivot-table function that allows users to customize tables to provide precisely the data they are looking for.
- Other software packages (such as Tableau) offer compelling tools for the analysis and visual presentation of data.
- Online analytical processing (OLAP) technology allows for multidimensional analysis of data and provides what is probably the most powerful alternative for creating dynamic tables.

Presenting Quantitative Data in Graphs

As institutional researchers, one of our greatest challenges is to turn data into insights, and one of the most effective techniques for doing this is through visual presentation of quantitative data—the graph. After all, as the saying goes, a picture is worth a thousand words. But a picture is worth a thousand words only if the reader can decipher it (Kosslyn, 2006). Good graphics take time, creativity, and patience.

Principles of Effective Graphics

What is an effective graphical display? Certainly, it is one that a reader can easily understand. After all, "it is a psychological, not a moral, fact that people do not like to expend effort and often will not bother to do so, particularly if they are not sure in advance that the effort will be rewarded" (Kosslyn, 2006, p. 20). Tufte's (2001) fundamental principle for effective statistical graphics is "Above all else, show the data" (Tufte, 2001, p. 92). Tufte defines graphical excellence as having the following characteristics:

- *Substance, statistics, and design*—The presentation of the data must be well-designed and interesting.
- *Clarity, precision, and efficiency*—Complex ideas are communicated clearly, with little extraneous or unnecessary information.
- *Parsimonious*—The graphic gives the viewer the greatest number of ideas in the shortest time with the least in the smallest spaces.
- *Multivariate*—Most graphics will review more than one variable at a time.
- *Truthful*—The graph tells the truth about the data.

When you graph data, focus on what is important. Prepare a visual display that will connect with the audience, direct and hold attention throughout the display, and promote understanding of the material and memory (Kosslyn, 2006). Kosslyn's eight psychological principles of effective graphics serve as a practical guide:

Principles related to connecting with the audience: Base what you deliver on what the audience needs.

- Principle of relevance: *Communication is most effective when neither too much nor too little information is presented.* This principle restrains us from including all the information that we, as analysts, might find interesting.
- Principle of appropriate knowledge: *Communication requires prior knowledge of relevant concepts, jargon, and symbols.* Using this principle, we would be unlikely to include standard deviations in a graph to a nonstatistical audience.

Principles related to directing and holding audience attention: Base what you deliver on the audience frame of reference.

- Principle of salience: *Attention is drawn to large perceptible differences;* for example, highlighting important information for the audience.
- Principle of discriminability: *Two properties must differ by a large enough proportion or they will not be distinguished.* Because we see things in a context, differences in the colors of the lines on a chart must be large enough to be noticed.

- Principle of perceptual organization: *People automatically group elements into units that they then can attend to and remember.* A long list of items in a graph, for example, should be broken down into smaller conceptual groupings.

Principles related to promoting understanding and memory: Base what you deliver on audience learning.

- Principle of compatibility: *A message is easiest to understand if its form is compatible with its meaning.* A common violation of this principle happens when we talk about proportions and graph numbers, or vice versa.
- Principle of informative changes: *People expect changes in properties to carry information.* Avoid using changes in color to merely enliven a graph; the audience expects that these changes signal something more meaningful.
- Principle of capacity limitations: *People have a limited capacity to retain and process information and will not understand a message if too much information must be retained or processed.* Research suggests that people remember about three or four pieces of information at a time, so avoid putting more than three or four lines on a graph or items in a list, unless grouped in meaningful ways.

Other Rules of Presentation

In addition to these overarching principles, we suggest the following design guidelines:

- Minimize ink that does not depict the data—that is, "chart junk." The grid-lines of a line graph, if they are necessary at all, should never overwhelm the lines showing the data in a line graph. Focus your time, effort, and toner on conveying the data, not the grid lines, frames, and ticks.
- Don't use 3D graphs—they distort the data.
- Sort data in graphs in the most meaningful way in order to show the reader the data trend that is important.
- Keep in mind that some people have trouble with graphs that use two *y*-axes. Try using two graphs side-by-side (two-panel displays) to avoid the confusion of axes.
- The size of features in a graph—such as bubbles, markers, and the like—communicates relative quantitative information, but it is not good for precise information.
- A good rule of thumb is to use a sans serif font for material that is projected. For material that is shared in written format, a serif font may work just fine.
- Don't use the software's default settings. Don't settle for a canned preparation of your data. Your data are too valuable, and you may have only one opportunity to connect with your audience.
- Don't settle for the first execution. Graph your data various ways to see what works best. Commit the time and effort to experiment. After all, a picture is worth a thousand words.

Dashboards and Special Graphic Displays

A dashboard is a special type of report that focuses on using multiple visual displays on a single page to convey, at a glance, information about what is currently going on. Driven by Tufte's concept of the value of providing adjacent contextual information to allow for nonlinear thinking (Tufte, 2001), dashboards provide new design challenges for the institutional researcher, but they remain at the core an analytical exercise. The research challenge is to understand the intellectual problems the dashboard is supposed to help the university community with, and to understand how it will be useful for the university. Armed with this information, the analyst can analyze the data and knit together on one page a series of meaningful tables and graphs that illuminate the data insights at a glance. The design challenges unique to dashboard development (Few, 2010; Goodman, 2008; Juice Analytics, 2009; Tufte, 2003) include the following:

- Using the one-page space efficiently, and populating it with only essential graphs and charts
- Organizing the information in the most meaningful way to emphasize how the information flows and how elements of the information are related, or at least how these elements group together
- Avoiding "chart junk" metaphors like rocket ship dials and strong or flashy colors that detract from the information
- Designing an effective page layout, starting with the most important information in the upper left corner, allowing for an "F" shaped visual scan of the page, and ending with the least important information in the lower right corner.

For a very useful three-part overview guide to dashboard development, see Juice Analytics (2009). (See Chapter 35 for additional discussion of performance indicators and dashboards.)

Reporting Qualitative Data

Although the bulk of this chapter addresses techniques for reporting quantitative data, we recognize that institutional researchers also collect data from open-ended survey questions and focus groups and may conduct qualitative research studies, and these qualitative data present unique challenges for reporting. These data provide both rich context and detail that may be worth providing in total to your client, and valuable and persuasive quotations to include in the final report summary. Often we also need to synthesize these data and reduce them into research insights for broader consumption—which at first may seem like a daunting task because of the sheer volume of information that has been gathered.

Several tools are available that can be helpful for analyzing qualitative data, including but not limited to products such as SPSS, QSR NVivo, ATLAS.ti, and RQDA. Once we have analyzed these qualitative data, the challenge is to find an effective way to present them. We can use more traditional graphic displays for qualitative data, essentially quantifying these qualitative findings. For some qualitative data, this approach is appropriate. You may choose, for example, to present the findings from your analysis on the important reasons student gave for choosing your college in a frequency table or a bar chart.

Another option is to use a tag cloud or word cloud. Much like a text-based scatter plot, the word cloud displays the content of your qualitative data as words in a text box, using font size to differentiate the relative importance of items cited in your analysis. For example, in the open-ended student satisfaction survey item on the important reason for choosing your college, often-cited words like "faculty" would appear much larger in your text box than those hardly mentioned, like "meal plans" (http://www.wordle.net/). Although word clouds can be visually effective, they present several real challenges. As Viegas and Wattenberg (2008) note, long words get more emphasis than short ones, font sizes may not effectively convey differences, and clouds that sort words alphabetically can separate related words, such as "east" and "west," making interpretation difficult.

Most visual displays are adequate at conveying quantitative information (what, where, and when), but not as effective with the qualitative results of "why" and "how" (Slone, 2009). Slone notes that for qualitative data that focus more on the "how" or "why" and the relationships between concepts, few techniques are more effective than the table, though tables are limited in that they can't graphically show patterns within the data or the structure of the relationships between variables. As in quantitative analysis, it is difficult to "see" the important data patterns in tables.

However, the research you have conducted may go beyond open-ended responses in an otherwise quantitative study; it may be a qualitative program evaluation, ethnography, or case study. In these cases, it is often difficult to separate the activities of data collection, analysis, and report writing (Cresswell, 2007). Although a full discussion of analysis techniques for qualitative inquiry is outside the scope of this chapter (for a more detailed discussion, see Cresswell, 2007; Guba, 1990; Patton, 1990), we offer a few practical considerations. First, writing an often lengthy qualitative research report requires the researcher to stay focused and strike a balance between description and interpretation (Patton, 1990). Second, it's important to remember the value of the executive summary. Patton notes that this one- to two-page document, written in plain language and focused on the essence of the evaluation or research study, may be the most widely read document you produce related to your study (Patton, 1990).

Distributing Information and Communicating Results

We've reached the final stage. We have written our report, replete with tables and graphs that make our findings about student engagement at our institution abundantly clear. Now we need to get this report into the hands of those who need to see it, which brings us to the matter of distribution. The purpose of distribution is to get it out there, get our findings percolating—to make sure the results of our labors contribute to these informed discussions.

Distribution of a report can take many forms, but all of them boil down to two basic strategies: pushing the report out to users or pulling the users into your information. You may push out a time-sensitive report via an email attachment or send out paper copies of your documents via campus mail. Other times you might post your report on a website and invite people to view it and additional resources at their leisure, thereby pulling them into the report. Although different reports will require different strategies, more often than not you will likely use both a push and a pull strategy for the distribution. In determining the best distribution plan, it is important to understand your audience and institutional culture.

The Role of the Internet

The way the IR office shares information has changed dramatically over the past ten years, thanks to the Internet. In 1996, *New Directions for Institutional Research* noted that forty-six institutions were known to have electronic fact books using the Web or gopher technologies, but no institution was known to have a completely online fact book (Jones, 1996). Today the situation is notably different. The ease with which websites can be created and maintained has been both a blessing and a curse to the IR office. The blessing comes from the ability to quickly post results of analyses, the multitude of tools and techniques for empowering users to conduct their own analyses, and the ability to market the wares of the IR office. The curse comes from the need to continually maintain links to current information and the belief that because something is up on our website, it is being used to inform decision making on campus. (See Chapter 26 for a discussion on business intelligence and analytics.)

Today, we rely heavily on the Web to help us reach our audiences, and it is an important piece of a broader strategy of information support, offering these benefits:

- Allowing users to request information via online data request forms.
- Providing access to data-cutting tools. We can allow end users to analyze our aggregated data sets while we still maintain a centralized control of the raw data.
- Providing training and retraining for tool users. In our experience, a handful of users take to the tools right away, becoming early adopting power users; the remaining bulk of the tools' eventual users need to be courted and coaxed.
- Serving as a living library. The IR website, with fresh information and working links to relevant resources, is a living library for the university community.

Conclusions

As an institutional researcher, your required skills go beyond analysis and statistics. You must be able to effectively communicate your findings to decision makers so that they can percolate in an environment of informed decision making. As most researchers do not have the time or resources to commit to a thorough review of the literature on effective presentation of quantitative data, it is our hope that this chapter, like the AIR monograph it was modeled after, will provide you with some encouragement, professional support, and validation for efforts that can often be seen as secondary to statistical analysis.

We value excellent graphs, well-designed tables, and dynamic research presentations. We think you should too. After all, an unread analysis sitting under a stack of papers on a vice president's desk is not an effective analysis, no matter what statistical technique was used. We encourage you to spend the extra time to graph the same data different ways, to take out the table gridlines, to run through presentations with colleagues, and to have a peer proofread a report. We have learned through experience that, as Bers and Seybert noted in 1999, when our work is enhanced by high-quality visual displays of quantitative information, it is received more favorably, travels farther, and touches more decision makers than a text-dense analytical report—and, yes, it is challenging and fun (yes, fun) to create good visual displays of data.

References

Allyn & Bacon Public Speaking. (n.d.). Pearson Education. Retrieved from http://wps .ablongman.com/ab_public_speaking_2/0,9651,1593249—t,00.html

Atkinson, C. (2008). *Beyond bullet points: Using Microsoft Office PowerPoint 2007 to create presentations that inform, motivate, and inspire.* Redmond, WA: Microsoft Press.

Bers, T., & Seybert, J. (1999). *Effective reporting.* Tallahassee, FL: Association for Institutional Research.

Cresswell, J. (2007). *Qualitative inquiry & research design: Choosing among five approaches* (2nd ed.). Thousand Oaks, CA: SAGE.

Few, S. (2004). *Show me the numbers: Designing tables and graphs to enlighten.* Oakland, CA: Analytics Press.

Few, S. (2010). *Information dashboard design.* Sebastopol, CA: O'Reilly.

Goodman, A. (2008, November). The science of site seeing. Retrieved from http://www .agoodmanonline.com/pdf/free_range_2008_11.pdf

Guba, E. (1990). *The paradigm dialog.* Thousand Oaks, CA: SAGE.

Jones, L. (1996). *Campus fact books: Keeping pace with new institutional needs and challenges.* New Directions for Institutional Research, no. 91. San Francisco: Jossey-Bass.

Juice Analytics, Inc. (2009). A guide to creating dashboards people love to use. Retrieved from http://media.juiceanalytics.com/downloads/Dashboard_Design_Part_1_v1.pdf

Kosslyn, S. (2006). *Graph design for the eye and mind.* New York: Oxford University Press.

Kosslyn, S. (2007). *Clear and to the point: 8 psychological principles for compelling PowerPoint presentations.* New York: Oxford University Press.

Patton, M. (1990). *Qualitative evaluation and research methods* (2nd ed.). Thousand Oaks, CA: SAGE.

Saupe, J. (1990). *The function of institutional research* (2nd ed.). Retrieved from http://www .airweb.org/page.asp?page=85

Slone, D. J. (2009). Visualizing qualitative information. *Qualitative Report, 14*(3), 488–497. Retrieved from http://www.nova.edu/ssss/QR/QR14-3/slone.pdf

Toastmasters International. (n.d.). Retrieved from http://www.toastmasters.org/

Tufte, E. (2001). *The visual display of quantitative information* (2nd ed.). Cheshire, CT: Graphics Press.

Tufte, E. (2003). *Executive dashboards: Ideas for monitoring business and other processes.* Retrieved from http://www.edwardtufte.com/bboard/q-and-a-fetch-msg?msg_id=0000bx

Tufte, E. (2006). *The cognitive style of PowerPoint: Pitching out corrupts within* (2nd ed.). Cheshire, CT: Graphics Press.

Viegas, F., & Wattenberg, M. (2008). Tag clouds and the case for vernacular visualization. *Interactions, 15*(4), 49–52.

Weiss, C. (1980). *Social science research and decision making.* New York: Columbia University Press.

CHAPTER 34

TOOLS FOR SETTING STRATEGY

Jan W. Lyddon, Bruce E. McComb, and J. Patrick Mizak

Roles for institutional researchers are changing, and new expectations and tools are making it possible to respond more effectively. This chapter is designed to provide an overview of some of the most prominent tools to use in setting strategy, including how and when they are used and developed, who uses them, and why they are important.

The stage for strategic tools centers on the institution's strategy, ideally as expressed in its strategic plan. There are excellent resources on developing strategic plans in higher education—among them Norris and Poulton's (2008) *A Guide to Planning for Change*—so we will not replicate them here. Instead, this chapter is primarily focused on ways in which IR professionals support strategy formulation, either in advance of a formal strategic planning process or at other points.

IR roles in strategy formulation are increasingly dynamic. "Institutional research has an established role in the planning process: providing data to support it" according to Clagett (2004, p. 47). With additional tools in the IR repertoire, however, IR professionals can be even more integral to the institution's strategy development. And, as shown in Chapter 35, "Tools for Executing Strategy," strategy is used in many ways: as a plan; a pattern of behavior; a position, perspective, or philosophy; or a ploy or maneuver (Mintzberg, Ahlstrand, & Lampel, 1998). Strategy, for our purposes here, is choosing the market and stakeholder segments that the institution intends to serve and then identifying the critical internal processes at which it must excel to deliver value to the stakeholders in the targeted segments (adapted from Kaplan & Norton, 1996, p. 37). This includes actions in environmental scanning, assessing internal conditions, portfolio analysis, and benchmarking (see Chapter 35).

A vital capacity for IR professionals in this new climate is *strategic thinking*. Although not a tool per se, its elements can be learned. Indeed, we would argue they *must* be learned if IR professionals are to be effective in supporting strategy development and execution at a high level. Just what is strategic thinking? It is a particular *way* of thinking, with several elements:

- A systems perspective—in which the systems thinker "has a mental model of the complete system of value creation from beginning to end, and understands the interdependencies within the chain" (Lawrence, 1999, p. 4).
- Intent-focused and intent-driven—it conveys a sense of direction relative to achieving goals (Lawrence, 1999, p. 4).
- Intelligent opportunism—that is, openness to new experience. This includes measuring very different phenomena than institutions might traditionally have reported.
- Thinking in time—strategy is driven by the gap between current reality and intent for the future; this is articulated by Hamel and Prahalad (as cited in Lawrence, 1999). IR professionals recognize the predictive value of the past and increasingly may be involved with establishing goals for the future. This iterative process, constantly oscillating or comparing past to alternative futures, is a feature of thinking in time.
- Hypothesis-driven—". . . in an environment of ever-increasing information availability and decreasing time to think, the ability to develop good hypotheses and test them efficiently is critical . . ." (from Liedtka's "Strategic Thinking: Can It Be Taught?" as cited in Lawrence, 1999, p. 8).

In sum, strategic thinking is more abstract, seeing the big picture but understanding the links to details, with a view toward altering which details are measured and when. To describe this more simplistically, some individuals use terminology like "thirty-thousand-foot view."

Strategic Tools for Assessing the External Environment

Early in the strategic planning process, institutions usually conduct an environmental scan to identify factors—usually large-scale issues and trends that may affect the institution. Institutions may also conduct environmental scans on an ongoing basis to keep abreast of forces and trends that will affect them. External factors can be grouped in six categories: political, economic, social, technical, environmental, and legal (PESTEL)—hence the term "PESTEL analysis." In today's higher education environment, competitive issues and trends also need to be considered as part of the scanning process. Porter's Five Forces model for competitive analysis (2007) provides an effective tool for doing so.

PESTEL Analysis

An environmental scan begins by establishing a focus; for example, an institution or specific program looking at its market, or an institution examining how it fits in the community it serves. To conduct a PESTEL analysis, an IR professional or a team of people within the institution reviews and summarizes relevant sources of information for each of the following categories:

- Political—executive and legislative actions at the national, state, and local levels and also the concerns and possible actions of a wide variety of political action and issue groups.
- Economic—current and future appropriations, funding, and grants from government, foundations, and other sources. Also included here would be macro and micro economic trends affecting costs and income, the economic impact of labor and faculty contracts, and prices of other goods and services the institution uses.
- Social—demographic and social trends and issues.
- Technical—all types of technology trends and issues relevant to the institution.
- Environmental—energy and a wide variety of "green" issues and trends.
- Legal—federal, state, and local regulations and laws, court cases, and contracts that might affect the institution.

Each category is listed in the first column of the analysis table (Table 34.1). In each category, researchers list the key trends and summarize the nature and degree of impact, implication, and importance of the trend in the appropriate columns. This, then, largely constitutes the Opportunities and Threats components of SWOT (Strengths, Weaknesses, Opportunities, and Threats) analysis.

Useful information for the scanning process can be obtained from sources directly associated with higher education and from other fields. There are likely to be faculty and staff who have knowledge and expertise relevant to the PESTEL analysis; they may serve on an environmental scanning group or provide advice. Google or similar search engines can also turn up useful information.

TABLE 34.1   PESTEL ANALYSIS TABLE

PESTEL Analysis Factors	How each factor will affect the organization or program	Potential Impact (High, Medium, Low)	Implication and Importance			
			Time Frame	Type (Positive, Neutral or Negative)	Impact (Increasing, Unchanged, Decreasing)	Relative Importance (Critical, Important, Unimportant)

PESTEL is a particularly useful starting point for environmental scanning because it helps institutional personnel think about an array of trends and factors and offers a way to categorize them. This is an ongoing process that may be repeated periodically to help institutions remain abreast of key information. And as the analysis proceeds, there will likely be additional items that surface for each of the categories, not listed in the preceding summary, that should be included (Morrison, 2010).

Porter's Five Forces Model

Higher education is becoming increasingly competitive. An increasing number of community colleges are offering or seeking to offer bachelor's degrees. Organizations that are not traditional players in higher education are getting involved by offering online course and degree programs to meet a growing demand. Articulation agreements and other strategic alignments are multiplying to draw more students to transfer easily. This increasing competition suggests that environmental scanning include consideration of competitive issues and trends.

Porter's Five Forces model is a tool for competitive analysis that can be adapted for use in higher education. The five forces that Porter (1980) uses to explain the degree of competition in an industry are the *degree of rivalry, supplier power, buyer power, barriers to entry,* and the *threat of substitutes* (McLaughlin & McLaughlin, 2007; Porter, 1980).

The Five Forces model, adapted for higher education and presented in Table 34.2, summarizes how each force affects competition. To apply the model, IR professionals should obtain information to answer the questions in the Analysis Question column for their institution. Others at the institution, such as faculty members in business, may be good resources for assistance in using the model and answering the questions.

Tools for Assessing and Making Decisions About Strategy

There are numerous tools for assessing and making decisions about strategy, as you can see from looking at various college courses on the topic. This section discusses some of the most popular.

SWOT

SWOT (strengths, weaknesses, opportunities and threats) analysis is a commonly used tool for identifying and assessing the impact of external and internal factors that are likely to affect strategic plans and decisions. Internal factors are categorized as the organization's strengths and weaknesses. An institution may, for example, have some undergraduate programs that are considered to

TABLE 34.2 COMPETITIVE ANALYSIS QUESTIONS

Forces	Factors Involved	Impact on Competition	Analysis Questions
Degree of Rivalry	Exit barriers, concentration or number of competitors, size of competitors, demand for services, intermittent overcapacity, industry growth, program differences, fixed costs, switching costs, institution stakes, diversity of rivals, and brand identity	Degree of rivalry is an assessment of the current level and nature of competition.	What is the current level and nature of rivalry? Are the number, size, and programs of current competitors likely to change in the future? What impact will these changes have on the level and nature of future rivalry with current competitors?
Supplier Power Includes faculty and staff and may include feeder schools and colleges and alumni	Supplier concentration or number of suppliers, importance to institution, presence of substitute inputs, switching costs, impact on costs, costs relative to total purchases, and differentiation of inputs	The level and type of power of key suppliers can limit the flexibility of the institution in the future in terms of costs and ability to respond to demand for new programs or services or eliminate existing programs or services with little demand. Relationships with feeder schools and colleges and alumni affect recruiting.	What limit does the power of any current supplier place on the institution's ability to be competitive with rivals (controlling costs, increasing or decreasing programs or services, and the like, including non-education ancillary services)?
Buyer Power Includes government, such as appropriations	Bargaining leverage, buyer's incentives, available substitutes, price sensitivity, brand identity, and leverage-tuition dependency	The level and type of power possessed by buyers, especially government, may constrain the flexibility of an institution with respect to costs and revenue (tuition) and program and service offerings, which affects the institution's competitiveness.	What constraints on costs, revenues, programs, or services, directly or indirectly influenced by government or groups of students, affect the competitiveness of the institution?
Barriers to Entry	Government policy, access to students, capital requirements, brand identity, proprietary programs, switching costs, cost advantages, learning curve, and economies of scale (might also include accreditation requirements)	The degree of difficulty or ease of offering higher education products or services have a direct bearing on the level and nature of competition in the higher education sector.	What factors are making it easier or more difficult for new entrants into the higher education sector to offer competitive products and services? Overall, will this lead to more or less competition in the higher education sector?
Threat of Substitutes Apprenticeships, military service, niche employment in jobs not requiring college degrees, alternative auxiliary services (such as local housing versus dorms)	Switching costs, buyer inclination to choose substitutes, and price and performance relative to substitutes	The availability and affordability of substitutes for higher education services or auxiliary services has a direct impact on the competition in higher education.	To what extent are affordable alternatives to either direct higher education services or auxiliary services available?

Source: Adapted from McLaughlin & McLaughlin, 2007; Porter, 1980; Porter's Five Forces, 2007.

TABLE 34.3   STANDARD SWOT MATRIX

SWOT Matrix	Internal Perspective	External Perspective
Beneficial	List of Strengths	List of Opportunities
Detrimental	List of Weaknesses	List of Threats

be very strong and whose graduates are rapidly employed. The same institution may have weak orientation programs and a poor registration process.

A list of threats and opportunities for a SWOT analysis can be readily obtained by summarizing the results of both the environmental scanning process using PESTEL analysis and the Five Forces model.

Increasing market demand for graduates in a program the institution is working to improve and expand would be an opportunity. Declining demand for a program to which the institution has traditionally devoted significant resources would be a threat.

Table 34.3 shows a standard format that IR professionals can use to list the institution's strengths, weaknesses, threats, and opportunities. Testing each item listed against some form of evidence rather than simply providing opinions will strengthen the value of a SWOT analysis. Additionally, it is important to ensure that each item is a current strength or weakness or a current or potential opportunity or threat.

The value of SWOT can also be greatly enhanced by providing additional context. Kaplan and Norton (1996) recommend the use of a SWOT matrix organized by balanced scorecard perspectives. Typical balanced scorecard perspectives for a higher education institution are mission, stakeholders, process, learning and growth, and financial or other resources. IR professionals conducting a SWOT can use the table shown in Table 34.4 by answering the questions in the boxes.

Another variation of SWOT is TOWS (SWOT reversed), which "encourages decisions makers to go the next step—a dialogue about and choice of possible strategic alternatives" (McLaughlin & McLaughlin, 2007, p. 114). Moreover, using a nine-cell format, illustrated in Table 34.5, enables institutions to use the SWOT analysis to formulate and select appropriate strategies.

After strengths, weaknesses, opportunities, and threats have been listed, compare the list of strengths with the list of opportunities to identify a strategy that would use a specific strength and take advantage of a specific opportunity. List the strategy in cell 1; continue to identify additional strategies for cell 1 that use the same strengths or others to pursue other opportunities. Using techniques such as brainstorming, a group can identify a variety of potential strategies before selecting the best for inclusion in cell 1. Complete the table by selecting strategies for cells 2, 3, and 4. A large white board (or white wall) is ideal for identifying and considering strategies as an interactive process with several individuals participating.

TABLE 34.4 SWOT MATRIX ORGANIZED BY BALANCED SCORECARD PERSPECTIVES

	Internal Factors		External Factors	
	Strengths	**Weaknesses**	**Opportunities**	**Threats**
Mission	What are the strengths and weaknesses of our institution relative to our mission?		What are the opportunities that can help us achieve our mission?	What are the threats to achieving our mission?
Stakeholders Students, faculty and staff, alumni, community, funding sources	What are the strengths and weaknesses of our institution in satisfying the expectations of our stakeholders?		What are the opportunities that can help us satisfy stakeholder expectations?	What are the threats to satisfying stakeholder expectations?
Process Internal processes such as recruiting, registration, fundraising, instructional methods, and so on; initiatives designed to create new processes or improve existing processes	What are the strengths in our internal processes in which we excel?	What are the weaknesses in our internal processes?	How can we take advantage of internal process strengths or improve the processes to realize the opportunities?	How can we take advantage of internal process strengths or improve the processes to neutralize the threats?
Learning and Growth Developing and improving human, information—IT, databases and other information resources—and organizational (cultural) capabilities (sometimes referred to as human capital, information capital, and organizational capital)	What are the human, information, and cultural core competencies and strategic capability strengths?	What are the human, information, and cultural core competencies and strategic capability weaknesses?	What are the opportunities and how can we take advantage of our human, informational, and cultural core competencies and strategic strengths to successfully realize opportunities?	What are the most significant external threats due to our weaknesses in human, informational, and cultural core competencies and strategic strengths?
Financial and Other Resources	What are our financial and resource strengths?	What are our financial and resource weaknesses?	What opportunities will our financial and resource strengths allow us to successfully realize?	What are the most significant external threats, given our financial and resource weaknesses?

Source: Adapted from Kaplan & Norton, 2008, p. 51.

TABLE 34.5   TOWS MATRIX

	Strengths **List major strengths in this cell**	**Weaknesses** **List major weaknesses in this cell**
Opportunities	1. Strengths + Opportunities	2. Weaknesses + Opportunities
List important opportunities in this cell	List strategies that enable the institution to use its strengths to take advantage of opportunities.	List strategies that enable the institution to overcome its weaknesses by taking advantage of opportunities.
Threats	3. Strengths + Threats	4. Weaknesses + Threats
List important threats in this cell	List strategies that enable the institution to use its strengths to neutralize threats.	List strategies that enable the institution to overcome its weaknesses while simultaneously neutralizing a threat.

Source: McLaughlin & McLaughlin, 2007, p. 114. *The Information mosaic: Strategic decision making for universities and colleges.* Washington, DC: Association of Governing Boards of Universities and Colleges, p. 114. Reprinted with permission.

TABLE 34.6   ANSOFF MATRIX

	Existing Programs and Services	**New Programs and Services**
Existing Markets (students, corporate training clients, and so on)	List **Market Penetration** Strategies	List **Program/Service Development** Strategies
New Markets (new groups or types of students, corporate training clients, and so on)	List **Market Development** Strategies	List **Diversification** Strategies

Source: Adapted from Ansoff, 2010.

Portfolio Analysis Using the Ansoff Matrix

The Ansoff matrix compares markets with programs and services, as illustrated in Table 34.6; once completed, it can be used in combination with an effective SWOT analysis to identify suggested strategic directions. These can be used for the entire institution or for a particular unit or area. For example, a school might have conditions that suggest market development for one academic program but market penetration for another.

Using the Ansoff matrix and the completed SWOT analysis together, as shown in Figure 34.1, provides guidance about the types of strategic decisions institutions can make. As the figure illustrates, the Ansoff matrix combined with SWOT helps the institution develop and think through marketing strategies that can take advantage of the institution's strengths and weaknesses. The importance of neutralizing the threats or weaknesses that might inhibit effective pursuit of the identified marketing strategies also becomes more apparent.

FIGURE 34.1   SWOT AND ANSOFF MATRIX

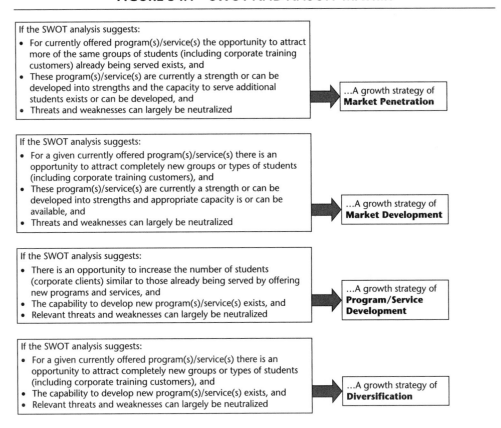

If the SWOT analysis suggests:
- For currently offered program(s)/service(s) the opportunity to attract more of the same groups of students (including corporate training customers) already being served exists, and
- These program(s)/service(s) are currently a strength or can be developed into strengths and the capacity to serve additional students exists or can be developed, and
- Threats and weaknesses can largely be neutralized

...A growth strategy of **Market Penetration**

If the SWOT analysis suggests:
- For a given currently offered program(s)/service(s) there is an opportunity to attract completely new groups or types of students (including corporate training customers), and
- These program(s)/service(s) are currently a strength or can be developed into strengths and appropriate capacity is or can be available, and
- Threats and weaknesses can largely be neutralized

...A growth strategy of **Market Development**

If the SWOT analysis suggests:
- There is an opportunity to increase the number of students (corporate clients) similar to those already being served by offering new programs and services, and
- The capability to develop new program(s)/service(s) exists, and
- Relevant threats and weaknesses can largely be neutralized

...A growth strategy of **Program/Service Development**

If the SWOT analysis suggests:
- For a given currently offered program(s)/service(s) there is an opportunity to attract completely new groups or types of students (including corporate training customers), and
- The capability to develop new program(s)/service(s) exists, and
- Relevant threats and weaknesses can largely be neutralized

...A growth strategy of **Diversification**

The analysis may reveal that an institution should consider more than one strategy (for example, market development and diversification). This is especially true if analysis is done at the college or school level, as an institution might use more than one strategy for its various colleges and schools (Ansoff, 2010).

Benchmarks and Benchmarking

Benchmarks and benchmarking can be used initially as an institution develops its strategy and again as it measures its results. "Benchmarks are the 'what' and benchmarking is the 'how'" (Stroud, 2010, p. 1). Benchmarks provide an overall standard of performance comparison, and benchmarking helps institutions identify the "process enablers that helped to develop the level of performance observed" (Watson, 1993, p. 17). "Benchmarking is an ongoing, systematic process" whose goal is "to provide key personnel, in charge of processes, with an external standard for measuring the quality and cost of internal activities, and to help identify where opportunities for improvement may reside" (Alstete, 1995, p. 5).

A common barrier in benchmarking is the widespread attitude among many in higher education that each institution is unique, with faculty and administrators quick to point out the ways in which their institution differs from others. Nonetheless, colleges and universities have much in common. They recruit and enroll students, hire faculty to develop and teach courses, and ultimately award degrees. These and many other attributes make benchmarking a valuable tool, whether for establishing or measuring goals or for understanding underlying processes. Colleges and universities hire and pay employees, operate physical spaces, and, in many cases, provide housing. These functions are common to other non–higher education organizations, which may be potential areas for benchmarking studies outside of higher education.

Given this common resistant attitude about institutional uniqueness, it may be understandable that benchmarking in higher education has focused more on cross-sectional measures to make comparisons such as size or growth of enrollment (Coughlin, 2009). Increasingly, datasets such as IPEDS and the IPEDS Data Feedback Report are readily available, and this makes overall outcomes or outputs comparisons easier. Additionally, there are other consortia that routinely share data on specific variables and/or results areas, including many listed near the end of this chapter (Table 34.7). (See Chapter 25 for more discussion on data exchanges.)

Benchmarking leads to two primary results: a measure of performance and information about the process enablers that helped lead to that performance level (Watson, 1993). Ultimately, benchmarking enables leaders "to make comparisons and draw inferences about their institutions based on objective sets of criteria" (McLaughlin & McLaughlin, 2007, p. 68).

Benchmarking Process

A benchmarking process may follow four phases, each with several steps (adapted from Alstete, 1995, and Mahalik, 2010). IR professionals may play a variety of roles in these processes, and their specific contributions will vary by institution and the process being benchmarked.

Phase I: Planning

- Identify and prioritize what to benchmark. Include primary stakeholders in the decisions at this early stage, so the priorities meet their needs and they will be more inclined to heed the results. A gap analysis may help identify the most important outcome to investigate.
- Decide who or which organizations—that is, peer institutions—to benchmark, and among these, which has superior performance. Internal benchmarking is an option for some processes. For example, if a large academic unit has

excellent student outcomes with similar students, other academic units may conduct benchmarking analyses to identify how they can achieve similar results.

Phase II: Information gathering and analysis

- Study the superior processes. This step may be the most time-consuming part of information gathering. Sometimes the information on processes is confidential or scattered among several units of the comparison institution. There may be significant costs involved in this step, including time and travel to comparison institutions to examine their processes. Guiding questions for this may include the following:
  - What are the primary inputs to the process and how do these compare with the inputs at the home institution? For example, a benchmarking study about certain student outcomes may depend heavily on the types of students involved.
  - What are the key processes or steps the comparison institution follows? For these steps, how long do they take and what resources do they require? What are the success factors or measures the institution uses to indicate that the steps were effective?
  - What are the outputs or measures of the overall process? These may include numbers of people served or similar near-term measures of results.
  - What are the outcomes or results of the process? These are usually the measures of the gap between the home institution's performance and the comparison institutions.
- Identify reasons for the superior performance compared with the performance at the home institution. Carefully examine the inputs and processes followed at the comparison institutions and the home institution to see where the differences occur.
- Set goals for improved processes. What needs to change in the home institution, and how and when can it change to achieve the desired results? What will it cost in time, equipment, talent, or other resources? Who needs to be involved, and who will lead the work?

Phase III: Integration

- Communicate the findings of the study and gain acceptance among key stakeholders. This step may be integrated with the information gathering and analysis phase, as many of the stakeholders will have been involved earlier. However, communicating beyond a project team to gain understanding and acceptance is critical in order to avoid obstruction as improvement processes move forward.
- Establish new functional goals. This involves setting both short- and mid-term goals to show progress toward meeting the longer-term desired outcome,

and it involves setting goals for specific units in the institution. For example, if a benchmarking process involves speeding up the process of hiring adjunct faculty, it may involve the human resources department as well as the academic units. Each of these units will have different tasks and thus will have its own functional goals.

Phase IV: Action

- Develop action plans for implementation. This step and establishing functional goals (part of the preceding Phase III) may occur almost simultaneously. The detailed action plans should include timelines, individuals responsible for carrying out the tasks, and targets.
- Keep the process continuous. Gains resulting from a one-time process improvement may be easily lost unless the process is one of continuous improvement.

"One of the biggest advantages of benchmarking is the extent of improvements the organization makes by learning from the processes of others. A better and proven process can be adapted, with suitable modifications . . . with less time invested for inventing new methodologies" (Mahalik, 2010). (See Chapter 37 for a discussion of applying benchmarking and Chapter 36 on comparative analyses.)

There are risks or limitations associated with benchmarking. McLaughlin and McLaughlin (2007) note several, including incorrect specification of the elements under consideration, not fully describing a standard against which comparison is made, and failing to use comparable units of analysis. Benchmarking can be expensive in terms of both staff time and money, and sometimes comparison institutions may be reluctant to share inside information with others.

Table 34.7 shows additional examples of benchmarking sources in higher education.

It is likely that benchmarking will continue as an important practice, and capabilities and opportunities to fully engage in this will increase.

Conclusion

IR professionals' roles are changing along with the array of tools available to assist them. Increasingly, IR professionals who can think strategically can be integral to institutional strategy development. IR can use these tools in an integrated way: starting with PESTEL analysis for environmental scanning, then brought into an effective SWOT analysis, and further deepened with a SWOT organized around strategic perspectives to effectively set the stage for strategy development. Carrying this further, into matching specific strengths or weaknesses with opportunities or threats through TOWS, helps point to potential strategies. Likewise, matching the results of a strong SWOT analysis with the

TABLE 34.7 EXAMPLES OF BENCHMARKING SOURCES IN HIGHER EDUCATION

Source Name	Type of Data	Specific School Information*	Web Address	Notes
IPEDS Executive Peer Tool	IPEDS	Yes	http://nces.ed.gov/IPEDSPAS/expt/	More recent data for IPEDS keyholders
NCCBP	Pseudo-IPEDS for CCs	Yes	http://www.nccbp.org/index.asp?IdS=000347–7C58080&~=	Paid subscription necessary
AAUDE	Assessment, Environmental Impact, Gender Equity, H1N1 policies, other external studies	Yes	http://aaude.org/home	Restricted to members only
CIC KIT	Basic IPEDS/Salary info	No	http://www.cic.edu/projects_services/infoservices/kit.asp	Restricted to members only
CIC FIT	Financial Information	No	http://www.cic.edu/projects_services/infoservices/fit/index.asp	Restricted to members only
WICHE	Demo, IPEDS info for West region	No	http://www.wiche.edu/resources/policy/297	For Western schools only
CUPA-HR	Salary Information	No	http://www.cupahr.org/index.aspx	Recent data available for a fee
AAUP	Salary Information	Yes	http://www.aaup.org/AAUP/pubsres/research/compensation.htm	More specific info available for a fee
College Board	Wide variety	No	http://professionals.collegeboard.com/educator/higher-ed	Advocacy data
HERI Freshman Survey	Incoming Freshman Survey	No	http://www.heri.ucla.edu/publications-brp.php	Additional data for participants
HERI YFCY	End of Year Freshman Survey	No	http://www.heri.ucla.edu/publications-brp.php	Additional data for participants
HERI Senior Survey	Graduating Senior Survey	No	http://www.heri.ucla.edu/publications-brp.php	Additional data for participants
HERI Faculty Survey	Faculty Survey	No	http://www.heri.ucla.edu/publications-brp.php	Additional data for participants
NSSE	Student Engagement	Yes	http://nsse.iub.edu/NSSE_2009_Results/order_ar.cfm	For purchase
FSSE	Faculty Engagement	No	http://fsse.iub.edu/	For purchase
BCSSE	Student Engagement	No	http://bcsse.iub.edu/	For purchase
CCSSE	Student Engagement	Yes	Http://www.ccsse.org/	For purchase
CCFSSE	Faculty Engagement	Yes	http://www.ccsse.org/CCFSSE/CCFSSE.cfm	For purchase
SENSE	Entering Student Engagement	Yes	http://www.ccsse.org/sense/	For purchase

* Specific school information is often available only to those who are members or who participate in some fashion in the study.

Ansoff matrix enables an institution to examine its portfolio of options. Finally, benchmarks and benchmarking provide effective comparisons of results and processes that help institutions look outside their boundaries. Each of these tools relies on data—but data and information used in increasingly strategic ways. IR professionals can be integral to supporting these tools.

References

Alstete, J. W. (1995). *Benchmarking in higher education.* ASHE-ERIC Higher Education Report no. 5. Washington, DC: The George Washington University Graduate School of Education and Human Development.

Ansoff, I. (2010). *Ansoff* matrix. QuickMBA. http://www.quickmba.com/strategy/matrix/ansoff/

Clagett, C. A. (2004, Fall). Applying ad hoc institutional research findings to college strategic planning. In M. J. Dooris, J. M. Kelley, & J. F. Trainer (Eds.), *Successful strategic planning* (pp. 33–48). New Directions for Institutional Research, no. 123. San Francisco: Jossey-Bass.

Coughlin, M. A. (2009). IPEDS Training Materials Module 1, *Using IPEDS data for benchmarking.* Tallahassee, FL: Association for Institutional Research, in cooperation with National Center for Education Statistics. Unpublished.

Kaplan, R. S., & Norton, D. P.. (1996). *The balanced scorecard: Translating strategy into action.* Boston: Harvard Business School Press.

Lawrence, E. (1999). *Strategic thinking: A discussion paper.* Prepared for the Research Directorate, Policy, Research and Communications Branch, Public Service Commission of Canada.

Mahalik, P. (2010). Benchmarking: Ten practical steps with review points. Retrieved from http://www.isixsigma.com

McLaughlin, G. W., & McLaughlin, J. S. (2007). *The information mosaic: Strategic decision making for universities and colleges.* Washington, DC: Association of Governing Boards of Universities and Colleges.

Mintzberg, H., Ahlstrand, B., and Lampel, J. (1998). *Strategy safari: A guided tour through the wilds of strategic management.* New York: The Free Press.

Morrison, M. (2010). RapidBI. Retrieved from http://rapidbi.com/pestle/

Norris, D. M., & Poulton, N. J. (2008). *A guide to planning for change.* Ann Arbor: Society for College and University Planning.

Porter, M. E. (1980). *Competitive strategy: Techniques for analyzing industries and competitors.* New York: Simon & Schuster.

Porter's Five Forces. (2007, March 23). *QuickMBA: Strategic management.* Retrieved from http:/www.QuickMBA.com/strategy/porter.shtml

Stroud, J. D. (2010, February 26). *Understanding the purpose and use of benchmarking.* Retrieved from http://www.isixsigma.com/methodology/benchmarking/understanding-purpose-and-use-benchmarking/

Watson, G. H. (1993). *Strategic benchmarking: How to rate your company's performance against the world's best.* New York: Wiley.

CHAPTER 35

TOOLS FOR EXECUTING STRATEGY

Jan W. Lyddon, Bruce E. McComb, and J. Patrick Mizak

Institutions expend a great deal of time and other resources to create strategic plans. Regrettably, many institutions put those documents on the shelf, dusting them off only when the accreditor inquires; others find that the grand schemes in the plans are so broad and general that doing almost anything would seem to fulfill the plan. Now, though, more is expected of higher education, including making a real effort to fulfill strategic plans and then providing evidence of having done so. This chapter addresses the primary tools for executing strategy, most of them originating in business, that are adapted for use in higher education. The chapter begins with measurements, but at a strategic level, and goes on to show how these are developed, displayed, and used in strategy execution.

Key Performance Indicators

As adapted by J. F. Rockart, key performance indicators (KPIs) are "the limited number of areas in which results, if they are satisfactory, will ensure successful competitive performance for the organization. They are the few key areas where 'things must go right' for the business to flourish" (as cited in Sapp, 1994, p. 1). The invocation of a "few" leads to the question: how many KPIs should an institution have? "To harness the power of the Balanced Scorecard as both a measurement and communication system, you have to keep the number of objectives [and their associated measures] to a manageable level. . . . Cap your objectives between 10 and 20" (Niven, 2003, p. 178). Moreover, it should be possible to display them on a single page or screen so that decision makers can see at a glance where they should direct their efforts (Few, 2006).

Types of KPIs

KPIs are typically measures or indicators of outputs or outcomes and also may be considered leading or lagging indicators. Output measures are immediate activity counts, such as number or percentage of students served, units produced, number of or percent of faculty and staff completing professional development. Outcomes, however, answer the "so what?" or result question. Although useful for some purposes, outputs typically do not provide information about whether students (or other stakeholders) are better off as a result of the services or education provided. However, outputs, as well as some outcomes, can be thought of as leading indicators that provide an institution with an early indication of whether or not a strategy is working. "A leading indicator looks at critical things that will help in the longer-term achievement of outcomes. For example, students' grades in certain courses may be a leading indicator of their graduation rates. If we were to wait and monitor only graduation rates we couldn't make corrections in the near-term to improve student success" (Lyddon & McComb, 2008, p. 139). Lagging indicators—which are usually outcome indicators—track the benefit received by stakeholders as a result of the institution's operations (Niven, 2003).

Categories of KPIs: A Balance of Perspectives

KPIs, whether they are output or outcome indicators, should also represent a balance of perspectives, typically four or five categories of perspectives which tie to a *balanced scorecard* (discussed later).

These categories (see Figure 35.1), adapted for higher education from those originally presented for businesses, are as follows:

- *Mission* perspective presents the institution's mission or *raison d'être.*
- *Stakeholder* indicators present what is important to or about the stakeholders. These are lagging outcome indicators and should be limited to just two to five.
- *Process* indicators show how well the institution's processes produce the outputs or outcomes that most directly affect the stakeholder indicators. KPIs in the process indicators and the next category, learning and innovation (also called learning and growth), most directly measure how an institution will implement its strategy (Kaplan & Norton, 2008).

Learning and innovation indicators show how well people, groups, and the institution as a whole are learning and innovating so they can achieve the desired process outcomes. Also called "learning and growth" measures, they identify "the infrastructure that the organization must build to create long-term growth and improvement. . . . Organizational learning and growth come from three principal sources: people, systems, and organizational procedures"

FIGURE 35.1 PERSPECTIVES FOR AN EDUCATIONAL INSTITUTION MODEL

Source: Adapted from Kaplan and Norton, 2004, 2008

(Kaplan & Norton, 1996, p. 28). Strategic investments in employee professional development, information technology and systems, and improving organizational procedures fall into this category. All institutions can benefit from an additional category, called *community capital,* which encompasses the non-monetary good will, support, promotion, encouragement, and volunteers provided by the community in which the institution is located as well as by alumni. *Resources indicators* show which resources are needed or will be increased or expended in relation to the work being done to produce the desired outcomes (Lyddon & McComb, 2008). These, too, are strategic rather than routine operational resources.

When selecting measures, it is important to distinguish between *vital* and *strategic* processes. "Vital processes are analogous to vital human processes such as those that determine body temperature, blood pressure, and heart rate. If any of these is erratic or out of control, the body cannot function and immediate corrective action must be taken" (Kaplan & Norton, 2008, p. 165). Strategic processes, on the other hand, are those that *differentiate* the institution's strategy and create a strategic difference. Being the best at the vital processes—such as filing reports on time, responding to student inquiries, and so on—will not *differentiate* the institution or create breakthrough performance.

The Importance of Having a Balance of Indicators

Balanced scorecards, discussed in more detail later in the chapter, give the institution information about how well its strategy is being executed. With a balance of indicators provided on a periodic basis, leaders can make necessary midcourse corrections and thereby better ensure that the goals will be achieved. A scorecard that consists of only outcome measurements, for example, may show how well the institution is doing in achieving its goals, but offers little useful or actionable information that can be used for midcourse adjustments. Moreover, scorecards with only one perspective may be similarly unbalanced and result in leaders missing some important factors in the institution's strategy. Finally, scorecards that use only existing measures, such as those found in traditional fact books, may miss important strategic directions. Thus a "balanced" scorecard (which is the display mechanism for KPIs) provides several viewpoints or perspectives as well as leading and lagging indicators (Kaplan & Norton, 1996, 2008).

Components of KPIs

Every KPI has several components: (1) the actual results for the indicator, (2) the target for which the indicator is striving, and (3) a mechanism to readily indicate whether the indicator is outside the bounds of normal variation. We call this last item "signal values," because on a display the color or symbol changes on a scorecard or dashboard when the results are outside the boundaries. Signal values, usually set at three levels within the range of the indicator's possible performance, enable the institution to easily differentiate results that are varying only slightly or are outside of normal. These can be results that are desirable or undesirable (beware of using the differentiators "up" or "down," because some measures are better if smaller, others better if larger). In a display of KPIs, often "good" or "desirable" results are displayed in green, undesirable but not significant problems in yellow, and very undesirable results in red: a "traffic light" system that everyone understands. No matter what values and displays are used, their meaning must be agreed on by stakeholders and communicated clearly to users.

Some institutions use other terminology for KPIs, such as critical performance indicators, key success factors, or end result measures. Whatever these important measures are called, they must be selected carefully, measured meaningfully, and communicated to stakeholders appropriately.

Changing or Updating KPIs

An important consideration is how often KPIs should be updated. The best advice is to update them as often as decisions can be effectively made about the things they're measuring. Also, some KPIs measure only data that change a few times a year (for example, KPIs tied to students' grades). There may be a temptation to establish real-time KPIs—that is, measures that change daily or even more often. But can institutions actually make strategic decisions and take action that rapidly? Not likely.

KPIs themselves may be changed. If the indicator is no longer valid, or if, for example, it's turning out to measure something that was an interim measure until a better one is developed, it should be changed. Moreover, if the institution's strategy changes, the measures associated with it will undoubtedly change. Working with the stakeholders for the strategy, IR professionals should recommend new KPIs.

IR Roles and Process for Developing KPIs

As advisors to strategists and operational leaders, IR professionals can research and recommend valid and reliable measures for strategies and collaborate with these stakeholders to establish reasonable targets and signal values. Working with those who are responsible for strategy to help them understand and use the indicators makes their understanding and use much more likely (Lyddon & McComb, 2008). Although we describe a general method of developing KPIs, there are other methods, including that described by Carpenter-Hubin and Hornsby (2005).

Identifying the KPIs requires not just measurement sense, but also diplomacy. A project champion or advocate at a senior level is vital, largely because the KPIs will use information from the entire institution. This person should be willing and able to persuade his or her colleagues to support the collection of data for KPIs and may set the overall tone for how the indicator will be used. The project champion may help educate senior administrators about the value of the measures and set a more team-oriented approach to using the results. Finally, a champion can help the IR office clear away other competing priorities to focus on the project.

There are a number of ways to select the measures or indices to use. Starting from the strategic plan of the institution, the IR professional can review the goals and ask, for each one, "What will change if we accomplish this goal, and how would we measure it?" By asking this question repeatedly and using strategic thinking skills (see Chapter 34), IR can identify a preliminary list of KPIs to share with stakeholders. Another method—developing a strategy map and translating the map into a scorecard—is discussed shortly. Finally, one popular method is to ask stakeholders to identify the measures they commonly report to their next higher level in the organization. There is a risk, however, as this latter method often results in listing measures that may not be strategic or may not be associated with the most important variables the institution should monitor and that could help spur strategic actions.

Using the resultant initial lists of potential KPIs, the IR professional can research options, including variations of the particular indicators. For example, if an institution wanted to have indicators of faculty quality, IR staff might identify options such as the percentage with terminal degrees, average compensation, research productivity, and so on. Using the variations, IR might work with stakeholders to identify which measure is the outcome of the strategy, or whether a combination of the measures might be used to create an index. Such an index might weight two or more variables so that a single measure results from the scoring of these. For example, a KPI of faculty quality might be composed of one-third from the percentage of those with terminal degrees and the remainder from an annual percentage of faculty with publications or other research activity. Given that hiring faculty with terminal degrees might not change rapidly but research output can vary annually, this may be a reasonably dynamic measure.

Ultimately, working with stakeholders, the institution should agree on the essential few KPIs—those fifteen to twenty that best represent the institution's strategy.

In addition to the project champion, other stakeholders in the process will vary according to each institution. Often the stakeholders are the top leadership group, perhaps a president's cabinet. Regardless of the titles, KPIs typically are of greatest value to those highest in the institution's leadership hierarchy.

KPIs are highly summarized but may have cascaded measures or details embedded within them. These details, including unit-by-unit measures or other variations, can be shown in such tools as cascading dashboards or reports pertinent to a particular school, department, or other group. A classic example of such details is enrollment components such as part-time and full-time enrollment.

Balanced Scorecards and Dashboards

The British scientist Lord Kelvin stated in 1883, "If you cannot measure it, you cannot improve it." More than a century later, Robert Kaplan and David Norton introduced the concept of the balanced scorecard for use in business. It has quickly been adapted to use by nonprofit organizations, including higher education institutions. The starting point, however, is *not* the measurements. Rather, it is the statement of strategy. What is it that the college or university intends to accomplish? What are the desired major outcomes or results of the institution?

"A well-constructed scorecard eloquently describes your strategy and makes the vague and imprecise world of visions and strategies come alive through the clear and objective performance measures you've chosen" (Niven, 2003, p. 22). A balanced scorecard, or simply a scorecard, usually represents the entire institution at a strategy level. It includes only those critical measures, as described in the preceding section on KPIs. Dashboards, on the other hand, often are specific views of operational items that indicate how well a segment of the institution is doing. A dashboard might, for example, include measures monitored by the chief development officer, like the endowment value, alumni giving rate, total gifts, and gifts from alumni. The development officer probably would not monitor things that a facilities director might monitor, so their dashboards would contain different measures. However, they both might serve on a president's cabinet and so would also see the institution's overall scorecard. With this distinction in mind, how is a scorecard or a dashboard developed?

Scorecard Development Process

A successful scorecard begins with the users, usually top leadership, and a project champion. Ultimately, it centers on the institution's strategy, translated into measurements. What indicators are most meaningful for the users of the scorecard, and how often will they use it? Some institutions update their scorecards monthly, others only quarterly or even less frequently.

If the IR office has a strong grasp of the KPIs, perhaps through creation of the strategy map and spreadsheet, the development process is already well under way. In this case, IR could hold a meeting with stakeholders to review the overall KPIs, including their types (leading versus lagging output or outcome), categories (stakeholder, process outcomes, learning and innovation, and resources), and components (the actual results, the target, and the "signal values"). It is likely that development of all KPIs to this level may require many months of effort, so the process of working with stakeholders is iterative and gradual, not a one-time meeting.

Assuming the institution's strategy and some or most KPIs have been identified, the primary steps in developing a balanced scorecard, along with roles for IR professionals, are delineated in Exhibit 35.1.

Users of Balanced Scorecards in Higher Education Institutions

Although the balanced scorecard originated in business, its use in higher education has been growing, particularly as a tool for top institutional leadership. Additionally, some states have adopted the scorecard as a means of depicting measures of policy initiatives; the audience for these includes general citizens, policy makers, and institutional leadership. Institutional examples include those reviewed by Terkla, Wiseman, and Cohen (2005), in which they noted that in almost all cases among the institutions they reviewed, the dashboard or scorecard was requested by the board, the president, or provost. "The primary audience . . . is upper management, consisting of the Board, the president, and/or the deans" (p. 15). Moreover, many among these same examples restrict access to a few users, likely the top management. More recently (2010), individual commentators to an online survey noted

EXHIBIT 35.1   IR PROFESSIONALS' ROLES IN BALANCED SCORECARDS

- Identify project partners: project champion, content providers, and technical support.
  - Project champion: someone high enough in administration to advocate for the scorecard and its uses with other leaders of the institution.
  - Content providers: may be primarily IR and also other knowledgeable people who use and report data associated with the KPIs.
  - Technical support: assists with obtaining and formatting data, and possibly with development of the scorecard display (Lyddon & McComb, 2008).
- Identify the KPIs, a step that usually occurs over several months.
- Work with process stakeholders to refine the KPIs.
  - Process stakeholders are those responsible for ensuring that a strategic process gets carried out and meet the objectives set in the strategy.
  - Process stakeholders can help refine the definition and even provide the data.
- Set benchmarks, targets, or signal values to provide the context for gauging whether the strategy is working by showing clearly whether the KPI's results are at acceptable levels.
- Design the display and delivery mechanism; the display must meet some important criteria, including the following:
  - Fit the data on a single page or computer screen; include hyperlinks or other means to drill down to appropriate detail. These might also become parts of cascaded dashboards (as depicted in Figure 35.3, later in the chapter).
  - Avoid clutter. Users must see the information at a glance, and clutter—including too many arrows, boxes, gauges, dials, or other elements—only distracts the viewer from the main message: is the strategy working?
  - Use colors or shapes that can be easily viewed in a variety of circumstances, including printing in black and white or being used by a color-blind person. Use columns, shapes, or other means of supplementing the colors in the display.
- Provide training and information to users of the scorecard. The purpose of the scorecard is to communicate, inform, and be used as an institutional learning system—not a punitive controlling system (Kaplan & Norton, 1996).
- Update the scorecard at predetermined and relevant times, including:
  - Frequency of primary users' decisions
  - Frequency of change in the measures themselves
- Review the scorecard at predetermined times, ideally two or more times annually.
  - Hold a strategy review meeting to present the scorecard results, in which leaders ask, "Is our strategy working?" and "Is this the right strategy?"
  - IR professionals can assist with such meetings by guiding the leadership through the measures and answering questions about underlying data.
- Revise the scorecard when the strategy changes.

that their scorecards were used as well by top leadership and/or the board (Mizak, 2010).

Other institutions that have adopted balanced scorecards also have adapted them, some by changing the perspectives to more closely align with their strategies or, perhaps, to have language that is more consistent with higher education terminology.

Others have adopted approaches that at least initially are very similar to their institutional fact books.

> However, the strength of the Balanced Scorecard is that it places before decision makers those presumably overlooked areas that are of concern to many faculty, staff, and students. The Balanced Scorecard can be used as a powerful tool to guide an institution toward its long-range goals. It allows administrators to view the institution from multiple perspectives, including (but not limited to) the financial. By also focusing on internal processes, customers, and employee development, the Balanced Scorecard can help a higher education institution continuously improve while achieving the goals that support its mission and vision for the future. . . . By forcing the institution to look at nontraditional metrics, the Balanced Scorecard makes visible the tensions that exist among competing priorities. (Ballentine & Eckles, 2009, p. 34)

Scorecard or Dashboard Display and Presentation: The Role of Technology

Readers may have noted that although, increasingly, there are technology solutions to help create displays, we did not discuss these technology options first. This is intentional, because the proper tool, whether advanced business intelligence systems (BI) or spreadsheets, should be chosen only after the uses, content, and other consideration have largely been settled.

Appropriately selecting scorecard or dashboard technology involves several steps and careful review, particularly if there is to be a large investment of time, money, or both. IR staff should begin the process by specifically defining and then prioritizing the functions the technology needs to perform from the perspective of the users. Inherent in this is the question of who the users are, including both those who put together the data (often IR staff or others) as well as end users of the system. Defining "users" broadly and carefully is important at the early stages of selecting a tool. Which users will use a technology tool and for what purpose(s)? How easy must it be for primary and secondary users to access and use the technology? Who will have access and by what method: Internet, intranet, or some other system? The system's complexity is important too: how many different scorecards or dashboards (in terms of content and focus) must the technology be capable of supporting? What, if any, drill down capability is required (for example, by clicking on a given data item it is possible to drill down into further detail). Do the scorecards and dashboards need to be cascaded, so that it is possible to link strategy level scorecards to operations level dashboards? What screen display capabilities should the technology have? We strongly recommend avoiding a lot of gauges, dials, and fancy graphs in favor of straightforward numerical and graphical displays, and it's important to remember that, in some cases, spreadsheets on paper are sufficient. Is the display visually appealing and easy to understand? What are the data sources for the scorecards and dashboards? Will the data be entered from automated sources, manual sources, or both? When must the scorecard and dashboard technology be installed and fully operational? (See Chapter 26 for more discussion of business intelligence and analytics.)

Once these and other user-based functional questions have been addressed, the answers can be translated into the specifications used for the institution's technology purchasing process. When considering proposals from technology vendors, it is critical to have in-depth conversations with other institutions using the technology. Ask how well the installation and use of the technology compared with the promises of the vendors. Did it take longer to get installed than promised? Was it more difficult or more costly than promised? Does it work as promised? When the inevitable problem arises, does the vendor fix the problem in a timely and cost-effective manner? Have there been difficulties with system upgrades? How much training did it take to support, maintain, and use the technology? What would you do differently, if you were to go through the technology selection process again?

Dig deeply and talk to users of the technology, not just the technical staff. Vendors usually give references only to institutions where their technology has been successfully installed in a timely manner and where users are happy. Seek out and talk with colleagues at other institutions and check with colleagues via online discussion groups to identify others who have purchased technology from the vendor and learn about the colleagues' experience.

Before going the route of purchasing new technology, consider developing and testing the basics of the scorecard and dashboard system, using readily available desktop software such as spreadsheets. Most permit use of hyperlinks to provide drill down capability. As the institution's users gain confidence that the scorecard and dashboard approach will work well for the institution, staff can then more confidently pursue the purchase of more advanced technology. A sample display using standard spreadsheet software is shown in Table 35.2.

Strategy Execution: An Emerging Role for Balanced Scorecards and Dashboards

Strategy maps, balanced scorecards, and dashboards are valuable tools for ensuring that an institution's strategies are effectively implemented. Many higher education institutions struggle to effectively execute their strategies. There is a perception that many institutions' strategic plans, once developed, are either put on the shelf and forgotten or just ignored. But increasingly, accrediting bodies are requiring institutions to demonstrate that the strategic planning loop has been closed—that is, the plan has been implemented and its impact evaluated, and appropriate adjustments have been made to ensure that the institution's strategic goals are attained. Often, too, institutions don't execute their strategies because their attention gets diverted from them.

FIGURE 35.2 STRATEGY MAP FOR A UNIVERSITY

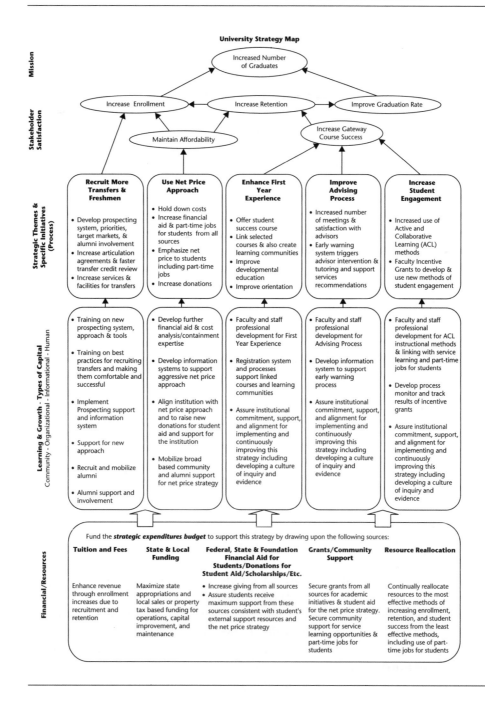

In this section, we outline six state-of-the-art practices that high-performing organizations use to help ensure that their strategies are effectively executed (Kaplan & Norton, 2008).

The first practice is to translate the strategy into measurements (Kaplan & Norton, 2008). Beckett and McComb (2009) note: "People pay attention to what is measured, people work on what they pay attention to and people improve what they work on. The measurement principle is simple, if you want people to improve a process, measure it and make the measurements known. . . . Balanced scorecards were developed by Kaplan and Norton to do exactly this: define strategic focus and objectives and measure the underlying success factors in terms of KPIs" (p. 9). The Balanced Scorecard Spreadsheet (Table 35.1) provides an example of how a strategy map (Figure 35.2) is translated into measurements.

The second practice is to manage a limited number of strategic initiatives (Kaplan & Norton, 2008). "The Pareto Principle states that roughly 80 percent of the effects come from 20% of the causes. Applied to organizations, this principle means 80% of success comes from 20% of actions. There is an inherent limit to the number of new initiatives any organization can effectively implement at one time. It's better to execute a limited number of strategic initiatives well and see significant impact than to attempt execution of too many initiatives, of which several will have a lesser impact" (Beckett & McComb, 2009, p. 13). The development of a strategy map is an effective way to limit the number of strategic initiatives. The discipline of using a strategy map effectively limits the number of strategic initiatives due to space considerations. Figure 35.2 shows an example of a strategy map for a university.

The third practice is aligning units with the strategy which requires that strategic plans be meaningfully linked to operational plans so that employees and units know how their work aligns with and contributes to the institution's strategic goals (Kaplan & Norton, 2008). "That means looking at how specific strategic initiatives will affect operations and what operational plans are necessary to support the strategy" (Beckett & McComb, 2009, p. 14). One means of presenting the data in aligned fashion is to use a scorecard display such as that in Table 35.2 and use hyperlinks to other segments with appropriate details by department or major unit. The display here was developed using commonly available desktop spreadsheet software, but as noted earlier, other technology is also available.

It is important to note the connections among the Cascading Alignment of Balanced Scorecard to Dashboards (shown in Figure 35.3), the strategy map (Figure 35.2), and the Balanced Scorecard Spreadsheet (Table 35.1). The spreadsheet serves as a bridge between the somewhat abstract strategy map and the summarized (and periodically updated) measures displayed in the scorecard.

Developing a cascading alignment of the institution's balanced scorecard (strategic focus) with operational dashboards (see Figure 35.3) provides a way to see how well work of units (dashboard measurements) aligns with the institution's strategic goals, as measured in the balanced scorecard (Table 35.2).

TABLE 35.1 BALANCED SCORECARD SPREADSHEET

	Strategy Map		Balanced Scorecard			Action Plan	
Perspective	Objectives	Measurement	Target (in four years)	Actual (current)	Initiative		Strategy Budget
Mission	Increase number of graduates.	Number of graduates	3,000	2,400	The Action Plan for each initiative covers four years. The **Target** for the measurements is what is to be achieved in 4 years. The **Actual** shows the current value of the measurements. The **Strategy Budget** (Strategic Expenditures Budget) shows funds required to support the Strategic Themes & Specific Initiatives, Learning & Growth, and obtaining Financial Support from all sources.		
Stakeholder Satisfaction	Increase enrollment.	Number of students enrolled	13,600	12,200			
	Improve the graduation rate.	Graduation rate	51%	48%			
	Increase retention.	Retention (fall to fall)	70%	65%			
	Maintain college affordability.	Rate of increase in average net cost per student	2.5%	4.5%			
	Increase gateway course success.	Percentage of students with C and above	75%	70%			
Strategic Themes and Specific Initiatives	Recruit more transfers.	# of transfers	1,600	1,000	**More** articulation agreements, fast transfer credit review, more recruiting.		$150,000
	Recruit more freshmen.	# of freshmen	4,500	4,000	**Improve** recruiting process and involve more alumni in recruiting.		$200,000
	Increase student support.	Student support as % of total yearly costs	18.3%	15%	**Contain** costs and increase student support from all sources.		$11,800,000
	Enhance first-year experience.	# students that took success course	2,000	0	**Phase** in success course requiring all potentially at-risk freshmen to take. Offer paired courses. Also create learning communities. Include some developmental education linked to credit courses. Improve orientation.		$8,900,000
	Improve academic advising process.	# students in paired or learning communication courses	3,500	0	**Restructure**, improve, and expand advising. Monitor student performance during semester and refer to tutoring and support services as needed.		$2,400,000

(continued)

TABLE 35.1 BALANCED SCORECARD SPREADSHEET (*Continued*)

	Strategy Map	Balanced Scorecard			Action Plan	
Perspective	Objectives	Measurement	Target (in four years)	Actual (current)	Initiative	Strategy Budget
	Increase student engagement.	Orientation satisfaction rate	95%	50%	**Professional** development programs and faculty incentive grants to encourage and support faculty development and use of active and collaborative learning (ACL) methods to increase student engagement. Supplement NSSE with frequent engagement surveys for all courses.	$700,000
		New student advising frequency/satisfaction rate	3/95%	1.5/60%		
		% referred that use tutor/support services	80%	N.A.		
		% faculty expanding use of student engagement methods	80%	40%		
		% students reporting active and collaborative learning	90%	40%		
Learning and Growth	Prepare faculty and staff to carry out initiatives.	# faculty prepared	800	200	**Professional** development programs for faculty and staff to develop capabilities required to initiate, encourage, and support initiatives.	Included above
	Assure planning, information, and analysis systems support initiatives.	#staff prepared Planning, information, and analysis systems capability index	500	100	**Technology,** training, and services to support initiatives.	$1,000,000
	Develop the support, alignment, and commitment of the entire institutional community with the strategy and continuous improvement.	Support, alignment, and commitment index	80	40	**Professional** development and workshops, support services.	$150,000

	Measure	Target	Actual	Initiative	Budget
Increase student engagement via community service learning.	Hours of community-based service learning	90	50	**Staffing** and related support for identifying and coordinating opportunities for both community service learning and community-based part-time jobs linked to courses and majors to increase student engagement.	$400,000
Create community based part-time student jobs.	Hours of community-based part-time student jobs	300,000 300,000	50,000 N.A.		
Financial and Resources Increase net revenue via retention and increased enrolment.	$ increase in net revenue	$1 million	$0.2 million	The items on the **left** show the sources of funding for the $23.6 million Strategic Expenditures Budget (target less actual). Budget allocations associated with increasing student support from all sources and obtaining grants for academic initiatives are shown on the right. The net revenue from increased retention and enrollment is a net figure: costs are reflected in regular operating budget, and there are no extra costs for reallocation of resources, so there is no budget allocation for these items.	
Increase funds for student support—all sources.	$ increase student support funds from all sources	$12 million	$1 million		Increasing student support: $200,000
Reallocate resources.	$ reallocated	$10 million	$0.5 million		
Obtain grants for academic initiatives.	$ received	$3 million	$0.7 million		Obtaining grants: $100,000

Source: Adapted from Kaplan and Norton, 2004.

TABLE 35.2 SAMPLE BALANCED SCORECARD DISPLAY USING DESKTOP SOFTWARE

Generic University Balanced Scorecard Perspectives and Measurements	At or Above Target	Below Target	Far Below Target	Score or Level	Target	Last Update
Mission						
Number of graduates	x			2,644	2,640	Spring 2011
Stakeholder Satisfaction						
Number of students enrolled	X			13,020	12,760	Spring 2011
Graduation rate	X			49.4%	49.2%	Spring 2011
Retention (fall to fall)	X			67.0%	67.0%	Spring 2011
Rate of increase in average net cost per student		X		3.9%	3.7%	Spring 2011
Percentage of students with C or better in gateway courses			X	70.5%	72.0%	Spring 2011
Strategic Themes and Specific Initiatives						
Number of transfers	X			1,400	1,240	Spring 2011
Number of freshmen	X			4,300	4,200	Spring 2011
Student support as a percentage of total yearly costs		X		16.1%	16.3%	Spring 2011
Number of students successfully completing student success course		X		822	1,000	Spring 2011
Number of students in paired or learning community courses		X		1,401	1,500	Spring 2011
Orientation satisfaction rate	X			85.0%	85.0%	Spring 2011
New student advising frequency /satisfaction rate	X			2/76%	2/75%	Spring 2011
Percentage of students referred that use tutoring or learning support services			X	59.0%	65.0%	Spring 2011
Percentage of faculty expanding use of student engagement pedagogy	X			57.0%	56.0%	Spring 2011
Percentage students reporting use of active and collaborative learning in class	X			61.0%	60.0%	Spring 2011

Learning and Growth					
Number of faculty prepared to implement specific initiatives	X		442	440	Spring 2011
Number of staff prepared to implement specific initiatives	X		265	260	Spring 2011
Planning, information, and analysis systems capability index	X		73.0%	70.0%	Spring 2011
Leadership support, unit alignment with goals and mission commitment index	X		84.0%	80.0%	Spring 2011
Hours of community-based service learning committed		X	155,000	150,000	Spring 2011
Hours of community-based part-time student jobs available			95,000	120,000	Spring 2011
Financial and Resources					
$ increase in net revenue from retention and enrollment increase	X		$.55 M	$.52 M	Spring 2011
$ increase in funds from all sources available to support students		X	$4.8 M	$5.4 M	Spring 2011
$ reallocated to support strategic initiatives	X		$3.5 M	$3.4 M	Spring 2011
$ in grants to support academic strategic initiatives	X		$.65 M	$.5 M	Spring 2011

**FIGURE 35.3   CASCADING ALIGNMENT OF BALANCED
SCORECARD TO DASHBOARDS**

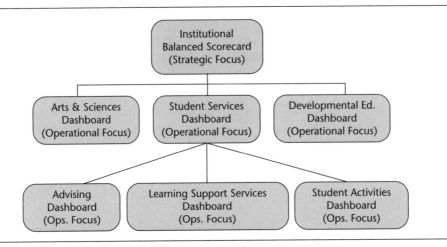

It is vitally important to communicate the strategy to stakeholders and the entire institution; the fourth practice. If people do not understand the strategy, they will not know how to align their work with the institution's strategic goals. The balanced scorecard, the operations dashboards, the strategy map, the BSC spreadsheet, a description of the strategic planning process, being involved in the developing operations plans for a strategic initiative—all of these are ways in which the strategy can be communicated to the organization. When the objective is to ensure that the entire organization understands the strategy, it is impossible to overcommunicate (Kaplan & Norton, 2008).

A fifth practice is to review the strategy (Kaplan & Norton, 2008). "Strategy reviews are essential for effective strategy execution. However, very few organizations have them. Operational reviews, in contrast, are fairly common. Because operational reviews take place within organizational silos, they are easier to conduct. In contrast, strategy reviews are cross-functional and require top leadership involvement. . . . A good performance management system makes it easy to do strategy reviews and link them to operational reviews through the use of drill downs. Presidents, vice presidents, academic leaders and analysts can all drill down to more detail as they see fit" (Beckett & McComb, 2009, p. 16). The balanced scorecard is the primary strategy review tool, and the operational dashboards are the primary operational review tools.

The sixth practice is to update the strategy (Kaplan & Norton, 2008). When the results of a strategy review or an operational review indicate that a change in the strategy is required, the strategy must be updated. Although simple and straightforward, the step is sometimes not carried out. Many institutions use a three- to five-year strategic plan horizon. However, updating the strategy annually and conducting a complete overhaul of the plan on a five-year basis is an effective way to balance a steady strategy with appropriate updates based on changing conditions.

Conclusion

Measuring at a strategic level through KPIs, strategy maps, and balanced scorecards or dashboards is a systematic approach that can assist an institution in executing its strategy. With the IR professional at the center of much of this development, such tools are enormously helpful to top leaders.

References

Ballentine, H., & Eckles, J. (2009). Dueling scorecards: How two colleges utilize the popular planning method. *Planning for Higher Education, 37*(3), 27–35.

Beckett, T., & McComb, B. E. (2009). *Increase enrollment, retention, and student success: Best practices for information delivery and strategic alignment.* An Expert Series White Paper: Information Builders, Inc. Retrieved from http://www.informationbuilders.com/cgi-shell/products/whitepaper/whitepaper_form.pl?Whitepaper_Code=8940

Carpenter-Hubin, J., & Hornsby, E. E. (2005, Fall). *Making measurement meaningful.* AIR Professional File, no. 97. Tallahassee, FL: Association for Institutional Research.

Few, S. (2006). *Information dashboard design: The effective visual communication of data.* Sebastopol, CA: O'Reilly.

Kaplan, R. S. (2010). Conceptual foundations of the balanced scorecard. Working paper 10–074.

Kaplan, R. S., & Norton, D. P. (1996). *The balanced scorecard: Translating strategy into action.* Boston: Harvard Business School Press.

Kaplan, R. S., & Norton, D. P. (2004). *Strategy maps: Converting intangible assets into tangible outcomes.* Boston: Harvard Business School Press.

Kaplan, R. S., & Norton, D. P. (2008). *The execution premium: Linking strategy to operations for competitive advantage.* Boston: Harvard Business Press.

Lyddon, J. W., & McComb, B. E. (2008, Spring). Strategic reporting tool: Balanced scorecards in higher education. *Journal of Applied Research in the Community College, 15*(2), 138–145.

Mizak, J. P. (2010, March). Results of survey of members of NEAIR, AJCU, and WNYIR communities regarding dashboards and balanced scorecards. Unpublished.

Niven, P. R. (2003). *Balanced scorecard step-by-step for government and nonprofit agencies.* New York: Wiley.

Sapp, M. M. (1994, Winter). *Setting up a key success index report: A how-to manual.* AIR Professional File. Tallahassee, FL: Association for Institutional Research.

Terkla, D. G., Wiseman, M., & Cohen, M. (2005, August). Institutional dashboards: Navigational tool for colleges and universities. Paper presented at the 27th annual EAIR Forum.

CHAPTER 36

DEVELOPING INSTITUTIONAL COMPARISONS

Glenn W. James

Institutional research includes analysis of the internal activity and operations of a higher education institution. Although some assessment and review are focused internally on the primary institution, there is value in comparing the information from internal institutional assessment and review with the corresponding information for one or more other institutions. This interinstitutional comparison and benchmarking process provides an important context in which to evaluate the information about the primary institution.

The comparison of primary institutional measures to appropriate corresponding measures from other institutions or groups of institutions can be a catalyst for examining reasons for the differences and for discussion of the meaning and usefulness of the comparison information. This type of comparative study can be a helpful input in the institutional process of measuring progress or of developing strategic direction for institutional improvement.

In contrast to methodologies in previous decades, data sources now are more extensive and accessible, and analytical tools are more powerful and easy to use. Nevertheless, in conducting interinstitutional analyses, the appropriate development of groups of comparison institutions is crucial (Teeter & Brinkman, 2003). Not only are interinstitutional comparisons useful in strategic planning and decision making, but comparative data also can be useful for developing budget requests and justifying adjustments to tuition, salaries, and teaching loads (Teeter & Brinkman, 2003). Interinstitutional comparisons also provide for evaluating institutional competitors, developing benchmarks, identifying areas of weakness, and guiding policy development (McLaughlin and Howard, 2005).

This chapter provides information about (1) sources of comparison data, (2) methods and tools for accessing and analyzing comparison data, (3) types of interinstitutional comparison groups, (4) methods for developing comparison groups, and (5) uses of group comparisons.

Institutional Data Sources

A variety of data sources are available for interinstitutional comparisons, with most of these sources being in one of three principal types: (1) national databases and web resources, (2) data exchanges and consortia, and (3) targeted data collections.

National Databases and Web Resources

In American higher education, the most available and most commonly used national database is the Integrated Postsecondary Education Data System (IPEDS), a comprehensive national institutional data source operated by the National Center for Education Statistics (NCES) in the Institute of Education Sciences of the United States Department of Education.

IPEDS contains data about institutional characteristics, enrollment, student retention rates, graduation rates, degree completions, financial aid, staffing, salaries, and finance. Selected data elements from IPEDS are available in a basic comparison web tool called College Navigator. NCES provides more powerful web tools for data selection, management, and analysis in the IPEDS Data Center, which is available in the IPEDS main website (http://nces.ed.gov/ipeds). NCES also provides a Data Feedback Report that displays information about a standard group of data elements and for a comparison group of institutions that is generated by NCES. In addition to receiving the standard Data Feedback Report, institutional users can request or produce Data Feedback Reports based on customized groups of institutions, as selected by the institutional user (National Center for Education Statistics, 2010). (More detailed information about NCES data and tools is available in this volume in Chapter 21.)

Other web tools and resources that use NCES and IPEDS data are available from the Association of Governing Boards (http://www.agb.org), the Education Trust (http://www.edtrust.org), the National Association of College and University Business Officers (NACUBO) (http://www.nacubo.org), and the National Center for Higher Education Management Systems (NCHEMS) (http://www.nchems.org). These and various higher education management consulting firms and other specialized users of IPEDS data either facilitate easier use of selected data elements, integrate data from other sources, and/or provide analyses using IPEDS data.

Certain college search information providers offer sources of national institutional comparison data, as well. Example providers or data sources include American College Testing (ACT), the College Board, the Common Data Set (CDS), and *U.S. News and World Report*.

Data Exchanges and Consortia

Data exchanges and consortia are a second source for data and analyses. For example, the Higher Education Data Sharing (HEDS) consortium (http://www.e-heds.org) comprises independent colleges and universities.

HEDS member institutions collect and share institutional comparative data that are used for internal assessment and benchmarking, as part of institutional efforts in effective strategic planning (Higher Education Data Sharing, 2010; Trainer, 1996). Similarly, the Association of American Universities Data Exchange (AAUDE) (http://www.aaude.org) comprises member institutions of the Association of American Universities (AAU). Another example is the Council of Independent Colleges (CIC) (http://www.cic.edu). Although data exchanges and consortia can be sources of useful data and analyses, Sapp (1996) warned about potential limitations and disadvantages associated with irregularities and inconsistencies in shared data.

In some states, the system of public higher education institutions serves as a delimited data-sharing consortium, with comparison of certain kinds of institutional data but perhaps with less useful institutional comparisons, because some of the institutions are not similar types of postsecondary education institutions. Correspondingly, some state associations of independent institutions provide limited data sharing for basic, general comparison purposes. (For more discussion of data exchanges, see Chapter 25.)

Targeted Data Collections

Similar to data exchanges and consortia, targeted data collections are focused on a specific subject or function, such as employee compensation, instructional costs, or student retention. Examples of targeted data collections are the annual compensation studies by the College and University Professional Association for Human Resources (CUPA-HR) (http://www.cupahr.org) and the American Association of University Professors (AAUP) (http://www.aaup.org).

National comparative information about instructional costs in four-year institutions is available from the National Study of Instructional Costs and Productivity, also known as the Delaware Study because the study is based at the University of Delaware (http://www.udel.edu/IR/cost). A national study about community colleges is the National Community College Benchmark Project (NCCBP) (http://www.nccbp.org), which is operated at Johnson County Community College in Overland Park, Kansas.

Another example of a targeted data collection is at the Consortium for Student Retention Data Exchange (CSRDE), based at the University of Oklahoma. CSRDE operates a national collection of institutional data regarding student retention and graduation rates (http://csrde.ou.edu). The Faculty Salary Survey of Institutions Belonging to the Association of Public and Land-Grant Universities also is called simply the Faculty Salary Survey by Discipline; it is operated by Oklahoma State University (http://vpaf.okstate.edu/irim/facultysalary.html). This survey provides faculty salary information from a targeted group of public universities. (Again, see Chapter 25 for more information about various data exchanges and consortia.)

Methods and Web Tools for Data Access and Analysis

NCES has developed and improved the availability of IPEDS data and the corresponding tools to access, select, and manage comparative data about higher education institutions. Basic comparative analyses can be performed with NCES online web tools, or data can be selected and downloaded for more extensive analysis. The following is a brief description of these tools; see Chapter 21 for more detailed descriptions.

College Navigator

College Navigator (http://nces.ed.gov/collegenavigator/), a college search web tool from NCES, is designed to assist prospective college students in exploring and comparing basic selected characteristics and information about postsecondary educational institutions in the United States. The simple selections in the user interface are easy to operate, and an array of IPEDS information can be compared across user-chosen institutions. Categories include General Information, Tuition/Fees/Estimated Student Expenses, Financial Aid, Enrollment, Admissions, Retention/Graduation Rates, Curricular Programs, Varsity Athletic Teams, Accreditation, Campus Security, and Federal Loans.

IPEDS Data Center

As indicated by the name, the IPEDS Data Center (http://nces.ed.gov/ipeds/datacenter), developed by NCES, provides access to institutional data and facilitates basic comparative analyses, allowing the user to create reports and to build and download customized data files. Data Center functions include comparing institutions, ranking institutions by one variable, viewing the trend for one variable, creating group statistics, generating predefined reports, downloading survey data files, downloading custom data files, analyzing data with the PowerStats tool, and downloading the IPEDS Data Feedback Report (DFR). The PowerStats data analysis tool provides access to nine NCES postsecondary education datasets and the thousands of variables in those datasets.

IPEDS Data Feedback Report

The Data Feedback Report (http://nces.ed.gov/ipeds/datacenter/) provides comparative information about such measures as fall enrollment, full-time equivalent (FTE) students, unduplicated headcount enrollment, graduation rates, degree completions, full-time equivalent staff, instructional staff salaries, core revenues and expenses, and tuition and fees. The Data Feedback Report provides comparative information about the primary institution and either (1) an automatically generated group of comparison institutions or (2) a custom-generated group of comparison institutions.

A customized comparison group can be developed by the primary institution and submitted to NCES by the IPEDS Keyholder, the principal IPEDS reporting official at the primary institution. Otherwise, NCES provides a group of comparison institutions through use of an algorithm developed by NCES. The selection criteria include institutional level, institutional control (regarding public or private institutions), Carnegie Classification, enrollment, and other variables.

A customized comparison group can be developed through use of a variety of general or specialized criterion variables available in the IPEDS data universe. The resulting customized comparison group is restricted to no more than one hundred institutions, but a useful final comparison group typically comprises considerably fewer than that. (For more discussion of NCES tools, see Chapter 21.)

Developing Institutional Comparison Groups

Use of a poorly developed comparison group can yield comparison information that is distorted or invalid; consequently, it can lead to poor decision making and policy development. Therefore it is important to seek to develop a strongly reasoned comparison group and to recognize the purpose and understand the relative strengths and limitations of using that comparison group.

Types of Groups

As described by Teeter and Brinkman (2003), typically there are four types of institutional comparison groups: competitor, aspirational, predetermined, and peer.

Competitor Comparison Group. The first type, the competitor comparison group, comprises institutions that compete with each other for students, faculty, or financial resources, even though the institutions may not be the same type. The basis for developing this type of group is the resource for which institutions are competing. For example, a frequently occurring competition is the recruitment and enrollment of students. In developing a competitor group of comparison institutions, the focal institution could seek to identify the institutions at which accepted but non-enrolling applicants of the focal institution had actually enrolled. The National Student Clearinghouse provides a service for this type of search. A technique for identifying other institutions to which students applied for admission is to obtain information about where applicants sent their entrance test scores, such as ACT or SAT scores.

Aspirational Comparison Group. A second type of institutional comparison group is the aspirational comparison group, which includes institutions that may have some similarities to the primary institution but also have characteristics that are worthy of emulation. For example, the aspirational comparison group could contain institutions that are somewhat similar to the primary institution but have a one-year freshman retention rate that is notably higher than that of the primary institution. The primary institution is seeking to improve its one-year freshman retention rate, and the group of aspirational comparison institutions was selected with this goal in mind. However, the primary institution must use the aspirational comparison group carefully and with appropriate labeling of "aspirational," so that the institutional group is not confused with a standard peer grouping. Such confusion could result in reduced credibility and cause political damage related to the use and perceived abuse of interinstitutional group comparisons.

Predetermined Comparison Group. A third type of comparison group is the predetermined group. Teeter and Brinkman (2003) described a predetermined comparison group as one in which the institutions are arranged for a purpose outside of the primary institution. They described four general categories of predetermined comparison groups: natural, traditional, jurisdictional, and classification-based.

- *Natural* predetermined groups are based on an existing institutional relationship, such as a location, a regional compact, or an athletic conference. The institutions already are in a visible group, and it is natural to consider the institutions to be appropriate for general comparisons. However, the specific type of comparison is crucial in determining whether the comparison is appropriate. Examples of natural groups are institutions in the Southern Universities Group (SUG), the Tennessee Board of Regents System, or the Big Ten Athletic Conference.
- *Traditional* predetermined groups are based on history. The traditional group can be familiar and perhaps has wide acceptance, but certain institutional comparisons may not be appropriate. An example of a traditional group is the Ivies, a group of eight independent institutions in the northeastern United States.
- *Jurisdictional* predetermined groups are composed of institutions with the same political or legal jurisdiction, even though some institutional comparisons might be dubious because the institutions are not particularly similar. For example, community colleges in an urban area might be identified as a comparison group. Establishing such a group can be appropriate regarding similar environment and context if the jurisdiction is sufficiently homogeneous, but establishing such a group also involves the risk of containing dramatically different institutions when the jurisdiction is defined too broadly and contains institutions that are radically different in key characteristics.
- *Classification-based* predetermined groups are those based on a national institutional classification, such as the taxonomy developed by the Carnegie Foundation for the Advancement of Teaching (2005). Use of

the Carnegie Classification provides a national grouping method that is commonly used and generally accepted, using the benefits of credibility and name recognition. The current classification has a basic category and five special-purpose categories that include all institutions (http://classifications.carnegie foundation.org). These six all-inclusive Carnegie categories also are part of the IPEDS data and provide a basic, general classification, as well as information about such dimensions as size and setting, enrollment profile, undergraduate profile, undergraduate instructional program, and graduate instructional program. One disadvantage of using classification-based groups is that the assignment to groups was based on a limited number of classification variables, which may not be pertinent to the application of the user. Teeter and Brinkman (2003) warned that classification-based groups may contain too much within-group variation for certain types of comparative analyses.

Peer Comparison Group. A fourth type of comparison group is the peer group. The peer comparison group consists of institutions with a similar mission and scope. Peer groups provide for the grouping of institutions that generally are similar but need not be nearly identical. The institutions can share certain categorical variables, such as "public land-grant university in the Western United States." However, the institutions can also have similar characteristics according to interval variables constructed to represent enrollment size, externally sponsored research expenditures, and educational and general expenditures per FTE student.

Methods for Developing Groups

As described by Teeter and Brinkman (2003), the spectrum of methods for developing groups can range from statistical approaches to approaches that are entirely dependent on judgment. The typology developed by Teeter and Brinkman classifies the most common procedures into four categories: (1) threshold, (2) cluster analysis, (3) panel review, and (4) hybrid.

Threshold Method. The threshold approach (sometimes called "nearest neighbor") establishes allowable ranges for the measures of specified institutional attributes (Teeter & Brinkman, 2003; Xu, 2008). This approach typically involves the use of both nominal variables and interval variables. Nominal variables are used to delimit the universe of higher education institutions to a more appropriate and useful set of comparison institutions. For example, in developing a group of prospective comparison institutions for a public university, "institutional control" could be used to select public institutions and not select private institutions. Similarly, an "institutional type" variable could be used to select universities and not select other types of postsecondary educational institutions. After a more useful subset of prospective institutions has been created by the use of nominal variables, then interval variables for a chosen set of attributes are used to rank order these remaining institutions in terms of the proximity to the measures of the primary institution. Examples of such attributes are the undergraduate percentage of enrollment, the part-time percentage of enrollment, and a curriculum indicator such as the engineering degree percentage of total degrees awarded. An allowable range is chosen for each attribute, and then a point system is used to provide for scoring of the prospective comparison institutions. If a prospective comparison institution is not similar to the primary institution on a certain attribute, then a score of zero could be assigned to the prospective comparison institution. If the prospective institution is somewhat similar to the primary institution, then a score of one point could be assigned. If the prospective institution is similar to the primary institution, then a score of two points could be assigned. Scores could then be summed to rank order the prospective institutions in terms of proximity of the measures to those of the primary institution. This point system can also be weighted by an importance criterion; based on this, decisions at the primary institution provide an importance value for each of the attributes.

Use of the threshold method identifies comparison institutions by determining the proximity of certain institutional characteristics to a chosen set of attributes. The resulting rank-ordered listing of institutions is then reviewed and final selection of the comparison institutions is made by the expert judgment of analysts and administrators at the primary institution. A detailed example of this process was provided by Xu (2008) in volume 110 of the *AIR Professional File*.

Teeter and Brinkman (2003) claimed that the threshold approach provides an ordered guide, but that the comparison criteria, ranges, and weights, as well as the final selection of comparison institutions, is made by judgment. They contend that the procedure is designed to use judgment built on the use of institutional characteristics and data. Although the transparency of the procedure is a positive feature, it also raises the risk of manipulation in the selection of comparison institutions. A variation of the threshold approach has been used extensively by the National Center for Higher Education Management Systems (NCHEMS) in its consultation with institutions and state systems of higher education institutions (Teeter & Brinkman, 2003; Brinkman & Teeter, 1987).

Cluster Analysis Method. Cluster analysis involves substantial use of multivariate statistics, with the inherent advantages of using a large number of institutional attributes and also developing the results in what may be the most objective way (Della Mea, 1989; Korb, 1982; Terenzini, Hartmark, Lorang, & Shirley, 1980). The disadvantage of this approach is the statistical complexity, which could be less than optimal in terms of (1) the necessary expertise to develop the results and (2) the political acceptance of those results at the primary institution (Teeter & Brinkman, 2003; Hurley, 2002). (For more information about cluster analysis, see the description by Luan, Kumar, Sujitparapitaya, & Bohannon in Chapter 28.)

Panel Review Method. Panel review is a method based on the informed judgment of a panel of reviewers. This method does not involve algorithms or statistical analytical techniques. Instead, a panel of institutional reviewers deliberates and develops consensus about the selection of an appropriate group of comparison institutions for the primary institution. Although the comparison group selection is developed by the judgment of knowledgeable reviewers, there nevertheless can be risk in the acceptance of the resulting comparison group, which may appear to reflect the suspected bias or manipulation of the reviewers (Teeter & Brinkman, 2003; Xu, 2008).

Hybrid Method. The hybrid method uses data, statistical analysis, and judgment to develop the group of comparison institutions (Teeter & Brinkman, 2003; Zhao & Dean, 1997). Because the hybrid approach incorporates the benefits of expert judgment and the empirical strength of data and statistical analysis, this method is considered to have the strength, balance, and benefits of both a judgment approach and a statistical analytical approach (Zhao & Dean, 1997; Xu, 2008; Ingram, 1995).

In using threshold or hybrid methods, the selection of appropriate variables is crucial (Teeter & Brinkman, 2003; Xu, 2008; Borden, 2005). The rationale for using the selected characteristics variables should be described and discussed, because the resulting group of comparison institutions will vary considerably depending on which institutional characteristic variables are used in the comparison group selection process. Several common types of institutional characteristic variables are important in the process of comparison group selection. Institutional size, often indicated by enrollment, has important implications for institutional structure, complexity, culture, finances, and other institutional aspects (Carnegie Foundation for the Advancement of Teaching, 2005; Xu, 2008). Enrollment intensity, or the differences in the proportions of undergraduate students in terms of full-time and part-time course load status, affects course scheduling, student services, extracurricular activities, time to degree, and other factors (Carnegie Foundation for the Advancement of Teaching, 2005; Xu, 2008). Student mix, research activity, and curricular program mix also have important implications for the development of a useful group of comparison institutions (Xu, 2008).

Xu (2008) provided these recommendations about the crucial process of variable selection:

1. Use clearly defined variables with reliable data.
2. Use percentages or ratios instead of absolute values, where applicable.
3. To avoid overweighting certain constructs in the statistical analysis, avoid duplicated or highly correlated measures.

Uses of Group Comparisons

As indicated previously in this chapter, the use of an appropriately developed comparison group is of considerable importance, so that subsequent comparison analyses can be conducted with reasonable confidence. Nevertheless, information that is developed from comparison analyses also must be used appropriately and carefully.

The development of comparison information is for improving the understanding of selected aspects of an institution and its operations. Comparative information should be a catalyst for review, discussion, and additional exploration and analysis. To illustrate this point, what does it mean when the primary institution has a measure that is either less than or greater than the mean value for the comparison group? Is that a positive or negative finding, and why? For example, for a given functional area of institutional operations, if average cost per FTE student is less at the primary institution than the mean value of that measure for the comparison group, is that a positive or a negative result for the primary institution? That is, does lower-than-average cost indicate that the primary institution is more efficient and perhaps more effective, or does it indicate that the primary institution has a weak, inadequate budget for that functional area? An answer to this question may not be immediately apparent. Therefore, interpretation and application of results from comparison analyses must be used very carefully and should, wherever feasible, be reviewed by those with expertise about that specific measure or functional area.

Benchmarking

Interinstitutional comparison information and analysis can be used for benchmarking the performance of the primary institution: to track progress, to compare performance of the primary institution with the performance of other institutions, and to develop a form of quality assurance (McLaughlin & Howard, 2005). (Benchmarking as part of setting strategy is discussed in Chapter 34.)

Decision Support

Another important application of interinstitutional comparison information and analysis is to inform the institutional decision-making process. Part of the standard role of institutional researchers is to provide information and analyses to support decision making at the institution. Use of interinstitutional comparison information and analysis adds to the existing body of information about internal comparison of current performance with previous performance at the institution. Although analysis focused only on the primary institution does have utility, the value of that analysis can be expanded when interinstitutional comparison information is also used. Instead of an isolated analysis about the primary institution, the expanded perspective has implications for developing greater understanding about the primary institution and for providing useful support to the decision-making process. This expanded perspective can be quite helpful to senior level administrators and decision makers.

Benefits and Limitations of Group Comparisons

As has been cited, the uses of group comparisons can enrich the benchmarking process and can expand and enlighten the decision-making process at higher education institutions. Comparison group information provides direct context and facilitates greater understanding of measures and processes at the primary institution. Nevertheless, there also are practical limitations to the information, the analyses, and the process of using comparison group results.

Fundamental concerns about the validity, accuracy, and reliability of shared institutional data are always an embedded part of interinstitutional comparisons (Teeter & Brinkman, 2003). However, improvements in standardizing data collection procedures and data definitions are an especially important characteristic of IPEDS, which has the advantage of greater completeness of data as well. Some data-sharing consortia and other data sources may use some of the same data elements as those found in IPEDS, but institutional researchers must continue to be vigilant and careful about using or combining data from multiple sources. Certain applications of comparison group analysis require greater precision in the underlying data, such as management control analyses; other applications, such as strategic planning, can perhaps tolerate somewhat less precision in the data without causing irregularities and problems (Teeter & Brinkman, 2003).

The evolving culture of accountability and analysis provides a certain imperative about interinstitutional comparisons. Therefore, institutional researchers must develop institutional comparison groups carefully, purposefully, and with an appropriate method that also will be acceptable to the users of the comparison analyses at the primary institution. Involving interested parties early in the process can be helpful in developing the necessary political support for comparison analyses to be useful at the primary institution (Teeter & Brinkman, 2003). The technical, data-driven parts and the judgment and political aspects are all important in the development of institutional comparison groups that will be applicable and useful at the institution.

References

Brinkman, P. T., & Teeter, D. J. (1987). Methods for selecting comparison groups. In P. T. Brinkman (Ed.), *Conducting interinstitutional comparisons* (pp. 5–23). New Directions for Institutional Research, no. 53. San Francisco: Jossey-Bass.

Borden, V.M.H. (2005). Identifying and analyzing group differences. In M. A. Coughlin (Ed.), *Application of intermediate/advanced statistics in institutional research.* Tallahassee, FL: Association for Institutional Research.

Carnegie Foundation for the Advancement of Teaching. (2005). The Carnegie Classification of institutions of higher education. Retrieved from http://classifications .carnegiefoundation.org/

Della Mea, C. L. (1989). A comparison of two procedures for peer group assignment of institutions of higher education (Doctoral dissertation, Virginia Polytechnic Institute and State University, 1989). *Dissertation Abstracts International, 50*(4), 838. (ProQuest No. 746594831)

Higher Education Data Sharing (HEDS) Consortium. (2010). HEDS website home page. Retrieved from http://www.e-heds.org/

Hurley, R. G. (2002, Spring). Identification and assessment of community college peer institution selection systems. *Community College Review, 29*(4), 1–27.

Ingram, J. A. (1995). *Using IPEDS data for selecting peer institutions.* Paper presentation at the annual meeting of the Association for Institutional Research, Boston, MA. (ERIC Document Reproduction Service No. ED 387 010)

Korb, R. (1982). *Clusters of colleges and universities: An empirically determined system.* Washington, DC: National Center for Education Statistics. (ERIC Document Reproduction Service No. ED 227 797)

Luan, J., Kumar, T., Sujitparapitaya, S., & Bohannon, T. (2012). Exploring and mining data. In R. D. Howard, W. E. Knight, & G. W. McLaughlin (Eds.), *The handbook of institutional research* (pp. 478–501). San Francisco: Jossey-Bass.

McLaughlin, G. W., & Howard, R. D. (2005, May). *Comparison groups: Data and decisions.* Workshop presented at the annual meeting of the Association for Institutional Research, San Diego, CA.

National Center for Education Statistics. (2010). Executive Peer Tool. Retrieved from http://nces.ed.gov/ipedspas/expt/

Sapp, M. M. (1996). Benefits and potential problems associated with effective data-sharing consortia. In J. F. Trainer (Ed.), *Inter-institutional data exchange: When to do it, what to look for, and how to make it work* (pp. 15–28). New Directions for Institutional Research, no. 89. San Francisco: Jossey-Bass.

Teeter, D. J., & Brinkman, P. T. (2003). Peer institutions. In W. E. Knight (Ed.), *The primer for institutional research.* Tallahassee, FL: Association for Institutional Research.

Terenzini, P. T., Hartmark, L., Lorang, W. G., & Shirley, R. C. (1980). A conceptual and methodological approach to the identification of peer institutions. *Research in Higher Education, 12*(4), 347–362.

Trainer, J. F. (Ed.). (1996). To share and share alike: The basic ground rules for inter-institutional data sharing. In J. F. Trainer (Ed.), *Inter-institutional data exchange: When to do it, what to look for, and how to make it work* (pp. 5–13). New Directions for Institutional Research, no. 89. San Francisco: Jossey-Bass.

Xu, J. (2008, Winter). Using the IPEDS Peer Analysis System in peer group selection. *AIR Professional File, 110.* Tallahassee, FL: Association for Institutional Research.

Zhao, J., & Dean, D. C. (1997, May). *Selecting peer institutions: A hybrid approach.* Paper presentation at the annual meeting of the Association for Institutional Research, Orlando, FL. (ERIC Document Reproduction Service No. ED 410 877)

CHAPTER 37

TOOLS FOR IMPROVING INSTITUTIONAL EFFECTIVENESS

Jonathan D. Fife and Stephen D. Spangehl

As a result of a decrease in both public and private funding of higher education institutions, institutional research professionals today find themselves in a position of growing importance in their institutions, facing new challenges that require new thinking, new tools, and a new proactive teaching role. These external pressures are demanding that institutions prove to the public that they are worthy of their support. These pressures come in two forms:

• *Accountability:* Institutions need to account for themselves—not just for what they earn and spend, but for what they accomplish for their students, employees, communities, states, and nation. It used to be sufficient to account for *outputs*—for example, the numbers of students passing courses and earning degrees—but now people want to know the *outcomes* as well: Did passing those courses teach students what they needed to know? Did earning those degrees provide the foundation for a fulfilling life and career? Measuring *outcomes* requires that we weigh competing and difficult-to-calculate values, and it is far more challenging than merely counting events. Yet virtually every institution turns first to their IR staff for guidance in assessing students' outputs rather than outcomes.

• *Effectiveness:* Compliance with accreditation and external reporting requirements is essential but not sufficient. Generating reports used to be enough to qualify one as a successful institutional researcher. The new expectation is that institutional researchers will take a more active role in identifying, collecting, analyzing , and applying data to assist the institution to more effectively achieve its ever-changing vision and mission—caused by increased international competition and student employment opportunities requiring greater critical thinking and technical skills, and as technology increases the transportability of work. The college or university that cannot find ways to improve its effectiveness—and ways to decrease its costs while doing so—will find itself a target for criticism.

IR professionals therefore have a major responsibility; they can no longer just impartially observe how well their institution works and report the data to insiders and outsiders; rather, they must be an active force in helping their institution improve its impact by lowering costs and increasing effectiveness. A major part of this is to educate their faculty and staff colleagues, imparting the knowledge and skill they need to use data intelligently to make the right decisions for the institution. To be able to do this, IR offices must understand the theoretical bases of creating an effective organization (Chaffee & Sherr, 1992).

Business Theory: Misunderstandings and Cultural Differences

There are a number of reasons why theories, concepts, and tools originating in the for-profit world have been rejected in the culture of higher education. The first is the belief that business theory is based on maximizing profits, which is not a goal of higher education. In fact, business theory is based on the concept of creating a sustainable organization that is continuously working to achieve and expand its vision, values, and goals, and, as a result, to create a fair return for the investors. This is the core of all enterprises, so these theories apply just as well to higher education institutions. The only difference is that higher education's return to its investors is the improvement and enlightenment of society through the creation, understanding, and transference of knowledge.

The second obstacle is a conflict with the language of business and that of higher education. Businesses are managed; higher education institutions are administered. Business employees' success depends on their responsiveness to the directions of upper-management; faculty are not employees in the traditional sense but often see themselves as independent scholars, part of a shared governance system that sets the academic policies for the administration of the organization. Businesses believe that everyone should be working for the common vision and values of the organization; faculty departments were established to protect their members from interference from other academic departments and the administration. Companies depend on the satisfaction of their customers; faculty often feel that they do not have customers—they teach students, create scholarship, and serve as equals with the other faculty members.

These language and organizational culture differences can be seen in the attempts to introduce the tools of total quality management (TQM) into higher education. The response by the faculty was uniformly negative because of the belief that: (1) nothing is ever total, (2) the institution they are at is already a quality organization, and (3) faculty are not managed, but have administrators whose job is to see that the organization functions effectively and gives them the freedom to pursue their intellectual areas of study.

The third obstacle is the lack of continuous development of skills in all parts of employees' sphere of responsibility. Large businesses spend between 3 to 5 percent of their *total personnel budget* on continuous education; small companies spend between 5 and 8 percent. Excluding the cost of sending faculty to academic conferences to give a paper, there are limited sources of data concerning what higher education spends on faculty and administrative staff training related to increasing their skills to further the core values of the institution. It has been estimated to be less than .5 percent of the total personnel budget.

One way to overcome these obstacles is to create new ways of measurement, *both quantitative and qualitative,* that are sensitive to the customs and language of higher education and help to advance ways to promote a more effective organization as defined by the resources needed to achieve the institution's mission.

The Power of the Underlying Concepts of an Effective Quality Institution

To use the tools of measuring the effectiveness of an institution and discover ways to make it more effective, it is necessary to understand the concepts central to organizational effectiveness.

The Organization as a Collection of Relationships and Processes

The following two concepts are central to understanding an organization as a whole. First, all organizations are made up of relationships that are both interrelated and interdependent. The larger the organization, the more complex these relationships become. These relationships are formed and linked through the organization's culture, which is the sum of individuals' beliefs about what the organization stands for (its core values) and how it should work (what the appropriate processes are).

Second, a change in one relationship eventually affects many other relationships. Because of this interconnectivity, it may take months or even years for the results of a change to be become observable. An example of this is when the faculty agrees to raise the admission standards in order to improve the institution's national ranking—the intended consequence. However, higher standards may mean fewer students are accepted, and therefore the institution receives lower revenues. This in turn may result in discontinuing programs, and staff and faculty reductions—the unintended consequences.

The Construct of an Institutional Culture

Organizations that have been able to be increasingly effective are those who recognize a hieratical interconnection among the major elements that form its organizational culture. If the organization does not recognize this hierarchy, there are usually major breakdowns in the organization's effectiveness. Figure 37.1 presents a conceptual design developed after an analysis of over three hundred books and articles related to effective organizations (Freed, Klugman, & Fife, 1997).

There are three components represented in this figure. First, the effectiveness of an institution is defined by the institution's ability to meet the expectations of it constituencies. Therefore the core values of an institution, as represented in its vision, mission, and outcomes statements, need to be based on the needs and expectations of its various constituencies. This is the heart and soul—the core values—of the institution. All activities need to be linked to the support and development of this core.

Second is an understanding that the effectiveness of an institution is determined by how well individuals' short- and long-term interactions consistently produce results that support the accomplishment of the long-term vision of the institution. For these interactions to be successful, there must be a common understanding of how these interactions will occur, the common values that are embodied in the interactions, and the desired results. This is represented

FIGURE 37.1 BASIC ELEMENTS OF AN EFFECTIVE ORGANIZATION

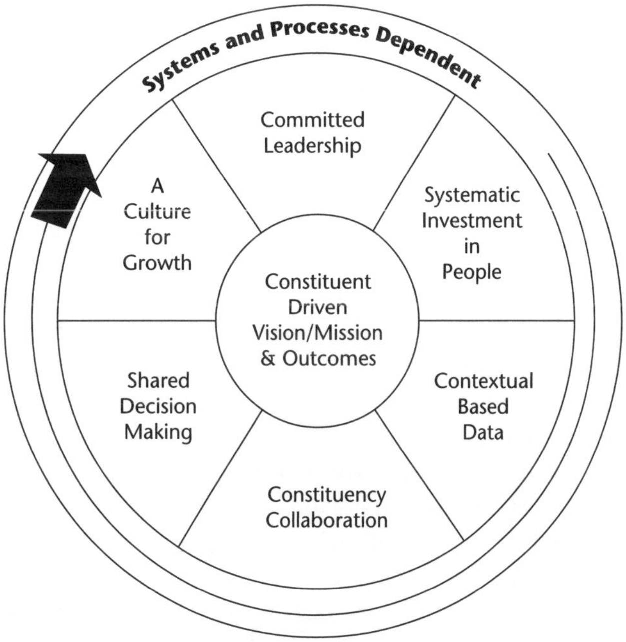

in the processes and systems of the organization as represented by the outer boundary of this model. This commonly held value-based boundary of systems and procedures is what holds the organization together.

Third, the interior, between the model's outer border and its core, are six essential elements that continuously link the core values with the institution's systems and processes, which produces the institution's culture. The effectiveness of these six elements depends on two conditions: the degree to which they are linked to both the institution's core and its processes, and how well the preceding activity has been developed.

These six elements are arranged in order of their interrelationship with each other.

• First, there must be *committed leadership* throughout the organization that supports the concept of developing an organizational culture dedicated to the institution's core values.

• Second, without a *systematic investment in people* that purposefully focuses on the knowledge and skills—related to fulfilling the vision, mission, and outcomes of the institution—of all the people who make up the institution, it is highly unlikely that the vision and mission of the institution will be accomplished. Fundamental to the systematic investment in people is understanding what skills are needed for each position and ensuring that there is an opportunity for individuals to get this training. Although this may be seen as the responsibility of the human resource office, IR offices can play a key role in identifying what type of training is needed.

• The third element—*context-based data*—is central to the IR office. One specific skill that institution decision makers need is how to interpret data collected by the IR office. One key to effective IR is being able to present data in the context of the institution's core values and processes (Terenzini, 1999). Many of the data requests IR offices receive have to deal with output data—for example, the number of students who failed, how many students are in a major, or the percentage of students graduating. Although this type of data is necessary for many reasons, it is the data that give context to fulfilling specific goals of the institution that make a difference in the future performance of the institution. To paraphrase Edwards Deming, data without context are just meaningless numbers and words. Context-based data make the difference in knowing how well the institution's core vision and mission are being met and which processes are not effectively contributing to increasing the effectiveness of the institution.

• Without contextually based data, the fourth element—*constituency collaboration*—is less likely to be achieved. Effective constituency collaboration depends on the identification of which constituencies a unit is most dependent on for its success and which constituencies are dependent on the unit for their success. When equipped with context-based data, units are better able to recognize these constituency relationships and work to make these relationships more effective. (For additional discussion of managing change and system thinking, see Chapter 7.)

• Because of the relationships in an organization whose major employees are professionals and who serve a multiple of different constituents, top-down decision making does not work. If the first four elements are functioning well, the fifth element—*shared decision making*—is more likely to develop, because an organizational culture that is trusting and willing to change has been created. For IR offices it is important to know these elements of an effective organization in order to develop quantitative and qualitative measurements that are contextually related to the institution, its organizational culture, and its processes.

The Closed System of Maintaining an Effective Organization

A closed system is a group of processes that continuously affect each other, directly or indirectly; therefore a change in one process will eventually affect all the processes. The continuous adaptation model (Figure 37.2), also known as the continuous improvement model, is an example of a closed, reinforcing process.

Figure 37.1 represents the essential elements needed to build an institutional culture that is based on linking core values with its systems and processes. Figure 37.2 represents a closed system that is used to regularly assess each process to ensure its focus on the institution's core values.

• *Approach process.* This is the articulation or planning of how each process is intended to function toward achieving the core outcomes of the institution. The institution's strategic plan usually articulates many of these links.

• *Deployment processes.* This represents the elements—organizational structure, policies, procedures, processes, and daily actions—that function together to accomplish the goals of the strategic plan.

• *Measurement and contextual analysis.* This is the point at which IR offices have the opportunity to play a major role in forwarding the goals of the institution. It also may be the most politically sensitive area of analysis. Here connections are

FIGURE 37.2   CYCLE OF CONTINUOUS ADAPTATION

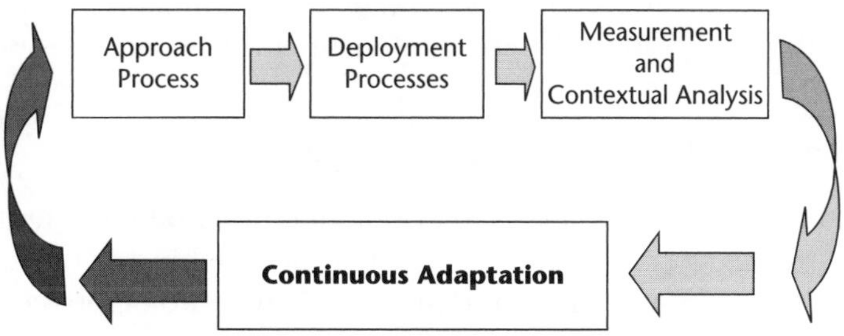

drawn between the outcomes and outputs of the deployment process and the events and interrelationships that have either aided in moving the institution toward its vision or hindered this progress.

- *Continuous adaptation.* Once the analyses are completed, it is decision time. What changes in the institution's approach and the related processes need to be reinforced, and what needs to be changed or eliminated? Although this is not the responsibility of an IR office, how the IR office presents the data will play a major role in decision making. Once the decisions are made, the approach process is modified, along with the related processes, and the cycle continues.

Tools for Improving Institutional Effectiveness

People—and therefore organizations—are reluctant to change unless they see a personal benefit to that change. An organization's culture is like a living organism: when something new (aka foreign) is introduced, if it senses a benefit, it accepts the change, but if it feels threatened, it rejects the change. The art of creating change is to emphasize the potential benefits of the change, identify the key change leaders, and ensure that these individuals have the appropriate skills and data to accent the positive in order to minimize the initial discomfort of change (Cameron & Quinn, 2006).

Developing a process begins with identifying a starting point. In many cases this can be done using the Pareto Principle. In the early 1900s an Italian economist, Vilfredo Pareto, discovered that 20 percent of the population held 80 percent of the country's wealth. In the 1940s Joseph M. Juran applied this observation to organizational performance. As a result, this principle also became known as the 20/80 rule. This rule can be applied to both ends of the continuum of organizational effectiveness: 20 percent of "x" produces 80 percent of "y"; 20 percent of the activities require 80 percent of the total expenditures; 20 percent of the students get 80 percent of the top grades; 20 percent of the faculty produce 80 percent of the scholarly writings. At the other end of institutional ineffectiveness, 20 percent of the staff produce 80 percent of administrative personnel issues and 20 percent of the processes addressing student academic performance may cause 80 percent of the dropouts. Therefore IR offices can greatly improve their effectiveness by identifying and examining the 20 percent of the activities that are creating 80 percent of the ineffective outcomes of the institutions.

Specific Tools for Identifying Where to Begin

The following tools are very valuable in helping to identify areas in which an institution can be more consistent in matching its decisions and processes to its core values, vision, and mission. Also, it should be recognized that although these tools are very useful, they are not listed in order of importance, and they are not the only tools. Appendix 37.1, at the end of this chapter, identifies additional resources that can help institutional researchers in their efforts to gather data that will help improve the effectiveness of their institutions. See also Brassard and Ritter (2010) and Tague (2005). Detailed explanations of each of the following tools can be found through an Internet search.

Baseline Assessment. As with any data gathering effort, it is essential to know where to begin in order to know the direction in which to go. A very useful and simple instrument to use is *Self-Assessment and Action Planning Using the Baldrige Organizational Profile for Education* (http://patapsco.nist.gov/eBaldrige/ Education_Profile.cfm). This survey examines perceptions of the organization in the following areas: organizational environment, organizational relationships, external environment, and the strategic context of the institution. It can be used to assess the entire institution or individual units. The Academic Quality Improvement Program (AQIP) of the Higher Learning Commission (HLC) has developed nine categories that can be used as a baseline structure to examine key processes related to the use of energy and resources that will help institutions achieve their goals (http://www.hlcommission.org/aqip-categories/aqip-categories.html).

Constituency Analysis. The effectiveness of a unit and an institution as a whole is demonstrated by how well they have met the needs and expectations of the people or organizations that form the reasons for their existence. For example, in business terms they are the employees, suppliers, customers, stakeholders, and investors; for higher education institutions, they include staff and faculty (employees); secondary education schools (suppliers); students, academic societies, and research funding organizations (customers); parents, the local community, and government regulatory agencies and employers (stakeholders); and state and federal governments, students and parents, foundations, and the alumni (investors). Because higher education is not measurement driven, assessment of the needs and expectations of the constituencies and how well the institution is meeting these needs is necessarily limited. Just identifying the most important 20 percent of these expectations would be a major step forward in increasing an institution's effectiveness, and it could well be associated with 80 percent of the institutional outcomes' effectiveness.

Specific Tools for Looking at the Process

Although many IR offices regularly survey the key external and internal constituencies about how well the institution is meeting their expectations, it is not clear how these data are used to make process-change decisions. If the survey questions lack a contextual base the results will be just a snapshot or census data that are difficult to use for decision making. For example, the question to an employer that asks "Would you continue to hire our graduates?" or "How do you rank our graduates in relation to the graduates you have hired from other institutions?" gives very little specific help in improving the institution's effectiveness. A question like "What additional skills or knowledge would make our graduates more attractive to you?" would provide actionable information.

Internal Unit Dependency Analysis. Because of the interrelationships and the consequential interdependencies between different units, it becomes necessary for a unit to understand which units are most critical for their success and to understand which units depend on them for their success. Few institutions regularly measure these relationships. In a course exercise at George Washington University, students interviewed seven different units concerning which two units they were most dependent on and which two units most depended on them. The students then interviewed those four units and asked the same questions. Not one unit mentioned any of the first units interviewed!

Cause and Effect Mapping. Once a process has been identified as not meeting the core objectives, there must be an analysis of the process with the objective of finding a way to permanently improve the process. To do this, it is necessary to find the fundamental or root cause of the problem (Andersen & Fagerhaug, 2006).

Detail Analysis. The initial solution is often a superficial action that may put out the fire but not ensure that the fire won't reignite. What is needed is a more detailed analysis that identifies the primary or root cause of the problem. The next four tools are useful in this type of analysis.

Brainstorming: The x plus five answers technique. This is just one of many forms of brainstorming (not to be confused with *blamestorming*). *The Quality Toolbox* (Tague, 2005) details six different forms of brainstorming. An Internet search will identify dozens more. This technique is important to highlight because it does not accept the most obvious answer to be the solution to the root cause. Instead, it requires that the participants list all the possibilities that they can think of (that's the *x*) and then identify five more. This additional step can be taken at the same meeting or at a subsequent meeting. The goal is to go beyond the obvious.

Fishbone Diagram. Also known as a cause-and-effect or Ishikawa diagram, this diagram allows all members of a group to identify, explore, and graphically display, in increasing detail, all of the possible causes related to a problem, sorted into categories. It enables a group to focus on the content of the problem rather than its history or the members' personal interests. By focusing the group broadly on causes, not symptoms, this tool can open up a group whose thinking has fallen into a rut. A common form of this diagram looks like the skeleton of a fish, hence the term *fishbone*. The process is to first identify the problem; for example, dissatisfaction with the campus food service. The next step is to identify what may be the major reasons for this dissatisfaction; in this example, it could be lack of variety in the menu, quality of the food, availability of ethnic or religious food choices, cleanness of the serving and eating areas, or the hours that the food service is available. After the major possibilities have been identified, a list is developed of all the possibilities for what may be creating student dissatisfaction. Next comes the hard part: determining which part of the resulting fishbone diagram is correct and which part is not. One response is to develop a detailed student survey based on the fishbone diagram and send it to all the students. However, student frustrations may differ from one food service location to another, and a campuswide survey may not find the solution to individual students' concerns. A more localized method would be to make comment cards available in all the food service facilities, review them every day, and post responses the next day. The key is to give the students feedback to recognize their contribution and then act on the data.

Decision Tree. This analytic tool is also known as a systematic diagram, tree analysis, hierarchy diagram, or analytical tree. The purpose is to move from an undesirable outcome backward through the various possibilities that may have turned what was thought to be a positive decision into negative results. For example, an institution is experiencing a decline in enrollments and therefore in revenue. There are many conditions and decisions that could cause this: an economic boom that makes additional education unnecessary for job seekers, an economic recession that makes more student aid necessary, low ranking in the national college rankings making other institutions more attractive, or course offerings that are not meeting the local community's needs. All of these can be measured and analyzed to estimate their possible impact on enrollment. An institution that was having an unexplainable enrollment decline constructed a decision tree and found out that, due to pressure from the board to increase the institution's national ranking, the admissions office had raised the minimum cutoff level for SAT and ACT scores. This decision did increase the average scores of those admitted, but it also excluded more students and hence had the unintended consequence of causing a decrease in enrollments and tuition revenues. A good source for more information about decision trees can be found in *The Quality Toolbox* (Tague, 2005, pp. 501–504.)

System Diagram. After identifying the parts of the problem, a further step is to develop a process relationship between the desired results and the different activities related to the processes that contribute to this end. An excellent introduction to process or system thinking can be found in *The Fifth Discipline: The Art and Practice of the Learning Organization* (Senge, 2006) and *A Culture for Academic Excellence: Implementing the Quality Principles in Higher Education* (Freed, Klugman, & Fife, 1997).

An analogy for looking at an organization as series of interlocking processes is to think of it as a symphony orchestra. Each musician has a critical role in performing the composition. Depending on the score, some musicians have a greater role than others; however, without each playing their parts at the right time in the right way, the performance will not meet the expectations of the audience.

Systems diagrams quickly display the interconnections between one single process or system and all of the others in an institution, and they let everyone understand why systems thinking—appreciating how each element operates in a larger context—is essential for effective problem solving. A completed systems diagram stimulates right-to-left discussion of requirements; to determine, for example, what system outputs are required in order to satisfy each customer, what inputs are required to make the each process successful, and what suppliers are needed to provide appropriate inputs.

Once the ideal system diagram is designed and fit together, an analysis of the parts can be conducted to identify which parts may not be functioning as expected or may not be present at all. This is part of the genius of a system diagram: the existence or absence of basic assumptions is easily identified.

Other Process Management Analytic Tools

There are many other tools being used to help in the analysis of managing the institution's processes. This section describes several of the most common tools. Many of these readers may already be familiar with; others may be new to them. More in-depth descriptions can be found from the resources listed in Appendix 37.1 or through an Internet search (Ewy & Gmitro, 2010).

Control Chart. This is a specific type of run chart used to detect and monitor process variations. Usually accepted limits of variation are established. If the outcomes remain within these limits, the process is considered to be working as expected; if there appear to be many points outside the variance limits, then the process needs further examination.

Run Chart. Using performance measures that, more often than not, are collected by IR offices, a trend or tracking chart is created to allow for clearer observation of the degree to which specific performance measures are meeting desired results. At least three measurement points are needed to create a trend line. The more points of measurement, the greater the reliability of a run chart. A run chart may be used, for example, to determine a specific goal established in a strategic plan; say, decreasing the time it takes to process maintenance requests. If the response time decreased for a short period of time just after this goal was announced and then reverted back to the previous level, then the chart would clearly indicate that this process needed to be examined to find out the basic cause of not meeting this goal.

Histogram. This is a vertical bar chart presenting the summary of data from a specific process over a period of time. A histogram has several advantages in helping to understand a large amount of data: it shows the relative frequency of occurrence of various data values; reveals the centering, variations, and shape of the data; helps to indicate changes in performance and therefore possible changes in the process; and gives an indication of the degree to which a process is supporting the institution's core.

Flowchart. This is a diagram of a process displaying the connections between events from the beginning to the end, using various symbols to illustrate the process steps, the inputs and outputs, and the conditional or decision point (if x happens, then the response is y.) Flowcharts are usually higher-level combinations of multiple systems diagrams—representations of work processes showing all the work steps in sequence, including handoffs, approvals, and process boundaries. A flowchart allows a group to capture and analyze the actual flow or sequence of events in a process that any product or service follows. Flowcharts compare and contrast the "as is" with the "as it should be." They highlight complexity, problem areas, redundancy, or unnecessary loops where simplification may be possible, and thus allow a team to come to agreement on the steps of a process.

Six Sigma (6σ). The Six Sigma process of improving organizational effectiveness was popularized in the 1980s by Motorola as a means to create a quality level that would be far superior to its Japanese competitors. It was designed to reach six standard deviations of quality, or processes that were 99.99966-percent free of defects (Pyzdek & Keller, 2010). The Six Sigma quality process was rejected by many people in higher education for two reasons: it was originally developed to improve manufacturing processes, and it set a standard of controlling variations that was unrealistic. However, some of the tools used in the Six Sigma process have been found to be very useful (see Figure 37.3).

FIGURE 37.3 PLAN-DO-STUDY-ACT

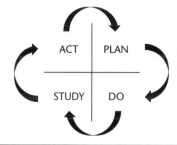

Plan-Do-Study-Act (PDSA). This is also known as Plan-Do-Check-Act (PDCA) and the Shewart Cycle. The value in PDSA can be summed up in an effective organization maxim that was developed after many costly mistakes: "Think big—act small." It also embraces the concept of the Cycle of Continuous Adaptation. The guiding principle is that when creating a new process or adjusting an old process, change needs to be tested on a small scale. Therefore *plan*—design a process change; *do*—implement that change on a small scale; *study*—review the results and, if needed, make adjustments; then *act*—implement the change on a slightly larger scale. This starts the PDSA cycle all over again. It is in the *study* phase that the skills of an IR offices can make a major contribution to organizational effectiveness.

Prioritization Matrices. This is a process of first creating L-shaped matrices that weigh the possible options of a process change and then systematically comparing these options by using specific criteria; for example, cost, ease of implementation, impact, skills needed, and risks. This process works best when representatives of all the directly affected constituencies are included in the development of a matrix. There are several possible benefits to using this tool:

- Basic disagreements become public.
- The best things to do are identified, and the "good" but less valuable ideas are eliminated.
- "Pet agendas" become more obvious and are tested against specific criteria.
- Follow-through is more likely, because each decision is made only after consensus has been reached.

Interrelationship Diagram. This tool provides another way to first examine cause-and-effect relationships that are major drivers or barriers to implementing change and to then create effective solutions. This process requires the involvement of both representatives of the constituencies as well as those who have the resources or data to verify personal opinions. Implementing the process of developing interrelationship diagrams offers the following advantages:

- It broadens the participants' perspectives, so they begin to think in multiple directions.
- It develops a more comprehensive examination of all the cause-and-effect relationships.
- It provides an atmosphere free of judgment, thereby allowing critical issues to emerge logically.
- Consequently, it also allows examination of what might be causing disagreement—such as false assumptions, fear of losing something, or territorial protection.
- It allows one to look for root causes to problems and to identify obstacles to solving them.

Affinity Diagram. This methodology concludes the list of techniques that can be used to increase the effectiveness of an institution. It is presented last in order to emphasize one of the major lessons learned by the organizations that have been recognized by receiving the Malcolm Baldrige National Quality Award. When asked "What did you first do wrong as you began implementing processes to increase your effectiveness?" the universal response was, "We spent too much time on the hard side of the data and not on the soft side—the people side."

Affinity diagrams are created through teams that are gathered to generate all possibilities of new ideas and thereby create an understanding of the core of a problem and create creative solutions. The steps are as follows:

- Clearly and succinctly define the issue.
- Brainstorm solutions, such as using the "*x* plus five" process previously discussed.
- Sort the ideas into related groupings.
- Finally, using consensus, classify each group and logically arrange the related ideas. The final result is an orderly presentation of creative ideas, overcoming the intellectual and emotional immobility caused by being besieged by so many possibilities.

As Figure 37.1 illustrates, an effective organization is driven by its central vision, mission, and goals that are the core of beliefs for both those within the organization and those outside it but directly affected by the organization's outcomes and outputs. The tools identified in this chapter can help develop measurements and observations that will give both quantitative and qualitative evidence of where the organization is being driven by its core values and where it is not (Revelle, 2004).

Conclusion

It's the people that make the difference. Effective IR professionals don't simply pile up collections of facts and then *hope* or *trust* that others will be able to use them to draw conclusions and formulate actions. IR must proactively help groups of faculty, administrators, and staff make sense of and act on what its research has found. The efforts to create effective organizations—CQI, TQM, Six Sigma, Lean, and other similar initiatives—provide valuable tools and techniques that can help facilitate discussion and analysis among academic colleagues.

Working with academic staff, IR offices should be aware of what may be major differences in perspective. Faculty scholars and researchers thrive on emphasizing distinctions that others have missed or ignored. Their discoveries and insights come as much from reinterpreting existing facts as from finding new ones. Their academic values and norms often do not include consensus and compromise, and many take "You're splitting hairs" or "That's nitpicking" as compliments, not criticisms. With groups of faculty, the IR professional who is sensitive to organizational culture employs techniques that keep personalities out of discussions, compensate for poor or out-of-practice listening skills, and create a process that moves a group toward consensus without giving its fiercely independent-minded members any inkling that they are being steered.

The goal for the groups that IR offices work with should be reaching consensus—that is, arriving at decisions that best reflect the thinking of all group members. *Consensus* means finding a proposal acceptable enough that all members can support it and no member actively opposes it. Reaching consensus requires time: all group members must actively participate, exhibit communication skills (listening, conflict resolution, discussion), and remain open-minded.

Consensus is not a majority vote. In a majority vote, only the majority winds up happy, and the minority may get something they do not want at all. Consensus recognizes that satisfying everyone completely, giving everyone everything he or she may want, is impossible. A consensus may not represent everyone's first priorities.

Not every decision needs *everyone's* support. IR staff should consult with leadership and decide ahead of time when to press for consensus, and how much is sufficient. Decisions that may have a major impact on the direction of a project or conduct of the entire group—such as major new goals or significant changes in current operations—need to be owned and supported broadly and therefore require consensus. But some decisions must be made quickly and cannot wait for a groundswell to materialize; one-person decisions (ideally made after seeking others' viewpoints and advice) are reasonable strategies in crises.

If time permits and support after the decision is critical, IR staff can work for consensus. Involving the entire group in making a decision reinforces everyone's ownership and responsibility. Broad-based decisions, with input from a diversity of sources, tend to be sounder, and implementing them becomes easier. However, IR needs to convince whatever groups they work with that not everyone will be satisfied with everything, and a reasonable goal is for nearly all group members to be 75–80 percent in agreement with the conclusions and decisions that emerge, so long as everyone commits to work 100 percent for whatever the group decides.

References

Andersen, B., & Fagerhaug, T. (2006). *Root cause analysis: Simplified tools and techniques* (2nd ed.). Milwaukee, WI: ASQ Quality Press.

Brassard, M., & Ritter, D. (2010). *The memory jogger II: A pocket guide of tools for continuous improvement and effective planning* (2nd ed.). Milwaukee, WI: ASQ Quality Press.

Cameron, K. S., & Quinn, R. E. (2006). *Diagnosing and changing organizational culture: Based on the competing values framework* (revised ed.). San Francisco: Jossey-Bass.

Chaffee, E. E., & Sherr, L. A. (1992). *Quality: Transforming postsecondary education.* ASHE-ERIC Higher Education Report, no. 3. Washington, DC: The George Washington University, Graduate School of Education and Human Development. (ERIC Document Number 351 922)

Ewy, R. W., & Gmitro, H. A. (2010). *Process management in education: How to design, measure, deploy, and improve educational processes.* Milwaukee, WI: ASQ Quality Press.

Freed, J. E., Klugman, M. R., & Fife, J. D. (1997). *A culture for academic excellence: Implementing the quality principles in higher education.* ASHE-ERIC Higher Education Report, *25*(1). Washington, DC: The George Washington University, Graduate School of Education and Human Development. (ERIC Document Number 406 963)

Pyzdek, T., & Keller, P. (2010). *The six sigma handbook* (3rd ed.). New York: McGraw-Hill.

Revelle, J. B. (2004). *Quality essentials: A reference guide from A to Z.* Milwaukee, WI: ASQ Quality Press.

Senge, P. M. (2006). *The fifth discipline: The art and practice of the learning organization* (rev. ed.). New York: Currency Doubleday.

Tague, N. R. (2005). *The quality toolbox* (2nd ed.). Milwaukee, WI: ASQ Quality Press.

Terenzini, P. T. (1999). On the nature of institutional research and the knowledge and skills it requires. In J. F. Volkwein (Ed.), *What is institutional research all about? A critical and comprehensive assessment of the profession* (pp. 21–29). New Directions for Institutional Research, no. 104. San Francisco: Jossey-Bass.

Appendix 37.1: Resources

American Society for Quality, P.O. Box 3005, Milwaukee 53201-3005, 877-713-0692 (United States and Canada only). http://www.asq.org. ASQ is a membership organization devoted to quality. They have an extensive publication department that offers topics on all areas of quality control tools.

Academic Quality Improvement Program (AQIP), The Higher Learning Commission, 230 South LaSalle Street, Suite 7-500, Chicago, IL 60604, 800-621-7440, http://www.hlcommission.org/aqip-home. "Launched in July 1999 with a generous grant from the Pew Charitable Trusts, the Commission's Academic Quality Improvement Program infuses the principles and benefits of continuous improvement into the culture of colleges and universities by providing an alternative process through which an already-accredited institution can maintain its accreditation. An institution in AQIP demonstrates how it meets accreditation standards and expectations through a sequence of events that align with the ongoing activities of an institution striving to improve its performance."

Baldrige National Quality Program, NIST, 100 Bureau Drive, M/S 1020, Gaithersburg, MD 20899-1020, 301-975-2036. The Baldrige Performance Excellence Program, following the loss of its federal funding, is in the process of transitioning to a new organization model. Their new website (http://www.nist.gov/baldrige/transition/index.cfm) details the progress of this evolving development: how it is transitioning to a sustainable, enterprise model, in which the Foundation for the Malcolm Baldrige National Quality Award, the Alliance for Performance Excellence, the American Society for Quality, and state and other performance excellence programs will work together toward a national, integrated model of excellence.

National Consortium for Continuous Improvement in Higher Education (NCCI), Jennifer Gentry, Association Administrator, NCCI, 342 North Main Street, West Hartford, CT 06117, 860-586-7567, jgentry@ncci-cu.org/http://www.ncci-cu.org. *Mission Statement:* "NCCI advances sustainable excellence in higher education by promoting the practice and discipline of continuous improvement across all academic and administrative functions."

CHAPTER 38

TOOLS FOR MEASURING THE EFFECTIVENESS OF INSTITUTIONAL RESEARCH

Sharron Ronco, Sandra Archer, and Patricia Ryan

As this expansive handbook demonstrates, the scope of responsibilities of an institutional researcher may cover a wide range of areas, from routine and ad hoc reporting to conducting sophisticated analyses in support of policy making. Institutional researchers often find themselves supporting various studies of institutional effectiveness, assisting other units in the institution to collect and analyze information on their performance and efforts toward continuous improvement. But what of the effectiveness of the institutional research office itself? How can IR turn its own tools inward to ensure that its operation is performing optimally?

How Do We Define "Effectiveness" In IR?

The IR profession benefits from a long history of self-reflection (Peterson, 1999). The profession's interest in evaluation for continuous improvement of its operations dates back almost to its inception. In their seminal statement on "The Nature and Role of Institutional Research—Memo to a College or University," Joe Saupe and James Montgomery (1970) wrote: "After institutional research is organized at a college or university and in whatever form this organization takes, it should be subject to careful and periodic evaluation. It should be organized for clearly understood reasons and purposes, and its performance can be judged on the basis of them. If one organization does not work, another can be tried" (p. 13).

Although there is no universally recognized measure or easy quantification of IR effectiveness, several decades of research have identified the characteristics of an effective IR office. Fundamentally, an effective IR office is one that has a tangible impact on decision making, planning, and policy formation (Knight, 2010). Studies of institutional researchers' self-reported perception of effectiveness and productivity suggest that it may be easier to identify the obstacles to effectiveness than it is to identify its properties. These obstacles often include inadequate staffing and material resources, lack of appreciation of data by top administrators, and poor organizational placement. Others define effective IR offices in terms of the effectiveness of their products (Chambers, 2007; Gerek, 2007).

A recurring theme in the literature on the characteristics of an effective IR office is that effective IR personnel possess "issues intelligence" and "context intelligence" (Terenzini, 1993). Often IR professionals have technical competence but lack the information on big-picture issues that they need to properly contextualize their research results (Chambers, 2007). It is clear that contextual intelligence, which may be gained only with time at the institution, is critical to an effective IR function. In fact, Knight, Moore, and Coperthwaite (1999) found that 88 percent of institutional researchers surveyed reported that on-the-job experience was their most important source of professional knowledge and skills. As Presley (1990) describes, an effective IR office is often led by a "generalist"; that is, a person with contextual intelligence, quantitative skills, and excellent communication skills. At the same time, the "specialists," or people with skills in computing, database administration, and assessment, are critical to the IR function.

Chambers (2007) may have summarized the characteristics for an effective IR office best, by providing these general suggestions for IR's effectiveness: (1) maintain objectivity, (2) "be ahead of the curve, not behind it," (3) stay aware of trends at the national, state, local, and institutional levels, (4) break out of the routine, (5) understand the context of your institution by collaborating with senior administrators, and (6) participate in self-assessment practices.

Not only is the evaluation of the effectiveness of the IR office a worthy practice, but all six of the regional accrediting agencies for colleges and universities require assessment of administrative functions, including the institutional research office (see Chapter 18 for a more detailed discussion of regional accreditation). The six agencies are as follows:

- Middle States Association of Colleges and Schools, Commission on Higher Education, Standard 5—Administration: "demonstrate . . . periodic assessment of the effectiveness of administrative structures and services" (Middle States Commission on Higher Education, 2009).
- New England Association of Schools and Colleges, Commission on Institutions of Higher Education, Standard 2.5: "The institution regularly and systematically evaluates the achievement of its mission and purposes. . . . Its system of evaluation is designed to provide relevant and trustworthy information to support institutional improvement" (New England Association of Schools and Colleges, Commission on Institutions of Higher Education, 2011, p. 6).

- North Central Association of Colleges and Schools, Higher Learning Commission, Core Component 5.D.1 "The institution develops and documents evidence of performance in its operations." (Higher Learning Commission, 2012, p. 8).
- Northwest Commission on Colleges and Universities, Standard 4.A.2: "The institution engages in an effective system of evaluation of its programs and services, wherever offered and however delivered, to evaluate achievement of clearly identified program goals or intended outcomes" (Northwest Commission on Colleges and Universities, 2010, p. 15).
- Southern Association of Colleges and Schools, Commission on Colleges Core principal 3.3.1: "identifies expected outcomes, assesses the extent to which it achieves these outcomes, and provides evidence of improvement based on analysis of the results in . . . administrative support services" (Southern Association of Colleges and Schools, Commission on Colleges, 2012, p. 27).
- Western Association of Schools and Colleges, Accrediting Commission for Senior Colleges and Universities Standard 4.5: "periodic reviews are conducted to ensure the effectiveness of the [institutional] research function and the suitability and usefulness of data" (Western Association of Schools and Colleges, 2008, p. 22).

The IR office has the opportunity to model the behavior it teaches, by turning the magnifying glass inward and conducting a study of its own effectiveness. Chambers (2007) asserts, "In order to present a credible persona on campus it is important that institutional research offices engage in the very practice that they purport to support." This section will equip institutional research offices with the tools necessary to demonstrate that "virtue begins at home" and lead others through example.

The IR Self-Study

"Cobbler's shoes wear worst!" Behind this adage is the assumption that the shoemaker is too busy to attend to his own needs or improve his lot. Institutional researchers must ensure that they are not too busy to keep their own "shops" in top condition. A useful tool for this is a self-study. Like those found in other venues, the self-study in IR provides for a comprehensive review of the current state of the office and identifies its strengths and weaknesses. By undertaking a self-study, the office can plan for improvement and emerge at the other end with enhanced efficiencies.

Exhibit 38.1 suggests a list of topics that could be included in an IR office's self-study. These are further described below. For an expanded treatment of these topics, see Gerek (2007) or contact Patricia Ryan.

EXHIBIT 38.1   SUGGESTED TOPIC LIST FOR IR SELF-STUDY

Office Mission
- Written mission statement
- Consistent with institutional mission
- Consistent with best practices in IR
- Communicated to internal and external constituents
- Periodically reviewed and updated as needed

Office Resources—Human
- Staffing levels sufficient to meet demand
- Possess competencies necessary to complete IR work
- Cross-trained
- Professional development opportunities for staff
- Equitable work assignments
- Clear job descriptions and regular staff evaluations
- Staff has time to reflect and ability to act proactively
- Effective working relationships with administrative and academic units

Office Resources—Other
- Adequate hardware and software to support office functions
- Adequate budget to meet IR needs
- Assistance available for programming needs, web design, statistical and research methodology consultation, document preparation

Workflow
- Process for submission of work requests to the IR office
- Process for acceptance, assignment, and prioritization of work requests
- Use of work-request log, calendar, or tracking system to monitor completion
- Automation of routine reports

Information access and retrieval
- Access to live/transactional data
- Access to archived/snapshot/warehoused data
- Availability of data dictionary and other documentation
- Processes for ensuring data reliability

Distribution of reports and other products
- Process for verifying accuracy before distribution
- Process for distribution of reports and other products
- Availability of information on the IR website
- Process for backup and security of data files and reports

Assessment
- Process for obtaining customer feedback
- Regular internal assessment of activities
- Identification of opportunities for enhancements or efficiencies with timetable for completion

Office Mission

The self-study begins with a review of the IR mission statement, which provides a foundation for the varied institutional needs served by the IR office and the scope of its responsibilities. Key considerations in mission statement review (or construction) include its support of institutional mission, its visibility to users, and congruence with activities actually performed by the office. Mission statements should be reviewed, at a minimum, every three years or whenever there is a change in the environment that affects the office's purpose, organization, or services.

Resources

Overall, the human resources assigned to IR must be sufficient to meet institutional demand. Adequate human resources will be evident when researchers have time to think beyond the tasks at hand and proactively "push out" important unsolicited information to the institution. In this phase of the self-study, the experience, education, cross-training, and workload of the staff are reviewed, together with processes for staff evaluation and opportunities for staff career development. Working relationships between IR and all units of the institution should be honestly assessed to ensure that these are functioning effectively.

Adequate material resources include a budget and technology sufficient to fully support IR functions. Depending on the skill set of the IR staff, the services of other institutional personnel—such as web designers, statisticians, or programmers—may need to be allocated to IR.

Workflow

Peter F. Drucker (1962) said that *efficiency* is doing things right; *effectiveness* is doing the right things. A thorough examination of workflow practices in the IR office, done against the backdrop of its mission within the institution, provides a review of both efficiency and effectiveness.

An effective tool for the review of workflow practices is the business process analysis developed by Darton and Darton (1997). Each individual work practice is mapped from its point of origin through completion and delivery of information. The review begins with an analysis of what occurs when a work task, whether routine or ad hoc, is received by the IR office. Is there a process for determining whether the task falls within the office's mission, for reassigning to another area if it does not, or for negotiating who will handle it? Processes for the equitable assignment of work in the office, consistent with staff competencies, should be made explicit. When workloads are heavy, it may be necessary to assign priority status and anticipated completion dates. Work request forms or an intake log can be used for recording assignments and tracking their completion status. Easily referenced documentation of work completed eliminates the duplication of requests and makes it easier to automate repeated requests for the same information or analysis. A shared calendar of routine requests can ensure that everyone is made aware of when reports are due or information will be available.

As data is the lifeblood of IR, it must be available, easily accessed, interpretable, and reliable. The self-study should explore the presence and availability of live and warehoused data and processes for capturing and storing snapshot data. Data dictionaries, documentation, verification, security, and back-up of data systems are relevant items for evaluation.

The self-study should undertake a thorough examination of the preparation, distribution, and publications of IR work products. When information is presented in a professional fashion, it not only satisfies institutional research needs but also conveys attention to detail, adeptness, and proficiency. Information disseminated throughout the institution can originate and be distributed from various venues. It is important that IR "informational products" have a visible brand—an identifying appearance. Distributed or published IR outcomes represent official and institutionally sanctioned data. Recipients should immediately recognize the appearance of IR informational products. The self-study should evaluate the extent to which IR uses uniform, professional, and office-identifiable templates for all information transmittals. Equally important areas to be examined with respect to IR products include the processes for the verification of information prior to distribution, and establishment of procedures and venues for the distribution and publication of research outcomes.

Cost-Effectiveness

Institutional research offices function in perpetual motion; rarely is there any down time or even slow time. It is essential, then, that part of the self-study include an analysis of cost-effectiveness. When a monetary value can be associated with a research request or product, the outcome can be seen as a responsible use of an institution's capital.

Begin by examining the annual budget, including allocations for personnel, operating expenditures, equipment, and other expenses. It is helpful to further distinguish salary differentials among employees to calculate an hourly rate for a director, professional staff, graduate assistant, or other types of employees. Operating and equipment costs can be equated to an hourly charge per employee hour. The result might be that one hour of professional staff research work costs the institution $50; an all-day project would cost $400. Graduate student or other student work might average $12 an hour.

Cost estimates can help put parameters around the acceptance and assignment of work.

Often IR offices are employed in deep sea fishing expeditions. When requestors are not completely sure what they want and ask the IR office to "run the numbers" or "see what you get," a better use of resources should be suggested. It is also important to consider the labor costs when assigning projects; make certain that labor grades are assigned appropriate level work. Common requests can be automated through establishment of program routines.

Assessment Processes

A vital component of the self-study is examining feedback from sources internal to the office, internal to the institution, and external to both the office and institution. It is recommended that, upon completion of a work assignment, the staff member charged with the assignment take time, albeit briefly, to reflect on the project. Summary comments, including problems encountered as well as suggestions for improving subsequent related efforts, can be noted on a digital work log. This information can provide valuable insight information to the office director and contribute to improving the work environment and outcomes. Procedures for incorporating feedback in the self-study from other internal constituents and from external reviewers are described in the next section.

The self-study should include a review of all routine work completed by IR staff. Over time, the number of requests for information grows, as does the number of regularly transmitted "reports." As the volume increases, "report creep" can set in. When this occurs, information is routinely transmitted that may no longer be required. From time to time it is important to reevaluate the need for this information, with an eye toward eliminating redundant or obsolete reporting.

It is recommended that self-studies be conducted every three to five years. The director or administrator responsible for IR functions should undertake this review, possibly with the assistance of one or two other institutional administrators. The involvement of those external to the IR office will bring an unbiased perspective. The work of the self-study team should be completed within a month. The ideal time for this effort is when work volume is lower, perhaps during the summer. The study results should be reviewed with the next supervisory level to increase the possibility that accomplishments can be recognized, inefficiencies addressed, and institutional commitments to support continuous improvement secured.

Getting Customer Feedback

To be fully in tune with its staff and constituents served, the IR office needs to know how its outcomes are both produced and received. With meaningful input, IR services can be taken to the next level and better meet demands. The first step is gaining insight into the voice of the IR customer.

A cornerstone of applying total quality management (TQM), which has been widely used in higher education (Quinn, 2009), is to focus on customer-driven quality. From this perspective, the customer is the principal judge of quality. To meet or exceed customer expectations, one must first build relationships with them and understand their needs. The customers of an IR office may include university leadership and decision makers, faculty, students, parents, media outlets, and the general public. Although it may be impossible to obtain feedback from all customers, IR offices can use a variety of techniques to understand the "voice of the customer."

One quick way to hear that voice is to attach a request for indicators of satisfaction with the actual transmission of an IR work product. The e-mail correspondence typically used to transmit the requested product can contain a hyperlink to an online survey site. There the recipient can provide immediate and anonymous feedback, and any problems or dissatisfactions reported can be readily addressed by the IR office before memory fades. Similarly, including links at the bottom of IR web pages that can be clicked to ask a question or "rate our service" can provide formative evaluation.

Summative techniques typically take place on an annual or periodic basis, and focus mostly on collecting input from institutional leadership or information recipients. Input may be collected via follow-up interviews with users to get more in-depth information on their satisfaction with IR products. No matter what method of feedback is employed, understanding the "critical to quality" needs of the customer is the key to achieving customer-driven quality. For example, an Excel PivotTable with drill down capability might be an appropriate deliverable for one customer, whereas a polished PowerPoint presentation with contextual information and explanations may be appropriate for another.

An annual or biennial customer service survey is a useful way for the IR office to obtain feedback from its internal customers. There are several good examples of IR office customer surveys available on various institutions' IR websites. Links to many of these IR office web pages are made available on the North Carolina State University office of University Planning and Analysis website (n.d.).

A typical survey asks users to rate their experience with the interaction with the IR office, and the quality of the products obtained. Asking users to rate their experience on a five-point Likert scale, from "strongly agree" to "strongly disagree" or from "excellent" to "poor," is a very effective way to gain insights in these two areas. Sample topics on the IR experience include:

- Website usability
- Timeliness of deliverables
- Knowledge of staff
- Responsiveness
- Staff professionalism
- Frequency of use of specific IR products

Sample topics on the quality of products include:

- Whether the customer was aware of an IR product and service
- Ease of use
- Accuracy and consistency
- Whether the product(s) meet customers' needs
- Level of product comprehensiveness

An effective survey tool will allow users to remain anonymous if desired, with the option to be contacted for follow-up on an expressed concern. The tool should also allow users to type in an explanation for any question marked with the lowest level of satisfaction, providing the IR office with ideas of the specific area that needs improvement. A typical survey will also include a section for general comments or suggestions for improvement.

A well-thought-out, well-designed survey will facilitate the collection of the most useful data from customers, with the least amount of questions—or inconvenience to the customer. A brief survey is ideal. An invitation to take the survey that ensures customers it is "only eight questions" or will take "only about five minutes" may encourage busy administrators to take the time to fill it out. For example, Pet-Armacost and Armacost (2007) define six aspects of "delivered quality"—aspects of the product (usability, value, and comprehensiveness) and aspects of the process (organization, user involvement, and responsiveness)—to address whether or not the office has met user needs for a desired product. These six aspects were determined to be critical to quality; therefore six simple questions on a customer feedback form is all that is needed to assess the success of the delivered product. (For a more detailed discussion of conducting surveys see Chapter 29.)

Even more important than the survey instrument itself is ensuring that the resulting information is used for improvement. Many IR offices post the results of their customers' surveys on their websites. Thad Allen, commandant of the U.S. Coast Guard, said "transparency of information breeds self-correcting behavior" (Linden, 2010). Making the survey results publicly available instills a sense of accountability in IR office personnel and inspires action to implement change. As changes to processes are put into place to address areas of weakness, tracking the survey results year over year will help the IR office determine whether efforts to implement these changes have been successful.

Seeking External Feedback

Although self-studies and internal reports of effectiveness are necessary and useful, an external review can bring objectivity and a fresh perspective to the IR operation and an independent assurance of quality. Perhaps because IR professionals often feel isolated within their institutions, it is natural for them to reach outside for validation and support. In fact, research has shown that institutional researchers who seek other professionals to advise them and who are a part of a strong professional network perceive themselves as more effective in bringing about changes at their institutions (Delaney, 2001).

Looking outside for help in assessing effectiveness can be a formal or informal process and can involve inviting others to the institution or visiting theirs. This section addresses tools and techniques for bringing an external view to the IR operation.

The Outside Consultant

Using consultants to solve problems and deliver new ideas and strategies is a time-honored tradition in higher education. Consultants can be helpful not only in assessing an existing IR operation but also in examining more broadly an institution's ability to (1) effectively engage in data-driven decision making, (2) identify what skills or expertise may be needed, or (3) help design an organizational structure that can get the work done.

Consultants typically have a multi-institution perspective, and their ability to suggest solutions that have worked for others is a real strength. But consultants are expensive—their fees plus travel and expenses add up quickly. And because they're "not from around here," they may seem like intruders rather than trusted outsiders. Consultants may rely on a standard bag of tricks instead of tailoring solutions for the particular institution. In addition, consultants are typically not around for follow-up questions unless that is built into the contract. Once the consultant leaves, it is up to the institutional rank and file to implement the solutions.

Because the ideal consultant will be someone with a solid IR background, look to the membership of the Association for Institutional Research and its affiliated groups for potential experts. A number of experienced IR professionals have formed independent consulting groups.

Volunteer Peer Audits

It has been sardonically claimed that a consultant is anyone who is more than two hundred miles away from home. However, it would be a mistake to overlook the assistance that colleagues from nearby institutions can offer, particularly those whose operations include aspects of best practices. The volunteer peer audit is a less formal and potentially useful strategy for bringing in an external perspective. This type of review is often done in preparation for a reaffirmation of accreditation, but it is appropriate at any time that an outside view is desired and willing peers can be found. Peer auditors can review the IR office's self-study or use that same template to check IR operations. Optionally, peer auditors can interview administrators, supervisors, and primary customers of IR products. Peer auditors bring a sympathetic and practical viewpoint, and the experience of sharing can be beneficial for all. The danger is that their expertise may be limited to what works in their own institutions.

Process Benchmarking

Many organizations engage in process benchmarking as a way to improve performance or production. Process benchmarking, historically associated with the TQM or Continuous Quality Improvement (CQI) movements, involves studying specific work procedures or processes in other institutions and adopting their successful practices to one's own advantage. It relies on open and honest sharing of information. Benchmarking can be a one-time event or an ongoing process.

McLaughlin, Howard, and McLaughlin (2009) describe a case study using process benchmarking to observe how other institutions define the responsibilities of IR. The processes that these institutions use can then be compared to the processes at one's own institution to form a basis for assessing effectiveness.

Process benchmarking starts with deciding what to benchmark. Is the office weak on being able to project enrollments in various categories? On doing surveys? Is it plagued with renegade databases whose elements contradict each other? Are the office staff passive responders when the leadership looks to them to translate campus discussions into proactive research?

A project team is created to include individuals who are knowledgeable about the activities to be benchmarked but generally not in charge of them. Potential institutions are identified based on their perceived effectiveness in carrying out the key activities. Comparator institutions need to be reduced to a manageable number, usually four to seven, and should be offered the opportunity to remain anonymous in any reporting. The project team assigns responsibility for key activities; determines what resources are required; sets timelines, standards, metrics, or methods by which the activities are evaluated; and identifies (1) preferred strategies for carrying out the activities and (2) major threats to the quality of the process. The process concludes with a report by the visiting project team, discussions of lessons learned, and recommendations for follow-up. The report is sent forward through regular decision-making processes at the institution for promulgating the appropriate institutional change.

Process benchmarking is difficult and expensive to implement and involves a major organizational commitment of resources. It requires a good deal of trust between institutions, an honest assessment of issues that surface, and recognition of limitations to the process. Crucial to the success of this strategy is acknowledgment that the processes that work well in one institution are not necessarily transportable to one with a different culture and organization.

Nonetheless, process benchmarking provides the most comprehensive and useful information for evaluating IR functions and effectiveness. Because of the significant investment of time and resources, it may be most appropriate in situations in which significant and widespread changes are needed within a short time frame.

A more informal kind of process benchmarking is a variation on the volunteer peer audit; it involves gathering with colleagues from other institutions expressly for the purpose of exchanging process information. This is a potentially useful strategy for IR staff who lack long histories in the profession, allowing them to partner with experienced staff in other institutions in planning and developing their operations.

Performance Benchmarking

IR professionals are "head-achingly" familiar with performance benchmarking, which compares a set of measured outcomes to a numerical criteria or data point (McLaughlin and McLaughlin, 2007). That criteria, or data point, could be another institution's (or group of institutions') performance on that same indicator. IR staffs typically spend significant amounts of time computing, describing, and explaining metrics that are used to benchmark their institutions on outcomes such as retention and graduation rates, student learning experiences, or fiscal indicators.

Can performance benchmarking be done for IR offices? Benchmarking against other institutions, for indicators such as turnaround times for data requests or customer satisfaction with services, is probably not a meaningful exercise. But it is possible that key performance indicators—those areas in which an IR unit must be successful in order to survive—can be developed by using survey tools such as the checklists developed by Gerek (2007) and Voorhees (2010). Survey items could be organized around major IR processes such as working with data and information systems, providing accurate and timely data, developing and administering surveys, conducting studies and disseminating results, supporting planning activities, and so on. By identifying a consortium of peer institutions willing to rate themselves on the survey dimensions, offices can compare their own capacity and effectiveness against others. This type of "performance benchmarking" is really a combination of process and outcome analysis, and it can be done at less cost than the visitations described earlier.

In another sense, IR professionals have ever-expanding opportunities to informally benchmark through the exchange of information afforded by web-logging, or "blogs." Virtual discussion on blogs dedicated to the Common Data Set, IPEDS, SACS, assessment, *U.S. News and World Report*, and other topics of IR interest keep practitioners constantly apprised of what others are doing. The use of benchmarking is discussed much more extensively in Chapter 34 as a means for setting strategy. Forming the groups that may be necessary for benchmarking is discussed in Chapter 36.

Putting the Results to Work

Once the IR office has gone through the exercise of a comprehensive self-study, obtained internal feedback, and solicited outside advice, it is time to put the results to work. Conducting an informal gap analysis can help set the direction for continuous improvement. The gap is the difference between the office's current situation and what it wants to achieve in the future. Analysis involves determining what specific actions must be taken to close the gap and achieve the office's goals. The plan for closing the gap includes the resources needed and timetable for completing each step of the plan.

Although many of the suggestions provided in this chapter for measuring the effectiveness of IR are more easily accomplished in larger operations, nothing precludes one- or two-person IR offices from undertaking efforts to improve. Customer feedback is particularly useful when resources are limited, as it can identify unmet needs and make the case for additional personnel. Volunteer peer audits and performance benchmarking with other small offices are helpful strategies for discovering how others have found creative solutions to dealing with the demands and challenges of the small IR office.

Implementing successful change starts with a frank dialogue within the IR office on the need for change and the direction that it will take. The results of customer feedback surveys and other tools described in this chapter provide evidence and spark the initial motivation for changes. Internal consensus on individual and collective workload, work assignments, and responsibilities will focus the vision for change and help move the process to the next step: approaching administration to secure additional resources.

To leverage requests for additional resources, it is useful to remind managers of IR's worth by increasing the visibility of IR's work. Posting an IR report card that summarizes self-study findings, key performance indicators, volume of work, customer comments, and the like can help accomplish this end. One successful tactic may be to demonstrate cost-effectiveness by comparing the direct costs of your operation to the benefits accrued by the institution as a result of your work.

Unfortunately, if the present era of budgetary constraints becomes a permanent way of life, additional staff or financial resources may not be an option. It may instead be necessary to find ways to implement needed efficiencies and work smarter. Evaluating the effectiveness of the IR operation using the tools and techniques outlined in this chapter can point the way.

References

Chambers, S. (2007). Insights from the Institutional Research Knowledge Base on understanding chief executive needs. IR Activities. IR Applications, vol. 12. Tallahassee, FL: Association for Institutional Research. Retrieved from http://www.airweb.org/page.asp?page=1154

Darton, G., & Darton, M. (1997). *Business process analysis.* London, UK: International Thomson Business Press.

Delaney, A. M. (2001). Institutional researchers' perceptions of effectiveness. *Research in Higher Education, 42*(2), 197–210.

Drucker, P. F. (1962). *The effective executive: The definitive guide to getting the right things done.* Oxford, UK: Elsevier.

Gerek, M. L. (2007). Appendix I, Institutional research activities inventory. IR Activities. IR Applications, vol. 12. Tallahassee, FL: Association for Institutional Research.

Higher Learning Commission (2012). *The New Criteria for Accreditation.* A Commission of the North Central Association of Colleges and Schools. Chicago, IL: The Higher Learning Commission. Retrieved from http://www.ncahlc.org/

Knight, W., (2010). In their own words: Effectiveness in institutional research. AIR Professional File, no. 115. Tallahassee, FL: Association for Institutional Research.

Knight, W., Moore, M., & Coperthwaite, C. (1999). *Knowledge, skills, and effectiveness in institutional research.* New Directions for Institutional Research, no. 104. San Francisco: Jossey-Bass.

Linden, R. (2010, January 13). *Governing.* Retrieved from http://www.governing.com/columns/mgmt-insights/Transparency-Breeds-Self-Correcting-Behavior.html

McLaughlin, G. W., Howard, R., & McLaughlin, J. S. (2009, June). *Assessing effectiveness of the IR function by visiting other institutions.* Paper presented at the Association for Institutional Research Annual Forum, Atlanta, GA.

McLaughlin, G. W., & McLaughlin, J. S. (2007). *The information mosaic: Strategic decision-making for universities and colleges.* Washington, DC: AGB Press.

Middle States Commission on Higher Education. (2009). *Characteristics of excellence in higher education.* Philadelphia, PA: Middle States Commission on Higher Education. Retrieved from http://www.msche.org/publications/CHX06_Aug08REVMarch09.pdf, p.19.

New England Association of Schools and Colleges Commission on Institutions of Higher Education. (2011). *Standards for accreditation.* Bedford, MA: New England Association of Schools and Colleges. Retrieved from http://cihe.neasc.org/standards_policies/standards/standards_html_version

North Carolina State University Office of University Planning and Analysis. (n.d.) Retrieved from http://www2.acs.ncsu.edu/upa/assmt/resource.htm

Northwest Commission on Colleges and Universities. (2010). *Standards for accreditation.* Retrieved from http://www.nwccu.org/Standards%20and%20Policies/Accreditation%20Standards/Accreditation%20Standards.htm

Pet-Armacost, J., & Armacost, R. L. (2007, November). *Performance-based assessment of quality and capability of educational support programs.* Paper presented at the 2007 Assessment Institute, Indianapolis, IN.

Peterson, M. W. (1999, Winter). The role of institutional research: From improvement to redesign. In J. F. Volkwein (series Ed. and vol. Ed.), *What is institutional research all about? A critical and comprehensive assessment of the profession* (pp. 83–103). New Directions for Institutional Research, no. 104. San Francisco: Jossey-Bass.

Presley, J. (Ed.). (1990, Summer). *Organizing effective institutional research offices.* New Directions for Institutional Research, no. 66. San Francisco: Jossey-Bass.

Quinn, A., et. al. (2009). Service quality in higher education. *Total Quality Management & Business Excellence, 20*(2), 139–152.

Saupe, J., & Montgomery, J. (1970). The nature and role of institutional research: Memo to a college or university. Tallahassee, FL: Association for Institutional Research. Retrieved from http://www3.airweb.org/page.asp?page=84

Southern Association of Colleges and Schools, Commission on Colleges. (2010). *The principles of accreditation: Foundations for quality enhancement 2010 edition.* Decatur, GA:

Southern Association of Colleges and Schools. Retrieved from http://www.sacscoc.org/principles.asp

Terenzini, P. T. (1993). On the nature of institutional research and the knowledge and skills it requires. *Research in Higher Education, 34*(1), 1–10.

Voorhees, R. (2010). *Institutional data readiness assessment tool.* Retrieved from http://www.voorheesgroup.org/

Western Association of Schools and Colleges, Accrediting Commission for Senior Colleges and Universities. (2008). *Handbook of accreditation.* Alameda, CA: Western Association of Schools and Colleges. Retrieved from http://www.wascsenior.org/resources

EPILOGUE

The changing functions of academic administration have been spurred by the organizational complexities of educational institutions and a somewhat radical shift in public attitudes, opinions, and sentiments. There is an intense dissatisfaction with traditional procedures in education, an increasing belief that our colleges and universities have been mismanaged, and a rising expectation that the adoption of management concepts and techniques from American industry and business can serve to alleviate or correct many of the difficulties experienced during the past decade. There is a firm insistence that our colleges become more efficient in their operations and that they become more effective in dealing with a complex of social, economic, and technological problems confronting the nation. (Fincher & McCord, 1973, p. 1)

These comments remind us of our legacy. The challenge to better manage our colleges and universities has been a constant companion to the growth and development of our profession of institutional research. In fact, in many ways this pressure has enabled our profession, as it "is an attitude of critical appraisal of all aspects of higher education" (Suslow, 1971, p. 1).

It Is Not Over Until It Is Over

We welcome you to this last component of this *Handbook*. You may have gotten here by starting at the first page and reading sequentially every section and every chapter, but we would find that hard to believe. We have been in IR for a combination of over a century, not necessarily evenly distributed. In that incredible length of time, we have observed very few events or activities that have been characterized by linear processes.

More likely, you got to this point in the *Handbook* after reading chapters that you found interesting or that sparked your curiosity. In that case, we want to encourage you to continue to examine those parts of the volume that address the challenges you face or that represent an area of interest.

It was our intention that this *Handbook* be about our profession in the context of our professional opportunities and responsibilities. The academic and professional interests and backgrounds of the intended audience are as varied as those who founded and built our profession. It provides a contextual background for those interested in the profession and the key components of that context. It looks at our typical responsibilities at colleges and universities. It provides a broad range of technical and analytic topics for the individual new to our profession, including students. The chapters' content and references act as portals to deeper knowing for others who are interested in new areas or advanced discussions of familiar topics. In other words, this is not simply a handbook of methodology or a handbook on assessment or a handbook of statistics, although it does contain many of those aspects. Our intent was to provide a framework to support a journey through the profession of institutional research.

DRIP: Data Rich, Information Poor

With the advent of the affordable mainframe and high-speed printer and low-cost punch cards, the profession spawned a generation of technologists and analysts. These tools made it feasible to provide data, and provide it we did. We produced so much data that we created the culture of DRIP, with tools such as PPBS, RRPM, and IEP. This was during that phase that Cameron Flincher and Michael McCord described in the quotation that opens this Epilogue.

This tendency to DRIP has carried forward to ERP, CRM, and MDM, to name a few. There was the rise of number crunchers. This was not unique to IR; it also engaged those in planning, in budgeting, in information technology, and in the various functions like the registrar, facilities, and business offices, to name a few examples. It also was reflected in the greater society, with funding formulae and calls for efficiency.

Sometimes You Are the Windshield, Sometimes You Are the Bug

It became apparent in the 1980s that data were not enough. The rise of the assessment movement came with the creation of the desktop computer, the Internet, and integrated institutional databases. The result was the democratization of data. We had the conceptual model of catastrophe theory and the emergence of TQM, CQI, and a series of models with names that word-processing software did not like. Academic assessment of learning became the welcome alternative to BRHC (bottom right hand corner) criteria. In this sequence of events the data handling skills of IR seemed to become less central to the discussion. In some cases IR offices were moved down in the organization, with a focus on meeting increasing demands for external accountability and internal data management. Other offices were able to take advantage of this new environment and became not only the campus resource for institutional data but also the campus resource in discussions of what the data meant and resulting implications. Accrediting agencies moved to a new and different set of criteria designed to measure the quality of our institutions' outcomes, in addition to academic and financial integrity. The rubrics of outcomes assessment and institutional effectiveness became the language of new discussions and the focus of their reviews.

Denial, Hostility, Bargaining, Depression, and Acceptance

You may well recognize this model from Kübler-Ross on death and dying (Kübler-Ross, 1969). It represents the likely stages of stressful change. We as a profession have changed. Much of this change came from the technology changes that eliminated the *Wizard of Oz* nature of computers and democratized data. With our efforts to put data back into the issues and institutional context, as done by those who founded the profession (Chapter 1), we got back to basics. The journey of the IR function is entering a level where our activities focus on placing information into context. Answers need to be judged in terms of their external and construct validity. Decisions need to be informed by data, not made by data. Our societies continue to expect higher education to be responsive to goals of access, affordability, and attainment, as noted in the quotation that opened this Epilogue. If we are to continue to add value, we will need to strengthen our ability as learners and move from novice to expert in all of Terenzini's tiers of intelligence.

Looking at the thoughts of the National Research Council, we see substantial differences between novices and experts. One of the key differences is that experts have metacognition—the ability to monitor one's problem-solving ability and to continually learn. A second key aspect that differentiates the "merely skilled" (artisans) from the "highly competent" (virtuosos) is adaptive expertise—being flexible and more adaptable to external demands. Adaptive expertise includes becoming metacognitive (National Research Council, 2000, p. 50). Metacognition and adaptive expertise enable us to challenge the rules and traditional wisdom that currently define our institutions, what they produce, and how they contribution to society. It is our hope, and we believe it is the hope of our colleagues who contributed to this *Handbook*, that these chapters will help institutional research professionals build and use the skills needed to be active and visible contributors on their campuses or agencies.

Quality Is a Verb, and Change Is a Journey

How do we see this *Handbook* contributing to our profession and to your journey? First, it is a part of a road map. We hope you have found aspects that have added value to your perspective of knowing. More than learning, we hope that you have identified a next step in your professional growth in which you can use the references provided in the volume. And even more, we hope you can use the conceptual maps provided here to frame a question or a phrase that will guide you through your next level of learning. The basic skills and knowledge of institutional research that your colleagues have shared have a great deal to contribute to the success of the journey; your opportunity is to use their efforts as a starting place.

We want to return to the thoughts of Terenzini at this point. The opportunities for becoming an expert in his highest tier of intelligence come from networking and *knowing* individuals. This is the key to continued professional development, to problem solving, and to survivability and sustainability (particularly when you find yourself the bug and not the windshield). The three editors of this *Handbook* can certainly identify those who have coached, mentored, and supported us through our professional lives and who continue to do so. Sometimes these are collegial relationships, sometimes they are mentoring relationships, sometimes they are coaching relationships, and many times they are personal friendships. Regardless of the relationship or the methodology or technology used to interact, these relationships are the means by which the journey continues and which, hopefully, this *Handbook* will support.

The purpose of the opening quotation was to remind us that after almost forty years the challenges continue to be real and dynamic, providing opportunities to those willing to learn and to contribute to solutions. As it was forty years ago, the future continues to be both exciting and challenging to the institutional research professional and scholar. Given the profession's history and the proven ability of institutional researchers to adapt, we reflect on the sentiment of Sidney Suslow when he spoke of the future of institutional research in 1971:

> As a field of higher education, institutional research will be fruitful and gather strength if the individual researcher neither allows himself to be intimidated by those who wish to save our institutions through pervasive management untempered by social conscience nor permits himself to ignore the value to be derived from management tools when aptly applied. . . . If we are pretentious in our pride for our achievements to date, then let us simply accept it; if we are satisfied to rest with this achievement then we are foolish, and, if we cannot accelerate and enlarge on our achievements then, I, for one, will be damned disappointed. (p. 3)

References

Fincher, C., & McCord, M. (1973). *Management concepts and academic administration.* Athens, GA: Institute of Higher Education, University of Georgia.

Kübler-Ross, E. (1969). *On death and dying.* New York: Scribner.

National Research Council. (2000). *How people learn: Brain, mind, experience, and school.* J. D. Bransford, A. L. Brown, R. R. Cocking, M. S. Donovan, and J. W. Pellegrino (Eds.).Washington, DC: National Academy Press.

Suslow, S. (1971), Presidential address: Present reality of institutional research. In C. T. Steward (Ed.), *Institutional research and institutional policy formulation,* Proceedings of the 11th Annual Forum of the Association for Institutional Research, Denver, CO, pp. 1–3.

NAME INDEX

A

Abdallah, H., 464
Abraham, S. Y., 209
Abramson, P., 258
Achtemeier, S., 429, 430
Adams, C. R., 206
Adams, J., 574
Adelman, C., 224, 377, 539
Ahlburg, D. A., 469
Ahlstrand, B., 611
Ahmed, A., 66
Allen, D., 467
Allen, J., 531, 536, 540
Allen, R. H., 205, 206, 209, 212
Allen, T., 681
Alstete, J. W., 317, 620
Altbach, P., 60, 64, 66, 69
Amoroso, L. M., 132, 268
Andersen, B., 664
Andrews, B. K., 317
Ansoff, I., 618, 619
Aráujo, L., 90
Archer, S., 457, 673
Argyris, C., 89, 91, 92, 93, 101
Ariyachandra, T., 445
Armacost, R. L., 681
Ashcroft, M. H., 327
Astin, A., 242, 537
Astin, A. W., 377

Atkinson, C., 602
Atwell, R. H., 541
Axt, R. G., 3–4

B

Bach, N., 574
Baer, L., 98
Bailey, T., 538
Baldridge, V., 231
Baldus, D., 346
Baldwin, J., 137
Balkan, L. A., 438, 439
Ballentine, H., 633
Banta, T. W., 320, 321
Barbezat, D., 341, 346, 465, 581, 582, 583, 589
Barbuti, S. M., 536
Bartunek, J. M., 146
Baum, S., 299
Bean, J., 228, 541
Becker, R., 66
Becker, W., 587, 588
Becker, W. E., 175
Beckett, T., 636, 642
Bedard, Y., 440, 446
Bell, A., 204, 234
Bender, K., 107, 126
Bensimon, E., 89
Berens, L., 48
Berg, B. L., 519

SUBJECT INDEX